SPIRAL-BOUND
JOURNALING BIBLE

SPIRAL-BOUND JOURNALING BIBLE

English Standard Version

HISTORY

WHEATON, ILLINOIS · ESV.ORG

ESV Spiral-Bound Journaling Bible, History
The Holy Bible, English Standard Version® (ESV®)
© 2001 by Crossway,
a publishing ministry of Good News Publishers
All rights reserved.

ESV Text Edition: 2025

Permissions notice: Crossway reserves all rights for all of the content of the *ESV Spiral-Bound Journaling Bible, History*, including but not limited to all print, electronic, and audio rights.

Crossway's Standard Use Guidelines allow for the ESV text to be quoted in print, digital, and audio formats up to and inclusive of five hundred (500) verses without express written permission of Crossway, provided that the verses quoted do not amount to more than one-half of any one book of the Bible or its equivalent measured in bytes, nor do the verses quoted account for twenty-five percent (25%) or more of the total text of the work in which they are quoted.

Notice of copyright must appear as follows on the title page or copyright page of printed works quoting from the ESV, or in a corresponding location when the ESV is quoted in other media:

"Scripture quotations are from the ESV® Bible (The Holy Bible, English Standard Version®), © 2001 by Crossway, a publishing ministry of Good News Publishers. ESV Text Edition: 2025. Used by permission. All rights reserved. The ESV text may not be quoted in any publication made available to the public by a Creative Commons license. The ESV may not be translated in whole or in part into any other language."

When more than one translation is quoted in printed works or other media, the foregoing notice of copyright should begin as follows:

"Unless otherwise indicated, all Scripture quotations are from . . . [etc.]"; or, "Scripture quotations marked (ESV) are from . . . [etc.]."

The "ESV" and "English Standard Version" are registered trademarks of Crossway. Use of either trademark requires the permission of Crossway.

When quotations from the ESV text are used in non-saleable print and digital media, such as church bulletins, orders of service, posters, transparencies, or similar media, a complete copyright notice is not required, but the initials (ESV) must appear at the end of the quotation. Permission requests that exceed Crossway's Standard Use Guidelines must be submitted to Crossway via https://www.crossway.org/permissions/.

The Holy Bible, English Standard Version (ESV) is adapted from the Revised Standard Version of the Bible, copyright Division of Christian Education of the National Council of the Churches of Christ in the U.S.A. All rights reserved.

Printed in China
Published by Crossway
Wheaton, Illinois 60187, USA
crossway.org

Crossway is a not-for-profit publishing ministry that exists solely for the purpose of publishing the Good News of the Gospel and the Truth of God's Word, the Bible.

The ESV Bible and related resources are available for free access online and on mobile devices everywhere worldwide at www.ESV.org.

RRDS		35	34	33	32	31	30	29	28	27	26	25
16	15	14	13	12	11	10	9	8	7	6	5	4

CONTENTS

Preface to the English Standard Version vii

Joshua 1
Judges 39
Ruth 79
1 Samuel 85
2 Samuel 135
1 Kings 179
2 Kings 227
1 Chronicles 275
2 Chronicles 319
Ezra 373
Nehemiah 389
Esther 411

Table of Weights and Measures 423

PREFACE
TO THE ENGLISH STANDARD VERSION

The Bible

"This Book [is] the most valuable thing that this world affords. Here is Wisdom; this is the royal Law; these are the lively Oracles of God." With these words the Moderator of the Church of Scotland hands a Bible to the new monarch in Britain's coronation service. These words echo the King James Bible translators, who wrote in 1611, "God's sacred Word . . . is that inestimable treasure that excelleth all the riches of the earth." This assessment of the Bible is the motivating force behind the publication of the English Standard Version.

Translation Legacy

The English Standard Version (ESV) stands in the classic mainstream of English Bible translations over the past half-millennium. The fountainhead of that stream was William Tyndale's New Testament of 1526; marking its course were the King James Version of 1611 (KJV), the English Revised Version of 1885 (RV), the American Standard Version of 1901 (ASV), and the Revised Standard Version of 1952 and 1971 (RSV). In that stream, faithfulness to the text and vigorous pursuit of precision were combined with simplicity, beauty, and dignity of expression. Our goal has been to carry forward this legacy for this generation and generations to come.

To this end each word and phrase in the ESV has been carefully weighed against the original Hebrew, Aramaic, and Greek, to ensure the fullest accuracy and clarity and to avoid under-translating or overlooking any nuance of the original text. The words and phrases themselves grow out of the Tyndale–King James legacy, and most recently out of the RSV, with the 1971 RSV text providing the starting point for our work. Archaic language has been brought into line with current usage and significant corrections have been made in the translation of key texts. But throughout, our goal has been to retain the depth of meaning and enduring quality of language that have made their indelible mark on the English-speaking world and have defined the life and doctrine of its church over the last five centuries.

Translation Philosophy

The ESV is an "essentially literal" translation that seeks as far as possible to reproduce the precise wording of the original text and the personal style of each Bible writer. As such, its emphasis is on "word-for-word" correspondence, at the same time taking full account of differences in grammar, syntax, and idiom between current literary English and the original languages. Thus it seeks to be transparent to the original text, letting the reader see as directly as possible the structure and exact force of the original.

PREFACE

In contrast to the ESV, some Bible versions have followed a "thought-for-thought" rather than "word-for-word" translation philosophy, emphasizing "dynamic equivalence" rather than the "essentially literal" meaning of the original. A "thought-for-thought" translation is of necessity more inclined to reflect the interpretive views of the translator and the influences of contemporary culture.

Every translation is at many points a trade-off between literal precision and readability, between "formal equivalence" in expression and "functional equivalence" in communication, and the ESV is no exception. Within this framework we have sought to be "as literal as possible" while maintaining clarity of expression and literary excellence. Therefore, to the extent that plain English permits and the meaning in each case allows, we have sought to use the same English word for important recurring words in the original; and, as far as grammar and syntax allow, we have rendered Old Testament passages cited in the New in ways that show their correspondence. Thus in each of these areas, as well as throughout the Bible as a whole, we have sought to capture all the echoes and overtones of meaning that are so abundantly present in the original texts.

As an essentially literal translation, taking into account grammar and syntax, the ESV thus seeks to carry over every possible nuance of meaning in the original words of Scripture into our own language. As such, the ESV is ideally suited for in-depth study of the Bible. Indeed, with its commitment to literary excellence, the ESV is equally well suited for public reading and preaching, for private reading and reflection, for both academic and devotional study, and for Scripture memorization.

Translation Principles and Style

The ESV also carries forward classic translation principles in its literary style. Accordingly it retains theological terminology—words such as grace, faith, justification, sanctification, redemption, regeneration, reconciliation, propitiation—because of their central importance for Christian doctrine and also because the underlying Greek words were already becoming key words and technical terms among Christians in New Testament times.

The ESV lets the stylistic variety of the biblical writers fully express itself—from the exalted prose that opens Genesis, to the flowing narratives of the historical books, to the rich metaphors and dramatic imagery of the poetic books, to the ringing rhetoric in the prophetic books, to the smooth elegance of Luke, to the profound simplicities of John, and the closely reasoned logic of Paul.

In punctuating, paragraphing, dividing long sentences, and rendering connectives, the ESV follows the path that seems to make the ongoing flow of thought clearest in English. The biblical languages regularly connect sentences by frequent repetition of words such as "and," "but," and "for," in a way that goes beyond the conventions of current literary English. Effective translation, however, requires that these links in the original be reproduced so that the flow of the argument will be transparent to the reader. We have therefore normally translated these connectives, though occasionally we have varied the rendering by using alternatives (such as "also," "however," "now," "so," "then," or "thus") when they better express the linkage in specific instances.

In the area of gender language, the goal of the ESV is to render literally what is in the original. For example, "anyone" replaces "any man" where there is no word corresponding to "man" in the original languages, and "people" rather than "men" is regularly used where the original languages refer to both men and women. But the words "man" and "men" are retained where a male meaning component is part of the original Greek or Hebrew. Likewise, the word "man" has been retained where the original text intends to convey a clear contrast between "God" on the one hand and "man" on the other hand, with "man" being used in the collective sense of the whole human race (see Luke 2:52). Similarly, the English word "brothers" (translating the Greek word *adelphoi*) is retained as an important familial form of address between fellow-Jews and fellow-Christians in the first century. A recurring note is included to indicate that the term "brothers" (*adelphoi*) was often used in Greek to refer to both men and women, and to indicate the specific instances in the text where this is the case. In addition, the English word "sons" (translating the Greek word *huioi*) is retained in specific instances because the underlying Greek term usually includes a male meaning component and it was used as a legal term in the adoption and inheritance laws of first-century Rome. As used by the apostle Paul, this term refers to the status of all Christians, both men and women, who, having been adopted into God's family, now enjoy all the privileges, obligations, and inheritance rights of God's children.

The inclusive use of the generic "he" has also regularly been retained, because this is consistent with similar usage in the original languages and because an essentially literal translation would be impossible without it.

In each case the objective has been transparency to the original text, allowing the reader to understand the original on its own terms rather than in the terms of our present-day Western culture.

The Translation of Specialized Terms

In the translation of biblical terms referring to God, the ESV takes great care to convey the specific nuances of meaning of the original Hebrew and Greek words. First, concerning terms that refer to God in the Old Testament: God, the Maker of heaven and earth, introduced himself to the people of Israel with a special personal name, the consonants for which are YHWH (see Exodus 3:14–15). Scholars call this the "Tetragrammaton," a Greek term referring to the four Hebrew letters YHWH. The exact pronunciation of YHWH is uncertain, because the Jewish people considered the personal name of God to be so holy that it should never be spoken aloud. Instead of reading the word YHWH, therefore, they would normally read the Hebrew word *'adonay* ("Lord"), and the ancient translations into Greek, Syriac, and Aramaic also followed this practice. When the vowels of the word *'adonay* are placed with the consonants of YHWH, this results in the familiar word *Jehovah* that was used in some earlier English Bible translations. As is common among English translations today, the ESV usually renders the personal name of God (YHWH) by the word Lord (printed in small capitals). An exception to this is when the Hebrew word *'adonay* appears together with YHWH, in which case the two words are rendered together as "the Lord [in lowercase] God [in small capitals]." In contrast to the personal name for God (YHWH), the more general name for God in Old Testament Hebrew is *'elohim* and its related forms of *'el* or *'eloah*, all of which are normally translated "God" (in lowercase letters). The use of these different ways to translate the Hebrew words for God is especially beneficial to English readers, enabling

PREFACE

them to see and understand the different ways that the *personal* name and the *general* name for God are both used to refer to the *One True God* of the Old Testament.

Second, in the New Testament, the Greek word *Christos* has been translated consistently as "Christ." Although the term originally meant simply "anointed," among Jews in New Testament times it had specifically come to designate the Messiah, the great Savior that God had promised to raise up. In other New Testament contexts, however, especially among Gentiles, *Christos* ("Christ") was on its way to becoming a proper name. It is important, therefore, to keep the context in mind in understanding the various ways that *Christos* ("Christ") is used in the New Testament. At the same time, in accord with its "essentially literal" translation philosophy, the ESV has retained consistency and concordance in the translation of *Christos* ("Christ") throughout the New Testament.

Third, a particular difficulty is presented when words in biblical Hebrew and Greek refer to ancient practices and institutions that do not correspond directly to those in the modern world. Such is the case in the translation of *'ebed* (Hebrew) and *doulos* (Greek), terms which are often rendered "slave." These terms, however, actually cover a range of relationships that requires a range of renderings—"slave," "bondservant," or "servant"—depending on the context. Further, the word "slave" currently carries associations with the often brutal and dehumanizing institution of slavery particularly in nineteenth-century America. For this reason, the ESV translation of the words *'ebed* and *doulos* has been undertaken with particular attention to their meaning in each specific context. Thus in Old Testament times, one might enter slavery either voluntarily (e.g., to escape poverty or to pay off a debt) or involuntarily (e.g., by birth, by being captured in battle, or by judicial sentence). Protection for all in servitude in ancient Israel was provided by the Mosaic Law, including specific provisions for release from slavery. In New Testament times, a *doulos* is often best described as a "bondservant"—that is, someone in the Roman Empire officially bound under contract to serve his master for seven years (except for those in Caesar's household in Rome who were contracted for fourteen years). When the contract expired, the person was freed, given his wage that had been saved by the master, and officially declared a freedman. The ESV usage thus seeks to express the most fitting nuance of meaning in each context. Where absolute ownership by a master is envisaged (as in Romans 6), "slave" is used; where a more limited form of servitude is in view, "bondservant" is used (as in 1 Corinthians 7:21–24); where the context indicates a wide range of freedom (as in John 4:51), "servant" is preferred. Footnotes are generally provided to identify the Hebrew or Greek and the range of meaning that these terms may carry in each case. The issues involved in translating the Greek word *doulos* apply also to the Greek word *sundoulos*, translated in the text as "fellow servant."

Fourth, it is sometimes suggested that Bible translations should capitalize pronouns referring to deity. It has seemed best not to capitalize deity pronouns in the ESV, however, for the following reasons: first, there is nothing in the original Hebrew and Greek manuscripts that corresponds to such capitalization; second, the practice of capitalizing deity pronouns in English Bible translations is a recent innovation, which began only in the mid-twentieth century; and, third, such capitalization is absent from the KJV Bible and the whole stream of Bible translations that the ESV carries forward.

A fifth specialized term, the word "behold," usually has been retained as the most common translation for the Hebrew word *hinneh* and the Greek word *idou*. Both of these words mean something like "Pay careful attention to what follows! This is important!" Other than the word "behold," there is no single word in English that fits well in most contexts. Although "Look!" and "See!" and "Listen!" would be workable in some contexts, in many others these words lack sufficient weight and dignity. Given the principles of "essentially literal" translation, it is important not to leave *hinneh* and *idou* completely untranslated and so to lose the intended emphasis in the original languages. The older and more formal word "behold" has usually been retained, therefore, as the best available option for conveying the original weight of meaning.

Textual Basis and Resources
The ESV is based on the Masoretic text of the Hebrew Bible as found in *Biblia Hebraica Stuttgartensia* (5th ed., 1997), and on the Greek text in the 2014 editions of the *Greek New Testament* (5th corrected ed.), published by the United Bible Societies (UBS), and *Novum Testamentum Graece* (28th ed., 2012), edited by Nestle and Aland. The currently renewed respect among Old Testament scholars for the Masoretic text is reflected in the ESV's attempt, wherever possible, to translate difficult Hebrew passages as they stand in the Masoretic text rather than resorting to emendations or to finding an alternative reading in the ancient versions. In exceptional, difficult cases, the Dead Sea Scrolls, the Septuagint, the Samaritan Pentateuch, the Syriac Peshitta, the Latin Vulgate, and other sources were consulted to shed possible light on the text, or, if necessary, to support a divergence from the Masoretic text. Similarly, in a few difficult cases in the New Testament, the ESV has followed a Greek text different from the text given preference in the UBS/Nestle-Aland 28th edition. Throughout, the translation team has benefited greatly from the massive textual resources that have become readily available recently, from new insights into biblical laws and culture, and from current advances in Hebrew and Greek lexicography and grammatical understanding.

Textual Footnotes
The footnotes that are included in most editions of the ESV are therefore an integral part of the ESV translation, informing the reader of textual variations and difficulties and showing how these have been resolved by the ESV translation team. In addition to this, the footnotes indicate significant alternative readings and occasionally provide an explanation for technical terms or for a difficult reading in the text.

Publishing Team
The ESV publishing team has included more than a hundred people. The fourteen-member Translation Oversight Committee benefited from the work of more than fifty biblical experts serving as Translation Review Scholars and from the comments of the more than fifty members of the Advisory Council, all of which was carried out under the auspices of the Crossway Board of Directors. This hundred-plus-member team shares a common commitment to the truth of God's Word and to historic Christian orthodoxy and is international in scope, including leaders in many denominations.

PREFACE

To God's Honor and Praise

We know that no Bible translation is perfect; but we also know that God uses imperfect and inadequate things to his honor and praise. So to our triune God and to his people we offer what we have done, with our prayers that it may prove useful, with gratitude for much help given, and with ongoing wonder that our God should ever have entrusted to us so momentous a task.

Soli Deo Gloria!—To God alone be the glory!
The Translation Oversight Committee

JOSHUA

God Commissions Joshua

1 After the death of Moses the servant of the Lord, the Lord said to Joshua the son of Nun, Moses' assistant, [2] "Moses my servant is dead. Now therefore arise, go over this Jordan, you and all this people, into the land that I am giving to them, to the people of Israel. [3] Every place that the sole of your foot will tread upon I have given to you, just as I promised to Moses. [4] From the wilderness and this Lebanon as far as the great river, the river Euphrates, all the land of the Hittites to the Great Sea toward the going down of the sun shall be your territory. [5] No man shall be able to stand before you all the days of your life. Just as I was with Moses, so I will be with you. I will not leave you or forsake you. [6] Be strong and courageous, for you shall cause this people to inherit the land that I swore to their fathers to give them. [7] Only be strong and very courageous, being careful to do according to all the law that Moses my servant commanded you. Do not turn from it to the right hand or to the left, that you may have good success[1] wherever you go. [8] This Book of the Law shall not depart from your mouth, but you shall meditate on it day and night, so that you may be careful to do according to all that is written in it. For then you will make your way prosperous, and then you will have good success. [9] Have I not commanded you? Be strong and courageous. Do not be frightened, and do not be dismayed, for the Lord your God is with you wherever you go."

Joshua Assumes Command

[10] And Joshua commanded the officers of the people, [11] "Pass through the midst of the camp and command the people, 'Prepare your provisions, for within three days you are to pass over this Jordan to go in to take possession of the land that the Lord your God is giving you to possess.'"

[12] And to the Reubenites, the Gadites, and the half-tribe of Manasseh Joshua said, [13] "Remember the word that Moses the servant of the Lord commanded you, saying, 'The Lord your God is providing you a place of rest and will give you this land.' [14] Your wives, your little ones, and your livestock shall

---

[1] Or *may act wisely*

remain in the land that Moses gave you beyond the Jordan, but all the men of valor among you shall pass over armed before your brothers and shall help them, ⁱ⁵ until the Lord gives rest to your brothers as he has to you, and they also take possession of the land that the Lord your God is giving them. Then you shall return to the land of your possession and shall possess it, the land that Moses the servant of the Lord gave you beyond the Jordan toward the sunrise."

¹⁶ And they answered Joshua, "All that you have commanded us we will do, and wherever you send us we will go. ¹⁷ Just as we obeyed Moses in all things, so we will obey you. Only may the Lord your God be with you, as he was with Moses! ¹⁸ Whoever rebels against your commandment and disobeys your words, whatever you command him, shall be put to death. Only be strong and courageous."

Rahab Hides the Spies

2 And Joshua the son of Nun sent[1] two men secretly from Shittim as spies, saying, "Go, view the land, especially Jericho." And they went and came into the house of a prostitute whose name was Rahab and lodged there. ² And it was told to the king of Jericho, "Behold, men of Israel have come here tonight to search out the land." ³ Then the king of Jericho sent to Rahab, saying, "Bring out the men who have come to you, who entered your house, for they have come to search out all the land." ⁴ But the woman had taken the two men and hidden them. And she said, "True, the men came to me, but I did not know where they were from. ⁵ And when the gate was about to be closed at dark, the men went out. I do not know where the men went. Pursue them quickly, for you will overtake them." ⁶ But she had brought them up to the roof and hid them with the stalks of flax that she had laid in order on the roof. ⁷ So the men pursued after them on the way to the Jordan as far as the fords. And the gate was shut as soon as the pursuers had gone out.

⁸ Before the men[2] lay down, she came up to them on the roof ⁹ and said to the men, "I know that the Lord has given you the land, and that the fear of you has fallen upon us, and that all the inhabitants of the land melt away before you. ¹⁰ For we have heard how the Lord dried up the water of the Red Sea before you when you came out of Egypt, and what you did to the two kings of the Amorites who were beyond the Jordan, to Sihon and Og, whom you devoted to destruction.[3] ¹¹ And as soon as we heard it, our hearts melted, and there was no spirit left in any man because of you, for the Lord your God, he is God in the heavens above and on the earth beneath. ¹² Now then,

[1] Or *had sent* [2] Hebrew *they* [3] That is, set apart (devoted) as an offering to the Lord (for destruction)

please swear to me by the Lord that, as I have dealt kindly with you, you also will deal kindly with my father's house, and give me a sure sign ¹³ that you will save alive my father and mother, my brothers and sisters, and all who belong to them, and deliver our lives from death." ¹⁴ And the men said to her, "Our life for yours even to death! If you do not tell this business of ours, then when the Lord gives us the land we will deal kindly and faithfully with you."

¹⁵ Then she let them down by a rope through the window, for her house was built into the city wall, so that she lived in the wall. ¹⁶ And she said[1] to them, "Go into the hills, or the pursuers will encounter you, and hide there three days until the pursuers have returned. Then afterward you may go your way." ¹⁷ The men said to her, "We will be guiltless with respect to this oath of yours that you have made us swear. ¹⁸ Behold, when we come into the land, you shall tie this scarlet cord in the window through which you let us down, and you shall gather into your house your father and mother, your brothers, and all your father's household. ¹⁹ Then if anyone goes out of the doors of your house into the street, his blood shall be on his own head, and we shall be guiltless. But if a hand is laid on anyone who is with you in the house, his blood shall be on our head. ²⁰ But if you tell this business of ours, then we shall be guiltless with respect to your oath that you have made us swear." ²¹ And she said, "According to your words, so be it." Then she sent them away, and they departed. And she tied the scarlet cord in the window.

²² They departed and went into the hills and remained there three days until the pursuers returned, and the pursuers searched all along the way and found nothing. ²³ Then the two men returned. They came down from the hills and passed over and came to Joshua the son of Nun, and they told him all that had happened to them. ²⁴ And they said to Joshua, "Truly the Lord has given all the land into our hands. And also, all the inhabitants of the land melt away because of us."

Israel Crosses the Jordan

3 Then Joshua rose early in the morning and they set out from Shittim. And they came to the Jordan, he and all the people of Israel, and lodged there before they passed over. ² At the end of three days the officers went through the camp ³ and commanded the people, "As soon as you see the ark of the covenant of the Lord your God being carried by the Levitical priests, then you shall set out from your place and follow it. ⁴ Yet there shall be a distance between you and it, about 2,000 cubits[2] in length. Do not come near it, in order that you may know the way you shall go, for you have not passed

---

[1] Or *had said* [2] A *cubit* was about 18 inches or 45 centimeters

this way before." ⁵ Then Joshua said to the people, "Consecrate yourselves, for tomorrow the Lord will do wonders among you." ⁶ And Joshua said to the priests, "Take up the ark of the covenant and pass on before the people." So they took up the ark of the covenant and went before the people.

⁷ The Lord said to Joshua, "Today I will begin to exalt you in the sight of all Israel, that they may know that, as I was with Moses, so I will be with you. ⁸ And as for you, command the priests who bear the ark of the covenant, 'When you come to the brink of the waters of the Jordan, you shall stand still in the Jordan.'" ⁹ And Joshua said to the people of Israel, "Come here and listen to the words of the Lord your God." ¹⁰ And Joshua said, "Here is how you shall know that the living God is among you and that he will without fail drive out from before you the Canaanites, the Hittites, the Hivites, the Perizzites, the Girgashites, the Amorites, and the Jebusites. ¹¹ Behold, the ark of the covenant of the Lord of all the earth[1] is passing over before you into the Jordan. ¹² Now therefore take twelve men from the tribes of Israel, from each tribe a man. ¹³ And when the soles of the feet of the priests bearing the ark of the Lord, the Lord of all the earth, shall rest in the waters of the Jordan, the waters of the Jordan shall be cut off from flowing, and the waters coming down from above shall stand in one heap."

¹⁴ So when the people set out from their tents to pass over the Jordan with the priests bearing the ark of the covenant before the people, ¹⁵ and as soon as those bearing the ark had come as far as the Jordan, and the feet of the priests bearing the ark were dipped in the brink of the water (now the Jordan overflows all its banks throughout the time of harvest), ¹⁶ the waters coming down from above stood and rose up in a heap very far away, at Adam, the city that is beside Zarethan, and those flowing down toward the Sea of the Arabah, the Salt Sea, were completely cut off. And the people passed over opposite Jericho. ¹⁷ Now the priests bearing the ark of the covenant of the Lord stood firmly on dry ground in the midst of the Jordan, and all Israel was passing over on dry ground until all the nation finished passing over the Jordan.

Twelve Memorial Stones from the Jordan

4 When all the nation had finished passing over the Jordan, the Lord said to Joshua, ² "Take twelve men from the people, from each tribe a man, ³ and command them, saying, 'Take twelve stones from here out of the midst of the Jordan, from the very place where the priests' feet stood firmly, and bring them over with you and lay them down in the place where you

[1] Hebrew *the ark of the covenant, the Lord of all the earth*

lodge tonight.'" ⁴Then Joshua called the twelve men from the people of Israel, whom he had appointed, a man from each tribe. ⁵And Joshua said to them, "Pass on before the ark of the Lord your God into the midst of the Jordan, and take up each of you a stone upon his shoulder, according to the number of the tribes of the people of Israel, ⁶that this may be a sign among you. When your children ask in time to come, 'What do those stones mean to you?' ⁷then you shall tell them that the waters of the Jordan were cut off before the ark of the covenant of the Lord. When it passed over the Jordan, the waters of the Jordan were cut off. So these stones shall be to the people of Israel a memorial forever."

⁸And the people of Israel did just as Joshua commanded and took up twelve stones out of the midst of the Jordan, according to the number of the tribes of the people of Israel, just as the Lord told Joshua. And they carried them over with them to the place where they lodged and laid them down[1] there. ⁹And Joshua set up[2] twelve stones in the midst of the Jordan, in the place where the feet of the priests bearing the ark of the covenant had stood; and they are there to this day. ¹⁰For the priests bearing the ark stood in the midst of the Jordan until everything was finished that the Lord commanded Joshua to tell the people, according to all that Moses had commanded Joshua.

The people passed over in haste. ¹¹And when all the people had finished passing over, the ark of the Lord and the priests passed over before the people. ¹²The sons of Reuben and the sons of Gad and the half-tribe of Manasseh passed over armed before the people of Israel, as Moses had told them. ¹³About 40,000 ready for war passed over before the Lord for battle, to the plains of Jericho. ¹⁴On that day the Lord exalted Joshua in the sight of all Israel, and they stood in awe of him just as they had stood in awe of Moses, all the days of his life.

¹⁵And the Lord said to Joshua, ¹⁶"Command the priests bearing the ark of the testimony to come up out of the Jordan." ¹⁷So Joshua commanded the priests, "Come up out of the Jordan." ¹⁸And when the priests bearing the ark of the covenant of the Lord came up from the midst of the Jordan, and the soles of the priests' feet were lifted up on dry ground, the waters of the Jordan returned to their place and overflowed all its banks, as before.

¹⁹The people came up out of the Jordan on the tenth day of the first month, and they encamped at Gilgal on the east border of Jericho. ²⁰And those twelve stones, which they took out of the Jordan, Joshua set up at Gilgal. ²¹And he said to the people of Israel, "When your children ask their fathers in times to come, 'What do these stones mean?' ²²then you shall let your children know,

---

[1] Or *to rest* [2] Or *Joshua had set up*

'Israel passed over this Jordan on dry ground.' ²³ For the LORD your God dried up the waters of the Jordan for you until you passed over, as the LORD your God did to the Red Sea, which he dried up for us until we passed over, ²⁴ so that all the peoples of the earth may know that the hand of the LORD is mighty, that you may fear the LORD your God forever."[1]

The New Generation Circumcised

5 As soon as all the kings of the Amorites who were beyond the Jordan to the west, and all the kings of the Canaanites who were by the sea, heard that the LORD had dried up the waters of the Jordan for the people of Israel until they had crossed over, their hearts melted and there was no longer any spirit in them because of the people of Israel.

² At that time the LORD said to Joshua, "Make flint knives and circumcise the sons of Israel a second time." ³ So Joshua made flint knives and circumcised the sons of Israel at Gibeath-haaraloth.[2] ⁴ And this is the reason why Joshua circumcised them: all the males of the people who came out of Egypt, all the men of war, had died in the wilderness on the way after they had come out of Egypt. ⁵ Though all the people who came out had been circumcised, yet all the people who were born on the way in the wilderness after they had come out of Egypt had not been circumcised. ⁶ For the people of Israel walked forty years in the wilderness, until all the nation, the men of war who came out of Egypt, perished, because they did not obey the voice of the LORD; the LORD swore to them that he would not let them see the land that the LORD had sworn to their fathers to give to us, a land flowing with milk and honey. ⁷ So it was their children, whom he raised up in their place, that Joshua circumcised. For they were uncircumcised, because they had not been circumcised on the way.

⁸ When the circumcising of the whole nation was finished, they remained in their places in the camp until they were healed. ⁹ And the LORD said to Joshua, "Today I have rolled away the reproach of Egypt from you." And so the name of that place is called Gilgal[3] to this day.

First Passover in Canaan

¹⁰ While the people of Israel were encamped at Gilgal, they kept the Passover on the fourteenth day of the month in the evening on the plains of Jericho. ¹¹ And the day after the Passover, on that very day, they ate of the produce of the land, unleavened cakes and parched grain. ¹² And the manna ceased the day after they ate of the produce of the land. And there was no longer manna for the people of Israel, but they ate of the fruit of the land of Canaan that year.

¹ Or *all the days* ² *Gibeath-haaraloth* means *the hill of the foreskins* ³ *Gilgal* sounds like the Hebrew for *to roll*

The Commander of the Lord's Army

¹³ When Joshua was by Jericho, he lifted up his eyes and looked, and behold, a man was standing before him with his drawn sword in his hand. And Joshua went to him and said to him, "Are you for us, or for our adversaries?" ¹⁴ And he said, "No; but I am the commander of the army of the Lord. Now I have come." And Joshua fell on his face to the earth and worshiped[1] and said to him, "What does my lord say to his servant?" ¹⁵ And the commander of the Lord's army said to Joshua, "Take off your sandals from your feet, for the place where you are standing is holy." And Joshua did so.

The Fall of Jericho

6 Now Jericho was shut up inside and outside because of the people of Israel. None went out, and none came in. ² And the Lord said to Joshua, "See, I have given Jericho into your hand, with its king and mighty men of valor. ³ You shall march around the city, all the men of war going around the city once. Thus shall you do for six days. ⁴ Seven priests shall bear seven trumpets of rams' horns before the ark. On the seventh day you shall march around the city seven times, and the priests shall blow the trumpets. ⁵ And when they make a long blast with the ram's horn, when you hear the sound of the trumpet, then all the people shall shout with a great shout, and the wall of the city will fall down flat,[2] and the people shall go up, everyone straight before him." ⁶ So Joshua the son of Nun called the priests and said to them, "Take up the ark of the covenant and let seven priests bear seven trumpets of rams' horns before the ark of the Lord." ⁷ And he said to the people, "Go forward. March around the city and let the armed men pass on before the ark of the Lord."

⁸ And just as Joshua had commanded the people, the seven priests bearing the seven trumpets of rams' horns before the Lord went forward, blowing the trumpets, with the ark of the covenant of the Lord following them. ⁹ The armed men were walking before the priests who were blowing the trumpets, and the rear guard was walking after the ark, while the trumpets blew continually. ¹⁰ But Joshua commanded the people, "You shall not shout or make your voice heard, neither shall any word go out of your mouth, until the day I tell you to shout. Then you shall shout." ¹¹ So he caused the ark of the Lord to circle the city, going about it once. And they came into the camp and spent the night in the camp.

¹² Then Joshua rose early in the morning, and the priests took up the ark of the Lord. ¹³ And the seven priests bearing the seven trumpets of rams' horns

---

[1] Or *and paid homage* [2] Hebrew *under itself*; also verse 20

before the ark of the Lord walked on, and they blew the trumpets continually. And the armed men were walking before them, and the rear guard was walking after the ark of the Lord, while the trumpets blew continually. ¹⁴ And the second day they marched around the city once, and returned into the camp. So they did for six days.

¹⁵ On the seventh day they rose early, at the dawn of day, and marched around the city in the same manner seven times. It was only on that day that they marched around the city seven times. ¹⁶ And at the seventh time, when the priests had blown the trumpets, Joshua said to the people, "Shout, for the Lord has given you the city. ¹⁷ And the city and all that is within it shall be devoted to the Lord for destruction.¹ Only Rahab the prostitute and all who are with her in her house shall live, because she hid the messengers whom we sent. ¹⁸ But you, keep yourselves from the things devoted to destruction, lest when you have devoted them you take any of the devoted things and make the camp of Israel a thing for destruction and bring trouble upon it. ¹⁹ But all silver and gold, and every vessel of bronze and iron, are holy to the Lord; they shall go into the treasury of the Lord." ²⁰ So the people shouted, and the trumpets were blown. As soon as the people heard the sound of the trumpet, the people shouted a great shout, and the wall fell down flat, so that the people went up into the city, every man straight before him, and they captured the city. ²¹ Then they devoted all in the city to destruction, both men and women, young and old, oxen, sheep, and donkeys, with the edge of the sword.

²² But to the two men who had spied out the land, Joshua said, "Go into the prostitute's house and bring out from there the woman and all who belong to her, as you swore to her." ²³ So the young men who had been spies went in and brought out Rahab and her father and mother and brothers and all who belonged to her. And they brought all her relatives and put them outside the camp of Israel. ²⁴ And they burned the city with fire, and everything in it. Only the silver and gold, and the vessels of bronze and of iron, they put into the treasury of the house of the Lord. ²⁵ But Rahab the prostitute and her father's household and all who belonged to her, Joshua saved alive. And she has lived in Israel to this day, because she hid the messengers whom Joshua sent to spy out Jericho.

²⁶ Joshua laid an oath on them at that time, saying, "Cursed before the Lord be the man who rises up and rebuilds this city, Jericho.

"At the cost of his firstborn
    shall he lay its foundation,

---

¹ That is, set apart (devoted) as an offering to the Lord (for destruction); also verses 18, 21

and at the cost of his youngest son
>shall he set up its gates."

⁲⁷ So the Lord was with Joshua, and his fame was in all the land.

Israel Defeated at Ai

7 But the people of Israel broke faith in regard to the devoted things, for Achan the son of Carmi, son of Zabdi, son of Zerah, of the tribe of Judah, took some of the devoted things. And the anger of the Lord burned against the people of Israel.

² Joshua sent men from Jericho to Ai, which is near Beth-aven, east of Bethel, and said to them, "Go up and spy out the land." And the men went up and spied out Ai. ³ And they returned to Joshua and said to him, "Do not have all the people go up, but let about two or three thousand men go up and attack Ai. Do not make the whole people toil up there, for they are few." ⁴ So about three thousand men went up there from the people. And they fled before the men of Ai, ⁵ and the men of Ai killed about thirty-six of their men and chased them before the gate as far as Shebarim and struck them at the descent. And the hearts of the people melted and became as water.

⁶ Then Joshua tore his clothes and fell to the earth on his face before the ark of the Lord until the evening, he and the elders of Israel. And they put dust on their heads. ⁷ And Joshua said, "Alas, O Lord God, why have you brought this people over the Jordan at all, to give us into the hands of the Amorites, to destroy us? Would that we had been content to dwell beyond the Jordan! ⁸ O Lord, what can I say, when Israel has turned their backs before their enemies! ⁹ For the Canaanites and all the inhabitants of the land will hear of it and will surround us and cut off our name from the earth. And what will you do for your great name?"

The Sin of Achan

¹⁰ The Lord said to Joshua, "Get up! Why have you fallen on your face? ¹¹ Israel has sinned; they have transgressed my covenant that I commanded them; they have taken some of the devoted things; they have stolen and lied and put them among their own belongings. ¹² Therefore the people of Israel cannot stand before their enemies. They turn their backs before their enemies, because they have become devoted for destruction.¹ I will be with you no more, unless you destroy the devoted things from among you. ¹³ Get up! Consecrate the people and say, 'Consecrate yourselves for tomorrow; for

---

¹ That is, set apart (devoted) as an offering to the Lord (for destruction)

thus says the LORD, God of Israel, "There are devoted things in your midst, O Israel. You cannot stand before your enemies until you take away the devoted things from among you." ¹⁴ In the morning therefore you shall be brought near by your tribes. And the tribe that the LORD takes by lot shall come near by clans. And the clan that the LORD takes shall come near by households. And the household that the LORD takes shall come near man by man. ¹⁵ And he who is taken with the devoted things shall be burned with fire, he and all that he has, because he has transgressed the covenant of the LORD, and because he has done an outrageous thing in Israel.'"

¹⁶ So Joshua rose early in the morning and brought Israel near tribe by tribe, and the tribe of Judah was taken. ¹⁷ And he brought near the clans of Judah, and the clan of the Zerahites was taken. And he brought near the clan of the Zerahites man by man, and Zabdi was taken. ¹⁸ And he brought near his household man by man, and Achan the son of Carmi, son of Zabdi, son of Zerah, of the tribe of Judah, was taken. ¹⁹ Then Joshua said to Achan, "My son, give glory to the LORD God of Israel and give praise[1] to him. And tell me now what you have done; do not hide it from me." ²⁰ And Achan answered Joshua, "Truly I have sinned against the LORD God of Israel, and this is what I did: ²¹ when I saw among the spoil a beautiful cloak from Shinar, and 200 shekels of silver, and a bar of gold weighing 50 shekels,[2] then I coveted them and took them. And see, they are hidden in the earth inside my tent, with the silver underneath."

²² So Joshua sent messengers, and they ran to the tent; and behold, it was hidden in his tent with the silver underneath. ²³ And they took them out of the tent and brought them to Joshua and to all the people of Israel. And they laid them down before the LORD. ²⁴ And Joshua and all Israel with him took Achan the son of Zerah, and the silver and the cloak and the bar of gold, and his sons and daughters and his oxen and donkeys and sheep and his tent and all that he had. And they brought them up to the Valley of Achor. ²⁵ And Joshua said, "Why did you bring trouble on us? The LORD brings trouble on you today." And all Israel stoned him with stones. They burned them with fire and stoned them with stones. ²⁶ And they raised over him a great heap of stones that remains to this day. Then the LORD turned from his burning anger. Therefore, to this day the name of that place is called the Valley of Achor.[3]

The Fall of Ai

8 And the LORD said to Joshua, "Do not fear and do not be dismayed. Take all the fighting men with you, and arise, go up to Ai. See, I have given into your hand the king of Ai, and his people, his city, and his land.

---

[1] Or *and make confession* [2] A *shekel* was about 2/5 ounce or 11 grams [3] *Achor* means *trouble*

² And you shall do to Ai and its king as you did to Jericho and its king. Only its spoil and its livestock you shall take as plunder for yourselves. Lay an ambush against the city, behind it."

³ So Joshua and all the fighting men arose to go up to Ai. And Joshua chose 30,000 mighty men of valor and sent them out by night. ⁴ And he commanded them, "Behold, you shall lie in ambush against the city, behind it. Do not go very far from the city, but all of you remain ready. ⁵ And I and all the people who are with me will approach the city. And when they come out against us just as before, we shall flee before them. ⁶ And they will come out after us, until we have drawn them away from the city. For they will say, 'They are fleeing from us, just as before.' So we will flee before them. ⁷ Then you shall rise up from the ambush and seize the city, for the Lord your God will give it into your hand. ⁸ And as soon as you have taken the city, you shall set the city on fire. You shall do according to the word of the Lord. See, I have commanded you." ⁹ So Joshua sent them out. And they went to the place of ambush and lay between Bethel and Ai, to the west of Ai, but Joshua spent that night among the people.

¹⁰ Joshua arose early in the morning and mustered the people and went up, he and the elders of Israel, before the people to Ai. ¹¹ And all the fighting men who were with him went up and drew near before the city and encamped on the north side of Ai, with a ravine between them and Ai. ¹² He took about 5,000 men and set them in ambush between Bethel and Ai, to the west of the city. ¹³ So they stationed the forces, the main encampment that was north of the city and its rear guard west of the city. But Joshua spent that night in the valley. ¹⁴ And as soon as the king of Ai saw this, he and all his people, the men of the city, hurried and went out early to the appointed place¹ toward the Arabah to meet Israel in battle. But he did not know that there was an ambush against him behind the city. ¹⁵ And Joshua and all Israel pretended to be beaten before them and fled in the direction of the wilderness. ¹⁶ So all the people who were in the city were called together to pursue them, and as they pursued Joshua they were drawn away from the city. ¹⁷ Not a man was left in Ai or Bethel who did not go out after Israel. They left the city open and pursued Israel.

¹⁸ Then the Lord said to Joshua, "Stretch out the javelin that is in your hand toward Ai, for I will give it into your hand." And Joshua stretched out the javelin that was in his hand toward the city. ¹⁹ And the men in the ambush rose quickly out of their place, and as soon as he had stretched out his hand, they ran and entered the city and captured it. And they hurried to set the city

---

¹ Hebrew *appointed time*

on fire. ²⁰ So when the men of Ai looked back, behold, the smoke of the city went up to heaven, and they had no power to flee this way or that, for the people who fled to the wilderness turned back against the pursuers. ²¹ And when Joshua and all Israel saw that the ambush had captured the city, and that the smoke of the city went up, then they turned back and struck down the men of Ai. ²² And the others came out from the city against them, so they were in the midst of Israel, some on this side, and some on that side. And Israel struck them down, until there was left none that survived or escaped. ²³ But the king of Ai they took alive, and brought him near to Joshua.

²⁴ When Israel had finished killing all the inhabitants of Ai in the open wilderness where they pursued them, and all of them to the very last had fallen by the edge of the sword, all Israel returned to Ai and struck it down with the edge of the sword. ²⁵ And all who fell that day, both men and women, were 12,000, all the people of Ai. ²⁶ But Joshua did not draw back his hand with which he stretched out the javelin until he had devoted all the inhabitants of Ai to destruction.¹ ²⁷ Only the livestock and the spoil of that city Israel took as their plunder, according to the word of the Lord that he commanded Joshua. ²⁸ So Joshua burned Ai and made it forever a heap of ruins, as it is to this day. ²⁹ And he hanged the king of Ai on a tree until evening. And at sunset Joshua commanded, and they took his body down from the tree and threw it at the entrance of the gate of the city and raised over it a great heap of stones, which stands there to this day.

Joshua Renews the Covenant

³⁰ At that time Joshua built an altar to the Lord, the God of Israel, on Mount Ebal, ³¹ just as Moses the servant of the Lord had commanded the people of Israel, as it is written in the Book of the Law of Moses, "an altar of uncut stones, upon which no man has wielded an iron tool." And they offered on it burnt offerings to the Lord and sacrificed peace offerings. ³² And there, in the presence of the people of Israel, he wrote on the stones a copy of the law of Moses, which he had written. ³³ And all Israel, sojourner as well as native born, with their elders and officers and their judges, stood on opposite sides of the ark before the Levitical priests who carried the ark of the covenant of the Lord, half of them in front of Mount Gerizim and half of them in front of Mount Ebal, just as Moses the servant of the Lord had commanded at the first, to bless the people of Israel. ³⁴ And afterward he read all the words of the law, the blessing and the curse, according to all that is written in the Book of the Law. ³⁵ There was not a word of all

¹ That is, set apart (devoted) as an offering to the Lord (for destruction)

that Moses commanded that Joshua did not read before all the assembly of Israel, and the women, and the little ones, and the sojourners who lived[1] among them.

The Gibeonite Deception

9 As soon as all the kings who were beyond the Jordan in the hill country and in the lowland all along the coast of the Great Sea toward Lebanon, the Hittites, the Amorites, the Canaanites, the Perizzites, the Hivites, and the Jebusites, heard of this, ² they gathered together as one to fight against Joshua and Israel.

³ But when the inhabitants of Gibeon heard what Joshua had done to Jericho and to Ai, ⁴ they on their part acted with cunning and went and made ready provisions and took worn-out sacks for their donkeys, and wineskins, worn-out and torn and mended, ⁵ with worn-out, patched sandals on their feet, and worn-out clothes. And all their provisions were dry and crumbly. ⁶ And they went to Joshua in the camp at Gilgal and said to him and to the men of Israel, "We have come from a distant country, so now make a covenant with us." ⁷ But the men of Israel said to the Hivites, "Perhaps you live among us; then how can we make a covenant with you?" ⁸ They said to Joshua, "We are your servants." And Joshua said to them, "Who are you? And where do you come from?" ⁹ They said to him, "From a very distant country your servants have come, because of the name of the Lord your God. For we have heard a report of him, and all that he did in Egypt, ¹⁰ and all that he did to the two kings of the Amorites who were beyond the Jordan, to Sihon the king of Heshbon, and to Og king of Bashan, who lived in Ashtaroth. ¹¹ So our elders and all the inhabitants of our country said to us, 'Take provisions in your hand for the journey and go to meet them and say to them, "We are your servants. Come now, make a covenant with us."' ¹² Here is our bread. It was still warm when we took it from our houses as our food for the journey on the day we set out to come to you, but now, behold, it is dry and crumbly. ¹³ These wineskins were new when we filled them, and behold, they have burst. And these garments and sandals of ours are worn out from the very long journey." ¹⁴ So the men took some of their provisions, but did not ask counsel from the Lord. ¹⁵ And Joshua made peace with them and made a covenant with them, to let them live, and the leaders of the congregation swore to them.

¹⁶ At the end of three days after they had made a covenant with them, they heard that they were their neighbors and that they lived among them. ¹⁷ And

[1] Or *traveled*

the people of Israel set out and reached their cities on the third day. Now their cities were Gibeon, Chephirah, Beeroth, and Kiriath-jearim. [18] But the people of Israel did not attack them, because the leaders of the congregation had sworn to them by the Lord, the God of Israel. Then all the congregation murmured against the leaders. [19] But all the leaders said to all the congregation, "We have sworn to them by the Lord, the God of Israel, and now we may not touch them. [20] This we will do to them: let them live, lest wrath be upon us, because of the oath that we swore to them." [21] And the leaders said to them, "Let them live." So they became cutters of wood and drawers of water for all the congregation, just as the leaders had said of them.

[22] Joshua summoned them, and he said to them, "Why did you deceive us, saying, 'We are very far from you,' when you dwell among us? [23] Now therefore you are cursed, and some of you shall never be anything but servants, cutters of wood and drawers of water for the house of my God." [24] They answered Joshua, "Because it was told to your servants for a certainty that the Lord your God had commanded his servant Moses to give you all the land and to destroy all the inhabitants of the land from before you—so we feared greatly for our lives because of you and did this thing. [25] And now, behold, we are in your hand. Whatever seems good and right in your sight to do to us, do it." [26] So he did this to them and delivered them out of the hand of the people of Israel, and they did not kill them. [27] But Joshua made them that day cutters of wood and drawers of water for the congregation and for the altar of the Lord, to this day, in the place that he should choose.

The Sun Stands Still

10 As soon as Adoni-zedek, king of Jerusalem, heard how Joshua had captured Ai and had devoted it to destruction,[1] doing to Ai and its king as he had done to Jericho and its king, and how the inhabitants of Gibeon had made peace with Israel and were among them, [2] he[2] feared greatly, because Gibeon was a great city, like one of the royal cities, and because it was greater than Ai, and all its men were warriors. [3] So Adoni-zedek king of Jerusalem sent to Hoham king of Hebron, to Piram king of Jarmuth, to Japhia king of Lachish, and to Debir king of Eglon, saying, [4] "Come up to me and help me, and let us strike Gibeon. For it has made peace with Joshua and with the people of Israel." [5] Then the five kings of the Amorites, the king of Jerusalem, the king of Hebron, the king of Jarmuth, the king of Lachish, and the king of Eglon, gathered their forces and went up with all their armies and encamped against Gibeon and made war against it.

---

[1] That is, set apart (devoted) as an offering to the Lord (for destruction); also verses 28, 35, 37, 39, 40
[2] One Hebrew manuscript, Vulgate (compare Syriac); most Hebrew manuscripts *they*

⁶ And the men of Gibeon sent to Joshua at the camp in Gilgal, saying, "Do not relax your hand from your servants. Come up to us quickly and save us and help us, for all the kings of the Amorites who dwell in the hill country are gathered against us." ⁷ So Joshua went up from Gilgal, he and all the people of war with him, and all the mighty men of valor. ⁸ And the Lord said to Joshua, "Do not fear them, for I have given them into your hands. Not a man of them shall stand before you." ⁹ So Joshua came upon them suddenly, having marched up all night from Gilgal. ¹⁰ And the Lord threw them into a panic before Israel, who¹ struck them with a great blow at Gibeon and chased them by the way of the ascent of Beth-horon and struck them as far as Azekah and Makkedah. ¹¹ And as they fled before Israel, while they were going down the ascent of Beth-horon, the Lord threw down large stones from heaven on them as far as Azekah, and they died. There were more who died because of the hailstones than the sons of Israel killed with the sword.

¹² At that time Joshua spoke to the Lord in the day when the Lord gave the Amorites over to the sons of Israel, and he said in the sight of Israel,

"Sun, stand still at Gibeon,
  and moon, in the Valley of Aijalon."
¹³ And the sun stood still, and the moon stopped,
  until the nation took vengeance on their enemies.

Is this not written in the Book of Jashar? The sun stopped in the midst of heaven and did not hurry to set for about a whole day. ¹⁴ There has been no day like it before or since, when the Lord heeded the voice of a man, for the Lord fought for Israel.

¹⁵ So Joshua returned, and all Israel with him, to the camp at Gilgal.

Five Amorite Kings Executed

¹⁶ These five kings fled and hid themselves in the cave at Makkedah. ¹⁷ And it was told to Joshua, "The five kings have been found, hidden in the cave at Makkedah." ¹⁸ And Joshua said, "Roll large stones against the mouth of the cave and set men by it to guard them, ¹⁹ but do not stay there yourselves. Pursue your enemies; attack their rear guard. Do not let them enter their cities, for the Lord your God has given them into your hand." ²⁰ When Joshua and the sons of Israel had finished striking them with a great blow until they were wiped out, and when the remnant that remained of them

¹ Or *and he*

had entered into the fortified cities, ²¹ then all the people returned safe to Joshua in the camp at Makkedah. Not a man moved his tongue against any of the people of Israel.

²² Then Joshua said, "Open the mouth of the cave and bring those five kings out to me from the cave." ²³ And they did so, and brought those five kings out to him from the cave, the king of Jerusalem, the king of Hebron, the king of Jarmuth, the king of Lachish, and the king of Eglon. ²⁴ And when they brought those kings out to Joshua, Joshua summoned all the men of Israel and said to the chiefs of the men of war who had gone with him, "Come near; put your feet on the necks of these kings." Then they came near and put their feet on their necks. ²⁵ And Joshua said to them, "Do not be afraid or dismayed; be strong and courageous. For thus the Lord will do to all your enemies against whom you fight." ²⁶ And afterward Joshua struck them and put them to death, and he hanged them on five trees. And they hung on the trees until evening. ²⁷ But at the time of the going down of the sun, Joshua commanded, and they took them down from the trees and threw them into the cave where they had hidden themselves, and they set large stones against the mouth of the cave, which remain to this very day.

²⁸ As for Makkedah, Joshua captured it on that day and struck it, and its king, with the edge of the sword. He devoted to destruction every person in it; he left none remaining. And he did to the king of Makkedah just as he had done to the king of Jericho.

Conquest of Southern Canaan

²⁹ Then Joshua and all Israel with him passed on from Makkedah to Libnah and fought against Libnah. ³⁰ And the Lord gave it also and its king into the hand of Israel. And he struck it with the edge of the sword, and every person in it; he left none remaining in it. And he did to its king as he had done to the king of Jericho.

³¹ Then Joshua and all Israel with him passed on from Libnah to Lachish and laid siege to it and fought against it. ³² And the Lord gave Lachish into the hand of Israel, and he captured it on the second day and struck it with the edge of the sword, and every person in it, as he had done to Libnah.

³³ Then Horam king of Gezer came up to help Lachish. And Joshua struck him and his people, until he left none remaining.

³⁴ Then Joshua and all Israel with him passed on from Lachish to Eglon. And they laid siege to it and fought against it. ³⁵ And they captured it on that day, and struck it with the edge of the sword. And he devoted every person in it to destruction that day, as he had done to Lachish.

⁶³⁶ Then Joshua and all Israel with him went up from Eglon to Hebron. And they fought against it ³⁷ and captured it and struck it with the edge of the sword, and its king and its towns, and every person in it. He left none remaining, as he had done to Eglon, and devoted it to destruction and every person in it.

³⁸ Then Joshua and all Israel with him turned back to Debir and fought against it ³⁹ and he captured it with its king and all its towns. And they struck them with the edge of the sword and devoted to destruction every person in it; he left none remaining. Just as he had done to Hebron and to Libnah and its king, so he did to Debir and to its king.

⁴⁰ So Joshua struck the whole land, the hill country and the Negeb and the lowland and the slopes, and all their kings. He left none remaining, but devoted to destruction all that breathed, just as the LORD God of Israel commanded. ⁴¹ And Joshua struck them from Kadesh-barnea as far as Gaza, and all the country of Goshen, as far as Gibeon. ⁴² And Joshua captured all these kings and their land at one time, because the LORD God of Israel fought for Israel. ⁴³ Then Joshua returned, and all Israel with him, to the camp at Gilgal.

Conquests in Northern Canaan

11 When Jabin, king of Hazor, heard of this, he sent to Jobab king of Madon, and to the king of Shimron, and to the king of Achshaph, ² and to the kings who were in the northern hill country, and in the Arabah south of Chinneroth, and in the lowland, and in Naphoth-dor on the west, ³ to the Canaanites in the east and the west, the Amorites, the Hittites, the Perizzites, and the Jebusites in the hill country, and the Hivites under Hermon in the land of Mizpah. ⁴ And they came out with all their troops, a great horde, in number like the sand that is on the seashore, with very many horses and chariots. ⁵ And all these kings joined their forces and came and encamped together at the waters of Merom to fight against Israel.

⁶ And the LORD said to Joshua, "Do not be afraid of them, for tomorrow at this time I will give over all of them, slain, to Israel. You shall hamstring their horses and burn their chariots with fire." ⁷ So Joshua and all his warriors came suddenly against them by the waters of Merom and fell upon them. ⁸ And the LORD gave them into the hand of Israel, who struck them and chased them as far as Great Sidon and Misrephoth-maim, and eastward as far as the Valley of Mizpeh. And they struck them until he left none remaining. ⁹ And Joshua did to them just as the LORD said to him: he hamstrung their horses and burned their chariots with fire.

¹⁰ And Joshua turned back at that time and captured Hazor and struck its king with the sword, for Hazor formerly was the head of all those kingdoms. ¹¹ And they struck with the sword all who were in it, devoting them to destruction;¹ there was none left that breathed. And he burned Hazor with fire. ¹² And all the cities of those kings, and all their kings, Joshua captured, and struck them with the edge of the sword, devoting them to destruction, just as Moses the servant of the LORD had commanded. ¹³ But none of the cities that stood on mounds did Israel burn, except Hazor alone; that Joshua burned. ¹⁴ And all the spoil of these cities and the livestock, the people of Israel took for their plunder. But every person they struck with the edge of the sword until they had destroyed them, and they did not leave any who breathed. ¹⁵ Just as the LORD had commanded Moses his servant, so Moses commanded Joshua, and so Joshua did. He left nothing undone of all that the LORD had commanded Moses.

¹⁶ So Joshua took all that land, the hill country and all the Negeb and all the land of Goshen and the lowland and the Arabah and the hill country of Israel and its lowland ¹⁷ from Mount Halak, which rises toward Seir, as far as Baal-gad in the Valley of Lebanon below Mount Hermon. And he captured all their kings and struck them and put them to death. ¹⁸ Joshua made war a long time with all those kings. ¹⁹ There was not a city that made peace with the people of Israel except the Hivites, the inhabitants of Gibeon. They took them all in battle. ²⁰ For it was the LORD's doing to harden their hearts that they should come against Israel in battle, in order that they should be devoted to destruction and should receive no mercy but be destroyed, just as the LORD commanded Moses.

²¹ And Joshua came at that time and cut off the Anakim from the hill country, from Hebron, from Debir, from Anab, and from all the hill country of Judah, and from all the hill country of Israel. Joshua devoted them to destruction with their cities. ²² There was none of the Anakim left in the land of the people of Israel. Only in Gaza, in Gath, and in Ashdod did some remain. ²³ So Joshua took the whole land, according to all that the LORD had spoken to Moses. And Joshua gave it for an inheritance to Israel according to their tribal allotments. And the land had rest from war.

Kings Defeated by Moses

12 Now these are the kings of the land whom the people of Israel defeated and took possession of their land beyond the Jordan toward the sunrise, from the Valley of the Arnon to Mount Hermon, with all the

---

¹ That is, setting apart (devoting) as an offering to the Lord (for destruction); also verses 12, 20, 21

Arabah eastward: ² Sihon king of the Amorites who lived at Heshbon and ruled from Aroer, which is on the edge of the Valley of the Arnon, and from the middle of the valley as far as the river Jabbok, the boundary of the Ammonites, that is, half of Gilead, ³ and the Arabah to the Sea of Chinneroth eastward, and in the direction of Beth-jeshimoth, to the Sea of the Arabah, the Salt Sea, southward to the foot of the slopes of Pisgah; ⁴ and Og[1] king of Bashan, one of the remnant of the Rephaim, who lived at Ashtaroth and at Edrei ⁵ and ruled over Mount Hermon and Salecah and all Bashan to the boundary of the Geshurites and the Maacathites, and over half of Gilead to the boundary of Sihon king of Heshbon. ⁶ Moses, the servant of the LORD, and the people of Israel defeated them. And Moses the servant of the LORD gave their land for a possession to the Reubenites and the Gadites and the half-tribe of Manasseh.

Kings Defeated by Joshua

⁷ And these are the kings of the land whom Joshua and the people of Israel defeated on the west side of the Jordan, from Baal-gad in the Valley of Lebanon to Mount Halak, that rises toward Seir (and Joshua gave their land to the tribes of Israel as a possession according to their allotments, ⁸ in the hill country, in the lowland, in the Arabah, in the slopes, in the wilderness, and in the Negeb, the land of the Hittites, the Amorites, the Canaanites, the Perizzites, the Hivites, and the Jebusites): ⁹ the king of Jericho, one; the king of Ai, which is beside Bethel, one; ¹⁰ the king of Jerusalem, one; the king of Hebron, one; ¹¹ the king of Jarmuth, one; the king of Lachish, one; ¹² the king of Eglon, one; the king of Gezer, one; ¹³ the king of Debir, one; the king of Geder, one; ¹⁴ the king of Hormah, one; the king of Arad, one; ¹⁵ the king of Libnah, one; the king of Adullam, one; ¹⁶ the king of Makkedah, one; the king of Bethel, one; ¹⁷ the king of Tappuah, one; the king of Hepher, one; ¹⁸ the king of Aphek, one; the king of Lasharon, one; ¹⁹ the king of Madon, one; the king of Hazor, one; ²⁰ the king of Shimron-meron, one; the king of Achshaph, one; ²¹ the king of Taanach, one; the king of Megiddo, one; ²² the king of Kedesh, one; the king of Jokneam in Carmel, one; ²³ the king of Dor in Naphath-dor, one; the king of Goiim in Galilee,[2] one; ²⁴ the king of Tirzah, one: in all, thirty-one kings.

Land Still to Be Conquered

13 Now Joshua was old and advanced in years, and the LORD said to him, "You are old and advanced in years, and there remains yet very much land to possess. ² This is the land that yet remains: all the regions of the

---
[1] Septuagint; Hebrew *the boundary of Og* [2] Septuagint; Hebrew *Gilgal*

Philistines, and all those of the Geshurites ³(from the Shihor, which is east of Egypt, northward to the boundary of Ekron, it is counted as Canaanite; there are five rulers of the Philistines, those of Gaza, Ashdod, Ashkelon, Gath, and Ekron), and those of the Avvim, ⁴in the south, all the land of the Canaanites, and Mearah that belongs to the Sidonians, to Aphek, to the boundary of the Amorites, ⁵and the land of the Gebalites, and all Lebanon, toward the sunrise, from Baal-gad below Mount Hermon to Lebo-hamath, ⁶all the inhabitants of the hill country from Lebanon to Misrephoth-maim, even all the Sidonians. I myself will drive them out from before the people of Israel. Only allot the land to Israel for an inheritance, as I have commanded you. ⁷Now therefore divide this land for an inheritance to the nine tribes and half the tribe of Manasseh."

The Inheritance East of the Jordan

⁸With the other half of the tribe of Manasseh[1] the Reubenites and the Gadites received their inheritance, which Moses gave them, beyond the Jordan eastward, as Moses the servant of the Lord gave them: ⁹from Aroer, which is on the edge of the Valley of the Arnon, and the city that is in the middle of the valley, and all the tableland of Medeba as far as Dibon; ¹⁰and all the cities of Sihon king of the Amorites, who reigned in Heshbon, as far as the boundary of the Ammonites; ¹¹and Gilead, and the region of the Geshurites and Maacathites, and all Mount Hermon, and all Bashan to Salecah; ¹²all the kingdom of Og in Bashan, who reigned in Ashtaroth and in Edrei (he alone was left of the remnant of the Rephaim); these Moses had struck and driven out. ¹³Yet the people of Israel did not drive out the Geshurites or the Maacathites, but Geshur and Maacath dwell in the midst of Israel to this day.

¹⁴To the tribe of Levi alone Moses gave no inheritance. The offerings by fire to the Lord God of Israel are their inheritance, as he said to him.

¹⁵And Moses gave an inheritance to the tribe of the people of Reuben according to their clans. ¹⁶So their territory was from Aroer, which is on the edge of the Valley of the Arnon, and the city that is in the middle of the valley, and all the tableland by Medeba; ¹⁷with Heshbon, and all its cities that are in the tableland; Dibon, and Bamoth-baal, and Beth-baal-meon, ¹⁸and Jahaz, and Kedemoth, and Mephaath, ¹⁹and Kiriathaim, and Sibmah, and Zereth-shahar on the hill of the valley, ²⁰and Beth-peor, and the slopes of Pisgah, and Beth-jeshimoth, ²¹that is, all the cities of the tableland, and all the kingdom of Sihon king of the Amorites, who reigned in Heshbon,

[1] Hebrew *With it*

whom Moses defeated with the leaders of Midian, Evi and Rekem and Zur and Hur and Reba, the princes of Sihon, who lived in the land. ²²Balaam also, the son of Beor, the one who practiced divination, was killed with the sword by the people of Israel among the rest of their slain. ²³And the border of the people of Reuben was the Jordan as a boundary. This was the inheritance of the people of Reuben, according to their clans with their cities and villages.

²⁴Moses gave an inheritance also to the tribe of Gad, to the people of Gad, according to their clans. ²⁵Their territory was Jazer, and all the cities of Gilead, and half the land of the Ammonites, to Aroer, which is east of Rabbah, ²⁶and from Heshbon to Ramath-mizpeh and Betonim, and from Mahanaim to the territory of Debir,¹ ²⁷and in the valley Beth-haram, Beth-nimrah, Succoth, and Zaphon, the rest of the kingdom of Sihon king of Heshbon, having the Jordan as a boundary, to the lower end of the Sea of Chinnereth, eastward beyond the Jordan. ²⁸This is the inheritance of the people of Gad according to their clans, with their cities and villages.

²⁹And Moses gave an inheritance to the half-tribe of Manasseh. It was allotted to the half-tribe of the people of Manasseh according to their clans. ³⁰Their region extended from Mahanaim, through all Bashan, the whole kingdom of Og king of Bashan, and all the towns of Jair, which are in Bashan, sixty cities, ³¹and half Gilead, and Ashtaroth, and Edrei, the cities of the kingdom of Og in Bashan. These were allotted to the people of Machir the son of Manasseh for the half of the people of Machir according to their clans.

³²These are the inheritances that Moses distributed in the plains of Moab, beyond the Jordan east of Jericho. ³³But to the tribe of Levi Moses gave no inheritance; the Lord God of Israel is their inheritance, just as he said to them.

The Inheritance West of the Jordan

14 These are the inheritances that the people of Israel received in the land of Canaan, which Eleazar the priest and Joshua the son of Nun and the heads of the fathers' houses of the tribes of the people of Israel gave them to inherit. ²Their inheritance was by lot, just as the Lord had commanded by the hand of Moses for the nine and one-half tribes. ³For Moses had given an inheritance to the two and one-half tribes beyond the Jordan, but to the Levites he gave no inheritance among them. ⁴For the people of Joseph were two tribes, Manasseh and Ephraim. And no portion was given to the Levites in the land, but only cities to dwell in, with their pasturelands for their livestock and their substance. ⁵The people of Israel did as the Lord commanded Moses; they allotted the land.

¹ Septuagint, Syriac, Vulgate; Hebrew *Lidebir*

Caleb's Request and Inheritance

⁶ Then the people of Judah came to Joshua at Gilgal. And Caleb the son of Jephunneh the Kenizzite said to him, "You know what the Lord said to Moses the man of God in Kadesh-barnea concerning you and me. ⁷ I was forty years old when Moses the servant of the Lord sent me from Kadesh-barnea to spy out the land, and I brought him word again as it was in my heart. ⁸ But my brothers who went up with me made the heart of the people melt; yet I wholly followed the Lord my God. ⁹ And Moses swore on that day, saying, 'Surely the land on which your foot has trodden shall be an inheritance for you and your children forever, because you have wholly followed the Lord my God.' ¹⁰ And now, behold, the Lord has kept me alive, just as he said, these forty-five years since the time that the Lord spoke this word to Moses, while Israel walked in the wilderness. And now, behold, I am this day eighty-five years old. ¹¹ I am still as strong today as I was in the day that Moses sent me; my strength now is as my strength was then, for war and for going and coming. ¹² So now give me this hill country of which the Lord spoke on that day, for you heard on that day how the Anakim were there, with great fortified cities. It may be that the Lord will be with me, and I shall drive them out just as the Lord said."

¹³ Then Joshua blessed him, and he gave Hebron to Caleb the son of Jephunneh for an inheritance. ¹⁴ Therefore Hebron became the inheritance of Caleb the son of Jephunneh the Kenizzite to this day, because he wholly followed the Lord, the God of Israel. ¹⁵ Now the name of Hebron formerly was Kiriath-arba.¹ (Arba² was the greatest man among the Anakim.) And the land had rest from war.

The Allotment for Judah

15 The allotment for the tribe of the people of Judah according to their clans reached southward to the boundary of Edom, to the wilderness of Zin at the farthest south. ² And their south boundary ran from the end of the Salt Sea, from the bay that faces southward. ³ It goes out southward of the ascent of Akrabbim, passes along to Zin, and goes up south of Kadesh-barnea, along by Hezron, up to Addar, turns about to Karka, ⁴ passes along to Azmon, goes out by the Brook of Egypt, and comes to its end at the sea. This shall be your south boundary. ⁵ And the east boundary is the Salt Sea, to the mouth of the Jordan. And the boundary on the north side runs from the bay of the sea at the mouth of the Jordan. ⁶ And the boundary goes up to Beth-hoglah and passes along north of Beth-arabah. And the boundary goes

---

¹ *Kiriath-arba* means *the city of Arba* ² Hebrew *He*

up to the stone of Bohan the son of Reuben. ⁷ And the boundary goes up to Debir from the Valley of Achor, and so northward, turning toward Gilgal, which is opposite the ascent of Adummim, which is on the south side of the valley. And the boundary passes along to the waters of En-shemesh and ends at En-rogel. ⁸ Then the boundary goes up by the Valley of the Son of Hinnom at the southern shoulder of the Jebusite (that is, Jerusalem). And the boundary goes up to the top of the mountain that lies over against the Valley of Hinnom, on the west, at the northern end of the Valley of Rephaim. ⁹ Then the boundary extends from the top of the mountain to the spring of the waters of Nephtoah, and from there to the cities of Mount Ephron. Then the boundary bends around to Baalah (that is, Kiriath-jearim). ¹⁰ And the boundary circles west of Baalah to Mount Seir, passes along to the northern shoulder of Mount Jearim (that is, Chesalon), and goes down to Beth-shemesh and passes along by Timnah. ¹¹ The boundary goes out to the shoulder of the hill north of Ekron, then the boundary bends around to Shikkeron and passes along to Mount Baalah and goes out to Jabneel. Then the boundary comes to an end at the sea. ¹² And the west boundary was the Great Sea with its coastline. This is the boundary around the people of Judah according to their clans.

¹³ According to the commandment of the Lord to Joshua, he gave to Caleb the son of Jephunneh a portion among the people of Judah, Kiriath-arba, that is, Hebron (Arba was the father of Anak). ¹⁴ And Caleb drove out from there the three sons of Anak, Sheshai and Ahiman and Talmai, the descendants of Anak. ¹⁵ And he went up from there against the inhabitants of Debir. Now the name of Debir formerly was Kiriath-sepher. ¹⁶ And Caleb said, "He who attacks Kiriath-sepher and captures it, I will give him Achsah my daughter as wife." ¹⁷ And Othniel the son of Kenaz, the brother of Caleb, captured it. And he gave him Achsah his daughter as wife. ¹⁸ When she came to him, she urged him to ask her father for a field. And she dismounted from her donkey, and Caleb said to her, "What do you want?" ¹⁹ She said to him, "Give me a blessing. Since you have given me the land of the Negeb, give me also springs of water." And he gave her the upper springs and the lower springs.

²⁰ This is the inheritance of the tribe of the people of Judah according to their clans. ²¹ The cities belonging to the tribe of the people of Judah in the extreme south, toward the boundary of Edom, were Kabzeel, Eder, Jagur, ²² Kinah, Dimonah, Adadah, ²³ Kedesh, Hazor, Ithnan, ²⁴ Ziph, Telem, Bealoth, ²⁵ Hazor-hadattah, Kerioth-hezron (that is, Hazor), ²⁶ Amam, Shema, Moladah, ²⁷ Hazar-gaddah, Heshmon, Beth-pelet, ²⁸ Hazar-shual, Beersheba, Biziothiah, ²⁹ Baalah, Iim, Ezem, ³⁰ Eltolad, Chesil, Hormah, ³¹ Ziklag, Madmannah,

Sansannah, ³²Lebaoth, Shilhim, Ain, and Rimmon: in all, twenty-nine cities with their villages.

³³And in the lowland, Eshtaol, Zorah, Ashnah, ³⁴Zanoah, En-gannim, Tappuah, Enam, ³⁵Jarmuth, Adullam, Socoh, Azekah, ³⁶Shaaraim, Adithaim, Gederah, Gederothaim: fourteen cities with their villages.

³⁷Zenan, Hadashah, Migdal-gad, ³⁸Dilean, Mizpeh, Joktheel, ³⁹Lachish, Bozkath, Eglon, ⁴⁰Cabbon, Lahmam, Chitlish, ⁴¹Gederoth, Beth-dagon, Naamah, and Makkedah: sixteen cities with their villages.

⁴²Libnah, Ether, Ashan, ⁴³Iphtah, Ashnah, Nezib, ⁴⁴Keilah, Achzib, and Mareshah: nine cities with their villages.

⁴⁵Ekron, with its towns and its villages; ⁴⁶from Ekron to the sea, all that were by the side of Ashdod, with their villages.

⁴⁷Ashdod, its towns and its villages; Gaza, its towns and its villages; to the Brook of Egypt, and the Great Sea with its coastline.

⁴⁸And in the hill country, Shamir, Jattir, Socoh, ⁴⁹Dannah, Kiriath-sannah (that is, Debir), ⁵⁰Anab, Eshtemoh, Anim, ⁵¹Goshen, Holon, and Giloh: eleven cities with their villages.

⁵²Arab, Dumah, Eshan, ⁵³Janim, Beth-tappuah, Aphekah, ⁵⁴Humtah, Kiriath-arba (that is, Hebron), and Zior: nine cities with their villages.

⁵⁵Maon, Carmel, Ziph, Juttah, ⁵⁶Jezreel, Jokdeam, Zanoah, ⁵⁷Kain, Gibeah, and Timnah: ten cities with their villages.

⁵⁸Halhul, Beth-zur, Gedor, ⁵⁹Maarath, Beth-anoth, and Eltekon: six cities with their villages.

⁶⁰Kiriath-baal (that is, Kiriath-jearim), and Rabbah: two cities with their villages.

⁶¹In the wilderness, Beth-arabah, Middin, Secacah, ⁶²Nibshan, the City of Salt, and Engedi: six cities with their villages.

⁶³But the Jebusites, the inhabitants of Jerusalem, the people of Judah could not drive out, so the Jebusites dwell with the people of Judah at Jerusalem to this day.

The Allotment for Ephraim and Manasseh

16 The allotment of the people of Joseph went from the Jordan by Jericho, east of the waters of Jericho, into the wilderness, going up from Jericho into the hill country to Bethel. ²Then going from Bethel to Luz, it passes along to Ataroth, the territory of the Archites. ³Then it goes down westward to the territory of the Japhletites, as far as the territory of Lower Beth-horon, then to Gezer, and it ends at the sea.

⁴The people of Joseph, Manasseh and Ephraim, received their inheritance.

⁵ The territory of the people of Ephraim by their clans was as follows: the boundary of their inheritance on the east was Ataroth-addar as far as Upper Beth-horon, ⁶ and the boundary goes from there to the sea. On the north is Michmethath. Then on the east the boundary turns around toward Taanath-shiloh and passes along beyond it on the east to Janoah, ⁷ then it goes down from Janoah to Ataroth and to Naarah, and touches Jericho, ending at the Jordan. ⁸ From Tappuah the boundary goes westward to the brook Kanah and ends at the sea. Such is the inheritance of the tribe of the people of Ephraim by their clans, ⁹ together with the towns that were set apart for the people of Ephraim within the inheritance of the Manassites, all those towns with their villages. ¹⁰ However, they did not drive out the Canaanites who lived in Gezer, so the Canaanites have lived in the midst of Ephraim to this day but have been made to do forced labor.

17

Then allotment was made to the people of Manasseh, for he was the firstborn of Joseph. To Machir the firstborn of Manasseh, the father of Gilead, were allotted Gilead and Bashan, because he was a man of war. ² And allotments were made to the rest of the people of Manasseh by their clans, Abiezer, Helek, Asriel, Shechem, Hepher, and Shemida. These were the male descendants of Manasseh the son of Joseph, by their clans.

³ Now Zelophehad the son of Hepher, son of Gilead, son of Machir, son of Manasseh, had no sons, but only daughters, and these are the names of his daughters: Mahlah, Noah, Hoglah, Milcah, and Tirzah. ⁴ They approached Eleazar the priest and Joshua the son of Nun and the leaders and said, "The Lord commanded Moses to give us an inheritance along with our brothers." So according to the mouth of the Lord he gave them an inheritance among the brothers of their father. ⁵ Thus there fell to Manasseh ten portions, besides the land of Gilead and Bashan, which is on the other side of the Jordan, ⁶ because the daughters of Manasseh received an inheritance along with his sons. The land of Gilead was allotted to the rest of the people of Manasseh.

⁷ The territory of Manasseh reached from Asher to Michmethath, which is east of Shechem. Then the boundary goes along southward to the inhabitants of En-tappuah. ⁸ The land of Tappuah belonged to Manasseh, but the town of Tappuah on the boundary of Manasseh belonged to the people of Ephraim. ⁹ Then the boundary went down to the brook Kanah. These cities, to the south of the brook, among the cities of Manasseh, belong to Ephraim. Then the boundary of Manasseh goes on the north side of the brook and ends at the sea, ¹⁰ the land to the south being Ephraim's and that to the north being Manasseh's, with the sea forming its boundary. On the north Asher is reached, and on the east Issachar. ¹¹ Also in Issachar and in Asher

Manasseh had Beth-shean and its villages, and Ibleam and its villages, and the inhabitants of Dor and its villages, and the inhabitants of En-dor and its villages, and the inhabitants of Taanach and its villages, and the inhabitants of Megiddo and its villages; the third is Naphath.[1] ¹² Yet the people of Manasseh could not take possession of those cities, but the Canaanites persisted in dwelling in that land. ¹³ Now when the people of Israel grew strong, they put the Canaanites to forced labor, but did not utterly drive them out.

¹⁴ Then the people of Joseph spoke to Joshua, saying, "Why have you given me but one lot and one portion as an inheritance, although I am a numerous people, since all along the LORD has blessed me?" ¹⁵ And Joshua said to them, "If you are a numerous people, go up by yourselves to the forest, and there clear ground for yourselves in the land of the Perizzites and the Rephaim, since the hill country of Ephraim is too narrow for you." ¹⁶ The people of Joseph said, "The hill country is not enough for us. Yet all the Canaanites who dwell in the plain have chariots of iron, both those in Beth-shean and its villages and those in the Valley of Jezreel." ¹⁷ Then Joshua said to the house of Joseph, to Ephraim and Manasseh, "You are a numerous people and have great power. You shall not have one allotment only, ¹⁸ but the hill country shall be yours, for though it is a forest, you shall clear it and possess it to its farthest borders. For you shall drive out the Canaanites, though they have chariots of iron, and though they are strong."

Allotment of the Remaining Land

18 Then the whole congregation of the people of Israel assembled at Shiloh and set up the tent of meeting there. The land lay subdued before them.

² There remained among the people of Israel seven tribes whose inheritance had not yet been apportioned. ³ So Joshua said to the people of Israel, "How long will you put off going in to take possession of the land, which the LORD, the God of your fathers, has given you? ⁴ Provide three men from each tribe, and I will send them out that they may set out and go up and down the land. They shall write a description of it with a view to their inheritances, and then come to me. ⁵ They shall divide it into seven portions. Judah shall continue in his territory on the south, and the house of Joseph shall continue in their territory on the north. ⁶ And you shall describe the land in seven divisions and bring the description here to me. And I will cast lots for you here before the LORD our God. ⁷ The Levites have no portion among you, for the priesthood

[1] The meaning of the Hebrew is uncertain

of the LORD is their heritage. And Gad and Reuben and half the tribe of Manasseh have received their inheritance beyond the Jordan eastward, which Moses the servant of the LORD gave them."

⁸ So the men arose and went, and Joshua charged those who went to write the description of the land, saying, "Go up and down in the land and write a description and return to me. And I will cast lots for you here before the LORD in Shiloh." ⁹ So the men went and passed up and down in the land and wrote in a book a description of it by towns in seven divisions. Then they came to Joshua to the camp at Shiloh, ¹⁰ and Joshua cast lots for them in Shiloh before the LORD. And there Joshua apportioned the land to the people of Israel, to each his portion.

The Inheritance for Benjamin

¹¹ The lot of the tribe of the people of Benjamin according to its clans came up, and the territory allotted to it fell between the people of Judah and the people of Joseph. ¹² On the north side their boundary began at the Jordan. Then the boundary goes up to the shoulder north of Jericho, then up through the hill country westward, and it ends at the wilderness of Beth-aven. ¹³ From there the boundary passes along southward in the direction of Luz, to the shoulder of Luz (that is, Bethel), then the boundary goes down to Ataroth-addar, on the mountain that lies south of Lower Beth-horon. ¹⁴ Then the boundary goes in another direction, turning on the western side southward from the mountain that lies to the south, opposite Beth-horon, and it ends at Kiriath-baal (that is, Kiriath-jearim), a city belonging to the people of Judah. This forms the western side. ¹⁵ And the southern side begins at the outskirts of Kiriath-jearim. And the boundary goes from there to Ephron,¹ to the spring of the waters of Nephtoah. ¹⁶ Then the boundary goes down to the border of the mountain that overlooks the Valley of the Son of Hinnom, which is at the north end of the Valley of Rephaim. And it then goes down the Valley of Hinnom, south of the shoulder of the Jebusites, and downward to En-rogel. ¹⁷ Then it bends in a northerly direction going on to En-shemesh, and from there goes to Geliloth, which is opposite the ascent of Adummim. Then it goes down to the stone of Bohan the son of Reuben, ¹⁸ and passing on to the north of the shoulder of Beth-arabah² it goes down to the Arabah. ¹⁹ Then the boundary passes on to the north of the shoulder of Beth-hoglah. And the boundary ends at the northern bay of the Salt Sea, at the south end of the Jordan: this is the southern border. ²⁰ The Jordan forms its boundary on the eastern side.

---

¹ See 15:9; Hebrew *westward* ² Septuagint; Hebrew *to the shoulder over against the Arabah*

This is the inheritance of the people of Benjamin, according to their clans, boundary by boundary all around.

²¹ Now the cities of the tribe of the people of Benjamin according to their clans were Jericho, Beth-hoglah, Emek-keziz, ²² Beth-arabah, Zemaraim, Bethel, ²³ Avvim, Parah, Ophrah, ²⁴ Chephar-ammoni, Ophni, Geba—twelve cities with their villages: ²⁵ Gibeon, Ramah, Beeroth, ²⁶ Mizpeh, Chephirah, Mozah, ²⁷ Rekem, Irpeel, Taralah, ²⁸ Zela, Haeleph, Jebus[1] (that is, Jerusalem), Gibeah[2] and Kiriath-jearim[3]—fourteen cities with their villages. This is the inheritance of the people of Benjamin according to its clans.

The Inheritance for Simeon

19

The second lot came out for Simeon, for the tribe of the people of Simeon, according to their clans, and their inheritance was in the midst of the inheritance of the people of Judah. ² And they had for their inheritance Beersheba, Sheba, Moladah, ³ Hazar-shual, Balah, Ezem, ⁴ Eltolad, Bethul, Hormah, ⁵ Ziklag, Beth-marcaboth, Hazar-susah, ⁶ Beth-lebaoth, and Sharuhen—thirteen cities with their villages; ⁷ Ain, Rimmon, Ether, and Ashan—four cities with their villages, ⁸ together with all the villages around these cities as far as Baalath-beer, Ramah of the Negeb. This was the inheritance of the tribe of the people of Simeon according to their clans. ⁹ The inheritance of the people of Simeon formed part of the territory of the people of Judah. Because the portion of the people of Judah was too large for them, the people of Simeon obtained an inheritance in the midst of their inheritance.

The Inheritance for Zebulun

¹⁰ The third lot came up for the people of Zebulun, according to their clans. And the territory of their inheritance reached as far as Sarid. ¹¹ Then their boundary goes up westward and on to Mareal and touches Dabbesheth, then the brook that is east of Jokneam. ¹² From Sarid it goes in the other direction eastward toward the sunrise to the boundary of Chisloth-tabor. From there it goes to Daberath, then up to Japhia. ¹³ From there it passes along on the east toward the sunrise to Gath-hepher, to Eth-kazin, and going on to Rimmon it bends toward Neah, ¹⁴ then on the north the boundary turns about to Hannathon, and it ends at the Valley of Iphtahel; ¹⁵ and Kattath, Nahalal, Shimron, Idalah, and Bethlehem—twelve cities with their villages. ¹⁶ This is the inheritance of the people of Zebulun, according to their clans—these cities with their villages.

[1] Septuagint, Syriac, Vulgate; Hebrew *the Jebusite* [2] Hebrew *Gibeath* [3] Septuagint; Hebrew *Kiriath*

The Inheritance for Issachar

¹⁷ The fourth lot came out for Issachar, for the people of Issachar, according to their clans. ¹⁸ Their territory included Jezreel, Chesulloth, Shunem, ¹⁹ Hapharaim, Shion, Anaharath, ²⁰ Rabbith, Kishion, Ebez, ²¹ Remeth, En-gannim, En-haddah, Beth-pazzez. ²² The boundary also touches Tabor, Shahazumah, and Beth-shemesh, and its boundary ends at the Jordan—sixteen cities with their villages. ²³ This is the inheritance of the tribe of the people of Issachar, according to their clans—the cities with their villages.

The Inheritance for Asher

²⁴ The fifth lot came out for the tribe of the people of Asher according to their clans. ²⁵ Their territory included Helkath, Hali, Beten, Achshaph, ²⁶ Allammelech, Amad, and Mishal. On the west it touches Carmel and Shihor-libnath, ²⁷ then it turns eastward, it goes to Beth-dagon, and touches Zebulun and the Valley of Iphtahel northward to Beth-emek and Neiel. Then it continues in the north to Cabul, ²⁸ Ebron, Rehob, Hammon, Kanah, as far as Sidon the Great. ²⁹ Then the boundary turns to Ramah, reaching to the fortified city of Tyre. Then the boundary turns to Hosah, and it ends at the sea; Mahalab,[1] Achzib, ³⁰ Ummah, Aphek and Rehob—twenty-two cities with their villages. ³¹ This is the inheritance of the tribe of the people of Asher according to their clans—these cities with their villages.

The Inheritance for Naphtali

³² The sixth lot came out for the people of Naphtali, for the people of Naphtali, according to their clans. ³³ And their boundary ran from Heleph, from the oak in Zaanannim, and Adami-nekeb, and Jabneel, as far as Lakkum, and it ended at the Jordan. ³⁴ Then the boundary turns westward to Aznoth-tabor and goes from there to Hukkok, touching Zebulun at the south and Asher on the west and Judah on the east at the Jordan. ³⁵ The fortified cities are Ziddim, Zer, Hammath, Rakkath, Chinnereth, ³⁶ Adamah, Ramah, Hazor, ³⁷ Kedesh, Edrei, En-hazor, ³⁸ Yiron, Migdal-el, Horem, Beth-anath, and Beth-shemesh—nineteen cities with their villages. ³⁹ This is the inheritance of the tribe of the people of Naphtali according to their clans—the cities with their villages.

The Inheritance for Dan

⁴⁰ The seventh lot came out for the tribe of the people of Dan, according to their clans. ⁴¹ And the territory of its inheritance included Zorah, Eshtaol,

---

[1] Compare Septuagint; Hebrew *Mehebel*

Ir-shemesh, ⁴²Shaalabbin, Aijalon, Ithlah, ⁴³Elon, Timnah, Ekron, ⁴⁴Eltekeh, Gibbethon, Baalath, ⁴⁵Jehud, Bene-berak, Gath-rimmon, ⁴⁶and Me-jarkon and Rakkon with the territory over against Joppa. ⁴⁷When the territory of the people of Dan was lost to them, the people of Dan went up and fought against Leshem, and after capturing it and striking it with the sword they took possession of it and settled in it, calling Leshem, Dan, after the name of Dan their ancestor. ⁴⁸This is the inheritance of the tribe of the people of Dan, according to their clans—these cities with their villages.

The Inheritance for Joshua

⁴⁹When they had finished distributing the several territories of the land as inheritances, the people of Israel gave an inheritance among them to Joshua the son of Nun. ⁵⁰By command of the Lord they gave him the city that he asked, Timnath-serah in the hill country of Ephraim. And he rebuilt the city and settled in it.

⁵¹These are the inheritances that Eleazar the priest and Joshua the son of Nun and the heads of the fathers' houses of the tribes of the people of Israel distributed by lot at Shiloh before the Lord, at the entrance of the tent of meeting. So they finished dividing the land.

The Cities of Refuge

20 Then the Lord said to Joshua, ²"Say to the people of Israel, 'Appoint the cities of refuge, of which I spoke to you through Moses, ³that the manslayer who strikes any person without intent or unknowingly may flee there. They shall be for you a refuge from the avenger of blood. ⁴He shall flee to one of these cities and shall stand at the entrance of the gate of the city and explain his case to the elders of that city. Then they shall take him into the city and give him a place, and he shall remain with them. ⁵And if the avenger of blood pursues him, they shall not give up the manslayer into his hand, because he struck his neighbor unknowingly, and did not hate him in the past. ⁶And he shall remain in that city until he has stood before the congregation for judgment, until the death of him who is high priest at the time. Then the manslayer may return to his own town and his own home, to the town from which he fled.'"

⁷So they set apart Kedesh in Galilee in the hill country of Naphtali, and Shechem in the hill country of Ephraim, and Kiriath-arba (that is, Hebron) in the hill country of Judah. ⁸And beyond the Jordan east of Jericho, they appointed Bezer in the wilderness on the tableland, from the tribe of Reuben, and Ramoth in Gilead, from the tribe of Gad, and Golan in Bashan, from

the tribe of Manasseh. ⁹These were the cities designated for all the people of Israel and for the stranger sojourning among them, that anyone who killed a person without intent could flee there, so that he might not die by the hand of the avenger of blood, till he stood before the congregation.

Cities and Pasturelands Allotted to Levi

21 Then the heads of the fathers' houses of the Levites came to Eleazar the priest and to Joshua the son of Nun and to the heads of the fathers' houses of the tribes of the people of Israel. ²And they said to them at Shiloh in the land of Canaan, "The Lord commanded through Moses that we be given cities to dwell in, along with their pasturelands for our livestock." ³So by command of the Lord the people of Israel gave to the Levites the following cities and pasturelands out of their inheritance.

⁴The lot came out for the clans of the Kohathites. So those Levites who were descendants of Aaron the priest received by lot from the tribes of Judah, Simeon, and Benjamin, thirteen cities.

⁵And the rest of the Kohathites received by lot from the clans of the tribe of Ephraim, from the tribe of Dan and the half-tribe of Manasseh, ten cities.

⁶The Gershonites received by lot from the clans of the tribe of Issachar, from the tribe of Asher, from the tribe of Naphtali, and from the half-tribe of Manasseh in Bashan, thirteen cities.

⁷The Merarites according to their clans received from the tribe of Reuben, the tribe of Gad, and the tribe of Zebulun, twelve cities.

⁸These cities and their pasturelands the people of Israel gave by lot to the Levites, as the Lord had commanded through Moses.

⁹Out of the tribe of the people of Judah and the tribe of the people of Simeon they gave the following cities mentioned by name, ¹⁰which went to the descendants of Aaron, one of the clans of the Kohathites who belonged to the people of Levi; since the lot fell to them first. ¹¹They gave them Kiriath-arba (Arba being the father of Anak), that is Hebron, in the hill country of Judah, along with the pasturelands around it. ¹²But the fields of the city and its villages had been given to Caleb the son of Jephunneh as his possession.

¹³And to the descendants of Aaron the priest they gave Hebron, the city of refuge for the manslayer, with its pasturelands, Libnah with its pasturelands, ¹⁴Jattir with its pasturelands, Eshtemoa with its pasturelands, ¹⁵Holon with its pasturelands, Debir with its pasturelands, ¹⁶Ain with its pasturelands, Juttah with its pasturelands, Beth-shemesh with its pasturelands—nine cities out of these two tribes; ¹⁷then out of the tribe of Benjamin, Gibeon with its pasturelands, Geba with its pasturelands, ¹⁸Anathoth with its pasturelands,

and Almon with its pasturelands—four cities. ¹⁹ The cities of the descendants of Aaron, the priests, were in all thirteen cities with their pasturelands.

²⁰ As to the rest of the Kohathites belonging to the Kohathite clans of the Levites, the cities allotted to them were out of the tribe of Ephraim. ²¹ To them were given Shechem, the city of refuge for the manslayer, with its pasturelands in the hill country of Ephraim, Gezer with its pasturelands, ²² Kibzaim with its pasturelands, Beth-horon with its pasturelands—four cities; ²³ and out of the tribe of Dan, Elteke with its pasturelands, Gibbethon with its pasturelands, ²⁴ Aijalon with its pasturelands, Gath-rimmon with its pasturelands—four cities; ²⁵ and out of the half-tribe of Manasseh, Taanach with its pasturelands, and Gath-rimmon with its pasturelands—two cities. ²⁶ The cities of the clans of the rest of the Kohathites were ten in all with their pasturelands.

²⁷ And to the Gershonites, one of the clans of the Levites, were given out of the half-tribe of Manasseh, Golan in Bashan with its pasturelands, the city of refuge for the manslayer, and Beeshterah with its pasturelands—two cities; ²⁸ and out of the tribe of Issachar, Kishion with its pasturelands, Daberath with its pasturelands, ²⁹ Jarmuth with its pasturelands, En-gannim with its pasturelands—four cities; ³⁰ and out of the tribe of Asher, Mishal with its pasturelands, Abdon with its pasturelands, ³¹ Helkath with its pasturelands, and Rehob with its pasturelands—four cities; ³² and out of the tribe of Naphtali, Kedesh in Galilee with its pasturelands, the city of refuge for the manslayer, Hammoth-dor with its pasturelands, and Kartan with its pasturelands—three cities. ³³ The cities of the several clans of the Gershonites were in all thirteen cities with their pasturelands.

³⁴ And to the rest of the Levites, the Merarite clans, were given out of the tribe of Zebulun, Jokneam with its pasturelands, Kartah with its pasturelands, ³⁵ Dimnah with its pasturelands, Nahalal with its pasturelands—four cities; ³⁶ and out of the tribe of Reuben, Bezer with its pasturelands, Jahaz with its pasturelands, ³⁷ Kedemoth with its pasturelands, and Mephaath with its pasturelands—four cities; ³⁸ and out of the tribe of Gad, Ramoth in Gilead with its pasturelands, the city of refuge for the manslayer, Mahanaim with its pasturelands, ³⁹ Heshbon with its pasturelands, Jazer with its pasturelands—four cities in all. ⁴⁰ As for the cities of the several Merarite clans, that is, the remainder of the clans of the Levites, those allotted to them were in all twelve cities.

⁴¹ The cities of the Levites in the midst of the possession of the people of Israel were in all forty-eight cities with their pasturelands. ⁴² These cities each had its pasturelands around it. So it was with all these cities.

⁴³ Thus the Lord gave to Israel all the land that he swore to give to their fathers. And they took possession of it, and they settled there. ⁴⁴ And the Lord gave them rest on every side just as he had sworn to their fathers. Not one of all their enemies had withstood them, for the Lord had given all their enemies into their hands. ⁴⁵ Not one word of all the good promises that the Lord had made to the house of Israel had failed; all came to pass.

The Eastern Tribes Return Home

22 At that time Joshua summoned the Reubenites and the Gadites and the half-tribe of Manasseh, ² and said to them, "You have kept all that Moses the servant of the Lord commanded you and have obeyed my voice in all that I have commanded you. ³ You have not forsaken your brothers these many days, down to this day, but have been careful to keep the charge of the Lord your God. ⁴ And now the Lord your God has given rest to your brothers, as he promised them. Therefore turn and go to your tents in the land where your possession lies, which Moses the servant of the Lord gave you on the other side of the Jordan. ⁵ Only be very careful to observe the commandment and the law that Moses the servant of the Lord commanded you, to love the Lord your God, and to walk in all his ways and to keep his commandments and to cling to him and to serve him with all your heart and with all your soul." ⁶ So Joshua blessed them and sent them away, and they went to their tents.

⁷ Now to the one half of the tribe of Manasseh Moses had given a possession in Bashan, but to the other half Joshua had given a possession beside their brothers in the land west of the Jordan. And when Joshua sent them away to their homes and blessed them, ⁸ he said to them, "Go back to your tents with much wealth and with very much livestock, with silver, gold, bronze, and iron, and with much clothing. Divide the spoil of your enemies with your brothers." ⁹ So the people of Reuben and the people of Gad and the half-tribe of Manasseh returned home, parting from the people of Israel at Shiloh, which is in the land of Canaan, to go to the land of Gilead, their own land of which they had possessed themselves by command of the Lord through Moses.

The Eastern Tribes' Altar of Witness

¹⁰ And when they came to the region of the Jordan that is in the land of Canaan, the people of Reuben and the people of Gad and the half-tribe of Manasseh built there an altar by the Jordan, an altar of imposing size. ¹¹ And the people of Israel heard it said, "Behold, the people of Reuben and

the people of Gad and the half-tribe of Manasseh have built the altar at the frontier of the land of Canaan, in the region about the Jordan, on the side that belongs to the people of Israel." ¹² And when the people of Israel heard of it, the whole assembly of the people of Israel gathered at Shiloh to make war against them.

¹³ Then the people of Israel sent to the people of Reuben and the people of Gad and the half-tribe of Manasseh, in the land of Gilead, Phinehas the son of Eleazar the priest, ¹⁴ and with him ten chiefs, one from each of the tribal families of Israel, every one of them the head of a family among the clans of Israel. ¹⁵ And they came to the people of Reuben, the people of Gad, and the half-tribe of Manasseh, in the land of Gilead, and they said to them, ¹⁶ "Thus says the whole congregation of the Lord, 'What is this breach of faith that you have committed against the God of Israel in turning away this day from following the Lord by building yourselves an altar this day in rebellion against the Lord? ¹⁷ Have we not had enough of the sin at Peor from which even yet we have not cleansed ourselves, and for which there came a plague upon the congregation of the Lord, ¹⁸ that you too must turn away this day from following the Lord? And if you too rebel against the Lord today then tomorrow he will be angry with the whole congregation of Israel. ¹⁹ But now, if the land of your possession is unclean, pass over into the Lord's land where the Lord's tabernacle stands, and take for yourselves a possession among us. Only do not rebel against the Lord or make us as rebels by building for yourselves an altar other than the altar of the Lord our God. ²⁰ Did not Achan the son of Zerah break faith in the matter of the devoted things, and wrath fell upon all the congregation of Israel? And he did not perish alone for his iniquity.'"

²¹ Then the people of Reuben, the people of Gad, and the half-tribe of Manasseh said in answer to the heads of the families of Israel, ²² "The Mighty One, God, the Lord! The Mighty One, God, the Lord! He knows; and let Israel itself know! If it was in rebellion or in breach of faith against the Lord, do not spare us today ²³ for building an altar to turn away from following the Lord. Or if we did so to offer burnt offerings or grain offerings or peace offerings on it, may the Lord himself take vengeance. ²⁴ No, but we did it from fear that in time to come your children might say to our children, 'What have you to do with the Lord, the God of Israel? ²⁵ For the Lord has made the Jordan a boundary between us and you, you people of Reuben and people of Gad. You have no portion in the Lord.' So your children might make our children cease to worship the Lord. ²⁶ Therefore we said, 'Let us now build an altar, not for burnt offering, nor for sacrifice, ²⁷ but

to be a witness between us and you, and between our generations after us, that we do perform the service of the Lord in his presence with our burnt offerings and sacrifices and peace offerings, so your children will not say to our children in time to come, "You have no portion in the Lord."' ²⁸ And we thought, 'If this should be said to us or to our descendants in time to come, we should say, "Behold, the copy of the altar of the Lord, which our fathers made, not for burnt offerings, nor for sacrifice, but to be a witness between us and you."' ²⁹ Far be it from us that we should rebel against the Lord and turn away this day from following the Lord by building an altar for burnt offering, grain offering, or sacrifice, other than the altar of the Lord our God that stands before his tabernacle!"

³⁰ When Phinehas the priest and the chiefs of the congregation, the heads of the families of Israel who were with him, heard the words that the people of Reuben and the people of Gad and the people of Manasseh spoke, it was good in their eyes. ³¹ And Phinehas the son of Eleazar the priest said to the people of Reuben and the people of Gad and the people of Manasseh, "Today we know that the Lord is in our midst, because you have not committed this breach of faith against the Lord. Now you have delivered the people of Israel from the hand of the Lord."

³² Then Phinehas the son of Eleazar the priest, and the chiefs, returned from the people of Reuben and the people of Gad in the land of Gilead to the land of Canaan, to the people of Israel, and brought back word to them. ³³ And the report was good in the eyes of the people of Israel. And the people of Israel blessed God and spoke no more of making war against them to destroy the land where the people of Reuben and the people of Gad were settled. ³⁴ The people of Reuben and the people of Gad called the altar Witness, "For," they said, "it is a witness between us that the Lord is God."

Joshua's Charge to Israel's Leaders

23 A long time afterward, when the Lord had given rest to Israel from all their surrounding enemies, and Joshua was old and well advanced in years, ² Joshua summoned all Israel, its elders and heads, its judges and officers, and said to them, "I am now old and well advanced in years. ³ And you have seen all that the Lord your God has done to all these nations for your sake, for it is the Lord your God who has fought for you. ⁴ Behold, I have allotted to you as an inheritance for your tribes those nations that remain, along with all the nations that I have already cut off, from the Jordan to the Great Sea in the west. ⁵ The Lord your God will push them back before you and drive them out of your sight. And you shall possess their land, just as the LORD your God promised you. ⁶ Therefore, be very strong to keep and to do all that is written in the Book of the Law of Moses, turning aside from it neither to the right hand nor to the left, ⁷ that you may not mix with these nations remaining among you or make mention of the names of their gods or swear by them or serve them or bow down to them, ⁸ but you shall cling to the LORD your God just as you have done to this day. ⁹ For the LORD has driven out before you great and strong nations. And as for you, no man has been able to stand before you to this day. ¹⁰ One man of you puts to flight a thousand, since it is the LORD your God who fights for you, just as he promised you. ¹¹ Be very careful, therefore, to love the LORD your God. ¹² For if you turn back and cling to the remnant of these nations remaining among you and make marriages with them, so that you associate with them and they with you, ¹³ know for certain that the LORD your God will no longer drive out these nations before you, but they shall be a snare and a trap for you, a whip on your sides and thorns in your eyes, until you perish from off this good ground that the LORD your God has given you.

¹⁴ "And now I am about to go the way of all the earth, and you know in your hearts and souls, all of you, that not one word has failed of all the good things[1] that the LORD your God promised concerning you. All have come to pass for you; not one of them has failed. ¹⁵ But just as all the good things that the LORD your God promised concerning you have been fulfilled for you, so the LORD will bring upon you all the evil things, until he has destroyed you from off this good land that the LORD your God has given you, ¹⁶ if you transgress the covenant of the LORD your God, which he commanded you, and go and serve other gods and bow down to them. Then the anger of the LORD will be kindled against you, and you shall perish quickly from off the good land that he has given to you."

The Covenant Renewal at Shechem

24 Joshua gathered all the tribes of Israel to Shechem and summoned the elders, the heads, the judges, and the officers of Israel. And they presented themselves before God. ² And Joshua said to all the people, "Thus says the LORD, the God of Israel, 'Long ago, your fathers lived beyond the Euphrates,[2] Terah, the father of Abraham and of Nahor; and they served other gods. ³ Then I took your father Abraham from beyond the River[3] and led him through all the land of Canaan, and made his offspring many. I gave him Isaac. ⁴ And to Isaac I gave Jacob and Esau. And I gave Esau the hill country of Seir to possess, but Jacob and his children went down to Egypt. ⁵ And I

---

[1] Or *words*; also twice in verse 15 [2] Hebrew *the River* [3] That is, the Euphrates; also verses 14, 15

sent Moses and Aaron, and I plagued Egypt with what I did in the midst of it, and afterward I brought you out.

⁶ "'Then I brought your fathers out of Egypt, and you came to the sea. And the Egyptians pursued your fathers with chariots and horsemen to the Red Sea. ⁷ And when they cried to the Lord, he put darkness between you and the Egyptians and made the sea come upon them and cover them; and your eyes saw what I did in Egypt. And you lived in the wilderness a long time. ⁸ Then I brought you to the land of the Amorites, who lived on the other side of the Jordan. They fought with you, and I gave them into your hand, and you took possession of their land, and I destroyed them before you. ⁹ Then Balak the son of Zippor, king of Moab, arose and fought against Israel. And he sent and invited Balaam the son of Beor to curse you, ¹⁰ but I would not listen to Balaam. Indeed, he blessed you. So I delivered you out of his hand. ¹¹ And you went over the Jordan and came to Jericho, and the leaders of Jericho fought against you, and also the Amorites, the Perizzites, the Canaanites, the Hittites, the Girgashites, the Hivites, and the Jebusites. And I gave them into your hand. ¹² And I sent the hornet before you, which drove them out before you, the two kings of the Amorites; it was not by your sword or by your bow. ¹³ I gave you a land on which you had not labored and cities that you had not built, and you dwell in them. You eat the fruit of vineyards and olive orchards that you did not plant.'

Choose Whom You Will Serve

¹⁴ "Now therefore fear the Lord and serve him in sincerity and in faithfulness. Put away the gods that your fathers served beyond the River and in Egypt, and serve the Lord. ¹⁵ And if it is evil in your eyes to serve the Lord, choose this day whom you will serve, whether the gods your fathers served in the region beyond the River, or the gods of the Amorites in whose land you dwell. But as for me and my house, we will serve the Lord."

¹⁶ Then the people answered, "Far be it from us that we should forsake the Lord to serve other gods, ¹⁷ for it is the Lord our God who brought us and our fathers up from the land of Egypt, out of the house of slavery, and who did those great signs in our sight and preserved us in all the way that we went, and among all the peoples through whom we passed. ¹⁸ And the Lord drove out before us all the peoples, the Amorites who lived in the land. Therefore we also will serve the Lord, for he is our God."

¹⁹ But Joshua said to the people, "You are not able to serve the Lord, for he is a holy God. He is a jealous God; he will not forgive your transgressions or your sins. ²⁰ If you forsake the Lord and serve foreign gods, then he will turn

and do you harm and consume you, after having done you good." ²¹ And the people said to Joshua, "No, but we will serve the Lord." ²² Then Joshua said to the people, "You are witnesses against yourselves that you have chosen the Lord, to serve him." And they said, "We are witnesses." ²³ He said, "Then put away the foreign gods that are among you, and incline your heart to the Lord, the God of Israel." ²⁴ And the people said to Joshua, "The Lord our God we will serve, and his voice we will obey." ²⁵ So Joshua made a covenant with the people that day, and put in place statutes and rules for them at Shechem. ²⁶ And Joshua wrote these words in the Book of the Law of God. And he took a large stone and set it up there under the terebinth that was by the sanctuary of the Lord. ²⁷ And Joshua said to all the people, "Behold, this stone shall be a witness against us, for it has heard all the words of the Lord that he spoke to us. Therefore it shall be a witness against you, lest you deal falsely with your God." ²⁸ So Joshua sent the people away, every man to his inheritance.

Joshua's Death and Burial

²⁹ After these things Joshua the son of Nun, the servant of the Lord, died, being 110 years old. ³⁰ And they buried him in his own inheritance at Timnath-serah, which is in the hill country of Ephraim, north of the mountain of Gaash.

³¹ Israel served the Lord all the days of Joshua, and all the days of the elders who outlived Joshua and had known all the work that the Lord did for Israel.

³² As for the bones of Joseph, which the people of Israel brought up from Egypt, they buried them at Shechem, in the piece of land that Jacob bought from the sons of Hamor the father of Shechem for a hundred pieces of money.¹ It became an inheritance of the descendants of Joseph.

³³ And Eleazar the son of Aaron died, and they buried him at Gibeah, the town of Phinehas his son, which had been given him in the hill country of Ephraim.

---

¹ Hebrew *for a hundred qesitah*; a unit of money of uncertain value

JUDGES

The Continuing Conquest of Canaan

1 After the death of Joshua, the people of Israel inquired of the Lord, "Who shall go up first for us against the Canaanites, to fight against them?" ²The Lord said, "Judah shall go up; behold, I have given the land into his hand." ³And Judah said to Simeon his brother, "Come up with me into the territory allotted to me, that we may fight against the Canaanites. And I likewise will go with you into the territory allotted to you." So Simeon went with him. ⁴Then Judah went up and the Lord gave the Canaanites and the Perizzites into their hand, and they defeated 10,000 of them at Bezek. ⁵They found Adoni-bezek at Bezek and fought against him and defeated the Canaanites and the Perizzites. ⁶Adoni-bezek fled, but they pursued him and caught him and cut off his thumbs and his big toes. ⁷And Adoni-bezek said, "Seventy kings with their thumbs and their big toes cut off used to pick up scraps under my table. As I have done, so God has repaid me." And they brought him to Jerusalem, and he died there.

⁸And the men of Judah fought against Jerusalem and captured it and struck it with the edge of the sword and set the city on fire. ⁹And afterward the men of Judah went down to fight against the Canaanites who lived in the hill country, in the Negeb, and in the lowland. ¹⁰And Judah went against the Canaanites who lived in Hebron (now the name of Hebron was formerly Kiriath-arba), and they defeated Sheshai and Ahiman and Talmai.

¹¹From there they went against the inhabitants of Debir. The name of Debir was formerly Kiriath-sepher. ¹²And Caleb said, "He who attacks Kiriath-sepher and captures it, I will give him Achsah my daughter as wife." ¹³And Othniel the son of Kenaz, Caleb's younger brother, captured it. And he gave him Achsah his daughter as wife. ¹⁴When she came to him, she urged him to ask her father for a field. And she dismounted from her donkey, and Caleb said to her, "What do you want?" ¹⁵She said to him, "Give me a blessing. Since you have given me the land of the Negeb, give me also springs of water." And Caleb gave her the upper springs and the lower springs.

¹⁶And the descendants of the Kenite, Moses' father-in-law, went up with the people of Judah from the city of palms into the wilderness of Judah, which

lies in the Negeb near Arad, and they went and settled with the people. ⁱ⁷ And Judah went with Simeon his brother, and they defeated the Canaanites who inhabited Zephath and devoted it to destruction. So the name of the city was called Hormah.¹ ¹⁸ Judah also captured Gaza with its territory, and Ashkelon with its territory, and Ekron with its territory. ¹⁹ And the Lord was with Judah, and he took possession of the hill country, but he could not drive out the inhabitants of the plain because they had chariots of iron. ²⁰ And Hebron was given to Caleb, as Moses had said. And he drove out from it the three sons of Anak. ²¹ But the people of Benjamin did not drive out the Jebusites who lived in Jerusalem, so the Jebusites have lived with the people of Benjamin in Jerusalem to this day.

²² The house of Joseph also went up against Bethel, and the Lord was with them. ²³ And the house of Joseph scouted out Bethel. (Now the name of the city was formerly Luz.) ²⁴ And the spies saw a man coming out of the city, and they said to him, "Please show us the way into the city, and we will deal kindly with you." ²⁵ And he showed them the way into the city. And they struck the city with the edge of the sword, but they let the man and all his family go. ²⁶ And the man went to the land of the Hittites and built a city and called its name Luz. That is its name to this day.

Failure to Complete the Conquest

²⁷ Manasseh did not drive out the inhabitants of Beth-shean and its villages, or Taanach and its villages, or the inhabitants of Dor and its villages, or the inhabitants of Ibleam and its villages, or the inhabitants of Megiddo and its villages, for the Canaanites persisted in dwelling in that land. ²⁸ When Israel grew strong, they put the Canaanites to forced labor, but did not drive them out completely.

²⁹ And Ephraim did not drive out the Canaanites who lived in Gezer, so the Canaanites lived in Gezer among them.

³⁰ Zebulun did not drive out the inhabitants of Kitron, or the inhabitants of Nahalol, so the Canaanites lived among them, but became subject to forced labor.

³¹ Asher did not drive out the inhabitants of Acco, or the inhabitants of Sidon or of Ahlab or of Achzib or of Helbah or of Aphik or of Rehob, ³² so the Asherites lived among the Canaanites, the inhabitants of the land, for they did not drive them out.

³³ Naphtali did not drive out the inhabitants of Beth-shemesh, or the inhabitants of Beth-anath, so they lived among the Canaanites, the inhabitants of the land. Nevertheless, the inhabitants of Beth-shemesh and of Beth-anath became subject to forced labor for them.

¹ *Hormah* means *utter destruction*

³⁴ The Amorites pressed the people of Dan back into the hill country, for they did not allow them to come down to the plain. ³⁵ The Amorites persisted in dwelling in Mount Heres, in Aijalon, and in Shaalbim, but the hand of the house of Joseph rested heavily on them, and they became subject to forced labor. ³⁶ And the border of the Amorites ran from the ascent of Akrabbim, from Sela and upward.

Israel's Disobedience

2 Now the angel of the Lord went up from Gilgal to Bochim. And he said, "I brought you up from Egypt and brought you into the land that I swore to give to your fathers. I said, 'I will never break my covenant with you, ² and you shall make no covenant with the inhabitants of this land; you shall break down their altars.' But you have not obeyed my voice. What is this you have done? ³ So now I say, I will not drive them out before you, but they shall become thorns in your sides, and their gods shall be a snare to you." ⁴ As soon as the angel of the Lord spoke these words to all the people of Israel, the people lifted up their voices and wept. ⁵ And they called the name of that place Bochim.¹ And they sacrificed there to the Lord.

The Death of Joshua

⁶ When Joshua dismissed the people, the people of Israel went each to his inheritance to take possession of the land. ⁷ And the people served the Lord all the days of Joshua, and all the days of the elders who outlived Joshua, who had seen all the great work that the Lord had done for Israel. ⁸ And Joshua the son of Nun, the servant of the Lord, died at the age of 110 years. ⁹ And they buried him within the boundaries of his inheritance in Timnath-heres, in the hill country of Ephraim, north of the mountain of Gaash. ¹⁰ And all that generation also were gathered to their fathers. And there arose another generation after them who did not know the Lord or the work that he had done for Israel.

Israel's Unfaithfulness

¹¹ And the people of Israel did what was evil in the sight of the Lord and served the Baals. ¹² And they abandoned the Lord, the God of their fathers, who had brought them out of the land of Egypt. They went after other gods, from among the gods of the peoples who were around them, and bowed down to them. And they provoked the Lord to anger. ¹³ They abandoned the Lord and served the Baals and the Ashtaroth. ¹⁴ So the anger of the Lord was kindled against Israel, and he gave them over to plunderers, who plundered them.

¹ *Bochim* means *weepers*

And he sold them into the hand of their surrounding enemies, so that they could no longer withstand their enemies. ¹⁵ Whenever they marched out, the hand of the Lord was against them for harm, as the Lord had warned, and as the Lord had sworn to them. And they were in terrible distress.

The Lord Raises Up Judges

¹⁶ Then the Lord raised up judges, who saved them out of the hand of those who plundered them. ¹⁷ Yet they did not listen to their judges, for they whored after other gods and bowed down to them. They soon turned aside from the way in which their fathers had walked, who had obeyed the commandments of the Lord, and they did not do so. ¹⁸ Whenever the Lord raised up judges for them, the Lord was with the judge, and he saved them from the hand of their enemies all the days of the judge. For the Lord was moved to pity by their groaning because of those who afflicted and oppressed them. ¹⁹ But whenever the judge died, they turned back and were more corrupt than their fathers, going after other gods, serving them and bowing down to them. They did not drop any of their practices or their stubborn ways. ²⁰ So the anger of the Lord was kindled against Israel, and he said, "Because this people have transgressed my covenant that I commanded their fathers and have not obeyed my voice, ²¹ I will no longer drive out before them any of the nations that Joshua left when he died, ²² in order to test Israel by them, whether they will take care to walk in the way of the Lord as their fathers did, or not." ²³ So the Lord left those nations, not driving them out quickly, and he did not give them into the hand of Joshua.

3 Now these are the nations that the Lord left, to test Israel by them, that is, all in Israel who had not experienced all the wars in Canaan. ² It was only in order that the generations of the people of Israel might know war, to teach war to those who had not known it before. ³ These are the nations: the five lords of the Philistines and all the Canaanites and the Sidonians and the Hivites who lived on Mount Lebanon, from Mount Baal-hermon as far as Lebo-hamath. ⁴ They were for the testing of Israel, to know whether Israel would obey the commandments of the Lord, which he commanded their fathers by the hand of Moses. ⁵ So the people of Israel lived among the Canaanites, the Hittites, the Amorites, the Perizzites, the Hivites, and the Jebusites. ⁶ And their daughters they took to themselves for wives, and their own daughters they gave to their sons, and they served their gods.

Othniel

⁷ And the people of Israel did what was evil in the sight of the Lord. They forgot the Lord their God and served the Baals and the Asheroth. ⁸ Therefore

the anger of the Lord was kindled against Israel, and he sold them into the hand of Cushan-rishathaim king of Mesopotamia. And the people of Israel served Cushan-rishathaim eight years. ⁹But when the people of Israel cried out to the Lord, the Lord raised up a deliverer for the people of Israel, who saved them, Othniel the son of Kenaz, Caleb's younger brother. ¹⁰The Spirit of the Lord was upon him, and he judged Israel. He went out to war, and the Lord gave Cushan-rishathaim king of Mesopotamia into his hand. And his hand prevailed over Cushan-rishathaim. ¹¹So the land had rest for forty years. Then Othniel the son of Kenaz died.

Ehud

¹²And the people of Israel again did what was evil in the sight of the Lord, and the Lord strengthened Eglon the king of Moab against Israel, because they had done what was evil in the sight of the Lord. ¹³He gathered to himself the Ammonites and the Amalekites, and went and defeated Israel. And they took possession of the city of palms. ¹⁴And the people of Israel served Eglon the king of Moab eighteen years.

¹⁵Then the people of Israel cried out to the Lord, and the Lord raised up for them a deliverer, Ehud, the son of Gera, the Benjaminite, a left-handed man. The people of Israel sent tribute by him to Eglon the king of Moab. ¹⁶And Ehud made for himself a sword with two edges, a cubit[1] in length, and he bound it on his right thigh under his clothes. ¹⁷And he presented the tribute to Eglon king of Moab. Now Eglon was a very fat man. ¹⁸And when Ehud had finished presenting the tribute, he sent away the people who carried the tribute. ¹⁹But he himself turned back at the idols near Gilgal and said, "I have a secret message for you, O king." And he commanded, "Silence." And all his attendants went out from his presence. ²⁰And Ehud came to him as he was sitting alone in his cool roof chamber. And Ehud said, "I have a message from God for you." And he arose from his seat. ²¹And Ehud reached with his left hand, took the sword from his right thigh, and thrust it into his belly. ²²And the hilt also went in after the blade, and the fat closed over the blade, for he did not pull the sword out of his belly; and the dung came out. ²³Then Ehud went out into the porch[2] and closed the doors of the roof chamber behind him and locked them.

²⁴When he had gone, the servants came, and when they saw that the doors of the roof chamber were locked, they thought, "Surely he is relieving himself in the closet of the cool chamber." ²⁵And they waited till they were embarrassed. But when he still did not open the doors of the roof chamber, they took the key and opened them, and there lay their lord dead on the floor.

[1] A *cubit* was about 18 inches or 45 centimeters [2] The meaning of the Hebrew word is uncertain

²⁶ Ehud escaped while they delayed, and he passed beyond the idols and escaped to Seirah. ²⁷ When he arrived, he sounded the trumpet in the hill country of Ephraim. Then the people of Israel went down with him from the hill country, and he was their leader. ²⁸ And he said to them, "Follow after me, for the Lord has given your enemies the Moabites into your hand." So they went down after him and seized the fords of the Jordan against the Moabites and did not allow anyone to pass over. ²⁹ And they killed at that time about 10,000 of the Moabites, all strong, able-bodied men; not a man escaped. ³⁰ So Moab was subdued that day under the hand of Israel. And the land had rest for eighty years.

Shamgar

³¹ After him was Shamgar the son of Anath, who killed 600 of the Philistines with an oxgoad, and he also saved Israel.

Deborah and Barak

4 And the people of Israel again did what was evil in the sight of the Lord after Ehud died. ² And the Lord sold them into the hand of Jabin king of Canaan, who reigned in Hazor. The commander of his army was Sisera, who lived in Harosheth-hagoyim. ³ Then the people of Israel cried out to the Lord for help, for he had 900 chariots of iron and he oppressed the people of Israel cruelly for twenty years.

⁴ Now Deborah, a prophetess, the wife of Lappidoth, was judging Israel at that time. ⁵ She used to sit under the palm of Deborah between Ramah and Bethel in the hill country of Ephraim, and the people of Israel came up to her for judgment. ⁶ She sent and summoned Barak the son of Abinoam from Kedesh-naphtali and said to him, "Has not the Lord, the God of Israel, commanded you, 'Go, gather your men at Mount Tabor, taking 10,000 from the people of Naphtali and the people of Zebulun. ⁷ And I will draw out Sisera, the general of Jabin's army, to meet you by the river Kishon with his chariots and his troops, and I will give him into your hand'?" ⁸ Barak said to her, "If you will go with me, I will go, but if you will not go with me, I will not go." ⁹ And she said, "I will surely go with you. Nevertheless, the road on which you are going will not lead to your glory, for the Lord will sell Sisera into the hand of a woman." Then Deborah arose and went with Barak to Kedesh. ¹⁰ And Barak called out Zebulun and Naphtali to Kedesh. And 10,000 men went up at his heels, and Deborah went up with him.

¹¹ Now Heber the Kenite had separated from the Kenites, the descendants of Hobab the father-in-law of Moses, and had pitched his tent as far away as the oak in Zaanannim, which is near Kedesh.

¹² When Sisera was told that Barak the son of Abinoam had gone up to Mount Tabor, ¹³ Sisera called out all his chariots, 900 chariots of iron, and all the men who were with him, from Harosheth-hagoyim to the river Kishon. ¹⁴ And Deborah said to Barak, "Up! For this is the day in which the Lord has given Sisera into your hand. Does not the Lord go out before you?" So Barak went down from Mount Tabor with 10,000 men following him. ¹⁵ And the Lord routed Sisera and all his chariots and all his army before Barak by the edge of the sword. And Sisera got down from his chariot and fled away on foot. ¹⁶ And Barak pursued the chariots and the army to Harosheth-hagoyim, and all the army of Sisera fell by the edge of the sword; not a man was left.

¹⁷ But Sisera fled away on foot to the tent of Jael, the wife of Heber the Kenite, for there was peace between Jabin the king of Hazor and the house of Heber the Kenite. ¹⁸ And Jael came out to meet Sisera and said to him, "Turn aside, my lord; turn aside to me; do not be afraid." So he turned aside to her into the tent, and she covered him with a rug. ¹⁹ And he said to her, "Please give me a little water to drink, for I am thirsty." So she opened a skin of milk and gave him a drink and covered him. ²⁰ And he said to her, "Stand at the opening of the tent, and if any man comes and asks you, 'Is anyone here?' say, 'No.'" ²¹ But Jael the wife of Heber took a tent peg, and took a hammer in her hand. Then she went softly to him and drove the peg into his temple until it went down into the ground while he was lying fast asleep from weariness. So he died. ²² And behold, as Barak was pursuing Sisera, Jael went out to meet him and said to him, "Come, and I will show you the man whom you are seeking." So he went in to her tent, and there lay Sisera dead, with the tent peg in his temple.

²³ So on that day God subdued Jabin the king of Canaan before the people of Israel. ²⁴ And the hand of the people of Israel pressed harder and harder against Jabin the king of Canaan, until they destroyed Jabin king of Canaan.

The Song of Deborah and Barak

5

Then sang Deborah and Barak the son of Abinoam on that day:

² "That the leaders took the lead in Israel,
    that the people offered themselves willingly,
    bless the Lord!

³ "Hear, O kings; give ear, O princes;
    to the Lord I will sing;
    I will make melody to the Lord, the God of Israel.

4 "Lord, when you went out from Seir,
    when you marched from the region of Edom,
  the earth trembled
    and the heavens dropped,
    yes, the clouds dropped water.
5   The mountains quaked before the Lord,
    even Sinai before the Lord,[1] the God of Israel.

6 "In the days of Shamgar, son of Anath,
    in the days of Jael, the highways were abandoned,
    and travelers kept to the byways.
7   The villagers ceased in Israel;
    they ceased to be until I arose;
    I, Deborah, arose as a mother in Israel.
8   When new gods were chosen,
    then war was in the gates.
  Was shield or spear to be seen
    among forty thousand in Israel?
9   My heart goes out to the commanders of Israel
    who offered themselves willingly among the people.
    Bless the Lord.

10 "Tell of it, you who ride on white donkeys,
    you who sit on rich carpets[2]
    and you who walk by the way.
11 To the sound of musicians[3] at the watering places,
    there they repeat the righteous triumphs of the Lord,
    the righteous triumphs of his villagers in Israel.

  "Then down to the gates marched the people of the Lord.

12 "Awake, awake, Deborah!
    Awake, awake, break out in a song!
  Arise, Barak, lead away your captives,
    O son of Abinoam.
13 Then down marched the remnant of the noble;
    the people of the Lord marched down for me against the mighty.

[1] Or *before the Lord, the One of Sinai, before the Lord* [2] The meaning of the Hebrew word is uncertain; it may connote *saddle blankets* [3] Or *archers*; the meaning of the Hebrew word is uncertain

14 From Ephraim their root they marched down into the valley,[1]
     following you, Benjamin, with your kinsmen;
  from Machir marched down the commanders,
     and from Zebulun those who bear the lieutenant's[2] staff;
15 the princes of Issachar came with Deborah,
     and Issachar faithful to Barak;
  into the valley they rushed at his heels.
  Among the clans of Reuben
     there were great searchings of heart.
16 Why did you sit still among the sheepfolds,
     to hear the whistling for the flocks?
  Among the clans of Reuben
     there were great searchings of heart.
17 Gilead stayed beyond the Jordan;
     and Dan, why did he stay with the ships?
  Asher sat still at the coast of the sea,
     staying by his landings.
18 Zebulun is a people who risked their lives to the death;
     Naphtali, too, on the heights of the field.

19 "The kings came, they fought;
     then fought the kings of Canaan,
  at Taanach, by the waters of Megiddo;
     they got no spoils of silver.
20 From heaven the stars fought,
     from their courses they fought against Sisera.
21 The torrent Kishon swept them away,
     the ancient torrent, the torrent Kishon.
     March on, my soul, with might!

22 "Then loud beat the horses' hoofs
     with the galloping, galloping of his steeds.

23 "Curse Meroz, says the angel of the Lord,
     curse its inhabitants thoroughly,
  because they did not come to the help of the Lord,
     to the help of the Lord against the mighty.

[1] Septuagint; Hebrew *in Amalek* [2] Hebrew *commander's*

²⁴ "Most blessed of women be Jael,

 the wife of Heber the Kenite,

 of tent-dwelling women most blessed.

²⁵ He asked for water and she gave him milk;

 she brought him curds in a noble's bowl.

²⁶ She sent her hand to the tent peg

 and her right hand to the workmen's mallet;

she struck Sisera;

 she crushed his head;

 she shattered and pierced his temple.

²⁷ Between her feet

 he sank, he fell, he lay still;

between her feet

 he sank, he fell;

where he sank,

 there he fell—dead.

²⁸ "Out of the window she peered,

 the mother of Sisera wailed through the lattice:

'Why is his chariot so long in coming?

 Why tarry the hoofbeats of his chariots?'

²⁹ Her wisest princesses answer,

 indeed, she answers herself,

³⁰ 'Have they not found and divided the spoil?—

 A womb or two for every man;

spoil of dyed materials for Sisera,

 spoil of dyed materials embroidered,

 two pieces of dyed work embroidered for the neck as spoil?'

³¹ "So may all your enemies perish, O Lord!

 But your friends be like the sun as he rises in his might."

And the land had rest for forty years.

Midian Oppresses Israel

6 The people of Israel did what was evil in the sight of the Lord, and the Lord gave them into the hand of Midian seven years. ² And the hand of Midian overpowered Israel, and because of Midian the people of Israel made for themselves the dens that are in the mountains and the caves and the strongholds. ³ For whenever the Israelites planted crops, the Midianites and the Amalekites and the people of the East would come up against them. ⁴ They would encamp against them and devour the produce of the land, as far as Gaza, and leave no sustenance in Israel and no sheep or ox or donkey. ⁵ For they would come up with their livestock and their tents; they would come like locusts in number—both they and their camels could not be counted—so that they laid waste the land as they came in. ⁶ And Israel was brought very low because of Midian. And the people of Israel cried out for help to the Lord.

⁷ When the people of Israel cried out to the Lord on account of the Midianites, ⁸ the Lord sent a prophet to the people of Israel. And he said to them, "Thus says the Lord, the God of Israel: I led you up from Egypt and brought you out of the house of slavery. ⁹ And I delivered you from the hand of the Egyptians and from the hand of all who oppressed you, and drove them out before you and gave you their land. ¹⁰ And I said to you, 'I am the Lord your God; you shall not fear the gods of the Amorites in whose land you dwell.' But you have not obeyed my voice."

The Call of Gideon

¹¹ Now the angel of the Lord came and sat under the terebinth at Ophrah, which belonged to Joash the Abiezrite, while his son Gideon was beating out wheat in the winepress to hide it from the Midianites. ¹² And the angel of the Lord appeared to him and said to him, "The Lord is with you, O mighty man of valor." ¹³ And Gideon said to him, "Please, my lord, if the Lord is with us, why then has all this happened to us? And where are all his wonderful deeds that our fathers recounted to us, saying, 'Did not the Lord bring us up from Egypt?' But now the Lord has forsaken us and given us into the hand of Midian." ¹⁴ And the Lord[1] turned to him and said, "Go in this might of yours and save Israel from the hand of Midian; do not I send you?" ¹⁵ And he said to him, "Please, Lord, how can I save Israel? Behold, my clan is the weakest in Manasseh, and I am the least in my father's house." ¹⁶ And the Lord said to him, "But I will be with you, and you shall strike the Midianites as one man." ¹⁷ And he said to him, "If now I have found favor in your eyes, then show me a sign that it is you who speak with me. ¹⁸ Please do not depart from here until I come to you and bring out my present and set it before you." And he said, "I will stay till you return."

¹⁹ So Gideon went into his house and prepared a young goat and unleavened cakes from an ephah[2] of flour. The meat he put in a basket, and the

---
[1] Septuagint *the angel of the Lord*; also verse 16 [2] An *ephah* was about 3/5 bushel or 22 liters

broth he put in a pot, and brought them to him under the terebinth and presented them. ²⁰ And the angel of God said to him, "Take the meat and the unleavened cakes, and put them on this rock, and pour the broth over them." And he did so. ²¹ Then the angel of the Lord reached out the tip of the staff that was in his hand and touched the meat and the unleavened cakes. And fire sprang up from the rock and consumed the meat and the unleavened cakes. And the angel of the Lord vanished from his sight. ²² Then Gideon perceived that he was the angel of the Lord. And Gideon said, "Alas, O Lord God! For now I have seen the angel of the Lord face to face." ²³ But the Lord said to him, "Peace be to you. Do not fear; you shall not die." ²⁴ Then Gideon built an altar there to the Lord and called it, The Lord Is Peace. To this day it still stands at Ophrah, which belongs to the Abiezrites.

²⁵ That night the Lord said to him, "Take your father's bull, and the second bull seven years old, and pull down the altar of Baal that your father has, and cut down the Asherah that is beside it ²⁶ and build an altar to the Lord your God on the top of the stronghold here, with stones laid in due order. Then take the second bull and offer it as a burnt offering with the wood of the Asherah that you shall cut down." ²⁷ So Gideon took ten men of his servants and did as the Lord had told him. But because he was too afraid of his family and the men of the town to do it by day, he did it by night.

Gideon Destroys the Altar of Baal

²⁸ When the men of the town rose early in the morning, behold, the altar of Baal was broken down, and the Asherah beside it was cut down, and the second bull was offered on the altar that had been built. ²⁹ And they said to one another, "Who has done this thing?" And after they had searched and inquired, they said, "Gideon the son of Joash has done this thing." ³⁰ Then the men of the town said to Joash, "Bring out your son, that he may die, for he has broken down the altar of Baal and cut down the Asherah beside it." ³¹ But Joash said to all who stood against him, "Will you contend for Baal? Or will you save him? Whoever contends for him shall be put to death by morning. If he is a god, let him contend for himself, because his altar has been broken down." ³² Therefore on that day Gideon[1] was called Jerubbaal, that is to say, "Let Baal contend against him," because he broke down his altar.

³³ Now all the Midianites and the Amalekites and the people of the East came together, and they crossed the Jordan and encamped in the Valley of Jezreel. ³⁴ But the Spirit of the Lord clothed Gideon, and he sounded the trumpet, and the Abiezrites were called out to follow him. ³⁵ And he sent

[1] Hebrew *he*

messengers throughout all Manasseh, and they too were called out to follow him. And he sent messengers to Asher, Zebulun, and Naphtali, and they went up to meet them.

The Sign of the Fleece

⁳⁶ Then Gideon said to God, "If you will save Israel by my hand, as you have said, ³⁷ behold, I am laying a fleece of wool on the threshing floor. If there is dew on the fleece alone, and it is dry on all the ground, then I shall know that you will save Israel by my hand, as you have said." ³⁸ And it was so. When he rose early next morning and squeezed the fleece, he wrung enough dew from the fleece to fill a bowl with water. ³⁹ Then Gideon said to God, "Let not your anger burn against me; let me speak just once more. Please let me test just once more with the fleece. Please let it be dry on the fleece only, and on all the ground let there be dew." ⁴⁰ And God did so that night; and it was dry on the fleece only, and on all the ground there was dew.

Gideon's Three Hundred Men

7 Then Jerubbaal (that is, Gideon) and all the people who were with him rose early and encamped beside the spring of Harod. And the camp of Midian was north of them, by the hill of Moreh, in the valley.

² The Lord said to Gideon, "The people with you are too many for me to give the Midianites into their hand, lest Israel boast over me, saying, 'My own hand has saved me.' ³ Now therefore proclaim in the ears of the people, saying, 'Whoever is fearful and trembling, let him return home and hurry away from Mount Gilead.'" Then 22,000 of the people returned, and 10,000 remained.

⁴ And the Lord said to Gideon, "The people are still too many. Take them down to the water, and I will test them for you there, and anyone of whom I say to you, 'This one shall go with you,' shall go with you, and anyone of whom I say to you, 'This one shall not go with you,' shall not go." ⁵ So he brought the people down to the water. And the Lord said to Gideon, "Every one who laps the water with his tongue, as a dog laps, you shall set by himself. Likewise, every one who kneels down to drink." ⁶ And the number of those who lapped, putting their hands to their mouths, was 300 men, but all the rest of the people knelt down to drink water. ⁷ And the Lord said to Gideon, "With the 300 men who lapped I will save you and give the Midianites into your hand, and let all the others go every man to his home." ⁸ So the people took provisions in their hands, and their trumpets. And he sent all the rest of Israel every man to his tent, but retained the 300 men. And the camp of Midian was below him in the valley.

⁹ That same night the Lord said to him, "Arise, go down against the camp, for I have given it into your hand. ¹⁰ But if you are afraid to go down, go down to the camp with Purah your servant. ¹¹ And you shall hear what they say, and afterward your hands shall be strengthened to go down against the camp." Then he went down with Purah his servant to the outposts of the armed men who were in the camp. ¹² And the Midianites and the Amalekites and all the people of the East lay along the valley like locusts in abundance, and their camels were without number, as the sand that is on the seashore in abundance. ¹³ When Gideon came, behold, a man was telling a dream to his comrade. And he said, "Behold, I dreamed a dream, and behold, a cake of barley bread tumbled into the camp of Midian and came to the tent and struck it so that it fell and turned it upside down, so that the tent lay flat." ¹⁴ And his comrade answered, "This is no other than the sword of Gideon the son of Joash, a man of Israel; God has given into his hand Midian and all the camp."

¹⁵ As soon as Gideon heard the telling of the dream and its interpretation, he worshiped. And he returned to the camp of Israel and said, "Arise, for the Lord has given the host of Midian into your hand." ¹⁶ And he divided the 300 men into three companies and put trumpets into the hands of all of them and empty jars, with torches inside the jars. ¹⁷ And he said to them, "Look at me, and do likewise. When I come to the outskirts of the camp, do as I do. ¹⁸ When I blow the trumpet, I and all who are with me, then blow the trumpets also on every side of all the camp and shout, 'For the Lord and for Gideon.'"

Gideon Defeats Midian

¹⁹ So Gideon and the hundred men who were with him came to the outskirts of the camp at the beginning of the middle watch, when they had just set the watch. And they blew the trumpets and smashed the jars that were in their hands. ²⁰ Then the three companies blew the trumpets and broke the jars. They held in their left hands the torches, and in their right hands the trumpets to blow. And they cried out, "A sword for the Lord and for Gideon!" ²¹ Every man stood in his place around the camp, and all the army ran. They cried out and fled. ²² When they blew the 300 trumpets, the Lord set every man's sword against his comrade and against all the army. And the army fled as far as Beth-shittah toward Zererah,¹ as far as the border of Abel-meholah, by Tabbath. ²³ And the men of Israel were called out from Naphtali and from Asher and from all Manasseh, and they pursued after Midian.

¹ Some Hebrew manuscripts *Zeredah*

⁴⁴ Gideon sent messengers throughout all the hill country of Ephraim, saying, "Come down against the Midianites and capture the waters against them, as far as Beth-barah, and also the Jordan." So all the men of Ephraim were called out, and they captured the waters as far as Beth-barah, and also the Jordan. ²⁵ And they captured the two princes of Midian, Oreb and Zeeb. They killed Oreb at the rock of Oreb, and Zeeb they killed at the winepress of Zeeb. Then they pursued Midian, and they brought the heads of Oreb and Zeeb to Gideon across the Jordan.

Gideon Defeats Zebah and Zalmunna

8 Then the men of Ephraim said to him, "What is this that you have done to us, not to call us when you went to fight against Midian?" And they accused him fiercely. ² And he said to them, "What have I done now in comparison with you? Is not the gleaning of the grapes of Ephraim better than the grape harvest of Abiezer? ³ God has given into your hands the princes of Midian, Oreb and Zeeb. What have I been able to do in comparison with you?" Then their anger[1] against him subsided when he said this.

⁴ And Gideon came to the Jordan and crossed over, he and the 300 men who were with him, exhausted yet pursuing. ⁵ So he said to the men of Succoth, "Please give loaves of bread to the people who follow me, for they are exhausted, and I am pursuing after Zebah and Zalmunna, the kings of Midian." ⁶ And the officials of Succoth said, "Are the hands of Zebah and Zalmunna already in your hand, that we should give bread to your army?" ⁷ So Gideon said, "Well then, when the Lord has given Zebah and Zalmunna into my hand, I will flail your flesh with the thorns of the wilderness and with briers." ⁸ And from there he went up to Penuel, and spoke to them in the same way, and the men of Penuel answered him as the men of Succoth had answered. ⁹ And he said to the men of Penuel, "When I come again in peace, I will break down this tower."

¹⁰ Now Zebah and Zalmunna were in Karkor with their army, about 15,000 men, all who were left of all the army of the people of the East, for there had fallen 120,000 men who drew the sword. ¹¹ And Gideon went up by the way of the tent dwellers east of Nobah and Jogbehah and attacked the army, for the army felt secure. ¹² And Zebah and Zalmunna fled, and he pursued them and captured the two kings of Midian, Zebah and Zalmunna, and he threw all the army into a panic.

¹³ Then Gideon the son of Joash returned from the battle by the ascent of Heres. ¹⁴ And he captured a young man of Succoth and questioned him. And

[1] Hebrew *their spirit*

he wrote down for him the officials and elders of Succoth, seventy-seven men. ¹⁵ And he came to the men of Succoth and said, "Behold Zebah and Zalmunna, about whom you taunted me, saying, 'Are the hands of Zebah and Zalmunna already in your hand, that we should give bread to your men who are exhausted?'" ¹⁶ And he took the elders of the city, and he took thorns of the wilderness and briers and with them taught the men of Succoth a lesson. ¹⁷ And he broke down the tower of Penuel and killed the men of the city.

¹⁸ Then he said to Zebah and Zalmunna, "Where are the men whom you killed at Tabor?" They answered, "As you are, so were they. Every one of them resembled the son of a king." ¹⁹ And he said, "They were my brothers, the sons of my mother. As the LORD lives, if you had saved them alive, I would not kill you." ²⁰ So he said to Jether his firstborn, "Rise and kill them!" But the young man did not draw his sword, for he was afraid, because he was still a young man. ²¹ Then Zebah and Zalmunna said, "Rise yourself and fall upon us, for as the man is, so is his strength." And Gideon arose and killed Zebah and Zalmunna, and he took the crescent ornaments that were on the necks of their camels.

Gideon's Ephod

²² Then the men of Israel said to Gideon, "Rule over us, you and your son and your grandson also, for you have saved us from the hand of Midian." ²³ Gideon said to them, "I will not rule over you, and my son will not rule over you; the LORD will rule over you." ²⁴ And Gideon said to them, "Let me make a request of you: every one of you give me the earrings from his spoil." (For they had golden earrings, because they were Ishmaelites.) ²⁵ And they answered, "We will willingly give them." And they spread a cloak, and every man threw in it the earrings of his spoil. ²⁶ And the weight of the golden earrings that he requested was 1,700 shekels¹ of gold, besides the crescent ornaments and the pendants and the purple garments worn by the kings of Midian, and besides the collars that were around the necks of their camels. ²⁷ And Gideon made an ephod of it and put it in his city, in Ophrah. And all Israel whored after it there, and it became a snare to Gideon and to his family. ²⁸ So Midian was subdued before the people of Israel, and they raised their heads no more. And the land had rest for forty years in the days of Gideon.

The Death of Gideon

²⁹ Jerubbaal the son of Joash went and lived in his own house. ³⁰ Now Gideon had seventy sons, his own offspring,² for he had many wives. ³¹ And

---

¹ A *shekel* was about 2/5 ounce or 11 grams ² Hebrew *who came from his own loins*

his concubine who was in Shechem also bore him a son, and he called his name Abimelech. ³² And Gideon the son of Joash died in a good old age and was buried in the tomb of Joash his father, at Ophrah of the Abiezrites.

³³ As soon as Gideon died, the people of Israel turned again and whored after the Baals and made Baal-berith their god. ³⁴ And the people of Israel did not remember the LORD their God, who had delivered them from the hand of all their enemies on every side, ³⁵ and they did not show steadfast love to the family of Jerubbaal (that is, Gideon) in return for all the good that he had done to Israel.

Abimelech's Conspiracy

9 Now Abimelech the son of Jerubbaal went to Shechem to his mother's relatives and said to them and to the whole clan of his mother's family, ² "Say in the ears of all the leaders of Shechem, 'Which is better for you, that all seventy of the sons of Jerubbaal rule over you, or that one rule over you?' Remember also that I am your bone and your flesh."

³ And his mother's relatives spoke all these words on his behalf in the ears of all the leaders of Shechem, and their hearts inclined to follow Abimelech, for they said, "He is our brother." ⁴ And they gave him seventy pieces of silver out of the house of Baal-berith with which Abimelech hired worthless and reckless fellows, who followed him. ⁵ And he went to his father's house at Ophrah and killed his brothers the sons of Jerubbaal, seventy men, on one stone. But Jotham the youngest son of Jerubbaal was left, for he hid himself. ⁶ And all the leaders of Shechem came together, and all Beth-millo, and they went and made Abimelech king, by the oak of the pillar at Shechem.

⁷ When it was told to Jotham, he went and stood on top of Mount Gerizim and cried aloud and said to them, "Listen to me, you leaders of Shechem, that God may listen to you. ⁸ The trees once went out to anoint a king over them, and they said to the olive tree, 'Reign over us.' ⁹ But the olive tree said to them, 'Shall I leave my abundance, by which gods and men are honored, and go hold sway over the trees?' ¹⁰ And the trees said to the fig tree, 'You come and reign over us.' ¹¹ But the fig tree said to them, 'Shall I leave my sweetness and my good fruit and go hold sway over the trees?' ¹² And the trees said to the vine, 'You come and reign over us.' ¹³ But the vine said to them, 'Shall I leave my wine that cheers God and men and go hold sway over the trees?' ¹⁴ Then all the trees said to the bramble, 'You come and reign over us.' ¹⁵ And the bramble said to the trees, 'If in good faith you are anointing me king over you, then come and take refuge in my shade, but if not, let fire come out of the bramble and devour the cedars of Lebanon.'

¹⁶ "Now therefore, if you acted in good faith and integrity when you made Abimelech king, and if you have dealt well with Jerubbaal and his house and have done to him as his deeds deserved— ¹⁷ for my father fought for you and risked his life and delivered you from the hand of Midian, ¹⁸ and you have risen up against my father's house this day and have killed his sons, seventy men on one stone, and have made Abimelech, the son of his female servant, king over the leaders of Shechem, because he is your relative— ¹⁹ if you then have acted in good faith and integrity with Jerubbaal and with his house this day, then rejoice in Abimelech, and let him also rejoice in you. ²⁰ But if not, let fire come out from Abimelech and devour the leaders of Shechem and Beth-millo; and let fire come out from the leaders of Shechem and from Beth-millo and devour Abimelech." ²¹ And Jotham ran away and fled and went to Beer and lived there, because of Abimelech his brother.

The Downfall of Abimelech

²² Abimelech ruled over Israel three years. ²³ And God sent an evil spirit between Abimelech and the leaders of Shechem, and the leaders of Shechem dealt treacherously with Abimelech, ²⁴ that the violence done to the seventy sons of Jerubbaal might come, and their blood be laid on Abimelech their brother, who killed them, and on the men of Shechem, who strengthened his hands to kill his brothers. ²⁵ And the leaders of Shechem put men in ambush against him on the mountaintops, and they robbed all who passed by them along that way. And it was told to Abimelech.

²⁶ And Gaal the son of Ebed moved into Shechem with his relatives, and the leaders of Shechem put confidence in him. ²⁷ And they went out into the field and gathered the grapes from their vineyards and trod them and held a festival; and they went into the house of their god and ate and drank and reviled Abimelech. ²⁸ And Gaal the son of Ebed said, "Who is Abimelech, and who are we of Shechem, that we should serve him? Is he not the son of Jerubbaal, and is not Zebul his officer? Serve the men of Hamor the father of Shechem; but why should we serve him? ²⁹ Would that this people were under my hand! Then I would remove Abimelech. I would say[1] to Abimelech, 'Increase your army, and come out.'"

³⁰ When Zebul the ruler of the city heard the words of Gaal the son of Ebed, his anger was kindled. ³¹ And he sent messengers to Abimelech secretly,[2] saying, "Behold, Gaal the son of Ebed and his relatives have come to Shechem, and they are stirring up[3] the city against you. ³² Now therefore, go by night, you and the people who are with you, and set an ambush in the field. ³³ Then

[1] Septuagint; Hebrew *and he said* [2] Or *at Tormah* [3] Hebrew *besieging*, or *closing up*

in the morning, as soon as the sun is up, rise early and rush upon the city. And when he and the people who are with him come out against you, you may do to them as your hand finds to do."

⁣³⁴ So Abimelech and all the men who were with him rose up by night and set an ambush against Shechem in four companies. ³⁵ And Gaal the son of Ebed went out and stood in the entrance of the gate of the city, and Abimelech and the people who were with him rose from the ambush. ³⁶ And when Gaal saw the people, he said to Zebul, "Look, people are coming down from the mountaintops!" And Zebul said to him, "You mistake[1] the shadow of the mountains for men." ³⁷ Gaal spoke again and said, "Look, people are coming down from the center of the land, and one company is coming from the direction of the Diviners' Oak." ³⁸ Then Zebul said to him, "Where is your mouth now, you who said, 'Who is Abimelech, that we should serve him?' Are not these the people whom you despised? Go out now and fight with them." ³⁹ And Gaal went out at the head of the leaders of Shechem and fought with Abimelech. ⁴⁰ And Abimelech chased him, and he fled before him. And many fell wounded, up to the entrance of the gate. ⁴¹ And Abimelech lived at Arumah, and Zebul drove out Gaal and his relatives, so that they could not dwell at Shechem.

⁴² On the following day, the people went out into the field, and Abimelech was told. ⁴³ He took his people and divided them into three companies and set an ambush in the fields. And he looked and saw the people coming out of the city. So he rose against them and killed them. ⁴⁴ Abimelech and the company that was with him rushed forward and stood at the entrance of the gate of the city, while the two companies rushed upon all who were in the field and killed them. ⁴⁵ And Abimelech fought against the city all that day. He captured the city and killed the people who were in it, and he razed the city and sowed it with salt.

⁴⁶ When all the leaders of the Tower of Shechem heard of it, they entered the stronghold of the house of El-berith. ⁴⁷ Abimelech was told that all the leaders of the Tower of Shechem were gathered together. ⁴⁸ And Abimelech went up to Mount Zalmon, he and all the people who were with him. And Abimelech took an axe in his hand and cut down a bundle of brushwood and took it up and laid it on his shoulder. And he said to the men who were with him, "What you have seen me do, hurry and do as I have done." ⁴⁹ So every one of the people cut down his bundle and following Abimelech put it against the stronghold, and they set the stronghold on fire over them, so that all the people of the Tower of Shechem also died, about 1,000 men and women.

⁵⁰ Then Abimelech went to Thebez and encamped against Thebez and captured it. ⁵¹ But there was a strong tower within the city, and all the men

[1] Hebrew *You see*

and women and all the leaders of the city fled to it and shut themselves in, and they went up to the roof of the tower. ⁵² And Abimelech came to the tower and fought against it and drew near to the door of the tower to burn it with fire. ⁵³ And a certain woman threw an upper millstone on Abimelech's head and crushed his skull. ⁵⁴ Then he called quickly to the young man his armor-bearer and said to him, "Draw your sword and kill me, lest they say of me, 'A woman killed him.'" And his young man thrust him through, and he died. ⁵⁵ And when the men of Israel saw that Abimelech was dead, everyone departed to his home. ⁵⁶ Thus God returned the evil of Abimelech, which he committed against his father in killing his seventy brothers. ⁵⁷ And God also made all the evil of the men of Shechem return on their heads, and upon them came the curse of Jotham the son of Jerubbaal.

Tola and Jair

10 After Abimelech there arose to save Israel Tola the son of Puah, son of Dodo, a man of Issachar, and he lived at Shamir in the hill country of Ephraim. ² And he judged Israel twenty-three years. Then he died and was buried at Shamir.

³ After him arose Jair the Gileadite, who judged Israel twenty-two years. ⁴ And he had thirty sons who rode on thirty donkeys, and they had thirty cities, called Havvoth-jair to this day, which are in the land of Gilead. ⁵ And Jair died and was buried in Kamon.

Further Disobedience and Oppression

⁶ The people of Israel again did what was evil in the sight of the Lord and served the Baals and the Ashtaroth, the gods of Syria, the gods of Sidon, the gods of Moab, the gods of the Ammonites, and the gods of the Philistines. And they forsook the Lord and did not serve him. ⁷ So the anger of the Lord was kindled against Israel, and he sold them into the hand of the Philistines and into the hand of the Ammonites, ⁸ and they crushed and oppressed the people of Israel that year. For eighteen years they oppressed all the people of Israel who were beyond the Jordan in the land of the Amorites, which is in Gilead. ⁹ And the Ammonites crossed the Jordan to fight also against Judah and against Benjamin and against the house of Ephraim, so that Israel was severely distressed.

¹⁰ And the people of Israel cried out to the Lord, saying, "We have sinned against you, because we have forsaken our God and have served the Baals." ¹¹ And the Lord said to the people of Israel, "Did I not save you from the Egyptians and from the Amorites, from the Ammonites and from the

Philistines? ¹² The Sidonians also, and the Amalekites and the Maonites oppressed you, and you cried out to me, and I saved you out of their hand. ¹³ Yet you have forsaken me and served other gods; therefore I will save you no more. ¹⁴ Go and cry out to the gods whom you have chosen; let them save you in the time of your distress." ¹⁵ And the people of Israel said to the Lord, "We have sinned; do to us whatever seems good to you. Only please deliver us this day." ¹⁶ So they put away the foreign gods from among them and served the Lord, and he became impatient over the misery of Israel.

¹⁷ Then the Ammonites were called to arms, and they encamped in Gilead. And the people of Israel came together, and they encamped at Mizpah. ¹⁸ And the people, the leaders of Gilead, said one to another, "Who is the man who will begin to fight against the Ammonites? He shall be head over all the inhabitants of Gilead."

Jephthah Delivers Israel

11 Now Jephthah the Gileadite was a mighty warrior, but he was the son of a prostitute. Gilead was the father of Jephthah. ² And Gilead's wife also bore him sons. And when his wife's sons grew up, they drove Jephthah out and said to him, "You shall not have an inheritance in our father's house, for you are the son of another woman." ³ Then Jephthah fled from his brothers and lived in the land of Tob, and worthless fellows collected around Jephthah and went out with him.

⁴ After a time the Ammonites made war against Israel. ⁵ And when the Ammonites made war against Israel, the elders of Gilead went to bring Jephthah from the land of Tob. ⁶ And they said to Jephthah, "Come and be our leader, that we may fight against the Ammonites." ⁷ But Jephthah said to the elders of Gilead, "Did you not hate me and drive me out of my father's house? Why have you come to me now when you are in distress?" ⁸ And the elders of Gilead said to Jephthah, "That is why we have turned to you now, that you may go with us and fight against the Ammonites and be our head over all the inhabitants of Gilead." ⁹ Jephthah said to the elders of Gilead, "If you bring me home again to fight against the Ammonites, and the Lord gives them over to me, I will be your head." ¹⁰ And the elders of Gilead said to Jephthah, "The Lord will be witness between us, if we do not do as you say." ¹¹ So Jephthah went with the elders of Gilead, and the people made him head and leader over them. And Jephthah spoke all his words before the Lord at Mizpah.

¹² Then Jephthah sent messengers to the king of the Ammonites and said, "What do you have against me, that you have come to me to fight against my land?" ¹³ And the king of the Ammonites answered the messengers of

Jephthah, "Because Israel on coming up from Egypt took away my land, from the Arnon to the Jabbok and to the Jordan; now therefore restore it peaceably." ¹⁴ Jephthah again sent messengers to the king of the Ammonites ¹⁵ and said to him, "Thus says Jephthah: Israel did not take away the land of Moab or the land of the Ammonites, ¹⁶ but when they came up from Egypt, Israel went through the wilderness to the Red Sea and came to Kadesh. ¹⁷ Israel then sent messengers to the king of Edom, saying, 'Please let us pass through your land,' but the king of Edom would not listen. And they sent also to the king of Moab, but he would not consent. So Israel remained at Kadesh.

¹⁸ "Then they journeyed through the wilderness and went around the land of Edom and the land of Moab and arrived on the east side of the land of Moab and camped on the other side of the Arnon. But they did not enter the territory of Moab, for the Arnon was the boundary of Moab. ¹⁹ Israel then sent messengers to Sihon king of the Amorites, king of Heshbon, and Israel said to him, 'Please let us pass through your land to our country,' ²⁰ but Sihon did not trust Israel to pass through his territory, so Sihon gathered all his people together and encamped at Jahaz and fought with Israel. ²¹ And the Lord, the God of Israel, gave Sihon and all his people into the hand of Israel, and they defeated them. So Israel took possession of all the land of the Amorites, who inhabited that country. ²² And they took possession of all the territory of the Amorites from the Arnon to the Jabbok and from the wilderness to the Jordan. ²³ So then the Lord, the God of Israel, dispossessed the Amorites from before his people Israel; and are you to take possession of them? ²⁴ Will you not possess what Chemosh your god gives you to possess? And all that the Lord our God has dispossessed before us, we will possess. ²⁵ Now are you any better than Balak the son of Zippor, king of Moab? Did he ever contend against Israel, or did he ever go to war with them? ²⁶ While Israel lived in Heshbon and its villages, and in Aroer and its villages, and in all the cities that are on the banks of the Arnon, 300 years, why did you not deliver them within that time? ²⁷ I therefore have not sinned against you, and you do me wrong by making war on me. The Lord, the Judge, decide this day between the people of Israel and the people of Ammon." ²⁸ But the king of the Ammonites did not listen to the words of Jephthah that he sent to him.

Jephthah's Tragic Vow

²⁹ Then the Spirit of the Lord was upon Jephthah, and he passed through Gilead and Manasseh and passed on to Mizpah of Gilead, and from Mizpah of Gilead he passed on to the Ammonites. ³⁰ And Jephthah made a vow to the Lord and said, "If you will give the Ammonites into my hand, ³¹ then

whatever¹ comes out from the doors of my house to meet me when I return in peace from the Ammonites shall be the Lord's, and I will offer it² up for a burnt offering." ³² So Jephthah crossed over to the Ammonites to fight against them, and the Lord gave them into his hand. ³³ And he struck them from Aroer to the neighborhood of Minnith, twenty cities, and as far as Abel-keramim, with a great blow. So the Ammonites were subdued before the people of Israel.

³⁴ Then Jephthah came to his home at Mizpah. And behold, his daughter came out to meet him with tambourines and with dances. She was his only child; besides her he had neither son nor daughter. ³⁵ And as soon as he saw her, he tore his clothes and said, "Alas, my daughter! You have brought me very low, and you have become the cause of great trouble to me. For I have opened my mouth to the Lord, and I cannot take back my vow." ³⁶ And she said to him, "My father, you have opened your mouth to the Lord; do to me according to what has gone out of your mouth, now that the Lord has avenged you on your enemies, on the Ammonites." ³⁷ So she said to her father, "Let this thing be done for me: leave me alone two months, that I may go up and down on the mountains and weep for my virginity, I and my companions." ³⁸ So he said, "Go." Then he sent her away for two months, and she departed, she and her companions, and wept for her virginity on the mountains. ³⁹ And at the end of two months, she returned to her father, who did with her according to his vow that he had made. She had never known a man, and it became a custom in Israel ⁴⁰ that the daughters of Israel went year by year to lament the daughter of Jephthah the Gileadite four days in the year.

Jephthah's Conflict with Ephraim

12 The men of Ephraim were called to arms, and they crossed to Zaphon and said to Jephthah, "Why did you cross over to fight against the Ammonites and did not call us to go with you? We will burn your house over you with fire." ² And Jephthah said to them, "I and my people had a great dispute with the Ammonites, and when I called you, you did not save me from their hand. ³ And when I saw that you would not save me, I took my life in my hand and crossed over against the Ammonites, and the Lord gave them into my hand. Why then have you come up to me this day to fight against me?" ⁴ Then Jephthah gathered all the men of Gilead and fought with Ephraim. And the men of Gilead struck Ephraim, because they said, "You are fugitives of Ephraim, you Gileadites, in the midst of Ephraim and Manasseh." ⁵ And the Gileadites captured the fords of the Jordan against the Ephraimites.

¹ Or *whoever* ² Or *him*

And when any of the fugitives of Ephraim said, "Let me go over," the men of Gilead said to him, "Are you an Ephraimite?" When he said, "No," ⁶ they said to him, "Then say Shibboleth," and he said, "Sibboleth," for he could not pronounce it right. Then they seized him and slaughtered him at the fords of the Jordan. At that time 42,000 of the Ephraimites fell.

⁷ Jephthah judged Israel six years. Then Jephthah the Gileadite died and was buried in his city in Gilead.¹

Ibzan, Elon, and Abdon

⁸ After him Ibzan of Bethlehem judged Israel. ⁹ He had thirty sons, and thirty daughters he gave in marriage outside his clan, and thirty daughters he brought in from outside for his sons. And he judged Israel seven years. ¹⁰ Then Ibzan died and was buried at Bethlehem.

¹¹ After him Elon the Zebulunite judged Israel, and he judged Israel ten years. ¹² Then Elon the Zebulunite died and was buried at Aijalon in the land of Zebulun.

¹³ After him Abdon the son of Hillel the Pirathonite judged Israel. ¹⁴ He had forty sons and thirty grandsons, who rode on seventy donkeys, and he judged Israel eight years. ¹⁵ Then Abdon the son of Hillel the Pirathonite died and was buried at Pirathon in the land of Ephraim, in the hill country of the Amalekites.

The Birth of Samson

13 And the people of Israel again did what was evil in the sight of the Lord, so the Lord gave them into the hand of the Philistines for forty years.

² There was a certain man of Zorah, of the tribe of the Danites, whose name was Manoah. And his wife was barren and had no children. ³ And the angel of the Lord appeared to the woman and said to her, "Behold, you are barren and have not borne children, but you shall conceive and bear a son. ⁴ Therefore be careful and drink no wine or strong drink, and eat nothing unclean, ⁵ for behold, you shall conceive and bear a son. No razor shall come upon his head, for the child shall be a Nazirite to God from the womb, and he shall begin to save Israel from the hand of the Philistines." ⁶ Then the woman came and told her husband, "A man of God came to me, and his appearance was like the appearance of the angel of God, very awesome. I did not ask him where he was from, and he did not tell me his name, ⁷ but he said to me, 'Behold, you shall conceive and bear a son. So then drink no wine or strong drink,

---

¹ Septuagint; Hebrew *in the cities of Gilead*

and eat nothing unclean, for the child shall be a Nazirite to God from the womb to the day of his death.'"

⁸ Then Manoah prayed to the Lord and said, "O Lord, please let the man of God whom you sent come again to us and teach us what we are to do with the child who will be born." ⁹ And God listened to the voice of Manoah, and the angel of God came again to the woman as she sat in the field. But Manoah her husband was not with her. ¹⁰ So the woman ran quickly and told her husband, "Behold, the man who came to me the other day has appeared to me." ¹¹ And Manoah arose and went after his wife and came to the man and said to him, "Are you the man who spoke to this woman?" And he said, "I am." ¹² And Manoah said, "Now when your words come true, what is to be the child's manner of life, and what is his mission?" ¹³ And the angel of the Lord said to Manoah, "Of all that I said to the woman let her be careful. ¹⁴ She may not eat of anything that comes from the vine, neither let her drink wine or strong drink, or eat any unclean thing. All that I commanded her let her observe."

¹⁵ Manoah said to the angel of the Lord, "Please let us detain you and prepare a young goat for you." ¹⁶ And the angel of the Lord said to Manoah, "If you detain me, I will not eat of your food. But if you prepare a burnt offering, then offer it to the Lord." (For Manoah did not know that he was the angel of the Lord.) ¹⁷ And Manoah said to the angel of the Lord, "What is your name, so that, when your words come true, we may honor you?" ¹⁸ And the angel of the Lord said to him, "Why do you ask my name, seeing it is wonderful?" ¹⁹ So Manoah took the young goat with the grain offering, and offered it on the rock to the Lord, to the one who works[1] wonders, and Manoah and his wife were watching. ²⁰ And when the flame went up toward heaven from the altar, the angel of the Lord went up in the flame of the altar. Now Manoah and his wife were watching, and they fell on their faces to the ground.

²¹ The angel of the Lord appeared no more to Manoah and to his wife. Then Manoah knew that he was the angel of the Lord. ²² And Manoah said to his wife, "We shall surely die, for we have seen God." ²³ But his wife said to him, "If the Lord had meant to kill us, he would not have accepted a burnt offering and a grain offering at our hands, or shown us all these things, or now announced to us such things as these." ²⁴ And the woman bore a son and called his name Samson. And the young man grew, and the Lord blessed him. ²⁵ And the Spirit of the Lord began to stir him in Mahaneh-dan, between Zorah and Eshtaol.

[1] Septuagint, Vulgate; Hebrew *Lord, and working*

Samson's Marriage

14 Samson went down to Timnah, and at Timnah he saw one of the daughters of the Philistines. ²Then he came up and told his father and mother, "I saw one of the daughters of the Philistines at Timnah. Now get her for me as my wife." ³But his father and mother said to him, "Is there not a woman among the daughters of your relatives, or among all our people, that you must go to take a wife from the uncircumcised Philistines?" But Samson said to his father, "Get her for me, for she is right in my eyes."

⁴His father and mother did not know that it was from the Lord, for he was seeking an opportunity against the Philistines. At that time the Philistines ruled over Israel.

⁵Then Samson went down with his father and mother to Timnah, and they came to the vineyards of Timnah. And behold, a young lion came toward him roaring. ⁶Then the Spirit of the Lord rushed upon him, and although he had nothing in his hand, he tore the lion in pieces as one tears a young goat. But he did not tell his father or his mother what he had done. ⁷Then he went down and talked with the woman, and she was right in Samson's eyes.

⁸After some days he returned to take her. And he turned aside to see the carcass of the lion, and behold, there was a swarm of bees in the body of the lion, and honey. ⁹He scraped it out into his hands and went on, eating as he went. And he came to his father and mother and gave some to them, and they ate. But he did not tell them that he had scraped the honey from the carcass of the lion.

¹⁰His father went down to the woman, and Samson prepared a feast there, for so the young men used to do. ¹¹As soon as the people saw him, they brought thirty companions to be with him. ¹²And Samson said to them, "Let me now put a riddle to you. If you can tell me what it is, within the seven days of the feast, and find it out, then I will give you thirty linen garments and thirty changes of clothes, ¹³but if you cannot tell me what it is, then you shall give me thirty linen garments and thirty changes of clothes." And they said to him, "Put your riddle, that we may hear it." ¹⁴And he said to them,

"Out of the eater came something to eat.
Out of the strong came something sweet."

And in three days they could not solve the riddle.

¹⁵On the fourth[1] day they said to Samson's wife, "Entice your husband to tell us what the riddle is, lest we burn you and your father's house with fire. Have you invited us here to impoverish us?" ¹⁶And Samson's wife wept over him

[1] Septuagint, Syriac; Hebrew *seventh*

and said, "You only hate me; you do not love me. You have put a riddle to my people, and you have not told me what it is." And he said to her, "Behold, I have not told my father nor my mother, and shall I tell you?" ¹⁷ She wept before him the seven days that their feast lasted, and on the seventh day he told her, because she pressed him hard. Then she told the riddle to her people. ¹⁸ And the men of the city said to him on the seventh day before the sun went down,

"What is sweeter than honey?
What is stronger than a lion?"

And he said to them,

"If you had not plowed with my heifer,
you would not have found out my riddle."

¹⁹ And the Spirit of the LORD rushed upon him, and he went down to Ashkelon and struck down thirty men of the town and took their spoil and gave the garments to those who had told the riddle. In hot anger he went back to his father's house. ²⁰ And Samson's wife was given to his companion, who had been his best man.

Samson Defeats the Philistines

15 After some days, at the time of wheat harvest, Samson went to visit his wife with a young goat. And he said, "I will go in to my wife in the chamber." But her father would not allow him to go in. ² And her father said, "I really thought that you utterly hated her, so I gave her to your companion. Is not her younger sister more beautiful than she? Please take her instead." ³ And Samson said to them, "This time I shall be innocent in regard to the Philistines, when I do them harm." ⁴ So Samson went and caught 300 foxes and took torches. And he turned them tail to tail and put a torch between each pair of tails. ⁵ And when he had set fire to the torches, he let the foxes go into the standing grain of the Philistines and set fire to the stacked grain and the standing grain, as well as the olive orchards. ⁶ Then the Philistines said, "Who has done this?" And they said, "Samson, the son-in-law of the Timnite, because he has taken his wife and given her to his companion." And the Philistines came up and burned her and her father with fire. ⁷ And Samson said to them, "If this is what you do, I swear I will be avenged on you, and after that I will quit." ⁸ And he struck them hip and thigh with a great blow, and he went down and stayed in the cleft of the rock of Etam.

⁹ Then the Philistines came up and encamped in Judah and made a raid on Lehi. ¹⁰ And the men of Judah said, "Why have you come up against us?" They said, "We have come up to bind Samson, to do to him as he did to us." ¹¹ Then 3,000 men of Judah went down to the cleft of the rock of Etam, and said to Samson, "Do you not know that the Philistines are rulers over us? What then is this that you have done to us?" And he said to them, "As they did to me, so have I done to them." ¹² And they said to him, "We have come down to bind you, that we may give you into the hands of the Philistines." And Samson said to them, "Swear to me that you will not attack me yourselves." ¹³ They said to him, "No; we will only bind you and give you into their hands. We will surely not kill you." So they bound him with two new ropes and brought him up from the rock.

¹⁴ When he came to Lehi, the Philistines came shouting to meet him. Then the Spirit of the Lord rushed upon him, and the ropes that were on his arms became as flax that has caught fire, and his bonds melted off his hands. ¹⁵ And he found a fresh jawbone of a donkey, and put out his hand and took it, and with it he struck 1,000 men. ¹⁶ And Samson said,

> "With the jawbone of a donkey,
>> heaps upon heaps,
> with the jawbone of a donkey
>> have I struck down a thousand men."

¹⁷ As soon as he had finished speaking, he threw away the jawbone out of his hand. And that place was called Ramath-lehi.[1]

¹⁸ And he was very thirsty, and he called upon the Lord and said, "You have granted this great salvation by the hand of your servant, and shall I now die of thirst and fall into the hands of the uncircumcised?" ¹⁹ And God split open the hollow place that is at Lehi, and water came out from it. And when he drank, his spirit returned, and he revived. Therefore the name of it was called En-hakkore;[2] it is at Lehi to this day. ²⁰ And he judged Israel in the days of the Philistines twenty years.

Samson and Delilah

16 Samson went to Gaza, and there he saw a prostitute, and he went in to her. ² The Gazites were told, "Samson has come here." And they surrounded the place and set an ambush for him all night at the gate of the city. They kept quiet all night, saying, "Let us wait till the light of

---

[1] *Ramath-lehi* means *the hill of the jawbone* [2] *En-hakkore* means *the spring of him who called*

the morning; then we will kill him." ³ But Samson lay till midnight, and at midnight he arose and took hold of the doors of the gate of the city and the two posts, and pulled them up, bar and all, and put them on his shoulders and carried them to the top of the hill that is in front of Hebron.

⁴ After this he loved a woman in the Valley of Sorek, whose name was Delilah. ⁵ And the lords of the Philistines came up to her and said to her, "Seduce him, and see where his great strength lies, and by what means we may overpower him, that we may bind him to humble him. And we will each give you 1,100 pieces of silver." ⁶ So Delilah said to Samson, "Please tell me where your great strength lies, and how you might be bound, that one could subdue you."

⁷ Samson said to her, "If they bind me with seven fresh bowstrings that have not been dried, then I shall become weak and be like any other man." ⁸ Then the lords of the Philistines brought up to her seven fresh bowstrings that had not been dried, and she bound him with them. ⁹ Now she had men lying in ambush in an inner chamber. And she said to him, "The Philistines are upon you, Samson!" But he snapped the bowstrings, as a thread of flax snaps when it touches the fire. So the secret of his strength was not known.

¹⁰ Then Delilah said to Samson, "Behold, you have mocked me and told me lies. Please tell me how you might be bound." ¹¹ And he said to her, "If they bind me with new ropes that have not been used, then I shall become weak and be like any other man." ¹² So Delilah took new ropes and bound him with them and said to him, "The Philistines are upon you, Samson!" And the men lying in ambush were in an inner chamber. But he snapped the ropes off his arms like a thread.

¹³ Then Delilah said to Samson, "Until now you have mocked me and told me lies. Tell me how you might be bound." And he said to her, "If you weave the seven locks of my head with the web and fasten it tight with the pin, then I shall become weak and be like any other man." ¹⁴ So while he slept, Delilah took the seven locks of his head and wove them into the web.[1] And she made them tight with the pin and said to him, "The Philistines are upon you, Samson!" But he awoke from his sleep and pulled away the pin, the loom, and the web.

¹⁵ And she said to him, "How can you say, 'I love you,' when your heart is not with me? You have mocked me these three times, and you have not told me where your great strength lies." ¹⁶ And when she pressed him hard with her words day after day, and urged him, his soul was vexed to death. ¹⁷ And he told her all his heart, and said to her, "A razor has never come upon my

---

[1] Compare Septuagint; Hebrew lacks *and fasten it tight . . . into the web*

head, for I have been a Nazirite to God from my mother's womb. If my head is shaved, then my strength will leave me, and I shall become weak and be like any other man."

ⁱ⁸ When Delilah saw that he had told her all his heart, she sent and called the lords of the Philistines, saying, "Come up again, for he has told me all his heart." Then the lords of the Philistines came up to her and brought the money in their hands. ¹⁹ She made him sleep on her knees. And she called a man and had him shave off the seven locks of his head. Then she began to torment him, and his strength left him. ²⁰ And she said, "The Philistines are upon you, Samson!" And he awoke from his sleep and said, "I will go out as at other times and shake myself free." But he did not know that the LORD had left him. ²¹ And the Philistines seized him and gouged out his eyes and brought him down to Gaza and bound him with bronze shackles. And he ground at the mill in the prison. ²² But the hair of his head began to grow again after it had been shaved.

The Death of Samson

²³ Now the lords of the Philistines gathered to offer a great sacrifice to Dagon their god and to rejoice, and they said, "Our god has given Samson our enemy into our hand." ²⁴ And when the people saw him, they praised their god. For they said, "Our god has given our enemy into our hand, the ravager of our country, who has killed many of us."[1] ²⁵ And when their hearts were merry, they said, "Call Samson, that he may entertain us." So they called Samson out of the prison, and he entertained them. They made him stand between the pillars. ²⁶ And Samson said to the young man who held him by the hand, "Let me feel the pillars on which the house rests, that I may lean against them." ²⁷ Now the house was full of men and women. All the lords of the Philistines were there, and on the roof there were about 3,000 men and women, who looked on while Samson entertained.

²⁸ Then Samson called to the LORD and said, "O Lord GOD, please remember me and please strengthen me only this once, O God, that I may be avenged on the Philistines for my two eyes." ²⁹ And Samson grasped the two middle pillars on which the house rested, and he leaned his weight against them, his right hand on the one and his left hand on the other. ³⁰ And Samson said, "Let me die with the Philistines." Then he bowed with all his strength, and the house fell upon the lords and upon all the people who were in it. So the dead whom he killed at his death were more than those whom he had killed during his life. ³¹ Then his brothers and all his family came down and took

[1] Or *who has multiplied our slain*

him and brought him up and buried him between Zorah and Eshtaol in the tomb of Manoah his father. He had judged Israel twenty years.

Micah and the Levite

17 There was a man of the hill country of Ephraim, whose name was Micah. ² And he said to his mother, "The 1,100 pieces of silver that were taken from you, about which you uttered a curse, and also spoke it in my ears, behold, the silver is with me; I took it." And his mother said, "Blessed be my son by the Lord." ³ And he restored the 1,100 pieces of silver to his mother. And his mother said, "I dedicate the silver to the Lord from my hand for my son, to make a carved image and a metal image. Now therefore I will restore it to you." ⁴ So when he restored the money to his mother, his mother took 200 pieces of silver and gave it to the silversmith, who made it into a carved image and a metal image. And it was in the house of Micah. ⁵ And the man Micah had a shrine, and he made an ephod and household gods, and ordained[1] one of his sons, who became his priest. ⁶ In those days there was no king in Israel. Everyone did what was right in his own eyes.

⁷ Now there was a young man of Bethlehem in Judah, of the family of Judah, who was a Levite, and he sojourned there. ⁸ And the man departed from the town of Bethlehem in Judah to sojourn where he could find a place. And as he journeyed, he came to the hill country of Ephraim to the house of Micah. ⁹ And Micah said to him, "Where do you come from?" And he said to him, "I am a Levite of Bethlehem in Judah, and I am going to sojourn where I may find a place." ¹⁰ And Micah said to him, "Stay with me, and be to me a father and a priest, and I will give you ten pieces of silver a year and a suit of clothes and your living." And the Levite went in. ¹¹ And the Levite was content to dwell with the man, and the young man became to him like one of his sons. ¹² And Micah ordained the Levite, and the young man became his priest, and was in the house of Micah. ¹³ Then Micah said, "Now I know that the Lord will prosper me, because I have a Levite as priest."

Danites Take the Levite and the Idol

18 In those days there was no king in Israel. And in those days the tribe of the people of Dan was seeking for itself an inheritance to dwell in, for until then no inheritance among the tribes of Israel had fallen to them. ² So the people of Dan sent five able men from the whole number of their tribe, from Zorah and from Eshtaol, to spy out the land and to explore it. And they said to them, "Go and explore the land." And they came to the hill

---

[1] Hebrew *filled the hand of;* also verse 12

country of Ephraim, to the house of Micah, and lodged there. ³ When they were by the house of Micah, they recognized the voice of the young Levite. And they turned aside and said to him, "Who brought you here? What are you doing in this place? What is your business here?" ⁴ And he said to them, "This is how Micah dealt with me: he has hired me, and I have become his priest." ⁵ And they said to him, "Inquire of God, please, that we may know whether the journey on which we are setting out will succeed." ⁶ And the priest said to them, "Go in peace. The journey on which you go is under the eye of the Lord."

⁷ Then the five men departed and came to Laish and saw the people who were there, how they lived in security, after the manner of the Sidonians, quiet and unsuspecting, lacking¹ nothing that is in the earth and possessing wealth, and how they were far from the Sidonians and had no dealings with anyone. ⁸ And when they came to their brothers at Zorah and Eshtaol, their brothers said to them, "What do you report?" ⁹ They said, "Arise, and let us go up against them, for we have seen the land, and behold, it is very good. And will you do nothing? Do not be slow to go, to enter in and possess the land. ¹⁰ As soon as you go, you will come to an unsuspecting people. The land is spacious, for God has given it into your hands, a place where there is no lack of anything that is in the earth."

¹¹ So 600 men of the tribe of Dan, armed with weapons of war, set out from Zorah and Eshtaol, ¹² and went up and encamped at Kiriath-jearim in Judah. On this account that place is called Mahaneh-dan² to this day; behold, it is west of Kiriath-jearim. ¹³ And they passed on from there to the hill country of Ephraim, and came to the house of Micah.

¹⁴ Then the five men who had gone to scout out the country of Laish said to their brothers, "Do you know that in these houses there are an ephod, household gods, a carved image, and a metal image? Now therefore consider what you will do." ¹⁵ And they turned aside there and came to the house of the young Levite, at the home of Micah, and asked him about his welfare. ¹⁶ Now the 600 men of the Danites, armed with their weapons of war, stood by the entrance of the gate. ¹⁷ And the five men who had gone to scout out the land went up and entered and took the carved image, the ephod, the household gods, and the metal image, while the priest stood by the entrance of the gate with the 600 men armed with weapons of war. ¹⁸ And when these went into Micah's house and took the carved image, the ephod, the household gods, and the metal image, the priest said to them, "What are you doing?" ¹⁹ And they said to him, "Keep quiet; put your hand on your mouth

¹ Compare 18:10; the meaning of the Hebrew word is uncertain   ² *Mahaneh-dan* means *camp of Dan*

and come with us and be to us a father and a priest. Is it better for you to be priest to the house of one man, or to be priest to a tribe and clan in Israel?" [20] And the priest's heart was glad. He took the ephod and the household gods and the carved image and went along with the people.

[21] So they turned and departed, putting the little ones and the livestock and the goods in front of them. [22] When they had gone a distance from the home of Micah, the men who were in the houses near Micah's house were called out, and they overtook the people of Dan. [23] And they shouted to the people of Dan, who turned around and said to Micah, "What is the matter with you, that you come with such a company?" [24] And he said, "You take my gods that I made and the priest, and go away, and what have I left? How then do you ask me, 'What is the matter with you?' " [25] And the people of Dan said to him, "Do not let your voice be heard among us, lest angry fellows fall upon you, and you lose your life with the lives of your household." [26] Then the people of Dan went their way. And when Micah saw that they were too strong for him, he turned and went back to his home.

[27] But the people of Dan took what Micah had made, and the priest who belonged to him, and they came to Laish, to a people quiet and unsuspecting, and struck them with the edge of the sword and burned the city with fire. [28] And there was no deliverer because it was far from Sidon, and they had no dealings with anyone. It was in the valley that belongs to Beth-rehob. Then they rebuilt the city and lived in it. [29] And they named the city Dan, after the name of Dan their ancestor, who was born to Israel; but the name of the city was Laish at the first. [30] And the people of Dan set up the carved image for themselves, and Jonathan the son of Gershom, son of Moses,[1] and his sons were priests to the tribe of the Danites until the day of the captivity of the land. [31] So they set up Micah's carved image that he made, as long as the house of God was at Shiloh.

A Levite and His Concubine

19 In those days, when there was no king in Israel, a certain Levite was sojourning in the remote parts of the hill country of Ephraim, who took to himself a concubine from Bethlehem in Judah. [2] And his concubine was unfaithful to[2] him, and she went away from him to her father's house at Bethlehem in Judah, and was there some four months. [3] Then her husband arose and went after her, to speak kindly to her and bring her back. He had with him his servant and a couple of donkeys. And she brought him into her father's house. And when the girl's father saw him, he came with joy to meet

---
[1] Or *Manasseh* [2] Septuagint, Old Latin *became angry with*

him. ⁴ And his father-in-law, the girl's father, made him stay, and he remained with him three days. So they ate and drank and spent the night there. ⁵ And on the fourth day they arose early in the morning, and he prepared to go, but the girl's father said to his son-in-law, "Strengthen your heart with a morsel of bread, and after that you may go." ⁶ So the two of them sat and ate and drank together. And the girl's father said to the man, "Be pleased to spend the night, and let your heart be merry." ⁷ And when the man rose up to go, his father-in-law pressed him, till he spent the night there again. ⁸ And on the fifth day he arose early in the morning to depart. And the girl's father said, "Strengthen your heart and wait until the day declines." So they ate, both of them. ⁹ And when the man and his concubine and his servant rose up to depart, his father-in-law, the girl's father, said to him, "Behold, now the day has waned toward evening. Please, spend the night. Behold, the day draws to its close. Lodge here and let your heart be merry, and tomorrow you shall arise early in the morning for your journey, and go home."

¹⁰ But the man would not spend the night. He rose up and departed and arrived opposite Jebus (that is, Jerusalem). He had with him a couple of saddled donkeys, and his concubine was with him. ¹¹ When they were near Jebus, the day was nearly over, and the servant said to his master, "Come now, let us turn aside to this city of the Jebusites and spend the night in it." ¹² And his master said to him, "We will not turn aside into the city of foreigners, who do not belong to the people of Israel, but we will pass on to Gibeah." ¹³ And he said to his young man, "Come and let us draw near to one of these places and spend the night at Gibeah or at Ramah." ¹⁴ So they passed on and went their way. And the sun went down on them near Gibeah, which belongs to Benjamin, ¹⁵ and they turned aside there, to go in and spend the night at Gibeah. And he went in and sat down in the open square of the city, for no one took them into his house to spend the night.

¹⁶ And behold, an old man was coming from his work in the field at evening. The man was from the hill country of Ephraim, and he was sojourning in Gibeah. The men of the place were Benjaminites. ¹⁷ And he lifted up his eyes and saw the traveler in the open square of the city. And the old man said, "Where are you going? And where do you come from?" ¹⁸ And he said to him, "We are passing from Bethlehem in Judah to the remote parts of the hill country of Ephraim, from which I come. I went to Bethlehem in Judah, and I am going to the house of the Lord,[1] but no one has taken me into his house. ¹⁹ We have straw and feed for our donkeys, with bread and wine for me and your female servant and the young man with your servants. There is

[1] Septuagint *my home*; compare verse 29

no lack of anything." ²⁰ And the old man said, "Peace be to you; I will care for all your wants. Only, do not spend the night in the square." ²¹ So he brought him into his house and gave the donkeys feed. And they washed their feet, and ate and drank.

Gibeah's Crime

²² As they were making their hearts merry, behold, the men of the city, worthless fellows, surrounded the house, beating on the door. And they said to the old man, the master of the house, "Bring out the man who came into your house, that we may know him." ²³ And the man, the master of the house, went out to them and said to them, "No, my brothers, do not act so wickedly; since this man has come into my house, do not do this vile thing. ²⁴ Behold, here are my virgin daughter and his concubine. Let me bring them out now. Violate them and do with them what seems good to you, but against this man do not do this outrageous thing." ²⁵ But the men would not listen to him. So the man seized his concubine and made her go out to them. And they knew her and abused her all night until the morning. And as the dawn began to break, they let her go. ²⁶ And as morning appeared, the woman came and fell down at the door of the man's house where her master was, until it was light.

²⁷ And her master rose up in the morning, and when he opened the doors of the house and went out to go on his way, behold, there was his concubine lying at the door of the house, with her hands on the threshold. ²⁸ He said to her, "Get up, let us be going." But there was no answer. Then he put her on the donkey, and the man rose up and went away to his home. ²⁹ And when he entered his house, he took a knife, and taking hold of his concubine he divided her, limb by limb, into twelve pieces, and sent her throughout all the territory of Israel. ³⁰ And all who saw it said, "Such a thing has never happened or been seen from the day that the people of Israel came up out of the land of Egypt until this day; consider it, take counsel, and speak."

Israel's War with the Tribe of Benjamin

20 Then all the people of Israel came out, from Dan to Beersheba, including the land of Gilead, and the congregation assembled as one man to the LORD at Mizpah. ² And the chiefs of all the people, of all the tribes of Israel, presented themselves in the assembly of the people of God, 400,000 men on foot that drew the sword. ³ (Now the people of Benjamin heard that the people of Israel had gone up to Mizpah.) And the people of Israel said, "Tell us, how did this evil happen?" ⁴ And the Levite, the husband of the woman who was murdered, answered and said, "I came to Gibeah that belongs to Benjamin, I and my concubine, to spend the night. ⁵ And the leaders of Gibeah rose against me and surrounded the house against me by night. They meant to kill me, and they violated my concubine, and she is dead. ⁶ So I took hold of my concubine and cut her in pieces and sent her throughout all the country of the inheritance of Israel, for they have committed abomination and outrage in Israel. ⁷ Behold, you people of Israel, all of you, give your advice and counsel here."

⁸ And all the people arose as one man, saying, "None of us will go to his tent, and none of us will return to his house. ⁹ But now this is what we will do to Gibeah: we will go up against it by lot, ¹⁰ and we will take ten men of a hundred throughout all the tribes of Israel, and a hundred of a thousand, and a thousand of ten thousand, to bring provisions for the people, that when they come they may repay Gibeah of Benjamin for all the outrage that they have committed in Israel." ¹¹ So all the men of Israel gathered against the city, united as one man.

¹² And the tribes of Israel sent men through all the tribe of Benjamin, saying, "What evil is this that has taken place among you? ¹³ Now therefore give up the men, the worthless fellows in Gibeah, that we may put them to death and purge evil from Israel." But the Benjaminites would not listen to the voice of their brothers, the people of Israel. ¹⁴ Then the people of Benjamin came together out of the cities to Gibeah to go out to battle against the people of Israel. ¹⁵ And the people of Benjamin mustered out of their cities on that day 26,000 men who drew the sword, besides the inhabitants of Gibeah, who mustered 700 chosen men. ¹⁶ Among all these were 700 chosen men who were left-handed; every one could sling a stone at a hair and not miss. ¹⁷ And the men of Israel, apart from Benjamin, mustered 400,000 men who drew the sword; all these were men of war.

¹⁸ The people of Israel arose and went up to Bethel and inquired of God, "Who shall go up first for us to fight against the people of Benjamin?" And the Lord said, "Judah shall go up first."

¹⁹ Then the people of Israel rose in the morning and encamped against Gibeah. ²⁰ And the men of Israel went out to fight against Benjamin, and the men of Israel drew up the battle line against them at Gibeah. ²¹ The people of Benjamin came out of Gibeah and destroyed on that day 22,000 men of the Israelites. ²² But the people, the men of Israel, took courage, and again formed the battle line in the same place where they had formed it on the first day. ²³ And the people of Israel went up and wept before the Lord until the evening. And they inquired of the Lord, "Shall we again draw near to fight against our brothers, the people of Benjamin?" And the Lord said, "Go up against them."

²⁴ So the people of Israel came near against the people of Benjamin the second day. ²⁵ And Benjamin went against them out of Gibeah the second day, and destroyed 18,000 men of the people of Israel. All these were men who drew the sword. ²⁶ Then all the people of Israel, the whole army, went up and came to Bethel and wept. They sat there before the Lord and fasted that day until evening, and offered burnt offerings and peace offerings before the Lord. ²⁷ And the people of Israel inquired of the Lord (for the ark of the covenant of God was there in those days, ²⁸ and Phinehas the son of Eleazar, son of Aaron, ministered before it in those days), saying, "Shall we go out once more to battle against our brothers, the people of Benjamin, or shall we cease?" And the Lord said, "Go up, for tomorrow I will give them into your hand."

²⁹ So Israel set men in ambush around Gibeah. ³⁰ And the people of Israel went up against the people of Benjamin on the third day and set themselves in array against Gibeah, as at other times. ³¹ And the people of Benjamin went out against the people and were drawn away from the city. And as at other times they began to strike and kill some of the people in the highways, one of which goes up to Bethel and the other to Gibeah, and in the open country, about thirty men of Israel. ³² And the people of Benjamin said, "They are routed before us, as at the first." But the people of Israel said, "Let us flee and draw them away from the city to the highways." ³³ And all the men of Israel rose up out of their place and set themselves in array at Baal-tamar, and the men of Israel who were in ambush rushed out of their place from Maareh-geba.¹ ³⁴ And there came against Gibeah 10,000 chosen men out of all Israel, and the battle was hard, but the Benjaminites did not know that disaster was close upon them. ³⁵ And the Lord defeated Benjamin before Israel, and the people of Israel destroyed 25,100 men of Benjamin that day. All these were men who drew the sword. ³⁶ So the people of Benjamin saw that they were defeated.

The men of Israel gave ground to Benjamin, because they trusted the men in ambush whom they had set against Gibeah. ³⁷ Then the men in ambush hurried and rushed against Gibeah; the men in ambush moved out and struck all the city with the edge of the sword. ³⁸ Now the appointed signal between the men of Israel and the men in the main ambush was that when they made a great cloud of smoke rise up out of the city ³⁹ the men of Israel should turn in battle. Now Benjamin had begun to strike and kill about thirty men of Israel. They said, "Surely they are defeated before us, as in the first battle." ⁴⁰ But when the signal began to rise out of the city in a column

---
¹ Some Septuagint manuscripts *place west of Geba*

of smoke, the Benjaminites looked behind them, and behold, the whole of the city went up in smoke to heaven. ⁴¹ Then the men of Israel turned, and the men of Benjamin were dismayed, for they saw that disaster was close upon them. ⁴² Therefore they turned their backs before the men of Israel in the direction of the wilderness, but the battle overtook them. And those who came out of the cities were destroying them in their midst. ⁴³ Surrounding the Benjaminites, they pursued them and trod them down from Nohah[1] as far as opposite Gibeah on the east. ⁴⁴ Eighteen thousand men of Benjamin fell, all of them men of valor. ⁴⁵ And they turned and fled toward the wilderness to the rock of Rimmon. Five thousand men of them were cut down in the highways. And they were pursued hard to Gidom, and 2,000 men of them were struck down. ⁴⁶ So all who fell that day of Benjamin were 25,000 men who drew the sword, all of them men of valor. ⁴⁷ But 600 men turned and fled toward the wilderness to the rock of Rimmon and remained at the rock of Rimmon four months. ⁴⁸ And the men of Israel turned back against the people of Benjamin and struck them with the edge of the sword, the city, men and beasts and all that they found. And all the towns that they found they set on fire.

Wives Provided for the Tribe of Benjamin

21 Now the men of Israel had sworn at Mizpah, "No one of us shall give his daughter in marriage to Benjamin." ² And the people came to Bethel and sat there till evening before God, and they lifted up their voices and wept bitterly. ³ And they said, "O Lord, the God of Israel, why has this happened in Israel, that today there should be one tribe lacking in Israel?" ⁴ And the next day the people rose early and built there an altar and offered burnt offerings and peace offerings. ⁵ And the people of Israel said, "Which of all the tribes of Israel did not come up in the assembly to the Lord?" For they had taken a great oath concerning him who did not come up to the Lord to Mizpah, saying, "He shall surely be put to death." ⁶ And the people of Israel had compassion for Benjamin their brother and said, "One tribe is cut off from Israel this day. ⁷ What shall we do for wives for those who are left, since we have sworn by the Lord that we will not give them any of our daughters for wives?"

⁸ And they said, "What one is there of the tribes of Israel that did not come up to the Lord to Mizpah?" And behold, no one had come to the camp from Jabesh-gilead, to the assembly. ⁹ For when the people were mustered, behold, not one of the inhabitants of Jabesh-gilead was there. ¹⁰ So the congregation

---

[1] Septuagint; Hebrew [at their] *resting place*

sent 12,000 of their bravest men there and commanded them, "Go and strike the inhabitants of Jabesh-gilead with the edge of the sword; also the women and the little ones. ¹¹ This is what you shall do: every male and every woman that has lain with a male you shall devote to destruction." ¹² And they found among the inhabitants of Jabesh-gilead 400 young virgins who had not known a man by lying with him, and they brought them to the camp at Shiloh, which is in the land of Canaan.

¹³ Then the whole congregation sent word to the people of Benjamin who were at the rock of Rimmon and proclaimed peace to them. ¹⁴ And Benjamin returned at that time. And they gave them the women whom they had saved alive of the women of Jabesh-gilead, but they were not enough for them. ¹⁵ And the people had compassion on Benjamin because the Lord had made a breach in the tribes of Israel.

¹⁶ Then the elders of the congregation said, "What shall we do for wives for those who are left, since the women are destroyed out of Benjamin?" ¹⁷ And they said, "There must be an inheritance for the survivors of Benjamin, that a tribe not be blotted out from Israel. ¹⁸ Yet we cannot give them wives from our daughters." For the people of Israel had sworn, "Cursed be he who gives a wife to Benjamin." ¹⁹ So they said, "Behold, there is the yearly feast of the Lord at Shiloh, which is north of Bethel, on the east of the highway that goes up from Bethel to Shechem, and south of Lebonah." ²⁰ And they commanded the people of Benjamin, saying, "Go and lie in ambush in the vineyards ²¹ and watch. If the daughters of Shiloh come out to dance in the dances, then come out of the vineyards and snatch each man his wife from the daughters of Shiloh, and go to the land of Benjamin. ²² And when their fathers or their brothers come to complain to us, we will say to them, 'Grant them graciously to us, because we did not take for each man of them his wife in battle, neither did you give them to them, else you would now be guilty.'" ²³ And the people of Benjamin did so and took their wives, according to their number, from the dancers whom they carried off. Then they went and returned to their inheritance and rebuilt the towns and lived in them. ²⁴ And the people of Israel departed from there at that time, every man to his tribe and family, and they went out from there every man to his inheritance.

²⁵ In those days there was no king in Israel. Everyone did what was right in his own eyes.

RUTH

Naomi Widowed

1 In the days when the judges ruled there was a famine in the land, and a man of Bethlehem in Judah went to sojourn in the country of Moab, he and his wife and his two sons. ²The name of the man was Elimelech and the name of his wife Naomi, and the names of his two sons were Mahlon and Chilion. They were Ephrathites from Bethlehem in Judah. They went into the country of Moab and remained there. ³But Elimelech, the husband of Naomi, died, and she was left with her two sons. ⁴These took Moabite wives; the name of the one was Orpah and the name of the other Ruth. They lived there about ten years, ⁵and both Mahlon and Chilion died, so that the woman was left without her two sons and her husband.

Ruth's Loyalty to Naomi

⁶Then she arose with her daughters-in-law to return from the country of Moab, for she had heard in the fields of Moab that the Lord had visited his people and given them food. ⁷So she set out from the place where she was with her two daughters-in-law, and they went on the way to return to the land of Judah. ⁸But Naomi said to her two daughters-in-law, "Go, return each of you to her mother's house. May the Lord deal kindly with you, as you have dealt with the dead and with me. ⁹The Lord grant that you may find rest, each of you in the house of her husband!" Then she kissed them, and they lifted up their voices and wept. ¹⁰And they said to her, "No, we will return with you to your people." ¹¹But Naomi said, "Turn back, my daughters; why will you go with me? Have I yet sons in my womb that they may become your husbands? ¹²Turn back, my daughters; go your way, for I am too old to have a husband. If I should say I have hope, even if I should have a husband this night and should bear sons, ¹³would you therefore wait till they were grown? Would you therefore refrain from marrying? No, my daughters, for it is exceedingly bitter to me for your sake that the hand of the Lord has gone out against me." ¹⁴Then they lifted up their voices and wept again. And Orpah kissed her mother-in-law, but Ruth clung to her.

ⁱ⁵ And she said, "See, your sister-in-law has gone back to her people and to her gods; return after your sister-in-law." ¹⁶ But Ruth said, "Do not urge me to leave you or to return from following you. For where you go I will go, and where you lodge I will lodge. Your people shall be my people, and your God my God. ¹⁷ Where you die I will die, and there will I be buried. May the Lord do so to me and more also if anything but death parts me from you." ¹⁸ And when Naomi saw that she was determined to go with her, she said no more.

Naomi and Ruth Return

¹⁹ So the two of them went on until they came to Bethlehem. And when they came to Bethlehem, the whole town was stirred because of them. And the women said, "Is this Naomi?" ²⁰ She said to them, "Do not call me Naomi;[1] call me Mara,[2] for the Almighty has dealt very bitterly with me. ²¹ I went away full, and the Lord has brought me back empty. Why call me Naomi, when the Lord has testified against me and the Almighty has brought calamity upon me?"

²² So Naomi returned, and Ruth the Moabite her daughter-in-law with her, who returned from the country of Moab. And they came to Bethlehem at the beginning of barley harvest.

Ruth Meets Boaz

2 Now Naomi had a relative of her husband's, a worthy man of the clan of Elimelech, whose name was Boaz. ² And Ruth the Moabite said to Naomi, "Let me go to the field and glean among the ears of grain after him in whose sight I shall find favor." And she said to her, "Go, my daughter." ³ So she set out and went and gleaned in the field after the reapers, and she happened to come to the part of the field belonging to Boaz, who was of the clan of Elimelech. ⁴ And behold, Boaz came from Bethlehem. And he said to the reapers, "The Lord be with you!" And they answered, "The Lord bless you." ⁵ Then Boaz said to his young man who was in charge of the reapers, "Whose young woman is this?" ⁶ And the servant who was in charge of the reapers answered, "She is the young Moabite woman, who came back with Naomi from the country of Moab. ⁷ She said, 'Please let me glean and gather among the sheaves after the reapers.' So she came, and she has continued from early morning until now, except for a short rest."[3]

⁸ Then Boaz said to Ruth, "Now, listen, my daughter, do not go to glean in another field or leave this one, but keep close to my young women. ⁹ Let your eyes be on the field that they are reaping, and go after them. Have I not charged the young men not to touch you? And when you are thirsty, go to

---

[1] *Naomi* means *pleasant* [2] *Mara* means *bitter* [3] Compare Septuagint, Vulgate; the meaning of the Hebrew phrase is uncertain

the vessels and drink what the young men have drawn." ¹⁰ Then she fell on her face, bowing to the ground, and said to him, "Why have I found favor in your eyes, that you should take notice of me, since I am a foreigner?" ¹¹ But Boaz answered her, "All that you have done for your mother-in-law since the death of your husband has been fully told to me, and how you left your father and mother and your native land and came to a people that you did not know before. ¹² The Lord repay you for what you have done, and a full reward be given you by the Lord, the God of Israel, under whose wings you have come to take refuge!" ¹³ Then she said, "I have found favor in your eyes, my lord, for you have comforted me and spoken kindly to your servant, though I am not one of your servants."

¹⁴ And at mealtime Boaz said to her, "Come here and eat some bread and dip your morsel in the wine." So she sat beside the reapers, and he passed to her roasted grain. And she ate until she was satisfied, and she had some left over. ¹⁵ When she rose to glean, Boaz instructed his young men, saying, "Let her glean even among the sheaves, and do not reproach her. ¹⁶ And also pull out some from the bundles for her and leave it for her to glean, and do not rebuke her."

¹⁷ So she gleaned in the field until evening. Then she beat out what she had gleaned, and it was about an ephah¹ of barley. ¹⁸ And she took it up and went into the city. Her mother-in-law saw what she had gleaned. She also brought out and gave her what food she had left over after being satisfied. ¹⁹ And her mother-in-law said to her, "Where did you glean today? And where have you worked? Blessed be the man who took notice of you." So she told her mother-in-law with whom she had worked and said, "The man's name with whom I worked today is Boaz." ²⁰ And Naomi said to her daughter-in-law, "May he be blessed by the Lord, whose kindness has not forsaken the living or the dead!" Naomi also said to her, "The man is a close relative of ours, one of our redeemers." ²¹ And Ruth the Moabite said, "Besides, he said to me, 'You shall keep close by my young men until they have finished all my harvest.'" ²² And Naomi said to Ruth, her daughter-in-law, "It is good, my daughter, that you go out with his young women, lest in another field you be assaulted." ²³ So she kept close to the young women of Boaz, gleaning until the end of the barley and wheat harvests. And she lived with her mother-in-law.

Ruth and Boaz at the Threshing Floor

3 Then Naomi her mother-in-law said to her, "My daughter, should I not seek rest for you, that it may be well with you? ² Is not Boaz our relative, with whose young women you were? See, he is winnowing barley tonight

---

¹ An *ephah* was about 3/5 bushel or 22 liters

at the threshing floor. ³ Wash therefore and anoint yourself, and put on your cloak and go down to the threshing floor, but do not make yourself known to the man until he has finished eating and drinking. ⁴ But when he lies down, observe the place where he lies. Then go and uncover his feet and lie down, and he will tell you what to do." ⁵ And she replied, "All that you say I will do."

⁶ So she went down to the threshing floor and did just as her mother-in-law had commanded her. ⁷ And when Boaz had eaten and drunk, and his heart was merry, he went to lie down at the end of the heap of grain. Then she came softly and uncovered his feet and lay down. ⁸ At midnight the man was startled and turned over, and behold, a woman lay at his feet! ⁹ He said, "Who are you?" And she answered, "I am Ruth, your servant. Spread your wings[1] over your servant, for you are a redeemer." ¹⁰ And he said, "May you be blessed by the Lord, my daughter. You have made this last kindness greater than the first in that you have not gone after young men, whether poor or rich. ¹¹ And now, my daughter, do not fear. I will do for you all that you ask, for all my fellow townsmen know that you are a worthy woman. ¹² And now it is true that I am a redeemer. Yet there is a redeemer nearer than I. ¹³ Remain tonight, and in the morning, if he will redeem you, good; let him do it. But if he is not willing to redeem you, then, as the Lord lives, I will redeem you. Lie down until the morning."

¹⁴ So she lay at his feet until the morning, but arose before one could recognize another. And he said, "Let it not be known that the woman came to the threshing floor." ¹⁵ And he said, "Bring the garment you are wearing and hold it out." So she held it, and he measured out six measures of barley and put it on her. Then she went into the city. ¹⁶ And when she came to her mother-in-law, she said, "How did you fare, my daughter?" Then she told her all that the man had done for her, ¹⁷ saying, "These six measures of barley he gave to me, for he said to me, 'You must not go back empty-handed to your mother-in-law.'" ¹⁸ She replied, "Wait, my daughter, until you learn how the matter turns out, for the man will not rest but will settle the matter today."

Boaz Redeems Ruth

4 Now Boaz had gone up to the gate and sat down there. And behold, the redeemer, of whom Boaz had spoken, came by. So Boaz said, "Turn aside, friend; sit down here." And he turned aside and sat down. ² And he took ten men of the elders of the city and said, "Sit down here." So they sat down. ³ Then he said to the redeemer, "Naomi, who has come back from the country

---

[1] Compare 2:12; the word for *wings* can also mean *corners of a garment*

of Moab, is selling the parcel of land that belonged to our relative Elimelech. ⁴ So I thought I would tell you of it and say, 'Buy it in the presence of those sitting here and in the presence of the elders of my people.' If you will redeem it, redeem it. But if you[1] will not, tell me, that I may know, for there is no one besides you to redeem it, and I come after you." And he said, "I will redeem it." ⁵ Then Boaz said, "The day you buy the field from the hand of Naomi, you also acquire Ruth[2] the Moabite, the widow of the dead, in order to perpetuate the name of the dead in his inheritance." ⁶ Then the redeemer said, "I cannot redeem it for myself, lest I impair my own inheritance. Take my right of redemption yourself, for I cannot redeem it."

⁷ Now this was the custom in former times in Israel concerning redeeming and exchanging: to confirm a transaction, the one drew off his sandal and gave it to the other, and this was the manner of attesting in Israel. ⁸ So when the redeemer said to Boaz, "Buy it for yourself," he drew off his sandal. ⁹ Then Boaz said to the elders and all the people, "You are witnesses this day that I have bought from the hand of Naomi all that belonged to Elimelech and all that belonged to Chilion and to Mahlon. ¹⁰ Also Ruth the Moabite, the widow of Mahlon, I have bought to be my wife, to perpetuate the name of the dead in his inheritance, that the name of the dead may not be cut off from among his brothers and from the gate of his native place. You are witnesses this day." ¹¹ Then all the people who were at the gate and the elders said, "We are witnesses. May the LORD make the woman, who is coming into your house, like Rachel and Leah, who together built up the house of Israel. May you act worthily in Ephrathah and be renowned in Bethlehem, ¹² and may your house be like the house of Perez, whom Tamar bore to Judah, because of the offspring that the LORD will give you by this young woman."

Ruth and Boaz Marry

¹³ So Boaz took Ruth, and she became his wife. And he went in to her, and the LORD gave her conception, and she bore a son. ¹⁴ Then the women said to Naomi, "Blessed be the LORD, who has not left you this day without a redeemer, and may his name be renowned in Israel! ¹⁵ He shall be to you a restorer of life and a nourisher of your old age, for your daughter-in-law who loves you, who is more to you than seven sons, has given birth to him." ¹⁶ Then Naomi took the child and laid him on her lap and became his nurse. ¹⁷ And the women of the neighborhood gave him a name, saying, "A son has been born to Naomi." They named him Obed. He was the father of Jesse, the father of David.

[1] Hebrew *he* [2] Masoretic Text *you also buy it from Ruth*

The Genealogy of David

[18] Now these are the generations of Perez: Perez fathered Hezron, [19] Hezron fathered Ram, Ram fathered Amminadab, [20] Amminadab fathered Nahshon, Nahshon fathered Salmon, [21] Salmon fathered Boaz, Boaz fathered Obed, [22] Obed fathered Jesse, and Jesse fathered David.

1 SAMUEL

The Birth of Samuel

1 There was a certain man of Ramathaim-zophim of the hill country of Ephraim whose name was Elkanah the son of Jeroham, son of Elihu, son of Tohu, son of Zuph, an Ephrathite. ²He had two wives. The name of the one was Hannah, and the name of the other, Peninnah. And Peninnah had children, but Hannah had no children.

³Now this man used to go up year by year from his city to worship and to sacrifice to the Lord of hosts at Shiloh, where the two sons of Eli, Hophni and Phinehas, were priests of the Lord. ⁴On the day when Elkanah sacrificed, he would give portions to Peninnah his wife and to all her sons and daughters. ⁵But to Hannah he gave a double portion, because he loved her, though the Lord had closed her womb.¹ ⁶And her rival used to provoke her grievously to irritate her, because the Lord had closed her womb. ⁷So it went on year by year. As often as she went up to the house of the Lord, she used to provoke her. Therefore Hannah wept and would not eat. ⁸And Elkanah, her husband, said to her, "Hannah, why do you weep? And why do you not eat? And why is your heart sad? Am I not more to you than ten sons?"

⁹After they had eaten and drunk in Shiloh, Hannah rose. Now Eli the priest was sitting on the seat beside the doorpost of the temple of the Lord. ¹⁰She was deeply distressed and prayed to the Lord and wept bitterly. ¹¹And she vowed a vow and said, "O Lord of hosts, if you will indeed look on the affliction of your servant and remember me and not forget your servant, but will give to your servant a son, then I will give him to the Lord all the days of his life, and no razor shall touch his head."

¹²As she continued praying before the Lord, Eli observed her mouth. ¹³Hannah was speaking in her heart; only her lips moved, and her voice was not heard. Therefore Eli took her to be a drunken woman. ¹⁴And Eli said to her, "How long will you go on being drunk? Put your wine away from you." ¹⁵But Hannah answered, "No, my lord, I am a woman troubled in spirit. I have drunk neither wine nor strong drink, but I have been pouring out my soul before the Lord. ¹⁶Do not regard your servant as a worthless woman, for

---

¹ Syriac; the meaning of the Hebrew is uncertain. Septuagint *And, although he loved Hannah, he would give Hannah only one portion, because the Lord had closed her womb*

all along I have been speaking out of my great anxiety and vexation." ¹⁷ Then Eli answered, "Go in peace, and the God of Israel grant your petition that you have made to him." ¹⁸ And she said, "Let your servant find favor in your eyes." Then the woman went her way and ate, and her face was no longer sad.

¹⁹ They rose early in the morning and worshiped before the Lord; then they went back to their house at Ramah. And Elkanah knew Hannah his wife, and the Lord remembered her. ²⁰ And in due time Hannah conceived and bore a son, and she called his name Samuel, for she said, "I have asked for him from the Lord."[1]

Samuel Given to the Lord

²¹ The man Elkanah and all his house went up to offer to the Lord the yearly sacrifice and to pay his vow. ²² But Hannah did not go up, for she said to her husband, "As soon as the child is weaned, I will bring him, so that he may appear in the presence of the Lord and dwell there forever." ²³ Elkanah her husband said to her, "Do what seems best to you; wait until you have weaned him; only, may the Lord establish his word." So the woman remained and nursed her son until she weaned him. ²⁴ And when she had weaned him, she took him up with her, along with a three-year-old bull,[2] an ephah[3] of flour, and a skin of wine, and she brought him to the house of the Lord at Shiloh. And the child was young. ²⁵ Then they slaughtered the bull, and they brought the child to Eli. ²⁶ And she said, "Oh, my lord! As you live, my lord, I am the woman who was standing here in your presence, praying to the Lord. ²⁷ For this child I prayed, and the Lord has granted me my petition that I made to him. ²⁸ Therefore I have lent him to the Lord. As long as he lives, he is lent to the Lord."

And he worshiped the Lord there.

Hannah's Prayer

2 And Hannah prayed and said,

"My heart exults in the Lord;
    my horn is exalted in the Lord.
My mouth derides my enemies,
    because I rejoice in your salvation.

² "There is none holy like the Lord:
    for there is none besides you;
    there is no rock like our God.

---

[1] *Samuel* sounds like the Hebrew for *heard of God* [2] Dead Sea Scroll, Septuagint, Syriac; Masoretic Text *three bulls* [3] An *ephah* was about 3/5 bushel or 22 liters

3 Talk no more so very proudly,
    let not arrogance come from your mouth;
for the LORD is a God of knowledge,
    and by him actions are weighed.
4 The bows of the mighty are broken,
    but the feeble bind on strength.
5 Those who were full have hired themselves out for bread,
    but those who were hungry have ceased to hunger.
The barren has borne seven,
    but she who has many children is forlorn.
6 The LORD kills and brings to life;
    he brings down to Sheol and raises up.
7 The LORD makes poor and makes rich;
    he brings low and he exalts.
8 He raises up the poor from the dust;
    he lifts the needy from the ash heap
to make them sit with princes
    and inherit a seat of honor.
For the pillars of the earth are the LORD's,
    and on them he has set the world.

9 "He will guard the feet of his faithful ones,
    but the wicked shall be cut off in darkness,
    for not by might shall a man prevail.
10 The adversaries of the LORD shall be broken to pieces;
    against them he will thunder in heaven.
The LORD will judge the ends of the earth;
    he will give strength to his king
    and exalt the horn of his anointed."

¹¹ Then Elkanah went home to Ramah. And the boy[1] was ministering to the LORD in the presence of Eli the priest.

Eli's Worthless Sons

¹² Now the sons of Eli were worthless men. They did not know the LORD. ¹³ The custom of the priests with the people was that when any man offered sacrifice, the priest's servant would come, while the meat was boiling, with a three-pronged fork in his hand, ¹⁴ and he would thrust it into the pan or

---

[1] Hebrew *na'ar* can be rendered *boy* (2:11, 18, 21, 26; 3:1, 8), *servant* (2:13, 15), or *young man* (2:17), depending on the context

kettle or cauldron or pot. All that the fork brought up the priest would take for himself. This is what they did at Shiloh to all the Israelites who came there. ¹⁵ Moreover, before the fat was burned, the priest's servant would come and say to the man who was sacrificing, "Give meat for the priest to roast, for he will not accept boiled meat from you but only raw." ¹⁶ And if the man said to him, "Let them burn the fat first, and then take as much as you wish," he would say, "No, you must give it now, and if not, I will take it by force." ¹⁷ Thus the sin of the young men was very great in the sight of the Lord, for the men treated the offering of the Lord with contempt.

¹⁸ Samuel was ministering before the Lord, a boy clothed with a linen ephod. ¹⁹ And his mother used to make for him a little robe and take it to him each year when she went up with her husband to offer the yearly sacrifice. ²⁰ Then Eli would bless Elkanah and his wife, and say, "May the Lord give you children by this woman for the petition she asked of the Lord." So then they would return to their home.

²¹ Indeed the Lord visited Hannah, and she conceived and bore three sons and two daughters. And the boy Samuel grew in the presence of the Lord.

Eli Rebukes His Sons

²² Now Eli was very old, and he kept hearing all that his sons were doing to all Israel, and how they lay with the women who were serving at the entrance to the tent of meeting. ²³ And he said to them, "Why do you do such things? For I hear of your evil dealings from all these people. ²⁴ No, my sons; it is no good report that I hear the people of the Lord spreading abroad. ²⁵ If someone sins against a man, God will mediate for him, but if someone sins against the Lord, who can intercede for him?" But they would not listen to the voice of their father, for it was the will of the Lord to put them to death.

²⁶ Now the boy Samuel continued to grow both in stature and in favor with the Lord and also with man.

The Lord Rejects Eli's Household

²⁷ And there came a man of God to Eli and said to him, "Thus says the Lord, 'Did I indeed reveal myself to the house of your father when they were in Egypt subject to the house of Pharaoh? ²⁸ Did I choose him out of all the tribes of Israel to be my priest, to go up to my altar, to burn incense, to wear an ephod before me? I gave to the house of your father all my offerings by fire from the people of Israel. ²⁹ Why then do you scorn[1] my sacrifices and my

[1] Hebrew *kick at*

offerings that I commanded for my dwelling, and honor your sons above me by fattening yourselves on the choicest parts of every offering of my people Israel?' ³⁰ Therefore the Lord, the God of Israel, declares: 'I promised that your house and the house of your father should go in and out before me forever,' but now the Lord declares: 'Far be it from me, for those who honor me I will honor, and those who despise me shall be lightly esteemed. ³¹ Behold, the days are coming when I will cut off your strength and the strength of your father's house, so that there will not be an old man in your house. ³² Then in distress you will look with envious eye on all the prosperity that shall be bestowed on Israel, and there shall not be an old man in your house forever. ³³ The only one of you whom I shall not cut off from my altar shall be spared to weep his¹ eyes out to grieve his heart, and all the descendants² of your house shall die by the sword of men.³ ³⁴ And this that shall come upon your two sons, Hophni and Phinehas, shall be the sign to you: both of them shall die on the same day. ³⁵ And I will raise up for myself a faithful priest, who shall do according to what is in my heart and in my mind. And I will build him a sure house, and he shall go in and out before my anointed forever. ³⁶ And everyone who is left in your house shall come to implore him for a piece of silver or a loaf of bread and shall say, "Please put me in one of the priests' places, that I may eat a morsel of bread."'"

The Lord Calls Samuel

3 Now the boy Samuel was ministering to the Lord in the presence of Eli. And the word of the Lord was rare in those days; there was no frequent vision.

² At that time Eli, whose eyesight had begun to grow dim so that he could not see, was lying down in his own place. ³ The lamp of God had not yet gone out, and Samuel was lying down in the temple of the Lord, where the ark of God was.

⁴ Then the Lord called Samuel, and he said, "Here I am!" ⁵ and ran to Eli and said, "Here I am, for you called me." But he said, "I did not call; lie down again." So he went and lay down.

⁶ And the Lord called again, "Samuel!" and Samuel arose and went to Eli and said, "Here I am, for you called me." But he said, "I did not call, my son; lie down again." ⁷ Now Samuel did not yet know the Lord, and the word of the Lord had not yet been revealed to him.

⁸ And the Lord called Samuel again the third time. And he arose and went to Eli and said, "Here I am, for you called me." Then Eli perceived that the

---

¹ Septuagint; Hebrew *your*; twice in this verse ² Hebrew *increase* ³ Septuagint; Hebrew *die as men*

Lord was calling the boy. ⁹ Therefore Eli said to Samuel, "Go, lie down, and if he calls you, you shall say, 'Speak, Lord, for your servant hears.'" So Samuel went and lay down in his place.

¹⁰ And the Lord came and stood, calling as at other times, "Samuel! Samuel!" And Samuel said, "Speak, for your servant hears." ¹¹ Then the Lord said to Samuel, "Behold, I am about to do a thing in Israel at which the two ears of everyone who hears it will tingle. ¹² On that day I will fulfill against Eli all that I have spoken concerning his house, from beginning to end. ¹³ And I declare to him that I am about to punish his house forever, for the iniquity that he knew, because his sons were blaspheming God,¹ and he did not restrain them. ¹⁴ Therefore I swear to the house of Eli that the iniquity of Eli's house shall not be atoned for by sacrifice or offering forever."

¹⁵ Samuel lay until morning; then he opened the doors of the house of the Lord. And Samuel was afraid to tell the vision to Eli. ¹⁶ But Eli called Samuel and said, "Samuel, my son." And he said, "Here I am." ¹⁷ And Eli said, "What was it that he told you? Do not hide it from me. May God do so to you and more also if you hide anything from me of all that he told you." ¹⁸ So Samuel told him everything and hid nothing from him. And he said, "It is the Lord. Let him do what seems good to him."

¹⁹ And Samuel grew, and the Lord was with him and let none of his words fall to the ground. ²⁰ And all Israel from Dan to Beersheba knew that Samuel was established as a prophet of the Lord. ²¹ And the Lord appeared again at Shiloh, for the Lord revealed himself to Samuel at Shiloh by the word of the Lord.

The Philistines Capture the Ark

4 And the word of Samuel came to all Israel.

Now Israel went out to battle against the Philistines. They encamped at Ebenezer, and the Philistines encamped at Aphek. ² The Philistines drew up in line against Israel, and when the battle spread, Israel was defeated before the Philistines, who killed about four thousand men on the field of battle. ³ And when the people came to the camp, the elders of Israel said, "Why has the Lord defeated us today before the Philistines? Let us bring the ark of the covenant of the Lord here from Shiloh, that it² may come among us and save us from the power of our enemies." ⁴ So the people sent to Shiloh and brought from there the ark of the covenant of the Lord of hosts, who is enthroned on the cherubim. And the two sons of Eli, Hophni and Phinehas, were there with the ark of the covenant of God.

¹ Or *blaspheming for themselves* ² Or *he*

⁵ As soon as the ark of the covenant of the Lord came into the camp, all Israel gave a mighty shout, so that the earth resounded. ⁶ And when the Philistines heard the noise of the shouting, they said, "What does this great shouting in the camp of the Hebrews mean?" And when they learned that the ark of the Lord had come to the camp, ⁷ the Philistines were afraid, for they said, "A god has come into the camp." And they said, "Woe to us! For nothing like this has happened before. ⁸ Woe to us! Who can deliver us from the power of these mighty gods? These are the gods who struck the Egyptians with every sort of plague in the wilderness. ⁹ Take courage, and be men, O Philistines, lest you become slaves to the Hebrews as they have been to you; be men and fight."

¹⁰ So the Philistines fought, and Israel was defeated, and they fled, every man to his home. And there was a very great slaughter, for thirty thousand foot soldiers of Israel fell. ¹¹ And the ark of God was captured, and the two sons of Eli, Hophni and Phinehas, died.

The Death of Eli

¹² A man of Benjamin ran from the battle line and came to Shiloh the same day, with his clothes torn and with dirt on his head. ¹³ When he arrived, Eli was sitting on his seat by the road watching, for his heart trembled for the ark of God. And when the man came into the city and told the news, all the city cried out. ¹⁴ When Eli heard the sound of the outcry, he said, "What is this uproar?" Then the man hurried and came and told Eli. ¹⁵ Now Eli was ninety-eight years old and his eyes were set so that he could not see. ¹⁶ And the man said to Eli, "I am he who has come from the battle; I fled from the battle today." And he said, "How did it go, my son?" ¹⁷ He who brought the news answered and said, "Israel has fled before the Philistines, and there has also been a great defeat among the people. Your two sons also, Hophni and Phinehas, are dead, and the ark of God has been captured." ¹⁸ As soon as he mentioned the ark of God, Eli fell over backward from his seat by the side of the gate, and his neck was broken and he died, for the man was old and heavy. He had judged Israel forty years.

¹⁹ Now his daughter-in-law, the wife of Phinehas, was pregnant, about to give birth. And when she heard the news that the ark of God was captured, and that her father-in-law and her husband were dead, she bowed and gave birth, for her pains came upon her. ²⁰ And about the time of her death the women attending her said to her, "Do not be afraid, for you have borne a son." But she did not answer or pay attention. ²¹ And she named the child Ichabod, saying, "The glory has departed[1] from Israel!" because the ark of

---

[1] Or *gone into exile*; also verse 22

God had been captured and because of her father-in-law and her husband. ²² And she said, "The glory has departed from Israel, for the ark of God has been captured."

The Philistines and the Ark

5 When the Philistines captured the ark of God, they brought it from Ebenezer to Ashdod. ² Then the Philistines took the ark of God and brought it into the house of Dagon and set it up beside Dagon. ³ And when the people of Ashdod rose early the next day, behold, Dagon had fallen face downward on the ground before the ark of the Lord. So they took Dagon and put him back in his place. ⁴ But when they rose early on the next morning, behold, Dagon had fallen face downward on the ground before the ark of the Lord, and the head of Dagon and both his hands were lying cut off on the threshold. Only the trunk of Dagon was left to him. ⁵ This is why the priests of Dagon and all who enter the house of Dagon do not tread on the threshold of Dagon in Ashdod to this day.

⁶ The hand of the Lord was heavy against the people of Ashdod, and he terrified and afflicted them with tumors, both Ashdod and its territory. ⁷ And when the men of Ashdod saw how things were, they said, "The ark of the God of Israel must not remain with us, for his hand is hard against us and against Dagon our god." ⁸ So they sent and gathered together all the lords of the Philistines and said, "What shall we do with the ark of the God of Israel?" They answered, "Let the ark of the God of Israel be brought around to Gath." So they brought the ark of the God of Israel there. ⁹ But after they had brought it around, the hand of the Lord was against the city, causing a very great panic, and he afflicted the men of the city, both young and old, so that tumors broke out on them. ¹⁰ So they sent the ark of God to Ekron. But as soon as the ark of God came to Ekron, the people of Ekron cried out, "They have brought around to us the ark of the God of Israel to kill us and our people." ¹¹ They sent therefore and gathered together all the lords of the Philistines and said, "Send away the ark of the God of Israel, and let it return to its own place, that it may not kill us and our people." For there was a deathly panic throughout the whole city. The hand of God was very heavy there. ¹² The men who did not die were struck with tumors, and the cry of the city went up to heaven.

The Ark Returned to Israel

6 The ark of the Lord was in the country of the Philistines seven months. ² And the Philistines called for the priests and the diviners and said, "What shall we do with the ark of the Lord? Tell us with what we shall

send it to its place." ³ They said, "If you send away the ark of the God of Israel, do not send it empty, but by all means return him a guilt offering. Then you will be healed, and it will be known to you why his hand does not turn away from you." ⁴ And they said, "What is the guilt offering that we shall return to him?" They answered, "Five golden tumors and five golden mice, according to the number of the lords of the Philistines, for the same plague was on all of you and on your lords. ⁵ So you must make images of your tumors and images of your mice that ravage the land, and give glory to the God of Israel. Perhaps he will lighten his hand from off you and your gods and your land. ⁶ Why should you harden your hearts as the Egyptians and Pharaoh hardened their hearts? After he had dealt severely with them, did they not send the people away, and they departed? ⁷ Now then, take and prepare a new cart and two milk cows on which there has never come a yoke, and yoke the cows to the cart, but take their calves home, away from them. ⁸ And take the ark of the Lord and place it on the cart and put in a box at its side the figures of gold, which you are returning to him as a guilt offering. Then send it off and let it go its way ⁹ and watch. If it goes up on the way to its own land, to Beth-shemesh, then it is he who has done us this great harm, but if not, then we shall know that it is not his hand that struck us; it happened to us by coincidence."

¹⁰ The men did so, and took two milk cows and yoked them to the cart and shut up their calves at home. ¹¹ And they put the ark of the Lord on the cart and the box with the golden mice and the images of their tumors. ¹² And the cows went straight in the direction of Beth-shemesh along one highway, lowing as they went. They turned neither to the right nor to the left, and the lords of the Philistines went after them as far as the border of Beth-shemesh. ¹³ Now the people of Beth-shemesh were reaping their wheat harvest in the valley. And when they lifted up their eyes and saw the ark, they rejoiced to see it. ¹⁴ The cart came into the field of Joshua of Beth-shemesh and stopped there. A great stone was there. And they split up the wood of the cart and offered the cows as a burnt offering to the Lord. ¹⁵ And the Levites took down the ark of the Lord and the box that was beside it, in which were the golden figures, and set them upon the great stone. And the men of Beth-shemesh offered burnt offerings and sacrificed sacrifices on that day to the Lord. ¹⁶ And when the five lords of the Philistines saw it, they returned that day to Ekron.

¹⁷ These are the golden tumors that the Philistines returned as a guilt offering to the Lord: one for Ashdod, one for Gaza, one for Ashkelon, one for Gath, one for Ekron, ¹⁸ and the golden mice, according to the number of

all the cities of the Philistines belonging to the five lords, both fortified cities and unwalled villages. The great stone beside which they set down the ark of the Lord is a witness to this day in the field of Joshua of Beth-shemesh.

¹⁹ And he struck some of the men of Beth-shemesh, because they looked upon the ark of the Lord. He struck seventy men of them,¹ and the people mourned because the Lord had struck the people with a great blow. ²⁰ Then the men of Beth-shemesh said, "Who is able to stand before the Lord, this holy God? And to whom shall he go up away from us?" ²¹ So they sent messengers to the inhabitants of Kiriath-jearim, saying, "The Philistines have returned the ark of the Lord. Come down and take it up to you."

7 And the men of Kiriath-jearim came and took up the ark of the Lord and brought it to the house of Abinadab on the hill. And they consecrated his son Eleazar to have charge of the ark of the Lord. ² From the day that the ark was lodged at Kiriath-jearim, a long time passed, some twenty years, and all the house of Israel lamented after the Lord.

Samuel Judges Israel

³ And Samuel said to all the house of Israel, "If you are returning to the Lord with all your heart, then put away the foreign gods and the Ashtaroth from among you and direct your heart to the Lord and serve him only, and he will deliver you out of the hand of the Philistines." ⁴ So the people of Israel put away the Baals and the Ashtaroth, and they served the Lord only.

⁵ Then Samuel said, "Gather all Israel at Mizpah, and I will pray to the Lord for you." ⁶ So they gathered at Mizpah and drew water and poured it out before the Lord and fasted on that day and said there, "We have sinned against the Lord." And Samuel judged the people of Israel at Mizpah. ⁷ Now when the Philistines heard that the people of Israel had gathered at Mizpah, the lords of the Philistines went up against Israel. And when the people of Israel heard of it, they were afraid of the Philistines. ⁸ And the people of Israel said to Samuel, "Do not cease to cry out to the Lord our God for us, that he may save us from the hand of the Philistines." ⁹ So Samuel took a nursing lamb and offered it as a whole burnt offering to the Lord. And Samuel cried out to the Lord for Israel, and the Lord answered him. ¹⁰ As Samuel was offering up the burnt offering, the Philistines drew near to attack Israel. But the Lord thundered with a mighty sound that day against the Philistines and threw them into confusion, and they were defeated before Israel. ¹¹ And the men of Israel went out from Mizpah and pursued the Philistines and struck them, as far as below Beth-car.

---

¹ Most Hebrew manuscripts *struck of the people seventy men, fifty thousand men*

¹² Then Samuel took a stone and set it up between Mizpah and Shen¹ and called its name Ebenezer;² for he said, "Till now the Lord has helped us." ¹³ So the Philistines were subdued and did not again enter the territory of Israel. And the hand of the Lord was against the Philistines all the days of Samuel. ¹⁴ The cities that the Philistines had taken from Israel were restored to Israel, from Ekron to Gath, and Israel delivered their territory from the hand of the Philistines. There was peace also between Israel and the Amorites.

¹⁵ Samuel judged Israel all the days of his life. ¹⁶ And he went on a circuit year by year to Bethel, Gilgal, and Mizpah. And he judged Israel in all these places. ¹⁷ Then he would return to Ramah, for his home was there, and there also he judged Israel. And he built there an altar to the Lord.

Israel Demands a King

8 When Samuel became old, he made his sons judges over Israel. ² The name of his firstborn son was Joel, and the name of his second, Abijah; they were judges in Beersheba. ³ Yet his sons did not walk in his ways but turned aside after gain. They took bribes and perverted justice.

⁴ Then all the elders of Israel gathered together and came to Samuel at Ramah ⁵ and said to him, "Behold, you are old and your sons do not walk in your ways. Now appoint for us a king to judge us like all the nations." ⁶ But the thing displeased Samuel when they said, "Give us a king to judge us." And Samuel prayed to the Lord. ⁷ And the Lord said to Samuel, "Obey the voice of the people in all that they say to you, for they have not rejected you, but they have rejected me from being king over them. ⁸ According to all the deeds that they have done, from the day I brought them up out of Egypt even to this day, forsaking me and serving other gods, so they are also doing to you. ⁹ Now then, obey their voice; only you shall solemnly warn them and show them the ways of the king who shall reign over them."

Samuel's Warning Against Kings

¹⁰ So Samuel told all the words of the Lord to the people who were asking for a king from him. ¹¹ He said, "These will be the ways of the king who will reign over you: he will take your sons and appoint them to his chariots and to be his horsemen and to run before his chariots. ¹² And he will appoint for himself commanders of thousands and commanders of fifties, and some to plow his ground and to reap his harvest, and to make his implements of war and the equipment of his chariots. ¹³ He will take your daughters to be perfumers and cooks and bakers. ¹⁴ He will take the best of your fields and

---

¹ Hebrew; Septuagint, Syriac *Jeshanah* ² *Ebenezer* means *stone of help*

vineyards and olive orchards and give them to his servants. ¹⁵ He will take the tenth of your grain and of your vineyards and give it to his officers and to his servants. ¹⁶ He will take your male servants and female servants and the best of your young men¹ and your donkeys, and put them to his work. ¹⁷ He will take the tenth of your flocks, and you shall be his slaves. ¹⁸ And in that day you will cry out because of your king, whom you have chosen for yourselves, but the Lord will not answer you in that day."

The Lord Grants Israel's Request

¹⁹ But the people refused to obey the voice of Samuel. And they said, "No! But there shall be a king over us, ²⁰ that we also may be like all the nations, and that our king may judge us and go out before us and fight our battles." ²¹ And when Samuel had heard all the words of the people, he repeated them in the ears of the Lord. ²² And the Lord said to Samuel, "Obey their voice and make them a king." Samuel then said to the men of Israel, "Go every man to his city."

Saul Chosen to Be King

9 There was a man of Benjamin whose name was Kish, the son of Abiel, son of Zeror, son of Becorath, son of Aphiah, a Benjaminite, a man of wealth. ² And he had a son whose name was Saul, a handsome young man. There was not a man among the people of Israel more handsome than he. From his shoulders upward he was taller than any of the people.

³ Now the donkeys of Kish, Saul's father, were lost. So Kish said to Saul his son, "Take one of the young men with you, and arise, go and look for the donkeys." ⁴ And he passed through the hill country of Ephraim and passed through the land of Shalishah, but they did not find them. And they passed through the land of Shaalim, but they were not there. Then they passed through the land of Benjamin, but did not find them.

⁵ When they came to the land of Zuph, Saul said to his servant² who was with him, "Come, let us go back, lest my father cease to care about the donkeys and become anxious about us." ⁶ But he said to him, "Behold, there is a man of God in this city, and he is a man who is held in honor; all that he says comes true. So now let us go there. Perhaps he can tell us the way we should go." ⁷ Then Saul said to his servant, "But if we go, what can we bring the man? For the bread in our sacks is gone, and there is no present to bring to the man of God. What do we have?" ⁸ The servant answered Saul again, "Here, I have with me a quarter of a shekel³ of silver, and I will give it to the

---

¹ Septuagint *cattle* ² Hebrew *young man*; also verses 7, 8, 10, 27 ³ A *shekel* was about 2/5 ounce or 11 grams

man of God to tell us our way." ⁹(Formerly in Israel, when a man went to inquire of God, he said, "Come, let us go to the seer," for today's "prophet" was formerly called a seer.) ¹⁰And Saul said to his servant, "Well said; come, let us go." So they went to the city where the man of God was.

¹¹As they went up the hill to the city, they met young women coming out to draw water and said to them, "Is the seer here?" ¹²They answered, "He is; behold, he is just ahead of you. Hurry. He has come just now to the city, because the people have a sacrifice today on the high place. ¹³As soon as you enter the city you will find him, before he goes up to the high place to eat. For the people will not eat till he comes, since he must bless the sacrifice; afterward those who are invited will eat. Now go up, for you will meet him immediately." ¹⁴So they went up to the city. As they were entering the city, they saw Samuel coming out toward them on his way up to the high place.

¹⁵Now the day before Saul came, the Lord had revealed to Samuel: ¹⁶"Tomorrow about this time I will send to you a man from the land of Benjamin, and you shall anoint him to be prince[1] over my people Israel. He shall save my people from the hand of the Philistines. For I have seen[2] my people, because their cry has come to me." ¹⁷When Samuel saw Saul, the Lord told him, "Here is the man of whom I spoke to you! He it is who shall restrain my people." ¹⁸Then Saul approached Samuel in the gate and said, "Tell me where is the house of the seer?" ¹⁹Samuel answered Saul, "I am the seer. Go up before me to the high place, for today you shall eat with me, and in the morning I will let you go and will tell you all that is on your mind. ²⁰As for your donkeys that were lost three days ago, do not set your mind on them, for they have been found. And for whom is all that is desirable in Israel? Is it not for you and for all your father's house?" ²¹Saul answered, "Am I not a Benjaminite, from the least of the tribes of Israel? And is not my clan the humblest of all the clans of the tribe of Benjamin? Why then have you spoken to me in this way?"

²²Then Samuel took Saul and his young man and brought them into the hall and gave them a place at the head of those who had been invited, who were about thirty persons. ²³And Samuel said to the cook, "Bring the portion I gave you, of which I said to you, 'Put it aside.'" ²⁴So the cook took up the leg and what was on it and set them before Saul. And Samuel said, "See, what was kept is set before you. Eat, because it was kept for you until the hour appointed, that you might eat with the guests."[3]

So Saul ate with Samuel that day. ²⁵And when they came down from the high place into the city, a bed was spread for Saul on the roof, and he lay

---

[1] Or *leader* [2] Septuagint adds *the affliction of* [3] Hebrew *appointed, saying, 'I have invited the people'*

down to sleep.¹ ²⁶ Then at the break of dawn² Samuel called to Saul on the roof, "Up, that I may send you on your way." So Saul arose, and both he and Samuel went out into the street.

²⁷ As they were going down to the outskirts of the city, Samuel said to Saul, "Tell the servant to pass on before us, and when he has passed on, stop here yourself for a while, that I may make known to you the word of God."

Saul Anointed King

10 Then Samuel took a flask of oil and poured it on his head and kissed him and said, "Has not the LORD anointed you to be prince³ over his people Israel? And you shall reign over the people of the LORD and you will save them from the hand of their surrounding enemies. And this shall be the sign to you that the LORD has anointed you to be prince⁴ over his heritage. ² When you depart from me today, you will meet two men by Rachel's tomb in the territory of Benjamin at Zelzah, and they will say to you, 'The donkeys that you went to seek are found, and now your father has ceased to care about the donkeys and is anxious about you, saying, "What shall I do about my son?"' ³ Then you shall go on from there farther and come to the oak of Tabor. Three men going up to God at Bethel will meet you there, one carrying three young goats, another carrying three loaves of bread, and another carrying a skin of wine. ⁴ And they will greet you and give you two loaves of bread, which you shall accept from their hand. ⁵ After that you shall come to Gibeath-elohim,⁵ where there is a garrison of the Philistines. And there, as soon as you come to the city, you will meet a group of prophets coming down from the high place with harp, tambourine, flute, and lyre before them, prophesying. ⁶ Then the Spirit of the LORD will rush upon you, and you will prophesy with them and be turned into another man. ⁷ Now when these signs meet you, do what your hand finds to do, for God is with you. ⁸ Then go down before me to Gilgal. And behold, I am coming down to you to offer burnt offerings and to sacrifice peace offerings. Seven days you shall wait, until I come to you and show you what you shall do."

⁹ When he turned his back to leave Samuel, God gave him another heart. And all these signs came to pass that day. ¹⁰ When they came to Gibeah,⁶ behold, a group of prophets met him, and the Spirit of God rushed upon him, and he prophesied among them. ¹¹ And when all who knew him previously saw how he prophesied with the prophets, the people said to one another, "What has come over the son of Kish? Is Saul also among the prophets?" ¹² And a man of the place answered, "And who is their father?"

---

¹ Septuagint; Hebrew *city, he spoke with Saul on the roof* ² Septuagint; Hebrew *And they arose early, and at the break of dawn* ³ Or *leader* ⁴ Septuagint; Hebrew lacks *over his people Israel? And you shall.... to be prince* ⁵ *Gibeath-elohim* means *the hill of God* ⁶ *Gibeah* means *the hill*

Therefore it became a proverb, "Is Saul also among the prophets?" [13] When he had finished prophesying, he came to the high place.

[14] Saul's uncle said to him and to his servant, "Where did you go?" And he said, "To seek the donkeys. And when we saw they were not to be found, we went to Samuel." [15] And Saul's uncle said, "Please tell me what Samuel said to you." [16] And Saul said to his uncle, "He told us plainly that the donkeys had been found." But about the matter of the kingdom, of which Samuel had spoken, he did not tell him anything.

Saul Proclaimed King

[17] Now Samuel called the people together to the Lord at Mizpah. [18] And he said to the people of Israel, "Thus says the Lord, the God of Israel, 'I brought up Israel out of Egypt, and I delivered you from the hand of the Egyptians and from the hand of all the kingdoms that were oppressing you.' [19] But today you have rejected your God, who saves you from all your calamities and your distresses, and you have said to him, 'Set a king over us.' Now therefore present yourselves before the Lord by your tribes and by your thousands."

[20] Then Samuel brought all the tribes of Israel near, and the tribe of Benjamin was taken by lot. [21] He brought the tribe of Benjamin near by its clans, and the clan of the Matrites was taken by lot;[1] and Saul the son of Kish was taken by lot. But when they sought him, he could not be found. [22] So they inquired again of the Lord, "Is there a man still to come?" and the Lord said, "Behold, he has hidden himself among the baggage." [23] Then they ran and took him from there. And when he stood among the people, he was taller than any of the people from his shoulders upward. [24] And Samuel said to all the people, "Do you see him whom the Lord has chosen? There is none like him among all the people." And all the people shouted, "Long live the king!"

[25] Then Samuel told the people the rights and duties of the kingship, and he wrote them in a book and laid it up before the Lord. Then Samuel sent all the people away, each one to his home. [26] Saul also went to his home at Gibeah, and with him went men of valor whose hearts God had touched. [27] But some worthless fellows said, "How can this man save us?" And they despised him and brought him no present. But he held his peace.

Saul Defeats the Ammonites

11 Then Nahash the Ammonite went up and besieged Jabesh-gilead, and all the men of Jabesh said to Nahash, "Make a treaty with us, and we will serve you." [2] But Nahash the Ammonite said to them, "On this condition

---

[1] Septuagint adds *finally he brought the family of the Matrites near, man by man*

I will make a treaty with you, that I gouge out all your right eyes, and thus bring disgrace on all Israel." ³The elders of Jabesh said to him, "Give us seven days' respite that we may send messengers through all the territory of Israel. Then, if there is no one to save us, we will give ourselves up to you." ⁴When the messengers came to Gibeah of Saul, they reported the matter in the ears of the people, and all the people wept aloud.

⁵Now, behold, Saul was coming from the field behind the oxen. And Saul said, "What is wrong with the people, that they are weeping?" So they told him the news of the men of Jabesh. ⁶And the Spirit of God rushed upon Saul when he heard these words, and his anger was greatly kindled. ⁷He took a yoke of oxen and cut them in pieces and sent them throughout all the territory of Israel by the hand of the messengers, saying, "Whoever does not come out after Saul and Samuel, so shall it be done to his oxen!" Then the dread of the Lord fell upon the people, and they came out as one man. ⁸When he mustered them at Bezek, the people of Israel were three hundred thousand, and the men of Judah thirty thousand. ⁹And they said to the messengers who had come, "Thus shall you say to the men of Jabesh-gilead: 'Tomorrow, by the time the sun is hot, you shall have salvation.'" When the messengers came and told the men of Jabesh, they were glad. ¹⁰Therefore the men of Jabesh said, "Tomorrow we will give ourselves up to you, and you may do to us whatever seems good to you." ¹¹And the next day Saul put the people in three companies. And they came into the midst of the camp in the morning watch and struck down the Ammonites until the heat of the day. And those who survived were scattered, so that no two of them were left together.

The Kingdom Is Renewed

¹²Then the people said to Samuel, "Who is it that said, 'Shall Saul reign over us?' Bring the men, that we may put them to death." ¹³But Saul said, "Not a man shall be put to death this day, for today the Lord has worked salvation in Israel." ¹⁴Then Samuel said to the people, "Come, let us go to Gilgal and there renew the kingdom." ¹⁵So all the people went to Gilgal, and there they made Saul king before the Lord in Gilgal. There they sacrificed peace offerings before the Lord, and there Saul and all the men of Israel rejoiced greatly.

Samuel's Farewell Address

12 And Samuel said to all Israel, "Behold, I have obeyed your voice in all that you have said to me and have made a king over you. ²And now, behold, the king walks before you, and I am old and gray; and behold, my sons are with you. I have walked before you from my youth until this day. ³ Here I am; testify against me before the Lord and before his anointed. Whose ox have I taken? Or whose donkey have I taken? Or whom have I defrauded? Whom have I oppressed? Or from whose hand have I taken a bribe to blind my eyes with it? Testify against me[1] and I will restore it to you." ⁴ They said, "You have not defrauded us or oppressed us or taken anything from any man's hand." ⁵ And he said to them, "The Lord is witness against you, and his anointed is witness this day, that you have not found anything in my hand." And they said, "He is witness."

⁶ And Samuel said to the people, "The Lord is witness,[2] who appointed Moses and Aaron and brought your fathers up out of the land of Egypt. ⁷ Now therefore stand still that I may plead with you before the Lord concerning all the righteous deeds of the Lord that he performed for you and for your fathers. ⁸ When Jacob went into Egypt, and the Egyptians oppressed them,[3] then your fathers cried out to the Lord and the Lord sent Moses and Aaron, who brought your fathers out of Egypt and made them dwell in this place. ⁹ But they forgot the Lord their God. And he sold them into the hand of Sisera, commander of the army of Hazor,[4] and into the hand of the Philistines, and into the hand of the king of Moab. And they fought against them. ¹⁰ And they cried out to the Lord and said, 'We have sinned, because we have forsaken the Lord and have served the Baals and the Ashtaroth. But now deliver us out of the hand of our enemies, that we may serve you.' ¹¹ And the Lord sent Jerubbaal and Barak[5] and Jephthah and Samuel and delivered you out of the hand of your enemies on every side, and you lived in safety. ¹² And when you saw that Nahash the king of the Ammonites came against you, you said to me, 'No, but a king shall reign over us,' when the Lord your God was your king. ¹³ And now behold the king whom you have chosen, for whom you have asked; behold, the Lord has set a king over you. ¹⁴ If you will fear the Lord and serve him and obey his voice and not rebel against the commandment of the Lord, and if both you and the king who reigns over you will follow the Lord your God, it will be well. ¹⁵ But if you will not obey the voice of the Lord, but rebel against the commandment of the Lord, then the hand of the Lord will be against you and your king.[6] ¹⁶ Now therefore stand still and see this great thing that the Lord will do before your eyes. ¹⁷ Is it not wheat harvest today? I will call upon the Lord, that he may send thunder and rain. And you shall know and see that your wickedness is great, which you have done in the sight of the Lord, in asking for yourselves a king." ¹⁸ So Samuel called upon the Lord, and the Lord sent thunder and rain that day, and all the people greatly feared the Lord and Samuel.

[1] Septuagint; Hebrew lacks *Testify against me* [2] Septuagint; Hebrew lacks *is witness* [3] Septuagint; Hebrew lacks *and the Egyptians oppressed them* [4] Septuagint *the army of Jabin king of Hazor* [5] Septuagint, Syriac; Hebrew *Bedan* [6] Septuagint; Hebrew *fathers*

¹⁹ And all the people said to Samuel, "Pray for your servants to the Lord your God, that we may not die, for we have added to all our sins this evil, to ask for ourselves a king." ²⁰ And Samuel said to the people, "Do not be afraid; you have done all this evil. Yet do not turn aside from following the Lord, but serve the Lord with all your heart. ²¹ And do not turn aside after empty things that cannot profit or deliver, for they are empty. ²² For the Lord will not forsake his people, for his great name's sake, because it has pleased the Lord to make you a people for himself. ²³ Moreover, as for me, far be it from me that I should sin against the Lord by ceasing to pray for you, and I will instruct you in the good and the right way. ²⁴ Only fear the Lord and serve him faithfully with all your heart. For consider what great things he has done for you. ²⁵ But if you still do wickedly, you shall be swept away, both you and your king."

Saul Fights the Philistines

13 Saul lived for one year and then became king, and when he had reigned for two years over Israel,¹ ² Saul chose three thousand men of Israel. Two thousand were with Saul in Michmash and the hill country of Bethel, and a thousand were with Jonathan in Gibeah of Benjamin. The rest of the people he sent home, every man to his tent. ³ Jonathan defeated the garrison of the Philistines that was at Geba, and the Philistines heard of it. And Saul blew the trumpet throughout all the land, saying, "Let the Hebrews hear." ⁴ And all Israel heard it said that Saul had defeated the garrison of the Philistines, and also that Israel had become a stench to the Philistines. And the people were called out to join Saul at Gilgal.

⁵ And the Philistines mustered to fight with Israel, thirty thousand chariots and six thousand horsemen and troops like the sand on the seashore in multitude. They came up and encamped in Michmash, to the east of Beth-aven. ⁶ When the men of Israel saw that they were in trouble (for the people were hard pressed), the people hid themselves in caves and in holes and in rocks and in tombs and in cisterns, ⁷ and some Hebrews crossed the fords of the Jordan to the land of Gad and Gilead. Saul was still at Gilgal, and all the people followed him trembling.

Saul's Unlawful Sacrifice

⁸ He waited seven days, the time appointed by Samuel. But Samuel did not come to Gilgal, and the people were scattering from him. ⁹ So Saul said, "Bring the burnt offering here to me, and the peace offerings." And he offered

¹ Hebrew *Saul was one year old when he became king, and he reigned two years over Israel;* some Greek manuscripts give Saul's age when he began to reign as thirty years

the burnt offering. ¹⁰ As soon as he had finished offering the burnt offering, behold, Samuel came. And Saul went out to meet him and greet him. ¹¹ Samuel said, "What have you done?" And Saul said, "When I saw that the people were scattering from me, and that you did not come within the days appointed, and that the Philistines had mustered at Michmash, ¹² I said, 'Now the Philistines will come down against me at Gilgal, and I have not sought the favor of the LORD.' So I forced myself, and offered the burnt offering." ¹³ And Samuel said to Saul, "You have done foolishly. You have not kept the command of the LORD your God, with which he commanded you. For then the LORD would have established your kingdom over Israel forever. ¹⁴ But now your kingdom shall not continue. The LORD has sought out a man after his own heart, and the LORD has commanded him to be prince[1] over his people, because you have not kept what the LORD commanded you." ¹⁵ And Samuel arose and went up from Gilgal. The rest of the people went up after Saul to meet the army; they went up from Gilgal[2] to Gibeah of Benjamin.

And Saul numbered the people who were present with him, about six hundred men. ¹⁶ And Saul and Jonathan his son and the people who were present with them stayed in Geba of Benjamin, but the Philistines encamped in Michmash. ¹⁷ And raiders came out of the camp of the Philistines in three companies. One company turned toward Ophrah, to the land of Shual; ¹⁸ another company turned toward Beth-horon; and another company turned toward the border that looks down on the Valley of Zeboim toward the wilderness.

¹⁹ Now there was no blacksmith to be found throughout all the land of Israel, for the Philistines said, "Lest the Hebrews make themselves swords or spears." ²⁰ But every one of the Israelites went down to the Philistines to sharpen his plowshare, his mattock, his axe, or his sickle,[3] ²¹ and the charge was two-thirds of a shekel[4] for the plowshares and for the mattocks, and a third of a shekel[5] for sharpening the axes and for setting the goads.[6] ²² So on the day of the battle there was neither sword nor spear found in the hand of any of the people with Saul and Jonathan, but Saul and Jonathan his son had them. ²³ And the garrison of the Philistines went out to the pass of Michmash.

Jonathan Defeats the Philistines

14 One day Jonathan the son of Saul said to the young man who carried his armor, "Come, let us go over to the Philistine garrison on the other side." But he did not tell his father. ² Saul was staying in the outskirts of Gibeah in the pomegranate cave[7] at Migron. The people who were with him

---

[1] Or *leader* [2] Septuagint; Hebrew lacks *The rest of the people . . . from Gilgal* [3] Septuagint; Hebrew *plowshare* [4] Hebrew *was a pim* [5] A *shekel* was about 2/5 ounce or 11 grams [6] The meaning of the Hebrew verse is uncertain [7] Or *under the pomegranate* [tree]

were about six hundred men, ³ including Ahijah the son of Ahitub, Ichabod's brother, son of Phinehas, son of Eli, the priest of the Lord in Shiloh, wearing an ephod. And the people did not know that Jonathan had gone. ⁴ Within the passes, by which Jonathan sought to go over to the Philistine garrison, there was a rocky crag on the one side and a rocky crag on the other side. The name of the one was Bozez, and the name of the other Seneh. ⁵ The one crag rose on the north in front of Michmash, and the other on the south in front of Geba.

⁶ Jonathan said to the young man who carried his armor, "Come, let us go over to the garrison of these uncircumcised. It may be that the Lord will work for us, for nothing can hinder the Lord from saving by many or by few." ⁷ And his armor-bearer said to him, "Do all that is in your heart. Do as you wish.¹ Behold, I am with you heart and soul." ⁸ Then Jonathan said, "Behold, we will cross over to the men, and we will show ourselves to them. ⁹ If they say to us, 'Wait until we come to you,' then we will stand still in our place, and we will not go up to them. ¹⁰ But if they say, 'Come up to us,' then we will go up, for the Lord has given them into our hand. And this shall be the sign to us." ¹¹ So both of them showed themselves to the garrison of the Philistines. And the Philistines said, "Look, Hebrews are coming out of the holes where they have hidden themselves." ¹² And the men of the garrison hailed Jonathan and his armor-bearer and said, "Come up to us, and we will show you a thing." And Jonathan said to his armor-bearer, "Come up after me, for the Lord has given them into the hand of Israel." ¹³ Then Jonathan climbed up on his hands and feet, and his armor-bearer after him. And they fell before Jonathan, and his armor-bearer killed them after him. ¹⁴ And that first strike, which Jonathan and his armor-bearer made, killed about twenty men within as it were half a furrow's length in an acre² of land. ¹⁵ And there was a panic in the camp, in the field, and among all the people. The garrison and even the raiders trembled, the earth quaked, and it became a very great panic.³

¹⁶ And the watchmen of Saul in Gibeah of Benjamin looked, and behold, the multitude was dispersing here and there.⁴ ¹⁷ Then Saul said to the people who were with him, "Count and see who has gone from us." And when they had counted, behold, Jonathan and his armor-bearer were not there. ¹⁸ So Saul said to Ahijah, "Bring the ark of God here." For the ark of God went at that time with the people⁵ of Israel. ¹⁹ Now while Saul was talking to the priest, the tumult in the camp of the Philistines increased more and more. So Saul said to the priest, "Withdraw your hand." ²⁰ Then Saul and all the people who were with him rallied and went into the battle. And behold, every Philistine's sword was against his fellow, and there was very great confusion. ²¹ Now

---

¹ Septuagint *Do all that your mind inclines to* ² Hebrew *a yoke* ³ Or *became a panic from God* ⁴ Septuagint; Hebrew *they went here and there* ⁵ Hebrew; Septuagint *"Bring the ephod." For at that time he wore the ephod before the people*

the Hebrews who had been with the Philistines before that time and who had gone up with them into the camp, even they also turned to be with the Israelites who were with Saul and Jonathan. ²² Likewise, when all the men of Israel who had hidden themselves in the hill country of Ephraim heard that the Philistines were fleeing, they too followed hard after them in the battle. ²³ So the Lord saved Israel that day. And the battle passed beyond Beth-aven.

Saul's Rash Vow

²⁴ And the men of Israel had been hard pressed that day, so Saul had laid an oath on the people, saying, "Cursed be the man who eats food until it is evening and I am avenged on my enemies." So none of the people had tasted food. ²⁵ Now when all the people[1] came to the forest, behold, there was honey on the ground. ²⁶ And when the people entered the forest, behold, the honey was dropping, but no one put his hand to his mouth, for the people feared the oath. ²⁷ But Jonathan had not heard his father charge the people with the oath, so he put out the tip of the staff that was in his hand and dipped it in the honeycomb and put his hand to his mouth, and his eyes became bright. ²⁸ Then one of the people said, "Your father strictly charged the people with an oath, saying, 'Cursed be the man who eats food this day.'" And the people were faint. ²⁹ Then Jonathan said, "My father has troubled the land. See how my eyes have become bright because I tasted a little of this honey. ³⁰ How much better if the people had eaten freely today of the spoil of their enemies that they found. For now the defeat among the Philistines has not been great."

³¹ They struck down the Philistines that day from Michmash to Aijalon. And the people were very faint. ³² The people pounced on the spoil and took sheep and oxen and calves and slaughtered them on the ground. And the people ate them with the blood. ³³ Then they told Saul, "Behold, the people are sinning against the Lord by eating with the blood." And he said, "You have dealt treacherously; roll a great stone to me here."[2] ³⁴ And Saul said, "Disperse yourselves among the people and say to them, 'Let every man bring his ox or his sheep and slaughter them here and eat, and do not sin against the Lord by eating with the blood.'" So every one of the people brought his ox with him that night and they slaughtered them there. ³⁵ And Saul built an altar to the Lord; it was the first altar that he built to the Lord.

³⁶ Then Saul said, "Let us go down after the Philistines by night and plunder them until the morning light; let us not leave a man of them." And they said, "Do whatever seems good to you." But the priest said, "Let us

[1] Hebrew *land* [2] Septuagint; Hebrew *this day*

draw near to God here." ³⁷ And Saul inquired of God, "Shall I go down after the Philistines? Will you give them into the hand of Israel?" But he did not answer him that day. ³⁸ And Saul said, "Come here, all you leaders of the people, and know and see how this sin has arisen today. ³⁹ For as the LORD lives who saves Israel, though it be in Jonathan my son, he shall surely die." But there was not a man among all the people who answered him. ⁴⁰ Then he said to all Israel, "You shall be on one side, and I and Jonathan my son will be on the other side." And the people said to Saul, "Do what seems good to you." ⁴¹ Therefore Saul said, "O LORD God of Israel, why have you not answered your servant this day? If this guilt is in me or in Jonathan my son, O LORD, God of Israel, give Urim. But if this guilt is in your people Israel, give Thummim."¹ And Jonathan and Saul were taken, but the people escaped. ⁴² Then Saul said, "Cast the lot between me and my son Jonathan." And Jonathan was taken.

⁴³ Then Saul said to Jonathan, "Tell me what you have done." And Jonathan told him, "I tasted a little honey with the tip of the staff that was in my hand. Here I am; I will die." ⁴⁴ And Saul said, "God do so to me and more also; you shall surely die, Jonathan." ⁴⁵ Then the people said to Saul, "Shall Jonathan die, who has worked this great salvation in Israel? Far from it! As the LORD lives, there shall not one hair of his head fall to the ground, for he has worked with God this day." So the people ransomed Jonathan, so that he did not die. ⁴⁶ Then Saul went up from pursuing the Philistines, and the Philistines went to their own place.

Saul Fights Israel's Enemies

⁴⁷ When Saul had taken the kingship over Israel, he fought against all his enemies on every side, against Moab, against the Ammonites, against Edom, against the kings of Zobah, and against the Philistines. Wherever he turned he routed them. ⁴⁸ And he did valiantly and struck the Amalekites and delivered Israel out of the hands of those who plundered them.

⁴⁹ Now the sons of Saul were Jonathan, Ishvi, and Malchi-shua. And the names of his two daughters were these: the name of the firstborn was Merab, and the name of the younger Michal. ⁵⁰ And the name of Saul's wife was Ahinoam the daughter of Ahimaaz. And the name of the commander of his army was Abner the son of Ner, Saul's uncle. ⁵¹ Kish was the father of Saul, and Ner the father of Abner was the son of Abiel.

⁵² There was hard fighting against the Philistines all the days of Saul. And when Saul saw any strong man, or any valiant man, he attached him to himself.

¹ Vulgate and Septuagint; Hebrew *Therefore Saul said to the LORD, the God of Israel, "Give Thummim."*

The Lord Rejects Saul

15 And Samuel said to Saul, "The Lord sent me to anoint you king over his people Israel; now therefore listen to the words of the Lord. ² Thus says the Lord of hosts, 'I have noted what Amalek did to Israel in opposing them on the way when they came up out of Egypt. ³ Now go and strike Amalek and devote to destruction[1] all that they have. Do not spare them, but kill both man and woman, child and infant, ox and sheep, camel and donkey.'"

⁴ So Saul summoned the people and numbered them in Telaim, two hundred thousand men on foot, and ten thousand men of Judah. ⁵ And Saul came to the city of Amalek and lay in wait in the valley. ⁶ Then Saul said to the Kenites, "Go, depart; go down from among the Amalekites, lest I destroy you with them. For you showed kindness to all the people of Israel when they came up out of Egypt." So the Kenites departed from among the Amalekites. ⁷ And Saul defeated the Amalekites from Havilah as far as Shur, which is east of Egypt. ⁸ And he took Agag the king of the Amalekites alive and devoted to destruction all the people with the edge of the sword. ⁹ But Saul and the people spared Agag and the best of the sheep and of the oxen and of the fattened calves[2] and the lambs, and all that was good, and would not utterly destroy them. All that was despised and worthless they devoted to destruction.

¹⁰ The word of the Lord came to Samuel: ¹¹ "I regret[3] that I have made Saul king, for he has turned back from following me and has not performed my commandments." And Samuel was angry, and he cried to the Lord all night. ¹² And Samuel rose early to meet Saul in the morning. And it was told Samuel, "Saul came to Carmel, and behold, he set up a monument for himself and turned and passed on and went down to Gilgal." ¹³ And Samuel came to Saul, and Saul said to him, "Blessed be you to the Lord. I have performed the commandment of the Lord." ¹⁴ And Samuel said, "What then is this bleating of the sheep in my ears and the lowing of the oxen that I hear?" ¹⁵ Saul said, "They have brought them from the Amalekites, for the people spared the best of the sheep and of the oxen to sacrifice to the Lord your God, and the rest we have devoted to destruction." ¹⁶ Then Samuel said to Saul, "Stop! I will tell you what the Lord said to me this night." And he said to him, "Speak."

¹⁷ And Samuel said, "Though you are little in your own eyes, are you not the head of the tribes of Israel? The Lord anointed you king over Israel. ¹⁸ And the Lord sent you on a mission and said, 'Go, devote to destruction the sinners, the Amalekites, and fight against them until they are consumed.' ¹⁹ Why then did you not obey the voice of the Lord? Why did you pounce on

---

[1] That is, set apart (devote) as an offering to the Lord (for destruction); also verses 8, 9, 15, 18, 20, 21
[2] The meaning of the Hebrew term is uncertain [3] See also verses 29, 35

the spoil and do what was evil in the sight of the Lord?" ²⁰ And Saul said to Samuel, "I have obeyed the voice of the Lord. I have gone on the mission on which the Lord sent me. I have brought Agag the king of Amalek, and I have devoted the Amalekites to destruction. ²¹ But the people took of the spoil, sheep and oxen, the best of the things devoted to destruction, to sacrifice to the Lord your God in Gilgal." ²² And Samuel said,

> "Has the Lord as great delight in burnt offerings and sacrifices,
>   as in obeying the voice of the Lord?
> Behold, to obey is better than sacrifice,
>   and to listen than the fat of rams.
> ²³ For rebellion is as the sin of divination,
>   and presumption is as iniquity and idolatry.
> Because you have rejected the word of the Lord,
>   he has also rejected you from being king."

²⁴ Saul said to Samuel, "I have sinned, for I have transgressed the commandment of the Lord and your words, because I feared the people and obeyed their voice. ²⁵ Now therefore, please pardon my sin and return with me that I may bow before the Lord." ²⁶ And Samuel said to Saul, "I will not return with you. For you have rejected the word of the Lord, and the Lord has rejected you from being king over Israel." ²⁷ As Samuel turned to go away, Saul seized the skirt of his robe, and it tore. ²⁸ And Samuel said to him, "The Lord has torn the kingdom of Israel from you this day and has given it to a neighbor of yours, who is better than you. ²⁹ And also the Glory of Israel will not lie or have regret, for he is not a man, that he should have regret." ³⁰ Then he said, "I have sinned; yet honor me now before the elders of my people and before Israel, and return with me, that I may bow before the Lord your God." ³¹ So Samuel turned back after Saul, and Saul bowed before the Lord.

³² Then Samuel said, "Bring here to me Agag the king of the Amalekites." And Agag came to him cheerfully.[1] Agag said, "Surely the bitterness of death is past." ³³ And Samuel said, "As your sword has made women childless, so shall your mother be childless among women." And Samuel hacked Agag to pieces before the Lord in Gilgal.

³⁴ Then Samuel went to Ramah, and Saul went up to his house in Gibeah of Saul. ³⁵ And Samuel did not see Saul again until the day of his death, but Samuel grieved over Saul. And the Lord regretted that he had made Saul king over Israel.

[1] Or *haltingly* (compare Septuagint); the Hebrew is uncertain

David Anointed King

16 The Lord said to Samuel, "How long will you grieve over Saul, since I have rejected him from being king over Israel? Fill your horn with oil, and go. I will send you to Jesse the Bethlehemite, for I have provided for myself a king among his sons." ² And Samuel said, "How can I go? If Saul hears it, he will kill me." And the Lord said, "Take a heifer with you and say, 'I have come to sacrifice to the Lord.' ³ And invite Jesse to the sacrifice, and I will show you what you shall do. And you shall anoint for me him whom I declare to you." ⁴ Samuel did what the Lord commanded and came to Bethlehem. The elders of the city came to meet him trembling and said, "Do you come peaceably?" ⁵ And he said, "Peaceably; I have come to sacrifice to the Lord. Consecrate yourselves, and come with me to the sacrifice." And he consecrated Jesse and his sons and invited them to the sacrifice.

⁶ When they came, he looked on Eliab and thought, "Surely the Lord's anointed is before him." ⁷ But the Lord said to Samuel, "Do not look on his appearance or on the height of his stature, because I have rejected him. For the Lord sees not as man sees: man looks on the outward appearance, but the Lord looks on the heart." ⁸ Then Jesse called Abinadab and made him pass before Samuel. And he said, "Neither has the Lord chosen this one." ⁹ Then Jesse made Shammah pass by. And he said, "Neither has the Lord chosen this one." ¹⁰ And Jesse made seven of his sons pass before Samuel. And Samuel said to Jesse, "The Lord has not chosen these." ¹¹ Then Samuel said to Jesse, "Are all your sons here?" And he said, "There remains yet the youngest,[1] but behold, he is keeping the sheep." And Samuel said to Jesse, "Send and get him, for we will not sit down till he comes here." ¹² And he sent and brought him in. Now he was ruddy and had beautiful eyes and was handsome. And the Lord said, "Arise, anoint him, for this is he." ¹³ Then Samuel took the horn of oil and anointed him in the midst of his brothers. And the Spirit of the Lord rushed upon David from that day forward. And Samuel rose up and went to Ramah.

David in Saul's Service

¹⁴ Now the Spirit of the Lord departed from Saul, and a harmful spirit from the Lord tormented him. ¹⁵ And Saul's servants said to him, "Behold now, a harmful spirit from God is tormenting you. ¹⁶ Let our lord now command your servants who are before you to seek out a man who is skillful in playing the lyre, and when the harmful spirit from God is upon you, he will play it, and you will be well." ¹⁷ So Saul said to his servants, "Provide for me a man

[1] Or *smallest*

who can play well and bring him to me." ¹⁸ One of the young men answered, "Behold, I have seen a son of Jesse the Bethlehemite, who is skillful in playing, a man of valor, a man of war, prudent in speech, and a man of good presence, and the LORD is with him." ¹⁹ Therefore Saul sent messengers to Jesse and said, "Send me David your son, who is with the sheep." ²⁰ And Jesse took a donkey laden with bread and a skin of wine and a young goat and sent them by David his son to Saul. ²¹ And David came to Saul and entered his service. And Saul loved him greatly, and he became his armor-bearer. ²² And Saul sent to Jesse, saying, "Let David remain in my service, for he has found favor in my sight." ²³ And whenever the harmful spirit from God was upon Saul, David took the lyre and played it with his hand. So Saul was refreshed and was well, and the harmful spirit departed from him.

David and Goliath

17 Now the Philistines gathered their armies for battle. And they were gathered at Socoh, which belongs to Judah, and encamped between Socoh and Azekah, in Ephes-dammim. ² And Saul and the men of Israel were gathered, and encamped in the Valley of Elah, and drew up in line of battle against the Philistines. ³ And the Philistines stood on the mountain on the one side, and Israel stood on the mountain on the other side, with a valley between them. ⁴ And there came out from the camp of the Philistines a champion named Goliath of Gath, whose height was six[1] cubits[2] and a span. ⁵ He had a helmet of bronze on his head, and he was armed with a coat of mail, and the weight of the coat was five thousand shekels[3] of bronze. ⁶ And he had bronze armor on his legs, and a javelin of bronze slung between his shoulders. ⁷ The shaft of his spear was like a weaver's beam, and his spear's head weighed six hundred shekels of iron. And his shield-bearer went before him. ⁸ He stood and shouted to the ranks of Israel, "Why have you come out to draw up for battle? Am I not a Philistine, and are you not servants of Saul? Choose a man for yourselves, and let him come down to me. ⁹ If he is able to fight with me and kill me, then we will be your servants. But if I prevail against him and kill him, then you shall be our servants and serve us." ¹⁰ And the Philistine said, "I defy the ranks of Israel this day. Give me a man, that we may fight together." ¹¹ When Saul and all Israel heard these words of the Philistine, they were dismayed and greatly afraid.

¹² Now David was the son of an Ephrathite of Bethlehem in Judah, named Jesse, who had eight sons. In the days of Saul the man was already old and advanced in years.[4] ¹³ The three oldest sons of Jesse had followed Saul to the

---

[1] Hebrew; Septuagint, Dead Sea Scroll and Josephus *four* [2] A *cubit* was about 18 inches or 45 centimeters [3] A *shekel* was about 2/5 ounce or 11 grams [4] Septuagint, Syriac; Hebrew *advanced among men*

battle. And the names of his three sons who went to the battle were Eliab the firstborn, and next to him Abinadab, and the third Shammah. ¹⁴ David was the youngest. The three eldest followed Saul, ¹⁵ but David went back and forth from Saul to feed his father's sheep at Bethlehem. ¹⁶ For forty days the Philistine came forward and took his stand, morning and evening.

¹⁷ And Jesse said to David his son, "Take for your brothers an ephah[1] of this parched grain, and these ten loaves, and carry them quickly to the camp to your brothers. ¹⁸ Also take these ten cheeses to the commander of their thousand. See if your brothers are well, and bring some token from them."

¹⁹ Now Saul and they and all the men of Israel were in the Valley of Elah, fighting with the Philistines. ²⁰ And David rose early in the morning and left the sheep with a keeper and took the provisions and went, as Jesse had commanded him. And he came to the encampment as the host was going out to the battle line, shouting the war cry. ²¹ And Israel and the Philistines drew up for battle, army against army. ²² And David left the things in charge of the keeper of the baggage and ran to the ranks and went and greeted his brothers. ²³ As he talked with them, behold, the champion, the Philistine of Gath, Goliath by name, came up out of the ranks of the Philistines and spoke the same words as before. And David heard him.

²⁴ All the men of Israel, when they saw the man, fled from him and were much afraid. ²⁵ And the men of Israel said, "Have you seen this man who has come up? Surely he has come up to defy Israel. And the king will enrich the man who kills him with great riches and will give him his daughter and make his father's house free in Israel." ²⁶ And David said to the men who stood by him, "What shall be done for the man who kills this Philistine and takes away the reproach from Israel? For who is this uncircumcised Philistine, that he should defy the armies of the living God?" ²⁷ And the people answered him in the same way, "So shall it be done to the man who kills him."

²⁸ Now Eliab his eldest brother heard when he spoke to the men. And Eliab's anger was kindled against David, and he said, "Why have you come down? And with whom have you left those few sheep in the wilderness? I know your presumption and the evil of your heart, for you have come down to see the battle." ²⁹ And David said, "What have I done now? Was it not but a word?" ³⁰ And he turned away from him toward another, and spoke in the same way, and the people answered him again as before.

³¹ When the words that David spoke were heard, they repeated them before Saul, and he sent for him. ³² And David said to Saul, "Let no man's heart fail because of him. Your servant will go and fight with this Philistine."

[1] An *ephah* was about 3/5 bushel or 22 liters

�philistine³³ And Saul said to David, "You are not able to go against this Philistine to fight with him, for you are but a youth, and he has been a man of war from his youth." ³⁴ But David said to Saul, "Your servant used to keep sheep for his father. And when there came a lion, or a bear, and took a lamb from the flock, ³⁵ I went after him and struck him and delivered it out of his mouth. And if he arose against me, I caught him by his beard and struck him and killed him. ³⁶ Your servant has struck down both lions and bears, and this uncircumcised Philistine shall be like one of them, for he has defied the armies of the living God." ³⁷ And David said, "The Lord who delivered me from the paw of the lion and from the paw of the bear will deliver me from the hand of this Philistine." And Saul said to David, "Go, and the Lord be with you!"

³⁸ Then Saul clothed David with his armor. He put a helmet of bronze on his head and clothed him with a coat of mail, ³⁹ and David strapped his sword over his armor. And he tried in vain to go, for he had not tested them. Then David said to Saul, "I cannot go with these, for I have not tested them." So David put them off. ⁴⁰ Then he took his staff in his hand and chose five smooth stones from the brook and put them in his shepherd's pouch. His sling was in his hand, and he approached the Philistine.

⁴¹ And the Philistine moved forward and came near to David, with his shield-bearer in front of him. ⁴² And when the Philistine looked and saw David, he disdained him, for he was but a youth, ruddy and handsome in appearance. ⁴³ And the Philistine said to David, "Am I a dog, that you come to me with sticks?" And the Philistine cursed David by his gods. ⁴⁴ The Philistine said to David, "Come to me, and I will give your flesh to the birds of the air and to the beasts of the field." ⁴⁵ Then David said to the Philistine, "You come to me with a sword and with a spear and with a javelin, but I come to you in the name of the Lord of hosts, the God of the armies of Israel, whom you have defied. ⁴⁶ This day the Lord will deliver you into my hand, and I will strike you down and cut off your head. And I will give the dead bodies of the host of the Philistines this day to the birds of the air and to the wild beasts of the earth, that all the earth may know that there is a God in Israel, ⁴⁷ and that all this assembly may know that the Lord saves not with sword and spear. For the battle is the Lord's, and he will give you into our hand."

⁴⁸ When the Philistine arose and came and drew near to meet David, David ran quickly toward the battle line to meet the Philistine. ⁴⁹ And David put his hand in his bag and took out a stone and slung it and struck the Philistine on his forehead. The stone sank into his forehead, and he fell on his face to the ground.

⁵⁰ So David prevailed over the Philistine with a sling and with a stone, and struck the Philistine and killed him. There was no sword in the hand of David. ⁵¹ Then David ran and stood over the Philistine and took his sword and drew it out of its sheath and killed him and cut off his head with it. When the Philistines saw that their champion was dead, they fled. ⁵² And the men of Israel and Judah rose with a shout and pursued the Philistines as far as Gath[1] and the gates of Ekron, so that the wounded Philistines fell on the way from Shaaraim as far as Gath and Ekron. ⁵³ And the people of Israel came back from chasing the Philistines, and they plundered their camp. ⁵⁴ And David took the head of the Philistine and brought it to Jerusalem, but he put his armor in his tent.

⁵⁵ As soon as Saul saw David go out against the Philistine, he said to Abner, the commander of the army, "Abner, whose son is this youth?" And Abner said, "As your soul lives, O king, I do not know." ⁵⁶ And the king said, "Inquire whose son the boy is." ⁵⁷ And as soon as David returned from the striking down of the Philistine, Abner took him, and brought him before Saul with the head of the Philistine in his hand. ⁵⁸ And Saul said to him, "Whose son are you, young man?" And David answered, "I am the son of your servant Jesse the Bethlehemite."

David and Jonathan's Friendship

18 As soon as he had finished speaking to Saul, the soul of Jonathan was knit to the soul of David, and Jonathan loved him as his own soul. ² And Saul took him that day and would not let him return to his father's house. ³ Then Jonathan made a covenant with David, because he loved him as his own soul. ⁴ And Jonathan stripped himself of the robe that was on him and gave it to David, and his armor, and even his sword and his bow and his belt. ⁵ And David went out and was successful wherever Saul sent him, so that Saul set him over the men of war. And this was good in the sight of all the people and also in the sight of Saul's servants.

Saul's Jealousy of David

⁶ As they were coming home, when David returned from striking down the Philistine, the women came out of all the cities of Israel, singing and dancing, to meet King Saul, with tambourines, with songs of joy, and with musical instruments.[2] ⁷ And the women sang to one another as they celebrated,

> "Saul has struck down his thousands,
>   and David his ten thousands."

---

[1] Septuagint; Hebrew *Gai* [2] Or *triangles*, or *three-stringed instruments*

⁸And Saul was very angry, and this saying displeased him. He said, "They have ascribed to David ten thousands, and to me they have ascribed thousands, and what more can he have but the kingdom?" ⁹And Saul eyed David from that day on.

¹⁰The next day a harmful spirit from God rushed upon Saul, and he raved within his house while David was playing the lyre, as he did day by day. Saul had his spear in his hand. ¹¹And Saul hurled the spear, for he thought, "I will pin David to the wall." But David evaded him twice.

¹²Saul was afraid of David because the Lord was with him but had departed from Saul. ¹³So Saul removed him from his presence and made him a commander of a thousand. And he went out and came in before the people. ¹⁴And David had success in all his undertakings, for the Lord was with him. ¹⁵And when Saul saw that he had great success, he stood in fearful awe of him. ¹⁶But all Israel and Judah loved David, for he went out and came in before them.

David Marries Michal

¹⁷Then Saul said to David, "Here is my elder daughter Merab. I will give her to you for a wife. Only be valiant for me and fight the Lord's battles." For Saul thought, "Let not my hand be against him, but let the hand of the Philistines be against him." ¹⁸And David said to Saul, "Who am I, and who are my relatives, my father's clan in Israel, that I should be son-in-law to the king?" ¹⁹But at the time when Merab, Saul's daughter, should have been given to David, she was given to Adriel the Meholathite for a wife.

²⁰Now Saul's daughter Michal loved David. And they told Saul, and the thing pleased him. ²¹Saul thought, "Let me give her to him, that she may be a snare for him and that the hand of the Philistines may be against him." Therefore Saul said to David a second time,¹ "You shall now be my son-in-law." ²²And Saul commanded his servants, "Speak to David in private and say, 'Behold, the king has delight in you, and all his servants love you. Now then become the king's son-in-law.'" ²³And Saul's servants spoke those words in the ears of David. And David said, "Does it seem to you a little thing to become the king's son-in-law, since I am a poor man and have no reputation?" ²⁴And the servants of Saul told him, "Thus and so did David speak." ²⁵Then Saul said, "Thus shall you say to David, 'The king desires no bride-price except a hundred foreskins of the Philistines, that he may be avenged of the king's enemies.'" Now Saul thought to make David fall by the hand of the Philistines. ²⁶And when his servants told David

---

¹ Hebrew *by two*

these words, it pleased David well to be the king's son-in-law. Before the time had expired, ²⁷ David arose and went, along with his men, and killed two hundred of the Philistines. And David brought their foreskins, which were given in full number to the king, that he might become the king's son-in-law. And Saul gave him his daughter Michal for a wife. ²⁸ But when Saul saw and knew that the Lord was with David, and that Michal, Saul's daughter, loved him, ²⁹ Saul was even more afraid of David. So Saul was David's enemy continually.

³⁰ Then the commanders of the Philistines came out to battle, and as often as they came out David had more success than all the servants of Saul, so that his name was highly esteemed.

Saul Tries to Kill David

19 And Saul spoke to Jonathan his son and to all his servants, that they should kill David. But Jonathan, Saul's son, delighted much in David. ² And Jonathan told David, "Saul my father seeks to kill you. Therefore be on your guard in the morning. Stay in a secret place and hide yourself. ³ And I will go out and stand beside my father in the field where you are, and I will speak to my father about you. And if I learn anything I will tell you." ⁴ And Jonathan spoke well of David to Saul his father and said to him, "Let not the king sin against his servant David, because he has not sinned against you, and because his deeds have brought good to you. ⁵ For he took his life in his hand and he struck down the Philistine, and the Lord worked a great salvation for all Israel. You saw it, and rejoiced. Why then will you sin against innocent blood by killing David without cause?" ⁶ And Saul listened to the voice of Jonathan. Saul swore, "As the Lord lives, he shall not be put to death." ⁷ And Jonathan called David, and Jonathan reported to him all these things. And Jonathan brought David to Saul, and he was in his presence as before.

⁸ And there was war again. And David went out and fought with the Philistines and struck them with a great blow, so that they fled before him. ⁹ Then a harmful spirit from the Lord came upon Saul, as he sat in his house with his spear in his hand. And David was playing the lyre. ¹⁰ And Saul sought to pin David to the wall with the spear, but he eluded Saul, so that he struck the spear into the wall. And David fled and escaped that night.

¹¹ Saul sent messengers to David's house to watch him, that he might kill him in the morning. But Michal, David's wife, told him, "If you do not escape with your life tonight, tomorrow you will be killed." ¹² So Michal let David down through the window, and he fled away and escaped. ¹³ Michal took an

image[1] and laid it on the bed and put a pillow of goats' hair at its head and covered it with the clothes. ⁱ⁴ And when Saul sent messengers to take David, she said, "He is sick." ¹⁵ Then Saul sent the messengers to see David, saying, "Bring him up to me in the bed, that I may kill him." ¹⁶ And when the messengers came in, behold, the image was in the bed, with the pillow of goats' hair at its head. ¹⁷ Saul said to Michal, "Why have you deceived me thus and let my enemy go, so that he has escaped?" And Michal answered Saul, "He said to me, 'Let me go. Why should I kill you?'"

¹⁸ Now David fled and escaped, and he came to Samuel at Ramah and told him all that Saul had done to him. And he and Samuel went and lived at Naioth. ¹⁹ And it was told Saul, "Behold, David is at Naioth in Ramah." ²⁰ Then Saul sent messengers to take David, and when they saw the company of the prophets prophesying, and Samuel standing as head over them, the Spirit of God came upon the messengers of Saul, and they also prophesied. ²¹ When it was told Saul, he sent other messengers, and they also prophesied. And Saul sent messengers again the third time, and they also prophesied. ²² Then he himself went to Ramah and came to the great well that is in Secu. And he asked, "Where are Samuel and David?" And one said, "Behold, they are at Naioth in Ramah." ²³ And he went there to Naioth in Ramah. And the Spirit of God came upon him also, and as he went he prophesied until he came to Naioth in Ramah. ²⁴ And he too stripped off his clothes, and he too prophesied before Samuel and lay naked all that day and all that night. Thus it is said, "Is Saul also among the prophets?"

Jonathan Warns David

20 Then David fled from Naioth in Ramah and came and said before Jonathan, "What have I done? What is my guilt? And what is my sin before your father, that he seeks my life?" ² And he said to him, "Far from it! You shall not die. Behold, my father does nothing either great or small without disclosing it to me. And why should my father hide this from me? It is not so." ³ But David vowed again, saying, "Your father knows well that I have found favor in your eyes, and he thinks, 'Do not let Jonathan know this, lest he be grieved.' But truly, as the LORD lives and as your soul lives, there is but a step between me and death." ⁴ Then Jonathan said to David, "Whatever you say, I will do for you." ⁵ David said to Jonathan, "Behold, tomorrow is the new moon, and I should not fail to sit at table with the king. But let me go, that I may hide myself in the field till the third day at evening. ⁶ If your father misses me at all, then say, 'David earnestly asked leave of me to run to

---

[1] Or *a household god*

Bethlehem his city, for there is a yearly sacrifice there for all the clan.' ⁷ If he says, 'Good!' it will be well with your servant, but if he is angry, then know that harm is determined by him. ⁸ Therefore deal kindly with your servant, for you have brought your servant into a covenant of the Lord with you. But if there is guilt in me, kill me yourself, for why should you bring me to your father?" ⁹ And Jonathan said, "Far be it from you! If I knew that it was determined by my father that harm should come to you, would I not tell you?" ¹⁰ Then David said to Jonathan, "Who will tell me if your father answers you roughly?" ¹¹ And Jonathan said to David, "Come, let us go out into the field." So they both went out into the field.

¹² And Jonathan said to David, "The Lord, the God of Israel, be witness!¹ When I have sounded out my father, about this time tomorrow, or the third day, behold, if he is well disposed toward David, shall I not then send and disclose it to you? ¹³ But should it please my father to do you harm, the Lord do so to Jonathan and more also if I do not disclose it to you and send you away, that you may go in safety. May the Lord be with you, as he has been with my father. ¹⁴ If I am still alive, show me the steadfast love of the Lord, that I may not die; ¹⁵ and do not cut off² your steadfast love from my house forever, when the Lord cuts off every one of the enemies of David from the face of the earth." ¹⁶ And Jonathan made a covenant with the house of David, saying, "May³ the Lord take vengeance on David's enemies." ¹⁷ And Jonathan made David swear again by his love for him, for he loved him as he loved his own soul.

¹⁸ Then Jonathan said to him, "Tomorrow is the new moon, and you will be missed, because your seat will be empty. ¹⁹ On the third day go down quickly to the place where you hid yourself when the matter was in hand, and remain beside the stone heap.⁴ ²⁰ And I will shoot three arrows to the side of it, as though I shot at a mark. ²¹ And behold, I will send the boy, saying, 'Go, find the arrows.' If I say to the boy, 'Look, the arrows are on this side of you, take them,' then you are to come, for, as the Lord lives, it is safe for you and there is no danger. ²² But if I say to the youth, 'Look, the arrows are beyond you,' then go, for the Lord has sent you away. ²³ And as for the matter of which you and I have spoken, behold, the Lord is between you and me forever."

²⁴ So David hid himself in the field. And when the new moon came, the king sat down to eat food. ²⁵ The king sat on his seat, as at other times, on the seat by the wall. Jonathan sat opposite,⁵ and Abner sat by Saul's side, but David's place was empty.

²⁶ Yet Saul did not say anything that day, for he thought, "Something has happened to him. He is not clean; surely he is not clean." ²⁷ But on the second

---

¹ Hebrew lacks *be witness* ² Or *but if I die, do not cut off* ³ Septuagint *earth,* ¹⁶*let not the name of Jonathan be cut off from the house of David. And may* ⁴ Septuagint; Hebrew *the stone Ezel* ⁵ Compare Septuagint; Hebrew *stood up*

day, the day after the new moon, David's place was empty. And Saul said to Jonathan his son, "Why has not the son of Jesse come to the meal, either yesterday or today?" ²⁸ Jonathan answered Saul, "David earnestly asked leave of me to go to Bethlehem. ²⁹ He said, 'Let me go, for our clan holds a sacrifice in the city, and my brother has commanded me to be there. So now, if I have found favor in your eyes, let me get away and see my brothers.' For this reason he has not come to the king's table."

³⁰ Then Saul's anger was kindled against Jonathan, and he said to him, "You son of a perverse, rebellious woman, do I not know that you have chosen the son of Jesse to your own shame, and to the shame of your mother's nakedness? ³¹ For as long as the son of Jesse lives on the earth, neither you nor your kingdom shall be established. Therefore send and bring him to me, for he shall surely die." ³² Then Jonathan answered Saul his father, "Why should he be put to death? What has he done?" ³³ But Saul hurled his spear at him to strike him. So Jonathan knew that his father was determined to put David to death. ³⁴ And Jonathan rose from the table in fierce anger and ate no food the second day of the month, for he was grieved for David, because his father had disgraced him.

³⁵ In the morning Jonathan went out into the field to the appointment with David, and with him a little boy. ³⁶ And he said to his boy, "Run and find the arrows that I shoot." As the boy ran, he shot an arrow beyond him. ³⁷ And when the boy came to the place of the arrow that Jonathan had shot, Jonathan called after the boy and said, "Is not the arrow beyond you?" ³⁸ And Jonathan called after the boy, "Hurry! Be quick! Do not stay!" So Jonathan's boy gathered up the arrows and came to his master. ³⁹ But the boy knew nothing. Only Jonathan and David knew the matter. ⁴⁰ And Jonathan gave his weapons to his boy and said to him, "Go and carry them to the city." ⁴¹ And as soon as the boy had gone, David rose from beside the stone heap¹ and fell on his face to the ground and bowed three times. And they kissed one another and wept with one another, David weeping the most. ⁴² Then Jonathan said to David, "Go in peace, because we have sworn both of us in the name of the LORD, saying, 'The LORD shall be between me and you, and between my offspring and your offspring, forever.'" And he rose and departed, and Jonathan went into the city.²

David and the Holy Bread

21 ³ Then David came to Nob, to Ahimelech the priest. And Ahimelech came to meet David, trembling, and said to him, "Why are you alone, and no one with you?" ² And David said to Ahimelech the priest,

¹ Septuagint; Hebrew *from beside the south* ² This sentence is 21:1 in Hebrew ³ Ch 21:2 in Hebrew

"The king has charged me with a matter and said to me, 'Let no one know anything of the matter about which I send you, and with which I have charged you.' I have made an appointment with the young men for such and such a place. ³ Now then, what do you have on hand? Give me five loaves of bread, or whatever is here." ⁴ And the priest answered David, "I have no common bread on hand, but there is holy bread—if the young men have kept themselves from women." ⁵ And David answered the priest, "Truly women have been kept from us as always when I go on an expedition. The vessels of the young men are holy even when it is an ordinary journey. How much more today will their vessels be holy?" ⁶ So the priest gave him the holy bread, for there was no bread there but the bread of the Presence, which is removed from before the Lord, to be replaced by hot bread on the day it is taken away.

⁷ Now a certain man of the servants of Saul was there that day, detained before the Lord. His name was Doeg the Edomite, the chief of Saul's herdsmen.

⁸ Then David said to Ahimelech, "Then have you not here a spear or a sword at hand? For I have brought neither my sword nor my weapons with me, because the king's business required haste." ⁹ And the priest said, "The sword of Goliath the Philistine, whom you struck down in the Valley of Elah, behold, it is here wrapped in a cloth behind the ephod. If you will take that, take it, for there is none but that here." And David said, "There is none like that; give it to me."

David Flees to Gath

¹⁰ And David rose and fled that day from Saul and went to Achish the king of Gath. ¹¹ And the servants of Achish said to him, "Is not this David the king of the land? Did they not sing to one another of him in dances,

'Saul has struck down his thousands,
  and David his ten thousands'?"

¹² And David took these words to heart and was much afraid of Achish the king of Gath. ¹³ So he changed his behavior before them and pretended to be insane in their hands and made marks on the doors of the gate and let his spittle run down his beard. ¹⁴ Then Achish said to his servants, "Behold, you see the man is mad. Why then have you brought him to me? ¹⁵ Do I lack madmen, that you have brought this fellow to behave as a madman in my presence? Shall this fellow come into my house?"

David at the Cave of Adullam

22 David departed from there and escaped to the cave of Adullam. And when his brothers and all his father's house heard it, they went down there to him. ² And everyone who was in distress, and everyone who was in debt, and everyone who was bitter in soul,[1] gathered to him. And he became commander over them. And there were with him about four hundred men.

³ And David went from there to Mizpeh of Moab. And he said to the king of Moab, "Please let my father and my mother stay[2] with you, till I know what God will do for me." ⁴ And he left them with the king of Moab, and they stayed with him all the time that David was in the stronghold. ⁵ Then the prophet Gad said to David, "Do not remain in the stronghold; depart, and go into the land of Judah." So David departed and went into the forest of Hereth.

Saul Kills the Priests at Nob

⁶ Now Saul heard that David was discovered, and the men who were with him. Saul was sitting at Gibeah under the tamarisk tree on the height with his spear in his hand, and all his servants were standing about him. ⁷ And Saul said to his servants who stood about him, "Hear now, people of Benjamin; will the son of Jesse give every one of you fields and vineyards, will he make you all commanders of thousands and commanders of hundreds, ⁸ that all of you have conspired against me? No one discloses to me when my son makes a covenant with the son of Jesse. None of you is sorry for me or discloses to me that my son has stirred up my servant against me, to lie in wait, as at this day." ⁹ Then answered Doeg the Edomite, who stood by the servants of Saul, "I saw the son of Jesse coming to Nob, to Ahimelech the son of Ahitub, ¹⁰ and he inquired of the LORD for him and gave him provisions and gave him the sword of Goliath the Philistine."

¹¹ Then the king sent to summon Ahimelech the priest, the son of Ahitub, and all his father's house, the priests who were at Nob, and all of them came to the king. ¹² And Saul said, "Hear now, son of Ahitub." And he answered, "Here I am, my lord." ¹³ And Saul said to him, "Why have you conspired against me, you and the son of Jesse, in that you have given him bread and a sword and have inquired of God for him, so that he has risen against me, to lie in wait, as at this day?" ¹⁴ Then Ahimelech answered the king, "And who among all your servants is so faithful as David, who is the king's son-in-law, and captain over[3] your bodyguard, and honored in your house? ¹⁵ Is today the first time that I have inquired of God for him? No! Let not the king impute

---

[1] Or *discontented* [2] Syriac, Vulgate; Hebrew *go out* [3] Septuagint, Targum; Hebrew *and has turned aside to*

anything to his servant or to all the house of my father, for your servant has known nothing of all this, much or little." ¹⁶ And the king said, "You shall surely die, Ahimelech, you and all your father's house." ¹⁷ And the king said to the guard who stood about him, "Turn and kill the priests of the Lord, because their hand also is with David, and they knew that he fled and did not disclose it to me." But the servants of the king would not put out their hand to strike the priests of the Lord. ¹⁸ Then the king said to Doeg, "You turn and strike the priests." And Doeg the Edomite turned and struck down the priests, and he killed on that day eighty-five persons who wore the linen ephod. ¹⁹ And Nob, the city of the priests, he put to the sword; both man and woman, child and infant, ox, donkey and sheep, he put to the sword.

²⁰ But one of the sons of Ahimelech the son of Ahitub, named Abiathar, escaped and fled after David. ²¹ And Abiathar told David that Saul had killed the priests of the Lord. ²² And David said to Abiathar, "I knew on that day, when Doeg the Edomite was there, that he would surely tell Saul. I have occasioned the death of all the persons of your father's house. ²³ Stay with me; do not be afraid, for he who seeks my life seeks your life. With me you shall be in safekeeping."

David Saves the City of Keilah

23 Now they told David, "Behold, the Philistines are fighting against Keilah and are robbing the threshing floors." ² Therefore David inquired of the Lord, "Shall I go and attack these Philistines?" And the Lord said to David, "Go and attack the Philistines and save Keilah." ³ But David's men said to him, "Behold, we are afraid here in Judah; how much more then if we go to Keilah against the armies of the Philistines?" ⁴ Then David inquired of the Lord again. And the Lord answered him, "Arise, go down to Keilah, for I will give the Philistines into your hand." ⁵ And David and his men went to Keilah and fought with the Philistines and brought away their livestock and struck them with a great blow. So David saved the inhabitants of Keilah.

⁶ When Abiathar the son of Ahimelech had fled to David to Keilah, he had come down with an ephod in his hand. ⁷ Now it was told Saul that David had come to Keilah. And Saul said, "God has given him into my hand, for he has shut himself in by entering a town that has gates and bars." ⁸ And Saul summoned all the people to war, to go down to Keilah, to besiege David and his men. ⁹ David knew that Saul was plotting harm against him. And he said to Abiathar the priest, "Bring the ephod here." ¹⁰ Then David said, "O Lord, the God of Israel, your servant has surely heard that Saul seeks to come to Keilah, to destroy the city on my account. ¹¹ Will the men of Keilah surrender

me into his hand? Will Saul come down, as your servant has heard? O Lord, the God of Israel, please tell your servant." And the Lord said, "He will come down." ¹² Then David said, "Will the men of Keilah surrender me and my men into the hand of Saul?" And the Lord said, "They will surrender you." ¹³ Then David and his men, who were about six hundred, arose and departed from Keilah, and they went wherever they could go. When Saul was told that David had escaped from Keilah, he gave up the expedition. ¹⁴ And David remained in the strongholds in the wilderness, in the hill country of the wilderness of Ziph. And Saul sought him every day, but God did not give him into his hand.

Saul Pursues David

¹⁵ David saw that Saul had come out to seek his life. David was in the wilderness of Ziph at Horesh. ¹⁶ And Jonathan, Saul's son, rose and went to David at Horesh, and strengthened his hand in God. ¹⁷ And he said to him, "Do not fear, for the hand of Saul my father shall not find you. You shall be king over Israel, and I shall be next to you. Saul my father also knows this." ¹⁸ And the two of them made a covenant before the Lord. David remained at Horesh, and Jonathan went home.

¹⁹ Then the Ziphites went up to Saul at Gibeah, saying, "Is not David hiding among us in the strongholds at Horesh, on the hill of Hachilah, which is south of Jeshimon? ²⁰ Now come down, O king, according to all your heart's desire to come down, and our part shall be to surrender him into the king's hand." ²¹ And Saul said, "May you be blessed by the Lord, for you have had compassion on me. ²² Go, make yet more sure. Know and see the place where his foot is, and who has seen him there, for it is told me that he is very cunning. ²³ See therefore and take note of all the lurking places where he hides, and come back to me with sure information. Then I will go with you. And if he is in the land, I will search him out among all the thousands of Judah." ²⁴ And they arose and went to Ziph ahead of Saul.

Now David and his men were in the wilderness of Maon, in the Arabah to the south of Jeshimon. ²⁵ And Saul and his men went to seek him. And David was told, so he went down to the rock and lived in the wilderness of Maon. And when Saul heard that, he pursued after David in the wilderness of Maon. ²⁶ Saul went on one side of the mountain, and David and his men on the other side of the mountain. And David was hurrying to get away from Saul. As Saul and his men were closing in on David and his men to capture them, ²⁷ a messenger came to Saul, saying, "Hurry and come, for the Philistines have made a raid against the land." ²⁸ So Saul returned from pursuing after David and went against the Philistines. Therefore that place was called the Rock of Escape.[1] [29] [2] And David went up from there and lived in the strongholds of Engedi.

David Spares Saul's Life

24 [3] When Saul returned from following the Philistines, he was told, "Behold, David is in the wilderness of Engedi." [2] Then Saul took three thousand chosen men out of all Israel and went to seek David and his men in front of the Wildgoats' Rocks. [3] And he came to the sheepfolds by the way, where there was a cave, and Saul went in to relieve himself.[4] Now David and his men were sitting in the innermost parts of the cave. [4] And the men of David said to him, "Here is the day of which the LORD said to you, 'Behold, I will give your enemy into your hand, and you shall do to him as it shall seem good to you.'" Then David arose and stealthily cut off a corner of Saul's robe. [5] And afterward David's heart struck him, because he had cut off a corner of Saul's robe. [6] He said to his men, "The LORD forbid that I should do this thing to my lord, the LORD's anointed, to put out my hand against him, seeing he is the LORD's anointed." [7] So David persuaded his men with these words and did not permit them to attack Saul. And Saul rose up and left the cave and went on his way.

[8] Afterward David also arose and went out of the cave, and called after Saul, "My lord the king!" And when Saul looked behind him, David bowed with his face to the earth and paid homage. [9] And David said to Saul, "Why do you listen to the words of men who say, 'Behold, David seeks your harm'? [10] Behold, this day your eyes have seen how the LORD gave you today into my hand in the cave. And some told me to kill you, but I spared you.[5] I said, 'I will not put out my hand against my lord, for he is the LORD's anointed.' [11] See, my father, see the corner of your robe in my hand. For by the fact that I cut off the corner of your robe and did not kill you, you may know and see that there is no wrong or treason in my hands. I have not sinned against you, though you hunt my life to take it. [12] May the LORD judge between me and you, may the LORD avenge me against you, but my hand shall not be against you. [13] As the proverb of the ancients says, 'Out of the wicked comes wickedness.' But my hand shall not be against you. [14] After whom has the king of Israel come out? After whom do you pursue? After a dead dog! After a flea! [15] May the LORD therefore be judge and give sentence between me and you, and see to it and plead my cause and deliver me from your hand."

[16] As soon as David had finished speaking these words to Saul, Saul said, "Is this your voice, my son David?" And Saul lifted up his voice and wept. [17] He

---

[1] Or *Rock of Divisions* [2] Ch 24:1 in Hebrew [3] Ch 24:2 in Hebrew [4] Hebrew *cover his feet* [5] Septuagint, Syriac, Targum; Hebrew *it [my eye] spared you*

said to David, "You are more righteous than I, for you have repaid me good, whereas I have repaid you evil. ¹⁸ And you have declared this day how you have dealt well with me, in that you did not kill me when the Lord put me into your hands. ¹⁹ For if a man finds his enemy, will he let him go away safe? So may the Lord reward you with good for what you have done to me this day. ²⁰ And now, behold, I know that you shall surely be king, and that the kingdom of Israel shall be established in your hand. ²¹ Swear to me therefore by the Lord that you will not cut off my offspring after me, and that you will not destroy my name out of my father's house." ²² And David swore this to Saul. Then Saul went home, but David and his men went up to the stronghold.

The Death of Samuel

25
Now Samuel died. And all Israel assembled and mourned for him, and they buried him in his house at Ramah.

David and Abigail

Then David rose and went down to the wilderness of Paran. ² And there was a man in Maon whose business was in Carmel. The man was very rich; he had three thousand sheep and a thousand goats. He was shearing his sheep in Carmel. ³ Now the name of the man was Nabal, and the name of his wife Abigail. The woman was discerning and beautiful, but the man was harsh and badly behaved; he was a Calebite. ⁴ David heard in the wilderness that Nabal was shearing his sheep. ⁵ So David sent ten young men. And David said to the young men, "Go up to Carmel, and go to Nabal and greet him in my name. ⁶ And thus you shall greet him:¹ 'Peace be to you, and peace be to your house, and peace be to all that you have. ⁷ I hear that you have shearers. Now your shepherds have been with us, and we did them no harm, and they missed nothing all the time they were in Carmel. ⁸ Ask your young men, and they will tell you. Therefore let my young men find favor in your eyes, for we come on a feast day. Please give whatever you have at hand to your servants and to your son David.'"

⁹ When David's young men came, they said all this to Nabal in the name of David, and then they waited. ¹⁰ And Nabal answered David's servants, "Who is David? Who is the son of Jesse? There are many servants these days who are breaking away from their masters. ¹¹ Shall I take my bread and my water and my meat that I have killed for my shearers and give it to men who come from I do not know where?" ¹² So David's young men turned away and came back and told him all this. ¹³ And David said to his men, "Every man strap

¹ Or *shall say to him who lives*

on his sword!" And every man of them strapped on his sword. David also strapped on his sword. And about four hundred men went up after David, while two hundred remained with the baggage.

¹⁴ But one of the young men told Abigail, Nabal's wife, "Behold, David sent messengers out of the wilderness to greet our master, and he railed at them. ¹⁵ Yet the men were very good to us, and we suffered no harm, and we did not miss anything when we were in the fields, as long as we went with them. ¹⁶ They were a wall to us both by night and by day, all the while we were with them keeping the sheep. ¹⁷ Now therefore know this and consider what you should do, for harm is determined against our master and against all his house, and he is such a worthless man that one cannot speak to him."

¹⁸ Then Abigail made haste and took two hundred loaves and two skins of wine and five sheep already prepared and five seahs¹ of parched grain and a hundred clusters of raisins and two hundred cakes of figs, and laid them on donkeys. ¹⁹ And she said to her young men, "Go on before me; behold, I come after you." But she did not tell her husband Nabal. ²⁰ And as she rode on the donkey and came down under cover of the mountain, behold, David and his men came down toward her, and she met them. ²¹ Now David had said, "Surely in vain have I guarded all that this fellow has in the wilderness, so that nothing was missed of all that belonged to him, and he has returned me evil for good. ²² God do so to the enemies of David² and more also, if by morning I leave so much as one male of all who belong to him."

²³ When Abigail saw David, she hurried and got down from the donkey and fell before David on her face and bowed to the ground. ²⁴ She fell at his feet and said, "On me alone, my lord, be the guilt. Please let your servant speak in your ears, and hear the words of your servant. ²⁵ Let not my lord regard this worthless fellow, Nabal, for as his name is, so is he. Nabal³ is his name, and folly is with him. But I your servant did not see the young men of my lord, whom you sent. ²⁶ Now then, my lord, as the Lord lives, and as your soul lives, because the Lord has restrained you from bloodguilt and from saving with your own hand, now then let your enemies and those who seek to do evil to my lord be as Nabal. ²⁷ And now let this present that your servant has brought to my lord be given to the young men who follow my lord. ²⁸ Please forgive the trespass of your servant. For the Lord will certainly make my lord a sure house, because my lord is fighting the battles of the Lord, and evil shall not be found in you so long as you live. ²⁹ If men rise up to pursue you and to seek your life, the life of my lord shall be bound in the bundle of the living in the care of the Lord your God. And the lives of your enemies he shall sling out as from the hollow

---

¹ A *seah* was about 7.7 quarts or 7.3 liters ² Septuagint *to David* ³ *Nabal* means *fool*

of a sling. ³⁰ And when the Lord has done to my lord according to all the good that he has spoken concerning you and has appointed you prince[1] over Israel, ³¹ my lord shall have no cause of grief or pangs of conscience for having shed blood without cause or for my lord working salvation himself. And when the Lord has dealt well with my lord, then remember your servant."

³² And David said to Abigail, "Blessed be the Lord, the God of Israel, who sent you this day to meet me! ³³ Blessed be your discretion, and blessed be you, who have kept me this day from bloodguilt and from working salvation with my own hand! ³⁴ For as surely as the Lord, the God of Israel, lives, who has restrained me from hurting you, unless you had hurried and come to meet me, truly by morning there had not been left to Nabal so much as one male." ³⁵ Then David received from her hand what she had brought him. And he said to her, "Go up in peace to your house. See, I have obeyed your voice, and I have granted your petition."

³⁶ And Abigail came to Nabal, and behold, he was holding a feast in his house, like the feast of a king. And Nabal's heart was merry within him, for he was very drunk. So she told him nothing at all until the morning light. ³⁷ In the morning, when the wine had gone out of Nabal, his wife told him these things, and his heart died within him, and he became as a stone. ³⁸ And about ten days later the Lord struck Nabal, and he died.

³⁹ When David heard that Nabal was dead, he said, "Blessed be the Lord who has avenged the insult I received at the hand of Nabal, and has kept back his servant from wrongdoing. The Lord has returned the evil of Nabal on his own head." Then David sent and spoke to Abigail, to take her as his wife. ⁴⁰ When the servants of David came to Abigail at Carmel, they said to her, "David has sent us to you to take you to him as his wife." ⁴¹ And she rose and bowed with her face to the ground and said, "Behold, your handmaid is a servant to wash the feet of the servants of my lord." ⁴² And Abigail hurried and rose and mounted a donkey, and her five young women attended her. She followed the messengers of David and became his wife.

⁴³ David also took Ahinoam of Jezreel, and both of them became his wives. ⁴⁴ Saul had given Michal his daughter, David's wife, to Palti the son of Laish, who was of Gallim.

David Spares Saul Again

26 Then the Ziphites came to Saul at Gibeah, saying, "Is not David hiding himself on the hill of Hachilah, which is on the east of Jeshimon?" ² So Saul arose and went down to the wilderness of Ziph with

[1] Or leader

three thousand chosen men of Israel to seek David in the wilderness of Ziph. ³ And Saul encamped on the hill of Hachilah, which is beside the road on the east of Jeshimon. But David remained in the wilderness. When he saw that Saul came after him into the wilderness, ⁴ David sent out spies and learned that Saul had indeed come. ⁵ Then David rose and came to the place where Saul had encamped. And David saw the place where Saul lay, with Abner the son of Ner, the commander of his army. Saul was lying within the encampment, while the army was encamped around him.

⁶ Then David said to Ahimelech the Hittite, and to Joab's brother Abishai the son of Zeruiah, "Who will go down with me into the camp to Saul?" And Abishai said, "I will go down with you." ⁷ So David and Abishai went to the army by night. And there lay Saul sleeping within the encampment, with his spear stuck in the ground at his head, and Abner and the army lay around him. ⁸ Then Abishai said to David, "God has given your enemy into your hand this day. Now please let me pin him to the earth with one stroke of the spear, and I will not strike him twice." ⁹ But David said to Abishai, "Do not destroy him, for who can put out his hand against the LORD's anointed and be guiltless?" ¹⁰ And David said, "As the LORD lives, the LORD will strike him, or his day will come to die, or he will go down into battle and perish. ¹¹ The LORD forbid that I should put out my hand against the LORD's anointed. But take now the spear that is at his head and the jar of water, and let us go." ¹² So David took the spear and the jar of water from Saul's head, and they went away. No man saw it or knew it, nor did any awake, for they were all asleep, because a deep sleep from the LORD had fallen upon them.

¹³ Then David went over to the other side and stood far off on the top of the hill, with a great space between them. ¹⁴ And David called to the army, and to Abner the son of Ner, saying, "Will you not answer, Abner?" Then Abner answered, "Who are you who calls to the king?" ¹⁵ And David said to Abner, "Are you not a man? Who is like you in Israel? Why then have you not kept watch over your lord the king? For one of the people came in to destroy the king your lord. ¹⁶ This thing that you have done is not good. As the LORD lives, you deserve to die, because you have not kept watch over your lord, the LORD's anointed. And now see where the king's spear is and the jar of water that was at his head."

¹⁷ Saul recognized David's voice and said, "Is this your voice, my son David?" And David said, "It is my voice, my lord, O king." ¹⁸ And he said, "Why does my lord pursue after his servant? For what have I done? What evil is on my hands? ¹⁹ Now therefore let my lord the king hear the words of his servant. If it is the LORD who has stirred you up against me, may he accept an offering,

but if it is men, may they be cursed before the Lord, for they have driven me out this day that I should have no share in the heritage of the Lord, saying, 'Go, serve other gods.' ²⁰ Now therefore, let not my blood fall to the earth away from the presence of the Lord, for the king of Israel has come out to seek a single flea like one who hunts a partridge in the mountains."

²¹ Then Saul said, "I have sinned. Return, my son David, for I will no more do you harm, because my life was precious in your eyes this day. Behold, I have acted foolishly, and have made a great mistake." ²² And David answered and said, "Here is the spear, O king! Let one of the young men come over and take it. ²³ The Lord rewards every man for his righteousness and his faithfulness, for the Lord gave you into my hand today, and I would not put out my hand against the Lord's anointed. ²⁴ Behold, as your life was precious this day in my sight, so may my life be precious in the sight of the Lord, and may he deliver me out of all tribulation." ²⁵ Then Saul said to David, "Blessed be you, my son David! You will do many things and will succeed in them." So David went his way, and Saul returned to his place.

David Flees to the Philistines

27 Then David said in his heart, "Now I shall perish one day by the hand of Saul. There is nothing better for me than that I should escape to the land of the Philistines. Then Saul will despair of seeking me any longer within the borders of Israel, and I shall escape out of his hand." ² So David arose and went over, he and the six hundred men who were with him, to Achish the son of Maoch, king of Gath. ³ And David lived with Achish at Gath, he and his men, every man with his household, and David with his two wives, Ahinoam of Jezreel, and Abigail of Carmel, Nabal's widow. ⁴ And when it was told Saul that David had fled to Gath, he no longer sought him.

⁵ Then David said to Achish, "If I have found favor in your eyes, let a place be given me in one of the country towns, that I may dwell there. For why should your servant dwell in the royal city with you?" ⁶ So that day Achish gave him Ziklag. Therefore Ziklag has belonged to the kings of Judah to this day. ⁷ And the number of the days that David lived in the country of the Philistines was a year and four months.

⁸ Now David and his men went up and made raids against the Geshurites, the Girzites, and the Amalekites, for these were the inhabitants of the land from of old, as far as Shur, to the land of Egypt. ⁹ And David would strike the land and would leave neither man nor woman alive, but would take away the sheep, the oxen, the donkeys, the camels, and the garments, and come back to Achish. ¹⁰ When Achish asked, "Where have you made a raid today?"

David would say, "Against the Negeb of Judah," or, "Against the Negeb of the Jerahmeelites," or, "Against the Negeb of the Kenites." ¹¹ And David would leave neither man nor woman alive to bring news to Gath, thinking, "lest they should tell about us and say, 'So David has done.'" Such was his custom all the while he lived in the country of the Philistines. ¹² And Achish trusted David, thinking, "He has made himself an utter stench to his people Israel; therefore he shall always be my servant."

Saul and the Medium of En-dor

28 In those days the Philistines gathered their forces for war, to fight against Israel. And Achish said to David, "Understand that you and your men are to go out with me in the army." ² David said to Achish, "Very well, you shall know what your servant can do." And Achish said to David, "Very well, I will make you my bodyguard for life."

³ Now Samuel had died, and all Israel had mourned for him and buried him in Ramah, his own city. And Saul had put the mediums and the necromancers out of the land. ⁴ The Philistines assembled and came and encamped at Shunem. And Saul gathered all Israel, and they encamped at Gilboa. ⁵ When Saul saw the army of the Philistines, he was afraid, and his heart trembled greatly. ⁶ And when Saul inquired of the Lord, the Lord did not answer him, either by dreams, or by Urim, or by prophets. ⁷ Then Saul said to his servants, "Seek out for me a woman who is a medium, that I may go to her and inquire of her." And his servants said to him, "Behold, there is a medium at En-dor."

⁸ So Saul disguised himself and put on other garments and went, he and two men with him. And they came to the woman by night. And he said, "Divine for me by a spirit and bring up for me whomever I shall name to you." ⁹ The woman said to him, "Surely you know what Saul has done, how he has cut off the mediums and the necromancers from the land. Why then are you laying a trap for my life to bring about my death?" ¹⁰ But Saul swore to her by the Lord, "As the Lord lives, no punishment shall come upon you for this thing." ¹¹ Then the woman said, "Whom shall I bring up for you?" He said, "Bring up Samuel for me." ¹² When the woman saw Samuel, she cried out with a loud voice. And the woman said to Saul, "Why have you deceived me? You are Saul." ¹³ The king said to her, "Do not be afraid. What do you see?" And the woman said to Saul, "I see a god coming up out of the earth." ¹⁴ He said to her, "What is his appearance?" And she said, "An old man is coming up, and he is wrapped in a robe." And Saul knew that it was Samuel, and he bowed with his face to the ground and paid homage.

¹⁵ Then Samuel said to Saul, "Why have you disturbed me by bringing me up?" Saul answered, "I am in great distress, for the Philistines are warring against me, and God has turned away from me and answers me no more, either by prophets or by dreams. Therefore I have summoned you to tell me what I shall do." ¹⁶ And Samuel said, "Why then do you ask me, since the Lord has turned from you and become your enemy? ¹⁷ The Lord has done to you as he spoke by me, for the Lord has torn the kingdom out of your hand and given it to your neighbor, David. ¹⁸ Because you did not obey the voice of the Lord and did not carry out his fierce wrath against Amalek, therefore the Lord has done this thing to you this day. ¹⁹ Moreover, the Lord will give Israel also with you into the hand of the Philistines, and tomorrow you and your sons shall be with me. The Lord will give the army of Israel also into the hand of the Philistines."

²⁰ Then Saul fell at once full length on the ground, filled with fear because of the words of Samuel. And there was no strength in him, for he had eaten nothing all day and all night. ²¹ And the woman came to Saul, and when she saw that he was terrified, she said to him, "Behold, your servant has obeyed you. I have taken my life in my hand and have listened to what you have said to me. ²² Now therefore, you also obey your servant. Let me set a morsel of bread before you; and eat, that you may have strength when you go on your way." ²³ He refused and said, "I will not eat." But his servants, together with the woman, urged him, and he listened to their words. So he arose from the earth and sat on the bed. ²⁴ Now the woman had a fattened calf in the house, and she quickly killed it, and she took flour and kneaded it and baked unleavened bread of it, ²⁵ and she put it before Saul and his servants, and they ate. Then they rose and went away that night.

The Philistines Reject David

29 Now the Philistines had gathered all their forces at Aphek. And the Israelites were encamped by the spring that is in Jezreel. ² As the lords of the Philistines were passing on by hundreds and by thousands, and David and his men were passing on in the rear with Achish, ³ the commanders of the Philistines said, "What are these Hebrews doing here?" And Achish said to the commanders of the Philistines, "Is this not David, the servant of Saul, king of Israel, who has been with me now for days and years, and since he deserted to me I have found no fault in him to this day." ⁴ But the commanders of the Philistines were angry with him. And the commanders of the Philistines said to him, "Send the man back, that he may return to the place to which you have assigned him. He shall not go down with us to battle, lest in the battle he become an adversary to us. For how could this fellow reconcile himself to his lord? Would it not be with the heads of the men here? ⁵ Is not this David, of whom they sing to one another in dances,

> 'Saul has struck down his thousands,
>   and David his ten thousands'?"

⁶ Then Achish called David and said to him, "As the LORD lives, you have been honest, and to me it seems right that you should march out and in with me in the campaign. For I have found nothing wrong in you from the day of your coming to me to this day. Nevertheless, the lords do not approve of you. ⁷ So go back now; and go peaceably, that you may not displease the lords of the Philistines." ⁸ And David said to Achish, "But what have I done? What have you found in your servant from the day I entered your service until now, that I may not go and fight against the enemies of my lord the king?" ⁹ And Achish answered David and said, "I know that you are as blameless in my sight as an angel of God. Nevertheless, the commanders of the Philistines have said, 'He shall not go up with us to the battle.' ¹⁰ Now then rise early in the morning with the servants of your lord who came with you, and start early in the morning, and depart as soon as you have light." ¹¹ So David set out with his men early in the morning to return to the land of the Philistines. But the Philistines went up to Jezreel.

David's Wives Are Captured

30 Now when David and his men came to Ziklag on the third day, the Amalekites had made a raid against the Negeb and against Ziklag. They had overcome Ziklag and burned it with fire ² and taken captive the women and all[1] who were in it, both small and great. They killed no one, but carried them off and went their way. ³ And when David and his men came to the city, they found it burned with fire, and their wives and sons and daughters taken captive. ⁴ Then David and the people who were with him raised their voices and wept until they had no more strength to weep. ⁵ David's two wives also had been taken captive, Ahinoam of Jezreel and Abigail the widow of Nabal of Carmel. ⁶ And David was greatly distressed, for the people spoke of stoning him, because all the people were bitter in soul,[2] each for his sons and daughters. But David strengthened himself in the LORD his God.

⁷ And David said to Abiathar the priest, the son of Ahimelech, "Bring me the ephod." So Abiathar brought the ephod to David. ⁸ And David inquired of the

---
[1] Septuagint; Hebrew lacks *and all* [2] Compare 22:2

LORD, "Shall I pursue after this band? Shall I overtake them?" He answered him, "Pursue, for you shall surely overtake and shall surely rescue." ⁹ So David set out, and the six hundred men who were with him, and they came to the brook Besor, where those who were left behind stayed. ¹⁰ But David pursued, he and four hundred men. Two hundred stayed behind, who were too exhausted to cross the brook Besor.

¹¹ They found an Egyptian in the open country and brought him to David. And they gave him bread and he ate. They gave him water to drink, ¹² and they gave him a piece of a cake of figs and two clusters of raisins. And when he had eaten, his spirit revived, for he had not eaten bread or drunk water for three days and three nights. ¹³ And David said to him, "To whom do you belong? And where are you from?" He said, "I am a young man of Egypt, servant to an Amalekite, and my master left me behind because I fell sick three days ago. ¹⁴ We had made a raid against the Negeb of the Cherethites and against that which belongs to Judah and against the Negeb of Caleb, and we burned Ziklag with fire." ¹⁵ And David said to him, "Will you take me down to this band?" And he said, "Swear to me by God that you will not kill me or deliver me into the hands of my master, and I will take you down to this band."

David Defeats the Amalekites

¹⁶ And when he had taken him down, behold, they were spread abroad over all the land, eating and drinking and dancing, because of all the great spoil they had taken from the land of the Philistines and from the land of Judah. ¹⁷ And David struck them down from twilight until the evening of the next day, and not a man of them escaped, except four hundred young men, who mounted camels and fled. ¹⁸ David recovered all that the Amalekites had taken, and David rescued his two wives. ¹⁹ Nothing was missing, whether small or great, sons or daughters, spoil or anything that had been taken. David brought back all. ²⁰ David also captured all the flocks and herds, and the people drove the livestock before him,¹ and said, "This is David's spoil."

²¹ Then David came to the two hundred men who had been too exhausted to follow David, and who had been left at the brook Besor. And they went out to meet David and to meet the people who were with him. And when David came near to the people he greeted them. ²² Then all the wicked and worthless fellows among the men who had gone with David said, "Because they did not go with us, we will not give them any of the spoil that we have recovered, except that each man may lead away his wife and children, and depart." ²³ But David said, "You shall not do so, my brothers, with what the

---

¹ The meaning of the Hebrew clause is uncertain

LORD has given us. He has preserved us and given into our hand the band that came against us. ²⁴ Who would listen to you in this matter? For as his share is who goes down into the battle, so shall his share be who stays by the baggage. They shall share alike." ²⁵ And he made it a statute and a rule for Israel from that day forward to this day.

²⁶ When David came to Ziklag, he sent part of the spoil to his friends, the elders of Judah, saying, "Here is a present for you from the spoil of the enemies of the LORD." ²⁷ It was for those in Bethel, in Ramoth of the Negeb, in Jattir, ²⁸ in Aroer, in Siphmoth, in Eshtemoa, ²⁹ in Racal, in the cities of the Jerahmeelites, in the cities of the Kenites, ³⁰ in Hormah, in Bor-ashan, in Athach, ³¹ in Hebron, for all the places where David and his men had roamed.

The Death of Saul

31 Now the Philistines were fighting against Israel, and the men of Israel fled before the Philistines and fell slain on Mount Gilboa. ² And the Philistines overtook Saul and his sons, and the Philistines struck down Jonathan and Abinadab and Malchi-shua, the sons of Saul. ³ The battle pressed hard against Saul, and the archers found him, and he was badly wounded by the archers. ⁴ Then Saul said to his armor-bearer, "Draw your sword, and thrust me through with it, lest these uncircumcised come and thrust me through, and mistreat me." But his armor-bearer would not, for he feared greatly. Therefore Saul took his own sword and fell upon it. ⁵ And when his armor-bearer saw that Saul was dead, he also fell upon his sword and died with him. ⁶ Thus Saul died, and his three sons, and his armor-bearer, and all his men, on the same day together. ⁷ And when the men of Israel who were on the other side of the valley and those beyond the Jordan saw that the men of Israel had fled and that Saul and his sons were dead, they abandoned their cities and fled. And the Philistines came and lived in them.

⁸ The next day, when the Philistines came to strip the slain, they found Saul and his three sons fallen on Mount Gilboa. ⁹ So they cut off his head and stripped off his armor and sent messengers throughout the land of the Philistines, to carry the good news to the house of their idols and to the people. ¹⁰ They put his armor in the temple of Ashtaroth, and they fastened his body to the wall of Beth-shan. ¹¹ But when the inhabitants of Jabesh-gilead heard what the Philistines had done to Saul, ¹² all the valiant men arose and went all night and took the body of Saul and the bodies of his sons from the wall of Beth-shan, and they came to Jabesh and burned them there. ¹³ And they took their bones and buried them under the tamarisk tree in Jabesh and fasted seven days.

2 SAMUEL

David Hears of Saul's Death

1 After the death of Saul, when David had returned from striking down the Amalekites, David remained two days in Ziklag. ²And on the third day, behold, a man came from Saul's camp, with his clothes torn and dirt on his head. And when he came to David, he fell to the ground and paid homage. ³David said to him, "Where do you come from?" And he said to him, "I have escaped from the camp of Israel." ⁴And David said to him, "How did it go? Tell me." And he answered, "The people fled from the battle, and also many of the people have fallen and are dead, and Saul and his son Jonathan are also dead." ⁵Then David said to the young man who told him, "How do you know that Saul and his son Jonathan are dead?" ⁶And the young man who told him said, "By chance I happened to be on Mount Gilboa, and there was Saul leaning on his spear, and behold, the chariots and the horsemen were close upon him. ⁷And when he looked behind him, he saw me, and called to me. And I answered, 'Here I am.' ⁸And he said to me, 'Who are you?' I answered him, 'I am an Amalekite.' ⁹And he said to me, 'Stand beside me and kill me, for anguish has seized me, and yet my life still lingers.' ¹⁰So I stood beside him and killed him, because I was sure that he could not live after he had fallen. And I took the crown that was on his head and the armlet that was on his arm, and I have brought them here to my lord."

¹¹Then David took hold of his clothes and tore them, and so did all the men who were with him. ¹²And they mourned and wept and fasted until evening for Saul and for Jonathan his son and for the people of the Lord and for the house of Israel, because they had fallen by the sword. ¹³And David said to the young man who told him, "Where do you come from?" And he answered, "I am the son of a sojourner, an Amalekite." ¹⁴David said to him, "How is it you were not afraid to put out your hand to destroy the Lord's anointed?" ¹⁵Then David called one of the young men and said, "Go, execute him." And he struck him down so that he died. ¹⁶And David said to him, "Your blood be on your head, for your own mouth has testified against you, saying, 'I have killed the Lord's anointed.'"

David's Lament for Saul and Jonathan

¹⁷ And David lamented with this lamentation over Saul and Jonathan his son, ¹⁸ and he said it[1] should be taught to the people of Judah; behold, it is written in the Book of Jashar.[2] He said:

¹⁹ "Your glory, O Israel, is slain on your high places!
　　　How the mighty have fallen!
²⁰ Tell it not in Gath,
　　　publish it not in the streets of Ashkelon,
　lest the daughters of the Philistines rejoice,
　　　lest the daughters of the uncircumcised exult.

²¹ "You mountains of Gilboa,
　　　let there be no dew or rain upon you,
　　　　nor fields of offerings![3]
　For there the shield of the mighty was defiled,
　　　the shield of Saul, not anointed with oil.

²² "From the blood of the slain,
　　　from the fat of the mighty,
　the bow of Jonathan turned not back,
　　　and the sword of Saul returned not empty.

²³ "Saul and Jonathan, beloved and lovely!
　　　In life and in death they were not divided;
　they were swifter than eagles;
　　　they were stronger than lions.

²⁴ "You daughters of Israel, weep over Saul,
　　　who clothed you luxuriously in scarlet,
　　　who put ornaments of gold on your apparel.

²⁵ "How the mighty have fallen
　　　in the midst of the battle!

　"Jonathan lies slain on your high places.
²⁶ 　　I am distressed for you, my brother Jonathan;
　very pleasant have you been to me;

---

[1] Septuagint; Hebrew *the Bow*, which may be the name of the lament's tune [2] Or *of the upright* [3] Septuagint *firstfruits*

> your love to me was extraordinary,
> surpassing the love of women.

27 "How the mighty have fallen,
and the weapons of war perished!"

David Anointed King of Judah

2 After this David inquired of the Lord, "Shall I go up into any of the cities of Judah?" And the Lord said to him, "Go up." David said, "To which shall I go up?" And he said, "To Hebron." ² So David went up there, and his two wives also, Ahinoam of Jezreel and Abigail the widow of Nabal of Carmel. ³ And David brought up his men who were with him, everyone with his household, and they lived in the towns of Hebron. ⁴ And the men of Judah came, and there they anointed David king over the house of Judah.

When they told David, "It was the men of Jabesh-gilead who buried Saul," ⁵ David sent messengers to the men of Jabesh-gilead and said to them, "May you be blessed by the Lord, because you showed this loyalty to Saul your lord and buried him. ⁶ Now may the Lord show steadfast love and faithfulness to you. And I will do good to you because you have done this thing. ⁷ Now therefore let your hands be strong, and be valiant, for Saul your lord is dead, and the house of Judah has anointed me king over them."

Ish-bosheth Made King of Israel

⁸ But Abner the son of Ner, commander of Saul's army, took Ish-bosheth the son of Saul and brought him over to Mahanaim, ⁹ and he made him king over Gilead and the Ashurites and Jezreel and Ephraim and Benjamin and all Israel. ¹⁰ Ish-bosheth, Saul's son, was forty years old when he began to reign over Israel, and he reigned two years. But the house of Judah followed David. ¹¹ And the time that David was king in Hebron over the house of Judah was seven years and six months.

The Battle of Gibeon

¹² Abner the son of Ner, and the servants of Ish-bosheth the son of Saul, went out from Mahanaim to Gibeon. ¹³ And Joab the son of Zeruiah and the servants of David went out and met them at the pool of Gibeon. And they sat down, the one on the one side of the pool, and the other on the other side of the pool. ¹⁴ And Abner said to Joab, "Let the young men arise and compete before us." And Joab said, "Let them arise." ¹⁵ Then they arose and passed over

by number, twelve for Benjamin and Ish-bosheth the son of Saul, and twelve of the servants of David. ¹⁶ And each caught his opponent by the head and thrust his sword in his opponent's side, so they fell down together. Therefore that place was called Helkath-hazzurim,¹ which is at Gibeon. ¹⁷ And the battle was very fierce that day. And Abner and the men of Israel were beaten before the servants of David.

¹⁸ And the three sons of Zeruiah were there, Joab, Abishai, and Asahel. Now Asahel was as swift of foot as a wild gazelle. ¹⁹ And Asahel pursued Abner, and as he went, he turned neither to the right hand nor to the left from following Abner. ²⁰ Then Abner looked behind him and said, "Is it you, Asahel?" And he answered, "It is I." ²¹ Abner said to him, "Turn aside to your right hand or to your left, and seize one of the young men and take his spoil." But Asahel would not turn aside from following him. ²² And Abner said again to Asahel, "Turn aside from following me. Why should I strike you to the ground? How then could I lift up my face to your brother Joab?" ²³ But he refused to turn aside. Therefore Abner struck him in the stomach with the butt of his spear, so that the spear came out at his back. And he fell there and died where he was. And all who came to the place where Asahel had fallen and died, stood still.

²⁴ But Joab and Abishai pursued Abner. And as the sun was going down they came to the hill of Ammah, which lies before Giah on the way to the wilderness of Gibeon. ²⁵ And the people of Benjamin gathered themselves together behind Abner and became one group and took their stand on the top of a hill. ²⁶ Then Abner called to Joab, "Shall the sword devour forever? Do you not know that the end will be bitter? How long will it be before you tell your people to turn from the pursuit of their brothers?" ²⁷ And Joab said, "As God lives, if you had not spoken, surely the men would not have given up the pursuit of their brothers until the morning." ²⁸ So Joab blew the trumpet, and all the men stopped and pursued Israel no more, nor did they fight anymore.

²⁹ And Abner and his men went all that night through the Arabah. They crossed the Jordan, and marching the whole morning, they came to Mahanaim. ³⁰ Joab returned from the pursuit of Abner. And when he had gathered all the people together, there were missing from David's servants nineteen men besides Asahel. ³¹ But the servants of David had struck down of Benjamin 360 of Abner's men. ³² And they took up Asahel and buried him in the tomb of his father, which was at Bethlehem. And Joab and his men marched all night, and the day broke upon them at Hebron.

¹ *Helkath-hazzurim* means *the field of sword-edges*

Abner Joins David

3 There was a long war between the house of Saul and the house of David. And David grew stronger and stronger, while the house of Saul became weaker and weaker.

² And sons were born to David at Hebron: his firstborn was Amnon, of Ahinoam of Jezreel; ³ and his second, Chileab, of Abigail the widow of Nabal of Carmel; and the third, Absalom the son of Maacah the daughter of Talmai king of Geshur; ⁴ and the fourth, Adonijah the son of Haggith; and the fifth, Shephatiah the son of Abital; ⁵ and the sixth, Ithream, of Eglah, David's wife. These were born to David in Hebron.

⁶ While there was war between the house of Saul and the house of David, Abner was making himself strong in the house of Saul. ⁷ Now Saul had a concubine whose name was Rizpah, the daughter of Aiah. And Ish-bosheth said to Abner, "Why have you gone in to my father's concubine?" ⁸ Then Abner was very angry over the words of Ish-bosheth and said, "Am I a dog's head of Judah? To this day I keep showing steadfast love to the house of Saul your father, to his brothers, and to his friends, and have not given you into the hand of David. And yet you charge me today with a fault concerning a woman. ⁹ God do so to Abner and more also, if I do not accomplish for David what the Lord has sworn to him, ¹⁰ to transfer the kingdom from the house of Saul and set up the throne of David over Israel and over Judah, from Dan to Beersheba." ¹¹ And Ish-bosheth could not answer Abner another word, because he feared him.

¹² And Abner sent messengers to David on his behalf,¹ saying, "To whom does the land belong? Make your covenant with me, and behold, my hand shall be with you to bring over all Israel to you." ¹³ And he said, "Good; I will make a covenant with you. But one thing I require of you; that is, you shall not see my face unless you first bring Michal, Saul's daughter, when you come to see my face." ¹⁴ Then David sent messengers to Ish-bosheth, Saul's son, saying, "Give me my wife Michal, for whom I paid the bridal price of a hundred foreskins of the Philistines." ¹⁵ And Ish-bosheth sent and took her from her husband Paltiel the son of Laish. ¹⁶ But her husband went with her, weeping after her all the way to Bahurim. Then Abner said to him, "Go, return." And he returned.

¹⁷ And Abner conferred with the elders of Israel, saying, "For some time past you have been seeking David as king over you. ¹⁸ Now then bring it about, for the Lord has promised David, saying, 'By the hand of my servant David I will save my people Israel from the hand of the Philistines, and from the

---
¹ Or *where he was*; Septuagint *at Hebron*

hand of all their enemies.'" ¹⁹ Abner also spoke to Benjamin. And then Abner went to tell David at Hebron all that Israel and the whole house of Benjamin thought good to do.

²⁰ When Abner came with twenty men to David at Hebron, David made a feast for Abner and the men who were with him. ²¹ And Abner said to David, "I will arise and go and will gather all Israel to my lord the king, that they may make a covenant with you, and that you may reign over all that your heart desires." So David sent Abner away, and he went in peace.

²² Just then the servants of David arrived with Joab from a raid, bringing much spoil with them. But Abner was not with David at Hebron, for he had sent him away, and he had gone in peace. ²³ When Joab and all the army that was with him came, it was told Joab, "Abner the son of Ner came to the king, and he has let him go, and he has gone in peace." ²⁴ Then Joab went to the king and said, "What have you done? Behold, Abner came to you. Why is it that you have sent him away, so that he is gone? ²⁵ You know that Abner the son of Ner came to deceive you and to know your going out and your coming in, and to know all that you are doing."

Joab Murders Abner

²⁶ When Joab came out from David's presence, he sent messengers after Abner, and they brought him back from the cistern of Sirah. But David did not know about it. ²⁷ And when Abner returned to Hebron, Joab took him aside into the midst of the gate to speak with him privately, and there he struck him in the stomach, so that he died, for the blood of Asahel his brother. ²⁸ Afterward, when David heard of it, he said, "I and my kingdom are forever guiltless before the Lord for the blood of Abner the son of Ner. ²⁹ May it fall upon the head of Joab and upon all his father's house, and may the house of Joab never be without one who has a discharge or who is leprous or who holds a spindle or who falls by the sword or who lacks bread!" ³⁰ So Joab and Abishai his brother killed Abner, because he had put their brother Asahel to death in the battle at Gibeon.

David Mourns Abner

³¹ Then David said to Joab and to all the people who were with him, "Tear your clothes and put on sackcloth and mourn before Abner." And King David followed the bier. ³² They buried Abner at Hebron. And the king lifted up his voice and wept at the grave of Abner, and all the people wept. ³³ And the king lamented for Abner, saying,

"Should Abner die as a fool dies?

³⁴ Your hands were not bound;
> your feet were not fettered;
as one falls before the wicked
> you have fallen."

And all the people wept again over him. ³⁵ Then all the people came to persuade David to eat bread while it was yet day. But David swore, saying, "God do so to me and more also, if I taste bread or anything else till the sun goes down!" ³⁶ And all the people took notice of it, and it pleased them, as everything that the king did pleased all the people. ³⁷ So all the people and all Israel understood that day that it had not been the king's will to put to death Abner the son of Ner. ³⁸ And the king said to his servants, "Do you not know that a prince and a great man has fallen this day in Israel? ³⁹ And I was gentle today, though anointed king. These men, the sons of Zeruiah, are more severe than I. The Lord repay the evildoer according to his wickedness!"

Ish-bosheth Murdered

4 When Ish-bosheth, Saul's son, heard that Abner had died at Hebron, his courage failed, and all Israel was dismayed. ² Now Saul's son had two men who were captains of raiding bands; the name of the one was Baanah, and the name of the other Rechab, sons of Rimmon a man of Benjamin from Beeroth (for Beeroth also is counted part of Benjamin; ³ the Beerothites fled to Gittaim and have been sojourners there to this day).

⁴ Jonathan, the son of Saul, had a son who was crippled in his feet. He was five years old when the news about Saul and Jonathan came from Jezreel, and his nurse took him up and fled, and as she fled in her haste, he fell and became lame. And his name was Mephibosheth.

⁵ Now the sons of Rimmon the Beerothite, Rechab and Baanah, set out, and about the heat of the day they came to the house of Ish-bosheth as he was taking his noonday rest. ⁶ And they came into the midst of the house as if to get wheat, and they stabbed him in the stomach. Then Rechab and Baanah his brother escaped.[1] ⁷ When they came into the house, as he lay on his bed in his bedroom, they struck him and put him to death and beheaded him. They took his head and went by the way of the Arabah all night, ⁸ and brought the head of Ish-bosheth to David at Hebron. And they said to the king, "Here is the head of Ish-bosheth, the son of Saul, your enemy, who sought your life. The Lord has avenged my lord the king this day on Saul and on his offspring." ⁹ But David answered Rechab and Baanah his brother,

---

[1] Septuagint *And behold, the doorkeeper of the house had been cleaning wheat, but she grew drowsy and slept. So Rechab and Baanah his brother slipped in*

the sons of Rimmon the Beerothite, "As the LORD lives, who has redeemed my life out of every adversity, ¹⁰ when one told me, 'Behold, Saul is dead,' and thought he was bringing good news, I seized him and killed him at Ziklag, which was the reward I gave him for his news. ¹¹ How much more, when wicked men have killed a righteous man in his own house on his bed, shall I not now require his blood at your hand and destroy you from the earth?" ¹² And David commanded his young men, and they killed them and cut off their hands and feet and hanged them beside the pool at Hebron. But they took the head of Ish-bosheth and buried it in the tomb of Abner at Hebron.

David Anointed King of Israel

5 Then all the tribes of Israel came to David at Hebron and said, "Behold, we are your bone and flesh. ² In times past, when Saul was king over us, it was you who led out and brought in Israel. And the LORD said to you, 'You shall be shepherd of my people Israel, and you shall be prince¹ over Israel.'" ³ So all the elders of Israel came to the king at Hebron, and King David made a covenant with them at Hebron before the LORD, and they anointed David king over Israel. ⁴ David was thirty years old when he began to reign, and he reigned forty years. ⁵ At Hebron he reigned over Judah seven years and six months, and at Jerusalem he reigned over all Israel and Judah thirty-three years.²

⁶ And the king and his men went to Jerusalem against the Jebusites, the inhabitants of the land, who said to David, "You will not come in here, but the blind and the lame will ward you off"—thinking, "David cannot come in here." ⁷ Nevertheless, David took the stronghold of Zion, that is, the city of David. ⁸ And David said on that day, "Whoever would strike the Jebusites, let him get up the water shaft to attack 'the lame and the blind,' who are hated by David's soul." Therefore it is said, "The blind and the lame shall not come into the house." ⁹ And David lived in the stronghold and called it the city of David. And David built the city all around from the Millo inward. ¹⁰ And David became greater and greater, for the LORD, the God of hosts, was with him.

¹¹ And Hiram king of Tyre sent messengers to David, and cedar trees, also carpenters and masons who built David a house. ¹² And David knew that the LORD had established him king over Israel, and that he had exalted his kingdom for the sake of his people Israel.

¹³ And David took more concubines and wives from Jerusalem, after he came from Hebron, and more sons and daughters were born to David. ¹⁴ And these are the names of those who were born to him in Jerusalem: Shammua,

¹ Or *leader* ² Dead Sea Scroll lacks verses 4–5

Shobab, Nathan, Solomon, ¹⁵ Ibhar, Elishua, Nepheg, Japhia, ¹⁶ Elishama, Eliada, and Eliphelet.

David Defeats the Philistines

¹⁷ When the Philistines heard that David had been anointed king over Israel, all the Philistines went up to search for David. But David heard of it and went down to the stronghold. ¹⁸ Now the Philistines had come and spread out in the Valley of Rephaim. ¹⁹ And David inquired of the LORD, "Shall I go up against the Philistines? Will you give them into my hand?" And the LORD said to David, "Go up, for I will certainly give the Philistines into your hand." ²⁰ And David came to Baal-perazim, and David defeated them there. And he said, "The LORD has broken through my enemies before me like a breaking flood." Therefore the name of that place is called Baal-perazim.¹ ²¹ And the Philistines left their idols there, and David and his men carried them away.

²² And the Philistines came up yet again and spread out in the Valley of Rephaim. ²³ And when David inquired of the LORD, he said, "You shall not go up; go around to their rear, and come against them opposite the balsam trees. ²⁴ And when you hear the sound of marching in the tops of the balsam trees, then rouse yourself, for then the LORD has gone out before you to strike down the army of the Philistines." ²⁵ And David did as the LORD commanded him, and struck down the Philistines from Geba to Gezer.

The Ark Brought to Jerusalem

6 David again gathered all the chosen men of Israel, thirty thousand. ² And David arose and went with all the people who were with him from Baale-judah to bring up from there the ark of God, which is called by the name of the LORD of hosts who sits enthroned on the cherubim. ³ And they carried the ark of God on a new cart and brought it out of the house of Abinadab, which was on the hill. And Uzzah and Ahio,² the sons of Abinadab, were driving the new cart, ⁴ with the ark of God,³ and Ahio went before the ark.

Uzzah and the Ark

⁵ And David and all the house of Israel were celebrating before the LORD, with songs⁴ and lyres and harps and tambourines and castanets and cymbals. ⁶ And when they came to the threshing floor of Nacon, Uzzah put out his hand to the ark of God and took hold of it, for the oxen stumbled. ⁷ And the anger of the LORD was kindled against Uzzah, and God struck him down

---

¹ *Baal-perazim* means *Lord of breaking through* ² Or *and his brother*; also verse 4 ³ Compare Septuagint; Hebrew *the new cart, ⁴and brought it out of the house of Abinadab, which was on the hill, with the ark of God* ⁴ Septuagint, 1 Chronicles 13:8; Hebrew *fir trees*

there because of his error, and he died there beside the ark of God. ⁸ And David was angry because the LORD had broken out against Uzzah. And that place is called Perez-uzzah¹ to this day. ⁹ And David was afraid of the LORD that day, and he said, "How can the ark of the LORD come to me?" ¹⁰ So David was not willing to take the ark of the LORD into the city of David. But David took it aside to the house of Obed-edom the Gittite. ¹¹ And the ark of the LORD remained in the house of Obed-edom the Gittite three months, and the LORD blessed Obed-edom and all his household.

¹² And it was told King David, "The LORD has blessed the household of Obed-edom and all that belongs to him, because of the ark of God." So David went and brought up the ark of God from the house of Obed-edom to the city of David with rejoicing. ¹³ And when those who bore the ark of the LORD had gone six steps, he sacrificed an ox and a fattened animal. ¹⁴ And David danced before the LORD with all his might. And David was wearing a linen ephod. ¹⁵ So David and all the house of Israel brought up the ark of the LORD with shouting and with the sound of the horn.

David and Michal

¹⁶ As the ark of the LORD came into the city of David, Michal the daughter of Saul looked out of the window and saw King David leaping and dancing before the LORD, and she despised him in her heart. ¹⁷ And they brought in the ark of the LORD and set it in its place, inside the tent that David had pitched for it. And David offered burnt offerings and peace offerings before the LORD. ¹⁸ And when David had finished offering the burnt offerings and the peace offerings, he blessed the people in the name of the LORD of hosts ¹⁹ and distributed among all the people, the whole multitude of Israel, both men and women, a cake of bread, a portion of meat,² and a cake of raisins to each one. Then all the people departed, each to his house.

²⁰ And David returned to bless his household. But Michal the daughter of Saul came out to meet David and said, "How the king of Israel honored himself today, uncovering himself today before the eyes of his servants' female servants, as one of the vulgar fellows shamelessly uncovers himself!" ²¹ And David said to Michal, "It was before the LORD, who chose me above your father and above all his house, to appoint me as prince³ over Israel, the people of the LORD—and I will celebrate before the LORD. ²² I will make myself yet more contemptible than this, and I will be abased in your⁴ eyes. But by the female servants of whom you have spoken, by them I shall be held in honor."
²³ And Michal the daughter of Saul had no child to the day of her death.

---

¹ *Perez-uzzah* means *the breaking out against Uzzah* ² Vulgate; the meaning of the Hebrew term is uncertain ³ Or *leader* ⁴ Septuagint; Hebrew *my*

The Lord's Covenant with David

7 Now when the king lived in his house and the Lord had given him rest from all his surrounding enemies, ² the king said to Nathan the prophet, "See now, I dwell in a house of cedar, but the ark of God dwells in a tent." ³ And Nathan said to the king, "Go, do all that is in your heart, for the Lord is with you."

⁴ But that same night the word of the Lord came to Nathan, ⁵ "Go and tell my servant David, 'Thus says the Lord: Would you build me a house to dwell in? ⁶ I have not lived in a house since the day I brought up the people of Israel from Egypt to this day, but I have been moving about in a tent for my dwelling. ⁷ In all places where I have moved with all the people of Israel, did I speak a word with any of the judges[1] of Israel, whom I commanded to shepherd my people Israel, saying, "Why have you not built me a house of cedar?"' ⁸ Now, therefore, thus you shall say to my servant David, 'Thus says the Lord of hosts, I took you from the pasture, from following the sheep, that you should be prince[2] over my people Israel. ⁹ And I have been with you wherever you went and have cut off all your enemies from before you. And I will make for you a great name, like the name of the great ones of the earth. ¹⁰ And I will appoint a place for my people Israel and will plant them, so that they may dwell in their own place and be disturbed no more. And violent men shall afflict them no more, as formerly, ¹¹ from the time that I appointed judges over my people Israel. And I will give you rest from all your enemies. Moreover, the Lord declares to you that the Lord will make you a house. ¹² When your days are fulfilled and you lie down with your fathers, I will raise up your offspring after you, who shall come from your body,[3] and I will establish his kingdom. ¹³ He shall build a house for my name, and I will establish the throne of his kingdom forever. ¹⁴ I will be to him a father, and he shall be to me a son. When he commits iniquity, I will discipline him with the rod of men, with the stripes of the sons of men, ¹⁵ but my steadfast love will not depart from him, as I took it from Saul, whom I put away from before you. ¹⁶ And your house and your kingdom shall be made sure forever before me.[4] Your throne shall be established forever.'" ¹⁷ In accordance with all these words, and in accordance with all this vision, Nathan spoke to David.

David's Prayer of Gratitude

¹⁸ Then King David went in and sat before the Lord and said, "Who am I, O Lord God, and what is my house, that you have brought me thus far? ¹⁹ And yet this was a small thing in your eyes, O Lord God. You have spoken also

---

[1] Compare 1 Chronicles 17:6; Hebrew *tribes* [2] Or *leader* [3] Hebrew *loins* [4] Septuagint; Hebrew *you*

of your servant's house for a great while to come, and this is instruction for mankind, O Lord God! ²⁰ And what more can David say to you? For you know your servant, O Lord God! ²¹ Because of your promise, and according to your own heart, you have brought about all this greatness, to make your servant know it. ²² Therefore you are great, O Lord God. For there is none like you, and there is no God besides you, according to all that we have heard with our ears. ²³ And who is like your people Israel, the one nation on earth whom God went to redeem to be his people, making himself a name and doing for them[1] great and awesome things by driving out before your people,[2] whom you redeemed for yourself from Egypt, a nation and its gods? ²⁴ And you established for yourself your people Israel to be your people forever. And you, O Lord, became their God. ²⁵ And now, O Lord God, confirm forever the word that you have spoken concerning your servant and concerning his house, and do as you have spoken. ²⁶ And your name will be magnified forever, saying, 'The Lord of hosts is God over Israel,' and the house of your servant David will be established before you. ²⁷ For you, O Lord of hosts, the God of Israel, have made this revelation to your servant, saying, 'I will build you a house.' Therefore your servant has found courage to pray this prayer to you. ²⁸ And now, O Lord God, you are God, and your words are true, and you have promised this good thing to your servant. ²⁹ Now therefore may it please you to bless the house of your servant, so that it may continue forever before you. For you, O Lord God, have spoken, and with your blessing shall the house of your servant be blessed forever."

David's Victories

8 After this David defeated the Philistines and subdued them, and David took Metheg-ammah out of the hand of the Philistines.

² And he defeated Moab and he measured them with a line, making them lie down on the ground. Two lines he measured to be put to death, and one full line to be spared. And the Moabites became servants to David and brought tribute.

³ David also defeated Hadadezer the son of Rehob, king of Zobah, as he went to restore his power at the river Euphrates. ⁴ And David took from him 1,700 horsemen, and 20,000 foot soldiers. And David hamstrung all the chariot horses but left enough for 100 chariots. ⁵ And when the Syrians of Damascus came to help Hadadezer king of Zobah, David struck down 22,000 men of the Syrians. ⁶ Then David put garrisons in Aram of Damascus, and the Syrians became servants to David and brought tribute. And the Lord gave

---

[1] With a few Targums, Vulgate, Syriac; Hebrew *you* [2] Septuagint (compare 1 Chronicles 17:21); Hebrew *awesome things for your land, before your people*

victory to David wherever he went. ⁷ And David took the shields of gold that were carried by the servants of Hadadezer and brought them to Jerusalem. ⁸ And from Betah and from Berothai, cities of Hadadezer, King David took very much bronze.

⁹ When Toi king of Hamath heard that David had defeated the whole army of Hadadezer, ¹⁰ Toi sent his son Joram to King David, to ask about his health and to bless him because he had fought against Hadadezer and defeated him, for Hadadezer had often been at war with Toi. And Joram brought with him articles of silver, of gold, and of bronze. ¹¹ These also King David dedicated to the Lord, together with the silver and gold that he dedicated from all the nations he subdued, ¹² from Edom, Moab, the Ammonites, the Philistines, Amalek, and from the spoil of Hadadezer the son of Rehob, king of Zobah.

¹³ And David made a name for himself when he returned from striking down 18,000 Edomites in the Valley of Salt. ¹⁴ Then he put garrisons in Edom; throughout all Edom he put garrisons, and all the Edomites became David's servants. And the Lord gave victory to David wherever he went.

David's Officials

¹⁵ So David reigned over all Israel. And David administered justice and equity to all his people. ¹⁶ Joab the son of Zeruiah was over the army, and Jehoshaphat the son of Ahilud was recorder, ¹⁷ and Zadok the son of Ahitub and Ahimelech the son of Abiathar were priests, and Seraiah was secretary, ¹⁸ and Benaiah the son of Jehoiada was over¹ the Cherethites and the Pelethites, and David's sons were priests.

David's Kindness to Mephibosheth

9 And David said, "Is there still anyone left of the house of Saul, that I may show him kindness for Jonathan's sake?" ² Now there was a servant of the house of Saul whose name was Ziba, and they called him to David. And the king said to him, "Are you Ziba?" And he said, "I am your servant." ³ And the king said, "Is there not still someone of the house of Saul, that I may show the kindness of God to him?" Ziba said to the king, "There is still a son of Jonathan; he is crippled in his feet." ⁴ The king said to him, "Where is he?" And Ziba said to the king, "He is in the house of Machir the son of Ammiel, at Lo-debar." ⁵ Then King David sent and brought him from the house of Machir the son of Ammiel, at Lo-debar. ⁶ And Mephibosheth the son of Jonathan, son of Saul, came to David and fell on his face and paid homage. And David said, "Mephibosheth!" And he answered, "Behold, I am

---

[1] Compare 20:23, 1 Chronicles 18:17, Syriac, Targum, Vulgate; Hebrew lacks *was over*

your servant." ⁷ And David said to him, "Do not fear, for I will show you kindness for the sake of your father Jonathan, and I will restore to you all the land of Saul your father, and you shall eat at my table always." ⁸ And he paid homage and said, "What is your servant, that you should show regard for a dead dog such as I?"

⁹ Then the king called Ziba, Saul's servant, and said to him, "All that belonged to Saul and to all his house I have given to your master's grandson. ¹⁰ And you and your sons and your servants shall till the land for him and shall bring in the produce, that your master's grandson may have bread to eat. But Mephibosheth your master's grandson shall always eat at my table." Now Ziba had fifteen sons and twenty servants. ¹¹ Then Ziba said to the king, "According to all that my lord the king commands his servant, so will your servant do." So Mephibosheth ate at David's¹ table, like one of the king's sons. ¹² And Mephibosheth had a young son, whose name was Mica. And all who lived in Ziba's house became Mephibosheth's servants. ¹³ So Mephibosheth lived in Jerusalem, for he ate always at the king's table. Now he was lame in both his feet.

David Defeats Ammon and Syria

10 After this the king of the Ammonites died, and Hanun his son reigned in his place. ² And David said, "I will deal loyally² with Hanun the son of Nahash, as his father dealt loyally with me." So David sent by his servants to console him concerning his father. And David's servants came into the land of the Ammonites. ³ But the princes of the Ammonites said to Hanun their lord, "Do you think, because David has sent comforters to you, that he is honoring your father? Has not David sent his servants to you to search the city and to spy it out and to overthrow it?" ⁴ So Hanun took David's servants and shaved off half the beard of each and cut off their garments in the middle, at their hips, and sent them away. ⁵ When it was told David, he sent to meet them, for the men were greatly ashamed. And the king said, "Remain at Jericho until your beards have grown and then return."

⁶ When the Ammonites saw that they had become a stench to David, the Ammonites sent and hired the Syrians of Beth-rehob, and the Syrians of Zobah, 20,000 foot soldiers, and the king of Maacah with 1,000 men, and the men of Tob, 12,000 men. ⁷ And when David heard of it, he sent Joab and all the host of the mighty men. ⁸ And the Ammonites came out and drew up in battle array at the entrance of the gate, and the Syrians of Zobah and of Rehob and the men of Tob and Maacah were by themselves in the open country.

¹ Septuagint; Hebrew *my* ² Or *kindly*; twice in this verse

⁹ When Joab saw that the battle was set against him both in front and in the rear, he chose some of the best men of Israel and arrayed them against the Syrians. ¹⁰ The rest of his men he put in the charge of Abishai his brother, and he arrayed them against the Ammonites. ¹¹ And he said, "If the Syrians are too strong for me, then you shall help me, but if the Ammonites are too strong for you, then I will come and help you. ¹² Be of good courage, and let us be courageous for our people, and for the cities of our God, and may the Lord do what seems good to him." ¹³ So Joab and the people who were with him drew near to battle against the Syrians, and they fled before him. ¹⁴ And when the Ammonites saw that the Syrians fled, they likewise fled before Abishai and entered the city. Then Joab returned from fighting against the Ammonites and came to Jerusalem.

¹⁵ But when the Syrians saw that they had been defeated by Israel, they gathered themselves together. ¹⁶ And Hadadezer sent and brought out the Syrians who were beyond the Euphrates.[1] They came to Helam, with Shobach the commander of the army of Hadadezer at their head. ¹⁷ And when it was told David, he gathered all Israel together and crossed the Jordan and came to Helam. The Syrians arrayed themselves against David and fought with him. ¹⁸ And the Syrians fled before Israel, and David killed of the Syrians the men of 700 chariots, and 40,000 horsemen, and wounded Shobach the commander of their army, so that he died there. ¹⁹ And when all the kings who were servants of Hadadezer saw that they had been defeated by Israel, they made peace with Israel and became subject to them. So the Syrians were afraid to save the Ammonites anymore.

David and Bathsheba

11 In the spring of the year, the time when kings go out to battle, David sent Joab, and his servants with him, and all Israel. And they ravaged the Ammonites and besieged Rabbah. But David remained at Jerusalem.

² It happened, late one afternoon, when David arose from his couch and was walking on the roof of the king's house, that he saw from the roof a woman bathing; and the woman was very beautiful. ³ And David sent and inquired about the woman. And one said, "Is not this Bathsheba, the daughter of Eliam, the wife of Uriah the Hittite?" ⁴ So David sent messengers and took her, and she came to him, and he lay with her. (Now she had been purifying herself from her uncleanness.) Then she returned to her house. ⁵ And the woman conceived, and she sent and told David, "I am pregnant."

[1] Hebrew *the River*

⁶ So David sent word to Joab, "Send me Uriah the Hittite." And Joab sent Uriah to David. ⁷ When Uriah came to him, David asked how Joab was doing and how the people were doing and how the war was going. ⁸ Then David said to Uriah, "Go down to your house and wash your feet." And Uriah went out of the king's house, and there followed him a present from the king. ⁹ But Uriah slept at the door of the king's house with all the servants of his lord, and did not go down to his house. ¹⁰ When they told David, "Uriah did not go down to his house," David said to Uriah, "Have you not come from a journey? Why did you not go down to your house?" ¹¹ Uriah said to David, "The ark and Israel and Judah dwell in booths, and my lord Joab and the servants of my lord are camping in the open field. Shall I then go to my house, to eat and to drink and to lie with my wife? As you live, and as your soul lives, I will not do this thing." ¹² Then David said to Uriah, "Remain here today also, and tomorrow I will send you back." So Uriah remained in Jerusalem that day and the next. ¹³ And David invited him, and he ate in his presence and drank, so that he made him drunk. And in the evening he went out to lie on his couch with the servants of his lord, but he did not go down to his house.

¹⁴ In the morning David wrote a letter to Joab and sent it by the hand of Uriah. ¹⁵ In the letter he wrote, "Set Uriah in the forefront of the hardest fighting, and then draw back from him, that he may be struck down, and die." ¹⁶ And as Joab was besieging the city, he assigned Uriah to the place where he knew there were valiant men. ¹⁷ And the men of the city came out and fought with Joab, and some of the servants of David among the people fell. Uriah the Hittite also died. ¹⁸ Then Joab sent and told David all the news about the fighting. ¹⁹ And he instructed the messenger, "When you have finished telling all the news about the fighting to the king, ²⁰ then, if the king's anger rises, and if he says to you, 'Why did you go so near the city to fight? Did you not know that they would shoot from the wall? ²¹ Who killed Abimelech the son of Jerubbesheth? Did not a woman cast an upper millstone on him from the wall, so that he died at Thebez? Why did you go so near the wall?' then you shall say, 'Your servant Uriah the Hittite is dead also.'"

²² So the messenger went and came and told David all that Joab had sent him to tell. ²³ The messenger said to David, "The men gained an advantage over us and came out against us in the field, but we drove them back to the entrance of the gate. ²⁴ Then the archers shot at your servants from the wall. Some of the king's servants are dead, and your servant Uriah the Hittite is dead also." ²⁵ David said to the messenger, "Thus shall you say to Joab, 'Do

not let this matter displease you, for the sword devours now one and now another. Strengthen your attack against the city and overthrow it.' And encourage him."

²⁶ When the wife of Uriah heard that Uriah her husband was dead, she lamented over her husband. ²⁷ And when the mourning was over, David sent and brought her to his house, and she became his wife and bore him a son. But the thing that David had done displeased the Lord.

Nathan Rebukes David

12 And the Lord sent Nathan to David. He came to him and said to him, "There were two men in a certain city, the one rich and the other poor. ² The rich man had very many flocks and herds, ³ but the poor man had nothing but one little ewe lamb, which he had bought. And he brought it up, and it grew up with him and with his children. It used to eat of his morsel and drink from his cup and lie in his arms,¹ and it was like a daughter to him. ⁴ Now there came a traveler to the rich man, and he was unwilling to take one of his own flock or herd to prepare for the guest who had come to him, but he took the poor man's lamb and prepared it for the man who had come to him." ⁵ Then David's anger was greatly kindled against the man, and he said to Nathan, "As the Lord lives, the man who has done this deserves to die, ⁶ and he shall restore the lamb fourfold, because he did this thing, and because he had no pity."

⁷ Nathan said to David, "You are the man! Thus says the Lord, the God of Israel, 'I anointed you king over Israel, and I delivered you out of the hand of Saul. ⁸ And I gave you your master's house and your master's wives into your arms and gave you the house of Israel and of Judah. And if this were too little, I would add to you as much more. ⁹ Why have you despised the word of the Lord, to do what is evil in his sight? You have struck down Uriah the Hittite with the sword and have taken his wife to be your wife and have killed him with the sword of the Ammonites. ¹⁰ Now therefore the sword shall never depart from your house, because you have despised me and have taken the wife of Uriah the Hittite to be your wife.' ¹¹ Thus says the Lord, 'Behold, I will raise up evil against you out of your own house. And I will take your wives before your eyes and give them to your neighbor, and he shall lie with your wives in the sight of this sun. ¹² For you did it secretly, but I will do this thing before all Israel and before the sun.'" ¹³ David said to Nathan, "I have sinned against the Lord." And Nathan said to David, "The Lord also has put away your sin; you shall not die. ¹⁴ Nevertheless, because

---

¹ Hebrew *bosom*; also verse 8

by this deed you have utterly scorned the Lord,¹ the child who is born to you shall die." ¹⁵ Then Nathan went to his house.

David's Child Dies

And the Lord afflicted the child that Uriah's wife bore to David, and he became sick. ¹⁶ David therefore sought God on behalf of the child. And David fasted and went in and lay all night on the ground. ¹⁷ And the elders of his house stood beside him, to raise him from the ground, but he would not, nor did he eat food with them. ¹⁸ On the seventh day the child died. And the servants of David were afraid to tell him that the child was dead, for they said, "Behold, while the child was yet alive, we spoke to him, and he did not listen to us. How then can we say to him the child is dead? He may do himself some harm." ¹⁹ But when David saw that his servants were whispering together, David understood that the child was dead. And David said to his servants, "Is the child dead?" They said, "He is dead." ²⁰ Then David arose from the earth and washed and anointed himself and changed his clothes. And he went into the house of the Lord and worshiped. He then went to his own house. And when he asked, they set food before him, and he ate. ²¹ Then his servants said to him, "What is this thing that you have done? You fasted and wept for the child while he was alive; but when the child died, you arose and ate food." ²² He said, "While the child was still alive, I fasted and wept, for I said, 'Who knows whether the Lord will be gracious to me, that the child may live?' ²³ But now he is dead. Why should I fast? Can I bring him back again? I shall go to him, but he will not return to me."

Solomon's Birth

²⁴ Then David comforted his wife, Bathsheba, and went in to her and lay with her, and she bore a son, and he called his name Solomon. And the Lord loved him ²⁵ and sent a message by Nathan the prophet. So he called his name Jedidiah,² because of the Lord.

Rabbah Is Captured

²⁶ Now Joab fought against Rabbah of the Ammonites and took the royal city. ²⁷ And Joab sent messengers to David and said, "I have fought against Rabbah; moreover, I have taken the city of waters. ²⁸ Now then gather the rest of the people together and encamp against the city and take it, lest I take the city and it be called by my name." ²⁹ So David gathered all the people together and went to Rabbah and fought against it and took it. ³⁰ And he took the

---

¹ Masoretic Text *the enemies of the Lord*; Dead Sea Scroll *the word of the Lord* ² *Jedidiah* means *beloved of the Lord*

crown of their king from his head. The weight of it was a talent[1] of gold, and in it was a precious stone, and it was placed on David's head. And he brought out the spoil of the city, a very great amount. ³¹ And he brought out the people who were in it and set them to labor with saws and iron picks and iron axes and made them toil at[2] the brick kilns. And thus he did to all the cities of the Ammonites. Then David and all the people returned to Jerusalem.

Amnon and Tamar

13 Now Absalom, David's son, had a beautiful sister, whose name was Tamar. And after a time Amnon, David's son, loved her. ² And Amnon was so tormented that he made himself ill because of his sister Tamar, for she was a virgin, and it seemed impossible to Amnon to do anything to her. ³ But Amnon had a friend, whose name was Jonadab, the son of Shimeah, David's brother. And Jonadab was a very crafty man. ⁴ And he said to him, "O son of the king, why are you so haggard morning after morning? Will you not tell me?" Amnon said to him, "I love Tamar, my brother Absalom's sister." ⁵ Jonadab said to him, "Lie down on your bed and pretend to be ill. And when your father comes to see you, say to him, 'Let my sister Tamar come and give me bread to eat, and prepare the food in my sight, that I may see it and eat it from her hand.'" ⁶ So Amnon lay down and pretended to be ill. And when the king came to see him, Amnon said to the king, "Please let my sister Tamar come and make a couple of cakes in my sight, that I may eat from her hand."

⁷ Then David sent home to Tamar, saying, "Go to your brother Amnon's house and prepare food for him." ⁸ So Tamar went to her brother Amnon's house, where he was lying down. And she took dough and kneaded it and made cakes in his sight and baked the cakes. ⁹ And she took the pan and emptied it out before him, but he refused to eat. And Amnon said, "Send out everyone from me." So everyone went out from him. ¹⁰ Then Amnon said to Tamar, "Bring the food into the chamber, that I may eat from your hand." And Tamar took the cakes she had made and brought them into the chamber to Amnon her brother. ¹¹ But when she brought them near him to eat, he took hold of her and said to her, "Come, lie with me, my sister." ¹² She answered him, "No, my brother, do not violate[3] me, for such a thing is not done in Israel; do not do this outrageous thing. ¹³ As for me, where could I carry my shame? And as for you, you would be as one of the outrageous fools in Israel. Now therefore, please speak to the king, for he will not withhold me from you." ¹⁴ But he would not listen to her, and being stronger than she, he violated her and lay with her.

[1] A *talent* was about 75 pounds or 34 kilograms [2] Hebrew *pass through* [3] Or *humiliate*; also verses 14, 22, 32

¹⁵ Then Amnon hated her with very great hatred, so that the hatred with which he hated her was greater than the love with which he had loved her. And Amnon said to her, "Get up! Go!" ¹⁶ But she said to him, "No, my brother, for this wrong in sending me away is greater than the other that you did to me."[1] But he would not listen to her. ¹⁷ He called the young man who served him and said, "Put this woman out of my presence and bolt the door after her." ¹⁸ Now she was wearing a long robe with sleeves,[2] for thus were the virgin daughters of the king dressed. So his servant put her out and bolted the door after her. ¹⁹ And Tamar put ashes on her head and tore the long robe that she wore. And she laid her hand on her head and went away, crying aloud as she went.

²⁰ And her brother Absalom said to her, "Has Amnon your brother been with you? Now hold your peace, my sister. He is your brother; do not take this to heart." So Tamar lived, a desolate woman, in her brother Absalom's house. ²¹ When King David heard of all these things, he was very angry.[3] ²² But Absalom spoke to Amnon neither good nor bad, for Absalom hated Amnon, because he had violated his sister Tamar.

Absalom Murders Amnon

²³ After two full years Absalom had sheepshearers at Baal-hazor, which is near Ephraim, and Absalom invited all the king's sons. ²⁴ And Absalom came to the king and said, "Behold, your servant has sheepshearers. Please let the king and his servants go with your servant." ²⁵ But the king said to Absalom, "No, my son, let us not all go, lest we be burdensome to you." He pressed him, but he would not go but gave him his blessing. ²⁶ Then Absalom said, "If not, please let my brother Amnon go with us." And the king said to him, "Why should he go with you?" ²⁷ But Absalom pressed him until he let Amnon and all the king's sons go with him. ²⁸ Then Absalom commanded his servants, "Mark when Amnon's heart is merry with wine, and when I say to you, 'Strike Amnon,' then kill him. Do not fear; have I not commanded you? Be courageous and be valiant." ²⁹ So the servants of Absalom did to Amnon as Absalom had commanded. Then all the king's sons arose, and each mounted his mule and fled.

³⁰ While they were on the way, news came to David, "Absalom has struck down all the king's sons, and not one of them is left." ³¹ Then the king arose and tore his garments and lay on the earth. And all his servants who were standing by tore their garments. ³² But Jonadab the son of Shimeah, David's brother, said, "Let not my lord suppose that they have killed all the young

---

[1] Compare Septuagint, Vulgate; the meaning of the Hebrew is uncertain [2] Or *a robe of many colors* (compare Genesis 37:3); compare *long robe*, verse 19 [3] Dead Sea Scroll, Septuagint add *But he would not punish his son Amnon, because he loved him, since he was his firstborn*

men, the king's sons, for Amnon alone is dead. For by the command of Absalom this has been determined from the day he violated his sister Tamar. ³³ Now therefore let not my lord the king so take it to heart as to suppose that all the king's sons are dead, for Amnon alone is dead."

Absalom Flees to Geshur

³⁴ But Absalom fled. And the young man who kept the watch lifted up his eyes and looked, and behold, many people were coming from the road behind him[1] by the side of the mountain. ³⁵ And Jonadab said to the king, "Behold, the king's sons have come; as your servant said, so it has come about." ³⁶ And as soon as he had finished speaking, behold, the king's sons came and lifted up their voice and wept. And the king also and all his servants wept very bitterly.

³⁷ But Absalom fled and went to Talmai the son of Ammihud, king of Geshur. And David mourned for his son day after day. ³⁸ So Absalom fled and went to Geshur, and was there three years. ³⁹ And the spirit of the king[2] longed to go out[3] to Absalom, because he was comforted about Amnon, since he was dead.

Absalom Returns to Jerusalem

14 Now Joab the son of Zeruiah knew that the king's heart went out to Absalom. ² And Joab sent to Tekoa and brought from there a wise woman and said to her, "Pretend to be a mourner and put on mourning garments. Do not anoint yourself with oil, but behave like a woman who has been mourning many days for the dead. ³ Go to the king and speak thus to him." So Joab put the words in her mouth.

⁴ When the woman of Tekoa came to the king, she fell on her face to the ground and paid homage and said, "Save me, O king." ⁵ And the king said to her, "What is your trouble?" She answered, "Alas, I am a widow; my husband is dead. ⁶ And your servant had two sons, and they quarreled with one another in the field. There was no one to separate them, and one struck the other and killed him. ⁷ And now the whole clan has risen against your servant, and they say, 'Give up the man who struck his brother, that we may put him to death for the life of his brother whom he killed.' And so they would destroy the heir also. Thus they would quench my coal that is left and leave to my husband neither name nor remnant on the face of the earth."

⁸ Then the king said to the woman, "Go to your house, and I will give orders concerning you." ⁹ And the woman of Tekoa said to the king, "On me be the

---

[1] Septuagint *the Horonaim Road* [2] Dead Sea Scroll, Septuagint; Hebrew *David* [3] Compare Vulgate *ceased to go out*

guilt, my lord the king, and on my father's house; let the king and his throne be guiltless." ¹⁰ The king said, "If anyone says anything to you, bring him to me, and he shall never touch you again." ¹¹ Then she said, "Please let the king invoke the Lord your God, that the avenger of blood kill no more, and my son be not destroyed." He said, "As the Lord lives, not one hair of your son shall fall to the ground."

¹² Then the woman said, "Please let your servant speak a word to my lord the king." He said, "Speak." ¹³ And the woman said, "Why then have you planned such a thing against the people of God? For in giving this decision the king convicts himself, inasmuch as the king does not bring his banished one home again. ¹⁴ We must all die; we are like water spilled on the ground, which cannot be gathered up again. But God will not take away life, and he devises means so that the banished one will not remain an outcast. ¹⁵ Now I have come to say this to my lord the king because the people have made me afraid, and your servant thought, 'I will speak to the king; it may be that the king will perform the request of his servant. ¹⁶ For the king will hear and deliver his servant from the hand of the man who would destroy me and my son together from the heritage of God.' ¹⁷ And your servant thought, 'The word of my lord the king will set me at rest,' for my lord the king is like the angel of God to discern good and evil. The Lord your God be with you!"

¹⁸ Then the king answered the woman, "Do not hide from me anything I ask you." And the woman said, "Let my lord the king speak." ¹⁹ The king said, "Is the hand of Joab with you in all this?" The woman answered and said, "As surely as you live, my lord the king, one cannot turn to the right hand or to the left from anything that my lord the king has said. It was your servant Joab who commanded me; it was he who put all these words in the mouth of your servant. ²⁰ In order to change the course of things your servant Joab did this. But my lord has wisdom like the wisdom of the angel of God to know all things that are on the earth."

²¹ Then the king said to Joab, "Behold now, I grant this; go, bring back the young man Absalom." ²² And Joab fell on his face to the ground and paid homage and blessed the king. And Joab said, "Today your servant knows that I have found favor in your sight, my lord the king, in that the king has granted the request of his servant." ²³ So Joab arose and went to Geshur and brought Absalom to Jerusalem. ²⁴ And the king said, "Let him dwell apart in his own house; he is not to come into my presence." So Absalom lived apart in his own house and did not come into the king's presence.

²⁵ Now in all Israel there was no one so much to be praised for his handsome appearance as Absalom. From the sole of his foot to the crown of his

head there was no blemish in him. ²⁶ And when he cut the hair of his head (for at the end of every year he used to cut it; when it was heavy on him, he cut it), he weighed the hair of his head, two hundred shekels¹ by the king's weight. ²⁷ There were born to Absalom three sons, and one daughter whose name was Tamar. She was a beautiful woman.

²⁸ So Absalom lived two full years in Jerusalem, without coming into the king's presence. ²⁹ Then Absalom sent for Joab, to send him to the king, but Joab would not come to him. And he sent a second time, but Joab would not come. ³⁰ Then he said to his servants, "See, Joab's field is next to mine, and he has barley there; go and set it on fire." So Absalom's servants set the field on fire.² ³¹ Then Joab arose and went to Absalom at his house and said to him, "Why have your servants set my field on fire?" ³² Absalom answered Joab, "Behold, I sent word to you, 'Come here, that I may send you to the king, to ask, "Why have I come from Geshur? It would be better for me to be there still." Now therefore let me go into the presence of the king, and if there is guilt in me, let him put me to death.'" ³³ Then Joab went to the king and told him, and he summoned Absalom. So he came to the king and bowed himself on his face to the ground before the king, and the king kissed Absalom.

Absalom's Conspiracy

15 After this Absalom got himself a chariot and horses, and fifty men to run before him. ² And Absalom used to rise early and stand beside the way of the gate. And when any man had a dispute to come before the king for judgment, Absalom would call to him and say, "From what city are you?" And when he said, "Your servant is of such and such a tribe in Israel," ³ Absalom would say to him, "See, your claims are good and right, but there is no man designated by the king to hear you." ⁴ Then Absalom would say, "Oh that I were judge in the land! Then every man with a dispute or cause might come to me, and I would give him justice." ⁵ And whenever a man came near to pay homage to him, he would put out his hand and take hold of him and kiss him. ⁶ Thus Absalom did to all of Israel who came to the king for judgment. So Absalom stole the hearts of the men of Israel.

⁷ And at the end of four³ years Absalom said to the king, "Please let me go and pay my vow, which I have vowed to the LORD, in Hebron. ⁸ For your servant vowed a vow while I lived at Geshur in Aram, saying, 'If the LORD will indeed bring me back to Jerusalem, then I will offer worship to⁴ the LORD.'" ⁹ The king said to him, "Go in peace." So he arose and went to Hebron. ¹⁰ But Absalom sent secret messengers throughout all the tribes of Israel, saying,

---

¹ A *shekel* was about 2/5 ounce or 11 grams ² Septuagint, Dead Sea Scroll add *So Joab's servants came to him with their clothes torn, and they said to him, "The servants of Absalom have set your field on fire."* ³ Septuagint, Syriac; Hebrew *forty* ⁴ Or *will serve*

"As soon as you hear the sound of the trumpet, then say, 'Absalom is king at Hebron!'" ¹¹ With Absalom went two hundred men from Jerusalem who were invited guests, and they went in their innocence and knew nothing. ¹² And while Absalom was offering the sacrifices, he sent for[1] Ahithophel the Gilonite, David's counselor, from his city Giloh. And the conspiracy grew strong, and the people with Absalom kept increasing.

David Flees Jerusalem

¹³ And a messenger came to David, saying, "The hearts of the men of Israel have gone after Absalom." ¹⁴ Then David said to all his servants who were with him at Jerusalem, "Arise, and let us flee, or else there will be no escape for us from Absalom. Go quickly, lest he overtake us quickly and bring down ruin on us and strike the city with the edge of the sword." ¹⁵ And the king's servants said to the king, "Behold, your servants are ready to do whatever my lord the king decides." ¹⁶ So the king went out, and all his household after him. And the king left ten concubines to keep the house. ¹⁷ And the king went out, and all the people after him. And they halted at the last house.

¹⁸ And all his servants passed by him, and all the Cherethites, and all the Pelethites, and all the six hundred Gittites who had followed him from Gath, passed on before the king. ¹⁹ Then the king said to Ittai the Gittite, "Why do you also go with us? Go back and stay with the king, for you are a foreigner and also an exile from your home. ²⁰ You came only yesterday, and shall I today make you wander about with us, since I go I know not where? Go back and take your brothers with you, and may the Lord show[2] steadfast love and faithfulness to you." ²¹ But Ittai answered the king, "As the Lord lives, and as my lord the king lives, wherever my lord the king shall be, whether for death or for life, there also will your servant be." ²² And David said to Ittai, "Go then, pass on." So Ittai the Gittite passed on with all his men and all the little ones who were with him. ²³ And all the land wept aloud as all the people passed by, and the king crossed the brook Kidron, and all the people passed on toward the wilderness.

²⁴ And Abiathar came up, and behold, Zadok came also with all the Levites, bearing the ark of the covenant of God. And they set down the ark of God until the people had all passed out of the city. ²⁵ Then the king said to Zadok, "Carry the ark of God back into the city. If I find favor in the eyes of the Lord, he will bring me back and let me see both it and his dwelling place. ²⁶ But if he says, 'I have no pleasure in you,' behold, here I am, let him do to me what seems good to him." ²⁷ The king also said to Zadok the priest, "Are you not a

---

[1] Or *sent* [2] Septuagint; Hebrew lacks *may the Lord show*

seer? Go back[1] to the city in peace, with your two sons, Ahimaaz your son, and Jonathan the son of Abiathar. ²⁸ See, I will wait at the fords of the wilderness until word comes from you to inform me." ²⁹ So Zadok and Abiathar carried the ark of God back to Jerusalem, and they remained there.

³⁰ But David went up the ascent of the Mount of Olives, weeping as he went, barefoot and with his head covered. And all the people who were with him covered their heads, and they went up, weeping as they went. ³¹ And it was told David, "Ahithophel is among the conspirators with Absalom." And David said, "O Lord, please turn the counsel of Ahithophel into foolishness."

³² While David was coming to the summit, where God was worshiped, behold, Hushai the Archite came to meet him with his coat torn and dirt on his head. ³³ David said to him, "If you go on with me, you will be a burden to me. ³⁴ But if you return to the city and say to Absalom, 'I will be your servant, O king; as I have been your father's servant in time past, so now I will be your servant,' then you will defeat for me the counsel of Ahithophel. ³⁵ Are not Zadok and Abiathar the priests with you there? So whatever you hear from the king's house, tell it to Zadok and Abiathar the priests. ³⁶ Behold, their two sons are with them there, Ahimaaz, Zadok's son, and Jonathan, Abiathar's son, and by them you shall send to me everything you hear." ³⁷ So Hushai, David's friend, came into the city, just as Absalom was entering Jerusalem.

David and Ziba

16 When David had passed a little beyond the summit, Ziba the servant of Mephibosheth met him, with a couple of donkeys saddled, bearing two hundred loaves of bread, a hundred bunches of raisins, a hundred of summer fruits, and a skin of wine. ² And the king said to Ziba, "Why have you brought these?" Ziba answered, "The donkeys are for the king's household to ride on, the bread and summer fruit for the young men to eat, and the wine for those who faint in the wilderness to drink." ³ And the king said, "And where is your master's son?" Ziba said to the king, "Behold, he remains in Jerusalem, for he said, 'Today the house of Israel will give me back the kingdom of my father.'" ⁴ Then the king said to Ziba, "Behold, all that belonged to Mephibosheth is now yours." And Ziba said, "I pay homage; let me ever find favor in your sight, my lord the king."

Shimei Curses David

⁵ When King David came to Bahurim, there came out a man of the family of the house of Saul, whose name was Shimei, the son of Gera, and as he came

---
[1] Septuagint *The king also said to Zadok the priest, "Look, go back*

he cursed continually. ⁶ And he threw stones at David and at all the servants of King David, and all the people and all the mighty men were on his right hand and on his left. ⁷ And Shimei said as he cursed, "Get out, get out, you man of blood, you worthless man! ⁸ The LORD has avenged on you all the blood of the house of Saul, in whose place you have reigned, and the LORD has given the kingdom into the hand of your son Absalom. See, your evil is on you, for you are a man of blood."

⁹ Then Abishai the son of Zeruiah said to the king, "Why should this dead dog curse my lord the king? Let me go over and take off his head." ¹⁰ But the king said, "What have I to do with you, you sons of Zeruiah? If he is cursing because the LORD has said to him, 'Curse David,' who then shall say, 'Why have you done so?'" ¹¹ And David said to Abishai and to all his servants, "Behold, my own son seeks my life; how much more now may this Benjaminite! Leave him alone, and let him curse, for the LORD has told him to. ¹² It may be that the LORD will look on the wrong done to me,[1] and that the LORD will repay me with good for his cursing today." ¹³ So David and his men went on the road, while Shimei went along on the hillside opposite him and cursed as he went and threw stones at him and flung dust. ¹⁴ And the king, and all the people who were with him, arrived weary at the Jordan.[2] And there he refreshed himself.

Absalom Enters Jerusalem

¹⁵ Now Absalom and all the people, the men of Israel, came to Jerusalem, and Ahithophel with him. ¹⁶ And when Hushai the Archite, David's friend, came to Absalom, Hushai said to Absalom, "Long live the king! Long live the king!" ¹⁷ And Absalom said to Hushai, "Is this your loyalty to your friend? Why did you not go with your friend?" ¹⁸ And Hushai said to Absalom, "No, for whom the LORD and this people and all the men of Israel have chosen, his I will be, and with him I will remain. ¹⁹ And again, whom should I serve? Should it not be his son? As I have served your father, so I will serve you."

²⁰ Then Absalom said to Ahithophel, "Give your counsel. What shall we do?" ²¹ Ahithophel said to Absalom, "Go in to your father's concubines, whom he has left to keep the house, and all Israel will hear that you have made yourself a stench to your father, and the hands of all who are with you will be strengthened." ²² So they pitched a tent for Absalom on the roof. And Absalom went in to his father's concubines in the sight of all Israel. ²³ Now in those days the counsel that Ahithophel gave was as if one consulted the word of God; so was all the counsel of Ahithophel esteemed, both by David and by Absalom.

---

[1] Septuagint, Vulgate *will look upon my affliction* [2] Septuagint; Hebrew lacks *at the Jordan*

Hushai Saves David

17

Moreover, Ahithophel said to Absalom, "Let me choose twelve thousand men, and I will arise and pursue David tonight. ² I will come upon him while he is weary and discouraged and throw him into a panic, and all the people who are with him will flee. I will strike down only the king, ³ and I will bring all the people back to you as a bride comes home to her husband. You seek the life of only one man,¹ and all the people will be at peace." ⁴ And the advice seemed right in the eyes of Absalom and all the elders of Israel.

⁵ Then Absalom said, "Call Hushai the Archite also, and let us hear what he has to say." ⁶ And when Hushai came to Absalom, Absalom said to him, "Thus has Ahithophel spoken; shall we do as he says? If not, you speak." ⁷ Then Hushai said to Absalom, "This time the counsel that Ahithophel has given is not good." ⁸ Hushai said, "You know that your father and his men are mighty men, and that they are enraged,² like a bear robbed of her cubs in the field. Besides, your father is expert in war; he will not spend the night with the people. ⁹ Behold, even now he has hidden himself in one of the pits or in some other place. And as soon as some of the people fall³ at the first attack, whoever hears it will say, 'There has been a slaughter among the people who follow Absalom.' ¹⁰ Then even the valiant man, whose heart is like the heart of a lion, will utterly melt with fear, for all Israel knows that your father is a mighty man, and that those who are with him are valiant men. ¹¹ But my counsel is that all Israel be gathered to you, from Dan to Beersheba, as the sand by the sea for multitude, and that you go to battle in person. ¹² So we shall come upon him in some place where he is to be found, and we shall light upon him as the dew falls on the ground, and of him and all the men with him not one will be left. ¹³ If he withdraws into a city, then all Israel will bring ropes to that city, and we shall drag it into the valley, until not even a pebble is to be found there." ¹⁴ And Absalom and all the men of Israel said, "The counsel of Hushai the Archite is better than the counsel of Ahithophel." For the Lord had ordained⁴ to defeat the good counsel of Ahithophel, so that the Lord might bring harm upon Absalom.

¹⁵ Then Hushai said to Zadok and Abiathar the priests, "Thus and so did Ahithophel counsel Absalom and the elders of Israel, and thus and so have I counseled. ¹⁶ Now therefore send quickly and tell David, 'Do not stay tonight at the fords of the wilderness, but by all means pass over, lest the king and all the people who are with him be swallowed up.'" ¹⁷ Now Jonathan and Ahimaaz were waiting at En-rogel. A female servant was to

---

¹ Septuagint; Hebrew *back to you. Like the return of the whole is the man whom you seek* ² Hebrew *bitter of soul* ³ Or *And as he falls on them* ⁴ Hebrew *commanded*

go and tell them, and they were to go and tell King David, for they were not to be seen entering the city. ⁱ⁸ But a young man saw them and told Absalom. So both of them went away quickly and came to the house of a man at Bahurim, who had a well in his courtyard. And they went down into it. ¹⁹ And the woman took and spread a covering over the well's mouth and scattered grain on it, and nothing was known of it. ²⁰ When Absalom's servants came to the woman at the house, they said, "Where are Ahimaaz and Jonathan?" And the woman said to them, "They have gone over the brook¹ of water." And when they had sought and could not find them, they returned to Jerusalem.

²¹ After they had gone, the men came up out of the well, and went and told King David. They said to David, "Arise, and go quickly over the water, for thus and so has Ahithophel counseled against you." ²² Then David arose, and all the people who were with him, and they crossed the Jordan. By daybreak not one was left who had not crossed the Jordan.

²³ When Ahithophel saw that his counsel was not followed, he saddled his donkey and went off home to his own city. He set his house in order and hanged himself, and he died and was buried in the tomb of his father.

²⁴ Then David came to Mahanaim. And Absalom crossed the Jordan with all the men of Israel. ²⁵ Now Absalom had set Amasa over the army instead of Joab. Amasa was the son of a man named Ithra the Ishmaelite,² who had married Abigal the daughter of Nahash, sister of Zeruiah, Joab's mother. ²⁶ And Israel and Absalom encamped in the land of Gilead.

²⁷ When David came to Mahanaim, Shobi the son of Nahash from Rabbah of the Ammonites, and Machir the son of Ammiel from Lo-debar, and Barzillai the Gileadite from Rogelim, ²⁸ brought beds, basins, and earthen vessels, wheat, barley, flour, parched grain, beans and lentils,³ ²⁹ honey and curds and sheep and cheese from the herd, for David and the people with him to eat, for they said, "The people are hungry and weary and thirsty in the wilderness."

Absalom Killed

18 Then David mustered the men who were with him and set over them commanders of thousands and commanders of hundreds. ² And David sent out the army, one third under the command of Joab, one third under the command of Abishai the son of Zeruiah, Joab's brother, and one third under the command of Ittai the Gittite. And the king said to the men, "I myself will also go out with you." ³ But the men said, "You shall not

---

¹ The meaning of the Hebrew word is uncertain ² Compare 1 Chronicles 2:17; Hebrew *Israelite* ³ Hebrew adds *and parched grain*

go out. For if we flee, they will not care about us. If half of us die, they will not care about us. But you are worth ten thousand of us. Therefore it is better that you send us help from the city." ⁴ The king said to them, "Whatever seems best to you I will do." So the king stood at the side of the gate, while all the army marched out by hundreds and by thousands. ⁵ And the king ordered Joab and Abishai and Ittai, "Deal gently for my sake with the young man Absalom." And all the people heard when the king gave orders to all the commanders about Absalom.

⁶ So the army went out into the field against Israel, and the battle was fought in the forest of Ephraim. ⁷ And the men of Israel were defeated there by the servants of David, and the loss there was great on that day, twenty thousand men. ⁸ The battle spread over the face of all the country, and the forest devoured more people that day than the sword.

⁹ And Absalom happened to meet the servants of David. Absalom was riding on his mule, and the mule went under the thick branches of a great oak,¹ and his head caught fast in the oak, and he was suspended between heaven and earth, while the mule that was under him went on. ¹⁰ And a certain man saw it and told Joab, "Behold, I saw Absalom hanging in an oak." ¹¹ Joab said to the man who told him, "What, you saw him! Why then did you not strike him there to the ground? I would have been glad to give you ten pieces of silver and a belt." ¹² But the man said to Joab, "Even if I felt in my hand the weight of a thousand pieces of silver, I would not reach out my hand against the king's son, for in our hearing the king commanded you and Abishai and Ittai, 'For my sake protect the young man Absalom.' ¹³ On the other hand, if I had dealt treacherously against his life² (and there is nothing hidden from the king), then you yourself would have stood aloof." ¹⁴ Joab said, "I will not waste time like this with you." And he took three javelins in his hand and thrust them into the heart of Absalom while he was still alive in the oak. ¹⁵ And ten young men, Joab's armor-bearers, surrounded Absalom and struck him and killed him.

¹⁶ Then Joab blew the trumpet, and the troops came back from pursuing Israel, for Joab restrained them. ¹⁷ And they took Absalom and threw him into a great pit in the forest and raised over him a very great heap of stones. And all Israel fled every one to his own home. ¹⁸ Now Absalom in his lifetime had taken and set up for himself the pillar that is in the King's Valley, for he said, "I have no son to keep my name in remembrance." He called the pillar after his own name, and it is called Absalom's monument³ to this day.

¹ Or *terebinth*; also verses 10, 14   ² Or *at the risk of my life*   ³ Or *Absalom's hand*

David Hears of Absalom's Death

¹⁹ Then Ahimaaz the son of Zadok said, "Let me run and carry news to the king that the Lord has delivered him from the hand of his enemies." ²⁰ And Joab said to him, "You are not to carry news today. You may carry news another day, but today you shall carry no news, because the king's son is dead." ²¹ Then Joab said to the Cushite, "Go, tell the king what you have seen." The Cushite bowed before Joab, and ran. ²² Then Ahimaaz the son of Zadok said again to Joab, "Come what may, let me also run after the Cushite." And Joab said, "Why will you run, my son, seeing that you will have no reward for the news?" ²³ "Come what may," he said, "I will run." So he said to him, "Run." Then Ahimaaz ran by the way of the plain, and outran the Cushite.

²⁴ Now David was sitting between the two gates, and the watchman went up to the roof of the gate by the wall, and when he lifted up his eyes and looked, he saw a man running alone. ²⁵ The watchman called out and told the king. And the king said, "If he is alone, there is news in his mouth." And he drew nearer and nearer. ²⁶ The watchman saw another man running. And the watchman called to the gate and said, "See, another man running alone!" The king said, "He also brings news." ²⁷ The watchman said, "I think the running of the first is like the running of Ahimaaz the son of Zadok." And the king said, "He is a good man and comes with good news."

²⁸ Then Ahimaaz cried out to the king, "All is well." And he bowed before the king with his face to the earth and said, "Blessed be the Lord your God, who has delivered up the men who raised their hand against my lord the king." ²⁹ And the king said, "Is it well with the young man Absalom?" Ahimaaz answered, "When Joab sent the king's servant, your servant, I saw a great commotion, but I do not know what it was." ³⁰ And the king said, "Turn aside and stand here." So he turned aside and stood still.

David's Grief

³¹ And behold, the Cushite came, and the Cushite said, "Good news for my lord the king! For the Lord has delivered you this day from the hand of all who rose up against you." ³² The king said to the Cushite, "Is it well with the young man Absalom?" And the Cushite answered, "May the enemies of my lord the king and all who rise up against you for evil be like that young man." ³³ ¹ And the king was deeply moved and went up to the chamber over the gate and wept. And as he went, he said, "O my son Absalom, my son, my son Absalom! Would I had died instead of you, O Absalom, my son, my son!"

¹ Ch 19:1 in Hebrew

Joab Rebukes David

19 It was told Joab, "Behold, the king is weeping and mourning for Absalom." ²So the victory that day was turned into mourning for all the people, for the people heard that day, "The king is grieving for his son." ³And the people stole into the city that day as people steal in who are ashamed when they flee in battle. ⁴The king covered his face, and the king cried with a loud voice, "O my son Absalom, O Absalom, my son, my son!" ⁵Then Joab came into the house to the king and said, "You have today covered with shame the faces of all your servants, who have this day saved your life and the lives of your sons and your daughters and the lives of your wives and your concubines, ⁶because you love those who hate you and hate those who love you. For you have made it clear today that commanders and servants are nothing to you, for today I know that if Absalom were alive and all of us were dead today, then you would be pleased. ⁷Now therefore arise, go out and speak kindly to your servants, for I swear by the Lord, if you do not go, not a man will stay with you this night, and this will be worse for you than all the evil that has come upon you from your youth until now." ⁸Then the king arose and took his seat in the gate. And the people were all told, "Behold, the king is sitting in the gate." And all the people came before the king.

David Returns to Jerusalem

Now Israel had fled every man to his own home. ⁹And all the people were arguing throughout all the tribes of Israel, saying, "The king delivered us from the hand of our enemies and saved us from the hand of the Philistines, and now he has fled out of the land from Absalom. ¹⁰But Absalom, whom we anointed over us, is dead in battle. Now therefore why do you say nothing about bringing the king back?"

¹¹And King David sent this message to Zadok and Abiathar the priests: "Say to the elders of Judah, 'Why should you be the last to bring the king back to his house, when the word of all Israel has come to the king?¹ ¹²You are my brothers; you are my bone and my flesh. Why then should you be the last to bring back the king?' ¹³And say to Amasa, 'Are you not my bone and my flesh? God do so to me and more also, if you are not commander of my army from now on in place of Joab.'" ¹⁴And he swayed the heart of all the men of Judah as one man, so that they sent word to the king, "Return, both you and all your servants." ¹⁵So the king came back to the Jordan, and Judah came to Gilgal to meet the king and to bring the king over the Jordan.

---

¹ Septuagint; Hebrew *to the king, to his house*

David Pardons His Enemies

¹⁶ And Shimei the son of Gera, the Benjaminite, from Bahurim, hurried to come down with the men of Judah to meet King David. ¹⁷ And with him were a thousand men from Benjamin. And Ziba the servant of the house of Saul, with his fifteen sons and his twenty servants, rushed down to the Jordan before the king, ¹⁸ and they crossed the ford to bring over the king's household and to do his pleasure. And Shimei the son of Gera fell down before the king, as he was about to cross the Jordan, ¹⁹ and said to the king, "Let not my lord hold me guilty or remember how your servant did wrong on the day my lord the king left Jerusalem. Do not let the king take it to heart. ²⁰ For your servant knows that I have sinned. Therefore, behold, I have come this day, the first of all the house of Joseph to come down to meet my lord the king." ²¹ Abishai the son of Zeruiah answered, "Shall not Shimei be put to death for this, because he cursed the LORD's anointed?" ²² But David said, "What have I to do with you, you sons of Zeruiah, that you should this day be as an adversary to me? Shall anyone be put to death in Israel this day? For do I not know that I am this day king over Israel?" ²³ And the king said to Shimei, "You shall not die." And the king gave him his oath.

²⁴ And Mephibosheth the son of Saul came down to meet the king. He had neither taken care of his feet nor trimmed his beard nor washed his clothes, from the day the king departed until the day he came back in safety. ²⁵ And when he came to Jerusalem to meet the king, the king said to him, "Why did you not go with me, Mephibosheth?" ²⁶ He answered, "My lord, O king, my servant deceived me, for your servant said to him, 'I will saddle a donkey for myself,¹ that I may ride on it and go with the king.' For your servant is lame. ²⁷ He has slandered your servant to my lord the king. But my lord the king is like the angel of God; do therefore what seems good to you. ²⁸ For all my father's house were but men doomed to death before my lord the king, but you set your servant among those who eat at your table. What further right have I, then, to cry to the king?" ²⁹ And the king said to him, "Why speak any more of your affairs? I have decided: you and Ziba shall divide the land." ³⁰ And Mephibosheth said to the king, "Oh, let him take it all, since my lord the king has come safely home."

³¹ Now Barzillai the Gileadite had come down from Rogelim, and he went on with the king to the Jordan, to escort him over the Jordan. ³² Barzillai was a very aged man, eighty years old. He had provided the king with food while he stayed at Mahanaim, for he was a very wealthy man. ³³ And the king said to Barzillai, "Come over with me, and I will provide for you with me in

---

¹ Septuagint, Syriac, Vulgate *Saddle a donkey for me*

Jerusalem." ³⁴ But Barzillai said to the king, "How many years have I still to live, that I should go up with the king to Jerusalem? ³⁵ I am this day eighty years old. Can I discern what is pleasant and what is not? Can your servant taste what he eats or what he drinks? Can I still listen to the voice of singing men and singing women? Why then should your servant be an added burden to my lord the king? ³⁶ Your servant will go a little way over the Jordan with the king. Why should the king repay me with such a reward? ³⁷ Please let your servant return, that I may die in my own city near the grave of my father and my mother. But here is your servant Chimham. Let him go over with my lord the king, and do for him whatever seems good to you." ³⁸ And the king answered, "Chimham shall go over with me, and I will do for him whatever seems good to you, and all that you desire of me I will do for you." ³⁹ Then all the people went over the Jordan, and the king went over. And the king kissed Barzillai and blessed him, and he returned to his own home. ⁴⁰ The king went on to Gilgal, and Chimham went on with him. All the people of Judah, and also half the people of Israel, brought the king on his way.

⁴¹ Then all the men of Israel came to the king and said to the king, "Why have our brothers the men of Judah stolen you away and brought the king and his household over the Jordan, and all David's men with him?" ⁴² All the men of Judah answered the men of Israel, "Because the king is our close relative. Why then are you angry over this matter? Have we eaten at all at the king's expense? Or has he given us any gift?" ⁴³ And the men of Israel answered the men of Judah, "We have ten shares in the king, and in David also we have more than you. Why then did you despise us? Were we not the first to speak of bringing back our king?" But the words of the men of Judah were fiercer than the words of the men of Israel.

The Rebellion of Sheba

20 Now there happened to be there a worthless man, whose name was Sheba, the son of Bichri, a Benjaminite. And he blew the trumpet and said,

> "We have no portion in David,
>   and we have no inheritance in the son of Jesse;
>   every man to his tents, O Israel!"

² So all the men of Israel withdrew from David and followed Sheba the son of Bichri. But the men of Judah followed their king steadfastly from the Jordan to Jerusalem.

³ And David came to his house at Jerusalem. And the king took the ten concubines whom he had left to care for the house and put them in a house under guard and provided for them, but did not go in to them. So they were shut up until the day of their death, living as if in widowhood.

⁴ Then the king said to Amasa, "Call the men of Judah together to me within three days, and be here yourself." ⁵ So Amasa went to summon Judah, but he delayed beyond the set time that had been appointed him. ⁶ And David said to Abishai, "Now Sheba the son of Bichri will do us more harm than Absalom. Take your lord's servants and pursue him, lest he get himself to fortified cities and escape from us."¹ ⁷ And there went out after him Joab's men and the Cherethites and the Pelethites, and all the mighty men. They went out from Jerusalem to pursue Sheba the son of Bichri. ⁸ When they were at the great stone that is in Gibeon, Amasa came to meet them. Now Joab was wearing a soldier's garment, and over it was a belt with a sword in its sheath fastened on his thigh, and as he went forward it fell out. ⁹ And Joab said to Amasa, "Is it well with you, my brother?" And Joab took Amasa by the beard with his right hand to kiss him. ¹⁰ But Amasa did not observe the sword that was in Joab's hand. So Joab struck him with it in the stomach and spilled his entrails to the ground without striking a second blow, and he died.

Then Joab and Abishai his brother pursued Sheba the son of Bichri. ¹¹ And one of Joab's young men took his stand by Amasa and said, "Whoever favors Joab, and whoever is for David, let him follow Joab." ¹² And Amasa lay wallowing in his blood in the highway. And anyone who came by, seeing him, stopped. And when the man saw that all the people stopped, he carried Amasa out of the highway into the field and threw a garment over him. ¹³ When he was taken out of the highway, all the people went on after Joab to pursue Sheba the son of Bichri.

¹⁴ And Sheba passed through all the tribes of Israel to Abel of Beth-maacah,² and all the Bichrites³ assembled and followed him in. ¹⁵ And all the men who were with Joab came and besieged him in Abel of Beth-maacah. They cast up a mound against the city, and it stood against the rampart, and they were battering the wall to throw it down. ¹⁶ Then a wise woman called from the city, "Listen! Listen! Tell Joab, 'Come here, that I may speak to you.'" ¹⁷ And he came near her, and the woman said, "Are you Joab?" He answered, "I am." Then she said to him, "Listen to the words of your servant." And he answered, "I am listening." ¹⁸ Then she said, "They used to say in former times, 'Let them but ask counsel at Abel,' and so they settled a matter. ¹⁹ I am one of those who are peaceable and faithful in Israel. You seek to destroy a

¹ Hebrew *and snatch away our eyes* ² Compare 20:15; Hebrew *and Beth-maacah* ³ Hebrew *Berites*

city that is a mother in Israel. Why will you swallow up the heritage of the Lord?" ²⁰ Joab answered, "Far be it from me, far be it, that I should swallow up or destroy! ²¹ That is not true. But a man of the hill country of Ephraim, called Sheba the son of Bichri, has lifted up his hand against King David. Give up him alone, and I will withdraw from the city." And the woman said to Joab, "Behold, his head shall be thrown to you over the wall." ²² Then the woman went to all the people in her wisdom. And they cut off the head of Sheba the son of Bichri and threw it out to Joab. So he blew the trumpet, and they dispersed from the city, every man to his home. And Joab returned to Jerusalem to the king.

²³ Now Joab was in command of all the army of Israel; and Benaiah the son of Jehoiada was in command of the Cherethites and the Pelethites; ²⁴ and Adoram was in charge of the forced labor; and Jehoshaphat the son of Ahilud was the recorder; ²⁵ and Sheva was secretary; and Zadok and Abiathar were priests; ²⁶ and Ira the Jairite was also David's priest.

David Avenges the Gibeonites

21 Now there was a famine in the days of David for three years, year after year. And David sought the face of the Lord. And the Lord said, "There is bloodguilt on Saul and on his house, because he put the Gibeonites to death." ² So the king called the Gibeonites and spoke to them. Now the Gibeonites were not of the people of Israel but of the remnant of the Amorites. Although the people of Israel had sworn to spare them, Saul had sought to strike them down in his zeal for the people of Israel and Judah. ³ And David said to the Gibeonites, "What shall I do for you? And how shall I make atonement, that you may bless the heritage of the Lord?" ⁴ The Gibeonites said to him, "It is not a matter of silver or gold between us and Saul or his house; neither is it for us to put any man to death in Israel." And he said, "What do you say that I shall do for you?" ⁵ They said to the king, "The man who consumed us and planned to destroy us, so that we should have no place in all the territory of Israel, ⁶ let seven of his sons be given to us, so that we may hang them before the Lord at Gibeah of Saul, the chosen of the Lord." And the king said, "I will give them."

⁷ But the king spared Mephibosheth, the son of Saul's son Jonathan, because of the oath of the Lord that was between them, between David and Jonathan the son of Saul. ⁸ The king took the two sons of Rizpah the daughter of Aiah, whom she bore to Saul, Armoni and Mephibosheth; and the five sons of Merab[1] the daughter of Saul, whom she bore to Adriel the

---

[1] Two Hebrew manuscripts, Septuagint; most Hebrew manuscripts *Michal*

son of Barzillai the Meholathite; ⁹and he gave them into the hands of the Gibeonites, and they hanged them on the mountain before the Lord, and the seven of them perished together. They were put to death in the first days of harvest, at the beginning of barley harvest.

¹⁰Then Rizpah the daughter of Aiah took sackcloth and spread it for herself on the rock, from the beginning of harvest until rain fell upon them from the heavens. And she did not allow the birds of the air to come upon them by day, or the beasts of the field by night. ¹¹When David was told what Rizpah the daughter of Aiah, the concubine of Saul, had done, ¹²David went and took the bones of Saul and the bones of his son Jonathan from the men of Jabesh-gilead, who had stolen them from the public square of Beth-shan, where the Philistines had hanged them, on the day the Philistines killed Saul on Gilboa. ¹³And he brought up from there the bones of Saul and the bones of his son Jonathan; and they gathered the bones of those who were hanged. ¹⁴And they buried the bones of Saul and his son Jonathan in the land of Benjamin in Zela, in the tomb of Kish his father. And they did all that the king commanded. And after that God responded to the plea for the land.

War with the Philistines

¹⁵There was war again between the Philistines and Israel, and David went down together with his servants, and they fought against the Philistines. And David grew weary. ¹⁶And Ishbi-benob, one of the descendants of the giants, whose spear weighed three hundred shekels[1] of bronze, and who was armed with a new sword, thought to kill David. ¹⁷But Abishai the son of Zeruiah came to his aid and attacked the Philistine and killed him. Then David's men swore to him, "You shall no longer go out with us to battle, lest you quench the lamp of Israel."

¹⁸After this there was again war with the Philistines at Gob. Then Sibbecai the Hushathite struck down Saph, who was one of the descendants of the giants. ¹⁹And there was again war with the Philistines at Gob, and Elhanan the son of Jaare-oregim, the Bethlehemite, struck down Goliath the Gittite, the shaft of whose spear was like a weaver's beam.[2] ²⁰And there was again war at Gath, where there was a man of great stature, who had six fingers on each hand, and six toes on each foot, twenty-four in number, and he also was descended from the giants. ²¹And when he taunted Israel, Jonathan the son of Shimei, David's brother, struck him down. ²²These four were descended from the giants in Gath, and they fell by the hand of David and by the hand of his servants.

[1] A *shekel* was about 2/5 ounce or 11 grams [2] Contrast 1 Chronicles 20:5, which may preserve the original reading

David's Song of Deliverance

22 And David spoke to the Lord the words of this song on the day when the Lord delivered him from the hand of all his enemies, and from the hand of Saul. ²He said,

"The Lord is my rock and my fortress and my deliverer,
3   my[1] God, my rock, in whom I take refuge,
  my shield, and the horn of my salvation,
     my stronghold and my refuge,
     my savior; you save me from violence.
4   I call upon the Lord, who is worthy to be praised,
     and I am saved from my enemies.

5   "For the waves of death encompassed me,
     the torrents of destruction assailed me;[2]
6   the cords of Sheol entangled me;
     the snares of death confronted me.

7   "In my distress I called upon the Lord;
     to my God I called.
  From his temple he heard my voice,
     and my cry came to his ears.

8   "Then the earth reeled and rocked;
     the foundations of the heavens trembled
     and quaked, because he was angry.
9   Smoke went up from his nostrils,[3]
     and devouring fire from his mouth;
     glowing coals flamed forth from him.
10 He bowed the heavens and came down;
     thick darkness was under his feet.
11 He rode on a cherub and flew;
     he was seen on the wings of the wind.
12 He made darkness around him his canopy,
     thick clouds, a gathering of water.
13 Out of the brightness before him
     coals of fire flamed forth.

[1] Septuagint (compare Psalm 18:2); Hebrew lacks *my* [2] Or *terrified me* [3] Or *in his wrath*

¹⁴ The Lord thundered from heaven,
 and the Most High uttered his voice.
¹⁵ And he sent out arrows and scattered them;
 lightning, and routed them.
¹⁶ Then the channels of the sea were seen;
 the foundations of the world were laid bare,
at the rebuke of the Lord,
 at the blast of the breath of his nostrils.

¹⁷ "He sent from on high, he took me;
 he drew me out of many waters.
¹⁸ He rescued me from my strong enemy,
 from those who hated me,
 for they were too mighty for me.
¹⁹ They confronted me in the day of my calamity,
 but the Lord was my support.
²⁰ He brought me out into a broad place;
 he rescued me, because he delighted in me.

²¹ "The Lord dealt with me according to my righteousness;
 according to the cleanness of my hands he rewarded me.
²² For I have kept the ways of the Lord
 and have not wickedly departed from my God.
²³ For all his rules were before me,
 and from his statutes I did not turn aside.
²⁴ I was blameless before him,
 and I kept myself from guilt.
²⁵ And the Lord has rewarded me according to my righteousness,
 according to my cleanness in his sight.

²⁶ "With the merciful you show yourself merciful;
 with the blameless man you show yourself blameless;
²⁷ with the purified you deal purely,
 and with the crooked you make yourself seem tortuous.
²⁸ You save a humble people,
 but your eyes are on the haughty to bring them down.
²⁹ For you are my lamp, O Lord,
 and my God lightens my darkness.

30 For by you I can run against a troop,
   and by my God I can leap over a wall.
31 This God—his way is perfect;
   the word of the LORD proves true;
   he is a shield for all those who take refuge in him.

32 "For who is God, but the LORD?
   And who is a rock, except our God?
33 This God is my strong refuge
   and has made my[1] way blameless.[2]
34 He made my feet like the feet of a deer
   and set me secure on the heights.
35 He trains my hands for war,
   so that my arms can bend a bow of bronze.
36 You have given me the shield of your salvation,
   and your gentleness made me great.
37 You gave a wide place for my steps under me,
   and my feet[3] did not slip;
38 I pursued my enemies and destroyed them,
   and did not turn back until they were consumed.
39 I consumed them; I thrust them through, so that they did not rise;
   they fell under my feet.
40 For you equipped me with strength for the battle;
   you made those who rise against me sink under me.
41 You made my enemies turn their backs to me,[4]
   those who hated me, and I destroyed them.
42 They looked, but there was none to save;
   they cried to the LORD, but he did not answer them.
43 I beat them fine as the dust of the earth;
   I crushed them and stamped them down like the mire of the streets.

44 "You delivered me from strife with my people;[5]
   you kept me as the head of the nations;
   people whom I had not known served me.
45 Foreigners came cringing to me;
   as soon as they heard of me, they obeyed me.

[1] Or *his*; also verse 34 [2] Compare Psalm 18:32; Hebrew *he has blamelessly set my way free*, or *he has made my way spring up blamelessly* [3] Hebrew *ankles* [4] Or *You gave me my enemies' necks* [5] Septuagint *with the peoples*

46 Foreigners lost heart
      and came trembling[1] out of their fortresses.

47 "The LORD lives, and blessed be my rock,
      and exalted be my God, the rock of my salvation,
48 the God who gave me vengeance
      and brought down peoples under me,
49 who brought me out from my enemies;
      you exalted me above those who rose against me;
      you delivered me from men of violence.

50 "For this I will praise you, O LORD, among the nations,
      and sing praises to your name.
51 Great salvation he brings[2] to his king,
      and shows steadfast love to his anointed,
      to David and his offspring forever."

The Last Words of David

23 Now these are the last words of David:

The oracle of David, the son of Jesse,
  the oracle of the man who was raised on high,
the anointed of the God of Jacob,
  the sweet psalmist of Israel:[3]

2 "The Spirit of the LORD speaks by me;
      his word is on my tongue.
3 The God of Israel has spoken;
      the Rock of Israel has said to me:
    When one rules justly over men,
      ruling in the fear of God,
4 he dawns on them like the morning light,
      like the sun shining forth on a cloudless morning,
      like rain[4] that makes grass to sprout from the earth.

5 "For does not my house stand so with God?
      For he has made with me an everlasting covenant,
      ordered in all things and secure.

[1] Compare Psalm 18:45; Hebrew *equipped themselves* [2] Or *He is a tower of salvation* [3] Or *the favorite of the songs of Israel* [4] Hebrew *from rain*

>   For will he not cause to prosper
>
>   > all my help and my desire?
>
> 6   But worthless men[1] are all like thorns that are thrown away,
>
>   > for they cannot be taken with the hand;
>
> 7   but the man who touches them
>
>   > arms himself with iron and the shaft of a spear,
>   >
>   > and they are utterly consumed with fire."[2]

David's Mighty Men

⁸ These are the names of the mighty men whom David had: Josheb-basshebeth a Tahchemonite; he was chief of the three.[3] He wielded his spear[4] against eight hundred whom he killed at one time.

⁹ And next to him among the three mighty men was Eleazar the son of Dodo, son of Ahohi. He was with David when they defied the Philistines who were gathered there for battle, and the men of Israel withdrew. ¹⁰ He rose and struck down the Philistines until his hand was weary, and his hand clung to the sword. And the Lord brought about a great victory that day, and the men returned after him only to strip the slain.

¹¹ And next to him was Shammah, the son of Agee the Hararite. The Philistines gathered together at Lehi,[5] where there was a plot of ground full of lentils, and the men fled from the Philistines. ¹² But he took his stand in the midst of the plot and defended it and struck down the Philistines, and the Lord worked a great victory.

¹³ And three of the thirty chief men went down and came about harvest time to David at the cave of Adullam, when a band of Philistines was encamped in the Valley of Rephaim. ¹⁴ David was then in the stronghold, and the garrison of the Philistines was then at Bethlehem. ¹⁵ And David said longingly, "Oh, that someone would give me water to drink from the well of Bethlehem that is by the gate!" ¹⁶ Then the three mighty men broke through the camp of the Philistines and drew water out of the well of Bethlehem that was by the gate and carried and brought it to David. But he would not drink of it. He poured it out to the Lord ¹⁷ and said, "Far be it from me, O Lord, that I should do this. Shall I drink the blood of the men who went at the risk of their lives?" Therefore he would not drink it. These things the three mighty men did.

¹⁸ Now Abishai, the brother of Joab, the son of Zeruiah, was chief of the thirty.[6] And he wielded his spear against three hundred men[7] and killed them and won a name beside the three. ¹⁹ He was the most renowned

---

[1] Hebrew *worthlessness* [2] Hebrew *consumed with fire in the sitting* [3] Or *of the captains* [4] Compare 1 Chronicles 11:11; the meaning of the Hebrew expression is uncertain [5] Or *gathered together as a camp* [6] Two Hebrew manuscripts, Syriac; most Hebrew manuscripts *three* [7] Or *slain ones*

of the thirty[1] and became their commander, but he did not attain to the three.

²⁰ And Benaiah the son of Jehoiada was a valiant man[2] of Kabzeel, a doer of great deeds. He struck down two ariels[3] of Moab. He also went down and struck down a lion in a pit on a day when snow had fallen. ²¹ And he struck down an Egyptian, a handsome man. The Egyptian had a spear in his hand, but Benaiah went down to him with a staff and snatched the spear out of the Egyptian's hand and killed him with his own spear. ²² These things did Benaiah the son of Jehoiada, and won a name beside the three mighty men. ²³ He was renowned among the thirty, but he did not attain to the three. And David set him over his bodyguard.

²⁴ Asahel the brother of Joab was one of the thirty; Elhanan the son of Dodo of Bethlehem, ²⁵ Shammah of Harod, Elika of Harod, ²⁶ Helez the Paltite, Ira the son of Ikkesh of Tekoa, ²⁷ Abiezer of Anathoth, Mebunnai the Hushathite, ²⁸ Zalmon the Ahohite, Maharai of Netophah, ²⁹ Heleb the son of Baanah of Netophah, Ittai the son of Ribai of Gibeah of the people of Benjamin, ³⁰ Benaiah of Pirathon, Hiddai of the brooks of Gaash, ³¹ Abi-albon the Arbathite, Azmaveth of Bahurim, ³² Eliahba the Shaalbonite, the sons of Jashen, Jonathan, ³³ Shammah the Hararite, Ahiam the son of Sharar the Hararite, ³⁴ Eliphelet the son of Ahasbai of Maacah, Eliam the son of Ahithophel the Gilonite, ³⁵ Hezro[4] of Carmel, Paarai the Arbite, ³⁶ Igal the son of Nathan of Zobah, Bani the Gadite, ³⁷ Zelek the Ammonite, Naharai of Beeroth, the armor-bearer of Joab the son of Zeruiah, ³⁸ Ira the Ithrite, Gareb the Ithrite, ³⁹ Uriah the Hittite: thirty-seven in all.

David's Census

24 Again the anger of the LORD was kindled against Israel, and he incited David against them, saying, "Go, number Israel and Judah." ² So the king said to Joab, the commander of the army,[5] who was with him, "Go through all the tribes of Israel, from Dan to Beersheba, and number the people, that I may know the number of the people." ³ But Joab said to the king, "May the LORD your God add to the people a hundred times as many as they are, while the eyes of my lord the king still see it, but why does my lord the king delight in this thing?" ⁴ But the king's word prevailed against Joab and the commanders of the army. So Joab and the commanders of the army went out from the presence of the king to number the people of Israel. ⁵ They crossed the Jordan and began from Aroer,[6] and from the city that is in the middle of the valley, toward Gad and on to Jazer. ⁶ Then they

---

[1] Compare 1 Chronicles 11:21; Hebrew *Was he the most renowned of the three?* [2] Or *the son of Ishhai*
[3] The meaning of the word *ariel* is uncertain [4] Or *Hezrai* [5] Septuagint *to Joab and the commanders of the army*
[6] Septuagint; Hebrew *encamped in Aroer*

came to Gilead, and to Kadesh in the land of the Hittites;[1] and they came to Dan, and from Dan[2] they went around to Sidon, ⁷ and came to the fortress of Tyre and to all the cities of the Hivites and Canaanites; and they went out to the Negeb of Judah at Beersheba. ⁸ So when they had gone through all the land, they came to Jerusalem at the end of nine months and twenty days. ⁹ And Joab gave the sum of the numbering of the people to the king: in Israel there were 800,000 valiant men who drew the sword, and the men of Judah were 500,000.

The Lord's Judgment of David's Sin

¹⁰ But David's heart struck him after he had numbered the people. And David said to the Lord, "I have sinned greatly in what I have done. But now, O Lord, please take away the iniquity of your servant, for I have done very foolishly." ¹¹ And when David arose in the morning, the word of the Lord came to the prophet Gad, David's seer, saying, ¹² "Go and say to David, 'Thus says the Lord, Three things I offer[3] you. Choose one of them, that I may do it to you.'" ¹³ So Gad came to David and told him, and said to him, "Shall three[4] years of famine come to you in your land? Or will you flee three months before your foes while they pursue you? Or shall there be three days' pestilence in your land? Now consider, and decide what answer I shall return to him who sent me." ¹⁴ Then David said to Gad, "I am in great distress. Let us fall into the hand of the Lord, for his mercy is great; but let me not fall into the hand of man."

¹⁵ So the Lord sent a pestilence on Israel from the morning until the appointed time. And there died of the people from Dan to Beersheba 70,000 men. ¹⁶ And when the angel stretched out his hand toward Jerusalem to destroy it, the Lord relented from the calamity and said to the angel who was working destruction among the people, "It is enough; now stay your hand." And the angel of the Lord was by the threshing floor of Araunah the Jebusite. ¹⁷ Then David spoke to the Lord when he saw the angel who was striking the people, and said, "Behold, I have sinned, and I have done wickedly. But these sheep, what have they done? Please let your hand be against me and against my father's house."

David Builds an Altar

¹⁸ And Gad came that day to David and said to him, "Go up, raise an altar to the Lord on the threshing floor of Araunah the Jebusite." ¹⁹ So David went up at Gad's word, as the Lord commanded. ²⁰ And when Araunah looked down,

---

[1] Septuagint; Hebrew *to the land of Tahtim-hodshi* [2] Septuagint; Hebrew *they came to Dan-jaan and* [3] Or *hold over* [4] Compare 1 Chronicles 21:12, Septuagint; Hebrew *seven*

he saw the king and his servants coming on toward him. And Araunah went out and paid homage to the king with his face to the ground. ²¹ And Araunah said, "Why has my lord the king come to his servant?" David said, "To buy the threshing floor from you, in order to build an altar to the Lord, that the plague may be averted from the people." ²² Then Araunah said to David, "Let my lord the king take and offer up what seems good to him. Here are the oxen for the burnt offering and the threshing sledges and the yokes of the oxen for the wood. ²³ All this, O king, Araunah gives to the king." And Araunah said to the king, "May the Lord your God accept you." ²⁴ But the king said to Araunah, "No, but I will buy it from you for a price. I will not offer burnt offerings to the Lord my God that cost me nothing." So David bought the threshing floor and the oxen for fifty shekels[1] of silver. ²⁵ And David built there an altar to the Lord and offered burnt offerings and peace offerings. So the Lord responded to the plea for the land, and the plague was averted from Israel.

---

[1] A *shekel* was about 2/5 ounce or 11 grams

1 KINGS

David in His Old Age

1 Now King David was old and advanced in years. And although they covered him with clothes, he could not get warm. ²Therefore his servants said to him, "Let a young woman be sought for my lord the king, and let her wait on the king and be in his service. Let her lie in your arms,[1] that my lord the king may be warm." ³So they sought for a beautiful young woman throughout all the territory of Israel, and found Abishag the Shunammite, and brought her to the king. ⁴The young woman was very beautiful, and she was of service to the king and attended to him, but the king knew her not.

Adonijah Sets Himself Up as King

⁵Now Adonijah the son of Haggith exalted himself, saying, "I will be king." And he prepared for himself chariots and horsemen, and fifty men to run before him. ⁶His father had never at any time displeased him by asking, "Why have you done thus and so?" He was also a very handsome man, and he was born next after Absalom. ⁷He conferred with Joab the son of Zeruiah and with Abiathar the priest. And they followed Adonijah and helped him. ⁸But Zadok the priest and Benaiah the son of Jehoiada and Nathan the prophet and Shimei and Rei and David's mighty men were not with Adonijah.

⁹Adonijah sacrificed sheep, oxen, and fattened cattle by the Serpent's Stone, which is beside En-rogel, and he invited all his brothers, the king's sons, and all the royal officials of Judah, ¹⁰but he did not invite Nathan the prophet or Benaiah or the mighty men or Solomon his brother.

Nathan and Bathsheba Before David

¹¹Then Nathan said to Bathsheba the mother of Solomon, "Have you not heard that Adonijah the son of Haggith has become king and David our lord does not know it? ¹²Now therefore come, let me give you advice, that you may save your own life and the life of your son Solomon. ¹³Go in at once to King David, and say to him, 'Did you not, my lord the king, swear to your servant, saying, "Solomon your son shall reign after me, and he shall sit on

[1] Or *in your bosom*

my throne"? Why then is Adonijah king?' ¹⁴ Then while you are still speaking with the king, I also will come in after you and confirm¹ your words."

¹⁵ So Bathsheba went to the king in his chamber (now the king was very old, and Abishag the Shunammite was attending to the king). ¹⁶ Bathsheba bowed and paid homage to the king, and the king said, "What do you desire?" ¹⁷ She said to him, "My lord, you swore to your servant by the LORD your God, saying, 'Solomon your son shall reign after me, and he shall sit on my throne.' ¹⁸ And now, behold, Adonijah is king, although you, my lord the king, do not know it. ¹⁹ He has sacrificed oxen, fattened cattle, and sheep in abundance, and has invited all the sons of the king, Abiathar the priest, and Joab the commander of the army, but Solomon your servant he has not invited. ²⁰ And now, my lord the king, the eyes of all Israel are on you, to tell them who shall sit on the throne of my lord the king after him. ²¹ Otherwise it will come to pass, when my lord the king sleeps with his fathers, that I and my son Solomon will be counted offenders."

²² While she was still speaking with the king, Nathan the prophet came in. ²³ And they told the king, "Here is Nathan the prophet." And when he came in before the king, he bowed before the king, with his face to the ground. ²⁴ And Nathan said, "My lord the king, have you said, 'Adonijah shall reign after me, and he shall sit on my throne'? ²⁵ For he has gone down this day and has sacrificed oxen, fattened cattle, and sheep in abundance, and has invited all the king's sons, the commanders² of the army, and Abiathar the priest. And behold, they are eating and drinking before him, and saying, 'Long live King Adonijah!' ²⁶ But me, your servant, and Zadok the priest, and Benaiah the son of Jehoiada, and your servant Solomon he has not invited. ²⁷ Has this thing been brought about by my lord the king and you have not told your servants who should sit on the throne of my lord the king after him?"

Solomon Anointed King

²⁸ Then King David answered, "Call Bathsheba to me." So she came into the king's presence and stood before the king. ²⁹ And the king swore, saying, "As the LORD lives, who has redeemed my soul out of every adversity, ³⁰ as I swore to you by the LORD, the God of Israel, saying, 'Solomon your son shall reign after me, and he shall sit on my throne in my place,' even so will I do this day." ³¹ Then Bathsheba bowed with her face to the ground and paid homage to the king and said, "May my lord King David live forever!"

³² King David said, "Call to me Zadok the priest, Nathan the prophet, and Benaiah the son of Jehoiada." So they came before the king. ³³ And the king

---

¹ Or *expand on* ² Hebrew; Septuagint *Joab the commander*

said to them, "Take with you the servants of your lord and have Solomon my son ride on my own mule, and bring him down to Gihon. ³⁴ And let Zadok the priest and Nathan the prophet there anoint him king over Israel. Then blow the trumpet and say, 'Long live King Solomon!' ³⁵ You shall then come up after him, and he shall come and sit on my throne, for he shall be king in my place. And I have appointed him to be ruler over Israel and over Judah." ³⁶ And Benaiah the son of Jehoiada answered the king, "Amen! May the Lord, the God of my lord the king, say so. ³⁷ As the Lord has been with my lord the king, even so may he be with Solomon, and make his throne greater than the throne of my lord King David."

³⁸ So Zadok the priest, Nathan the prophet, and Benaiah the son of Jehoiada, and the Cherethites and the Pelethites went down and had Solomon ride on King David's mule and brought him to Gihon. ³⁹ There Zadok the priest took the horn of oil from the tent and anointed Solomon. Then they blew the trumpet, and all the people said, "Long live King Solomon!" ⁴⁰ And all the people went up after him, playing on pipes, and rejoicing with great joy, so that the earth was split by their noise.

⁴¹ Adonijah and all the guests who were with him heard it as they finished feasting. And when Joab heard the sound of the trumpet, he said, "What does this uproar in the city mean?" ⁴² While he was still speaking, behold, Jonathan the son of Abiathar the priest came. And Adonijah said, "Come in, for you are a worthy man and bring good news." ⁴³ Jonathan answered Adonijah, "No, for our lord King David has made Solomon king, ⁴⁴ and the king has sent with him Zadok the priest, Nathan the prophet, and Benaiah the son of Jehoiada, and the Cherethites and the Pelethites. And they had him ride on the king's mule. ⁴⁵ And Zadok the priest and Nathan the prophet have anointed him king at Gihon, and they have gone up from there rejoicing, so that the city is in an uproar. This is the noise that you have heard. ⁴⁶ Solomon sits on the royal throne. ⁴⁷ Moreover, the king's servants came to congratulate our lord King David, saying, 'May your God make the name of Solomon more famous than yours, and make his throne greater than your throne.' And the king bowed himself on the bed. ⁴⁸ And the king also said, 'Blessed be the Lord, the God of Israel, who has granted someone[1] to sit on my throne this day, my own eyes seeing it.'"

⁴⁹ Then all the guests of Adonijah trembled and rose, and each went his own way. ⁵⁰ And Adonijah feared Solomon. So he arose and went and took hold of the horns of the altar. ⁵¹ Then it was told Solomon, "Behold, Adonijah fears King Solomon, for behold, he has laid hold of the horns of the altar,

[1] Septuagint *one of my offspring*

saying, 'Let King Solomon swear to me first that he will not put his servant to death with the sword.'" ⁵²And Solomon said, "If he will show himself a worthy man, not one of his hairs shall fall to the earth, but if wickedness is found in him, he shall die." ⁵³So King Solomon sent, and they brought him down from the altar. And he came and paid homage to King Solomon, and Solomon said to him, "Go to your house."

David's Instructions to Solomon

2 When David's time to die drew near, he commanded Solomon his son, saying, ²"I am about to go the way of all the earth. Be strong, and show yourself a man, ³and keep the charge of the LORD your God, walking in his ways and keeping his statutes, his commandments, his rules, and his testimonies, as it is written in the Law of Moses, that you may prosper in all that you do and wherever you turn, ⁴that the LORD may establish his word that he spoke concerning me, saying, 'If your sons pay close attention to their way, to walk before me in faithfulness with all their heart and with all their soul, you shall not lack[1] a man on the throne of Israel.'

⁵"Moreover, you also know what Joab the son of Zeruiah did to me, how he dealt with the two commanders of the armies of Israel, Abner the son of Ner, and Amasa the son of Jether, whom he killed, avenging[2] in time of peace for blood that had been shed in war, and putting the blood of war[3] on the belt around his[4] waist and on the sandals on his feet. ⁶Act therefore according to your wisdom, but do not let his gray head go down to Sheol in peace. ⁷But deal loyally with the sons of Barzillai the Gileadite, and let them be among those who eat at your table, for with such loyalty[5] they met me when I fled from Absalom your brother. ⁸And there is also with you Shimei the son of Gera, the Benjaminite from Bahurim, who cursed me with a grievous curse on the day when I went to Mahanaim. But when he came down to meet me at the Jordan, I swore to him by the LORD, saying, 'I will not put you to death with the sword.' ⁹Now therefore do not hold him guiltless, for you are a wise man. You will know what you ought to do to him, and you shall bring his gray head down with blood to Sheol."

The Death of David

¹⁰Then David slept with his fathers and was buried in the city of David. ¹¹And the time that David reigned over Israel was forty years. He reigned seven years in Hebron and thirty-three years in Jerusalem. ¹²So Solomon sat on the throne of David his father, and his kingdom was firmly established.

---

[1] Hebrew *there shall not be cut off for you* [2] Septuagint; Hebrew *placing* [3] Septuagint *innocent blood* [4] Septuagint *my*; twice in this verse [5] Or *steadfast love*

Solomon's Reign Established

¹³ Then Adonijah the son of Haggith came to Bathsheba the mother of Solomon. And she said, "Do you come peacefully?" He said, "Peacefully." ¹⁴ Then he said, "I have something to say to you." She said, "Speak." ¹⁵ He said, "You know that the kingdom was mine, and that all Israel fully expected me to reign. However, the kingdom has turned about and become my brother's, for it was his from the Lord. ¹⁶ And now I have one request to make of you; do not refuse me." She said to him, "Speak." ¹⁷ And he said, "Please ask King Solomon—he will not refuse you—to give me Abishag the Shunammite as my wife." ¹⁸ Bathsheba said, "Very well; I will speak for you to the king."

¹⁹ So Bathsheba went to King Solomon to speak to him on behalf of Adonijah. And the king rose to meet her and bowed down to her. Then he sat on his throne and had a seat brought for the king's mother, and she sat on his right. ²⁰ Then she said, "I have one small request to make of you; do not refuse me." And the king said to her, "Make your request, my mother, for I will not refuse you." ²¹ She said, "Let Abishag the Shunammite be given to Adonijah your brother as his wife." ²² King Solomon answered his mother, "And why do you ask Abishag the Shunammite for Adonijah? Ask for him the kingdom also, for he is my older brother, and on his side are Abiathar[1] the priest and Joab the son of Zeruiah." ²³ Then King Solomon swore by the Lord, saying, "God do so to me and more also if this word does not cost Adonijah his life! ²⁴ Now therefore as the Lord lives, who has established me and placed me on the throne of David my father, and who has made me a house, as he promised, Adonijah shall be put to death today." ²⁵ So King Solomon sent Benaiah the son of Jehoiada, and he struck him down, and he died.

²⁶ And to Abiathar the priest the king said, "Go to Anathoth, to your estate, for you deserve death. But I will not at this time put you to death, because you carried the ark of the Lord God before David my father, and because you shared in all my father's affliction." ²⁷ So Solomon expelled Abiathar from being priest to the Lord, thus fulfilling the word of the Lord that he had spoken concerning the house of Eli in Shiloh.

²⁸ When the news came to Joab—for Joab had supported Adonijah although he had not supported Absalom—Joab fled to the tent of the Lord and caught hold of the horns of the altar. ²⁹ And when it was told King Solomon, "Joab has fled to the tent of the Lord, and behold, he is beside the altar," Solomon sent Benaiah the son of Jehoiada, saying, "Go, strike him down." ³⁰ So Benaiah came to the tent of the Lord and said to him, "The king commands, 'Come out.'" But he said, "No, I will die here." Then Benaiah

---

[1] Septuagint, Syriac, Vulgate; Hebrew *and for him and for Abiathar*

brought the king word again, saying, "Thus said Joab, and thus he answered me." ³¹ The king replied to him, "Do as he has said, strike him down and bury him, and thus take away from me and from my father's house the guilt for the blood that Joab shed without cause. ³² The LORD will bring back his bloody deeds on his own head, because, without the knowledge of my father David, he attacked and killed with the sword two men more righteous and better than himself, Abner the son of Ner, commander of the army of Israel, and Amasa the son of Jether, commander of the army of Judah. ³³ So shall their blood come back on the head of Joab and on the head of his descendants forever. But for David and for his descendants and for his house and for his throne there shall be peace from the LORD forevermore." ³⁴ Then Benaiah the son of Jehoiada went up and struck him down and put him to death. And he was buried in his own house in the wilderness. ³⁵ The king put Benaiah the son of Jehoiada over the army in place of Joab, and the king put Zadok the priest in the place of Abiathar.

³⁶ Then the king sent and summoned Shimei and said to him, "Build yourself a house in Jerusalem and dwell there, and do not go out from there to any place whatever. ³⁷ For on the day you go out and cross the brook Kidron, know for certain that you shall die. Your blood shall be on your own head." ³⁸ And Shimei said to the king, "What you say is good; as my lord the king has said, so will your servant do." So Shimei lived in Jerusalem many days.

³⁹ But it happened at the end of three years that two of Shimei's servants ran away to Achish, son of Maacah, king of Gath. And when it was told Shimei, "Behold, your servants are in Gath," ⁴⁰ Shimei arose and saddled a donkey and went to Gath to Achish to seek his servants. Shimei went and brought his servants from Gath. ⁴¹ And when Solomon was told that Shimei had gone from Jerusalem to Gath and returned, ⁴² the king sent and summoned Shimei and said to him, "Did I not make you swear by the LORD and solemnly warn you, saying, 'Know for certain that on the day you go out and go to any place whatever, you shall die'? And you said to me, 'What you say is good; I will obey.' ⁴³ Why then have you not kept your oath to the LORD and the commandment with which I commanded you?" ⁴⁴ The king also said to Shimei, "You know in your own heart all the harm that you did to David my father. So the LORD will bring back your harm on your own head. ⁴⁵ But King Solomon shall be blessed, and the throne of David shall be established before the LORD forever." ⁴⁶ Then the king commanded Benaiah the son of Jehoiada, and he went out and struck him down, and he died.

So the kingdom was established in the hand of Solomon.

Solomon's Prayer for Wisdom

3 Solomon made a marriage alliance with Pharaoh king of Egypt. He took Pharaoh's daughter and brought her into the city of David until he had finished building his own house and the house of the Lord and the wall around Jerusalem. ²The people were sacrificing at the high places, however, because no house had yet been built for the name of the Lord.

³Solomon loved the Lord, walking in the statutes of David his father, only he sacrificed and made offerings at the high places. ⁴And the king went to Gibeon to sacrifice there, for that was the great high place. Solomon used to offer a thousand burnt offerings on that altar. ⁵At Gibeon the Lord appeared to Solomon in a dream by night, and God said, "Ask what I shall give you." ⁶And Solomon said, "You have shown great and steadfast love to your servant David my father, because he walked before you in faithfulness, in righteousness, and in uprightness of heart toward you. And you have kept for him this great and steadfast love and have given him a son to sit on his throne this day. ⁷And now, O Lord my God, you have made your servant king in place of David my father, although I am but a little child. I do not know how to go out or come in. ⁸And your servant is in the midst of your people whom you have chosen, a great people, too many to be numbered or counted for multitude. ⁹Give your servant therefore an understanding mind to govern your people, that I may discern between good and evil, for who is able to govern this your great people?"

¹⁰It pleased the Lord that Solomon had asked this. ¹¹And God said to him, "Because you have asked this, and have not asked for yourself long life or riches or the life of your enemies, but have asked for yourself understanding to discern what is right, ¹²behold, I now do according to your word. Behold, I give you a wise and discerning mind, so that none like you has been before you and none like you shall arise after you. ¹³I give you also what you have not asked, both riches and honor, so that no other king shall compare with you, all your days. ¹⁴And if you will walk in my ways, keeping my statutes and my commandments, as your father David walked, then I will lengthen your days."

¹⁵And Solomon awoke, and behold, it was a dream. Then he came to Jerusalem and stood before the ark of the covenant of the Lord, and offered up burnt offerings and peace offerings, and made a feast for all his servants.

Solomon's Wisdom

¹⁶Then two prostitutes came to the king and stood before him. ¹⁷The one woman said, "Oh, my lord, this woman and I live in the same house, and

I gave birth to a child while she was in the house. ⁱ⁸ Then on the third day after I gave birth, this woman also gave birth. And we were alone. There was no one else with us in the house; only we two were in the house. ¹⁹ And this woman's son died in the night, because she lay on him. ²⁰ And she arose at midnight and took my son from beside me, while your servant slept, and laid him at her breast, and laid her dead son at my breast. ²¹ When I rose in the morning to nurse my child, behold, he was dead. But when I looked at him closely in the morning, behold, he was not the child that I had borne." ²² But the other woman said, "No, the living child is mine, and the dead child is yours." The first said, "No, the dead child is yours, and the living child is mine." Thus they spoke before the king.

²³ Then the king said, "The one says, 'This is my son that is alive, and your son is dead'; and the other says, 'No; but your son is dead, and my son is the living one.'" ²⁴ And the king said, "Bring me a sword." So a sword was brought before the king. ²⁵ And the king said, "Divide the living child in two, and give half to the one and half to the other." ²⁶ Then the woman whose son was alive said to the king, because her heart yearned for her son, "Oh, my lord, give her the living child, and by no means put him to death." But the other said, "He shall be neither mine nor yours; divide him." ²⁷ Then the king answered and said, "Give the living child to the first woman, and by no means put him to death; she is his mother." ²⁸ And all Israel heard of the judgment that the king had rendered, and they stood in awe of the king, because they perceived that the wisdom of God was in him to do justice.

Solomon's Officials

4 King Solomon was king over all Israel, ² and these were his high officials: Azariah the son of Zadok was the priest; ³ Elihoreph and Ahijah the sons of Shisha were secretaries; Jehoshaphat the son of Ahilud was recorder; ⁴ Benaiah the son of Jehoiada was in command of the army; Zadok and Abiathar were priests; ⁵ Azariah the son of Nathan was over the officers; Zabud the son of Nathan was priest and king's friend; ⁶ Ahishar was in charge of the palace; and Adoniram the son of Abda was in charge of the forced labor.

⁷ Solomon had twelve officers over all Israel, who provided food for the king and his household. Each man had to make provision for one month in the year. ⁸ These were their names: Ben-hur, in the hill country of Ephraim; ⁹ Ben-deker, in Makaz, Shaalbim, Beth-shemesh, and Elonbeth-hanan; ¹⁰ Ben-hesed, in Arubboth (to him belonged Socoh and all the land of Hepher); ¹¹ Ben-abinadab, in all Naphath-dor (he had Taphath the daughter of Solomon as his wife); ¹² Baana the son of Ahilud, in Taanach, Megiddo, and all Beth-shean

that is beside Zarethan below Jezreel, and from Beth-shean to Abel-meholah, as far as the other side of Jokmeam; [13] Ben-geber, in Ramoth-gilead (he had the villages of Jair the son of Manasseh, which are in Gilead, and he had the region of Argob, which is in Bashan, sixty great cities with walls and bronze bars); [14] Ahinadab the son of Iddo, in Mahanaim; [15] Ahimaaz, in Naphtali (he had taken Basemath the daughter of Solomon as his wife); [16] Baana the son of Hushai, in Asher and Bealoth; [17] Jehoshaphat the son of Paruah, in Issachar; [18] Shimei the son of Ela, in Benjamin; [19] Geber the son of Uri, in the land of Gilead, the country of Sihon king of the Amorites and of Og king of Bashan. And there was one governor who was over the land.

Solomon's Wealth and Wisdom

[20] Judah and Israel were as many as the sand by the sea. They ate and drank and were happy. [21] [1] Solomon ruled over all the kingdoms from the Euphrates[2] to the land of the Philistines and to the border of Egypt. They brought tribute and served Solomon all the days of his life.

[22] Solomon's provision for one day was thirty cors[3] of fine flour and sixty cors of meal, [23] ten fat oxen, and twenty pasture-fed cattle, a hundred sheep, besides deer, gazelles, roebucks, and fattened fowl. [24] For he had dominion over all the region west of the Euphrates[4] from Tiphsah to Gaza, over all the kings west of the Euphrates. And he had peace on all sides around him. [25] And Judah and Israel lived in safety, from Dan even to Beersheba, every man under his vine and under his fig tree, all the days of Solomon. [26] Solomon also had 40,000[5] stalls of horses for his chariots, and 12,000 horsemen. [27] And those officers supplied provisions for King Solomon, and for all who came to King Solomon's table, each one in his month. They let nothing be lacking. [28] Barley also and straw for the horses and swift steeds they brought to the place where it was required, each according to his duty.

[29] And God gave Solomon wisdom and understanding beyond measure, and breadth of mind like the sand on the seashore, [30] so that Solomon's wisdom surpassed the wisdom of all the people of the east and all the wisdom of Egypt. [31] For he was wiser than all other men, wiser than Ethan the Ezrahite, and Heman, Calcol, and Darda, the sons of Mahol, and his fame was in all the surrounding nations. [32] He also spoke 3,000 proverbs, and his songs were 1,005. [33] He spoke of trees, from the cedar that is in Lebanon to the hyssop that grows out of the wall. He spoke also of beasts, and of birds, and of reptiles, and of fish. [34] And people of all nations came to hear the wisdom of Solomon, and from all the kings of the earth, who had heard of his wisdom.

---

[1] Ch 5:1 in Hebrew [2] Hebrew *the River* [3] A *cor* was about 6 bushels or 220 liters [4] Hebrew *the River*; twice in this verse [5] Hebrew; one Hebrew manuscript (see 2 Chronicles 9:25 and Septuagint of 1 Kings 10:26) *4,000*

Preparations for Building the Temple

5 ¹ Now Hiram king of Tyre sent his servants to Solomon when he heard that they had anointed him king in place of his father, for Hiram always loved David. ² And Solomon sent word to Hiram, ³ "You know that David my father could not build a house for the name of the Lord his God because of the warfare with which his enemies surrounded him, until the Lord put them under the soles of his feet. ⁴ But now the Lord my God has given me rest on every side. There is neither adversary nor misfortune. ⁵ And so I intend to build a house for the name of the Lord my God, as the Lord said to David my father, 'Your son, whom I will set on your throne in your place, shall build the house for my name.' ⁶ Now therefore command that cedars of Lebanon be cut for me. And my servants will join your servants, and I will pay you for your servants such wages as you set, for you know that there is no one among us who knows how to cut timber like the Sidonians."

⁷ As soon as Hiram heard the words of Solomon, he rejoiced greatly and said, "Blessed be the Lord this day, who has given to David a wise son to be over this great people." ⁸ And Hiram sent to Solomon, saying, "I have heard the message that you have sent to me. I am ready to do all you desire in the matter of cedar and cypress timber. ⁹ My servants shall bring it down to the sea from Lebanon, and I will make it into rafts to go by sea to the place you direct. And I will have them broken up there, and you shall receive it. And you shall meet my wishes by providing food for my household." ¹⁰ So Hiram supplied Solomon with all the timber of cedar and cypress that he desired, ¹¹ while Solomon gave Hiram 20,000 cors[2] of wheat as food for his household, and 20,000[3] cors of beaten oil. Solomon gave this to Hiram year by year. ¹² And the Lord gave Solomon wisdom, as he promised him. And there was peace between Hiram and Solomon, and the two of them made a treaty.

¹³ King Solomon drafted forced labor out of all Israel, and the draft numbered 30,000 men. ¹⁴ And he sent them to Lebanon, 10,000 a month in shifts. They would be a month in Lebanon and two months at home. Adoniram was in charge of the draft. ¹⁵ Solomon also had 70,000 burden-bearers and 80,000 stonecutters in the hill country, ¹⁶ besides Solomon's 3,300 chief officers who were over the work, who had charge of the people who carried on the work. ¹⁷ At the king's command they quarried out great, costly stones in order to lay the foundation of the house with dressed stones. ¹⁸ So Solomon's builders and Hiram's builders and the men of Gebal did the cutting and prepared the timber and the stone to build the house.

[1] Ch 5:15 in Hebrew [2] A *cor* was about 6 bushels or 220 liters [3] Septuagint; Hebrew *twenty*

Solomon Builds the Temple

6 In the four hundred and eightieth year after the people of Israel came out of the land of Egypt, in the fourth year of Solomon's reign over Israel, in the month of Ziv, which is the second month, he began to build the house of the Lord. [2] The house that King Solomon built for the Lord was sixty cubits[1] long, twenty cubits wide, and thirty cubits high. [3] The vestibule in front of the nave of the house was twenty cubits long, equal to the width of the house, and ten cubits deep in front of the house. [4] And he made for the house windows with recessed frames.[2] [5] He also built a structure[3] against the wall of the house, running around the walls of the house, both the nave and the inner sanctuary. And he made side chambers all around. [6] The lowest story[4] was five cubits broad, the middle one was six cubits broad, and the third was seven cubits broad. For around the outside of the house he made offsets on the wall in order that the supporting beams should not be inserted into the walls of the house.

[7] When the house was built, it was with stone prepared at the quarry, so that neither hammer nor axe nor any tool of iron was heard in the house while it was being built.

[8] The entrance for the lowest[5] story was on the south side of the house, and one went up by stairs to the middle story, and from the middle story to the third. [9] So he built the house and finished it, and he made the ceiling of the house of beams and planks of cedar. [10] He built the structure against the whole house, five cubits high, and it was joined to the house with timbers of cedar.

[11] Now the word of the Lord came to Solomon, [12] "Concerning this house that you are building, if you will walk in my statutes and obey my rules and keep all my commandments and walk in them, then I will establish my word with you, which I spoke to David your father. [13] And I will dwell among the children of Israel and will not forsake my people Israel."

[14] So Solomon built the house and finished it. [15] He lined the walls of the house on the inside with boards of cedar. From the floor of the house to the walls of the ceiling, he covered them on the inside with wood, and he covered the floor of the house with boards of cypress. [16] He built twenty cubits of the rear of the house with boards of cedar from the floor to the walls, and he built this within as an inner sanctuary, as the Most Holy Place. [17] The house, that is, the nave in front of the inner sanctuary, was forty cubits long. [18] The cedar within the house was carved in the form of gourds and open flowers. All was cedar; no stone was seen. [19] The inner sanctuary he prepared in the innermost part of the house, to set there the ark of the covenant of the Lord. [20] The inner sanctuary[6] was twenty cubits long, twenty cubits wide, and twenty cubits high,

---

[1] A *cubit* was about 18 inches or 45 centimeters [2] Or *blocked lattice windows* [3] Or *platform*; also verse 10
[4] Septuagint; Hebrew *structure, or platform* [5] Septuagint, Targum; Hebrew *middle* [6] Vulgate; Hebrew *And before the inner sanctuary*

and he overlaid it with pure gold. He also overlaid[1] an altar of cedar. ²¹ And Solomon overlaid the inside of the house with pure gold, and he drew chains of gold across, in front of the inner sanctuary, and overlaid it with gold. ²² And he overlaid the whole house with gold, until all the house was finished. Also the whole altar that belonged to the inner sanctuary he overlaid with gold.

²³ In the inner sanctuary he made two cherubim of olivewood, each ten cubits high. ²⁴ Five cubits was the length of one wing of the cherub, and five cubits the length of the other wing of the cherub; it was ten cubits from the tip of one wing to the tip of the other. ²⁵ The other cherub also measured ten cubits; both cherubim had the same measure and the same form. ²⁶ The height of one cherub was ten cubits, and so was that of the other cherub. ²⁷ He put the cherubim in the innermost part of the house. And the wings of the cherubim were spread out so that a wing of one touched the one wall, and a wing of the other cherub touched the other wall; their other wings touched each other in the middle of the house. ²⁸ And he overlaid the cherubim with gold.

²⁹ Around all the walls of the house he carved engraved figures of cherubim and palm trees and open flowers, in the inner and outer rooms. ³⁰ The floor of the house he overlaid with gold in the inner and outer rooms.

³¹ For the entrance to the inner sanctuary he made doors of olivewood; the lintel and the doorposts were five-sided.[2] ³² He covered the two doors of olivewood with carvings of cherubim, palm trees, and open flowers. He overlaid them with gold and spread gold on the cherubim and on the palm trees.

³³ So also he made for the entrance to the nave doorposts of olivewood, in the form of a square, ³⁴ and two doors of cypress wood. The two leaves of the one door were folding, and the two leaves of the other door were folding. ³⁵ On them he carved cherubim and palm trees and open flowers, and he overlaid them with gold evenly applied on the carved work. ³⁶ He built the inner court with three courses of cut stone and one course of cedar beams.

³⁷ In the fourth year the foundation of the house of the LORD was laid, in the month of Ziv. ³⁸ And in the eleventh year, in the month of Bul, which is the eighth month, the house was finished in all its parts, and according to all its specifications. He was seven years in building it.

Solomon Builds His Palace

7 Solomon was building his own house thirteen years, and he finished his entire house.

² He built the House of the Forest of Lebanon. Its length was a hundred cubits[3] and its breadth fifty cubits and its height thirty cubits, and it was

---

[1] Septuagint *made* [2] The meaning of the Hebrew phrase is uncertain [3] A *cubit* was about 18 inches or 45 centimeters

built on four[1] rows of cedar pillars, with cedar beams on the pillars. ³ And it was covered with cedar above the chambers that were on the forty-five pillars, fifteen in each row. ⁴ There were window frames in three rows, and window opposite window in three tiers. ⁵ All the doorways and windows[2] had square frames, and window was opposite window in three tiers.

⁶ And he made the Hall of Pillars; its length was fifty cubits, and its breadth thirty cubits. There was a porch in front with pillars, and a canopy in front of them.

⁷ And he made the Hall of the Throne where he was to pronounce judgment, even the Hall of Judgment. It was finished with cedar from floor to rafters.[3]

⁸ His own house where he was to dwell, in the other court at the back of the hall, was of like workmanship. Solomon also made a house like this hall for Pharaoh's daughter whom he had taken in marriage.

⁹ All these were made of costly stones, cut according to measure, sawed with saws, back and front, even from the foundation to the coping, and from the outside to the great court. ¹⁰ The foundation was of costly stones, huge stones, stones of eight and ten cubits. ¹¹ And above were costly stones, cut according to measurement, and cedar. ¹² The great court had three courses of cut stone all around, and a course of cedar beams; so had the inner court of the house of the LORD and the vestibule of the house.

The Temple Furnishings

¹³ And King Solomon sent and brought Hiram from Tyre. ¹⁴ He was the son of a widow of the tribe of Naphtali, and his father was a man of Tyre, a worker in bronze. And he was full of wisdom, understanding, and skill for making any work in bronze. He came to King Solomon and did all his work.

¹⁵ He cast two pillars of bronze. Eighteen cubits was the height of one pillar, and a line of twelve cubits measured its circumference. It was hollow, and its thickness was four fingers. The second pillar was the same.[4] ¹⁶ He also made two capitals of cast bronze to set on the tops of the pillars. The height of the one capital was five cubits, and the height of the other capital was five cubits. ¹⁷ There were lattices of checker work with wreaths of chain work for the capitals on the tops of the pillars, a lattice[5] for the one capital and a lattice for the other capital. ¹⁸ Likewise he made pomegranates[6] in two rows around the one latticework to cover the capital that was on the top of the pillar, and he did the same with the other capital. ¹⁹ Now the capitals that were on the tops of the pillars in the vestibule were of lily-work, four cubits.

²⁰ The capitals were on the two pillars and also above the rounded projection

---

[1] Septuagint *three* [2] Septuagint; Hebrew *posts* [3] Syriac, Vulgate; Hebrew *floor* [4] Targum, Syriac (compare Septuagint and Jeremiah 52:21); Hebrew *and a line of twelve cubits measured the circumference of the second pillar* [5] Septuagint; Hebrew *seven*; twice in this verse [6] Two manuscripts (compare Septuagint); Hebrew *pillars*

which was beside the latticework. There were two hundred pomegranates in two rows all around, and so with the other capital. ²¹ He set up the pillars at the vestibule of the temple. He set up the pillar on the south and called its name Jachin, and he set up the pillar on the north and called its name Boaz. ²² And on the tops of the pillars was lily-work. Thus the work of the pillars was finished.

²³ Then he made the sea of cast metal. It was round, ten cubits from brim to brim, and five cubits high, and a line of thirty cubits measured its circumference. ²⁴ Under its brim were gourds, for ten cubits, compassing the sea all around. The gourds were in two rows, cast with it when it was cast. ²⁵ It stood on twelve oxen, three facing north, three facing west, three facing south, and three facing east. The sea was set on them, and all their rear parts were inward. ²⁶ Its thickness was a handbreadth,¹ and its brim was made like the brim of a cup, like the flower of a lily. It held two thousand baths.²

²⁷ He also made the ten stands of bronze. Each stand was four cubits long, four cubits wide, and three cubits high. ²⁸ This was the construction of the stands: they had panels, and the panels were set in the frames, ²⁹ and on the panels that were set in the frames were lions, oxen, and cherubim. On the frames, both above and below the lions and oxen, there were wreaths of beveled work. ³⁰ Moreover, each stand had four bronze wheels and axles of bronze, and at the four corners were supports for a basin. The supports were cast with wreaths at the side of each. ³¹ Its opening was within a crown that projected upward one cubit. Its opening was round, as a pedestal is made, a cubit and a half deep. At its opening there were carvings, and its panels were square, not round. ³² And the four wheels were underneath the panels. The axles of the wheels were of one piece with the stands, and the height of a wheel was a cubit and a half. ³³ The wheels were made like a chariot wheel; their axles, their rims, their spokes, and their hubs were all cast. ³⁴ There were four supports at the four corners of each stand. The supports were of one piece with the stands. ³⁵ And on the top of the stand there was a round band half a cubit high; and on the top of the stand its stays and its panels were of one piece with it. ³⁶ And on the surfaces of its stays and on its panels, he carved cherubim, lions, and palm trees, according to the space of each, with wreaths all around. ³⁷ After this manner he made the ten stands. All of them were cast alike, of the same measure and the same form.

³⁸ And he made ten basins of bronze. Each basin held forty baths, each basin measured four cubits, and there was a basin for each of the ten stands. ³⁹ And

---

¹ A *handbreadth* was about 3 inches or 7.5 centimeters ² A *bath* was about 6 gallons or 22 liters

he set the stands, five on the south side of the house, and five on the north side of the house. And he set the sea at the southeast corner of the house.

⁴⁰ Hiram also made the pots, the shovels, and the basins. So Hiram finished all the work that he did for King Solomon on the house of the Lord: ⁴¹ the two pillars, the two bowls of the capitals that were on the tops of the pillars, and the two latticeworks to cover the two bowls of the capitals that were on the tops of the pillars; ⁴² and the four hundred pomegranates for the two latticeworks, two rows of pomegranates for each latticework, to cover the two bowls of the capitals that were on the pillars; ⁴³ the ten stands, and the ten basins on the stands; ⁴⁴ and the one sea, and the twelve oxen underneath the sea.

⁴⁵ Now the pots, the shovels, and the basins, all these vessels in the house of the Lord, which Hiram made for King Solomon, were of burnished bronze. ⁴⁶ In the plain of the Jordan the king cast them, in the clay ground between Succoth and Zarethan. ⁴⁷ And Solomon left all the vessels unweighed, because there were so many of them; the weight of the bronze was not ascertained.

⁴⁸ So Solomon made all the vessels that were in the house of the Lord: the golden altar, the golden table for the bread of the Presence, ⁴⁹ the lampstands of pure gold, five on the south side and five on the north, before the inner sanctuary; the flowers, the lamps, and the tongs, of gold; ⁵⁰ the cups, snuffers, basins, dishes for incense, and fire pans, of pure gold; and the sockets of gold, for the doors of the innermost part of the house, the Most Holy Place, and for the doors of the nave of the temple.

⁵¹ Thus all the work that King Solomon did on the house of the Lord was finished. And Solomon brought in the things that David his father had dedicated, the silver, the gold, and the vessels, and stored them in the treasuries of the house of the Lord.

The Ark Brought into the Temple

8 Then Solomon assembled the elders of Israel and all the heads of the tribes, the leaders of the fathers' houses of the people of Israel, before King Solomon in Jerusalem, to bring up the ark of the covenant of the Lord out of the city of David, which is Zion. ² And all the men of Israel assembled to King Solomon at the feast in the month Ethanim, which is the seventh month. ³ And all the elders of Israel came, and the priests took up the ark. ⁴ And they brought up the ark of the Lord, the tent of meeting, and all the holy vessels that were in the tent; the priests and the Levites brought them up. ⁵ And King Solomon and all the congregation of Israel, who had assembled before him, were with him before the ark, sacrificing so many sheep and

oxen that they could not be counted or numbered. ⁶ Then the priests brought the ark of the covenant of the LORD to its place in the inner sanctuary of the house, in the Most Holy Place, underneath the wings of the cherubim. ⁷ For the cherubim spread out their wings over the place of the ark, so that the cherubim overshadowed the ark and its poles. ⁸ And the poles were so long that the ends of the poles were seen from the Holy Place before the inner sanctuary; but they could not be seen from outside. And they are there to this day. ⁹ There was nothing in the ark except the two tablets of stone that Moses put there at Horeb, where the LORD made a covenant with the people of Israel, when they came out of the land of Egypt. ¹⁰ And when the priests came out of the Holy Place, a cloud filled the house of the LORD, ¹¹ so that the priests could not stand to minister because of the cloud, for the glory of the LORD filled the house of the LORD.

Solomon Blesses the LORD

¹² Then Solomon said, "The LORD[1] has said that he would dwell in thick darkness. ¹³ I have indeed built you an exalted house, a place for you to dwell in forever." ¹⁴ Then the king turned around and blessed all the assembly of Israel, while all the assembly of Israel stood. ¹⁵ And he said, "Blessed be the LORD, the God of Israel, who with his hand has fulfilled what he promised with his mouth to David my father, saying, ¹⁶ 'Since the day that I brought my people Israel out of Egypt, I chose no city out of all the tribes of Israel in which to build a house, that my name might be there. But I chose David to be over my people Israel.' ¹⁷ Now it was in the heart of David my father to build a house for the name of the LORD, the God of Israel. ¹⁸ But the LORD said to David my father, 'Whereas it was in your heart to build a house for my name, you did well that it was in your heart. ¹⁹ Nevertheless, you shall not build the house, but your son who shall be born to you shall build the house for my name.' ²⁰ Now the LORD has fulfilled his promise that he made. For I have risen in the place of David my father, and sit on the throne of Israel, as the LORD promised, and I have built the house for the name of the LORD, the God of Israel. ²¹ And there I have provided a place for the ark, in which is the covenant of the LORD that he made with our fathers, when he brought them out of the land of Egypt."

Solomon's Prayer of Dedication

²² Then Solomon stood before the altar of the LORD in the presence of all the assembly of Israel and spread out his hands toward heaven, ²³ and said, "O LORD, God of Israel, there is no God like you, in heaven above or on earth

[1] Septuagint *The LORD has set the sun in the heavens, but*

beneath, keeping covenant and showing steadfast love to your servants who walk before you with all their heart; ²⁴ you have kept with your servant David my father what you declared to him. You spoke with your mouth, and with your hand have fulfilled it this day. ²⁵ Now therefore, O Lord, God of Israel, keep for your servant David my father what you have promised him, saying, 'You shall not lack a man to sit before me on the throne of Israel, if only your sons pay close attention to their way, to walk before me as you have walked before me.' ²⁶ Now therefore, O God of Israel, let your word be confirmed, which you have spoken to your servant David my father.

²⁷ "But will God indeed dwell on the earth? Behold, heaven and the highest heaven cannot contain you; how much less this house that I have built! ²⁸ Yet have regard to the prayer of your servant and to his plea, O Lord my God, listening to the cry and to the prayer that your servant prays before you this day, ²⁹ that your eyes may be open night and day toward this house, the place of which you have said, 'My name shall be there,' that you may listen to the prayer that your servant offers toward this place. ³⁰ And listen to the plea of your servant and of your people Israel, when they pray toward this place. And listen in heaven your dwelling place, and when you hear, forgive.

³¹ "If a man sins against his neighbor and is made to take an oath and comes and swears his oath before your altar in this house, ³² then hear in heaven and act and judge your servants, condemning the guilty by bringing his conduct on his own head, and vindicating the righteous by rewarding him according to his righteousness.

³³ "When your people Israel are defeated before the enemy because they have sinned against you, and if they turn again to you and acknowledge your name and pray and plead with you in this house, ³⁴ then hear in heaven and forgive the sin of your people Israel and bring them again to the land that you gave to their fathers.

³⁵ "When heaven is shut up and there is no rain because they have sinned against you, if they pray toward this place and acknowledge your name and turn from their sin, when you afflict them, ³⁶ then hear in heaven and forgive the sin of your servants, your people Israel, when you teach them the good way in which they should walk, and grant rain upon your land, which you have given to your people as an inheritance.

³⁷ "If there is famine in the land, if there is pestilence or blight or mildew or locust or caterpillar, if their enemy besieges them in the land at their gates,¹ whatever plague, whatever sickness there is, ³⁸ whatever prayer, whatever plea is made by any man or by all your people Israel, each knowing the affliction

¹ Septuagint, Syriac *in any of their cities*

of his own heart and stretching out his hands toward this house, ³⁹ then hear in heaven your dwelling place and forgive and act and render to each whose heart you know, according to all his ways (for you, you only, know the hearts of all the children of mankind), ⁴⁰ that they may fear you all the days that they live in the land that you gave to our fathers.

⁴¹ "Likewise, when a foreigner, who is not of your people Israel, comes from a far country for your name's sake ⁴² (for they shall hear of your great name and your mighty hand, and of your outstretched arm), when he comes and prays toward this house, ⁴³ hear in heaven your dwelling place and do according to all for which the foreigner calls to you, in order that all the peoples of the earth may know your name and fear you, as do your people Israel, and that they may know that this house that I have built is called by your name.

⁴⁴ "If your people go out to battle against their enemy, by whatever way you shall send them, and they pray to the Lord toward the city that you have chosen and the house that I have built for your name, ⁴⁵ then hear in heaven their prayer and their plea, and maintain their cause.

⁴⁶ "If they sin against you—for there is no one who does not sin—and you are angry with them and give them to an enemy, so that they are carried away captive to the land of the enemy, far off or near, ⁴⁷ yet if they turn their heart in the land to which they have been carried captive, and repent and plead with you in the land of their captors, saying, 'We have sinned and have acted perversely and wickedly,' ⁴⁸ if they repent with all their heart and with all their soul in the land of their enemies, who carried them captive, and pray to you toward their land, which you gave to their fathers, the city that you have chosen, and the house that I have built for your name, ⁴⁹ then hear in heaven your dwelling place their prayer and their plea, and maintain their cause ⁵⁰ and forgive your people who have sinned against you, and all their transgressions that they have committed against you, and grant them compassion in the sight of those who carried them captive, that they may have compassion on them ⁵¹ (for they are your people, and your heritage, which you brought out of Egypt, from the midst of the iron furnace). ⁵² Let your eyes be open to the plea of your servant and to the plea of your people Israel, giving ear to them whenever they call to you. ⁵³ For you separated them from among all the peoples of the earth to be your heritage, as you declared through Moses your servant, when you brought our fathers out of Egypt, O Lord God."

Solomon's Benediction

⁵⁴ Now as Solomon finished offering all this prayer and plea to the Lord, he arose from before the altar of the Lord, where he had knelt with hands

outstretched toward heaven. ⁵⁵ And he stood and blessed all the assembly of Israel with a loud voice, saying, ⁵⁶ "Blessed be the Lord who has given rest to his people Israel, according to all that he promised. Not one word has failed of all his good promise, which he spoke by Moses his servant. ⁵⁷ The Lord our God be with us, as he was with our fathers. May he not leave us or forsake us, ⁵⁸ that he may incline our hearts to him, to walk in all his ways and to keep his commandments, his statutes, and his rules, which he commanded our fathers. ⁵⁹ Let these words of mine, with which I have pleaded before the Lord, be near to the Lord our God day and night, and may he maintain the cause of his servant and the cause of his people Israel, as each day requires, ⁶⁰ that all the peoples of the earth may know that the Lord is God; there is no other. ⁶¹ Let your heart therefore be wholly true to the Lord our God, walking in his statutes and keeping his commandments, as at this day."

Solomon's Sacrifices

⁶² Then the king, and all Israel with him, offered sacrifice before the Lord. ⁶³ Solomon offered as peace offerings to the Lord 22,000 oxen and 120,000 sheep. So the king and all the people of Israel dedicated the house of the Lord. ⁶⁴ The same day the king consecrated the middle of the court that was before the house of the Lord, for there he offered the burnt offering and the grain offering and the fat pieces of the peace offerings, because the bronze altar that was before the Lord was too small to receive the burnt offering and the grain offering and the fat pieces of the peace offerings.

⁶⁵ So Solomon held the feast at that time, and all Israel with him, a great assembly, from Lebo-hamath to the Brook of Egypt, before the Lord our God, seven days.¹ ⁶⁶ On the eighth day he sent the people away, and they blessed the king and went to their homes joyful and glad of heart for all the goodness that the Lord had shown to David his servant and to Israel his people.

The Lord Appears to Solomon

9 As soon as Solomon had finished building the house of the Lord and the king's house and all that Solomon desired to build, ² the Lord appeared to Solomon a second time, as he had appeared to him at Gibeon. ³ And the Lord said to him, "I have heard your prayer and your plea, which you have made before me. I have consecrated this house that you have built, by putting my name there forever. My eyes and my heart will be there for all time. ⁴ And as for you, if you will walk before me, as David your father

---

¹ Septuagint; Hebrew *seven days and seven days, fourteen days*

walked, with integrity of heart and uprightness, doing according to all that I have commanded you, and keeping my statutes and my rules, ⁵ then I will establish your royal throne over Israel forever, as I promised David your father, saying, 'You shall not lack a man on the throne of Israel.' ⁶ But if you turn aside from following me, you or your children, and do not keep my commandments and my statutes that I have set before you, but go and serve other gods and worship them, ⁷ then I will cut off Israel from the land that I have given them, and the house that I have consecrated for my name I will cast out of my sight, and Israel will become a proverb and a byword among all peoples. ⁸ And this house will become a heap of ruins.[1] Everyone passing by it will be astonished and will hiss, and they will say, 'Why has the LORD done thus to this land and to this house?' ⁹ Then they will say, 'Because they abandoned the LORD their God who brought their fathers out of the land of Egypt and laid hold on other gods and worshiped them and served them. Therefore the LORD has brought all this disaster on them.'"

Solomon's Other Acts

¹⁰ At the end of twenty years, in which Solomon had built the two houses, the house of the LORD and the king's house, ¹¹ and Hiram king of Tyre had supplied Solomon with cedar and cypress timber and gold, as much as he desired, King Solomon gave to Hiram twenty cities in the land of Galilee. ¹² But when Hiram came from Tyre to see the cities that Solomon had given him, they did not please him. ¹³ Therefore he said, "What kind of cities are these that you have given me, my brother?" So they are called the land of Cabul to this day. ¹⁴ Hiram had sent to the king 120 talents[2] of gold.

¹⁵ And this is the account of the forced labor that King Solomon drafted to build the house of the LORD and his own house and the Millo and the wall of Jerusalem and Hazor and Megiddo and Gezer ¹⁶ (Pharaoh king of Egypt had gone up and captured Gezer and burned it with fire, and had killed the Canaanites who lived in the city, and had given it as dowry to his daughter, Solomon's wife; ¹⁷ so Solomon rebuilt Gezer) and Lower Beth-horon ¹⁸ and Baalath and Tamar in the wilderness, in the land of Judah,[3] ¹⁹ and all the store cities that Solomon had, and the cities for his chariots, and the cities for his horsemen, and whatever Solomon desired to build in Jerusalem, in Lebanon, and in all the land of his dominion. ²⁰ All the people who were left of the Amorites, the Hittites, the Perizzites, the Hivites, and the Jebusites, who were not of the people of Israel— ²¹ their descendants who were left after them in the land, whom the people of Israel were unable to devote to

---

[1] Syriac, Old Latin; Hebrew *will become high* [2] A *talent* was about 75 pounds or 34 kilograms [3] Hebrew lacks *of Judah*

destruction[1]—these Solomon drafted to be slaves, and so they are to this day. ²² But of the people of Israel Solomon made no slaves. They were the soldiers, they were his officials, his commanders, his captains, his chariot commanders and his horsemen.

²³ These were the chief officers who were over Solomon's work: 550 who had charge of the people who carried on the work.

²⁴ But Pharaoh's daughter went up from the city of David to her own house that Solomon had built for her. Then he built the Millo.

²⁵ Three times a year Solomon used to offer up burnt offerings and peace offerings on the altar that he built to the LORD, making offerings with it[2] before the LORD. So he finished the house.

²⁶ King Solomon built a fleet of ships at Ezion-geber, which is near Eloth on the shore of the Red Sea, in the land of Edom. ²⁷ And Hiram sent with the fleet his servants, seamen who were familiar with the sea, together with the servants of Solomon. ²⁸ And they went to Ophir and brought from there gold, 420 talents, and they brought it to King Solomon.

The Queen of Sheba

10 Now when the queen of Sheba heard of the fame of Solomon concerning the name of the LORD, she came to test him with hard questions. ² She came to Jerusalem with a very great retinue, with camels bearing spices and very much gold and precious stones. And when she came to Solomon, she told him all that was on her mind. ³ And Solomon answered all her questions; there was nothing hidden from the king that he could not explain to her. ⁴ And when the queen of Sheba had seen all the wisdom of Solomon, the house that he had built, ⁵ the food of his table, the seating of his officials, and the attendance of his servants, their clothing, his cupbearers, and his burnt offerings that he offered at the house of the LORD, there was no more breath in her.

⁶ And she said to the king, "The report was true that I heard in my own land of your words and of your wisdom, ⁷ but I did not believe the reports until I came and my own eyes had seen it. And behold, the half was not told me. Your wisdom and prosperity surpass the report that I heard. ⁸ Happy are your men! Happy are your servants, who continually stand before you and hear your wisdom! ⁹ Blessed be the LORD your God, who has delighted in you and set you on the throne of Israel! Because the LORD loved Israel forever, he has made you king, that you may execute justice and righteousness." ¹⁰ Then she gave the king 120 talents[3] of gold, and a very great quantity of spices and

---

[1] That is, set apart (devote) as an offering to the Lord (for destruction) [2] Septuagint lacks *with it* [3] A *talent* was about 75 pounds or 34 kilograms

precious stones. Never again came such an abundance of spices as these that the queen of Sheba gave to King Solomon.

11 Moreover, the fleet of Hiram, which brought gold from Ophir, brought from Ophir a very great amount of almug wood and precious stones. 12 And the king made of the almug wood supports for the house of the Lord and for the king's house, also lyres and harps for the singers. No such almug wood has come or been seen to this day.

13 And King Solomon gave to the queen of Sheba all that she desired, whatever she asked besides what was given her by the bounty of King Solomon. So she turned and went back to her own land with her servants.

Solomon's Great Wealth

14 Now the weight of gold that came to Solomon in one year was 666 talents of gold, 15 besides that which came from the explorers and from the business of the merchants, and from all the kings of the west and from the governors of the land. 16 King Solomon made 200 large shields of beaten gold; 600 shekels[1] of gold went into each shield. 17 And he made 300 shields of beaten gold; three minas[2] of gold went into each shield. And the king put them in the House of the Forest of Lebanon. 18 The king also made a great ivory throne and overlaid it with the finest gold. 19 The throne had six steps, and the throne had a round top,[3] and on each side of the seat were armrests and two lions standing beside the armrests, 20 while twelve lions stood there, one on each end of a step on the six steps. The like of it was never made in any kingdom. 21 All King Solomon's drinking vessels were of gold, and all the vessels of the House of the Forest of Lebanon were of pure gold. None were of silver; silver was not considered as anything in the days of Solomon. 22 For the king had a fleet of ships of Tarshish at sea with the fleet of Hiram. Once every three years the fleet of ships of Tarshish used to come bringing gold, silver, ivory, apes, and peacocks.[4]

23 Thus King Solomon excelled all the kings of the earth in riches and in wisdom. 24 And the whole earth sought the presence of Solomon to hear his wisdom, which God had put into his mind. 25 Every one of them brought his present, articles of silver and gold, garments, myrrh,[5] spices, horses, and mules, so much year by year.

26 And Solomon gathered together chariots and horsemen. He had 1,400 chariots and 12,000 horsemen, whom he stationed in the chariot cities and with the king in Jerusalem. 27 And the king made silver as common in Jerusalem as stone, and he made cedar as plentiful as the sycamore of the

---

[1] A *shekel* was about 2/5 ounce or 11 grams [2] A *mina* was about 1 1/4 pounds or 0.6 kilogram [3] Or *and at the back of the throne was a calf's head* [4] Or *baboons* [5] Or *armor*

Shephelah. ²⁸ And Solomon's import of horses was from Egypt and Kue, and the king's traders received them from Kue at a price. ²⁹ A chariot could be imported from Egypt for 600 shekels of silver and a horse for 150, and so through the king's traders they were exported to all the kings of the Hittites and the kings of Syria.

Solomon Turns from the Lord

11 Now King Solomon loved many foreign women, along with the daughter of Pharaoh: Moabite, Ammonite, Edomite, Sidonian, and Hittite women, ² from the nations concerning which the Lord had said to the people of Israel, "You shall not enter into marriage with them, neither shall they with you, for surely they will turn away your heart after their gods." Solomon clung to these in love. ³ He had 700 wives, who were princesses, and 300 concubines. And his wives turned away his heart. ⁴ For when Solomon was old his wives turned away his heart after other gods, and his heart was not wholly true to the Lord his God, as was the heart of David his father. ⁵ For Solomon went after Ashtoreth the goddess of the Sidonians, and after Milcom the abomination of the Ammonites. ⁶ So Solomon did what was evil in the sight of the Lord and did not wholly follow the Lord, as David his father had done. ⁷ Then Solomon built a high place for Chemosh the abomination of Moab, and for Molech the abomination of the Ammonites, on the mountain east of Jerusalem. ⁸ And so he did for all his foreign wives, who made offerings and sacrificed to their gods.

The Lord Raises Adversaries

⁹ And the Lord was angry with Solomon, because his heart had turned away from the Lord, the God of Israel, who had appeared to him twice ¹⁰ and had commanded him concerning this thing, that he should not go after other gods. But he did not keep what the Lord commanded. ¹¹ Therefore the Lord said to Solomon, "Since this has been your practice and you have not kept my covenant and my statutes that I have commanded you, I will surely tear the kingdom from you and will give it to your servant. ¹² Yet for the sake of David your father I will not do it in your days, but I will tear it out of the hand of your son. ¹³ However, I will not tear away all the kingdom, but I will give one tribe to your son, for the sake of David my servant and for the sake of Jerusalem that I have chosen."

¹⁴ And the Lord raised up an adversary against Solomon, Hadad the Edomite. He was of the royal house in Edom. ¹⁵ For when David was in Edom, and Joab the commander of the army went up to bury the slain, he

struck down every male in Edom ¹⁶ (for Joab and all Israel remained there six months, until he had cut off every male in Edom). ¹⁷ But Hadad fled to Egypt, together with certain Edomites of his father's servants, Hadad still being a little child. ¹⁸ They set out from Midian and came to Paran and took men with them from Paran and came to Egypt, to Pharaoh king of Egypt, who gave him a house and assigned him an allowance of food and gave him land. ¹⁹ And Hadad found great favor in the sight of Pharaoh, so that he gave him in marriage the sister of his own wife, the sister of Tahpenes the queen. ²⁰ And the sister of Tahpenes bore him Genubath his son, whom Tahpenes weaned in Pharaoh's house. And Genubath was in Pharaoh's house among the sons of Pharaoh. ²¹ But when Hadad heard in Egypt that David slept with his fathers and that Joab the commander of the army was dead, Hadad said to Pharaoh, "Let me depart, that I may go to my own country." ²² But Pharaoh said to him, "What have you lacked with me that you are now seeking to go to your own country?" And he said to him, "Only let me depart."

²³ God also raised up as an adversary to him, Rezon the son of Eliada, who had fled from his master Hadadezer king of Zobah. ²⁴ And he gathered men about him and became leader of a marauding band, after the killing by David. And they went to Damascus and lived there and made him king in Damascus. ²⁵ He was an adversary of Israel all the days of Solomon, doing harm as Hadad did. And he loathed Israel and reigned over Syria.

²⁶ Jeroboam the son of Nebat, an Ephraimite of Zeredah, a servant of Solomon, whose mother's name was Zeruah, a widow, also lifted up his hand against the king. ²⁷ And this was the reason why he lifted up his hand against the king. Solomon built the Millo, and closed up the breach of the city of David his father. ²⁸ The man Jeroboam was very able, and when Solomon saw that the young man was industrious he gave him charge over all the forced labor of the house of Joseph. ²⁹ And at that time, when Jeroboam went out of Jerusalem, the prophet Ahijah the Shilonite found him on the road. Now Ahijah had dressed himself in a new garment, and the two of them were alone in the open country. ³⁰ Then Ahijah laid hold of the new garment that was on him, and tore it into twelve pieces. ³¹ And he said to Jeroboam, "Take for yourself ten pieces, for thus says the Lord, the God of Israel, 'Behold, I am about to tear the kingdom from the hand of Solomon and will give you ten tribes ³² (but he shall have one tribe, for the sake of my servant David and for the sake of Jerusalem, the city that I have chosen out of all the tribes of Israel), ³³ because they have[1] forsaken me and worshiped Ashtoreth the goddess of the Sidonians, Chemosh the god of Moab, and

---

[1] Septuagint, Syriac, Vulgate *he has*; twice in this verse

Milcom the god of the Ammonites, and they have not walked in my ways, doing what is right in my sight and keeping my statutes and my rules, as David his father did. ³⁴ Nevertheless, I will not take the whole kingdom out of his hand, but I will make him ruler all the days of his life, for the sake of David my servant whom I chose, who kept my commandments and my statutes. ³⁵ But I will take the kingdom out of his son's hand and will give it to you, ten tribes. ³⁶ Yet to his son I will give one tribe, that David my servant may always have a lamp before me in Jerusalem, the city where I have chosen to put my name. ³⁷ And I will take you, and you shall reign over all that your soul desires, and you shall be king over Israel. ³⁸ And if you will listen to all that I command you, and will walk in my ways, and do what is right in my eyes by keeping my statutes and my commandments, as David my servant did, I will be with you and will build you a sure house, as I built for David, and I will give Israel to you. ³⁹ And I will afflict the offspring of David because of this, but not forever.'" ⁴⁰ Solomon sought therefore to kill Jeroboam. But Jeroboam arose and fled into Egypt, to Shishak king of Egypt, and was in Egypt until the death of Solomon.

⁴¹ Now the rest of the acts of Solomon, and all that he did, and his wisdom, are they not written in the Book of the Acts of Solomon? ⁴² And the time that Solomon reigned in Jerusalem over all Israel was forty years. ⁴³ And Solomon slept with his fathers and was buried in the city of David his father. And Rehoboam his son reigned in his place.

Rehoboam's Folly

12 Rehoboam went to Shechem, for all Israel had come to Shechem to make him king. ² And as soon as Jeroboam the son of Nebat heard of it (for he was still in Egypt, where he had fled from King Solomon), then Jeroboam returned from[1] Egypt. ³ And they sent and called him, and Jeroboam and all the assembly of Israel came and said to Rehoboam, ⁴ "Your father made our yoke heavy. Now therefore lighten the hard service of your father and his heavy yoke on us, and we will serve you." ⁵ He said to them, "Go away for three days, then come again to me." So the people went away.

⁶ Then King Rehoboam took counsel with the old men, who had stood before Solomon his father while he was yet alive, saying, "How do you advise me to answer this people?" ⁷ And they said to him, "If you will be a servant to this people today and serve them, and speak good words to them when you answer them, then they will be your servants forever." ⁸ But he abandoned the counsel that the old men gave him and took counsel with the young men who

---

[1] Septuagint, Vulgate (compare 2 Chronicles 10:2); Hebrew *lived in*

had grown up with him and stood before him. ⁹ And he said to them, "What do you advise that we answer this people who have said to me, 'Lighten the yoke that your father put on us'?" ¹⁰ And the young men who had grown up with him said to him, "Thus shall you speak to this people who said to you, 'Your father made our yoke heavy, but you lighten it for us,' thus shall you say to them, 'My little finger is thicker than my father's thighs. ¹¹ And now, whereas my father laid on you a heavy yoke, I will add to your yoke. My father disciplined you with whips, but I will discipline you with scorpions.'"

¹² So Jeroboam and all the people came to Rehoboam the third day, as the king said, "Come to me again the third day." ¹³ And the king answered the people harshly, and forsaking the counsel that the old men had given him, ¹⁴ he spoke to them according to the counsel of the young men, saying, "My father made your yoke heavy, but I will add to your yoke. My father disciplined you with whips, but I will discipline you with scorpions." ¹⁵ So the king did not listen to the people, for it was a turn of affairs brought about by the Lord that he might fulfill his word, which the Lord spoke by Ahijah the Shilonite to Jeroboam the son of Nebat.

The Kingdom Divided

¹⁶ And when all Israel saw that the king did not listen to them, the people answered the king, "What portion do we have in David? We have no inheritance in the son of Jesse. To your tents, O Israel! Look now to your own house, David." So Israel went to their tents. ¹⁷ But Rehoboam reigned over the people of Israel who lived in the cities of Judah. ¹⁸ Then King Rehoboam sent Adoram, who was taskmaster over the forced labor, and all Israel stoned him to death with stones. And King Rehoboam hurried to mount his chariot to flee to Jerusalem. ¹⁹ So Israel has been in rebellion against the house of David to this day. ²⁰ And when all Israel heard that Jeroboam had returned, they sent and called him to the assembly and made him king over all Israel. There was none that followed the house of David but the tribe of Judah only.

²¹ When Rehoboam came to Jerusalem, he assembled all the house of Judah and the tribe of Benjamin, 180,000 chosen warriors, to fight against the house of Israel, to restore the kingdom to Rehoboam the son of Solomon. ²² But the word of God came to Shemaiah the man of God: ²³ "Say to Rehoboam the son of Solomon, king of Judah, and to all the house of Judah and Benjamin, and to the rest of the people, ²⁴ 'Thus says the Lord, You shall not go up or fight against your relatives the people of Israel. Every man return to his home, for this thing is from me.'" So they listened to the word of the Lord and went home again, according to the word of the Lord.

Jeroboam's Golden Calves

²⁵ Then Jeroboam built Shechem in the hill country of Ephraim and lived there. And he went out from there and built Penuel. ²⁶ And Jeroboam said in his heart, "Now the kingdom will turn back to the house of David. ²⁷ If this people go up to offer sacrifices in the temple of the Lord at Jerusalem, then the heart of this people will turn again to their lord, to Rehoboam king of Judah, and they will kill me and return to Rehoboam king of Judah." ²⁸ So the king took counsel and made two calves of gold. And he said to the people, "You have gone up to Jerusalem long enough. Behold your gods, O Israel, who brought you up out of the land of Egypt." ²⁹ And he set one in Bethel, and the other he put in Dan. ³⁰ Then this thing became a sin, for the people went as far as Dan to be before one.¹ ³¹ He also made temples on high places and appointed priests from among all the people, who were not of the Levites. ³² And Jeroboam appointed a feast on the fifteenth day of the eighth month like the feast that was in Judah, and he offered sacrifices on the altar. So he did in Bethel, sacrificing to the calves that he made. And he placed in Bethel the priests of the high places that he had made. ³³ He went up to the altar that he had made in Bethel on the fifteenth day in the eighth month, in the month that he had devised from his own heart. And he instituted a feast for the people of Israel and went up to the altar to make offerings.

A Man of God Confronts Jeroboam

13 And behold, a man of God came out of Judah by the word of the Lord to Bethel. Jeroboam was standing by the altar to make offerings. ² And the man cried against the altar by the word of the Lord and said, "O altar, altar, thus says the Lord: 'Behold, a son shall be born to the house of David, Josiah by name, and he shall sacrifice on you the priests of the high places who make offerings on you, and human bones shall be burned on you.'" ³ And he gave a sign the same day, saying, "This is the sign that the Lord has spoken: 'Behold, the altar shall be torn down, and the ashes that are on it shall be poured out.'" ⁴ And when the king heard the saying of the man of God, which he cried against the altar at Bethel, Jeroboam stretched out his hand from the altar, saying, "Seize him." And his hand, which he stretched out against him, dried up, so that he could not draw it back to himself. ⁵ The altar also was torn down, and the ashes poured out from the altar, according to the sign that the man of God had given by the word of the Lord. ⁶ And the king said to the man of God, "Entreat now the favor of the Lord your God, and pray for me, that my hand may be restored to me." And the man of God

---
¹ Septuagint *went to the one at Bethel and to the other as far as Dan*

entreated the Lord, and the king's hand was restored to him and became as it was before. ⁷ And the king said to the man of God, "Come home with me, and refresh yourself, and I will give you a reward." ⁸ And the man of God said to the king, "If you give me half your house, I will not go in with you. And I will not eat bread or drink water in this place, ⁹ for so was it commanded me by the word of the Lord, saying, 'You shall neither eat bread nor drink water nor return by the way that you came.'" ¹⁰ So he went another way and did not return by the way that he came to Bethel.

The Prophet's Disobedience

¹¹ Now an old prophet lived in Bethel. And his sons[1] came and told him all that the man of God had done that day in Bethel. They also told to their father the words that he had spoken to the king. ¹² And their father said to them, "Which way did he go?" And his sons showed him the way that the man of God who came from Judah had gone. ¹³ And he said to his sons, "Saddle the donkey for me." So they saddled the donkey for him and he mounted it. ¹⁴ And he went after the man of God and found him sitting under an oak. And he said to him, "Are you the man of God who came from Judah?" And he said, "I am." ¹⁵ Then he said to him, "Come home with me and eat bread." ¹⁶ And he said, "I may not return with you, or go in with you, neither will I eat bread nor drink water with you in this place, ¹⁷ for it was said to me by the word of the Lord, 'You shall neither eat bread nor drink water there, nor return by the way that you came.'" ¹⁸ And he said to him, "I also am a prophet as you are, and an angel spoke to me by the word of the Lord, saying, 'Bring him back with you into your house that he may eat bread and drink water.'" But he lied to him. ¹⁹ So he went back with him and ate bread in his house and drank water.

²⁰ And as they sat at the table, the word of the Lord came to the prophet who had brought him back. ²¹ And he cried to the man of God who came from Judah, "Thus says the Lord, 'Because you have disobeyed the word of the Lord and have not kept the command that the Lord your God commanded you, ²² but have come back and have eaten bread and drunk water in the place of which he said to you, "Eat no bread and drink no water," your body shall not come to the tomb of your fathers.'" ²³ And after he had eaten bread and drunk, he saddled the donkey for the prophet whom he had brought back. ²⁴ And as he went away a lion met him on the road and killed him. And his body was thrown in the road, and the donkey stood beside it; the lion also stood beside the body. ²⁵ And behold, men passed by and saw the body thrown

---

[1] Septuagint, Syriac, Vulgate; Hebrew *son*

in the road and the lion standing by the body. And they came and told it in the city where the old prophet lived.

⁲⁶ And when the prophet who had brought him back from the way heard of it, he said, "It is the man of God who disobeyed the word of the Lord; therefore the Lord has given him to the lion, which has torn him and killed him, according to the word that the Lord spoke to him." ²⁷ And he said to his sons, "Saddle the donkey for me." And they saddled it. ²⁸ And he went and found his body thrown in the road, and the donkey and the lion standing beside the body. The lion had not eaten the body or torn the donkey. ²⁹ And the prophet took up the body of the man of God and laid it on the donkey and brought it back to the city¹ to mourn and to bury him. ³⁰ And he laid the body in his own grave. And they mourned over him, saying, "Alas, my brother!" ³¹ And after he had buried him, he said to his sons, "When I die, bury me in the grave in which the man of God is buried; lay my bones beside his bones. ³² For the saying that he called out by the word of the Lord against the altar in Bethel and against all the houses of the high places that are in the cities of Samaria shall surely come to pass."

³³ After this thing Jeroboam did not turn from his evil way, but made priests for the high places again from among all the people. Any who would, he ordained to be priests of the high places. ³⁴ And this thing became sin to the house of Jeroboam, so as to cut it off and to destroy it from the face of the earth.

Prophecy Against Jeroboam

14 At that time Abijah the son of Jeroboam fell sick. ² And Jeroboam said to his wife, "Arise, and disguise yourself, that it not be known that you are the wife of Jeroboam, and go to Shiloh. Behold, Ahijah the prophet is there, who said of me that I should be king over this people. ³ Take with you ten loaves, some cakes, and a jar of honey, and go to him. He will tell you what shall happen to the child."

⁴ Jeroboam's wife did so. She arose and went to Shiloh and came to the house of Ahijah. Now Ahijah could not see, for his eyes were dim because of his age. ⁵ And the Lord said to Ahijah, "Behold, the wife of Jeroboam is coming to inquire of you concerning her son, for he is sick. Thus and thus shall you say to her."

When she came, she pretended to be another woman. ⁶ But when Ahijah heard the sound of her feet, as she came in at the door, he said, "Come in, wife of Jeroboam. Why do you pretend to be another? For I am charged

---

¹ Septuagint; Hebrew *he came to the city of the old prophet*

with unbearable news for you. ⁷ Go, tell Jeroboam, 'Thus says the LORD, the God of Israel: "Because I exalted you from among the people and made you leader over my people Israel ⁸ and tore the kingdom away from the house of David and gave it to you, and yet you have not been like my servant David, who kept my commandments and followed me with all his heart, doing only that which was right in my eyes, ⁹ but you have done evil above all who were before you and have gone and made for yourself other gods and metal images, provoking me to anger, and have cast me behind your back, ¹⁰ therefore behold, I will bring harm upon the house of Jeroboam and will cut off from Jeroboam every male, both bond and free in Israel, and will burn up the house of Jeroboam, as a man burns up dung until it is all gone. ¹¹ Anyone belonging to Jeroboam who dies in the city the dogs shall eat, and anyone who dies in the open country the birds of the heavens shall eat, for the LORD has spoken it."' ¹² Arise therefore, go to your house. When your feet enter the city, the child shall die. ¹³ And all Israel shall mourn for him and bury him, for he only of Jeroboam shall come to the grave, because in him there is found something pleasing to the LORD, the God of Israel, in the house of Jeroboam. ¹⁴ Moreover, the LORD will raise up for himself a king over Israel who shall cut off the house of Jeroboam today. And henceforth, ¹⁵ the LORD will strike Israel as a reed is shaken in the water, and root up Israel out of this good land that he gave to their fathers and scatter them beyond the Euphrates,[1] because they have made their Asherim, provoking the LORD to anger. ¹⁶ And he will give Israel up because of the sins of Jeroboam, which he sinned and made Israel to sin."

¹⁷ Then Jeroboam's wife arose and departed and came to Tirzah. And as she came to the threshold of the house, the child died. ¹⁸ And all Israel buried him and mourned for him, according to the word of the LORD, which he spoke by his servant Ahijah the prophet.

The Death of Jeroboam

¹⁹ Now the rest of the acts of Jeroboam, how he warred and how he reigned, behold, they are written in the Book of the Chronicles of the Kings of Israel. ²⁰ And the time that Jeroboam reigned was twenty-two years. And he slept with his fathers, and Nadab his son reigned in his place.

Rehoboam Reigns in Judah

²¹ Now Rehoboam the son of Solomon reigned in Judah. Rehoboam was forty-one years old when he began to reign, and he reigned seventeen years

[1] Hebrew *the River*

in Jerusalem, the city that the LORD had chosen out of all the tribes of Israel, to put his name there. His mother's name was Naamah the Ammonite. ²² And Judah did what was evil in the sight of the LORD, and they provoked him to jealousy with their sins that they committed, more than all that their fathers had done. ²³ For they also built for themselves high places and pillars and Asherim on every high hill and under every green tree, ²⁴ and there were also male cult prostitutes in the land. They did according to all the abominations of the nations that the LORD drove out before the people of Israel.

²⁵ In the fifth year of King Rehoboam, Shishak king of Egypt came up against Jerusalem. ²⁶ He took away the treasures of the house of the LORD and the treasures of the king's house. He took away everything. He also took away all the shields of gold that Solomon had made, ²⁷ and King Rehoboam made in their place shields of bronze, and committed them to the hands of the officers of the guard, who kept the door of the king's house. ²⁸ And as often as the king went into the house of the LORD, the guard carried them and brought them back to the guardroom.

²⁹ Now the rest of the acts of Rehoboam and all that he did, are they not written in the Book of the Chronicles of the Kings of Judah? ³⁰ And there was war between Rehoboam and Jeroboam continually. ³¹ And Rehoboam slept with his fathers and was buried with his fathers in the city of David. His mother's name was Naamah the Ammonite. And Abijam his son reigned in his place.

Abijam Reigns in Judah

15 Now in the eighteenth year of King Jeroboam the son of Nebat, Abijam began to reign over Judah. ² He reigned for three years in Jerusalem. His mother's name was Maacah the daughter of Abishalom. ³ And he walked in all the sins that his father did before him, and his heart was not wholly true to the LORD his God, as the heart of David his father. ⁴ Nevertheless, for David's sake the LORD his God gave him a lamp in Jerusalem, setting up his son after him, and establishing Jerusalem, ⁵ because David did what was right in the eyes of the LORD and did not turn aside from anything that he commanded him all the days of his life, except in the matter of Uriah the Hittite. ⁶ Now there was war between Rehoboam and Jeroboam all the days of his life. ⁷ The rest of the acts of Abijam and all that he did, are they not written in the Book of the Chronicles of the Kings of Judah? And there was war between Abijam and Jeroboam. ⁸ And Abijam slept with his fathers, and they buried him in the city of David. And Asa his son reigned in his place.

Asa Reigns in Judah

⁹ In the twentieth year of Jeroboam king of Israel, Asa began to reign over Judah, ¹⁰ and he reigned forty-one years in Jerusalem. His mother's name was Maacah the daughter of Abishalom. ¹¹ And Asa did what was right in the eyes of the Lord, as David his father had done. ¹² He put away the male cult prostitutes out of the land and removed all the idols that his fathers had made. ¹³ He also removed Maacah his mother from being queen mother because she had made an abominable image for Asherah. And Asa cut down her image and burned it at the brook Kidron. ¹⁴ But the high places were not taken away. Nevertheless, the heart of Asa was wholly true to the Lord all his days. ¹⁵ And he brought into the house of the Lord the sacred gifts of his father and his own sacred gifts, silver, and gold, and vessels.

¹⁶ And there was war between Asa and Baasha king of Israel all their days. ¹⁷ Baasha king of Israel went up against Judah and built Ramah, that he might permit no one to go out or come in to Asa king of Judah. ¹⁸ Then Asa took all the silver and the gold that were left in the treasures of the house of the Lord and the treasures of the king's house and gave them into the hands of his servants. And King Asa sent them to Ben-hadad the son of Tabrimmon, the son of Hezion, king of Syria, who lived in Damascus, saying, ¹⁹ "Let there be a covenant[1] between me and you, as there was between my father and your father. Behold, I am sending to you a present of silver and gold. Go, break your covenant with Baasha king of Israel, that he may withdraw from me." ²⁰ And Ben-hadad listened to King Asa and sent the commanders of his armies against the cities of Israel and conquered Ijon, Dan, Abel-beth-maacah, and all Chinneroth, with all the land of Naphtali. ²¹ And when Baasha heard of it, he stopped building Ramah, and he lived in Tirzah. ²² Then King Asa made a proclamation to all Judah, none was exempt, and they carried away the stones of Ramah and its timber, with which Baasha had been building, and with them King Asa built Geba of Benjamin and Mizpah. ²³ Now the rest of all the acts of Asa, all his might, and all that he did, and the cities that he built, are they not written in the Book of the Chronicles of the Kings of Judah? But in his old age he was diseased in his feet. ²⁴ And Asa slept with his fathers and was buried with his fathers in the city of David his father, and Jehoshaphat his son reigned in his place.

Nadab Reigns in Israel

²⁵ Nadab the son of Jeroboam began to reign over Israel in the second year of Asa king of Judah, and he reigned over Israel two years. ²⁶ He did what was

---

[1] Or *treaty*; twice in this verse

evil in the sight of the Lord and walked in the way of his father, and in his sin which he made Israel to sin.

²⁷ Baasha the son of Ahijah, of the house of Issachar, conspired against him. And Baasha struck him down at Gibbethon, which belonged to the Philistines, for Nadab and all Israel were laying siege to Gibbethon. ²⁸ So Baasha killed him in the third year of Asa king of Judah and reigned in his place. ²⁹ And as soon as he was king, he killed all the house of Jeroboam. He left to the house of Jeroboam not one that breathed, until he had destroyed it, according to the word of the Lord that he spoke by his servant Ahijah the Shilonite. ³⁰ It was for the sins of Jeroboam that he sinned and that he made Israel to sin, and because of the anger to which he provoked the Lord, the God of Israel.

³¹ Now the rest of the acts of Nadab and all that he did, are they not written in the Book of the Chronicles of the Kings of Israel? ³² And there was war between Asa and Baasha king of Israel all their days.

Baasha Reigns in Israel

³³ In the third year of Asa king of Judah, Baasha the son of Ahijah began to reign over all Israel at Tirzah, and he reigned twenty-four years. ³⁴ He did what was evil in the sight of the Lord and walked in the way of Jeroboam and in his sin which he made Israel to sin.

16 And the word of the Lord came to Jehu the son of Hanani against Baasha, saying, ² "Since I exalted you out of the dust and made you leader over my people Israel, and you have walked in the way of Jeroboam and have made my people Israel to sin, provoking me to anger with their sins, ³ behold, I will utterly sweep away Baasha and his house, and I will make your house like the house of Jeroboam the son of Nebat. ⁴ Anyone belonging to Baasha who dies in the city the dogs shall eat, and anyone of his who dies in the field the birds of the heavens shall eat."

⁵ Now the rest of the acts of Baasha and what he did, and his might, are they not written in the Book of the Chronicles of the Kings of Israel? ⁶ And Baasha slept with his fathers and was buried at Tirzah, and Elah his son reigned in his place. ⁷ Moreover, the word of the Lord came by the prophet Jehu the son of Hanani against Baasha and his house, both because of all the evil that he did in the sight of the Lord, provoking him to anger with the work of his hands, in being like the house of Jeroboam, and also because he destroyed it.

Elah Reigns in Israel

⁸ In the twenty-sixth year of Asa king of Judah, Elah the son of Baasha began to reign over Israel in Tirzah, and he reigned two years. ⁹ But his servant

Zimri, commander of half his chariots, conspired against him. When he was at Tirzah, drinking himself drunk in the house of Arza, who was over the household in Tirzah, [10] Zimri came in and struck him down and killed him, in the twenty-seventh year of Asa king of Judah, and reigned in his place.

[11] When he began to reign, as soon as he had seated himself on his throne, he struck down all the house of Baasha. He did not leave him a single male of his relatives or his friends. [12] Thus Zimri destroyed all the house of Baasha, according to the word of the Lord, which he spoke against Baasha by Jehu the prophet, [13] for all the sins of Baasha and the sins of Elah his son, which they sinned and which they made Israel to sin, provoking the Lord God of Israel to anger with their idols. [14] Now the rest of the acts of Elah and all that he did, are they not written in the Book of the Chronicles of the Kings of Israel?

Zimri Reigns in Israel

[15] In the twenty-seventh year of Asa king of Judah, Zimri reigned seven days in Tirzah. Now the troops were encamped against Gibbethon, which belonged to the Philistines, [16] and the troops who were encamped heard it said, "Zimri has conspired, and he has killed the king." Therefore all Israel made Omri, the commander of the army, king over Israel that day in the camp. [17] So Omri went up from Gibbethon, and all Israel with him, and they besieged Tirzah. [18] And when Zimri saw that the city was taken, he went into the citadel of the king's house and burned the king's house over him with fire and died, [19] because of his sins that he committed, doing evil in the sight of the Lord, walking in the way of Jeroboam, and for his sin which he committed, making Israel to sin. [20] Now the rest of the acts of Zimri, and the conspiracy that he made, are they not written in the Book of the Chronicles of the Kings of Israel?

Omri Reigns in Israel

[21] Then the people of Israel were divided into two parts. Half of the people followed Tibni the son of Ginath, to make him king, and half followed Omri. [22] But the people who followed Omri overcame the people who followed Tibni the son of Ginath. So Tibni died, and Omri became king. [23] In the thirty-first year of Asa king of Judah, Omri began to reign over Israel, and he reigned for twelve years; six years he reigned in Tirzah. [24] He bought the hill of Samaria from Shemer for two talents[1] of silver, and he fortified the hill and called the name of the city that he built Samaria, after the name of Shemer, the owner of the hill.

---

[1] A *talent* was about 75 pounds or 34 kilograms

⁲⁵ Omri did what was evil in the sight of the Lord, and did more evil than all who were before him. ²⁶ For he walked in all the way of Jeroboam the son of Nebat, and in the sins that he made Israel to sin, provoking the Lord, the God of Israel, to anger by their idols. ²⁷ Now the rest of the acts of Omri that he did, and the might that he showed, are they not written in the Book of the Chronicles of the Kings of Israel? ²⁸ And Omri slept with his fathers and was buried in Samaria, and Ahab his son reigned in his place.

Ahab Reigns in Israel

²⁹ In the thirty-eighth year of Asa king of Judah, Ahab the son of Omri began to reign over Israel, and Ahab the son of Omri reigned over Israel in Samaria twenty-two years. ³⁰ And Ahab the son of Omri did evil in the sight of the Lord, more than all who were before him. ³¹ And as if it had been a light thing for him to walk in the sins of Jeroboam the son of Nebat, he took for his wife Jezebel the daughter of Ethbaal king of the Sidonians, and went and served Baal and worshiped him. ³² He erected an altar for Baal in the house of Baal, which he built in Samaria. ³³ And Ahab made an Asherah. Ahab did more to provoke the Lord, the God of Israel, to anger than all the kings of Israel who were before him. ³⁴ In his days Hiel of Bethel built Jericho. He laid its foundation at the cost of Abiram his firstborn, and set up its gates at the cost of his youngest son Segub, according to the word of the Lord, which he spoke by Joshua the son of Nun.

Elijah Predicts a Drought

17 Now Elijah the Tishbite, of Tishbe[1] in Gilead, said to Ahab, "As the Lord, the God of Israel, lives, before whom I stand, there shall be neither dew nor rain these years, except by my word." ² And the word of the Lord came to him: ³ "Depart from here and turn eastward and hide yourself by the brook Cherith, which is east of the Jordan. ⁴ You shall drink from the brook, and I have commanded the ravens to feed you there." ⁵ So he went and did according to the word of the Lord. He went and lived by the brook Cherith that is east of the Jordan. ⁶ And the ravens brought him bread and meat in the morning, and bread and meat in the evening, and he drank from the brook. ⁷ And after a while the brook dried up, because there was no rain in the land.

The Widow of Zarephath

⁸ Then the word of the Lord came to him, ⁹ "Arise, go to Zarephath, which belongs to Sidon, and dwell there. Behold, I have commanded a widow there

[1] Septuagint; Hebrew *of the settlers*

to feed you." ¹⁰ So he arose and went to Zarephath. And when he came to the gate of the city, behold, a widow was there gathering sticks. And he called to her and said, "Bring me a little water in a vessel, that I may drink." ¹¹ And as she was going to bring it, he called to her and said, "Bring me a morsel of bread in your hand." ¹² And she said, "As the LORD your God lives, I have nothing baked, only a handful of flour in a jar and a little oil in a jug. And now I am gathering a couple of sticks that I may go in and prepare it for myself and my son, that we may eat it and die." ¹³ And Elijah said to her, "Do not fear; go and do as you have said. But first make me a little cake of it and bring it to me, and afterward make something for yourself and your son. ¹⁴ For thus says the LORD, the God of Israel, 'The jar of flour shall not be spent, and the jug of oil shall not be empty, until the day that the LORD sends rain upon the earth.'" ¹⁵ And she went and did as Elijah said. And she and he and her household ate for many days. ¹⁶ The jar of flour was not spent, neither did the jug of oil become empty, according to the word of the LORD that he spoke by Elijah.

Elijah Raises the Widow's Son

¹⁷ After this the son of the woman, the mistress of the house, became ill. And his illness was so severe that there was no breath left in him. ¹⁸ And she said to Elijah, "What have you against me, O man of God? You have come to me to bring my sin to remembrance and to cause the death of my son!" ¹⁹ And he said to her, "Give me your son." And he took him from her arms and carried him up into the upper chamber where he lodged, and laid him on his own bed. ²⁰ And he cried to the LORD, "O LORD my God, have you brought calamity even upon the widow with whom I sojourn, by killing her son?" ²¹ Then he stretched himself upon the child three times and cried to the LORD, "O LORD my God, let this child's life¹ come into him again." ²² And the LORD listened to the voice of Elijah. And the life of the child came into him again, and he revived. ²³ And Elijah took the child and brought him down from the upper chamber into the house and delivered him to his mother. And Elijah said, "See, your son lives." ²⁴ And the woman said to Elijah, "Now I know that you are a man of God, and that the word of the LORD in your mouth is truth."

Elijah Confronts Ahab

18 After many days the word of the LORD came to Elijah, in the third year, saying, "Go, show yourself to Ahab, and I will send rain upon the earth." ² So Elijah went to show himself to Ahab. Now the famine was

¹ Or *soul*; also verse 22

severe in Samaria. ³ And Ahab called Obadiah, who was over the household. (Now Obadiah feared the Lord greatly, ⁴ and when Jezebel cut off the prophets of the Lord, Obadiah took a hundred prophets and hid them by fifties in a cave and fed them with bread and water.) ⁵ And Ahab said to Obadiah, "Go through the land to all the springs of water and to all the valleys. Perhaps we may find grass and save the horses and mules alive, and not lose some of the animals." ⁶ So they divided the land between them to pass through it. Ahab went in one direction by himself, and Obadiah went in another direction by himself.

⁷ And as Obadiah was on the way, behold, Elijah met him. And Obadiah recognized him and fell on his face and said, "Is it you, my lord Elijah?" ⁸ And he answered him, "It is I. Go, tell your lord, 'Behold, Elijah is here.'" ⁹ And he said, "How have I sinned, that you would give your servant into the hand of Ahab, to kill me? ¹⁰ As the Lord your God lives, there is no nation or kingdom where my lord has not sent to seek you. And when they would say, 'He is not here,' he would take an oath of the kingdom or nation, that they had not found you. ¹¹ And now you say, 'Go, tell your lord, "Behold, Elijah is here."' ¹² And as soon as I have gone from you, the Spirit of the Lord will carry you I know not where. And so, when I come and tell Ahab and he cannot find you, he will kill me, although I your servant have feared the Lord from my youth. ¹³ Has it not been told my lord what I did when Jezebel killed the prophets of the Lord, how I hid a hundred men of the Lord's prophets by fifties in a cave and fed them with bread and water? ¹⁴ And now you say, 'Go, tell your lord, "Behold, Elijah is here"'; and he will kill me." ¹⁵ And Elijah said, "As the Lord of hosts lives, before whom I stand, I will surely show myself to him today." ¹⁶ So Obadiah went to meet Ahab, and told him. And Ahab went to meet Elijah.

¹⁷ When Ahab saw Elijah, Ahab said to him, "Is it you, you troubler of Israel?" ¹⁸ And he answered, "I have not troubled Israel, but you have, and your father's house, because you have abandoned the commandments of the Lord and followed the Baals. ¹⁹ Now therefore send and gather all Israel to me at Mount Carmel, and the 450 prophets of Baal and the 400 prophets of Asherah, who eat at Jezebel's table."

The Prophets of Baal Defeated

²⁰ So Ahab sent to all the people of Israel and gathered the prophets together at Mount Carmel. ²¹ And Elijah came near to all the people and said, "How long will you go limping between two different opinions? If the Lord is God, follow him; but if Baal, then follow him." And the people did not

answer him a word. ²² Then Elijah said to the people, "I, even I only, am left a prophet of the Lord, but Baal's prophets are 450 men. ²³ Let two bulls be given to us, and let them choose one bull for themselves and cut it in pieces and lay it on the wood, but put no fire to it. And I will prepare the other bull and lay it on the wood and put no fire to it. ²⁴ And you call upon the name of your god, and I will call upon the name of the Lord, and the God who answers by fire, he is God." And all the people answered, "It is well spoken." ²⁵ Then Elijah said to the prophets of Baal, "Choose for yourselves one bull and prepare it first, for you are many, and call upon the name of your god, but put no fire to it." ²⁶ And they took the bull that was given them, and they prepared it and called upon the name of Baal from morning until noon, saying, "O Baal, answer us!" But there was no voice, and no one answered. And they limped around the altar that they had made. ²⁷ And at noon Elijah mocked them, saying, "Cry aloud, for he is a god. Either he is musing, or he is relieving himself, or he is on a journey, or perhaps he is asleep and must be awakened." ²⁸ And they cried aloud and cut themselves after their custom with swords and lances, until the blood gushed out upon them. ²⁹ And as midday passed, they raved on until the time of the offering of the oblation, but there was no voice. No one answered; no one paid attention.

³⁰ Then Elijah said to all the people, "Come near to me." And all the people came near to him. And he repaired the altar of the Lord that had been thrown down. ³¹ Elijah took twelve stones, according to the number of the tribes of the sons of Jacob, to whom the word of the Lord came, saying, "Israel shall be your name," ³² and with the stones he built an altar in the name of the Lord. And he made a trench about the altar, as great as would contain two seahs¹ of seed. ³³ And he put the wood in order and cut the bull in pieces and laid it on the wood. And he said, "Fill four jars with water and pour it on the burnt offering and on the wood." ³⁴ And he said, "Do it a second time." And they did it a second time. And he said, "Do it a third time." And they did it a third time. ³⁵ And the water ran around the altar and filled the trench also with water.

³⁶ And at the time of the offering of the oblation, Elijah the prophet came near and said, "O Lord, God of Abraham, Isaac, and Israel, let it be known this day that you are God in Israel, and that I am your servant, and that I have done all these things at your word. ³⁷ Answer me, O Lord, answer me, that this people may know that you, O Lord, are God, and that you have turned their hearts back." ³⁸ Then the fire of the Lord fell and consumed the burnt offering and the wood and the stones and the dust, and licked up the water that was in the trench. ³⁹ And when all the people saw it, they fell on their faces and said,

---

¹ A *seah* was about 7.7 quarts or 7.3 liters

"The Lord, he is God; the Lord, he is God." ⁴⁰ And Elijah said to them, "Seize the prophets of Baal; let not one of them escape." And they seized them. And Elijah brought them down to the brook Kishon and slaughtered them there.

The Lord Sends Rain

⁴¹ And Elijah said to Ahab, "Go up, eat and drink, for there is a sound of the rushing of rain." ⁴² So Ahab went up to eat and to drink. And Elijah went up to the top of Mount Carmel. And he bowed himself down on the earth and put his face between his knees. ⁴³ And he said to his servant, "Go up now, look toward the sea." And he went up and looked and said, "There is nothing." And he said, "Go again," seven times. ⁴⁴ And at the seventh time he said, "Behold, a little cloud like a man's hand is rising from the sea." And he said, "Go up, say to Ahab, 'Prepare your chariot and go down, lest the rain stop you.'" ⁴⁵ And in a little while the heavens grew black with clouds and wind, and there was a great rain. And Ahab rode and went to Jezreel. ⁴⁶ And the hand of the Lord was on Elijah, and he gathered up his garment and ran before Ahab to the entrance of Jezreel.

Elijah Flees Jezebel

19 Ahab told Jezebel all that Elijah had done, and how he had killed all the prophets with the sword. ² Then Jezebel sent a messenger to Elijah, saying, "So may the gods do to me and more also, if I do not make your life as the life of one of them by this time tomorrow." ³ Then he was afraid, and he arose and ran for his life and came to Beersheba, which belongs to Judah, and left his servant there.

⁴ But he himself went a day's journey into the wilderness and came and sat down under a broom tree. And he asked that he might die, saying, "It is enough; now, O Lord, take away my life, for I am no better than my fathers." ⁵ And he lay down and slept under a broom tree. And behold, an angel touched him and said to him, "Arise and eat." ⁶ And he looked, and behold, there was at his head a cake baked on hot stones and a jar of water. And he ate and drank and lay down again. ⁷ And the angel of the Lord came again a second time and touched him and said, "Arise and eat, for the journey is too great for you." ⁸ And he arose and ate and drank, and went in the strength of that food forty days and forty nights to Horeb, the mount of God.

The Lord Speaks to Elijah

⁹ There he came to a cave and lodged in it. And behold, the word of the Lord came to him, and he said to him, "What are you doing here, Elijah?"

¹⁰ He said, "I have been very jealous for the Lord, the God of hosts. For the people of Israel have forsaken your covenant, thrown down your altars, and killed your prophets with the sword, and I, even I only, am left, and they seek my life, to take it away." ¹¹ And he said, "Go out and stand on the mount before the Lord." And behold, the Lord passed by, and a great and strong wind tore the mountains and broke in pieces the rocks before the Lord, but the Lord was not in the wind. And after the wind an earthquake, but the Lord was not in the earthquake. ¹² And after the earthquake a fire, but the Lord was not in the fire. And after the fire the sound of a low whisper.[1] ¹³ And when Elijah heard it, he wrapped his face in his cloak and went out and stood at the entrance of the cave. And behold, there came a voice to him and said, "What are you doing here, Elijah?" ¹⁴ He said, "I have been very jealous for the Lord, the God of hosts. For the people of Israel have forsaken your covenant, thrown down your altars, and killed your prophets with the sword, and I, even I only, am left, and they seek my life, to take it away." ¹⁵ And the Lord said to him, "Go, return on your way to the wilderness of Damascus. And when you arrive, you shall anoint Hazael to be king over Syria. ¹⁶ And Jehu the son of Nimshi you shall anoint to be king over Israel, and Elisha the son of Shaphat of Abel-meholah you shall anoint to be prophet in your place. ¹⁷ And the one who escapes from the sword of Hazael shall Jehu put to death, and the one who escapes from the sword of Jehu shall Elisha put to death. ¹⁸ Yet I will leave seven thousand in Israel, all the knees that have not bowed to Baal, and every mouth that has not kissed him."

The Call of Elisha

¹⁹ So he departed from there and found Elisha the son of Shaphat, who was plowing with twelve yoke of oxen in front of him, and he was with the twelfth. Elijah passed by him and cast his cloak upon him. ²⁰ And he left the oxen and ran after Elijah and said, "Let me kiss my father and my mother, and then I will follow you." And he said to him, "Go back again, for what have I done to you?" ²¹ And he returned from following him and took the yoke of oxen and sacrificed them and boiled their flesh with the yokes of the oxen and gave it to the people, and they ate. Then he arose and went after Elijah and assisted him.

Ahab's Wars with Syria

20 Ben-hadad the king of Syria gathered all his army together. Thirty-two kings were with him, and horses and chariots. And he went up and closed in on Samaria and fought against it. ² And he sent messengers

---

[1] Or *a sound, a thin silence*

into the city to Ahab king of Israel and said to him, "Thus says Ben-hadad: ³'Your silver and your gold are mine; your best wives and children also are mine.'" ⁴And the king of Israel answered, "As you say, my lord, O king, I am yours, and all that I have." ⁵The messengers came again and said, "Thus says Ben-hadad: 'I sent to you, saying, "Deliver to me your silver and your gold, your wives and your children." ⁶Nevertheless I will send my servants to you tomorrow about this time, and they shall search your house and the houses of your servants and lay hands on whatever pleases you and take it away.'"

⁷Then the king of Israel called all the elders of the land and said, "Mark, now, and see how this man is seeking trouble, for he sent to me for my wives and my children, and for my silver and my gold, and I did not refuse him." ⁸And all the elders and all the people said to him, "Do not listen or consent." ⁹So he said to the messengers of Ben-hadad, "Tell my lord the king, 'All that you first demanded of your servant I will do, but this thing I cannot do.'" And the messengers departed and brought him word again. ¹⁰Ben-hadad sent to him and said, "The gods do so to me and more also, if the dust of Samaria shall suffice for handfuls for all the people who follow me." ¹¹And the king of Israel answered, "Tell him, 'Let not him who straps on his armor boast himself as he who takes it off.'" ¹²When Ben-hadad heard this message as he was drinking with the kings in the booths, he said to his men, "Take your positions." And they took their positions against the city.

Ahab Defeats Ben-hadad

¹³And behold, a prophet came near to Ahab king of Israel and said, "Thus says the Lord, Have you seen all this great multitude? Behold, I will give it into your hand this day, and you shall know that I am the Lord." ¹⁴And Ahab said, "By whom?" He said, "Thus says the Lord, By the servants of the governors of the districts." Then he said, "Who shall begin the battle?" He answered, "You." ¹⁵Then he mustered the servants of the governors of the districts, and they were 232. And after them he mustered all the people of Israel, seven thousand.

¹⁶And they went out at noon, while Ben-hadad was drinking himself drunk in the booths, he and the thirty-two kings who helped him. ¹⁷The servants of the governors of the districts went out first. And Ben-hadad sent out scouts, and they reported to him, "Men are coming out from Samaria." ¹⁸He said, "If they have come out for peace, take them alive. Or if they have come out for war, take them alive."

¹⁹So these went out of the city, the servants of the governors of the districts and the army that followed them. ²⁰And each struck down his man. The

Syrians fled, and Israel pursued them, but Ben-hadad king of Syria escaped on a horse with horsemen. ²¹ And the king of Israel went out and struck the horses and chariots, and struck the Syrians with a great blow.

²² Then the prophet came near to the king of Israel and said to him, "Come, strengthen yourself, and consider well what you have to do, for in the spring the king of Syria will come up against you."

²³ And the servants of the king of Syria said to him, "Their gods are gods of the hills, and so they were stronger than we. But let us fight against them in the plain, and surely we shall be stronger than they. ²⁴ And do this: remove the kings, each from his post, and put commanders in their places, ²⁵ and muster an army like the army that you have lost, horse for horse, and chariot for chariot. Then we will fight against them in the plain, and surely we shall be stronger than they." And he listened to their voice and did so.

Ahab Defeats Ben-hadad Again

²⁶ In the spring, Ben-hadad mustered the Syrians and went up to Aphek to fight against Israel. ²⁷ And the people of Israel were mustered and were provisioned and went against them. The people of Israel encamped before them like two little flocks of goats, but the Syrians filled the country. ²⁸ And a man of God came near and said to the king of Israel, "Thus says the LORD, 'Because the Syrians have said, "The LORD is a god of the hills but he is not a god of the valleys," therefore I will give all this great multitude into your hand, and you shall know that I am the LORD.'" ²⁹ And they encamped opposite one another seven days. Then on the seventh day the battle was joined. And the people of Israel struck down of the Syrians 100,000 foot soldiers in one day. ³⁰ And the rest fled into the city of Aphek, and the wall fell upon 27,000 men who were left.

Ben-hadad also fled and entered an inner chamber in the city. ³¹ And his servants said to him, "Behold now, we have heard that the kings of the house of Israel are merciful kings. Let us put sackcloth around our waists and ropes on our heads and go out to the king of Israel. Perhaps he will spare your life." ³² So they tied sackcloth around their waists and put ropes on their heads and went to the king of Israel and said, "Your servant Ben-hadad says, 'Please, let me live.'" And he said, "Does he still live? He is my brother." ³³ Now the men were watching for a sign, and they quickly took it up from him and said, "Yes, your brother Ben-hadad." Then he said, "Go and bring him." Then Ben-hadad came out to him, and he caused him to come up into the chariot. ³⁴ And Ben-hadad said to him, "The cities that my father took from your father I will restore, and you may establish bazaars for yourself in Damascus, as my father did in Samaria." And Ahab said, "I will let you go on these terms." So he made a covenant with him and let him go.

A Prophet Condemns Ben-hadad's Release

⁣³⁵ And a certain man of the sons of the prophets said to his fellow at the command of the Lord, "Strike me, please." But the man refused to strike him. ³⁶ Then he said to him, "Because you have not obeyed the voice of the Lord, behold, as soon as you have gone from me, a lion shall strike you down." And as soon as he had departed from him, a lion met him and struck him down. ³⁷ Then he found another man and said, "Strike me, please." And the man struck him—struck him and wounded him. ³⁸ So the prophet departed and waited for the king by the way, disguising himself with a bandage over his eyes. ³⁹ And as the king passed, he cried to the king and said, "Your servant went out into the midst of the battle, and behold, a soldier turned and brought a man to me and said, 'Guard this man; if by any means he is missing, your life shall be for his life, or else you shall pay a talent[1] of silver.' ⁴⁰ And as your servant was busy here and there, he was gone." The king of Israel said to him, "So shall your judgment be; you yourself have decided it." ⁴¹ Then he hurried to take the bandage away from his eyes, and the king of Israel recognized him as one of the prophets. ⁴² And he said to him, "Thus says the Lord, 'Because you have let go out of your hand the man whom I had devoted to destruction,[2] therefore your life shall be for his life, and your people for his people.'" ⁴³ And the king of Israel went to his house vexed and sullen and came to Samaria.

Naboth's Vineyard

21 Now Naboth the Jezreelite had a vineyard in Jezreel, beside the palace of Ahab king of Samaria. ² And after this Ahab said to Naboth, "Give me your vineyard, that I may have it for a vegetable garden, because it is near my house, and I will give you a better vineyard for it; or, if it seems good to you, I will give you its value in money." ³ But Naboth said to Ahab, "The Lord forbid that I should give you the inheritance of my fathers." ⁴ And Ahab went into his house vexed and sullen because of what Naboth the Jezreelite had said to him, for he had said, "I will not give you the inheritance of my fathers." And he lay down on his bed and turned away his face and would eat no food.

⁵ But Jezebel his wife came to him and said to him, "Why is your spirit so vexed that you eat no food?" ⁶ And he said to her, "Because I spoke to Naboth

---

[1] A *talent* was about 75 pounds or 34 kilograms [2] That is, set apart (devoted) as an offering to the Lord (for destruction)

the Jezreelite and said to him, 'Give me your vineyard for money, or else, if it please you, I will give you another vineyard for it.' And he answered, 'I will not give you my vineyard.'" ⁷ And Jezebel his wife said to him, "Do you now govern Israel? Arise and eat bread and let your heart be cheerful; I will give you the vineyard of Naboth the Jezreelite."

⁸ So she wrote letters in Ahab's name and sealed them with his seal, and she sent the letters to the elders and the leaders who lived with Naboth in his city. ⁹ And she wrote in the letters, "Proclaim a fast, and set Naboth at the head of the people. ¹⁰ And set two worthless men opposite him, and let them bring a charge against him, saying, 'You have cursed[1] God and the king.' Then take him out and stone him to death." ¹¹ And the men of his city, the elders and the leaders who lived in his city, did as Jezebel had sent word to them. As it was written in the letters that she had sent to them, ¹² they proclaimed a fast and set Naboth at the head of the people. ¹³ And the two worthless men came in and sat opposite him. And the worthless men brought a charge against Naboth in the presence of the people, saying, "Naboth cursed God and the king." So they took him outside the city and stoned him to death with stones. ¹⁴ Then they sent to Jezebel, saying, "Naboth has been stoned; he is dead."

¹⁵ As soon as Jezebel heard that Naboth had been stoned and was dead, Jezebel said to Ahab, "Arise, take possession of the vineyard of Naboth the Jezreelite, which he refused to give you for money, for Naboth is not alive, but dead." ¹⁶ And as soon as Ahab heard that Naboth was dead, Ahab arose to go down to the vineyard of Naboth the Jezreelite, to take possession of it.

The Lord Condemns Ahab

¹⁷ Then the word of the Lord came to Elijah the Tishbite, saying, ¹⁸ "Arise, go down to meet Ahab king of Israel, who is in Samaria; behold, he is in the vineyard of Naboth, where he has gone to take possession. ¹⁹ And you shall say to him, 'Thus says the Lord, "Have you killed and also taken possession?"' And you shall say to him, 'Thus says the Lord: "In the place where dogs licked up the blood of Naboth shall dogs lick your own blood."'"

²⁰ Ahab said to Elijah, "Have you found me, O my enemy?" He answered, "I have found you, because you have sold yourself to do what is evil in the sight of the Lord. ²¹ Behold, I will bring disaster upon you. I will utterly burn you up, and will cut off from Ahab every male, bond or free, in Israel. ²² And I will make your house like the house of Jeroboam the son of Nebat, and like the house of Baasha the son of Ahijah, for the anger to which you have provoked me, and because you have made Israel to sin. ²³ And of

---

[1] Hebrew *blessed*; also verse 13

Jezebel the Lord also said, 'The dogs shall eat Jezebel within the walls of Jezreel.' ²⁴ Anyone belonging to Ahab who dies in the city the dogs shall eat, and anyone of his who dies in the open country the birds of the heavens shall eat."

Ahab's Repentance

²⁵ (There was none who sold himself to do what was evil in the sight of the Lord like Ahab, whom Jezebel his wife incited. ²⁶ He acted very abominably in going after idols, as the Amorites had done, whom the Lord cast out before the people of Israel.)

²⁷ And when Ahab heard those words, he tore his clothes and put sackcloth on his flesh and fasted and lay in sackcloth and went about dejectedly. ²⁸ And the word of the Lord came to Elijah the Tishbite, saying, ²⁹ "Have you seen how Ahab has humbled himself before me? Because he has humbled himself before me, I will not bring the disaster in his days; but in his son's days I will bring the disaster upon his house."

Ahab and the False Prophets

22 For three years Syria and Israel continued without war. ² But in the third year Jehoshaphat the king of Judah came down to the king of Israel. ³ And the king of Israel said to his servants, "Do you know that Ramoth-gilead belongs to us, and we keep quiet and do not take it out of the hand of the king of Syria?" ⁴ And he said to Jehoshaphat, "Will you go with me to battle at Ramoth-gilead?" And Jehoshaphat said to the king of Israel, "I am as you are, my people as your people, my horses as your horses."

⁵ And Jehoshaphat said to the king of Israel, "Inquire first for the word of the Lord." ⁶ Then the king of Israel gathered the prophets together, about four hundred men, and said to them, "Shall I go to battle against Ramoth-gilead, or shall I refrain?" And they said, "Go up, for the Lord will give it into the hand of the king." ⁷ But Jehoshaphat said, "Is there not here another prophet of the Lord of whom we may inquire?" ⁸ And the king of Israel said to Jehoshaphat, "There is yet one man by whom we may inquire of the Lord, Micaiah the son of Imlah, but I hate him, for he never prophesies good concerning me, but evil." And Jehoshaphat said, "Let not the king say so." ⁹ Then the king of Israel summoned an officer and said, "Bring quickly Micaiah the son of Imlah." ¹⁰ Now the king of Israel and Jehoshaphat the king of Judah were sitting on their thrones, arrayed in their robes, at the threshing floor at the entrance of the gate of Samaria, and all the prophets were prophesying before them. ¹¹ And Zedekiah the son of Chenaanah made for himself

horns of iron and said, "Thus says the Lord, 'With these you shall push the Syrians until they are destroyed.'" ¹² And all the prophets prophesied so and said, "Go up to Ramoth-gilead and triumph; the Lord will give it into the hand of the king."

Micaiah Prophesies Against Ahab

¹³ And the messenger who went to summon Micaiah said to him, "Behold, the words of the prophets with one accord are favorable to the king. Let your word be like the word of one of them, and speak favorably." ¹⁴ But Micaiah said, "As the Lord lives, what the Lord says to me, that I will speak." ¹⁵ And when he had come to the king, the king said to him, "Micaiah, shall we go to Ramoth-gilead to battle, or shall we refrain?" And he answered him, "Go up and triumph; the Lord will give it into the hand of the king." ¹⁶ But the king said to him, "How many times shall I make you swear that you speak to me nothing but the truth in the name of the Lord?" ¹⁷ And he said, "I saw all Israel scattered on the mountains, as sheep that have no shepherd. And the Lord said, 'These have no master; let each return to his home in peace.'" ¹⁸ And the king of Israel said to Jehoshaphat, "Did I not tell you that he would not prophesy good concerning me, but evil?" ¹⁹ And Micaiah said, "Therefore hear the word of the Lord: I saw the Lord sitting on his throne, and all the host of heaven standing beside him on his right hand and on his left; ²⁰ and the Lord said, 'Who will entice Ahab, that he may go up and fall at Ramoth-gilead?' And one said one thing, and another said another. ²¹ Then a spirit came forward and stood before the Lord, saying, 'I will entice him.' ²² And the Lord said to him, 'By what means?' And he said, 'I will go out, and will be a lying spirit in the mouth of all his prophets.' And he said, 'You are to entice him, and you shall succeed; go out and do so.' ²³ Now therefore behold, the Lord has put a lying spirit in the mouth of all these your prophets; the Lord has declared disaster for you."

²⁴ Then Zedekiah the son of Chenaanah came near and struck Micaiah on the cheek and said, "How did the Spirit of the Lord go from me to speak to you?" ²⁵ And Micaiah said, "Behold, you shall see on that day when you go into an inner chamber to hide yourself." ²⁶ And the king of Israel said, "Seize Micaiah, and take him back to Amon the governor of the city and to Joash the king's son, ²⁷ and say, 'Thus says the king, "Put this fellow in prison and feed him meager rations of bread and water, until I come in peace."'" ²⁸ And Micaiah said, "If you return in peace, the Lord has not spoken by me." And he said, "Hear, all you peoples!"

Ahab Killed in Battle

²⁹ So the king of Israel and Jehoshaphat the king of Judah went up to Ramoth-gilead. ³⁰ And the king of Israel said to Jehoshaphat, "I will disguise myself and go into battle, but you wear your robes." And the king of Israel disguised himself and went into battle. ³¹ Now the king of Syria had commanded the thirty-two captains of his chariots, "Fight with neither small nor great, but only with the king of Israel." ³² And when the captains of the chariots saw Jehoshaphat, they said, "It is surely the king of Israel." So they turned to fight against him. And Jehoshaphat cried out. ³³ And when the captains of the chariots saw that it was not the king of Israel, they turned back from pursuing him. ³⁴ But a certain man drew his bow at random¹ and struck the king of Israel between the scale armor and the breastplate. Therefore he said to the driver of his chariot, "Turn around and carry me out of the battle, for I am wounded." ³⁵ And the battle continued that day, and the king was propped up in his chariot facing the Syrians, until at evening he died. And the blood of the wound flowed into the bottom of the chariot. ³⁶ And about sunset a cry went through the army, "Every man to his city, and every man to his country!"

³⁷ So the king died, and was brought to Samaria. And they buried the king in Samaria. ³⁸ And they washed the chariot by the pool of Samaria, and the dogs licked up his blood, and the prostitutes washed themselves in it, according to the word of the Lord that he had spoken. ³⁹ Now the rest of the acts of Ahab and all that he did, and the ivory house that he built and all the cities that he built, are they not written in the Book of the Chronicles of the Kings of Israel? ⁴⁰ So Ahab slept with his fathers, and Ahaziah his son reigned in his place.

Jehoshaphat Reigns in Judah

⁴¹ Jehoshaphat the son of Asa began to reign over Judah in the fourth year of Ahab king of Israel. ⁴² Jehoshaphat was thirty-five years old when he began to reign, and he reigned twenty-five years in Jerusalem. His mother's name was Azubah the daughter of Shilhi. ⁴³ He walked in all the way of Asa his father. He did not turn aside from it, doing what was right in the sight of the Lord. Yet the high places were not taken away, and the people still sacrificed and made offerings on the high places. ⁴⁴ Jehoshaphat also made peace with the king of Israel.

⁴⁵ Now the rest of the acts of Jehoshaphat, and his might that he showed, and how he warred, are they not written in the Book of the Chronicles of the

---

¹ Hebrew *in his innocence*

Kings of Judah? ⁴⁶ And from the land he exterminated the remnant of the male cult prostitutes who remained in the days of his father Asa.

⁴⁷ There was no king in Edom; a deputy was king. ⁴⁸ Jehoshaphat made ships of Tarshish to go to Ophir for gold, but they did not go, for the ships were wrecked at Ezion-geber. ⁴⁹ Then Ahaziah the son of Ahab said to Jehoshaphat, "Let my servants go with your servants in the ships," but Jehoshaphat was not willing. ⁵⁰ And Jehoshaphat slept with his fathers and was buried with his fathers in the city of David his father, and Jehoram his son reigned in his place.

Ahaziah Reigns in Israel

⁵¹ Ahaziah the son of Ahab began to reign over Israel in Samaria in the seventeenth year of Jehoshaphat king of Judah, and he reigned two years over Israel. ⁵² He did what was evil in the sight of the Lord and walked in the way of his father and in the way of his mother and in the way of Jeroboam the son of Nebat, who made Israel to sin. ⁵³ He served Baal and worshiped him and provoked the Lord, the God of Israel, to anger in every way that his father had done.

2 KINGS

Elijah Denounces Ahaziah

1 After the death of Ahab, Moab rebelled against Israel. ² Now Ahaziah fell through the lattice in his upper chamber in Samaria, and lay sick; so he sent messengers, telling them, "Go, inquire of Baal-zebub, the god of Ekron, whether I shall recover from this sickness." ³ But the angel of the LORD said to Elijah the Tishbite, "Arise, go up to meet the messengers of the king of Samaria, and say to them, 'Is it because there is no God in Israel that you are going to inquire of Baal-zebub, the god of Ekron? ⁴ Now therefore thus says the LORD, You shall not come down from the bed to which you have gone up, but you shall surely die.'" So Elijah went.

⁵ The messengers returned to the king, and he said to them, "Why have you returned?" ⁶ And they said to him, "There came a man to meet us, and said to us, 'Go back to the king who sent you, and say to him, Thus says the LORD, Is it because there is no God in Israel that you are sending to inquire of Baal-zebub, the god of Ekron? Therefore you shall not come down from the bed to which you have gone up, but you shall surely die.'" ⁷ He said to them, "What kind of man was he who came to meet you and told you these things?" ⁸ They answered him, "He wore a garment of hair, with a belt of leather about his waist." And he said, "It is Elijah the Tishbite."

⁹ Then the king sent to him a captain of fifty men with his fifty. He went up to Elijah, who was sitting on the top of a hill, and said to him, "O man of God, the king says, 'Come down.'" ¹⁰ But Elijah answered the captain of fifty, "If I am a man of God, let fire come down from heaven and consume you and your fifty." Then fire came down from heaven and consumed him and his fifty.

¹¹ Again the king sent to him another captain of fifty men with his fifty. And he answered and said to him, "O man of God, this is the king's order, 'Come down quickly!'" ¹² But Elijah answered them, "If I am a man of God, let fire come down from heaven and consume you and your fifty." Then the fire of God came down from heaven and consumed him and his fifty.

¹³ Again the king sent the captain of a third fifty with his fifty. And the third captain of fifty went up and came and fell on his knees before Elijah and entreated him, "O man of God, please let my life, and the life of these

fifty servants of yours, be precious in your sight. ¹⁴ Behold, fire came down from heaven and consumed the two former captains of fifty men with their fifties, but now let my life be precious in your sight." ¹⁵ Then the angel of the Lord said to Elijah, "Go down with him; do not be afraid of him." So he arose and went down with him to the king ¹⁶ and said to him, "Thus says the Lord, 'Because you have sent messengers to inquire of Baal-zebub, the god of Ekron—is it because there is no God in Israel to inquire of his word?—therefore you shall not come down from the bed to which you have gone up, but you shall surely die.'"

¹⁷ So he died according to the word of the Lord that Elijah had spoken. Jehoram became king in his place in the second year of Jehoram the son of Jehoshaphat, king of Judah, because Ahaziah had no son. ¹⁸ Now the rest of the acts of Ahaziah that he did, are they not written in the Book of the Chronicles of the Kings of Israel?

Elijah Taken to Heaven

2 Now when the Lord was about to take Elijah up to heaven by a whirlwind, Elijah and Elisha were on their way from Gilgal. ² And Elijah said to Elisha, "Please stay here, for the Lord has sent me as far as Bethel." But Elisha said, "As the Lord lives, and as you yourself live, I will not leave you." So they went down to Bethel. ³ And the sons of the prophets who were in Bethel came out to Elisha and said to him, "Do you know that today the Lord will take away your master from over you?" And he said, "Yes, I know it; keep quiet."

⁴ Elijah said to him, "Elisha, please stay here, for the Lord has sent me to Jericho." But he said, "As the Lord lives, and as you yourself live, I will not leave you." So they came to Jericho. ⁵ The sons of the prophets who were at Jericho drew near to Elisha and said to him, "Do you know that today the Lord will take away your master from over you?" And he answered, "Yes, I know it; keep quiet."

⁶ Then Elijah said to him, "Please stay here, for the Lord has sent me to the Jordan." But he said, "As the Lord lives, and as you yourself live, I will not leave you." So the two of them went on. ⁷ Fifty men of the sons of the prophets also went and stood at some distance from them, as they both were standing by the Jordan. ⁸ Then Elijah took his cloak and rolled it up and struck the water, and the water was parted to the one side and to the other, till the two of them could go over on dry ground.

⁹ When they had crossed, Elijah said to Elisha, "Ask what I shall do for you, before I am taken from you." And Elisha said, "Please let there be a double

portion of your spirit on me." ¹⁰ And he said, "You have asked a hard thing; yet, if you see me as I am being taken from you, it shall be so for you, but if you do not see me, it shall not be so." ¹¹ And as they still went on and talked, behold, chariots of fire and horses of fire separated the two of them. And Elijah went up by a whirlwind into heaven. ¹² And Elisha saw it and he cried, "My father, my father! The chariots of Israel and its horsemen!" And he saw him no more.

Then he took hold of his own clothes and tore them in two pieces. ¹³ And he took up the cloak of Elijah that had fallen from him and went back and stood on the bank of the Jordan. ¹⁴ Then he took the cloak of Elijah that had fallen from him and struck the water, saying, "Where is the LORD, the God of Elijah?" And when he had struck the water, the water was parted to the one side and to the other, and Elisha went over.

Elisha Succeeds Elijah

¹⁵ Now when the sons of the prophets who were at Jericho saw him opposite them, they said, "The spirit of Elijah rests on Elisha." And they came to meet him and bowed to the ground before him. ¹⁶ And they said to him, "Behold now, there are with your servants fifty strong men. Please let them go and seek your master. It may be that the Spirit of the LORD has caught him up and cast him upon some mountain or into some valley." And he said, "You shall not send." ¹⁷ But when they urged him till he was ashamed, he said, "Send." They sent therefore fifty men. And for three days they sought him but did not find him. ¹⁸ And they came back to him while he was staying at Jericho, and he said to them, "Did I not say to you, 'Do not go'?"

¹⁹ Now the men of the city said to Elisha, "Behold, the situation of this city is pleasant, as my lord sees, but the water is bad, and the land is unfruitful." ²⁰ He said, "Bring me a new bowl, and put salt in it." So they brought it to him. ²¹ Then he went to the spring of water and threw salt in it and said, "Thus says the LORD, I have healed this water; from now on neither death nor miscarriage shall come from it." ²² So the water has been healed to this day, according to the word that Elisha spoke.

²³ He went up from there to Bethel, and while he was going up on the way, some small boys came out of the city and jeered at him, saying, "Go up, you baldhead! Go up, you baldhead!" ²⁴ And he turned around, and when he saw them, he cursed them in the name of the LORD. And two she-bears came out of the woods and tore forty-two of the boys. ²⁵ From there he went on to Mount Carmel, and from there he returned to Samaria.

Moab Rebels Against Israel

3 In the eighteenth year of Jehoshaphat king of Judah, Jehoram the son of Ahab became king over Israel in Samaria, and he reigned twelve years. ² He did what was evil in the sight of the Lord, though not like his father and mother, for he put away the pillar of Baal that his father had made. ³ Nevertheless, he clung to the sin of Jeroboam the son of Nebat, which he made Israel to sin; he did not depart from it.

⁴ Now Mesha king of Moab was a sheep breeder, and he had to deliver to the king of Israel 100,000 lambs and the wool of 100,000 rams. ⁵ But when Ahab died, the king of Moab rebelled against the king of Israel. ⁶ So King Jehoram marched out of Samaria at that time and mustered all Israel. ⁷ And he went and sent word to Jehoshaphat king of Judah: "The king of Moab has rebelled against me. Will you go with me to battle against Moab?" And he said, "I will go. I am as you are, my people as your people, my horses as your horses." ⁸ Then he said, "By which way shall we march?" Jehoram answered, "By the way of the wilderness of Edom."

⁹ So the king of Israel went with the king of Judah and the king of Edom. And when they had made a circuitous march of seven days, there was no water for the army or for the animals that followed them. ¹⁰ Then the king of Israel said, "Alas! The Lord has called these three kings to give them into the hand of Moab." ¹¹ And Jehoshaphat said, "Is there no prophet of the Lord here, through whom we may inquire of the Lord?" Then one of the king of Israel's servants answered, "Elisha the son of Shaphat is here, who poured water on the hands of Elijah." ¹² And Jehoshaphat said, "The word of the Lord is with him." So the king of Israel and Jehoshaphat and the king of Edom went down to him.

¹³ And Elisha said to the king of Israel, "What have I to do with you? Go to the prophets of your father and to the prophets of your mother." But the king of Israel said to him, "No; it is the Lord who has called these three kings to give them into the hand of Moab." ¹⁴ And Elisha said, "As the Lord of hosts lives, before whom I stand, were it not that I have regard for Jehoshaphat the king of Judah, I would neither look at you nor see you. ¹⁵ But now bring me a musician." And when the musician played, the hand of the Lord came upon him. ¹⁶ And he said, "Thus says the Lord, 'I will make this dry streambed full of pools.' ¹⁷ For thus says the Lord, 'You shall not see wind or rain, but that streambed shall be filled with water, so that you shall drink, you, your livestock, and your animals.' ¹⁸ This is a light thing in the sight of the Lord. He will also give the Moabites into your hand, ¹⁹ and you shall attack every fortified city and every choice city, and shall fell every

good tree and stop up all springs of water and ruin every good piece of land with stones." [20] The next morning, about the time of offering the sacrifice, behold, water came from the direction of Edom, till the country was filled with water.

[21] When all the Moabites heard that the kings had come up to fight against them, all who were able to put on armor, from the youngest to the oldest, were called out and were drawn up at the border. [22] And when they rose early in the morning and the sun shone on the water, the Moabites saw the water opposite them as red as blood. [23] And they said, "This is blood; the kings have surely fought together and struck one another down. Now then, Moab, to the spoil!" [24] But when they came to the camp of Israel, the Israelites rose and struck the Moabites, till they fled before them. And they went forward, striking the Moabites as they went.[1] [25] And they overthrew the cities, and on every good piece of land every man threw a stone until it was covered. They stopped every spring of water and felled all the good trees, till only its stones were left in Kir-hareseth, and the slingers surrounded and attacked it. [26] When the king of Moab saw that the battle was going against him, he took with him 700 swordsmen to break through, opposite the king of Edom, but they could not. [27] Then he took his oldest son who was to reign in his place and offered him for a burnt offering on the wall. And there came great wrath against Israel. And they withdrew from him and returned to their own land.

Elisha and the Widow's Oil

4 Now the wife of one of the sons of the prophets cried to Elisha, "Your servant my husband is dead, and you know that your servant feared the LORD, but the creditor has come to take my two children to be his slaves." [2] And Elisha said to her, "What shall I do for you? Tell me; what have you in the house?" And she said, "Your servant has nothing in the house except a jar of oil." [3] Then he said, "Go outside, borrow vessels from all your neighbors, empty vessels and not too few. [4] Then go in and shut the door behind yourself and your sons and pour into all these vessels. And when one is full, set it aside." [5] So she went from him and shut the door behind herself and her sons. And as she poured they brought the vessels to her. [6] When the vessels were full, she said to her son, "Bring me another vessel." And he said to her, "There is not another." Then the oil stopped flowing. [7] She came and told the man of God, and he said, "Go, sell the oil and pay your debts, and you and your sons can live on the rest."

[1] Septuagint; the meaning of the Hebrew is uncertain

Elisha and the Shunammite Woman

⁸ One day Elisha went on to Shunem, where a wealthy woman lived, who urged him to eat some food. So whenever he passed that way, he would turn in there to eat food. ⁹ And she said to her husband, "Behold now, I know that this is a holy man of God who is continually passing our way. ¹⁰ Let us make a small room on the roof with walls and put there for him a bed, a table, a chair, and a lamp, so that whenever he comes to us, he can go in there."

¹¹ One day he came there, and he turned into the chamber and rested there. ¹² And he said to Gehazi his servant, "Call this Shunammite." When he had called her, she stood before him. ¹³ And he said to him, "Say now to her, 'See, you have taken all this trouble for us; what is to be done for you? Would you have a word spoken on your behalf to the king or to the commander of the army?'" She answered, "I dwell among my own people." ¹⁴ And he said, "What then is to be done for her?" Gehazi answered, "Well, she has no son, and her husband is old." ¹⁵ He said, "Call her." And when he had called her, she stood in the doorway. ¹⁶ And he said, "At this season, about this time next year, you shall embrace a son." And she said, "No, my lord, O man of God; do not lie to your servant." ¹⁷ But the woman conceived, and she bore a son about that time the following spring, as Elisha had said to her.

Elisha Raises the Shunammite's Son

¹⁸ When the child had grown, he went out one day to his father among the reapers. ¹⁹ And he said to his father, "Oh, my head, my head!" The father said to his servant, "Carry him to his mother." ²⁰ And when he had lifted him and brought him to his mother, the child sat on her lap till noon, and then he died. ²¹ And she went up and laid him on the bed of the man of God and shut the door behind him and went out. ²² Then she called to her husband and said, "Send me one of the servants and one of the donkeys, that I may quickly go to the man of God and come back again." ²³ And he said, "Why will you go to him today? It is neither new moon nor Sabbath." She said, "All is well." ²⁴ Then she saddled the donkey, and she said to her servant, "Urge the animal on; do not slacken the pace for me unless I tell you." ²⁵ So she set out and came to the man of God at Mount Carmel.

When the man of God saw her coming, he said to Gehazi his servant, "Look, there is the Shunammite. ²⁶ Run at once to meet her and say to her, 'Is all well with you? Is all well with your husband? Is all well with the child?'" And she answered, "All is well." ²⁷ And when she came to the mountain to the man of God, she caught hold of his feet. And Gehazi came to push her away. But the man of God said, "Leave her alone, for she is in bitter distress, and the LORD has hidden it from me and has not told me." ²⁸ Then she said, "Did I ask my lord for a son? Did I not say, 'Do not deceive me?'" ²⁹ He said to Gehazi, "Tie up your garment and take my staff in your hand and go. If you meet anyone, do not greet him, and if anyone greets you, do not reply. And lay my staff on the face of the child." ³⁰ Then the mother of the child said, "As the LORD lives and as you yourself live, I will not leave you." So he arose and followed her. ³¹ Gehazi went on ahead and laid the staff on the face of the child, but there was no sound or sign of life. Therefore he returned to meet him and told him, "The child has not awakened."

³² When Elisha came into the house, he saw the child lying dead on his bed. ³³ So he went in and shut the door behind the two of them and prayed to the LORD. ³⁴ Then he went up and lay on the child, putting his mouth on his mouth, his eyes on his eyes, and his hands on his hands. And as he stretched himself upon him, the flesh of the child became warm. ³⁵ Then he got up again and walked once back and forth in the house, and went up and stretched himself upon him. The child sneezed seven times, and the child opened his eyes. ³⁶ Then he summoned Gehazi and said, "Call this Shunammite." So he called her. And when she came to him, he said, "Pick up your son." ³⁷ She came and fell at his feet, bowing to the ground. Then she picked up her son and went out.

Elisha Purifies the Deadly Stew

³⁸ And Elisha came again to Gilgal when there was a famine in the land. And as the sons of the prophets were sitting before him, he said to his servant, "Set on the large pot, and boil stew for the sons of the prophets." ³⁹ One of them went out into the field to gather herbs, and found a wild vine and gathered from it his lap full of wild gourds, and came and cut them up into the pot of stew, not knowing what they were. ⁴⁰ And they poured out some for the men to eat. But while they were eating of the stew, they cried out, "O man of God, there is death in the pot!" And they could not eat it. ⁴¹ He said, "Then bring flour." And he threw it into the pot and said, "Pour some out for the men, that they may eat." And there was no harm in the pot.

⁴² A man came from Baal-shalishah, bringing the man of God bread of the firstfruits, twenty loaves of barley and fresh ears of grain in his sack. And Elisha said, "Give to the men, that they may eat." ⁴³ But his servant said, "How can I set this before a hundred men?" So he repeated, "Give them to the men, that they may eat, for thus says the LORD, 'They shall eat and have some left.'" ⁴⁴ So he set it before them. And they ate and had some left, according to the word of the LORD.

Naaman Healed of Leprosy

5 Naaman, commander of the army of the king of Syria, was a great man with his master and in high favor, because by him the Lord had given victory to Syria. He was a mighty man of valor, but he was a leper.[1] ² Now the Syrians on one of their raids had carried off a little girl from the land of Israel, and she worked in the service of Naaman's wife. ³ She said to her mistress, "Would that my lord were with the prophet who is in Samaria! He would cure him of his leprosy." ⁴ So Naaman went in and told his lord, "Thus and so spoke the girl from the land of Israel." ⁵ And the king of Syria said, "Go now, and I will send a letter to the king of Israel."

So he went, taking with him ten talents of silver, six thousand shekels[2] of gold, and ten changes of clothing. ⁶ And he brought the letter to the king of Israel, which read, "When this letter reaches you, know that I have sent to you Naaman my servant, that you may cure him of his leprosy." ⁷ And when the king of Israel read the letter, he tore his clothes and said, "Am I God, to kill and to make alive, that this man sends word to me to cure a man of his leprosy? Only consider, and see how he is seeking a quarrel with me."

⁸ But when Elisha the man of God heard that the king of Israel had torn his clothes, he sent to the king, saying, "Why have you torn your clothes? Let him come now to me, that he may know that there is a prophet in Israel." ⁹ So Naaman came with his horses and chariots and stood at the door of Elisha's house. ¹⁰ And Elisha sent a messenger to him, saying, "Go and wash in the Jordan seven times, and your flesh shall be restored, and you shall be clean." ¹¹ But Naaman was angry and went away, saying, "Behold, I thought that he would surely come out to me and stand and call upon the name of the Lord his God, and wave his hand over the place and cure the leper. ¹² Are not Abana[3] and Pharpar, the rivers of Damascus, better than all the waters of Israel? Could I not wash in them and be clean?" So he turned and went away in a rage. ¹³ But his servants came near and said to him, "My father, it is a great word the prophet has spoken to you; will you not do it? Has he actually said to you, 'Wash, and be clean'?" ¹⁴ So he went down and dipped himself seven times in the Jordan, according to the word of the man of God, and his flesh was restored like the flesh of a little child, and he was clean.

Gehazi's Greed and Punishment

¹⁵ Then he returned to the man of God, he and all his company, and he came and stood before him. And he said, "Behold, I know that there is no God in all the earth but in Israel; so accept now a present from your servant." ¹⁶ But

---

[1] *Leprosy* was a term for several skin diseases; see Leviticus 13 [2] A *talent* was about 75 pounds or 34 kilograms; a *shekel* was about 2/5 ounce or 11 grams [3] Or *Amana*

he said, "As the Lord lives, before whom I stand, I will receive none." And he urged him to take it, but he refused. ⁱ⁷ Then Naaman said, "If not, please let there be given to your servant two mule loads of earth, for from now on your servant will not offer burnt offering or sacrifice to any god but the Lord. ¹⁸ In this matter may the Lord pardon your servant: when my master goes into the house of Rimmon to worship there, leaning on my arm, and I bow myself in the house of Rimmon, when I bow myself in the house of Rimmon, the Lord pardon your servant in this matter." ¹⁹ He said to him, "Go in peace."

But when Naaman had gone from him a short distance, ²⁰ Gehazi, the servant of Elisha the man of God, said, "See, my master has spared this Naaman the Syrian, in not accepting from his hand what he brought. As the Lord lives, I will run after him and get something from him." ²¹ So Gehazi followed Naaman. And when Naaman saw someone running after him, he got down from the chariot to meet him and said, "Is all well?" ²² And he said, "All is well. My master has sent me to say, 'There have just now come to me from the hill country of Ephraim two young men of the sons of the prophets. Please give them a talent of silver and two changes of clothing.'" ²³ And Naaman said, "Be pleased to accept two talents." And he urged him and tied up two talents of silver in two bags, with two changes of clothing, and laid them on two of his servants. And they carried them before Gehazi. ²⁴ And when he came to the hill, he took them from their hand and put them in the house, and he sent the men away, and they departed. ²⁵ He went in and stood before his master, and Elisha said to him, "Where have you been, Gehazi?" And he said, "Your servant went nowhere." ²⁶ But he said to him, "Did not my heart go when the man turned from his chariot to meet you? Was it a time to accept money and garments, olive orchards and vineyards, sheep and oxen, male servants and female servants? ²⁷ Therefore the leprosy of Naaman shall cling to you and to your descendants forever." So he went out from his presence a leper, like snow.

The Axe Head Recovered

6 Now the sons of the prophets said to Elisha, "See, the place where we dwell under your charge is too small for us. ² Let us go to the Jordan and each of us get there a log, and let us make a place for us to dwell there." And he answered, "Go." ³ Then one of them said, "Be pleased to go with your servants." And he answered, "I will go." ⁴ So he went with them. And when they came to the Jordan, they cut down trees. ⁵ But as one was felling a log, his axe head fell into the water, and he cried out, "Alas, my master! It was borrowed." ⁶ Then the man of God said, "Where did it fall?" When he showed

him the place, he cut off a stick and threw it in there and made the iron float. ⁷ And he said, "Take it up." So he reached out his hand and took it.

Horses and Chariots of Fire

⁸ Once when the king of Syria was warring against Israel, he took counsel with his servants, saying, "At such and such a place shall be my camp." ⁹ But the man of God sent word to the king of Israel, "Beware that you do not pass this place, for the Syrians are going down there." ¹⁰ And the king of Israel sent to the place about which the man of God told him. Thus he used to warn him, so that he saved himself there more than once or twice.

¹¹ And the mind of the king of Syria was greatly troubled because of this thing, and he called his servants and said to them, "Will you not show me who of us is for the king of Israel?" ¹² And one of his servants said, "None, my lord, O king; but Elisha, the prophet who is in Israel, tells the king of Israel the words that you speak in your bedroom." ¹³ And he said, "Go and see where he is, that I may send and seize him." It was told him, "Behold, he is in Dothan." ¹⁴ So he sent there horses and chariots and a great army, and they came by night and surrounded the city.

¹⁵ When the servant of the man of God rose early in the morning and went out, behold, an army with horses and chariots was all around the city. And the servant said, "Alas, my master! What shall we do?" ¹⁶ He said, "Do not be afraid, for those who are with us are more than those who are with them." ¹⁷ Then Elisha prayed and said, "O Lord, please open his eyes that he may see." So the Lord opened the eyes of the young man, and he saw, and behold, the mountain was full of horses and chariots of fire all around Elisha. ¹⁸ And when the Syrians came down against him, Elisha prayed to the Lord and said, "Please strike this people with blindness." So he struck them with blindness in accordance with the prayer of Elisha. ¹⁹ And Elisha said to them, "This is not the way, and this is not the city. Follow me, and I will bring you to the man whom you seek." And he led them to Samaria.

²⁰ As soon as they entered Samaria, Elisha said, "O Lord, open the eyes of these men, that they may see." So the Lord opened their eyes and they saw, and behold, they were in the midst of Samaria. ²¹ As soon as the king of Israel saw them, he said to Elisha, "My father, shall I strike them down? Shall I strike them down?" ²² He answered, "You shall not strike them down. Would you strike down those whom you have taken captive with your sword and with your bow? Set bread and water before them, that they may eat and drink and go to their master." ²³ So he prepared for them a great feast, and when they had eaten and drunk, he sent them away, and

they went to their master. And the Syrians did not come again on raids into the land of Israel.

Ben-hadad's Siege of Samaria

²⁴ Afterward Ben-hadad king of Syria mustered his entire army and went up and besieged Samaria. ²⁵ And there was a great famine in Samaria, as they besieged it, until a donkey's head was sold for eighty shekels of silver, and the fourth part of a kab[1] of dove's dung for five shekels of silver. ²⁶ Now as the king of Israel was passing by on the wall, a woman cried out to him, saying, "Help, my lord, O king!" ²⁷ And he said, "If the Lord will not help you, how shall I help you? From the threshing floor, or from the winepress?" ²⁸ And the king asked her, "What is your trouble?" She answered, "This woman said to me, 'Give your son, that we may eat him today, and we will eat my son tomorrow.' ²⁹ So we boiled my son and ate him. And on the next day I said to her, 'Give your son, that we may eat him.' But she has hidden her son." ³⁰ When the king heard the words of the woman, he tore his clothes—now he was passing by on the wall—and the people looked, and behold, he had sackcloth beneath on his body— ³¹ and he said, "May God do so to me and more also, if the head of Elisha the son of Shaphat remains on his shoulders today."

³² Elisha was sitting in his house, and the elders were sitting with him. Now the king had dispatched a man from his presence, but before the messenger arrived Elisha said to the elders, "Do you see how this murderer has sent to take off my head? Look, when the messenger comes, shut the door and hold the door fast against him. Is not the sound of his master's feet behind him?" ³³ And while he was still speaking with them, the messenger came down to him and said, "This trouble is from the Lord! Why should I wait for the Lord any longer?"

Elisha Promises Food

7 But Elisha said, "Hear the word of the Lord: thus says the Lord, Tomorrow about this time a seah[2] of fine flour shall be sold for a shekel,[3] and two seahs of barley for a shekel, at the gate of Samaria." ² Then the captain on whose hand the king leaned said to the man of God, "If the Lord himself should make windows in heaven, could this thing be?" But he said, "You shall see it with your own eyes, but you shall not eat of it."

The Syrians Flee

³ Now there were four men who were lepers[4] at the entrance to the gate. And they said to one another, "Why are we sitting here until we die? ⁴ If we

---

[1] A *shekel* was about 2/5 ounce or 11 grams; a *kab* was about 1 quart or 1 liter [2] A *seah* was about 7.7 quarts or 7.3 liters [3] A *shekel* was about 2/5 ounce or 11 grams [4] *Leprosy* was a term for several skin diseases; see Leviticus 13

say, 'Let us enter the city,' the famine is in the city, and we shall die there. And if we sit here, we die also. So now come, let us go over to the camp of the Syrians. If they spare our lives we shall live, and if they kill us we shall but die." ⁵ So they arose at twilight to go to the camp of the Syrians. But when they came to the edge of the camp of the Syrians, behold, there was no one there. ⁶ For the Lord had made the army of the Syrians hear the sound of chariots and of horses, the sound of a great army, so that they said to one another, "Behold, the king of Israel has hired against us the kings of the Hittites and the kings of Egypt to come against us." ⁷ So they fled away in the twilight and abandoned their tents, their horses, and their donkeys, leaving the camp as it was, and fled for their lives. ⁸ And when these lepers came to the edge of the camp, they went into a tent and ate and drank, and they carried off silver and gold and clothing and went and hid them. Then they came back and entered another tent and carried off things from it and went and hid them.

⁹ Then they said to one another, "We are not doing right. This day is a day of good news. If we are silent and wait until the morning light, punishment will overtake us. Now therefore come; let us go and tell the king's household." ¹⁰ So they came and called to the gatekeepers of the city and told them, "We came to the camp of the Syrians, and behold, there was no one to be seen or heard there, nothing but the horses tied and the donkeys tied and the tents as they were." ¹¹ Then the gatekeepers called out, and it was told within the king's household. ¹² And the king rose in the night and said to his servants, "I will tell you what the Syrians have done to us. They know that we are hungry. Therefore they have gone out of the camp to hide themselves in the open country, thinking, 'When they come out of the city, we shall take them alive and get into the city.'" ¹³ And one of his servants said, "Let some men take five of the remaining horses, seeing that those who are left here will fare like the whole multitude of Israel who have already perished. Let us send and see." ¹⁴ So they took two horsemen, and the king sent them after the army of the Syrians, saying, "Go and see." ¹⁵ So they went after them as far as the Jordan, and behold, all the way was littered with garments and equipment that the Syrians had thrown away in their haste. And the messengers returned and told the king.

¹⁶ Then the people went out and plundered the camp of the Syrians. So a seah of fine flour was sold for a shekel, and two seahs of barley for a shekel, according to the word of the Lord. ¹⁷ Now the king had appointed the captain on whose hand he leaned to have charge of the gate. And the people trampled him in the gate, so that he died, as the man of God had said when the king came down to him. ¹⁸ For when the man of God had said to the king,

"Two seahs of barley shall be sold for a shekel, and a seah of fine flour for a shekel, about this time tomorrow in the gate of Samaria," ¹⁹ the captain had answered the man of God, "If the LORD himself should make windows in heaven, could such a thing be?" And he had said, "You shall see it with your own eyes, but you shall not eat of it." ²⁰ And so it happened to him, for the people trampled him in the gate and he died.

The Shunammite's Land Restored

8 Now Elisha had said to the woman whose son he had restored to life, "Arise, and depart with your household, and sojourn wherever you can, for the LORD has called for a famine, and it will come upon the land for seven years." ² So the woman arose and did according to the word of the man of God. She went with her household and sojourned in the land of the Philistines seven years. ³ And at the end of the seven years, when the woman returned from the land of the Philistines, she went to appeal to the king for her house and her land. ⁴ Now the king was talking with Gehazi the servant of the man of God, saying, "Tell me all the great things that Elisha has done." ⁵ And while he was telling the king how Elisha had restored the dead to life, behold, the woman whose son he had restored to life appealed to the king for her house and her land. And Gehazi said, "My lord, O king, here is the woman, and here is her son whom Elisha restored to life." ⁶ And when the king asked the woman, she told him. So the king appointed an official for her, saying, "Restore all that was hers, together with all the produce of the fields from the day that she left the land until now."

Hazael Murders Ben-hadad

⁷ Now Elisha came to Damascus. Ben-hadad the king of Syria was sick. And when it was told him, "The man of God has come here," ⁸ the king said to Hazael, "Take a present with you and go to meet the man of God, and inquire of the LORD through him, saying, 'Shall I recover from this sickness?'" ⁹ So Hazael went to meet him, and took a present with him, all kinds of goods of Damascus, forty camels' loads. When he came and stood before him, he said, "Your son Ben-hadad king of Syria has sent me to you, saying, 'Shall I recover from this sickness?'" ¹⁰ And Elisha said to him, "Go, say to him, 'You shall certainly recover,' but[1] the LORD has shown me that he shall certainly die." ¹¹ And he fixed his gaze and stared at him, until he was embarrassed. And the man of God wept. ¹² And Hazael said, "Why does my lord weep?" He answered, "Because I know the evil that you will do to the people of Israel.

---

[1] Some manuscripts *say, 'You shall certainly not recover,' for*

You will set on fire their fortresses, and you will kill their young men with the sword and dash in pieces their little ones and rip open their pregnant women." ¹³ And Hazael said, "What is your servant, who is but a dog, that he should do this great thing?" Elisha answered, "The LORD has shown me that you are to be king over Syria." ¹⁴ Then he departed from Elisha and came to his master, who said to him, "What did Elisha say to you?" And he answered, "He told me that you would certainly recover." ¹⁵ But the next day he took the bed cloth[1] and dipped it in water and spread it over his face, till he died. And Hazael became king in his place.

Jehoram Reigns in Judah

¹⁶ In the fifth year of Joram the son of Ahab, king of Israel, when Jehoshaphat was king of Judah,[2] Jehoram the son of Jehoshaphat, king of Judah, began to reign. ¹⁷ He was thirty-two years old when he became king, and he reigned eight years in Jerusalem. ¹⁸ And he walked in the way of the kings of Israel, as the house of Ahab had done, for the daughter of Ahab was his wife. And he did what was evil in the sight of the LORD. ¹⁹ Yet the LORD was not willing to destroy Judah, for the sake of David his servant, since he promised to give a lamp to him and to his sons forever.

²⁰ In his days Edom revolted from the rule of Judah and set up a king of their own. ²¹ Then Joram[3] passed over to Zair with all his chariots and rose by night, and he and his chariot commanders struck the Edomites who had surrounded him, but his army fled home. ²² So Edom revolted from the rule of Judah to this day. Then Libnah revolted at the same time. ²³ Now the rest of the acts of Joram, and all that he did, are they not written in the Book of the Chronicles of the Kings of Judah? ²⁴ So Joram slept with his fathers and was buried with his fathers in the city of David, and Ahaziah his son reigned in his place.

Ahaziah Reigns in Judah

²⁵ In the twelfth year of Joram the son of Ahab, king of Israel, Ahaziah the son of Jehoram, king of Judah, began to reign. ²⁶ Ahaziah was twenty-two years old when he began to reign, and he reigned one year in Jerusalem. His mother's name was Athaliah; she was a granddaughter of Omri king of Israel. ²⁷ He also walked in the way of the house of Ahab and did what was evil in the sight of the LORD, as the house of Ahab had done, for he was son-in-law to the house of Ahab.

²⁸ He went with Joram the son of Ahab to make war against Hazael king of Syria at Ramoth-gilead, and the Syrians wounded Joram. ²⁹ And King Joram

---

[1] The meaning of the Hebrew is uncertain [2] Septuagint, Syriac lack *when Jehoshaphat was king of Judah* [3] *Joram* (also verses 23, 24) is an alternate spelling of *Jehoram* (son of Jehoshaphat), mentioned in verses 16, 25, 29

returned to be healed in Jezreel of the wounds that the Syrians had given him at Ramah, when he fought against Hazael king of Syria. And Ahaziah the son of Jehoram king of Judah went down to see Joram the son of Ahab in Jezreel, because he was sick.

Jehu Anointed King of Israel

9 Then Elisha the prophet called one of the sons of the prophets and said to him, "Tie up your garments, and take this flask of oil in your hand, and go to Ramoth-gilead. ²And when you arrive, look there for Jehu the son of Jehoshaphat, son of Nimshi. And go in and have him rise from among his fellows, and lead him to an inner chamber. ³Then take the flask of oil and pour it on his head and say, 'Thus says the Lord, I anoint you king over Israel.' Then open the door and flee; do not linger."

⁴So the young man, the servant of the prophet, went to Ramoth-gilead. ⁵And when he came, behold, the commanders of the army were in council. And he said, "I have a word for you, O commander." And Jehu said, "To which of us all?" And he said, "To you, O commander." ⁶So he arose and went into the house. And the young man poured the oil on his head, saying to him, "Thus says the Lord, the God of Israel, I anoint you king over the people of the Lord, over Israel. ⁷And you shall strike down the house of Ahab your master, so that I may avenge on Jezebel the blood of my servants the prophets, and the blood of all the servants of the Lord. ⁸For the whole house of Ahab shall perish, and I will cut off from Ahab every male, bond or free, in Israel. ⁹And I will make the house of Ahab like the house of Jeroboam the son of Nebat, and like the house of Baasha the son of Ahijah. ¹⁰And the dogs shall eat Jezebel in the territory of Jezreel, and none shall bury her." Then he opened the door and fled.

¹¹When Jehu came out to the servants of his master, they said to him, "Is all well? Why did this mad fellow come to you?" And he said to them, "You know the fellow and his talk." ¹²And they said, "That is not true; tell us now." And he said, "Thus and so he spoke to me, saying, 'Thus says the Lord, I anoint you king over Israel.'" ¹³Then in haste every man of them took his garment and put it under him on the bare¹ steps, and they blew the trumpet and proclaimed, "Jehu is king."

Jehu Assassinates Joram and Ahaziah

¹⁴Thus Jehu the son of Jehoshaphat the son of Nimshi conspired against Joram. (Now Joram with all Israel had been on guard at Ramoth-gilead

¹ The meaning of the Hebrew word is uncertain

against Hazael king of Syria, ⁱ⁵ but King Joram had returned to be healed in Jezreel of the wounds that the Syrians had given him, when he fought with Hazael king of Syria.) So Jehu said, "If this is your decision, then let no one slip out of the city to go and tell the news in Jezreel." ⁱ⁶ Then Jehu mounted his chariot and went to Jezreel, for Joram lay there. And Ahaziah king of Judah had come down to visit Joram.

¹⁷ Now the watchman was standing on the tower in Jezreel, and he saw the company of Jehu as he came and said, "I see a company." And Joram said, "Take a horseman and send to meet them, and let him say, 'Is it peace?'" ¹⁸ So a man on horseback went to meet him and said, "Thus says the king, 'Is it peace?'" And Jehu said, "What do you have to do with peace? Turn around and ride behind me." And the watchman reported, saying, "The messenger reached them, but he is not coming back." ¹⁹ Then he sent out a second horseman, who came to them and said, "Thus the king has said, 'Is it peace?'" And Jehu answered, "What do you have to do with peace? Turn around and ride behind me." ²⁰ Again the watchman reported, "He reached them, but he is not coming back. And the driving is like the driving of Jehu the son of Nimshi, for he drives furiously."

²¹ Joram said, "Make ready." And they made ready his chariot. Then Joram king of Israel and Ahaziah king of Judah set out, each in his chariot, and went to meet Jehu, and met him at the property of Naboth the Jezreelite. ²² And when Joram saw Jehu, he said, "Is it peace, Jehu?" He answered, "What peace can there be, so long as the whorings and the sorceries of your mother Jezebel are so many?" ²³ Then Joram reined about and fled, saying to Ahaziah, "Treachery, O Ahaziah!" ²⁴ And Jehu drew his bow with his full strength, and shot Joram between the shoulders, so that the arrow pierced his heart, and he sank in his chariot. ²⁵ Jehu said to Bidkar his aide, "Take him up and throw him on the plot of ground belonging to Naboth the Jezreelite. For remember, when you and I rode side by side behind Ahab his father, how the Lord made this pronouncement against him: ²⁶ 'As surely as I saw yesterday the blood of Naboth and the blood of his sons—declares the Lord—I will repay you on this plot of ground.' Now therefore take him up and throw him on the plot of ground, in accordance with the word of the Lord."

²⁷ When Ahaziah the king of Judah saw this, he fled in the direction of Beth-haggan. And Jehu pursued him and said, "Shoot him also." And they shot him[1] in the chariot at the ascent of Gur, which is by Ibleam. And he fled to Megiddo and died there. ²⁸ His servants carried him in a chariot to Jerusalem, and buried him in his tomb with his fathers in the city of David.

[1] Syriac, Vulgate (compare Septuagint); Hebrew lacks *and they shot him*

²⁹ In the eleventh year of Joram the son of Ahab, Ahaziah began to reign over Judah.

Jehu Executes Jezebel

³⁰ When Jehu came to Jezreel, Jezebel heard of it. And she painted her eyes and adorned her head and looked out of the window. ³¹ And as Jehu entered the gate, she said, "Is it peace, you Zimri, murderer of your master?" ³² And he lifted up his face to the window and said, "Who is on my side? Who?" Two or three eunuchs looked out at him. ³³ He said, "Throw her down." So they threw her down. And some of her blood spattered on the wall and on the horses, and they trampled on her. ³⁴ Then he went in and ate and drank. And he said, "See now to this cursed woman and bury her, for she is a king's daughter." ³⁵ But when they went to bury her, they found no more of her than the skull and the feet and the palms of her hands. ³⁶ When they came back and told him, he said, "This is the word of the LORD, which he spoke by his servant Elijah the Tishbite: 'In the territory of Jezreel the dogs shall eat the flesh of Jezebel, ³⁷ and the corpse of Jezebel shall be as dung on the face of the field in the territory of Jezreel, so that no one can say, This is Jezebel.'"

Jehu Slaughters Ahab's Descendants

10 Now Ahab had seventy sons in Samaria. So Jehu wrote letters and sent them to Samaria, to the rulers of the city,¹ to the elders, and to the guardians of the sons² of Ahab, saying, ² "Now then, as soon as this letter comes to you, seeing your master's sons are with you, and there are with you chariots and horses, fortified cities also, and weapons, ³ select the best and fittest of your master's sons and set him on his father's throne and fight for your master's house." ⁴ But they were exceedingly afraid and said, "Behold, the two kings could not stand before him. How then can we stand?" ⁵ So he who was over the palace, and he who was over the city, together with the elders and the guardians, sent to Jehu, saying, "We are your servants, and we will do all that you tell us. We will not make anyone king. Do whatever is good in your eyes." ⁶ Then he wrote to them a second letter, saying, "If you are on my side, and if you are ready to obey me, take the heads of your master's sons and come to me at Jezreel tomorrow at this time." Now the king's sons, seventy persons, were with the great men of the city, who were bringing them up. ⁷ And as soon as the letter came to them, they took the king's sons and slaughtered them, seventy persons, and put their heads in baskets and sent them to him at Jezreel. ⁸ When the messenger came and told him, "They

---

¹ Septuagint, Vulgate; Hebrew *rulers of Jezreel* ² Hebrew lacks *of the sons*

have brought the heads of the king's sons," he said, "Lay them in two heaps at the entrance of the gate until the morning." ⁹ Then in the morning, when he went out, he stood and said to all the people, "You are innocent. It was I who conspired against my master and killed him, but who struck down all these? ¹⁰ Know then that there shall fall to the earth nothing of the word of the Lord, which the Lord spoke concerning the house of Ahab, for the Lord has done what he said by his servant Elijah." ¹¹ So Jehu struck down all who remained of the house of Ahab in Jezreel, all his great men and his close friends and his priests, until he left him none remaining.

¹² Then he set out and went to Samaria. On the way, when he was at Beth-eked of the Shepherds, ¹³ Jehu met the relatives of Ahaziah king of Judah, and he said, "Who are you?" And they answered, "We are the relatives of Ahaziah, and we came down to visit the royal princes and the sons of the queen mother." ¹⁴ He said, "Take them alive." And they took them alive and slaughtered them at the pit of Beth-eked, forty-two persons, and he spared none of them.

¹⁵ And when he departed from there, he met Jehonadab the son of Rechab coming to meet him. And he greeted him and said to him, "Is your heart true to my heart as mine is to yours?" And Jehonadab answered, "It is." Jehu said,¹ "If it is, give me your hand." So he gave him his hand. And Jehu took him up with him into the chariot. ¹⁶ And he said, "Come with me, and see my zeal for the Lord." So he² had him ride in his chariot. ¹⁷ And when he came to Samaria, he struck down all who remained to Ahab in Samaria, till he had wiped them out, according to the word of the Lord that he spoke to Elijah.

Jehu Strikes Down the Prophets of Baal

¹⁸ Then Jehu assembled all the people and said to them, "Ahab served Baal a little, but Jehu will serve him much. ¹⁹ Now therefore call to me all the prophets of Baal, all his worshipers and all his priests. Let none be missing, for I have a great sacrifice to offer to Baal. Whoever is missing shall not live." But Jehu did it with cunning in order to destroy the worshipers of Baal. ²⁰ And Jehu ordered, "Sanctify a solemn assembly for Baal." So they proclaimed it. ²¹ And Jehu sent throughout all Israel, and all the worshipers of Baal came, so that there was not a man left who did not come. And they entered the house of Baal, and the house of Baal was filled from one end to the other. ²² He said to him who was in charge of the wardrobe, "Bring out the vestments for all the worshipers of Baal." So he brought out the vestments for them. ²³ Then Jehu went into the house of Baal with Jehonadab the son of Rechab, and he

---

¹ Septuagint; Hebrew lacks *Jehu said* ² Septuagint, Syriac, Targum; Hebrew *they*

said to the worshipers of Baal, "Search, and see that there is no servant of the Lord here among you, but only the worshipers of Baal." ²⁴ Then they¹ went in to offer sacrifices and burnt offerings.

Now Jehu had stationed eighty men outside and said, "The man who allows any of those whom I give into your hands to escape shall forfeit his life." ²⁵ So as soon as he had made an end of offering the burnt offering, Jehu said to the guard and to the officers, "Go in and strike them down; let not a man escape." So when they put them to the sword, the guard and the officers cast them out and went into the inner room of the house of Baal, ²⁶ and they brought out the pillar that was in the house of Baal and burned it. ²⁷ And they demolished the pillar of Baal, and demolished the house of Baal, and made it a latrine to this day.

Jehu Reigns in Israel

²⁸ Thus Jehu wiped out Baal from Israel. ²⁹ But Jehu did not turn aside from the sins of Jeroboam the son of Nebat, which he made Israel to sin—that is, the golden calves that were in Bethel and in Dan. ³⁰ And the Lord said to Jehu, "Because you have done well in carrying out what is right in my eyes, and have done to the house of Ahab according to all that was in my heart, your sons of the fourth generation shall sit on the throne of Israel." ³¹ But Jehu was not careful to walk in the law of the Lord, the God of Israel, with all his heart. He did not turn from the sins of Jeroboam, which he made Israel to sin.

³² In those days the Lord began to cut off parts of Israel. Hazael defeated them throughout the territory of Israel: ³³ from the Jordan eastward, all the land of Gilead, the Gadites, and the Reubenites, and the Manassites, from Aroer, which is by the Valley of the Arnon, that is, Gilead and Bashan. ³⁴ Now the rest of the acts of Jehu and all that he did, and all his might, are they not written in the Book of the Chronicles of the Kings of Israel? ³⁵ So Jehu slept with his fathers, and they buried him in Samaria. And Jehoahaz his son reigned in his place. ³⁶ The time that Jehu reigned over Israel in Samaria was twenty-eight years.

Athaliah Reigns in Judah

11 Now when Athaliah the mother of Ahaziah saw that her son was dead, she arose and destroyed all the royal family. ² But Jehosheba, the daughter of King Joram, sister of Ahaziah, took Joash the son of Ahaziah and stole him away from among the king's sons who were being put to death, and she put² him and his nurse in a bedroom. Thus they³ hid him from Athaliah,

---

¹ Septuagint *he* (compare verse 25) ² Compare 2 Chronicles 22:11; Hebrew lacks *and she put* ³ Septuagint, Syriac, Vulgate (compare 2 Chronicles 22:11) *she*

so that he was not put to death. ³ And he remained with her six years, hidden in the house of the Lord, while Athaliah reigned over the land.

Joash Anointed King in Judah

⁴ But in the seventh year Jehoiada sent and brought the captains of the Carites and of the guards, and had them come to him in the house of the Lord. And he made a covenant with them and put them under oath in the house of the Lord, and he showed them the king's son. ⁵ And he commanded them, "This is the thing that you shall do: one third of you, those who come off duty on the Sabbath and guard the king's house ⁶ (another third being at the gate Sur and a third at the gate behind the guards) shall guard the palace.¹ ⁷ And the two divisions of you, which come on duty in force on the Sabbath and guard the house of the Lord on behalf of the king, ⁸ shall surround the king, each with his weapons in his hand. And whoever approaches the ranks is to be put to death. Be with the king when he goes out and when he comes in."

⁹ The captains did according to all that Jehoiada the priest commanded, and they each brought his men who were to go off duty on the Sabbath, with those who were to come on duty on the Sabbath, and came to Jehoiada the priest. ¹⁰ And the priest gave to the captains the spears and shields that had been King David's, which were in the house of the Lord. ¹¹ And the guards stood, every man with his weapons in his hand, from the south side of the house to the north side of the house, around the altar and the house on behalf of the king. ¹² Then he brought out the king's son and put the crown on him and gave him the testimony. And they proclaimed him king and anointed him, and they clapped their hands and said, "Long live the king!"

¹³ When Athaliah heard the noise of the guard and of the people, she went into the house of the Lord to the people. ¹⁴ And when she looked, there was the king standing by the pillar, according to the custom, and the captains and the trumpeters beside the king, and all the people of the land rejoicing and blowing trumpets. And Athaliah tore her clothes and cried, "Treason! Treason!" ¹⁵ Then Jehoiada the priest commanded the captains who were set over the army, "Bring her out between the ranks, and put to death with the sword anyone who follows her." For the priest said, "Let her not be put to death in the house of the Lord." ¹⁶ So they laid hands on her; and she went through the horses' entrance to the king's house, and there she was put to death.

¹⁷ And Jehoiada made a covenant between the Lord and the king and people, that they should be the Lord's people, and also between the king and the

---

¹ The meaning of the Hebrew word is uncertain

people. ⁱ⁸ Then all the people of the land went to the house of Baal and tore it down; his altars and his images they broke in pieces, and they killed Mattan the priest of Baal before the altars. And the priest posted watchmen over the house of the Lord. ¹⁹ And he took the captains, the Carites, the guards, and all the people of the land, and they brought the king down from the house of the Lord, marching through the gate of the guards to the king's house. And he took his seat on the throne of the kings. ²⁰ So all the people of the land rejoiced, and the city was quiet after Athaliah had been put to death with the sword at the king's house.

Jehoash Reigns in Judah

²¹ ¹ Jehoash² was seven years old when he began to reign.

12 In the seventh year of Jehu, Jehoash³ began to reign, and he reigned forty years in Jerusalem. His mother's name was Zibiah of Beersheba. ² And Jehoash did what was right in the eyes of the Lord all his days, because Jehoiada the priest instructed him. ³ Nevertheless, the high places were not taken away; the people continued to sacrifice and make offerings on the high places.

Jehoash Repairs the Temple

⁴ Jehoash said to the priests, "All the money of the holy things that is brought into the house of the Lord, the money for which each man is assessed—the money from the assessment of persons—and the money that a man's heart prompts him to bring into the house of the Lord, ⁵ let the priests take, each from his donor, and let them repair the house wherever any need of repairs is discovered." ⁶ But by the twenty-third year of King Jehoash, the priests had made no repairs on the house. ⁷ Therefore King Jehoash summoned Jehoiada the priest and the other priests and said to them, "Why are you not repairing the house? Now therefore take no more money from your donors, but hand it over for the repair of the house." ⁸ So the priests agreed that they should take no more money from the people, and that they should not repair the house.

⁹ Then Jehoiada the priest took a chest and bored a hole in the lid of it and set it beside the altar on the right side as one entered the house of the Lord. And the priests who guarded the threshold put in it all the money that was brought into the house of the Lord. ¹⁰ And whenever they saw that there was much money in the chest, the king's secretary and the high priest came up and they bagged and counted the money that was found in the house of the

---

¹ Ch 12:1 in Hebrew ² *Jehoash* is an alternate spelling of *Joash* (son of Ahaziah) as in verse 2 ³ *Jehoash* is an alternate spelling of *Joash* (son of Ahaziah) as in 11:2; also verses 2, 4, 6, 7, 18

Lord. ¹¹ Then they would give the money that was weighed out into the hands of the workmen who had the oversight of the house of the Lord. And they paid it out to the carpenters and the builders who worked on the house of the Lord, ¹² and to the masons and the stonecutters, as well as to buy timber and quarried stone for making repairs on the house of the Lord, and for any outlay for the repairs of the house. ¹³ But there were not made for the house of the Lord basins of silver, snuffers, bowls, trumpets, or any vessels of gold, or of silver, from the money that was brought into the house of the Lord, ¹⁴ for that was given to the workmen who were repairing the house of the Lord with it. ¹⁵ And they did not ask for an accounting from the men into whose hand they delivered the money to pay out to the workmen, for they dealt honestly. ¹⁶ The money from the guilt offerings and the money from the sin offerings was not brought into the house of the Lord; it belonged to the priests.

¹⁷ At that time Hazael king of Syria went up and fought against Gath and took it. But when Hazael set his face to go up against Jerusalem, ¹⁸ Jehoash king of Judah took all the sacred gifts that Jehoshaphat and Jehoram and Ahaziah his fathers, the kings of Judah, had dedicated, and his own sacred gifts, and all the gold that was found in the treasuries of the house of the Lord and of the king's house, and sent these to Hazael king of Syria. Then Hazael went away from Jerusalem.

The Death of Joash

¹⁹ Now the rest of the acts of Joash and all that he did, are they not written in the Book of the Chronicles of the Kings of Judah? ²⁰ His servants arose and made a conspiracy and struck down Joash in the house of Millo, on the way that goes down to Silla. ²¹ It was Jozacar the son of Shimeath and Jehozabad the son of Shomer, his servants, who struck him down, so that he died. And they buried him with his fathers in the city of David, and Amaziah his son reigned in his place.

Jehoahaz Reigns in Israel

13 In the twenty-third year of Joash the son of Ahaziah, king of Judah, Jehoahaz the son of Jehu began to reign over Israel in Samaria, and he reigned seventeen years. ² He did what was evil in the sight of the Lord and followed the sins of Jeroboam the son of Nebat, which he made Israel to sin; he did not depart from them. ³ And the anger of the Lord was kindled against Israel, and he gave them continually into the hand of Hazael king of Syria and into the hand of Ben-hadad the son of Hazael. ⁴ Then Jehoahaz sought the favor of the Lord, and the Lord listened to him, for he saw the oppression of Israel, how the king of Syria oppressed them. ⁵(Therefore the LORD gave Israel a savior, so that they escaped from the hand of the Syrians, and the people of Israel lived in their homes as formerly. ⁶Nevertheless, they did not depart from the sins of the house of Jeroboam, which he made Israel to sin, but walked¹ in them; and the Asherah also remained in Samaria.) ⁷For there was not left to Jehoahaz an army of more than fifty horsemen and ten chariots and ten thousand footmen, for the king of Syria had destroyed them and made them like the dust at threshing. ⁸Now the rest of the acts of Jehoahaz and all that he did, and his might, are they not written in the Book of the Chronicles of the Kings of Israel? ⁹So Jehoahaz slept with his fathers, and they buried him in Samaria, and Joash his son reigned in his place.

Jehoash Reigns in Israel

¹⁰In the thirty-seventh year of Joash king of Judah, Jehoash² the son of Jehoahaz began to reign over Israel in Samaria, and he reigned sixteen years. ¹¹He also did what was evil in the sight of the LORD. He did not depart from all the sins of Jeroboam the son of Nebat, which he made Israel to sin, but he walked in them. ¹²Now the rest of the acts of Joash and all that he did, and the might with which he fought against Amaziah king of Judah, are they not written in the Book of the Chronicles of the Kings of Israel? ¹³So Joash slept with his fathers, and Jeroboam sat on his throne. And Joash was buried in Samaria with the kings of Israel.

The Death of Elisha

¹⁴Now when Elisha had fallen sick with the illness of which he was to die, Joash king of Israel went down to him and wept before him, crying, "My father, my father! The chariots of Israel and its horsemen!" ¹⁵And Elisha said to him, "Take a bow and arrows." So he took a bow and arrows. ¹⁶Then he said to the king of Israel, "Draw the bow," and he drew it. And Elisha laid his hands on the king's hands. ¹⁷And he said, "Open the window eastward," and he opened it. Then Elisha said, "Shoot," and he shot. And he said, "The LORD's arrow of victory, the arrow of victory over Syria! For you shall fight the Syrians in Aphek until you have made an end of them." ¹⁸And he said, "Take the arrows," and he took them. And he said to the king of Israel, "Strike the ground with them." And he struck three times and stopped. ¹⁹Then the man of God was angry with him and said, "You should have struck five or six times; then you would have struck down Syria until you had made an end of it, but now you will strike down Syria only three times."

---

¹ Septuagint, Syriac, Targum, Vulgate; Hebrew *he walked* ² *Jehoash* is an alternate spelling of *Joash* (son of Jehoahaz) as in verses 9, 12–14; also verse 25

²⁰ So Elisha died, and they buried him. Now bands of Moabites used to invade the land in the spring of the year. ²¹ And as a man was being buried, behold, a marauding band was seen and the man was thrown into the grave of Elisha, and as soon as the man touched the bones of Elisha, he revived and stood on his feet.

²² Now Hazael king of Syria oppressed Israel all the days of Jehoahaz. ²³ But the LORD was gracious to them and had compassion on them, and he turned toward them, because of his covenant with Abraham, Isaac, and Jacob, and would not destroy them, nor has he cast them from his presence until now.

²⁴ When Hazael king of Syria died, Ben-hadad his son became king in his place. ²⁵ Then Jehoash the son of Jehoahaz took again from Ben-hadad the son of Hazael the cities that he had taken from Jehoahaz his father in war. Three times Joash defeated him and recovered the cities of Israel.

Amaziah Reigns in Judah

14 In the second year of Joash the son of Joahaz, king of Israel, Amaziah the son of Joash, king of Judah, began to reign. ² He was twenty-five years old when he began to reign, and he reigned twenty-nine years in Jerusalem. His mother's name was Jehoaddin of Jerusalem. ³ And he did what was right in the eyes of the LORD, yet not like David his father. He did in all things as Joash his father had done. ⁴ But the high places were not removed; the people still sacrificed and made offerings on the high places. ⁵ And as soon as the royal power was firmly in his hand, he struck down his servants who had struck down the king his father. ⁶ But he did not put to death the children of the murderers, according to what is written in the Book of the Law of Moses, where the LORD commanded, "Fathers shall not be put to death because of their children, nor shall children be put to death because of their fathers. But each one shall die for his own sin."

⁷ He struck down ten thousand Edomites in the Valley of Salt and took Sela by storm, and called it Joktheel, which is its name to this day.

⁸ Then Amaziah sent messengers to Jehoash[1] the son of Jehoahaz, son of Jehu, king of Israel, saying, "Come, let us look one another in the face." ⁹ And Jehoash king of Israel sent word to Amaziah king of Judah, "A thistle on Lebanon sent to a cedar on Lebanon, saying, 'Give your daughter to my son for a wife,' and a wild beast of Lebanon passed by and trampled down the thistle. ¹⁰ You have indeed struck down Edom, and your heart has lifted you up. Be content with your glory, and stay at home, for why should you provoke trouble so that you fall, you and Judah with you?"

---

[1] *Jehoash* is an alternate spelling of *Joash* (son of Jehoahaz) as in 13:9, 12–14; also verses 9, 11–16

¹¹ But Amaziah would not listen. So Jehoash king of Israel went up, and he and Amaziah king of Judah faced one another in battle at Beth-shemesh, which belongs to Judah. ¹² And Judah was defeated by Israel, and every man fled to his home. ¹³ And Jehoash king of Israel captured Amaziah king of Judah, the son of Jehoash, son of Ahaziah, at Beth-shemesh, and came to Jerusalem and broke down the wall of Jerusalem for four hundred cubits,[1] from the Ephraim Gate to the Corner Gate. ¹⁴ And he seized all the gold and silver, and all the vessels that were found in the house of the Lord and in the treasuries of the king's house, also hostages, and he returned to Samaria.

¹⁵ Now the rest of the acts of Jehoash that he did, and his might, and how he fought with Amaziah king of Judah, are they not written in the Book of the Chronicles of the Kings of Israel? ¹⁶ And Jehoash slept with his fathers and was buried in Samaria with the kings of Israel, and Jeroboam his son reigned in his place.

¹⁷ Amaziah the son of Joash, king of Judah, lived fifteen years after the death of Jehoash son of Jehoahaz, king of Israel. ¹⁸ Now the rest of the deeds of Amaziah, are they not written in the Book of the Chronicles of the Kings of Judah? ¹⁹ And they made a conspiracy against him in Jerusalem, and he fled to Lachish. But they sent after him to Lachish and put him to death there. ²⁰ And they brought him on horses; and he was buried in Jerusalem with his fathers in the city of David. ²¹ And all the people of Judah took Azariah, who was sixteen years old, and made him king instead of his father Amaziah. ²² He built Elath and restored it to Judah, after the king slept with his fathers.

Jeroboam II Reigns in Israel

²³ In the fifteenth year of Amaziah the son of Joash, king of Judah, Jeroboam the son of Joash, king of Israel, began to reign in Samaria, and he reigned forty-one years. ²⁴ And he did what was evil in the sight of the Lord. He did not depart from all the sins of Jeroboam the son of Nebat, which he made Israel to sin. ²⁵ He restored the border of Israel from Lebo-hamath as far as the Sea of the Arabah, according to the word of the Lord, the God of Israel, which he spoke by his servant Jonah the son of Amittai, the prophet, who was from Gath-hepher. ²⁶ For the Lord saw that the affliction of Israel was very bitter, for there was none left, bond or free, and there was none to help Israel. ²⁷ But the Lord had not said that he would blot out the name of Israel from under heaven, so he saved them by the hand of Jeroboam the son of Joash.

²⁸ Now the rest of the acts of Jeroboam and all that he did, and his might, how he fought, and how he restored Damascus and Hamath to Judah in

---

[1] A *cubit* was about 18 inches or 45 centimeters

Israel, are they not written in the Book of the Chronicles of the Kings of Israel? ²⁹ And Jeroboam slept with his fathers, the kings of Israel, and Zechariah his son reigned in his place.

Azariah Reigns in Judah

15 In the twenty-seventh year of Jeroboam king of Israel, Azariah the son of Amaziah, king of Judah, began to reign. ² He was sixteen years old when he began to reign, and he reigned fifty-two years in Jerusalem. His mother's name was Jecoliah of Jerusalem. ³ And he did what was right in the eyes of the LORD, according to all that his father Amaziah had done. ⁴ Nevertheless, the high places were not taken away. The people still sacrificed and made offerings on the high places. ⁵ And the LORD touched the king, so that he was a leper[1] to the day of his death, and he lived in a separate house.[2] And Jotham the king's son was over the household, governing the people of the land. ⁶ Now the rest of the acts of Azariah, and all that he did, are they not written in the Book of the Chronicles of the Kings of Judah? ⁷ And Azariah slept with his fathers, and they buried him with his fathers in the city of David, and Jotham his son reigned in his place.

Zechariah Reigns in Israel

⁸ In the thirty-eighth year of Azariah king of Judah, Zechariah the son of Jeroboam reigned over Israel in Samaria six months. ⁹ And he did what was evil in the sight of the LORD, as his fathers had done. He did not depart from the sins of Jeroboam the son of Nebat, which he made Israel to sin. ¹⁰ Shallum the son of Jabesh conspired against him and struck him down at Ibleam and put him to death and reigned in his place. ¹¹ Now the rest of the deeds of Zechariah, behold, they are written in the Book of the Chronicles of the Kings of Israel. ¹² (This was the promise of the LORD that he gave to Jehu, "Your sons shall sit on the throne of Israel to the fourth generation." And so it came to pass.)

Shallum Reigns in Israel

¹³ Shallum the son of Jabesh began to reign in the thirty-ninth year of Uzziah[3] king of Judah, and he reigned one month in Samaria. ¹⁴ Then Menahem the son of Gadi came up from Tirzah and came to Samaria, and he struck down Shallum the son of Jabesh in Samaria and put him to death and reigned in his place. ¹⁵ Now the rest of the deeds of Shallum, and the conspiracy that he made, behold, they are written in the Book of the

---

[1] *Leprosy* was a term for several skin diseases; see Leviticus 13 [2] The meaning of the Hebrew word is uncertain [3] Another name for *Azariah*

Chronicles of the Kings of Israel. ¹⁶ At that time Menahem sacked Tiphsah and all who were in it and its territory from Tirzah on, because they did not open it to him. Therefore he sacked it, and he ripped open all the women in it who were pregnant.

Menahem Reigns in Israel

¹⁷ In the thirty-ninth year of Azariah king of Judah, Menahem the son of Gadi began to reign over Israel, and he reigned ten years in Samaria. ¹⁸ And he did what was evil in the sight of the Lord. He did not depart all his days from all the sins of Jeroboam the son of Nebat, which he made Israel to sin. ¹⁹ Pul[1] the king of Assyria came against the land, and Menahem gave Pul a thousand talents[2] of silver, that he might help him to confirm his hold on the royal power. ²⁰ Menahem exacted the money from Israel, that is, from all the wealthy men, fifty shekels[3] of silver from every man, to give to the king of Assyria. So the king of Assyria turned back and did not stay there in the land. ²¹ Now the rest of the deeds of Menahem and all that he did, are they not written in the Book of the Chronicles of the Kings of Israel? ²² And Menahem slept with his fathers, and Pekahiah his son reigned in his place.

Pekahiah Reigns in Israel

²³ In the fiftieth year of Azariah king of Judah, Pekahiah the son of Menahem began to reign over Israel in Samaria, and he reigned two years. ²⁴ And he did what was evil in the sight of the Lord. He did not turn away from the sins of Jeroboam the son of Nebat, which he made Israel to sin. ²⁵ And Pekah the son of Remaliah, his captain, conspired against him with fifty men of the people of Gilead, and struck him down in Samaria, in the citadel of the king's house with Argob and Arieh; he put him to death and reigned in his place. ²⁶ Now the rest of the deeds of Pekahiah and all that he did, behold, they are written in the Book of the Chronicles of the Kings of Israel.

Pekah Reigns in Israel

²⁷ In the fifty-second year of Azariah king of Judah, Pekah the son of Remaliah began to reign over Israel in Samaria, and he reigned twenty years. ²⁸ And he did what was evil in the sight of the Lord. He did not depart from the sins of Jeroboam the son of Nebat, which he made Israel to sin.

²⁹ In the days of Pekah king of Israel, Tiglath-pileser king of Assyria came and captured Ijon, Abel-beth-maacah, Janoah, Kedesh, Hazor, Gilead, and Galilee, all the land of Naphtali, and he carried the people captive to Assyria.

---

[1] Another name for *Tiglath-pileser III* (compare verse 29) [2] A *talent* was about 75 pounds or 34 kilograms
[3] A *shekel* was about 2/5 ounce or 11 grams

³⁰ Then Hoshea the son of Elah made a conspiracy against Pekah the son of Remaliah and struck him down and put him to death and reigned in his place, in the twentieth year of Jotham the son of Uzziah. ³¹ Now the rest of the acts of Pekah and all that he did, behold, they are written in the Book of the Chronicles of the Kings of Israel.

Jotham Reigns in Judah

³² In the second year of Pekah the son of Remaliah, king of Israel, Jotham the son of Uzziah, king of Judah, began to reign. ³³ He was twenty-five years old when he began to reign, and he reigned sixteen years in Jerusalem. His mother's name was Jerusha the daughter of Zadok. ³⁴ And he did what was right in the eyes of the LORD, according to all that his father Uzziah had done. ³⁵ Nevertheless, the high places were not removed. The people still sacrificed and made offerings on the high places. He built the upper gate of the house of the LORD. ³⁶ Now the rest of the acts of Jotham and all that he did, are they not written in the Book of the Chronicles of the Kings of Judah? ³⁷ In those days the LORD began to send Rezin the king of Syria and Pekah the son of Remaliah against Judah. ³⁸ Jotham slept with his fathers and was buried with his fathers in the city of David his father, and Ahaz his son reigned in his place.

Ahaz Reigns in Judah

16 In the seventeenth year of Pekah the son of Remaliah, Ahaz the son of Jotham, king of Judah, began to reign. ² Ahaz was twenty years old when he began to reign, and he reigned sixteen years in Jerusalem. And he did not do what was right in the eyes of the LORD his God, as his father David had done, ³ but he walked in the way of the kings of Israel. He even burned his son as an offering,¹ according to the despicable practices of the nations whom the LORD drove out before the people of Israel. ⁴ And he sacrificed and made offerings on the high places and on the hills and under every green tree.

⁵ Then Rezin king of Syria and Pekah the son of Remaliah, king of Israel, came up to wage war on Jerusalem, and they besieged Ahaz but could not conquer him. ⁶ At that time Rezin the king of Syria recovered Elath for Syria and drove the men of Judah from Elath, and the Edomites came to Elath, where they dwell to this day. ⁷ So Ahaz sent messengers to Tiglath-pileser king of Assyria, saying, "I am your servant and your son. Come up and rescue me from the hand of the king of Syria and from the hand of the king of Israel, who are attacking me." ⁸ Ahaz also took the silver and gold that was found

¹ Or *made his son pass through the fire*

in the house of the LORD and in the treasures of the king's house and sent a present to the king of Assyria. ⁹ And the king of Assyria listened to him. The king of Assyria marched up against Damascus and took it, carrying its people captive to Kir, and he killed Rezin.

¹⁰ When King Ahaz went to Damascus to meet Tiglath-pileser king of Assyria, he saw the altar that was at Damascus. And King Ahaz sent to Uriah the priest a model of the altar, and its pattern, exact in all its details. ¹¹ And Uriah the priest built the altar; in accordance with all that King Ahaz had sent from Damascus, so Uriah the priest made it, before King Ahaz arrived from Damascus. ¹² And when the king came from Damascus, the king viewed the altar. Then the king drew near to the altar and went up on it ¹³ and burned his burnt offering and his grain offering and poured his drink offering and threw the blood of his peace offerings on the altar. ¹⁴ And the bronze altar that was before the LORD he removed from the front of the house, from the place between his altar and the house of the LORD, and put it on the north side of his altar. ¹⁵ And King Ahaz commanded Uriah the priest, saying, "On the great altar burn the morning burnt offering and the evening grain offering and the king's burnt offering and his grain offering, with the burnt offering of all the people of the land, and their grain offering and their drink offering. And throw on it all the blood of the burnt offering and all the blood of the sacrifice, but the bronze altar shall be for me to inquire by." ¹⁶ Uriah the priest did all this, as King Ahaz commanded.

¹⁷ And King Ahaz cut off the frames of the stands and removed the basin from them, and he took down the sea¹ from off the bronze oxen that were under it and put it on a stone pedestal. ¹⁸ And the covered way for the Sabbath that had been built inside the house and the outer entrance for the king he caused to go around the house of the LORD, because of the king of Assyria. ¹⁹ Now the rest of the acts of Ahaz that he did, are they not written in the Book of the Chronicles of the Kings of Judah? ²⁰ And Ahaz slept with his fathers and was buried with his fathers in the city of David, and Hezekiah his son reigned in his place.

Hoshea Reigns in Israel

17 In the twelfth year of Ahaz king of Judah, Hoshea the son of Elah began to reign in Samaria over Israel, and he reigned nine years. ² And he did what was evil in the sight of the LORD, yet not as the kings of Israel who were before him. ³ Against him came up Shalmaneser king of Assyria. And Hoshea became his vassal and paid him tribute. ⁴ But the king

---
¹ Compare 1 Kings 7:23

of Assyria found treachery in Hoshea, for he had sent messengers to So, king of Egypt, and offered no tribute to the king of Assyria, as he had done year by year. Therefore the king of Assyria shut him up and bound him in prison. ⁵ Then the king of Assyria invaded all the land and came to Samaria, and for three years he besieged it.

The Fall of Israel

⁶ In the ninth year of Hoshea, the king of Assyria captured Samaria, and he carried the Israelites away to Assyria and placed them in Halah, and on the Habor, the river of Gozan, and in the cities of the Medes.

Exile Because of Idolatry

⁷ And this occurred because the people of Israel had sinned against the LORD their God, who had brought them up out of the land of Egypt from under the hand of Pharaoh king of Egypt, and had feared other gods ⁸ and walked in the customs of the nations whom the LORD drove out before the people of Israel, and in the customs that the kings of Israel had practiced. ⁹ And the people of Israel did secretly against the LORD their God things that were not right. They built for themselves high places in all their towns, from watchtower to fortified city. ¹⁰ They set up for themselves pillars and Asherim on every high hill and under every green tree, ¹¹ and there they made offerings on all the high places, as the nations did whom the LORD carried away before them. And they did wicked things, provoking the LORD to anger, ¹² and they served idols, of which the LORD had said to them, "You shall not do this." ¹³ Yet the LORD warned Israel and Judah by every prophet and every seer, saying, "Turn from your evil ways and keep my commandments and my statutes, in accordance with all the Law that I commanded your fathers, and that I sent to you by my servants the prophets."

¹⁴ But they would not listen, but were stubborn, as their fathers had been, who did not believe in the LORD their God. ¹⁵ They despised his statutes and his covenant that he made with their fathers and the warnings that he gave them. They went after false idols and became false, and they followed the nations that were around them, concerning whom the LORD had commanded them that they should not do like them. ¹⁶ And they abandoned all the commandments of the LORD their God, and made for themselves metal images of two calves; and they made an Asherah and worshiped all the host of heaven and served Baal. ¹⁷ And they burned their sons and their daughters as offerings[1] and used divination and omens and sold themselves to do evil

---

[1] Or *made their sons and their daughters pass through the fire*

in the sight of the Lord, provoking him to anger. ¹⁸ Therefore the Lord was very angry with Israel and removed them out of his sight. None was left but the tribe of Judah only.

¹⁹ Judah also did not keep the commandments of the Lord their God, but walked in the customs that Israel had introduced. ²⁰ And the Lord rejected all the descendants of Israel and afflicted them and gave them into the hand of plunderers, until he had cast them out of his sight.

²¹ When he had torn Israel from the house of David, they made Jeroboam the son of Nebat king. And Jeroboam drove Israel from following the Lord and made them commit great sin. ²² The people of Israel walked in all the sins that Jeroboam did. They did not depart from them, ²³ until the Lord removed Israel out of his sight, as he had spoken by all his servants the prophets. So Israel was exiled from their own land to Assyria until this day.

Assyria Resettles Samaria

²⁴ And the king of Assyria brought people from Babylon, Cuthah, Avva, Hamath, and Sepharvaim, and placed them in the cities of Samaria instead of the people of Israel. And they took possession of Samaria and lived in its cities. ²⁵ And at the beginning of their dwelling there, they did not fear the Lord. Therefore the Lord sent lions among them, which killed some of them. ²⁶ So the king of Assyria was told, "The nations that you have carried away and placed in the cities of Samaria do not know the law of the god of the land. Therefore he has sent lions among them, and behold, they are killing them, because they do not know the law of the god of the land." ²⁷ Then the king of Assyria commanded, "Send there one of the priests whom you carried away from there, and let him¹ go and dwell there and teach them the law of the god of the land." ²⁸ So one of the priests whom they had carried away from Samaria came and lived in Bethel and taught them how they should fear the Lord.

²⁹ But every nation still made gods of its own and put them in the shrines of the high places that the Samaritans had made, every nation in the cities in which they lived. ³⁰ The men of Babylon made Succoth-benoth, the men of Cuth made Nergal, the men of Hamath made Ashima, ³¹ and the Avvites made Nibhaz and Tartak; and the Sepharvites burned their children in the fire to Adrammelech and Anammelech, the gods of Sepharvaim. ³² They also feared the Lord and appointed from among themselves all sorts of people as priests of the high places, who sacrificed for them in the shrines of the high places. ³³ So they feared the Lord but also served their own gods, after the manner of the nations from among whom they had been carried away.

¹ Syriac, Vulgate; Hebrew *them*

⁣³⁴ To this day they do according to the former manner. They do not fear the Lord, and they do not follow the statutes or the rules or the law or the commandment that the Lord commanded the children of Jacob, whom he named Israel. ³⁵ The Lord made a covenant with them and commanded them, "You shall not fear other gods or bow yourselves to them or serve them or sacrifice to them, ³⁶ but you shall fear the Lord, who brought you out of the land of Egypt with great power and with an outstretched arm. You shall bow yourselves to him, and to him you shall sacrifice. ³⁷ And the statutes and the rules and the law and the commandment that he wrote for you, you shall always be careful to do. You shall not fear other gods, ³⁸ and you shall not forget the covenant that I have made with you. You shall not fear other gods, ³⁹ but you shall fear the Lord your God, and he will deliver you out of the hand of all your enemies." ⁴⁰ However, they would not listen, but they did according to their former manner.

⁴¹ So these nations feared the Lord and also served their carved images. Their children did likewise, and their children's children—as their fathers did, so they do to this day.

Hezekiah Reigns in Judah

18 In the third year of Hoshea son of Elah, king of Israel, Hezekiah the son of Ahaz, king of Judah, began to reign. ² He was twenty-five years old when he began to reign, and he reigned twenty-nine years in Jerusalem. His mother's name was Abi the daughter of Zechariah. ³ And he did what was right in the eyes of the Lord, according to all that David his father had done. ⁴ He removed the high places and broke the pillars and cut down the Asherah. And he broke in pieces the bronze serpent that Moses had made, for until those days the people of Israel had made offerings to it (it was called Nehushtan).¹ ⁵ He trusted in the Lord, the God of Israel, so that there was none like him among all the kings of Judah after him, nor among those who were before him. ⁶ For he held fast to the Lord. He did not depart from following him, but kept the commandments that the Lord commanded Moses. ⁷ And the Lord was with him; wherever he went out, he prospered. He rebelled against the king of Assyria and would not serve him. ⁸ He struck down the Philistines as far as Gaza and its territory, from watchtower to fortified city.

⁹ In the fourth year of King Hezekiah, which was the seventh year of Hoshea son of Elah, king of Israel, Shalmaneser king of Assyria came up against Samaria and besieged it, ¹⁰ and at the end of three years he took it.

---

¹ *Nehushtan* sounds like the Hebrew for both *bronze* and *serpent*

In the sixth year of Hezekiah, which was the ninth year of Hoshea king of Israel, Samaria was taken. ¹¹ The king of Assyria carried the Israelites away to Assyria and put them in Halah, and on the Habor, the river of Gozan, and in the cities of the Medes, ¹² because they did not obey the voice of the Lord their God but transgressed his covenant, even all that Moses the servant of the Lord commanded. They neither listened nor obeyed.

Sennacherib Attacks Judah

¹³ In the fourteenth year of King Hezekiah, Sennacherib king of Assyria came up against all the fortified cities of Judah and took them. ¹⁴ And Hezekiah king of Judah sent to the king of Assyria at Lachish, saying, "I have done wrong; withdraw from me. Whatever you impose on me I will bear." And the king of Assyria required of Hezekiah king of Judah three hundred talents[1] of silver and thirty talents of gold. ¹⁵ And Hezekiah gave him all the silver that was found in the house of the Lord and in the treasuries of the king's house. ¹⁶ At that time Hezekiah stripped the gold from the doors of the temple of the Lord and from the doorposts that Hezekiah king of Judah had overlaid and gave it to the king of Assyria. ¹⁷ And the king of Assyria sent the Tartan, the Rab-saris, and the Rabshakeh with a great army from Lachish to King Hezekiah at Jerusalem. And they went up and came to Jerusalem. When they arrived, they came and stood by the conduit of the upper pool, which is on the highway to the Washer's Field. ¹⁸ And when they called for the king, there came out to them Eliakim the son of Hilkiah, who was over the household, and Shebnah the secretary, and Joah the son of Asaph, the recorder.

¹⁹ And the Rabshakeh said to them, "Say to Hezekiah, 'Thus says the great king, the king of Assyria: On what do you rest this trust of yours? ²⁰ Do you think that mere words are strategy and power for war? In whom do you now trust, that you have rebelled against me? ²¹ Behold, you are trusting now in Egypt, that broken reed of a staff, which will pierce the hand of any man who leans on it. Such is Pharaoh king of Egypt to all who trust in him. ²² But if you say to me, "We trust in the Lord our God," is it not he whose high places and altars Hezekiah has removed, saying to Judah and to Jerusalem, "You shall worship before this altar in Jerusalem"? ²³ Come now, make a wager with my master the king of Assyria: I will give you two thousand horses, if you are able on your part to set riders on them. ²⁴ How then can you repulse a single captain among the least of my master's servants, when you trust in Egypt for chariots and for horsemen? ²⁵ Moreover, is it without the Lord that

---

[1] A *talent* was about 75 pounds or 34 kilograms

I have come up against this place to destroy it? The Lord said to me, "Go up against this land and destroy it."'"

26 Then Eliakim the son of Hilkiah, and Shebnah, and Joah, said to the Rabshakeh, "Please speak to your servants in Aramaic, for we understand it. Do not speak to us in the language of Judah within the hearing of the people who are on the wall." 27 But the Rabshakeh said to them, "Has my master sent me to speak these words to your master and to you, and not to the men sitting on the wall, who are doomed with you to eat their own dung and to drink their own urine?"

28 Then the Rabshakeh stood and called out in a loud voice in the language of Judah: "Hear the word of the great king, the king of Assyria! 29 Thus says the king: 'Do not let Hezekiah deceive you, for he will not be able to deliver you out of my[1] hand. 30 Do not let Hezekiah make you trust in the Lord by saying, The Lord will surely deliver us, and this city will not be given into the hand of the king of Assyria.' 31 Do not listen to Hezekiah, for thus says the king of Assyria: 'Make your peace with me[2] and come out to me. Then each one of you will eat of his own vine, and each one of his own fig tree, and each one of you will drink the water of his own cistern, 32 until I come and take you away to a land like your own land, a land of grain and wine, a land of bread and vineyards, a land of olive trees and honey, that you may live, and not die. And do not listen to Hezekiah when he misleads you by saying, "The Lord will deliver us." 33 Has any of the gods of the nations ever delivered his land out of the hand of the king of Assyria? 34 Where are the gods of Hamath and Arpad? Where are the gods of Sepharvaim, Hena, and Ivvah? Have they delivered Samaria out of my hand? 35 Who among all the gods of the lands have delivered their lands out of my hand, that the Lord should deliver Jerusalem out of my hand?'"

36 But the people were silent and answered him not a word, for the king's command was, "Do not answer him." 37 Then Eliakim the son of Hilkiah, who was over the household, and Shebna the secretary, and Joah the son of Asaph, the recorder, came to Hezekiah with their clothes torn and told him the words of the Rabshakeh.

Isaiah Reassures Hezekiah

19 As soon as King Hezekiah heard it, he tore his clothes and covered himself with sackcloth and went into the house of the Lord. 2 And he sent Eliakim, who was over the household, and Shebna the secretary, and the senior priests, covered with sackcloth, to the prophet Isaiah the son of

---

[1] Hebrew *his* [2] Hebrew *Make a blessing with me*

Amoz. ³They said to him, "Thus says Hezekiah, This day is a day of distress, of rebuke, and of disgrace; children have come to the point of birth, and there is no strength to bring them forth. ⁴It may be that the Lord your God heard all the words of the Rabshakeh, whom his master the king of Assyria has sent to mock the living God, and will rebuke the words that the Lord your God has heard; therefore lift up your prayer for the remnant that is left." ⁵When the servants of King Hezekiah came to Isaiah, ⁶Isaiah said to them, "Say to your master, 'Thus says the Lord: Do not be afraid because of the words that you have heard, with which the servants of the king of Assyria have reviled me. ⁷Behold, I will put a spirit in him, so that he shall hear a rumor and return to his own land, and I will make him fall by the sword in his own land.'"

Sennacherib Defies the Lord

⁸The Rabshakeh returned, and found the king of Assyria fighting against Libnah, for he heard that the king had left Lachish. ⁹Now the king heard concerning Tirhakah king of Cush, "Behold, he has set out to fight against you." So he sent messengers again to Hezekiah, saying, ¹⁰"Thus shall you speak to Hezekiah king of Judah: 'Do not let your God in whom you trust deceive you by promising that Jerusalem will not be given into the hand of the king of Assyria. ¹¹Behold, you have heard what the kings of Assyria have done to all lands, devoting them to destruction. And shall you be delivered? ¹²Have the gods of the nations delivered them, the nations that my fathers destroyed, Gozan, Haran, Rezeph, and the people of Eden who were in Telassar? ¹³Where is the king of Hamath, the king of Arpad, the king of the city of Sepharvaim, the king of Hena, or the king of Ivvah?'"

Hezekiah's Prayer

¹⁴Hezekiah received the letter from the hand of the messengers and read it; and Hezekiah went up to the house of the Lord and spread it before the Lord. ¹⁵And Hezekiah prayed before the Lord and said: "O Lord, the God of Israel, enthroned above the cherubim, you are the God, you alone, of all the kingdoms of the earth; you have made the heavens and the earth. ¹⁶Incline your ear, O Lord, and hear; open your eyes, O Lord, and see; and hear the words of Sennacherib, which he has sent to mock the living God. ¹⁷Truly, O Lord, the kings of Assyria have laid waste the nations and their lands ¹⁸and have cast their gods into the fire, for they were not gods, but the work of men's hands, wood and stone. Therefore they were destroyed. ¹⁹So now, O Lord our God, save us, please, from his hand, that all the kingdoms of the earth may know that you, O Lord, are God alone."

Isaiah Prophesies Sennacherib's Fall

²⁰ Then Isaiah the son of Amoz sent to Hezekiah, saying, "Thus says the Lord, the God of Israel: Your prayer to me about Sennacherib king of Assyria I have heard. ²¹ This is the word that the Lord has spoken concerning him:

"She despises you, she scorns you—
    the virgin daughter of Zion;
she wags her head behind you—
    the daughter of Jerusalem.

²² "Whom have you mocked and reviled?
    Against whom have you raised your voice
and lifted your eyes to the heights?
    Against the Holy One of Israel!
²³ By your messengers you have mocked the Lord,
    and you have said, 'With my many chariots
I have gone up the heights of the mountains,
    to the far recesses of Lebanon;
I felled its tallest cedars,
    its choicest cypresses;
I entered its farthest lodging place,
    its most fruitful forest.
²⁴ I dug wells
    and drank foreign waters,
and I dried up with the sole of my foot
    all the streams of Egypt.'

²⁵ "Have you not heard
    that I determined it long ago?
I planned from days of old
    what now I bring to pass,
that you should turn fortified cities
    into heaps of ruins,
²⁶ while their inhabitants, shorn of strength,
    are dismayed and confounded,
and have become like plants of the field
    and like tender grass,
like grass on the housetops,
    blighted before it is grown.

27 "But I know your sitting down
    and your going out and coming in,
    and your raging against me.
28 Because you have raged against me
    and your complacency has come into my ears,
    I will put my hook in your nose
    and my bit in your mouth,
  and I will turn you back on the way
    by which you came.

²⁹ "And this shall be the sign for you: this year eat what grows of itself, and in the second year what springs of the same. Then in the third year sow and reap and plant vineyards, and eat their fruit. ³⁰ And the surviving remnant of the house of Judah shall again take root downward and bear fruit upward. ³¹ For out of Jerusalem shall go a remnant, and out of Mount Zion a band of survivors. The zeal of the LORD will do this.

³² "Therefore thus says the LORD concerning the king of Assyria: He shall not come into this city or shoot an arrow there, or come before it with a shield or cast up a siege mound against it. ³³ By the way that he came, by the same he shall return, and he shall not come into this city, declares the LORD. ³⁴ For I will defend this city to save it, for my own sake and for the sake of my servant David."

³⁵ And that night the angel of the LORD went out and struck down 185,000 in the camp of the Assyrians. And when people arose early in the morning, behold, these were all dead bodies. ³⁶ Then Sennacherib king of Assyria departed and went home and lived at Nineveh. ³⁷ And as he was worshiping in the house of Nisroch his god, Adrammelech and Sharezer, his sons, struck him down with the sword and escaped into the land of Ararat. And Esarhaddon his son reigned in his place.

Hezekiah's Illness and Recovery

20 In those days Hezekiah became sick and was at the point of death. And Isaiah the prophet the son of Amoz came to him and said to him, "Thus says the LORD, 'Set your house in order, for you shall die; you shall not recover.'" ² Then Hezekiah turned his face to the wall and prayed to the LORD, saying, ³ "Now, O LORD, please remember how I have walked before you in faithfulness and with a whole heart, and have done what is good in your sight." And Hezekiah wept bitterly. ⁴ And before Isaiah had gone out of the middle court, the word of the LORD came to him:

⁵ "Turn back, and say to Hezekiah the leader of my people, Thus says the Lord, the God of David your father: I have heard your prayer; I have seen your tears. Behold, I will heal you. On the third day you shall go up to the house of the Lord, ⁶ and I will add fifteen years to your life. I will deliver you and this city out of the hand of the king of Assyria, and I will defend this city for my own sake and for my servant David's sake." ⁷ And Isaiah said, "Bring a cake of figs. And let them take and lay it on the boil, that he may recover."

⁸ And Hezekiah said to Isaiah, "What shall be the sign that the Lord will heal me, and that I shall go up to the house of the Lord on the third day?" ⁹ And Isaiah said, "This shall be the sign to you from the Lord, that the Lord will do the thing that he has promised: shall the shadow go forward ten steps, or go back ten steps?" ¹⁰ And Hezekiah answered, "It is an easy thing for the shadow to lengthen ten steps. Rather let the shadow go back ten steps." ¹¹ And Isaiah the prophet called to the Lord, and he brought the shadow back ten steps, by which it had gone down on the steps of Ahaz.

Hezekiah and the Babylonian Envoys

¹² At that time Merodach-baladan the son of Baladan, king of Babylon, sent envoys with letters and a present to Hezekiah, for he heard that Hezekiah had been sick. ¹³ And Hezekiah welcomed them, and he showed them all his treasure house, the silver, the gold, the spices, the precious oil, his armory, all that was found in his storehouses. There was nothing in his house or in all his realm that Hezekiah did not show them. ¹⁴ Then Isaiah the prophet came to King Hezekiah, and said to him, "What did these men say? And from where did they come to you?" And Hezekiah said, "They have come from a far country, from Babylon." ¹⁵ He said, "What have they seen in your house?" And Hezekiah answered, "They have seen all that is in my house; there is nothing in my storehouses that I did not show them."

¹⁶ Then Isaiah said to Hezekiah, "Hear the word of the Lord: ¹⁷ Behold, the days are coming, when all that is in your house, and that which your fathers have stored up till this day, shall be carried to Babylon. Nothing shall be left, says the Lord. ¹⁸ And some of your own sons, who will come from you, whom you will father, shall be taken away, and they shall be eunuchs in the palace of the king of Babylon." ¹⁹ Then Hezekiah said to Isaiah, "The word of the Lord that you have spoken is good." For he thought, "Why not, if there will be peace and security in my days?"

²⁰ The rest of the deeds of Hezekiah and all his might and how he made the pool and the conduit and brought water into the city, are they not written

in the Book of the Chronicles of the Kings of Judah? ²¹ And Hezekiah slept with his fathers, and Manasseh his son reigned in his place.

Manasseh Reigns in Judah

21 Manasseh was twelve years old when he began to reign, and he reigned fifty-five years in Jerusalem. His mother's name was Hephzibah. ² And he did what was evil in the sight of the LORD, according to the despicable practices of the nations whom the LORD drove out before the people of Israel. ³ For he rebuilt the high places that Hezekiah his father had destroyed, and he erected altars for Baal and made an Asherah, as Ahab king of Israel had done, and worshiped all the host of heaven and served them. ⁴ And he built altars in the house of the LORD, of which the LORD had said, "In Jerusalem will I put my name." ⁵ And he built altars for all the host of heaven in the two courts of the house of the LORD. ⁶ And he burned his son as an offering[1] and used fortune-telling and omens and dealt with mediums and with necromancers. He did much evil in the sight of the LORD, provoking him to anger. ⁷ And the carved image of Asherah that he had made he set in the house of which the LORD said to David and to Solomon his son, "In this house, and in Jerusalem, which I have chosen out of all the tribes of Israel, I will put my name forever. ⁸ And I will not cause the feet of Israel to wander anymore out of the land that I gave to their fathers, if only they will be careful to do according to all that I have commanded them, and according to all the Law that my servant Moses commanded them." ⁹ But they did not listen, and Manasseh led them astray to do more evil than the nations had done whom the LORD destroyed before the people of Israel.

Manasseh's Idolatry Denounced

¹⁰ And the LORD said by his servants the prophets, ¹¹ "Because Manasseh king of Judah has committed these abominations and has done things more evil than all that the Amorites did, who were before him, and has made Judah also to sin with his idols, ¹² therefore thus says the LORD, the God of Israel: Behold, I am bringing upon Jerusalem and Judah such disaster[2] that the ears of everyone who hears of it will tingle. ¹³ And I will stretch over Jerusalem the measuring line of Samaria, and the plumb line of the house of Ahab, and I will wipe Jerusalem as one wipes a dish, wiping it and turning it upside down. ¹⁴ And I will forsake the remnant of my heritage and give them into the hand of their enemies, and they shall become a prey and a spoil to all their enemies, ¹⁵ because they have done what is evil in my

---

[1] Hebrew *made his son pass through the fire* [2] Or *evil*

sight and have provoked me to anger, since the day their fathers came out of Egypt, even to this day."

[16] Moreover, Manasseh shed very much innocent blood, till he had filled Jerusalem from one end to another, besides the sin that he made Judah to sin so that they did what was evil in the sight of the Lord.

[17] Now the rest of the acts of Manasseh and all that he did, and the sin that he committed, are they not written in the Book of the Chronicles of the Kings of Judah? [18] And Manasseh slept with his fathers and was buried in the garden of his house, in the garden of Uzza, and Amon his son reigned in his place.

Amon Reigns in Judah

[19] Amon was twenty-two years old when he began to reign, and he reigned two years in Jerusalem. His mother's name was Meshullemeth the daughter of Haruz of Jotbah. [20] And he did what was evil in the sight of the Lord, as Manasseh his father had done. [21] He walked in all the way in which his father walked and served the idols that his father served and worshiped them. [22] He abandoned the Lord, the God of his fathers, and did not walk in the way of the Lord. [23] And the servants of Amon conspired against him and put the king to death in his house. [24] But the people of the land struck down all those who had conspired against King Amon, and the people of the land made Josiah his son king in his place. [25] Now the rest of the acts of Amon that he did, are they not written in the Book of the Chronicles of the Kings of Judah? [26] And he was buried in his tomb in the garden of Uzza, and Josiah his son reigned in his place.

Josiah Reigns in Judah

22 Josiah was eight years old when he began to reign, and he reigned thirty-one years in Jerusalem. His mother's name was Jedidah the daughter of Adaiah of Bozkath. [2] And he did what was right in the eyes of the Lord and walked in all the way of David his father, and he did not turn aside to the right or to the left.

Josiah Repairs the Temple

[3] In the eighteenth year of King Josiah, the king sent Shaphan the son of Azaliah, son of Meshullam, the secretary, to the house of the Lord, saying, [4] "Go up to Hilkiah the high priest, that he may count the money that has been brought into the house of the Lord, which the keepers of the threshold have collected from the people. [5] And let it be given into the hand of the workmen who have the oversight of the house of the Lord, and let them

give it to the workmen who are at the house of the Lord, repairing the house ⁶ (that is, to the carpenters, and to the builders, and to the masons), and let them use it for buying timber and quarried stone to repair the house. ⁷ But no accounting shall be asked from them for the money that is delivered into their hand, for they deal honestly."

Hilkiah Finds the Book of the Law

⁸ And Hilkiah the high priest said to Shaphan the secretary, "I have found the Book of the Law in the house of the Lord." And Hilkiah gave the book to Shaphan, and he read it. ⁹ And Shaphan the secretary came to the king, and reported to the king, "Your servants have emptied out the money that was found in the house and have delivered it into the hand of the workmen who have the oversight of the house of the Lord." ¹⁰ Then Shaphan the secretary told the king, "Hilkiah the priest has given me a book." And Shaphan read it before the king.

¹¹ When the king heard the words of the Book of the Law, he tore his clothes. ¹² And the king commanded Hilkiah the priest, and Ahikam the son of Shaphan, and Achbor the son of Micaiah, and Shaphan the secretary, and Asaiah the king's servant, saying, ¹³ "Go, inquire of the Lord for me, and for the people, and for all Judah, concerning the words of this book that has been found. For great is the wrath of the Lord that is kindled against us, because our fathers have not obeyed the words of this book, to do according to all that is written concerning us."

¹⁴ So Hilkiah the priest, and Ahikam, and Achbor, and Shaphan, and Asaiah went to Huldah the prophetess, the wife of Shallum the son of Tikvah, son of Harhas, keeper of the wardrobe (now she lived in Jerusalem in the Second Quarter), and they talked with her. ¹⁵ And she said to them, "Thus says the Lord, the God of Israel: 'Tell the man who sent you to me, ¹⁶ Thus says the Lord, Behold, I will bring disaster upon this place and upon its inhabitants, all the words of the book that the king of Judah has read. ¹⁷ Because they have forsaken me and have made offerings to other gods, that they might provoke me to anger with all the work of their hands, therefore my wrath will be kindled against this place, and it will not be quenched. ¹⁸ But to the king of Judah, who sent you to inquire of the Lord, thus shall you say to him, Thus says the Lord, the God of Israel: Regarding the words that you have heard, ¹⁹ because your heart was penitent, and you humbled yourself before the Lord, when you heard how I spoke against this place and against its inhabitants, that they should become a desolation and a curse, and you have torn your clothes and wept before me, I also have heard you, declares

the Lord. ²⁰ Therefore, behold, I will gather you to your fathers, and you shall be gathered to your grave in peace, and your eyes shall not see all the disaster that I will bring upon this place.'" And they brought back word to the king.

Josiah's Reforms

23 Then the king sent, and all the elders of Judah and Jerusalem were gathered to him. ² And the king went up to the house of the Lord, and with him all the men of Judah and all the inhabitants of Jerusalem and the priests and the prophets, all the people, both small and great. And he read in their hearing all the words of the Book of the Covenant that had been found in the house of the Lord. ³ And the king stood by the pillar and made a covenant before the Lord, to walk after the Lord and to keep his commandments and his testimonies and his statutes with all his heart and all his soul, to perform the words of this covenant that were written in this book. And all the people joined in the covenant.

⁴ And the king commanded Hilkiah the high priest and the priests of the second order and the keepers of the threshold to bring out of the temple of the Lord all the vessels made for Baal, for Asherah, and for all the host of heaven. He burned them outside Jerusalem in the fields of the Kidron and carried their ashes to Bethel. ⁵ And he deposed the priests whom the kings of Judah had ordained to make offerings in the high places at the cities of Judah and around Jerusalem; those also who burned incense to Baal, to the sun and the moon and the constellations and all the host of the heavens. ⁶ And he brought out the Asherah from the house of the Lord, outside Jerusalem, to the brook Kidron, and burned it at the brook Kidron and beat it to dust and cast the dust of it upon the graves of the common people. ⁷ And he broke down the houses of the male cult prostitutes who were in the house of the Lord, where the women wove hangings for the Asherah. ⁸ And he brought all the priests out of the cities of Judah, and defiled the high places where the priests had made offerings, from Geba to Beersheba. And he broke down the high places of the gates that were at the entrance of the gate of Joshua the governor of the city, which were on one's left at the gate of the city. ⁹ However, the priests of the high places did not come up to the altar of the Lord in Jerusalem, but they ate unleavened bread among their brothers. ¹⁰ And he defiled Topheth, which is in the Valley of the Son of Hinnom, that no one might burn his son or his daughter as an offering to Molech.¹ ¹¹ And he removed the horses that the kings of Judah had dedicated to the sun, at the entrance to the house of the Lord, by the chamber of

---

¹ Hebrew *might cause his son or daughter to pass through the fire for Molech*

Nathan-melech the chamberlain, which was in the precincts.[1] And he burned the chariots of the sun with fire. ¹² And the altars on the roof of the upper chamber of Ahaz, which the kings of Judah had made, and the altars that Manasseh had made in the two courts of the house of the LORD, he pulled down and broke in pieces[2] and cast the dust of them into the brook Kidron. ¹³ And the king defiled the high places that were east of Jerusalem, to the south of the mount of corruption, which Solomon the king of Israel had built for Ashtoreth the abomination of the Sidonians, and for Chemosh the abomination of Moab, and for Milcom the abomination of the Ammonites. ¹⁴ And he broke in pieces the pillars and cut down the Asherim and filled their places with the bones of men.

¹⁵ Moreover, the altar at Bethel, the high place erected by Jeroboam the son of Nebat, who made Israel to sin, that altar with the high place he pulled down and burned,[3] reducing it to dust. He also burned the Asherah. ¹⁶ And as Josiah turned, he saw the tombs there on the mount. And he sent and took the bones out of the tombs and burned them on the altar and defiled it, according to the word of the LORD that the man of God proclaimed, who had predicted these things. ¹⁷ Then he said, "What is that monument that I see?" And the men of the city told him, "It is the tomb of the man of God who came from Judah and predicted[4] these things that you have done against the altar at Bethel." ¹⁸ And he said, "Let him be; let no man move his bones." So they let his bones alone, with the bones of the prophet who came out of Samaria. ¹⁹ And Josiah removed all the shrines also of the high places that were in the cities of Samaria, which kings of Israel had made, provoking the LORD to anger. He did to them according to all that he had done at Bethel. ²⁰ And he sacrificed all the priests of the high places who were there, on the altars, and burned human bones on them. Then he returned to Jerusalem.

Josiah Restores the Passover

²¹ And the king commanded all the people, "Keep the Passover to the LORD your God, as it is written in this Book of the Covenant." ²² For no such Passover had been kept since the days of the judges who judged Israel, or during all the days of the kings of Israel or of the kings of Judah. ²³ But in the eighteenth year of King Josiah this Passover was kept to the LORD in Jerusalem.

²⁴ Moreover, Josiah put away the mediums and the necromancers and the household gods and the idols and all the abominations that were seen in the land of Judah and in Jerusalem, that he might establish the words of the law that were written in the book that Hilkiah the priest found in the house of

---

[1] The meaning of the Hebrew word is uncertain [2] Hebrew *pieces from there* [3] Septuagint *broke in pieces its stones* [4] Hebrew *called*

the LORD. ²⁵ Before him there was no king like him, who turned to the LORD with all his heart and with all his soul and with all his might, according to all the Law of Moses, nor did any like him arise after him.

²⁶ Still the LORD did not turn from the burning of his great wrath, by which his anger was kindled against Judah, because of all the provocations with which Manasseh had provoked him. ²⁷ And the LORD said, "I will remove Judah also out of my sight, as I have removed Israel, and I will cast off this city that I have chosen, Jerusalem, and the house of which I said, My name shall be there."

Josiah's Death in Battle

²⁸ Now the rest of the acts of Josiah and all that he did, are they not written in the Book of the Chronicles of the Kings of Judah? ²⁹ In his days Pharaoh Neco king of Egypt went up to the king of Assyria to the river Euphrates. King Josiah went to meet him, and Pharaoh Neco killed him at Megiddo, as soon as he saw him. ³⁰ And his servants carried him dead in a chariot from Megiddo and brought him to Jerusalem and buried him in his own tomb. And the people of the land took Jehoahaz the son of Josiah, and anointed him, and made him king in his father's place.

Jehoahaz's Reign and Captivity

³¹ Jehoahaz was twenty-three years old when he began to reign, and he reigned three months in Jerusalem. His mother's name was Hamutal the daughter of Jeremiah of Libnah. ³² And he did what was evil in the sight of the LORD, according to all that his fathers had done. ³³ And Pharaoh Neco put him in bonds at Riblah in the land of Hamath, that he might not reign in Jerusalem, and laid on the land a tribute of a hundred talents[1] of silver and a talent of gold. ³⁴ And Pharaoh Neco made Eliakim the son of Josiah king in the place of Josiah his father, and changed his name to Jehoiakim. But he took Jehoahaz away, and he came to Egypt and died there. ³⁵ And Jehoiakim gave the silver and the gold to Pharaoh, but he taxed the land to give the money according to the command of Pharaoh. He exacted the silver and the gold of the people of the land, from everyone according to his assessment, to give it to Pharaoh Neco.

Jehoiakim Reigns in Judah

³⁶ Jehoiakim was twenty-five years old when he began to reign, and he reigned eleven years in Jerusalem. His mother's name was Zebidah the

---

[1] A *talent* was about 75 pounds or 34 kilograms

daughter of Pedaiah of Rumah. ³⁷ And he did what was evil in the sight of the Lord, according to all that his fathers had done.

24 In his days, Nebuchadnezzar king of Babylon came up, and Jehoiakim became his servant for three years. Then he turned and rebelled against him. ² And the Lord sent against him bands of the Chaldeans and bands of the Syrians and bands of the Moabites and bands of the Ammonites, and sent them against Judah to destroy it, according to the word of the Lord that he spoke by his servants the prophets. ³ Surely this came upon Judah at the command of the Lord, to remove them out of his sight, for the sins of Manasseh, according to all that he had done, ⁴ and also for the innocent blood that he had shed. For he filled Jerusalem with innocent blood, and the Lord would not pardon. ⁵ Now the rest of the deeds of Jehoiakim and all that he did, are they not written in the Book of the Chronicles of the Kings of Judah? ⁶ So Jehoiakim slept with his fathers, and Jehoiachin his son reigned in his place. ⁷ And the king of Egypt did not come again out of his land, for the king of Babylon had taken all that belonged to the king of Egypt from the Brook of Egypt to the river Euphrates.

Jehoiachin Reigns in Judah

⁸ Jehoiachin was eighteen years old when he became king, and he reigned three months in Jerusalem. His mother's name was Nehushta the daughter of Elnathan of Jerusalem. ⁹ And he did what was evil in the sight of the Lord, according to all that his father had done.

Jerusalem Captured

¹⁰ At that time the servants of Nebuchadnezzar king of Babylon came up to Jerusalem, and the city was besieged. ¹¹ And Nebuchadnezzar king of Babylon came to the city while his servants were besieging it, ¹² and Jehoiachin the king of Judah gave himself up to the king of Babylon, himself and his mother and his servants and his officials and his palace officials. The king of Babylon took him prisoner in the eighth year of his reign ¹³ and carried off all the treasures of the house of the Lord and the treasures of the king's house, and cut in pieces all the vessels of gold in the temple of the Lord, which Solomon king of Israel had made, as the Lord had foretold. ¹⁴ He carried away all Jerusalem and all the officials and all the mighty men of valor, 10,000 captives, and all the craftsmen and the smiths. None remained, except the poorest people of the land. ¹⁵ And he carried away Jehoiachin to Babylon. The king's mother, the king's wives, his officials, and the chief men of the land he took into captivity from Jerusalem to Babylon. ¹⁶ And the king

of Babylon brought captive to Babylon all the men of valor, 7,000, and the craftsmen and the metal workers, 1,000, all of them strong and fit for war. [17] And the king of Babylon made Mattaniah, Jehoiachin's uncle, king in his place, and changed his name to Zedekiah.

Zedekiah Reigns in Judah

[18] Zedekiah was twenty-one years old when he became king, and he reigned eleven years in Jerusalem. His mother's name was Hamutal the daughter of Jeremiah of Libnah. [19] And he did what was evil in the sight of the Lord, according to all that Jehoiakim had done. [20] For because of the anger of the Lord it came to the point in Jerusalem and Judah that he cast them out from his presence.

And Zedekiah rebelled against the king of Babylon.

Fall and Captivity of Judah

25 And in the ninth year of his reign, in the tenth month, on the tenth day of the month, Nebuchadnezzar king of Babylon came with all his army against Jerusalem and laid siege to it. And they built siegeworks all around it. [2] So the city was besieged till the eleventh year of King Zedekiah. [3] On the ninth day of the fourth month the famine was so severe in the city that there was no food for the people of the land. [4] Then a breach was made in the city, and all the men of war fled by night by the way of the gate between the two walls, by the king's garden, and the Chaldeans were around the city. And they went in the direction of the Arabah. [5] But the army of the Chaldeans pursued the king and overtook him in the plains of Jericho, and all his army was scattered from him. [6] Then they captured the king and brought him up to the king of Babylon at Riblah, and they passed sentence on him. [7] They slaughtered the sons of Zedekiah before his eyes, and put out the eyes of Zedekiah and bound him in chains and took him to Babylon.

[8] In the fifth month, on the seventh day of the month—that was the nineteenth year of King Nebuchadnezzar, king of Babylon—Nebuzaradan, the captain of the bodyguard, a servant of the king of Babylon, came to Jerusalem. [9] And he burned the house of the Lord and the king's house and all the houses of Jerusalem; every great house he burned down. [10] And all the army of the Chaldeans, who were with the captain of the guard, broke down the walls around Jerusalem. [11] And the rest of the people who were left in the city and the deserters who had deserted to the king of Babylon, together with the rest of the multitude, Nebuzaradan the captain of the guard carried into

exile. ¹² But the captain of the guard left some of the poorest of the land to be vinedressers and plowmen.

¹³ And the pillars of bronze that were in the house of the Lord, and the stands and the bronze sea that were in the house of the Lord, the Chaldeans broke in pieces and carried the bronze to Babylon. ¹⁴ And they took away the pots and the shovels and the snuffers and the dishes for incense and all the vessels of bronze used in the temple service, ¹⁵ the fire pans also and the bowls. What was of gold the captain of the guard took away as gold, and what was of silver, as silver. ¹⁶ As for the two pillars, the one sea, and the stands that Solomon had made for the house of the Lord, the bronze of all these vessels was beyond weight. ¹⁷ The height of the one pillar was eighteen cubits,¹ and on it was a capital of bronze. The height of the capital was three cubits. A latticework and pomegranates, all of bronze, were all around the capital. And the second pillar had the same, with the latticework.

¹⁸ And the captain of the guard took Seraiah the chief priest and Zephaniah the second priest and the three keepers of the threshold; ¹⁹ and from the city he took an officer who had been in command of the men of war, and five men of the king's council who were found in the city; and the secretary of the commander of the army, who mustered the people of the land; and sixty men of the people of the land, who were found in the city. ²⁰ And Nebuzaradan the captain of the guard took them and brought them to the king of Babylon at Riblah. ²¹ And the king of Babylon struck them down and put them to death at Riblah in the land of Hamath. So Judah was taken into exile out of its land.

Gedaliah Made Governor of Judah

²² And over the people who remained in the land of Judah, whom Nebuchadnezzar king of Babylon had left, he appointed Gedaliah the son of Ahikam, son of Shaphan, governor. ²³ Now when all the captains and their men heard that the king of Babylon had appointed Gedaliah governor, they came with their men to Gedaliah at Mizpah, namely, Ishmael the son of Nethaniah, and Johanan the son of Kareah, and Seraiah the son of Tanhumeth the Netophathite, and Jaazaniah the son of the Maacathite. ²⁴ And Gedaliah swore to them and their men, saying, "Do not be afraid because of the Chaldean officials. Live in the land and serve the king of Babylon, and it shall be well with you." ²⁵ But in the seventh month, Ishmael the son of Nethaniah, son of Elishama, of the royal family, came with ten men and struck down Gedaliah and put him to death along with the Jews and the Chaldeans who were with him at Mizpah. ²⁶ Then all the people, both

---

¹ A *cubit* was about 18 inches or 45 centimeters

small and great, and the captains of the forces arose and went to Egypt, for they were afraid of the Chaldeans.

Jehoiachin Released from Prison

²⁷ And in the thirty-seventh year of the exile of Jehoiachin king of Judah, in the twelfth month, on the twenty-seventh day of the month, Evil-merodach king of Babylon, in the year that he began to reign, graciously freed[1] Jehoiachin king of Judah from prison. ²⁸ And he spoke kindly to him and gave him a seat above the seats of the kings who were with him in Babylon. ²⁹ So Jehoiachin put off his prison garments. And every day of his life he dined regularly at the king's table, ³⁰ and for his allowance, a regular allowance was given him by the king, according to his daily needs, as long as he lived.

---

[1] Hebrew *reign, lifted up the head of*

1 CHRONICLES

From Adam to Abraham

1 ¹ Adam, Seth, Enosh; ² Kenan, Mahalalel, Jared; ³ Enoch, Methuselah, Lamech; ⁴ Noah, Shem, Ham, and Japheth.

⁵ The sons of Japheth: Gomer, Magog, Madai, Javan, Tubal, Meshech, and Tiras. ⁶ The sons of Gomer: Ashkenaz, Riphath,² and Togarmah. ⁷ The sons of Javan: Elishah, Tarshish, Kittim, and Rodanim.

⁸ The sons of Ham: Cush, Egypt, Put, and Canaan. ⁹ The sons of Cush: Seba, Havilah, Sabta, Raamah, and Sabteca. The sons of Raamah: Sheba and Dedan. ¹⁰ Cush fathered Nimrod. He was the first on earth to be a mighty man.³

¹¹ Egypt fathered Ludim, Anamim, Lehabim, Naphtuhim, ¹² Pathrusim, Casluhim (from whom the Philistines came), and Caphtorim.

¹³ Canaan fathered Sidon his firstborn and Heth, ¹⁴ and the Jebusites, the Amorites, the Girgashites, ¹⁵ the Hivites, the Arkites, the Sinites, ¹⁶ the Arvadites, the Zemarites, and the Hamathites.

¹⁷ The sons of Shem: Elam, Asshur, Arpachshad, Lud, and Aram. And the sons of Aram:⁴ Uz, Hul, Gether, and Meshech. ¹⁸ Arpachshad fathered Shelah, and Shelah fathered Eber. ¹⁹ To Eber were born two sons: the name of the one was Peleg⁵ (for in his days the earth was divided), and his brother's name was Joktan. ²⁰ Joktan fathered Almodad, Sheleph, Hazarmaveth, Jerah, ²¹ Hadoram, Uzal, Diklah, ²² Obal,⁶ Abimael, Sheba, ²³ Ophir, Havilah, and Jobab; all these were the sons of Joktan.

²⁴ Shem, Arpachshad, Shelah; ²⁵ Eber, Peleg, Reu; ²⁶ Serug, Nahor, Terah; ²⁷ Abram, that is, Abraham.

From Abraham to Jacob

²⁸ The sons of Abraham: Isaac and Ishmael. ²⁹ These are their genealogies: the firstborn of Ishmael, Nebaioth, and Kedar, Adbeel, Mibsam, ³⁰ Mishma, Dumah, Massa, Hadad, Tema, ³¹ Jetur, Naphish, and Kedemah. These are the sons of Ishmael. ³² The sons of Keturah, Abraham's concubine: she bore Zimran, Jokshan, Medan, Midian, Ishbak, and Shuah. The sons of Jokshan:

---

¹ Many names in these genealogies are spelled differently in other biblical books ² Septuagint; Hebrew *Diphath* ³ Or *He began to be a mighty man on the earth* ⁴ Septuagint; Hebrew lacks *And the sons of Aram* ⁵ *Peleg* means *division* ⁶ Septuagint, Syriac (compare Genesis 10:28); Hebrew *Ebal*

Sheba and Dedan. ³³ The sons of Midian: Ephah, Epher, Hanoch, Abida, and Eldaah. All these were the descendants of Keturah.

³⁴ Abraham fathered Isaac. The sons of Isaac: Esau and Israel. ³⁵ The sons of Esau: Eliphaz, Reuel, Jeush, Jalam, and Korah. ³⁶ The sons of Eliphaz: Teman, Omar, Zepho, Gatam, Kenaz, and of Timna,¹ Amalek. ³⁷ The sons of Reuel: Nahath, Zerah, Shammah, and Mizzah.

³⁸ The sons of Seir: Lotan, Shobal, Zibeon, Anah, Dishon, Ezer, and Dishan. ³⁹ The sons of Lotan: Hori and Hemam;² and Lotan's sister was Timna. ⁴⁰ The sons of Shobal: Alvan,³ Manahath, Ebal, Shepho,⁴ and Onam. The sons of Zibeon: Aiah and Anah. ⁴¹ The son⁵ of Anah: Dishon. The sons of Dishon: Hemdan,⁶ Eshban, Ithran, and Cheran. ⁴² The sons of Ezer: Bilhan, Zaavan, and Akan.⁷ The sons of Dishan: Uz and Aran.

⁴³ These are the kings who reigned in the land of Edom before any king reigned over the people of Israel: Bela the son of Beor, the name of his city being Dinhabah. ⁴⁴ Bela died, and Jobab the son of Zerah of Bozrah reigned in his place. ⁴⁵ Jobab died, and Husham of the land of the Temanites reigned in his place. ⁴⁶ Husham died, and Hadad the son of Bedad, who defeated Midian in the country of Moab, reigned in his place, the name of his city being Avith. ⁴⁷ Hadad died, and Samlah of Masrekah reigned in his place. ⁴⁸ Samlah died, and Shaul of Rehoboth on the Euphrates⁸ reigned in his place. ⁴⁹ Shaul died, and Baal-hanan, the son of Achbor, reigned in his place. ⁵⁰ Baal-hanan died, and Hadad reigned in his place, the name of his city being Pai; and his wife's name was Mehetabel, the daughter of Matred, the daughter of Mezahab. ⁵¹ And Hadad died.

The chiefs of Edom were: chiefs Timna, Alvah, Jetheth, ⁵² Oholibamah, Elah, Pinon, ⁵³ Kenaz, Teman, Mibzar, ⁵⁴ Magdiel, and Iram; these are the chiefs of Edom.

A Genealogy of David

2 These are the sons of Israel: Reuben, Simeon, Levi, Judah, Issachar, Zebulun, ² Dan, Joseph, Benjamin, Naphtali, Gad, and Asher. ³ The sons of Judah: Er, Onan and Shelah; these three Bath-shua the Canaanite bore to him. Now Er, Judah's firstborn, was evil in the sight of the LORD, and he put him to death. ⁴ His daughter-in-law Tamar also bore him Perez and Zerah. Judah had five sons in all.

⁵ The sons of Perez: Hezron and Hamul. ⁶ The sons of Zerah: Zimri, Ethan, Heman, Calcol, and Dara, five in all. ⁷ The son⁹ of Carmi: Achan, the troubler

---

¹ Septuagint (compare Genesis 36:12); Hebrew lacks *and of* ² Septuagint (compare Genesis 36:22); Hebrew *Homam* ³ Septuagint (compare Genesis 36:23); Hebrew *Alian* ⁴ Septuagint (compare Genesis 36:23); Hebrew *Shephi* ⁵ Hebrew *sons* ⁶ Septuagint (compare Genesis 36:26); Hebrew *Hamran* ⁷ Septuagint (compare Genesis 36:27); Hebrew *Jaakan* ⁸ Hebrew *the River* ⁹ Hebrew *sons*

of Israel, who broke faith in the matter of the devoted thing; ⁸ and Ethan's son was Azariah.

⁹ The sons of Hezron that were born to him: Jerahmeel, Ram, and Chelubai. ¹⁰ Ram fathered Amminadab, and Amminadab fathered Nahshon, prince of the sons of Judah. ¹¹ Nahshon fathered Salmon,¹ Salmon fathered Boaz, ¹² Boaz fathered Obed, Obed fathered Jesse. ¹³ Jesse fathered Eliab his firstborn, Abinadab the second, Shimea the third, ¹⁴ Nethanel the fourth, Raddai the fifth, ¹⁵ Ozem the sixth, David the seventh. ¹⁶ And their sisters were Zeruiah and Abigail. The sons of Zeruiah: Abishai, Joab, and Asahel, three. ¹⁷ Abigail bore Amasa, and the father of Amasa was Jether the Ishmaelite.

¹⁸ Caleb the son of Hezron fathered children by his wife Azubah, and by Jerioth; and these were her sons: Jesher, Shobab, and Ardon. ¹⁹ When Azubah died, Caleb married Ephrath, who bore him Hur. ²⁰ Hur fathered Uri, and Uri fathered Bezalel.

²¹ Afterward Hezron went in to the daughter of Machir the father of Gilead, whom he married when he was sixty years old, and she bore him Segub. ²² And Segub fathered Jair, who had twenty-three cities in the land of Gilead. ²³ But Geshur and Aram took from them Havvoth-jair, Kenath, and its villages, sixty towns. All these were descendants of Machir, the father of Gilead. ²⁴ After the death of Hezron, Caleb went in to Ephrathah,² the wife of Hezron his father, and she bore him Ashhur, the father of Tekoa.

²⁵ The sons of Jerahmeel, the firstborn of Hezron: Ram, his firstborn, Bunah, Oren, Ozem, and Ahijah. ²⁶ Jerahmeel also had another wife, whose name was Atarah; she was the mother of Onam. ²⁷ The sons of Ram, the firstborn of Jerahmeel: Maaz, Jamin, and Eker. ²⁸ The sons of Onam: Shammai and Jada. The sons of Shammai: Nadab and Abishur. ²⁹ The name of Abishur's wife was Abihail, and she bore him Ahban and Molid. ³⁰ The sons of Nadab: Seled and Appaim; and Seled died childless. ³¹ The son³ of Appaim: Ishi. The son of Ishi: Sheshan. The son of Sheshan: Ahlai. ³² The sons of Jada, Shammai's brother: Jether and Jonathan; and Jether died childless. ³³ The sons of Jonathan: Peleth and Zaza. These were the descendants of Jerahmeel. ³⁴ Now Sheshan had no sons, only daughters, but Sheshan had an Egyptian slave whose name was Jarha. ³⁵ So Sheshan gave his daughter in marriage to Jarha his slave, and she bore him Attai. ³⁶ Attai fathered Nathan, and Nathan fathered Zabad. ³⁷ Zabad fathered Ephlal, and Ephlal fathered Obed. ³⁸ Obed fathered Jehu, and Jehu fathered Azariah. ³⁹ Azariah fathered Helez, and Helez fathered Eleasah. ⁴⁰ Eleasah fathered Sismai, and Sismai fathered Shallum. ⁴¹ Shallum fathered Jekamiah, and Jekamiah fathered Elishama.

---

¹ Septuagint (compare Ruth 4:21); Hebrew *Salma* ² Septuagint, Vulgate; Hebrew *in Caleb Ephrathah* ³ Hebrew *sons*; three times in this verse

⁴² The sons of Caleb the brother of Jerahmeel: Mareshah[1] his firstborn, who fathered Ziph. The son[2] of Mareshah: Hebron.[3] ⁴³ The sons of Hebron: Korah, Tappuah, Rekem and Shema. ⁴⁴ Shema fathered Raham, the father of Jorkeam; and Rekem fathered Shammai. ⁴⁵ The son of Shammai: Maon; and Maon fathered Beth-zur. ⁴⁶ Ephah also, Caleb's concubine, bore Haran, Moza, and Gazez; and Haran fathered Gazez. ⁴⁷ The sons of Jahdai: Regem, Jotham, Geshan, Pelet, Ephah, and Shaaph. ⁴⁸ Maacah, Caleb's concubine, bore Sheber and Tirhanah. ⁴⁹ She also bore Shaaph the father of Madmannah, Sheva the father of Machbenah and the father of Gibea; and the daughter of Caleb was Achsah. ⁵⁰ These were the descendants of Caleb.

The sons[4] of Hur the firstborn of Ephrathah: Shobal the father of Kiriath-jearim, ⁵¹ Salma, the father of Bethlehem, and Hareph the father of Beth-gader. ⁵² Shobal the father of Kiriath-jearim had other sons: Haroeh, half of the Menuhoth. ⁵³ And the clans of Kiriath-jearim: the Ithrites, the Puthites, the Shumathites, and the Mishraites; from these came the Zorathites and the Eshtaolites. ⁵⁴ The sons of Salma: Bethlehem, the Netophathites, Atroth-beth-joab and half of the Manahathites, the Zorites. ⁵⁵ The clans also of the scribes who lived at Jabez: the Tirathites, the Shimeathites and the Sucathites. These are the Kenites who came from Hammath, the father of the house of Rechab.

Descendants of David

3 These are the sons of David who were born to him in Hebron: the firstborn, Amnon, by Ahinoam the Jezreelite; the second, Daniel, by Abigail the Carmelite, ² the third, Absalom, whose mother was Maacah, the daughter of Talmai, king of Geshur; the fourth, Adonijah, whose mother was Haggith; ³ the fifth, Shephatiah, by Abital; the sixth, Ithream, by his wife Eglah; ⁴ six were born to him in Hebron, where he reigned for seven years and six months. And he reigned thirty-three years in Jerusalem. ⁵ These were born to him in Jerusalem: Shimea, Shobab, Nathan and Solomon, four by Bath-shua, the daughter of Ammiel; ⁶ then Ibhar, Elishama, Eliphelet, ⁷ Nogah, Nepheg, Japhia, ⁸ Elishama, Eliada, and Eliphelet, nine. ⁹ All these were David's sons, besides the sons of the concubines, and Tamar was their sister.

¹⁰ The son of Solomon was Rehoboam, Abijah his son, Asa his son, Jehoshaphat his son, ¹¹ Joram his son, Ahaziah his son, Joash his son, ¹² Amaziah his son, Azariah his son, Jotham his son, ¹³ Ahaz his son, Hezekiah his son, Manasseh his son, ¹⁴ Amon his son, Josiah his son. ¹⁵ The sons of Josiah: Johanan the firstborn, the second Jehoiakim, the third Zedekiah, the fourth Shallum. ¹⁶ The descendants of Jehoiakim: Jeconiah his son, Zedekiah his

---

[1] Septuagint; Hebrew *Mesha* [2] Hebrew *sons* [3] Hebrew *the father of Hebron* [4] Septuagint, Vulgate; Hebrew *son*

son; ¹⁷ and the sons of Jeconiah, the captive: Shealtiel his son, ¹⁸ Malchiram, Pedaiah, Shenazzar, Jekamiah, Hoshama and Nedabiah; ¹⁹ and the sons of Pedaiah: Zerubbabel and Shimei; and the sons of Zerubbabel: Meshullam and Hananiah, and Shelomith was their sister; ²⁰ and Hashubah, Ohel, Berechiah, Hasadiah, and Jushab-hesed, five. ²¹ The sons of Hananiah: Pelatiah and Jeshaiah, his son[1] Rephaiah, his son Arnan, his son Obadiah, his son Shecaniah. ²² The son[2] of Shecaniah: Shemaiah. And the sons of Shemaiah: Hattush, Igal, Bariah, Neariah, and Shaphat, six. ²³ The sons of Neariah: Elioenai, Hizkiah, and Azrikam, three. ²⁴ The sons of Elioenai: Hodaviah, Eliashib, Pelaiah, Akkub, Johanan, Delaiah, and Anani, seven.

Descendants of Judah

4 The sons of Judah: Perez, Hezron, Carmi, Hur, and Shobal. ² Reaiah the son of Shobal fathered Jahath, and Jahath fathered Ahumai and Lahad. These were the clans of the Zorathites. ³ These were the sons[3] of Etam: Jezreel, Ishma, and Idbash; and the name of their sister was Hazzelelponi, ⁴ and Penuel fathered Gedor, and Ezer fathered Hushah. These were the sons of Hur, the firstborn of Ephrathah, the father of Bethlehem. ⁵ Ashhur, the father of Tekoa, had two wives, Helah and Naarah; ⁶ Naarah bore him Ahuzzam, Hepher, Temeni, and Haahashtari. These were the sons of Naarah. ⁷ The sons of Helah: Zereth, Izhar, and Ethnan. ⁸ Koz fathered Anub, Zobebah, and the clans of Aharhel, the son of Harum. ⁹ Jabez was more honorable than his brothers; and his mother called his name Jabez, saying, "Because I bore him in pain."[4] ¹⁰ Jabez called upon the God of Israel, saying, "Oh that you would bless me and enlarge my border, and that your hand might be with me, and that you would keep me from harm[5] so that it might not bring me pain!" And God granted what he asked. ¹¹ Chelub, the brother of Shuhah, fathered Mehir, who fathered Eshton. ¹² Eshton fathered Beth-rapha, Paseah, and Tehinnah, the father of Ir-nahash. These are the men of Recah. ¹³ The sons of Kenaz: Othniel and Seraiah; and the sons of Othniel: Hathath and Meonothai.[6] ¹⁴ Meonothai fathered Ophrah; and Seraiah fathered Joab, the father of Ge-harashim,[7] so-called because they were craftsmen. ¹⁵ The sons of Caleb the son of Jephunneh: Iru, Elah, and Naam; and the son[8] of Elah: Kenaz. ¹⁶ The sons of Jehallelel: Ziph, Ziphah, Tiria, and Asarel. ¹⁷ The sons of Ezrah: Jether, Mered, Epher, and Jalon. These are the sons of Bithiah, the daughter of Pharaoh, whom Mered married;[9] and she conceived and bore[10] Miriam, Shammai, and Ishbah, the father of Eshtemoa. ¹⁸ And his Judahite

---

[1] Septuagint (compare Syriac, Vulgate); Hebrew *sons of*; four times in this verse [2] Hebrew *sons* [3] Septuagint (compare Vulgate); Hebrew *father* [4] *Jabez* sounds like the Hebrew for *pain* [5] Or *evil* [6] Septuagint, Vulgate; Hebrew lacks *Meonothai* [7] *Ge-harashim* means *valley of craftsmen* [8] Hebrew *sons* [9] The clause *These are . . . married* is transposed from verse 18 [10] Hebrew lacks *and bore*

wife bore Jered the father of Gedor, Heber the father of Soco, and Jekuthiel the father of Zanoah. [19] The sons of the wife of Hodiah, the sister of Naham, were the fathers of Keilah the Garmite and Eshtemoa the Maacathite. [20] The sons of Shimon: Amnon, Rinnah, Ben-hanan, and Tilon. The sons of Ishi: Zoheth and Ben-zoheth. [21] The sons of Shelah the son of Judah: Er the father of Lecah, Laadah the father of Mareshah, and the clans of the house of linen workers at Beth-ashbea; [22] and Jokim, and the men of Cozeba, and Joash, and Saraph, who ruled in Moab and returned to Lehem[1] (now the records[2] are ancient). [23] These were the potters who were inhabitants of Netaim and Gederah. They lived there in the king's service.

Descendants of Simeon

[24] The sons of Simeon: Nemuel, Jamin, Jarib, Zerah, Shaul; [25] Shallum was his son, Mibsam his son, Mishma his son. [26] The sons of Mishma: Hammuel his son, Zaccur his son, Shimei his son. [27] Shimei had sixteen sons and six daughters; but his brothers did not have many children, nor did all their clan multiply like the men of Judah. [28] They lived in Beersheba, Moladah, Hazar-shual, [29] Bilhah, Ezem, Tolad, [30] Bethuel, Hormah, Ziklag, [31] Beth-marcaboth, Hazar-susim, Beth-biri, and Shaaraim. These were their cities until David reigned. [32] And their villages were Etam, Ain, Rimmon, Tochen, and Ashan, five cities, [33] along with all their villages that were around these cities as far as Baal. These were their settlements, and they kept a genealogical record.

[34] Meshobab, Jamlech, Joshah the son of Amaziah, [35] Joel, Jehu the son of Joshibiah, son of Seraiah, son of Asiel, [36] Elioenai, Jaakobah, Jeshohaiah, Asaiah, Adiel, Jesimiel, Benaiah, [37] Ziza the son of Shiphi, son of Allon, son of Jedaiah, son of Shimri, son of Shemaiah— [38] these mentioned by name were princes in their clans, and their fathers' houses increased greatly. [39] They journeyed to the entrance of Gedor, to the east side of the valley, to seek pasture for their flocks, [40] where they found rich, good pasture, and the land was very broad, quiet, and peaceful, for the former inhabitants there belonged to Ham. [41] These, registered by name, came in the days of Hezekiah, king of Judah, and destroyed their tents and the Meunites who were found there, and marked them for destruction to this day, and settled in their place, because there was pasture there for their flocks. [42] And some of them, five hundred men of the Simeonites, went to Mount Seir, having as their leaders Pelatiah, Neariah, Rephaiah, and Uzziel, the sons of Ishi. [43] And they defeated the remnant of the Amalekites who had escaped, and they have lived there to this day.

[1] Vulgate (compare Septuagint); Hebrew *and Jashubi-lahem* [2] Or *matters*

Descendants of Reuben

5 The sons of Reuben the firstborn of Israel (for he was the firstborn, but because he defiled his father's couch, his birthright was given to the sons of Joseph the son of Israel, so that he could not be enrolled as the oldest son; ² though Judah became strong among his brothers and a chief came from him, yet the birthright belonged to Joseph), ³ the sons of Reuben, the firstborn of Israel: Hanoch, Pallu, Hezron, and Carmi. ⁴ The sons of Joel: Shemaiah his son, Gog his son, Shimei his son, ⁵ Micah his son, Reaiah his son, Baal his son, ⁶ Beerah his son, whom Tiglath-pileser[1] king of Assyria carried away into exile; he was a chief of the Reubenites. ⁷ And his kinsmen by their clans, when the genealogy of their generations was recorded: the chief, Jeiel, and Zechariah, ⁸ and Bela the son of Azaz, son of Shema, son of Joel, who lived in Aroer, as far as Nebo and Baal-meon. ⁹ He also lived to the east as far as the entrance of the desert this side of the Euphrates, because their livestock had multiplied in the land of Gilead. ¹⁰ And in the days of Saul they waged war against the Hagrites, who fell into their hand. And they lived in their tents throughout all the region east of Gilead.

Descendants of Gad

¹¹ The sons of Gad lived over against them in the land of Bashan as far as Salecah: ¹² Joel the chief, Shapham the second, Janai, and Shaphat in Bashan. ¹³ And their kinsmen according to their fathers' houses: Michael, Meshullam, Sheba, Jorai, Jacan, Zia and Eber, seven. ¹⁴ These were the sons of Abihail the son of Huri, son of Jaroah, son of Gilead, son of Michael, son of Jeshishai, son of Jahdo, son of Buz. ¹⁵ Ahi the son of Abdiel, son of Guni, was chief in their fathers' houses, ¹⁶ and they lived in Gilead, in Bashan and in its towns, and in all the pasturelands of Sharon to their limits. ¹⁷ All of these were recorded in genealogies in the days of Jotham king of Judah, and in the days of Jeroboam king of Israel.

¹⁸ The Reubenites, the Gadites, and the half-tribe of Manasseh had valiant men who carried shield and sword, and drew the bow, expert in war, 44,760, able to go to war. ¹⁹ They waged war against the Hagrites, Jetur, Naphish, and Nodab. ²⁰ And when they prevailed[2] over them, the Hagrites and all who were with them were given into their hands, for they cried out to God in the battle, and he granted their urgent plea because they trusted in him. ²¹ They carried off their livestock: 50,000 of their camels, 250,000 sheep, 2,000 donkeys, and 100,000 men alive. ²² For many fell, because the war was of God. And they lived in their place until the exile.

[1] Hebrew *Tilgath-pilneser*; also verse 26 [2] Or *they were helped to prevail*

The Half-Tribe of Manasseh

23 The members of the half-tribe of Manasseh lived in the land. They were very numerous from Bashan to Baal-hermon, Senir, and Mount Hermon. 24 These were the heads of their fathers' houses: Epher,[1] Ishi, Eliel, Azriel, Jeremiah, Hodaviah, and Jahdiel, mighty warriors, famous men, heads of their fathers' houses. 25 But they broke faith with the God of their fathers, and whored after the gods of the peoples of the land, whom God had destroyed before them. 26 So the God of Israel stirred up the spirit of Pul king of Assyria, the spirit of Tiglath-pileser king of Assyria, and he took them into exile, namely, the Reubenites, the Gadites, and the half-tribe of Manasseh, and brought them to Halah, Habor, Hara, and the river Gozan, to this day.

Descendants of Levi

6 [2] The sons of Levi: Gershon, Kohath, and Merari. 2 The sons of Kohath: Amram, Izhar, Hebron, and Uzziel. 3 The children of Amram: Aaron, Moses, and Miriam. The sons of Aaron: Nadab, Abihu, Eleazar, and Ithamar. 4 Eleazar fathered Phinehas, Phinehas fathered Abishua, 5 Abishua fathered Bukki, Bukki fathered Uzzi, 6 Uzzi fathered Zerahiah, Zerahiah fathered Meraioth, 7 Meraioth fathered Amariah, Amariah fathered Ahitub, 8 Ahitub fathered Zadok, Zadok fathered Ahimaaz, 9 Ahimaaz fathered Azariah, Azariah fathered Johanan, 10 and Johanan fathered Azariah (it was he who served as priest in the house that Solomon built in Jerusalem). 11 Azariah fathered Amariah, Amariah fathered Ahitub, 12 Ahitub fathered Zadok, Zadok fathered Shallum, 13 Shallum fathered Hilkiah, Hilkiah fathered Azariah, 14 Azariah fathered Seraiah, Seraiah fathered Jehozadak; 15 and Jehozadak went into exile when the LORD sent Judah and Jerusalem into exile by the hand of Nebuchadnezzar.

16 [3] The sons of Levi: Gershom, Kohath, and Merari. 17 And these are the names of the sons of Gershom: Libni and Shimei. 18 The sons of Kohath: Amram, Izhar, Hebron and Uzziel. 19 The sons of Merari: Mahli and Mushi. These are the clans of the Levites according to their fathers. 20 Of Gershom: Libni his son, Jahath his son, Zimmah his son, 21 Joah his son, Iddo his son, Zerah his son, Jeatherai his son. 22 The sons of Kohath: Amminadab his son, Korah his son, Assir his son, 23 Elkanah his son, Ebiasaph his son, Assir his son, 24 Tahath his son, Uriel his son, Uzziah his son, and Shaul his son. 25 The sons of Elkanah: Amasai and Ahimoth, 26 Elkanah his son, Zophai his son, Nahath his son, 27 Eliab his son, Jeroham his son, Elkanah his son. 28 The sons of Samuel: Joel[4] his firstborn, the second Abijah.[5] 29 The sons of Merari: Mahli,

---

[1] Septuagint, Vulgate; Hebrew *and Epher* [2] Ch 5:27 in Hebrew [3] Ch 6:1 in Hebrew [4] Septuagint, Syriac (compare verse 33 and 1 Samuel 8:2); Hebrew lacks *Joel* [5] Hebrew *and Abijah*

Libni his son, Shimei his son, Uzzah his son, ³⁰ Shimea his son, Haggiah his son, and Asaiah his son.

³¹ These are the men whom David put in charge of the service of song in the house of the LORD after the ark rested there. ³² They ministered with song before the tabernacle of the tent of meeting until Solomon built the house of the LORD in Jerusalem, and they performed their service according to their order. ³³ These are the men who served and their sons. Of the sons of the Kohathites: Heman the singer the son of Joel, son of Samuel, ³⁴ son of Elkanah, son of Jeroham, son of Eliel, son of Toah, ³⁵ son of Zuph, son of Elkanah, son of Mahath, son of Amasai, ³⁶ son of Elkanah, son of Joel, son of Azariah, son of Zephaniah, ³⁷ son of Tahath, son of Assir, son of Ebiasaph, son of Korah, ³⁸ son of Izhar, son of Kohath, son of Levi, son of Israel; ³⁹ and his brother Asaph, who stood on his right hand, namely, Asaph the son of Berechiah, son of Shimea, ⁴⁰ son of Michael, son of Baaseiah, son of Malchijah, ⁴¹ son of Ethni, son of Zerah, son of Adaiah, ⁴² son of Ethan, son of Zimmah, son of Shimei, ⁴³ son of Jahath, son of Gershom, son of Levi. ⁴⁴ On the left hand were their brothers, the sons of Merari: Ethan the son of Kishi, son of Abdi, son of Malluch, ⁴⁵ son of Hashabiah, son of Amaziah, son of Hilkiah, ⁴⁶ son of Amzi, son of Bani, son of Shemer, ⁴⁷ son of Mahli, son of Mushi, son of Merari, son of Levi. ⁴⁸ And their brothers the Levites were appointed for all the service of the tabernacle of the house of God.

⁴⁹ But Aaron and his sons made offerings on the altar of burnt offering and on the altar of incense for all the work of the Most Holy Place, and to make atonement for Israel, according to all that Moses the servant of God had commanded. ⁵⁰ These are the sons of Aaron: Eleazar his son, Phinehas his son, Abishua his son, ⁵¹ Bukki his son, Uzzi his son, Zerahiah his son, ⁵² Meraioth his son, Amariah his son, Ahitub his son, ⁵³ Zadok his son, Ahimaaz his son.

⁵⁴ These are their dwelling places according to their settlements within their borders: to the sons of Aaron of the clans of Kohathites, for theirs was the first lot, ⁵⁵ to them they gave Hebron in the land of Judah and its surrounding pasturelands, ⁵⁶ but the fields of the city and its villages they gave to Caleb the son of Jephunneh. ⁵⁷ To the sons of Aaron they gave the cities of refuge: Hebron, Libnah with its pasturelands, Jattir, Eshtemoa with its pasturelands, ⁵⁸ Hilen with its pasturelands, Debir with its pasturelands, ⁵⁹ Ashan with its pasturelands, and Beth-shemesh with its pasturelands; ⁶⁰ and from the tribe of Benjamin, Gibeon,¹ Geba with its pasturelands, Alemeth with its pasturelands, and Anathoth with its pasturelands. All their cities throughout their clans were thirteen.

---
¹ Septuagint, Syriac (compare Joshua 21:17); Hebrew lacks *Gibeon*

⁶¹ To the rest of the Kohathites were given by lot out of the clan of the tribe, out of the half-tribe, the half of Manasseh, ten cities. ⁶² To the Gershomites according to their clans were allotted thirteen cities out of the tribes of Issachar, Asher, Naphtali and Manasseh in Bashan. ⁶³ To the Merarites according to their clans were allotted twelve cities out of the tribes of Reuben, Gad, and Zebulun. ⁶⁴ So the people of Israel gave the Levites the cities with their pasturelands. ⁶⁵ They gave by lot out of the tribes of Judah, Simeon, and Benjamin these cities that are mentioned by name.

⁶⁶ And some of the clans of the sons of Kohath had cities of their territory out of the tribe of Ephraim. ⁶⁷ They were given the cities of refuge: Shechem with its pasturelands in the hill country of Ephraim, Gezer with its pasturelands, ⁶⁸ Jokmeam with its pasturelands, Beth-horon with its pasturelands, ⁶⁹ Aijalon with its pasturelands, Gath-rimmon with its pasturelands, ⁷⁰ and out of the half-tribe of Manasseh, Aner with its pasturelands, and Bileam with its pasturelands, for the rest of the clans of the Kohathites.

⁷¹ To the Gershomites were given out of the clan of the half-tribe of Manasseh: Golan in Bashan with its pasturelands and Ashtaroth with its pasturelands; ⁷² and out of the tribe of Issachar: Kedesh with its pasturelands, Daberath with its pasturelands, ⁷³ Ramoth with its pasturelands, and Anem with its pasturelands; ⁷⁴ out of the tribe of Asher: Mashal with its pasturelands, Abdon with its pasturelands, ⁷⁵ Hukok with its pasturelands, and Rehob with its pasturelands; ⁷⁶ and out of the tribe of Naphtali: Kedesh in Galilee with its pasturelands, Hammon with its pasturelands, and Kiriathaim with its pasturelands. ⁷⁷ To the rest of the Merarites were allotted out of the tribe of Zebulun: Rimmono with its pasturelands, Tabor with its pasturelands, ⁷⁸ and beyond the Jordan at Jericho, on the east side of the Jordan, out of the tribe of Reuben: Bezer in the wilderness with its pasturelands, Jahzah with its pasturelands, ⁷⁹ Kedemoth with its pasturelands, and Mephaath with its pasturelands; ⁸⁰ and out of the tribe of Gad: Ramoth in Gilead with its pasturelands, Mahanaim with its pasturelands, ⁸¹ Heshbon with its pasturelands, and Jazer with its pasturelands.

Descendants of Issachar

7 The sons[1] of Issachar: Tola, Puah, Jashub, and Shimron, four. ² The sons of Tola: Uzzi, Rephaiah, Jeriel, Jahmai, Ibsam, and Shemuel, heads of their fathers' houses, namely of Tola, mighty warriors of their generations, their number in the days of David being 22,600. ³ The son[2] of Uzzi: Izrahiah. And the sons of Izrahiah: Michael, Obadiah, Joel, and Isshiah, all five of them

---

[1] Syriac (compare Vulgate); Hebrew *And to the sons* [2] Hebrew *sons*; also verses 10, 12, 17

were chief men. ⁴And along with them, by their generations, according to their fathers' houses, were units of the army for war, 36,000, for they had many wives and sons. ⁵Their kinsmen belonging to all the clans of Issachar were in all 87,000 mighty warriors, enrolled by genealogy.

Descendants of Benjamin

⁶The sons of Benjamin: Bela, Becher, and Jediael, three. ⁷The sons of Bela: Ezbon, Uzzi, Uzziel, Jerimoth, and Iri, five, heads of fathers' houses, mighty warriors. And their enrollment by genealogies was 22,034. ⁸The sons of Becher: Zemirah, Joash, Eliezer, Elioenai, Omri, Jeremoth, Abijah, Anathoth, and Alemeth. All these were the sons of Becher. ⁹And their enrollment by genealogies, according to their generations, as heads of their fathers' houses, mighty warriors, was 20,200. ¹⁰The son of Jediael: Bilhan. And the sons of Bilhan: Jeush, Benjamin, Ehud, Chenaanah, Zethan, Tarshish, and Ahishahar. ¹¹All these were the sons of Jediael according to the heads of their fathers' houses, mighty warriors, 17,200, able to go to war. ¹²And Shuppim and Huppim were the sons of Ir, Hushim the son of Aher.

Descendants of Naphtali

¹³The sons of Naphtali: Jahziel, Guni, Jezer and Shallum, the descendants of Bilhah.

Descendants of Manasseh

¹⁴The sons of Manasseh: Asriel, whom his Aramean concubine bore; she bore Machir the father of Gilead. ¹⁵And Machir took a wife for Huppim and for Shuppim. The name of his sister was Maacah. And the name of the second was Zelophehad, and Zelophehad had daughters. ¹⁶And Maacah the wife of Machir bore a son, and she called his name Peresh; and the name of his brother was Sheresh; and his sons were Ulam and Rakem. ¹⁷The son of Ulam: Bedan. These were the sons of Gilead the son of Machir, son of Manasseh. ¹⁸And his sister Hammolecheth bore Ishhod, Abiezer, and Mahlah. ¹⁹The sons of Shemida were Ahian, Shechem, Likhi, and Aniam.

Descendants of Ephraim

²⁰The sons of Ephraim: Shuthelah, and Bered his son, Tahath his son, Eleadah his son, Tahath his son, ²¹Zabad his son, Shuthelah his son, and Ezer and Elead, whom the men of Gath who were born in the land killed, because they came down to raid their livestock. ²²And Ephraim their father mourned many days, and his brothers came to comfort him. ²³And Ephraim

went in to his wife, and she conceived and bore a son. And he called his name Beriah, because disaster had befallen his house.[1] [24] His daughter was Sheerah, who built both Lower and Upper Beth-horon, and Uzzen-sheerah. [25] Rephah was his son, Resheph his son, Telah his son, Tahan his son, [26] Ladan his son, Ammihud his son, Elishama his son, [27] Nun[2] his son, Joshua his son. [28] Their possessions and settlements were Bethel and its towns, and to the east Naaran, and to the west Gezer and its towns, Shechem and its towns, and Ayyah and its towns; [29] also in possession of the Manassites, Beth-shean and its towns, Taanach and its towns, Megiddo and its towns, Dor and its towns. In these lived the sons of Joseph the son of Israel.

Descendants of Asher

[30] The sons of Asher: Imnah, Ishvah, Ishvi, Beriah, and their sister Serah. [31] The sons of Beriah: Heber, and Malchiel, who fathered Birzaith. [32] Heber fathered Japhlet, Shomer, Hotham, and their sister Shua. [33] The sons of Japhlet: Pasach, Bimhal, and Ashvath. These are the sons of Japhlet. [34] The sons of Shemer his brother: Rohgah, Jehubbah, and Aram. [35] The sons of Helem his brother: Zophah, Imna, Shelesh, and Amal. [36] The sons of Zophah: Suah, Harnepher, Shual, Beri, Imrah. [37] Bezer, Hod, Shamma, Shilshah, Ithran, and Beera. [38] The sons of Jether: Jephunneh, Pispa, and Ara. [39] The sons of Ulla: Arah, Hanniel, and Rizia. [40] All of these were men of Asher, heads of fathers' houses, approved, mighty warriors, chiefs of the princes. Their number enrolled by genealogies, for service in war, was 26,000 men.

A Genealogy of Saul

8 Benjamin fathered Bela his firstborn, Ashbel the second, Aharah the third, [2] Nohah the fourth, and Rapha the fifth. [3] And Bela had sons: Addar, Gera, Abihud, [4] Abishua, Naaman, Ahoah, [5] Gera, Shephuphan, and Huram. [6] These are the sons of Ehud (they were heads of fathers' houses of the inhabitants of Geba, and they were carried into exile to Manahath): [7] Naaman,[3] Ahijah, and Gera, that is, Heglam, who fathered[4] Uzza and Ahihud. [8] And Shaharaim fathered sons in the country of Moab after he had sent away Hushim and Baara his wives. [9] He fathered sons by Hodesh his wife: Jobab, Zibia, Mesha, Malcam, [10] Jeuz, Sachia, and Mirmah. These were his sons, heads of fathers' houses. [11] He also fathered sons by Hushim: Abitub and Elpaal. [12] The sons of Elpaal: Eber, Misham, and Shemed, who built Ono and Lod with its towns, [13] and Beriah and Shema (they were heads of fathers' houses of the inhabitants of Aijalon, who caused the inhabitants

---

[1] *Beriah* sounds like the Hebrew for *disaster* [2] Hebrew *Non* [3] Hebrew *and Naaman* [4] Or *Gera; he carried them into exile and fathered*

of Gath to flee); ¹⁴ and Ahio, Shashak, and Jeremoth. ¹⁵ Zebadiah, Arad, Eder, ¹⁶ Michael, Ishpah, and Joha were sons of Beriah. ¹⁷ Zebadiah, Meshullam, Hizki, Heber, ¹⁸ Ishmerai, Izliah, and Jobab were the sons of Elpaal. ¹⁹ Jakim, Zichri, Zabdi, ²⁰ Elienai, Zillethai, Eliel, ²¹ Adaiah, Beraiah, and Shimrath were the sons of Shimei. ²² Ishpan, Eber, Eliel, ²³ Abdon, Zichri, Hanan, ²⁴ Hananiah, Elam, Anthothijah, ²⁵ Iphdeiah, and Penuel were the sons of Shashak. ²⁶ Shamsherai, Shehariah, Athaliah, ²⁷ Jaareshiah, Elijah, and Zichri were the sons of Jeroham. ²⁸ These were the heads of fathers' houses, according to their generations, chief men. These lived in Jerusalem.

²⁹ Jeiel[1] the father of Gibeon lived in Gibeon, and the name of his wife was Maacah. ³⁰ His firstborn son: Abdon, then Zur, Kish, Baal, Nadab, ³¹ Gedor, Ahio, Zecher, ³² and Mikloth (he fathered Shimeah). Now these also lived opposite their kinsmen in Jerusalem, with their kinsmen. ³³ Ner was the father of Kish, Kish of Saul, Saul of Jonathan, Malchi-shua, Abinadab and Eshbaal; ³⁴ and the son of Jonathan was Merib-baal; and Merib-baal was the father of Micah. ³⁵ The sons of Micah: Pithon, Melech, Tarea, and Ahaz. ³⁶ Ahaz fathered Jehoaddah, and Jehoaddah fathered Alemeth, Azmaveth, and Zimri. Zimri fathered Moza. ³⁷ Moza fathered Binea; Raphah was his son, Eleasah his son, Azel his son. ³⁸ Azel had six sons, and these are their names: Azrikam, Bocheru, Ishmael, Sheariah, Obadiah, and Hanan. All these were the sons of Azel. ³⁹ The sons of Eshek his brother: Ulam his firstborn, Jeush the second, and Eliphelet the third. ⁴⁰ The sons of Ulam were men who were mighty warriors, bowmen, having many sons and grandsons, 150. All these were Benjaminites.

A Genealogy of the Returned Exiles

9 So all Israel was recorded in genealogies, and these are written in the Book of the Kings of Israel. And Judah was taken into exile in Babylon because of their breach of faith. ² Now the first to dwell again in their possessions in their cities were Israel, the priests, the Levites, and the temple servants. ³ And some of the people of Judah, Benjamin, Ephraim, and Manasseh lived in Jerusalem: ⁴ Uthai the son of Ammihud, son of Omri, son of Imri, son of Bani, from the sons of Perez the son of Judah. ⁵ And of the Shilonites: Asaiah the firstborn, and his sons. ⁶ Of the sons of Zerah: Jeuel and their kinsmen, 690. ⁷ Of the Benjaminites: Sallu the son of Meshullam, son of Hodaviah, son of Hassenuah, ⁸ Ibneiah the son of Jeroham, Elah the son of Uzzi, son of Michri, and Meshullam the son of Shephatiah, son of Reuel, son of Ibnijah; ⁹ and their kinsmen according to their generations, 956. All these were heads of fathers' houses according to their fathers' houses.

[1] Compare 9:35; Hebrew lacks *Jeiel*

¹⁰ Of the priests: Jedaiah, Jehoiarib, Jachin, ¹¹ and Azariah the son of Hilkiah, son of Meshullam, son of Zadok, son of Meraioth, son of Ahitub, the chief officer of the house of God; ¹² and Adaiah the son of Jeroham, son of Pashhur, son of Malchijah, and Maasai the son of Adiel, son of Jahzerah, son of Meshullam, son of Meshillemith, son of Immer; ¹³ besides their kinsmen, heads of their fathers' houses, 1,760, mighty men for the work of the service of the house of God.

¹⁴ Of the Levites: Shemaiah the son of Hasshub, son of Azrikam, son of Hashabiah, of the sons of Merari; ¹⁵ and Bakbakkar, Heresh, Galal and Mattaniah the son of Mica, son of Zichri, son of Asaph; ¹⁶ and Obadiah the son of Shemaiah, son of Galal, son of Jeduthun, and Berechiah the son of Asa, son of Elkanah, who lived in the villages of the Netophathites.

¹⁷ The gatekeepers were Shallum, Akkub, Talmon, Ahiman, and their kinsmen (Shallum was the chief); ¹⁸ until then they were in the king's gate on the east side as the gatekeepers of the camps of the Levites. ¹⁹ Shallum the son of Kore, son of Ebiasaph, son of Korah, and his kinsmen of his fathers' house, the Korahites, were in charge of the work of the service, keepers of the thresholds of the tent, as their fathers had been in charge of the camp of the Lord, keepers of the entrance. ²⁰ And Phinehas the son of Eleazar was the chief officer over them in time past; the Lord was with him. ²¹ Zechariah the son of Meshelemiah was gatekeeper at the entrance of the tent of meeting. ²² All these, who were chosen as gatekeepers at the thresholds, were 212. They were enrolled by genealogies in their villages. David and Samuel the seer established them in their office of trust. ²³ So they and their sons were in charge of the gates of the house of the Lord, that is, the house of the tent, as guards. ²⁴ The gatekeepers were on the four sides, east, west, north, and south. ²⁵ And their kinsmen who were in their villages were obligated to come in every seven days, in turn, to be with these, ²⁶ for the four chief gatekeepers, who were Levites, were entrusted to be over the chambers and the treasures of the house of God. ²⁷ And they lodged around the house of God, for on them lay the duty of watching, and they had charge of opening it every morning.

²⁸ Some of them had charge of the utensils of service, for they were required to count them when they were brought in and taken out. ²⁹ Others of them were appointed over the furniture and over all the holy utensils, also over the fine flour, the wine, the oil, the incense, and the spices. ³⁰ Others, of the sons of the priests, prepared the mixing of the spices, ³¹ and Mattithiah, one of the Levites, the firstborn of Shallum the Korahite, was entrusted with making the flat cakes. ³² Also some of their kinsmen of the Kohathites had charge of the showbread, to prepare it every Sabbath.

³³ Now these, the singers, the heads of fathers' houses of the Levites, were in the chambers of the temple free from other service, for they were on duty day and night. ³⁴ These were heads of fathers' houses of the Levites, according to their generations, leaders. These lived in Jerusalem.

Saul's Genealogy Repeated

³⁵ In Gibeon lived the father of Gibeon, Jeiel, and the name of his wife was Maacah, ³⁶ and his firstborn son Abdon, then Zur, Kish, Baal, Ner, Nadab, ³⁷ Gedor, Ahio, Zechariah, and Mikloth; ³⁸ and Mikloth was the father of Shimeam; and these also lived opposite their kinsmen in Jerusalem, with their kinsmen. ³⁹ Ner fathered Kish, Kish fathered Saul, Saul fathered Jonathan, Malchi-shua, Abinadab, and Eshbaal. ⁴⁰ And the son of Jonathan was Merib-baal, and Merib-baal fathered Micah. ⁴¹ The sons of Micah: Pithon, Melech, Tahrea, and Ahaz.[1] ⁴² And Ahaz fathered Jarah, and Jarah fathered Alemeth, Azmaveth, and Zimri. And Zimri fathered Moza. ⁴³ Moza fathered Binea, and Rephaiah was his son, Eleasah his son, Azel his son. ⁴⁴ Azel had six sons and these are their names: Azrikam, Bocheru, Ishmael, Sheariah, Obadiah, and Hanan; these were the sons of Azel.

The Death of Saul and His Sons

10 Now the Philistines fought against Israel, and the men of Israel fled before the Philistines and fell slain on Mount Gilboa. ² And the Philistines overtook Saul and his sons, and the Philistines struck down Jonathan and Abinadab and Malchi-shua, the sons of Saul. ³ The battle pressed hard against Saul, and the archers found him, and he was wounded by the archers. ⁴ Then Saul said to his armor-bearer, "Draw your sword and thrust me through with it, lest these uncircumcised come and mistreat me." But his armor-bearer would not, for he feared greatly. Therefore Saul took his own sword and fell upon it. ⁵ And when his armor-bearer saw that Saul was dead, he also fell upon his sword and died. ⁶ Thus Saul died; he and his three sons and all his house died together. ⁷ And when all the men of Israel who were in the valley saw that the army[2] had fled and that Saul and his sons were dead, they abandoned their cities and fled, and the Philistines came and lived in them.

⁸ The next day, when the Philistines came to strip the slain, they found Saul and his sons fallen on Mount Gilboa. ⁹ And they stripped him and took his head and his armor, and sent messengers throughout the land of the Philistines to carry the good news to their idols and to the people. ¹⁰ And

---

[1] Compare 8:35; Hebrew lacks *and Ahaz* [2] Hebrew *they*

they put his armor in the temple of their gods and fastened his head in the temple of Dagon. ⁱⁱ But when all Jabesh-gilead heard all that the Philistines had done to Saul, ¹² all the valiant men arose and took away the body of Saul and the bodies of his sons, and brought them to Jabesh. And they buried their bones under the oak in Jabesh and fasted seven days.

¹³ So Saul died for his breach of faith. He broke faith with the Lord in that he did not keep the command of the Lord, and also consulted a medium, seeking guidance. ¹⁴ He did not seek guidance from the Lord. Therefore the Lord put him to death and turned the kingdom over to David the son of Jesse.

David Anointed King

11 Then all Israel gathered together to David at Hebron and said, "Behold, we are your bone and flesh. ² In times past, even when Saul was king, it was you who led out and brought in Israel. And the Lord your God said to you, 'You shall be shepherd of my people Israel, and you shall be prince over my people Israel.'" ³ So all the elders of Israel came to the king at Hebron, and David made a covenant with them at Hebron before the Lord. And they anointed David king over Israel, according to the word of the Lord by Samuel.

David Takes Jerusalem

⁴ And David and all Israel went to Jerusalem, that is, Jebus, where the Jebusites were, the inhabitants of the land. ⁵ The inhabitants of Jebus said to David, "You will not come in here." Nevertheless, David took the stronghold of Zion, that is, the city of David. ⁶ David said, "Whoever strikes the Jebusites first shall be chief and commander." And Joab the son of Zeruiah went up first, so he became chief. ⁷ And David lived in the stronghold; therefore it was called the city of David. ⁸ And he built the city all around from the Millo in complete circuit, and Joab repaired the rest of the city. ⁹ And David became greater and greater, for the Lord of hosts was with him.

David's Mighty Men

¹⁰ Now these are the chiefs of David's mighty men, who gave him strong support in his kingdom, together with all Israel, to make him king, according to the word of the Lord concerning Israel. ¹¹ This is an account of David's mighty men: Jashobeam, a Hachmonite, was chief of the three.¹ He wielded his spear against 300 whom he killed at one time.

¹ Compare 2 Samuel 23:8; Hebrew *thirty*, or *captains*

¹² And next to him among the three mighty men was Eleazar the son of Dodo, the Ahohite. ¹³ He was with David at Pas-dammim when the Philistines were gathered there for battle. There was a plot of ground full of barley, and the men fled from the Philistines. ¹⁴ But he took his[1] stand in the midst of the plot and defended it and killed the Philistines. And the LORD saved them by a great victory.

¹⁵ Three of the thirty chief men went down to the rock to David at the cave of Adullam, when the army of Philistines was encamped in the Valley of Rephaim. ¹⁶ David was then in the stronghold, and the garrison of the Philistines was then at Bethlehem. ¹⁷ And David said longingly, "Oh that someone would give me water to drink from the well of Bethlehem that is by the gate!" ¹⁸ Then the three mighty men broke through the camp of the Philistines and drew water out of the well of Bethlehem that was by the gate and took it and brought it to David. But David would not drink it. He poured it out to the LORD ¹⁹ and said, "Far be it from me before my God that I should do this. Shall I drink the lifeblood of these men? For at the risk of their lives they brought it." Therefore he would not drink it. These things did the three mighty men.

²⁰ Now Abishai, the brother of Joab, was chief of the thirty.[2] And he wielded his spear against 300 men and killed them and won a name beside the three. ²¹ He was the most renowned[3] of the thirty[4] and became their commander, but he did not attain to the three.

²² And Benaiah the son of Jehoiada was a valiant man[5] of Kabzeel, a doer of great deeds. He struck down two heroes of Moab. He also went down and struck down a lion in a pit on a day when snow had fallen. ²³ And he struck down an Egyptian, a man of great stature, five cubits[6] tall. The Egyptian had in his hand a spear like a weaver's beam, but Benaiah went down to him with a staff and snatched the spear out of the Egyptian's hand and killed him with his own spear. ²⁴ These things did Benaiah the son of Jehoiada and won a name beside the three mighty men. ²⁵ He was renowned among the thirty, but he did not attain to the three. And David set him over his bodyguard.

²⁶ The mighty men were Asahel the brother of Joab, Elhanan the son of Dodo of Bethlehem, ²⁷ Shammoth of Harod,[7] Helez the Pelonite, ²⁸ Ira the son of Ikkesh of Tekoa, Abiezer of Anathoth, ²⁹ Sibbecai the Hushathite, Ilai the Ahohite, ³⁰ Maharai of Netophah, Heled the son of Baanah of Netophah, ³¹ Ithai the son of Ribai of Gibeah of the people of Benjamin, Benaiah of Pirathon, ³² Hurai of the brooks of Gaash, Abiel the Arbathite, ³³ Azmaveth of Baharum, Eliahba the Shaalbonite, ³⁴ Hashem[8] the Gizonite, Jonathan the

---

[1] Compare 2 Samuel 23:12; Hebrew *they...their* [2] Syriac; Hebrew *three* [3] Compare 2 Samuel 23:19; Hebrew *more renowned among the two* [4] Syriac; Hebrew *three* [5] Syriac; Hebrew *the son of a valiant man* [6] A *cubit* was about 18 inches or 45 centimeters [7] Compare 2 Samuel 23:25; Hebrew *the Harorite* [8] Compare Septuagint and 2 Samuel 23:32; Hebrew *the sons of Hashem*

son of Shagee the Hararite, ³⁵ Ahiam the son of Sachar the Hararite, Eliphal the son of Ur, ³⁶ Hepher the Mecherathite, Ahijah the Pelonite, ³⁷ Hezro of Carmel, Naarai the son of Ezbai, ³⁸ Joel the brother of Nathan, Mibhar the son of Hagri, ³⁹ Zelek the Ammonite, Naharai of Beeroth, the armor-bearer of Joab the son of Zeruiah, ⁴⁰ Ira the Ithrite, Gareb the Ithrite, ⁴¹ Uriah the Hittite, Zabad the son of Ahlai, ⁴² Adina the son of Shiza the Reubenite, a leader of the Reubenites, and thirty with him, ⁴³ Hanan the son of Maacah, and Joshaphat the Mithnite, ⁴⁴ Uzzia the Ashterathite, Shama and Jeiel the sons of Hotham the Aroerite, ⁴⁵ Jediael the son of Shimri, and Joha his brother, the Tizite, ⁴⁶ Eliel the Mahavite, and Jeribai, and Joshaviah, the sons of Elnaam, and Ithmah the Moabite, ⁴⁷ Eliel, and Obed, and Jaasiel the Mezobaite.

The Mighty Men Join David

12 Now these are the men who came to David at Ziklag, while he could not move about freely because of Saul the son of Kish. And they were among the mighty men who helped him in war. ² They were bowmen and could shoot arrows and sling stones with either the right or the left hand; they were Benjaminites, Saul's kinsmen. ³ The chief was Ahiezer, then Joash, both sons of Shemaah of Gibeah; also Jeziel and Pelet, the sons of Azmaveth; Beracah, Jehu of Anathoth, ⁴ Ishmaiah of Gibeon, a mighty man among the thirty and a leader over the thirty; Jeremiah,¹ Jahaziel, Johanan, Jozabad of Gederah, ⁵ Eluzai,² Jerimoth, Bealiah, Shemariah, Shephatiah the Haruphite; ⁶ Elkanah, Isshiah, Azarel, Joezer, and Jashobeam, the Korahites; ⁷ And Joelah and Zebadiah, the sons of Jeroham of Gedor.

⁸ From the Gadites there went over to David at the stronghold in the wilderness mighty and experienced warriors, expert with shield and spear, whose faces were like the faces of lions and who were swift as gazelles upon the mountains: ⁹ Ezer the chief, Obadiah second, Eliab third, ¹⁰ Mishmannah fourth, Jeremiah fifth, ¹¹ Attai sixth, Eliel seventh, ¹² Johanan eighth, Elzabad ninth, ¹³ Jeremiah tenth, Machbannai eleventh. ¹⁴ These Gadites were officers of the army; the least was a match for a hundred men and the greatest for a thousand. ¹⁵ These are the men who crossed the Jordan in the first month, when it was overflowing all its banks, and put to flight all those in the valleys, to the east and to the west.

¹⁶ And some of the men of Benjamin and Judah came to the stronghold to David. ¹⁷ David went out to meet them and said to them, "If you have come to me in friendship to help me, my heart will be joined to you; but if to betray me to my adversaries, although there is no wrong in my hands, then may the

¹ Hebrew verse 5 ² Hebrew verse 6

God of our fathers see and rebuke you." [18] Then the Spirit clothed Amasai, chief of the thirty, and he said,

"We are yours, O David,
 and with you, O son of Jesse!
Peace, peace to you,
 and peace to your helpers!
 For your God helps you."

Then David received them and made them officers of his troops.

[19] Some of the men of Manasseh deserted to David when he came with the Philistines for the battle against Saul. (Yet he did not help them, for the rulers of the Philistines took counsel and sent him away, saying, "At peril to our heads he will desert to his master Saul.") [20] As he went to Ziklag, these men of Manasseh deserted to him: Adnah, Jozabad, Jediael, Michael, Jozabad, Elihu, and Zillethai, chiefs of thousands in Manasseh. [21] They helped David against the band of raiders, for they were all mighty men of valor and were commanders in the army. [22] For from day to day men came to David to help him, until there was a great army, like an army of God.

[23] These are the numbers of the divisions of the armed troops who came to David in Hebron to turn the kingdom of Saul over to him, according to the word of the Lord. [24] The men of Judah bearing shield and spear were 6,800 armed troops. [25] Of the Simeonites, mighty men of valor for war, 7,100. [26] Of the Levites 4,600. [27] The prince Jehoiada, of the house of Aaron, and with him 3,700. [28] Zadok, a young man mighty in valor, and twenty-two commanders from his own fathers' house. [29] Of the Benjaminites, the kinsmen of Saul, 3,000, of whom the majority had to that point kept their allegiance to the house of Saul. [30] Of the Ephraimites 20,800, mighty men of valor, famous men in their fathers' houses. [31] Of the half-tribe of Manasseh 18,000, who were expressly named to come and make David king. [32] Of Issachar, men who had understanding of the times, to know what Israel ought to do, 200 chiefs, and all their kinsmen under their command. [33] Of Zebulun 50,000 seasoned troops, equipped for battle with all the weapons of war, to help David[1] with singleness of purpose. [34] Of Naphtali 1,000 commanders with whom were 37,000 men armed with shield and spear. [35] Of the Danites 28,600 men equipped for battle. [36] Of Asher 40,000 seasoned troops ready for battle. [37] Of the Reubenites and Gadites and the half-tribe of Manasseh from beyond the Jordan, 120,000 men armed with all the weapons of war.

[1] Septuagint; Hebrew lacks *David*

⁣³⁸ All these, men of war, arrayed in battle order, came to Hebron with a whole heart to make David king over all Israel. Likewise, all the rest of Israel were of a single mind to make David king. ³⁹ And they were there with David for three days, eating and drinking, for their brothers had made preparation for them. ⁴⁰ And also their relatives, from as far as Issachar and Zebulun and Naphtali, came bringing food on donkeys and on camels and on mules and on oxen, abundant provisions of flour, cakes of figs, clusters of raisins, and wine and oil, oxen and sheep, for there was joy in Israel.

The Ark Brought from Kiriath-Jearim

13 David consulted with the commanders of thousands and of hundreds, with every leader. ² And David said to all the assembly of Israel, "If it seems good to you and from the Lord our God, let us send abroad to our brothers who remain in all the lands of Israel, as well as to the priests and Levites in the cities that have pasturelands, that they may be gathered to us. ³ Then let us bring again the ark of our God to us, for we did not seek it[1] in the days of Saul." ⁴ All the assembly agreed to do so, for the thing was right in the eyes of all the people.

Uzzah and the Ark

⁵ So David assembled all Israel from the Nile[2] of Egypt to Lebo-hamath, to bring the ark of God from Kiriath-jearim. ⁶ And David and all Israel went up to Baalah, that is, to Kiriath-jearim that belongs to Judah, to bring up from there the ark of God, which is called by the name of the Lord who sits enthroned above the cherubim. ⁷ And they carried the ark of God on a new cart, from the house of Abinadab, and Uzzah and Ahio[3] were driving the cart. ⁸ And David and all Israel were celebrating before God with all their might, with song and lyres and harps and tambourines and cymbals and trumpets.

⁹ And when they came to the threshing floor of Chidon, Uzzah put out his hand to take hold of the ark, for the oxen stumbled. ¹⁰ And the anger of the Lord was kindled against Uzzah, and he struck him down because he put out his hand to the ark, and he died there before God. ¹¹ And David was angry because the Lord had broken out against Uzzah. And that place is called Perez-uzza[4] to this day. ¹² And David was afraid of God that day, and he said, "How can I bring the ark of God home to me?" ¹³ So David did not take the ark home into the city of David, but took it aside to the house of Obed-edom the Gittite. ¹⁴ And the ark of God remained with the household of Obed-edom in his house three months. And the Lord blessed the household of Obed-edom and all that he had.

[1] Or *him* [2] Hebrew *Shihor* [3] Or *and his brother* [4] *Perez-uzza* means *the breaking out against Uzzah*

David's Wives and Children

14 And Hiram king of Tyre sent messengers to David, and cedar trees, also masons and carpenters to build a house for him. ² And David knew that the Lord had established him as king over Israel, and that his kingdom was highly exalted for the sake of his people Israel.

³ And David took more wives in Jerusalem, and David fathered more sons and daughters. ⁴ These are the names of the children born to him in Jerusalem: Shammua, Shobab, Nathan, Solomon, ⁵ Ibhar, Elishua, Elpelet, ⁶ Nogah, Nepheg, Japhia, ⁷ Elishama, Beeliada and Eliphelet.

Philistines Defeated

⁸ When the Philistines heard that David had been anointed king over all Israel, all the Philistines went up to search for David. But David heard of it and went out against them. ⁹ Now the Philistines had come and made a raid in the Valley of Rephaim. ¹⁰ And David inquired of God, "Shall I go up against the Philistines? Will you give them into my hand?" And the Lord said to him, "Go up, and I will give them into your hand." ¹¹ And he went up to Baal-perazim, and David struck them down there. And David said, "God has broken through[1] my enemies by my hand, like a bursting flood." Therefore the name of that place is called Baal-perazim. ¹² And they left their gods there, and David gave command, and they were burned.

¹³ And the Philistines yet again made a raid in the valley. ¹⁴ And when David again inquired of God, God said to him, "You shall not go up after them; go around and come against them opposite the balsam trees. ¹⁵ And when you hear the sound of marching in the tops of the balsam trees, then go out to battle, for God has gone out before you to strike down the army of the Philistines." ¹⁶ And David did as God commanded him, and they struck down the Philistine army from Gibeon to Gezer. ¹⁷ And the fame of David went out into all lands, and the Lord brought the fear of him upon all nations.

The Ark Brought to Jerusalem

15 David[2] built houses for himself in the city of David. And he prepared a place for the ark of God and pitched a tent for it. ² Then David said that no one but the Levites may carry the ark of God, for the Lord had chosen them to carry the ark of the Lord and to minister to him forever. ³ And David assembled all Israel at Jerusalem to bring up the ark of the Lord to its place, which he had prepared for it. ⁴ And David gathered together the sons of Aaron and the Levites: ⁵ of the sons of Kohath, Uriel the chief, with 120 of his brothers;

---

[1] *Baal-perazim* means *Lord of breaking through* [2] Hebrew *He*

⁶ of the sons of Merari, Asaiah the chief, with 220 of his brothers; ⁷ of the sons of Gershom, Joel the chief, with 130 of his brothers; ⁸ of the sons of Elizaphan, Shemaiah the chief, with 200 of his brothers; ⁹ of the sons of Hebron, Eliel the chief, with 80 of his brothers; ¹⁰ of the sons of Uzziel, Amminadab the chief, with 112 of his brothers. ¹¹ Then David summoned the priests Zadok and Abiathar, and the Levites Uriel, Asaiah, Joel, Shemaiah, Eliel, and Amminadab, ¹² and said to them, "You are the heads of the fathers' houses of the Levites. Consecrate yourselves, you and your brothers, so that you may bring up the ark of the Lord, the God of Israel, to the place that I have prepared for it. ¹³ Because you did not carry it the first time, the Lord our God broke out against us, because we did not seek him according to the rule." ¹⁴ So the priests and the Levites consecrated themselves to bring up the ark of the Lord, the God of Israel. ¹⁵ And the Levites carried the ark of God on their shoulders with the poles, as Moses had commanded according to the word of the Lord.

¹⁶ David also commanded the chiefs of the Levites to appoint their brothers as the singers who should play loudly on musical instruments, on harps and lyres and cymbals, to raise sounds of joy. ¹⁷ So the Levites appointed Heman the son of Joel; and of his brothers Asaph the son of Berechiah; and of the sons of Merari, their brothers, Ethan the son of Kushaiah; ¹⁸ and with them their brothers of the second order, Zechariah, Jaaziel, Shemiramoth, Jehiel, Unni, Eliab, Benaiah, Maaseiah, Mattithiah, Eliphelehu, and Mikneiah, and the gatekeepers Obed-edom and Jeiel. ¹⁹ The singers, Heman, Asaph, and Ethan, were to sound bronze cymbals; ²⁰ Zechariah, Aziel, Shemiramoth, Jehiel, Unni, Eliab, Maaseiah, and Benaiah were to play harps according to Alamoth; ²¹ but Mattithiah, Eliphelehu, Mikneiah, Obed-edom, Jeiel, and Azaziah were to lead with lyres according to the Sheminith. ²² Chenaniah, leader of the Levites in music, should direct the music, for he understood it. ²³ Berechiah and Elkanah were to be gatekeepers for the ark. ²⁴ Shebaniah, Joshaphat, Nethanel, Amasai, Zechariah, Benaiah, and Eliezer, the priests, should blow the trumpets before the ark of God. Obed-edom and Jehiah were to be gatekeepers for the ark.

²⁵ So David and the elders of Israel and the commanders of thousands went to bring up the ark of the covenant of the Lord from the house of Obed-edom with rejoicing. ²⁶ And because God helped the Levites who were carrying the ark of the covenant of the Lord, they sacrificed seven bulls and seven rams. ²⁷ David was clothed with a robe of fine linen, as also were all the Levites who were carrying the ark, and the singers and Chenaniah the leader of the music of the singers. And David wore a linen ephod. ²⁸ So all Israel brought up the ark of the covenant of the Lord with shouting, to the sound of the horn, trumpets, and cymbals, and made loud music on harps and lyres.

²⁹ And as the ark of the covenant of the Lord came to the city of David, Michal the daughter of Saul looked out of the window and saw King David dancing and celebrating, and she despised him in her heart.

The Ark Placed in a Tent

16 And they brought in the ark of God and set it inside the tent that David had pitched for it, and they offered burnt offerings and peace offerings before God. ² And when David had finished offering the burnt offerings and the peace offerings, he blessed the people in the name of the Lord ³ and distributed to all Israel, both men and women, to each a loaf of bread, a portion of meat,¹ and a cake of raisins.

⁴ Then he appointed some of the Levites as ministers before the ark of the Lord, to invoke, to thank, and to praise the Lord, the God of Israel. ⁵ Asaph was the chief, and second to him were Zechariah, Jeiel, Shemiramoth, Jehiel, Mattithiah, Eliab, Benaiah, Obed-edom, and Jeiel, who were to play harps and lyres; Asaph was to sound the cymbals, ⁶ and Benaiah and Jahaziel the priests were to blow trumpets regularly before the ark of the covenant of God. ⁷ Then on that day David first appointed that thanksgiving be sung to the Lord by Asaph and his brothers.

David's Song of Thanks

8   Oh give thanks to the Lord; call upon his name;
     make known his deeds among the peoples!
9   Sing to him, sing praises to him;
     tell of all his wondrous works!
10   Glory in his holy name;
     let the hearts of those who seek the Lord rejoice!
11   Seek the Lord and his strength;
     seek his presence continually!
12   Remember the wondrous works that he has done,
     his miracles and the judgments he uttered,
13   O offspring of Israel his servant,
     children of Jacob, his chosen ones!

14   He is the Lord our God;
     his judgments are in all the earth.
15   Remember his covenant forever,
     the word that he commanded, for a thousand generations,

---

¹ Compare Septuagint, Syriac, Vulgate; the meaning of the Hebrew is uncertain

¹⁶ the covenant that he made with Abraham,
   his sworn promise to Isaac,
¹⁷ which he confirmed to Jacob as a statute,
   to Israel as an everlasting covenant,
¹⁸ saying, "To you I will give the land of Canaan,
   as your portion for an inheritance."

¹⁹ When you were few in number,
   of little account, and sojourners in it,
²⁰ wandering from nation to nation,
   from one kingdom to another people,
²¹ he allowed no one to oppress them;
   he rebuked kings on their account,
²² saying, "Touch not my anointed ones,
   do my prophets no harm!"

²³ Sing to the Lord, all the earth!
   Tell of his salvation from day to day.
²⁴ Declare his glory among the nations,
   his marvelous works among all the peoples!
²⁵ For great is the Lord, and greatly to be praised,
   and he is to be feared above all gods.
²⁶ For all the gods of the peoples are worthless idols,
   but the Lord made the heavens.
²⁷ Splendor and majesty are before him;
   strength and joy are in his place.

²⁸ Ascribe to the Lord, O families of the peoples,
   ascribe to the Lord glory and strength!
²⁹ Ascribe to the Lord the glory due his name;
   bring an offering and come before him!
   Worship the Lord in the splendor of holiness;[1]
³⁰   tremble before him, all the earth;
   yes, the world is established; it shall never be moved.
³¹ Let the heavens be glad, and let the earth rejoice,
   and let them say among the nations, "The Lord reigns!"
³² Let the sea roar, and all that fills it;
   let the field exult, and everything in it!

[1] Or *in holy attire*

33 Then shall the trees of the forest sing for joy
> before the Lord, for he comes to judge the earth.
34 Oh give thanks to the Lord, for he is good;
> for his steadfast love endures forever!

³⁵ Say also:

"Save us, O God of our salvation,
> and gather and deliver us from among the nations,
that we may give thanks to your holy name
> and glory in your praise.
36 Blessed be the Lord, the God of Israel,
> from everlasting to everlasting!"

Then all the people said, "Amen!" and praised the Lord.

Worship Before the Ark

³⁷ So David left Asaph and his brothers there before the ark of the covenant of the Lord to minister regularly before the ark as each day required, ³⁸ and also Obed-edom and his[1] sixty-eight brothers, while Obed-edom, the son of Jeduthun, and Hosah were to be gatekeepers. ³⁹ And he left Zadok the priest and his brothers the priests before the tabernacle of the Lord in the high place that was at Gibeon ⁴⁰ to offer burnt offerings to the Lord on the altar of burnt offering regularly morning and evening, to do all that is written in the Law of the Lord that he commanded Israel. ⁴¹ With them were Heman and Jeduthun and the rest of those chosen and expressly named to give thanks to the Lord, for his steadfast love endures forever. ⁴² Heman and Jeduthun had trumpets and cymbals for the music and instruments for sacred song. The sons of Jeduthun were appointed to the gate.

⁴³ Then all the people departed each to his house, and David went home to bless his household.

The Lord's Covenant with David

17 Now when David lived in his house, David said to Nathan the prophet, "Behold, I dwell in a house of cedar, but the ark of the covenant of the Lord is under a tent." ² And Nathan said to David, "Do all that is in your heart, for God is with you."

[1] Hebrew *their*

³ But that same night the word of the Lord came to Nathan, ⁴ "Go and tell my servant David, 'Thus says the Lord: It is not you who will build me a house to dwell in. ⁵ For I have not lived in a house since the day I brought up Israel to this day, but I have gone from tent to tent and from dwelling to dwelling. ⁶ In all places where I have moved with all Israel, did I speak a word with any of the judges of Israel, whom I commanded to shepherd my people, saying, "Why have you not built me a house of cedar?"' ⁷ Now, therefore, thus shall you say to my servant David, 'Thus says the Lord of hosts, I took you from the pasture, from following the sheep, to be prince over my people Israel, ⁸ and I have been with you wherever you have gone and have cut off all your enemies from before you. And I will make for you a name, like the name of the great ones of the earth. ⁹ And I will appoint a place for my people Israel and will plant them, that they may dwell in their own place and be disturbed no more. And violent men shall waste them no more, as formerly, ¹⁰ from the time that I appointed judges over my people Israel. And I will subdue all your enemies. Moreover, I declare to you that the Lord will build you a house. ¹¹ When your days are fulfilled to walk with your fathers, I will raise up your offspring after you, one of your own sons, and I will establish his kingdom. ¹² He shall build a house for me, and I will establish his throne forever. ¹³ I will be to him a father, and he shall be to me a son. I will not take my steadfast love from him, as I took it from him who was before you, ¹⁴ but I will confirm him in my house and in my kingdom forever, and his throne shall be established forever.'" ¹⁵ In accordance with all these words, and in accordance with all this vision, Nathan spoke to David.

David's Prayer

¹⁶ Then King David went in and sat before the Lord and said, "Who am I, O Lord God, and what is my house, that you have brought me thus far? ¹⁷ And this was a small thing in your eyes, O God. You have also spoken of your servant's house for a great while to come, and have shown me future generations,¹ O Lord God! ¹⁸ And what more can David say to you for honoring your servant? For you know your servant. ¹⁹ For your servant's sake, O Lord, and according to your own heart, you have done all this greatness, in making known all these great things. ²⁰ There is none like you, O Lord, and there is no God besides you, according to all that we have heard with our ears. ²¹ And who is like your people Israel, the one² nation on earth whom God went to redeem to be his people, making for yourself a name for great and awesome things, in driving out nations before your people whom you

---

¹ Or *and you look upon me as a man of high rank* ² Septuagint, Vulgate *other*

redeemed from Egypt? ²² And you made your people Israel to be your people forever, and you, O Lord, became their God. ²³ And now, O Lord, let the word that you have spoken concerning your servant and concerning his house be established forever, and do as you have spoken, ²⁴ and your name will be established and magnified forever, saying, 'The Lord of hosts, the God of Israel, is Israel's God,' and the house of your servant David will be established before you. ²⁵ For you, my God, have revealed to your servant that you will build a house for him. Therefore your servant has found courage to pray before you. ²⁶ And now, O Lord, you are God, and you have promised this good thing to your servant. ²⁷ Now you have been pleased to bless the house of your servant, that it may continue forever before you, for it is you, O Lord, who have blessed, and it is blessed forever."

David Defeats His Enemies

18 After this David defeated the Philistines and subdued them, and he took Gath and its villages out of the hand of the Philistines.

² And he defeated Moab, and the Moabites became servants to David and brought tribute.

³ David also defeated Hadadezer king of Zobah-Hamath, as he went to set up his monument¹ at the river Euphrates. ⁴ And David took from him 1,000 chariots, 7,000 horsemen, and 20,000 foot soldiers. And David hamstrung all the chariot horses, but left enough for 100 chariots. ⁵ And when the Syrians of Damascus came to help Hadadezer king of Zobah, David struck down 22,000 men of the Syrians. ⁶ Then David put garrisons² in Syria of Damascus, and the Syrians became servants to David and brought tribute. And the Lord gave victory to David³ wherever he went. ⁷ And David took the shields of gold that were carried by the servants of Hadadezer and brought them to Jerusalem. ⁸ And from Tibhath and from Cun, cities of Hadadezer, David took a large amount of bronze. With it Solomon made the bronze sea and the pillars and the vessels of bronze.

⁹ When Tou king of Hamath heard that David had defeated the whole army of Hadadezer, king of Zobah, ¹⁰ he sent his son Hadoram to King David, to ask about his health and to bless him because he had fought against Hadadezer and defeated him; for Hadadezer had often been at war with Tou. And he sent all sorts of articles of gold, of silver, and of bronze. ¹¹ These also King David dedicated to the Lord, together with the silver and gold that he had carried off from all the nations, from Edom, Moab, the Ammonites, the Philistines, and Amalek.

---

¹ Hebrew *hand* ² Septuagint, Vulgate, 2 Samuel 8:6 (compare Syriac); Hebrew lacks *garrisons* ³ Hebrew *the Lord saved David*; also verse 13

¹² And Abishai, the son of Zeruiah, killed 18,000 Edomites in the Valley of Salt. ¹³ Then he put garrisons in Edom, and all the Edomites became David's servants. And the Lord gave victory to David wherever he went.

David's Administration

¹⁴ So David reigned over all Israel, and he administered justice and equity to all his people. ¹⁵ And Joab the son of Zeruiah was over the army; and Jehoshaphat the son of Ahilud was recorder; ¹⁶ and Zadok the son of Ahitub and Ahimelech the son of Abiathar were priests; and Shavsha was secretary; ¹⁷ and Benaiah the son of Jehoiada was over the Cherethites and the Pelethites; and David's sons were the chief officials in the service of the king.

The Ammonites Disgrace David's Men

19 Now after this Nahash the king of the Ammonites died, and his son reigned in his place. ² And David said, "I will deal kindly with Hanun the son of Nahash, for his father dealt kindly with me." So David sent messengers to console him concerning his father. And David's servants came to the land of the Ammonites to Hanun to console him. ³ But the princes of the Ammonites said to Hanun, "Do you think, because David has sent comforters to you, that he is honoring your father? Have not his servants come to you to search and to overthrow and to spy out the land?" ⁴ So Hanun took David's servants and shaved them and cut off their garments in the middle, at their hips, and sent them away; ⁵ and they departed. When David was told concerning the men, he sent messengers to meet them, for the men were greatly ashamed. And the king said, "Remain at Jericho until your beards have grown and then return."

⁶ When the Ammonites saw that they had become a stench to David, Hanun and the Ammonites sent 1,000 talents[1] of silver to hire chariots and horsemen from Mesopotamia, from Aram-maacah, and from Zobah. ⁷ They hired 32,000 chariots and the king of Maacah with his army, who came and encamped before Medeba. And the Ammonites were mustered from their cities and came to battle. ⁸ When David heard of it, he sent Joab and all the army of the mighty men. ⁹ And the Ammonites came out and drew up in battle array at the entrance of the city, and the kings who had come were by themselves in the open country.

Ammonites and Syrians Defeated

¹⁰ When Joab saw that the battle was set against him both in front and in the rear, he chose some of the best men of Israel and arrayed them against

---

[1] A *talent* was about 75 pounds or 34 kilograms

the Syrians. ¹¹ The rest of his men he put in the charge of Abishai his brother, and they were arrayed against the Ammonites. ¹² And he said, "If the Syrians are too strong for me, then you shall help me, but if the Ammonites are too strong for you, then I will help you. ¹³ Be strong, and let us use our strength for our people and for the cities of our God, and may the Lord do what seems good to him." ¹⁴ So Joab and the people who were with him drew near before the Syrians for battle, and they fled before him. ¹⁵ And when the Ammonites saw that the Syrians fled, they likewise fled before Abishai, Joab's brother, and entered the city. Then Joab came to Jerusalem.

¹⁶ But when the Syrians saw that they had been defeated by Israel, they sent messengers and brought out the Syrians who were beyond the Euphrates,[1] with Shophach the commander of the army of Hadadezer at their head. ¹⁷ And when it was told to David, he gathered all Israel together and crossed the Jordan and came to them and drew up his forces against them. And when David set the battle in array against the Syrians, they fought with him. ¹⁸ And the Syrians fled before Israel, and David killed of the Syrians the men of 7,000 chariots and 40,000 foot soldiers, and put to death also Shophach the commander of their army. ¹⁹ And when the servants of Hadadezer saw that they had been defeated by Israel, they made peace with David and became subject to him. So the Syrians were not willing to save the Ammonites anymore.

The Capture of Rabbah

20 In the spring of the year, the time when kings go out to battle, Joab led out the army and ravaged the country of the Ammonites and came and besieged Rabbah. But David remained at Jerusalem. And Joab struck down Rabbah and overthrew it. ² And David took the crown of their king from his head. He found that it weighed a talent[2] of gold, and in it was a precious stone. And it was placed on David's head. And he brought out the spoil of the city, a very great amount. ³ And he brought out the people who were in it and set them to labor[3] with saws and iron picks and axes.[4] And thus David did to all the cities of the Ammonites. Then David and all the people returned to Jerusalem.

Philistine Giants Killed

⁴ And after this there arose war with the Philistines at Gezer. Then Sibbecai the Hushathite struck down Sippai, who was one of the descendants of the giants, and the Philistines were subdued. ⁵ And there was again war with the Philistines, and Elhanan the son of Jair struck down Lahmi the brother

---

[1] Hebrew *the River* [2] A *talent* was about 75 pounds or 34 kilograms [3] Compare 2 Samuel 12:31; Hebrew *he sawed* [4] Compare 2 Samuel 12:31; Hebrew *saws*

of Goliath the Gittite, the shaft of whose spear was like a weaver's beam. ⁶ And there was again war at Gath, where there was a man of great stature, who had six fingers on each hand and six toes on each foot, twenty-four in number, and he also was descended from the giants. ⁷ And when he taunted Israel, Jonathan the son of Shimea, David's brother, struck him down. ⁸ These were descended from the giants in Gath, and they fell by the hand of David and by the hand of his servants.

David's Census Brings Pestilence

21 Then Satan stood against Israel and incited David to number Israel. ² So David said to Joab and the commanders of the army, "Go, number Israel, from Beersheba to Dan, and bring me a report, that I may know their number." ³ But Joab said, "May the Lord add to his people a hundred times as many as they are! Are they not, my lord the king, all of them my lord's servants? Why then should my lord require this? Why should it be a cause of guilt for Israel?" ⁴ But the king's word prevailed against Joab. So Joab departed and went throughout all Israel and came back to Jerusalem. ⁵ And Joab gave the sum of the numbering of the people to David. In all Israel there were 1,100,000 men who drew the sword, and in Judah 470,000 who drew the sword. ⁶ But he did not include Levi and Benjamin in the numbering, for the king's command was abhorrent to Joab.

⁷ But God was displeased with this thing, and he struck Israel. ⁸ And David said to God, "I have sinned greatly in that I have done this thing. But now, please take away the iniquity of your servant, for I have acted very foolishly." ⁹ And the Lord spoke to Gad, David's seer, saying, ¹⁰ "Go and say to David, 'Thus says the Lord, Three things I offer you; choose one of them, that I may do it to you.'" ¹¹ So Gad came to David and said to him, "Thus says the Lord, 'Choose what you will: ¹² either three years of famine, or three months of devastation by your foes while the sword of your enemies overtakes you, or else three days of the sword of the Lord, pestilence on the land, with the angel of the Lord destroying throughout all the territory of Israel.' Now decide what answer I shall return to him who sent me." ¹³ Then David said to Gad, "I am in great distress. Let me fall into the hand of the Lord, for his mercy is very great, but do not let me fall into the hand of man."

¹⁴ So the Lord sent a pestilence on Israel, and 70,000 men of Israel fell. ¹⁵ And God sent the angel to Jerusalem to destroy it, but as he was about to destroy it, the Lord saw, and he relented from the calamity. And he said to the angel who was working destruction, "It is enough; now stay your hand." And the angel of the Lord was standing by the threshing floor of

Ornan the Jebusite. ¹⁶ And David lifted his eyes and saw the angel of the Lord standing between earth and heaven, and in his hand a drawn sword stretched out over Jerusalem. Then David and the elders, clothed in sackcloth, fell upon their faces. ¹⁷ And David said to God, "Was it not I who gave command to number the people? It is I who have sinned and done great evil. But these sheep, what have they done? Please let your hand, O Lord my God, be against me and against my father's house. But do not let the plague be on your people."

David Builds an Altar

¹⁸ Now the angel of the Lord had commanded Gad to say to David that David should go up and raise an altar to the Lord on the threshing floor of Ornan the Jebusite. ¹⁹ So David went up at Gad's word, which he had spoken in the name of the Lord. ²⁰ Now Ornan was threshing wheat. He turned and saw the angel, and his four sons who were with him hid themselves. ²¹ As David came to Ornan, Ornan looked and saw David and went out from the threshing floor and paid homage to David with his face to the ground. ²² And David said to Ornan, "Give me the site of the threshing floor that I may build on it an altar to the Lord—give it to me at its full price—that the plague may be averted from the people." ²³ Then Ornan said to David, "Take it, and let my lord the king do what seems good to him. See, I give the oxen for burnt offerings and the threshing sledges for the wood and the wheat for a grain offering; I give it all." ²⁴ But King David said to Ornan, "No, but I will buy them for the full price. I will not take for the Lord what is yours, nor offer burnt offerings that cost me nothing." ²⁵ So David paid Ornan 600 shekels[1] of gold by weight for the site. ²⁶ And David built there an altar to the Lord and presented burnt offerings and peace offerings and called on the Lord, and the Lord[2] answered him with fire from heaven upon the altar of burnt offering. ²⁷ Then the Lord commanded the angel, and he put his sword back into its sheath.

²⁸ At that time, when David saw that the Lord had answered him at the threshing floor of Ornan the Jebusite, he sacrificed there. ²⁹ For the tabernacle of the Lord, which Moses had made in the wilderness, and the altar of burnt offering were at that time in the high place at Gibeon, ³⁰ but David could not go before it to inquire of God, for he was afraid of the sword of the angel of the Lord.

22

Then David said, "Here shall be the house of the Lord God and here the altar of burnt offering for Israel."

[1] A *shekel* was about 2/5 ounce or 11 grams [2] Hebrew *he*

David Prepares for Temple Building

² David commanded to gather together the resident aliens who were in the land of Israel, and he set stonecutters to prepare dressed stones for building the house of God. ³ David also provided great quantities of iron for nails for the doors of the gates and for clamps, as well as bronze in quantities beyond weighing, ⁴ and cedar timbers without number, for the Sidonians and Tyrians brought great quantities of cedar to David. ⁵ For David said, "Solomon my son is young and inexperienced, and the house that is to be built for the Lord must be exceedingly magnificent, of fame and glory throughout all lands. I will therefore make preparation for it." So David provided materials in great quantity before his death.

Solomon Charged to Build the Temple

⁶ Then he called for Solomon his son and charged him to build a house for the Lord, the God of Israel. ⁷ David said to Solomon, "My son, I had it in my heart to build a house to the name of the Lord my God. ⁸ But the word of the Lord came to me, saying, 'You have shed much blood and have waged great wars. You shall not build a house to my name, because you have shed so much blood before me on the earth. ⁹ Behold, a son shall be born to you who shall be a man of rest. I will give him rest from all his surrounding enemies. For his name shall be Solomon, and I will give peace and quiet to Israel in his days. ¹⁰ He shall build a house for my name. He shall be my son, and I will be his father, and I will establish his royal throne in Israel forever.'

¹¹ "Now, my son, the Lord be with you, so that you may succeed in building the house of the Lord your God, as he has spoken concerning you. ¹² Only, may the Lord grant you discretion and understanding, that when he gives you charge over Israel you may keep the law of the Lord your God. ¹³ Then you will prosper if you are careful to observe the statutes and the rules that the Lord commanded Moses for Israel. Be strong and courageous. Fear not; do not be dismayed. ¹⁴ With great pains I have provided for the house of the Lord 100,000 talents[1] of gold, a million talents of silver, and bronze and iron beyond weighing, for there is so much of it; timber and stone, too, I have provided. To these you must add. ¹⁵ You have an abundance of workmen: stonecutters, masons, carpenters, and all kinds of craftsmen without number, skilled in working ¹⁶ gold, silver, bronze, and iron. Arise and work! The Lord be with you!"

¹⁷ David also commanded all the leaders of Israel to help Solomon his son, saying, ¹⁸ "Is not the Lord your God with you? And has he not given you

---

[1] A *talent* was about 75 pounds or 34 kilograms

peace[1] on every side? For he has delivered the inhabitants of the land into my hand, and the land is subdued before the LORD and his people. ⁱ⁹ Now set your mind and heart to seek the LORD your God. Arise and build the sanctuary of the LORD God, so that the ark of the covenant of the LORD and the holy vessels of God may be brought into a house built for the name of the LORD."

David Organizes the Levites

23 When David was old and full of days, he made Solomon his son king over Israel.

² David[2] assembled all the leaders of Israel and the priests and the Levites. ³ The Levites, thirty years old and upward, were numbered, and the total was 38,000 men. ⁴ "Twenty-four thousand of these," David said,[3] "shall have charge of the work in the house of the LORD, 6,000 shall be officers and judges, ⁵ 4,000 gatekeepers, and 4,000 shall offer praises to the LORD with the instruments that I have made for praise." ⁶ And David organized them in divisions corresponding to the sons of Levi: Gershon, Kohath, and Merari.

⁷ The sons of Gershon[4] were Ladan and Shimei. ⁸ The sons of Ladan: Jehiel the chief, and Zetham, and Joel, three. ⁹ The sons of Shimei: Shelomoth, Haziel, and Haran, three. These were the heads of the fathers' houses of Ladan. ¹⁰ And the sons of Shimei: Jahath, Zina, and Jeush and Beriah. These four were the sons of Shimei. ¹¹ Jahath was the chief, and Zizah the second; but Jeush and Beriah did not have many sons, therefore they became counted as a single father's house.

¹² The sons of Kohath: Amram, Izhar, Hebron, and Uzziel, four. ¹³ The sons of Amram: Aaron and Moses. Aaron was set apart to dedicate the most holy things, that he and his sons forever should make offerings before the LORD and minister to him and pronounce blessings in his name forever. ¹⁴ But the sons of Moses the man of God were named among the tribe of Levi. ¹⁵ The sons of Moses: Gershom and Eliezer. ¹⁶ The sons of Gershom: Shebuel the chief. ¹⁷ The sons of Eliezer: Rehabiah the chief. Eliezer had no other sons, but the sons of Rehabiah were very many. ¹⁸ The sons of Izhar: Shelomith the chief. ¹⁹ The sons of Hebron: Jeriah the chief, Amariah the second, Jahaziel the third, and Jekameam the fourth. ²⁰ The sons of Uzziel: Micah the chief and Isshiah the second.

²¹ The sons of Merari: Mahli and Mushi. The sons of Mahli: Eleazar and Kish. ²² Eleazar died having no sons, but only daughters; their kinsmen, the sons of Kish, married them. ²³ The sons of Mushi: Mahli, Eder, and Jeremoth, three.

---

[1] Or *rest* (see 22:9) [2] Hebrew *He* [3] Hebrew lacks *David said* [4] Vulgate (compare Septuagint, Syriac); Hebrew *to the Gershonite*

²⁴ These were the sons of Levi by their fathers' houses, the heads of fathers' houses as they were listed according to the number of the names of the individuals from twenty years old and upward who were to do the work for the service of the house of the LORD. ²⁵ For David said, "The LORD, the God of Israel, has given rest to his people, and he dwells in Jerusalem forever. ²⁶ And so the Levites no longer need to carry the tabernacle or any of the things for its service." ²⁷ For by the last words of David the sons of Levi were numbered from twenty years old and upward. ²⁸ For their duty was to assist the sons of Aaron for the service of the house of the LORD, having the care of the courts and the chambers, the cleansing of all that is holy, and any work for the service of the house of God. ²⁹ Their duty was also to assist with the showbread, the flour for the grain offering, the wafers of unleavened bread, the baked offering, the offering mixed with oil, and all measures of quantity or size. ³⁰ And they were to stand every morning, thanking and praising the LORD, and likewise at evening, ³¹ and whenever burnt offerings were offered to the LORD on Sabbaths, new moons, and feast days, according to the number required of them, regularly before the LORD. ³² Thus they were to keep charge of the tent of meeting and the sanctuary, and to attend the sons of Aaron, their brothers, for the service of the house of the LORD.

David Organizes the Priests

24 The divisions of the sons of Aaron were these. The sons of Aaron: Nadab, Abihu, Eleazar, and Ithamar. ² But Nadab and Abihu died before their father and had no children, so Eleazar and Ithamar became the priests. ³ With the help of Zadok of the sons of Eleazar, and Ahimelech of the sons of Ithamar, David organized them according to the appointed duties in their service. ⁴ Since more chief men were found among the sons of Eleazar than among the sons of Ithamar, they organized them under sixteen heads of fathers' houses of the sons of Eleazar, and eight of the sons of Ithamar. ⁵ They divided them by lot, all alike, for there were sacred officers and officers of God among both the sons of Eleazar and the sons of Ithamar. ⁶ And the scribe Shemaiah, the son of Nethanel, a Levite, recorded them in the presence of the king and the princes and Zadok the priest and Ahimelech the son of Abiathar and the heads of the fathers' houses of the priests and of the Levites, one father's house being chosen for Eleazar and one chosen for Ithamar.

⁷ The first lot fell to Jehoiarib, the second to Jedaiah, ⁸ the third to Harim, the fourth to Seorim, ⁹ the fifth to Malchijah, the sixth to Mijamin, ¹⁰ the seventh to Hakkoz, the eighth to Abijah, ¹¹ the ninth to Jeshua, the tenth to Shecaniah, ¹² the eleventh to Eliashib, the twelfth to Jakim, ¹³ the thirteenth

to Huppah, the fourteenth to Jeshebeab, ¹⁴ the fifteenth to Bilgah, the sixteenth to Immer, ¹⁵ the seventeenth to Hezir, the eighteenth to Happizzez, ¹⁶ the nineteenth to Pethahiah, the twentieth to Jehezkel, ¹⁷ the twenty-first to Jachin, the twenty-second to Gamul, ¹⁸ the twenty-third to Delaiah, the twenty-fourth to Maaziah. ¹⁹ These had as their appointed duty in their service to come into the house of the Lord according to the procedure established for them by Aaron their father, as the Lord God of Israel had commanded him.

²⁰ And of the rest of the sons of Levi: of the sons of Amram, Shubael; of the sons of Shubael, Jehdeiah. ²¹ Of Rehabiah: of the sons of Rehabiah, Isshiah the chief. ²² Of the Izharites, Shelomoth; of the sons of Shelomoth, Jahath. ²³ The sons of Hebron:¹ Jeriah the chief,² Amariah the second, Jahaziel the third, Jekameam the fourth. ²⁴ The sons of Uzziel, Micah; of the sons of Micah, Shamir. ²⁵ The brother of Micah, Isshiah; of the sons of Isshiah, Zechariah. ²⁶ The sons of Merari: Mahli and Mushi. The sons of Jaaziah: Beno.³ ²⁷ The sons of Merari: of Jaaziah, Beno, Shoham, Zaccur, and Ibri. ²⁸ Of Mahli: Eleazar, who had no sons. ²⁹ Of Kish, the sons of Kish: Jerahmeel. ³⁰ The sons of Mushi: Mahli, Eder, and Jerimoth. These were the sons of the Levites according to their fathers' houses. ³¹ These also, the head of each father's house and his younger brother alike, cast lots, just as their brothers the sons of Aaron, in the presence of King David, Zadok, Ahimelech, and the heads of fathers' houses of the priests and of the Levites.

David Organizes the Musicians

25 David and the chiefs of the service also set apart for the service the sons of Asaph, and of Heman, and of Jeduthun, who prophesied with lyres, with harps, and with cymbals. The list of those who did the work and of their duties was: ² Of the sons of Asaph: Zaccur, Joseph, Nethaniah, and Asharelah, sons of Asaph, under the direction of Asaph, who prophesied under the direction of the king. ³ Of Jeduthun, the sons of Jeduthun: Gedaliah, Zeri, Jeshaiah, Shimei,⁴ Hashabiah, and Mattithiah, six, under the direction of their father Jeduthun, who prophesied with the lyre in thanksgiving and praise to the Lord. ⁴ Of Heman, the sons of Heman: Bukkiah, Mattaniah, Uzziel, Shebuel and Jerimoth, Hananiah, Hanani, Eliathah, Giddalti, and Romamti-ezer, Joshbekashah, Mallothi, Hothir, Mahazioth. ⁵ All these were the sons of Heman the king's seer, according to the promise of God to exalt him, for God had given Heman fourteen sons and three daughters. ⁶ They were all under the direction of their father in the music in

---

¹ Compare 23:19; Hebrew lacks *Hebron* ² Compare 23:19; Hebrew lacks *the chief* ³ Or *his son*; also verse 27
⁴ One Hebrew manuscript, Septuagint; most Hebrew manuscripts lack *Shimei*

the house of the LORD with cymbals, harps, and lyres for the service of the house of God. Asaph, Jeduthun, and Heman were under the order of the king. ⁷ The number of them along with their brothers, who were trained in singing to the LORD, all who were skillful, was 288. ⁸ And they cast lots for their duties, small and great, teacher and pupil alike.

⁹ The first lot fell for Asaph to Joseph; the second to Gedaliah, to him and his brothers and his sons, twelve; ¹⁰ the third to Zaccur, his sons and his brothers, twelve; ¹¹ the fourth to Izri, his sons and his brothers, twelve; ¹² the fifth to Nethaniah, his sons and his brothers, twelve; ¹³ the sixth to Bukkiah, his sons and his brothers, twelve; ¹⁴ the seventh to Jesharelah, his sons and his brothers, twelve; ¹⁵ the eighth to Jeshaiah, his sons and his brothers, twelve; ¹⁶ the ninth to Mattaniah, his sons and his brothers, twelve; ¹⁷ the tenth to Shimei, his sons and his brothers, twelve; ¹⁸ the eleventh to Azarel, his sons and his brothers, twelve; ¹⁹ the twelfth to Hashabiah, his sons and his brothers, twelve; ²⁰ to the thirteenth, Shubael, his sons and his brothers, twelve; ²¹ to the fourteenth, Mattithiah, his sons and his brothers, twelve; ²² to the fifteenth, to Jeremoth, his sons and his brothers, twelve; ²³ to the sixteenth, to Hananiah, his sons and his brothers, twelve; ²⁴ to the seventeenth, to Joshbekashah, his sons and his brothers, twelve; ²⁵ to the eighteenth, to Hanani, his sons and his brothers, twelve; ²⁶ to the nineteenth, to Mallothi, his sons and his brothers, twelve; ²⁷ to the twentieth, to Eliathah, his sons and his brothers, twelve; ²⁸ to the twenty-first, to Hothir, his sons and his brothers, twelve; ²⁹ to the twenty-second, to Giddalti, his sons and his brothers, twelve; ³⁰ to the twenty-third, to Mahazioth, his sons and his brothers, twelve; ³¹ to the twenty-fourth, to Romamti-ezer, his sons and his brothers, twelve.

Divisions of the Gatekeepers

26 As for the divisions of the gatekeepers: of the Korahites, Meshelemiah the son of Kore, of the sons of Asaph. ² And Meshelemiah had sons: Zechariah the firstborn, Jediael the second, Zebadiah the third, Jathniel the fourth, ³ Elam the fifth, Jehohanan the sixth, Eliehoenai the seventh. ⁴ And Obed-edom had sons: Shemaiah the firstborn, Jehozabad the second, Joah the third, Sachar the fourth, Nethanel the fifth, ⁵ Ammiel the sixth, Issachar the seventh, Peullethai the eighth, for God blessed him. ⁶ Also to his son Shemaiah were sons born who were rulers in their fathers' houses, for they were men of great ability. ⁷ The sons of Shemaiah: Othni, Rephael, Obed and Elzabad, whose brothers were able men, Elihu and Semachiah. ⁸ All these were of the sons of Obed-edom with their sons and brothers, able men qualified for the service; sixty-two of Obed-edom. ⁹ And Meshelemiah had

sons and brothers, able men, eighteen. ¹⁰ And Hosah, of the sons of Merari, had sons: Shimri the chief (for though he was not the firstborn, his father made him chief), ¹¹ Hilkiah the second, Tebaliah the third, Zechariah the fourth: all the sons and brothers of Hosah were thirteen.

¹² These divisions of the gatekeepers, corresponding to their chief men, had duties, just as their brothers did, ministering in the house of the Lord. ¹³ And they cast lots by fathers' houses, small and great alike, for their gates. ¹⁴ The lot for the east fell to Shelemiah. They cast lots also for his son Zechariah, a shrewd counselor, and his lot came out for the north. ¹⁵ Obed-edom's came out for the south, and to his sons was allotted the gatehouse. ¹⁶ For Shuppim and Hosah it came out for the west, at the gate of Shallecheth on the road that goes up. Watch corresponded to watch. ¹⁷ On the east there were six each day,¹ on the north four each day, on the south four each day, as well as two and two at the gatehouse. ¹⁸ And for the colonnade² on the west there were four at the road and two at the colonnade. ¹⁹ These were the divisions of the gatekeepers among the Korahites and the sons of Merari.

Treasurers and Other Officials

²⁰ And of the Levites, Ahijah had charge of the treasuries of the house of God and the treasuries of the dedicated gifts. ²¹ The sons of Ladan, the sons of the Gershonites belonging to Ladan, the heads of the fathers' houses belonging to Ladan the Gershonite: Jehieli.³

²² The sons of Jehieli, Zetham, and Joel his brother, were in charge of the treasuries of the house of the Lord. ²³ Of the Amramites, the Izharites, the Hebronites, and the Uzzielites— ²⁴ and Shebuel the son of Gershom, son of Moses, was chief officer in charge of the treasuries. ²⁵ His brothers: from Eliezer were his son Rehabiah, and his son Jeshaiah, and his son Joram, and his son Zichri, and his son Shelomoth. ²⁶ This Shelomoth and his brothers were in charge of all the treasuries of the dedicated gifts that David the king and the heads of the fathers' houses and the officers of the thousands and the hundreds and the commanders of the army had dedicated. ²⁷ From spoil won in battles they dedicated gifts for the maintenance of the house of the Lord. ²⁸ Also all that Samuel the seer and Saul the son of Kish and Abner the son of Ner and Joab the son of Zeruiah had dedicated—all dedicated gifts were in the care of Shelomoth⁴ and his brothers.

²⁹ Of the Izharites, Chenaniah and his sons were appointed to external duties for Israel, as officers and judges. ³⁰ Of the Hebronites, Hashabiah and his brothers, 1,700 men of ability, had the oversight of Israel westward of

---

¹ Septuagint; Hebrew *six Levites* ² Or *court*; Hebrew *parbar* (meaning uncertain); twice in this verse
³ The Hebrew of verse 21 is uncertain ⁴ Hebrew *Shelomith*

the Jordan for all the work of the LORD and for the service of the king. ³¹ Of the Hebronites, Jerijah was chief of the Hebronites of whatever genealogy or fathers' houses. (In the fortieth year of David's reign search was made and men of great ability among them were found at Jazer in Gilead.) ³² King David appointed him and his brothers, 2,700 men of ability, heads of fathers' houses, to have the oversight of the Reubenites, the Gadites and the half-tribe of the Manassites for everything pertaining to God and for the affairs of the king.

Military Divisions

27 This is the number of the people of Israel, the heads of fathers' houses, the commanders of thousands and hundreds, and their officers who served the king in all matters concerning the divisions that came and went, month after month throughout the year, each division numbering 24,000:

² Jashobeam the son of Zabdiel was in charge of the first division in the first month; in his division were 24,000. ³ He was a descendant of Perez and was chief of all the commanders. He served for the first month. ⁴ Dodai the Ahohite[1] was in charge of the division of the second month; in his division were 24,000. ⁵ The third commander, for the third month, was Benaiah, the son of Jehoiada the chief priest; in his division were 24,000. ⁶ This is the Benaiah who was a mighty man of the thirty and in command of the thirty; Ammizabad his son was in charge of his division.[2] ⁷ Asahel the brother of Joab was fourth, for the fourth month, and his son Zebadiah after him; in his division were 24,000. ⁸ The fifth commander, for the fifth month, was Shamhuth the Izrahite; in his division were 24,000. ⁹ Sixth, for the sixth month, was Ira, the son of Ikkesh the Tekoite; in his division were 24,000. ¹⁰ Seventh, for the seventh month, was Helez the Pelonite, of the sons of Ephraim; in his division were 24,000. ¹¹ Eighth, for the eighth month, was Sibbecai the Hushathite, of the Zerahites; in his division were 24,000. ¹² Ninth, for the ninth month, was Abiezer of Anathoth, a Benjaminite; in his division were 24,000. ¹³ Tenth, for the tenth month, was Maharai of Netophah, of the Zerahites; in his division were 24,000. ¹⁴ Eleventh, for the eleventh month, was Benaiah of Pirathon, of the sons of Ephraim; in his division were 24,000. ¹⁵ Twelfth, for the twelfth month, was Heldai the Netophathite, of Othniel; in his division were 24,000.

Leaders of Tribes

¹⁶ Over the tribes of Israel, for the Reubenites, Eliezer the son of Zichri was chief officer; for the Simeonites, Shephatiah the son of Maacah; ¹⁷ for Levi,

---

[1] Septuagint; Hebrew *Ahohite and his division and Mikloth the chief officer* [2] Septuagint, Vulgate; Hebrew *was his division*

Hashabiah the son of Kemuel; for Aaron, Zadok; ¹⁸ for Judah, Elihu, one of David's brothers; for Issachar, Omri the son of Michael; ¹⁹ for Zebulun, Ishmaiah the son of Obadiah; for Naphtali, Jeremoth the son of Azriel; ²⁰ for the Ephraimites, Hoshea the son of Azaziah; for the half-tribe of Manasseh, Joel the son of Pedaiah; ²¹ for the half-tribe of Manasseh in Gilead, Iddo the son of Zechariah; for Benjamin, Jaasiel the son of Abner; ²² for Dan, Azarel the son of Jeroham. These were the leaders of the tribes of Israel. ²³ David did not count those below twenty years of age, for the LORD had promised to make Israel as many as the stars of heaven. ²⁴ Joab the son of Zeruiah began to count, but did not finish. Yet wrath came upon Israel for this, and the number was not entered in the chronicles of King David.

²⁵ Over the king's treasuries was Azmaveth the son of Adiel; and over the treasuries in the country, in the cities, in the villages, and in the towers, was Jonathan the son of Uzziah; ²⁶ and over those who did the work of the field for tilling the soil was Ezri the son of Chelub; ²⁷ and over the vineyards was Shimei the Ramathite; and over the produce of the vineyards for the wine cellars was Zabdi the Shiphmite. ²⁸ Over the olive and sycamore trees in the Shephelah was Baal-hanan the Gederite; and over the stores of oil was Joash. ²⁹ Over the herds that pastured in Sharon was Shitrai the Sharonite; over the herds in the valleys was Shaphat the son of Adlai. ³⁰ Over the camels was Obil the Ishmaelite; and over the donkeys was Jehdeiah the Meronothite. ³¹ Over the flocks was Jaziz the Hagrite. All these were stewards of King David's property.

³² Jonathan, David's uncle, was a counselor, being a man of understanding and a scribe. He and Jehiel the son of Hachmoni attended the king's sons. ³³ Ahithophel was the king's counselor, and Hushai the Archite was the king's friend. ³⁴ Ahithophel was succeeded by Jehoiada the son of Benaiah, and Abiathar. Joab was commander of the king's army.

David's Charge to Israel

28 David assembled at Jerusalem all the officials of Israel, the officials of the tribes, the officers of the divisions that served the king, the commanders of thousands, the commanders of hundreds, the stewards of all the property and livestock of the king and his sons, together with the palace officials, the mighty men and all the seasoned warriors. ² Then King David rose to his feet and said: "Hear me, my brothers and my people. I had it in my heart to build a house of rest for the ark of the covenant of the LORD and for the footstool of our God, and I made preparations for building. ³ But God said to me, 'You may not build a house for my name, for you are a man of war and have shed blood.' ⁴ Yet the LORD God of Israel chose me from all my father's house to be king over Israel forever. For he chose Judah as leader, and in the house of Judah my father's house, and among my father's sons he took pleasure in me to make me king over all Israel. ⁵ And of all my sons (for the LORD has given me many sons) he has chosen Solomon my son to sit on the throne of the kingdom of the LORD over Israel. ⁶ He said to me, 'It is Solomon your son who shall build my house and my courts, for I have chosen him to be my son, and I will be his father. ⁷ I will establish his kingdom forever if he continues strong in keeping my commandments and my rules, as he is today.' ⁸ Now therefore in the sight of all Israel, the assembly of the LORD, and in the hearing of our God, observe and seek out all the commandments of the LORD your God, that you may possess this good land and leave it for an inheritance to your children after you forever.

David's Charge to Solomon

⁹ "And you, Solomon my son, know the God of your father and serve him with a whole heart and with a willing mind, for the LORD searches all hearts and understands every plan and thought. If you seek him, he will be found by you, but if you forsake him, he will cast you off forever. ¹⁰ Be careful now, for the LORD has chosen you to build a house for the sanctuary; be strong and do it."

¹¹ Then David gave Solomon his son the plan of the vestibule of the temple,¹ and of its houses, its treasuries, its upper rooms, and its inner chambers, and of the room for the mercy seat; ¹² and the plan of all that he had in mind for the courts of the house of the LORD, all the surrounding chambers, the treasuries of the house of God, and the treasuries for dedicated gifts; ¹³ for the divisions of the priests and of the Levites, and all the work of the service in the house of the LORD; for all the vessels for the service in the house of the LORD, ¹⁴ the weight of gold for all golden vessels for each service, the weight of silver vessels for each service, ¹⁵ the weight of the golden lampstands and their lamps, the weight of gold for each lampstand and its lamps, the weight of silver for a lampstand and its lamps, according to the use of each lampstand in the service, ¹⁶ the weight of gold for each table for the showbread, the silver for the silver tables, ¹⁷ and pure gold for the forks, the basins and the cups; for the golden bowls and the weight of each; for the silver bowls and the weight of each; ¹⁸ for the altar of incense made of refined gold, and its weight; also his plan for the golden chariot of the cherubim that spread their wings and covered the ark of the covenant of the LORD. ¹⁹ "All this he made clear to me in writing from the hand of the LORD, all the work to be done according to the plan."

¹ Hebrew lacks *of the temple*

20 Then David said to Solomon his son, "Be strong and courageous and do it. Do not be afraid and do not be dismayed, for the Lord God, even my God, is with you. He will not leave you or forsake you, until all the work for the service of the house of the Lord is finished. 21 And behold the divisions of the priests and the Levites for all the service of the house of God; and with you in all the work will be every willing man who has skill for any kind of service; also the officers and all the people will be wholly at your command."

Offerings for the Temple

29 And David the king said to all the assembly, "Solomon my son, whom alone God has chosen, is young and inexperienced, and the work is great, for the palace will not be for man but for the Lord God. 2 So I have provided for the house of my God, so far as I was able, the gold for the things of gold, the silver for the things of silver, and the bronze for the things of bronze, the iron for the things of iron, and wood for the things of wood, besides great quantities of onyx and stones for setting, antimony, colored stones, all sorts of precious stones and marble. 3 Moreover, in addition to all that I have provided for the holy house, I have a treasure of my own of gold and silver, and because of my devotion to the house of my God I give it to the house of my God: 4 3,000 talents[1] of gold, of the gold of Ophir, and 7,000 talents of refined silver, for overlaying the walls of the house,[2] 5 and for all the work to be done by craftsmen, gold for the things of gold and silver for the things of silver. Who then will offer willingly, consecrating himself[3] today to the Lord?"

6 Then the leaders of fathers' houses made their freewill offerings, as did also the leaders of the tribes, the commanders of thousands and of hundreds, and the officers over the king's work. 7 They gave for the service of the house of God 5,000 talents and 10,000 darics[4] of gold, 10,000 talents of silver, 18,000 talents of bronze and 100,000 talents of iron. 8 And whoever had precious stones gave them to the treasury of the house of the Lord, in the care of Jehiel the Gershonite. 9 Then the people rejoiced because they had given willingly, for with a whole heart they had offered freely to the Lord. David the king also rejoiced greatly.

David Prays in the Assembly

10 Therefore David blessed the Lord in the presence of all the assembly. And David said: "Blessed are you, O Lord, the God of Israel our father, forever and ever. 11 Yours, O Lord, is the greatness and the power and the

---

[1] A *talent* was about 75 pounds or 34 kilograms [2] Septuagint; Hebrew *houses* [3] Or *ordaining himself*; Hebrew *filling his hand* [4] A *daric* was a coin weighing about 1/4 ounce or 8.5 grams

glory and the victory and the majesty, for all that is in the heavens and in the earth is yours. Yours is the kingdom, O Lord, and you are exalted as head above all. ¹² Both riches and honor come from you, and you rule over all. In your hand are power and might, and in your hand it is to make great and to give strength to all. ¹³ And now we thank you, our God, and praise your glorious name.

¹⁴ "But who am I, and what is my people, that we should be able thus to offer willingly? For all things come from you, and of your own have we given you. ¹⁵ For we are strangers before you and sojourners, as all our fathers were. Our days on the earth are like a shadow, and there is no abiding.¹ ¹⁶ O Lord our God, all this abundance that we have provided for building you a house for your holy name comes from your hand and is all your own. ¹⁷ I know, my God, that you test the heart and have pleasure in uprightness. In the uprightness of my heart I have freely offered all these things, and now I have seen your people, who are present here, offering freely and joyously to you. ¹⁸ O Lord, the God of Abraham, Isaac, and Israel, our fathers, keep forever such purposes and thoughts in the hearts of your people, and direct their hearts toward you. ¹⁹ Grant to Solomon my son a whole heart that he may keep your commandments, your testimonies, and your statutes, performing all, and that he may build the palace for which I have made provision."

²⁰ Then David said to all the assembly, "Bless the Lord your God." And all the assembly blessed the Lord, the God of their fathers, and bowed their heads and paid homage to the Lord and to the king. ²¹ And they offered sacrifices to the Lord, and on the next day offered burnt offerings to the Lord, 1,000 bulls, 1,000 rams, and 1,000 lambs, with their drink offerings, and sacrifices in abundance for all Israel. ²² And they ate and drank before the Lord on that day with great gladness.

Solomon Anointed King

And they made Solomon the son of David king the second time, and they anointed him as prince for the Lord, and Zadok as priest.

²³ Then Solomon sat on the throne of the Lord as king in place of David his father. And he prospered, and all Israel obeyed him. ²⁴ All the leaders and the mighty men, and also all the sons of King David, pledged their allegiance to King Solomon. ²⁵ And the Lord made Solomon very great in the sight of all Israel and bestowed on him such royal majesty as had not been on any king before him in Israel.

---

¹ Septuagint, Vulgate; Hebrew *hope*, or *prospect*

The Death of David

²⁶ Thus David the son of Jesse reigned over all Israel. ²⁷ The time that he reigned over Israel was forty years. He reigned seven years in Hebron and thirty-three years in Jerusalem. ²⁸ Then he died at a good age, full of days, riches, and honor. And Solomon his son reigned in his place. ²⁹ Now the acts of King David, from first to last, are written in the Chronicles of Samuel the seer, and in the Chronicles of Nathan the prophet, and in the Chronicles of Gad the seer, ³⁰ with accounts of all his rule and his might and of the circumstances that came upon him and upon Israel and upon all the kingdoms of the countries.

2 CHRONICLES

Solomon Worships at Gibeon

1 Solomon the son of David established himself in his kingdom, and the LORD his God was with him and made him exceedingly great.

² Solomon spoke to all Israel, to the commanders of thousands and of hundreds, to the judges, and to all the leaders in all Israel, the heads of fathers' houses. ³ And Solomon, and all the assembly with him, went to the high place that was at Gibeon, for the tent of meeting of God, which Moses the servant of the LORD had made in the wilderness, was there. ⁴ (But David had brought up the ark of God from Kiriath-jearim to the place that David had prepared for it, for he had pitched a tent for it in Jerusalem.) ⁵ Moreover, the bronze altar that Bezalel the son of Uri, son of Hur, had made, was there before the tabernacle of the LORD. And Solomon and the assembly sought it¹ out. ⁶ And Solomon went up there to the bronze altar before the LORD, which was at the tent of meeting, and offered a thousand burnt offerings on it.

Solomon Prays for Wisdom

⁷ In that night God appeared to Solomon, and said to him, "Ask what I shall give you." ⁸ And Solomon said to God, "You have shown great and steadfast love to David my father, and have made me king in his place. ⁹ O LORD God, let your word to David my father be now fulfilled, for you have made me king over a people as numerous as the dust of the earth. ¹⁰ Give me now wisdom and knowledge to go out and come in before this people, for who can govern this people of yours, which is so great?" ¹¹ God answered Solomon, "Because this was in your heart, and you have not asked for possessions, wealth, honor, or the life of those who hate you, and have not even asked for long life, but have asked for wisdom and knowledge for yourself that you may govern my people over whom I have made you king, ¹² wisdom and knowledge are granted to you. I will also give you riches, possessions, and honor, such as none of the kings had who were before you, and none after you shall have the like." ¹³ So Solomon came from² the high place at Gibeon, from before the tent of meeting, to Jerusalem. And he reigned over Israel.

¹ Or *him* ² Septuagint, Vulgate; Hebrew *to*

Solomon Given Wealth

[14] Solomon gathered together chariots and horsemen. He had 1,400 chariots and 12,000 horsemen, whom he stationed in the chariot cities and with the king in Jerusalem. [15] And the king made silver and gold as common in Jerusalem as stone, and he made cedar as plentiful as the sycamore of the Shephelah. [16] And Solomon's import of horses was from Egypt and Kue, and the king's traders would buy them from Kue for a price. [17] They imported a chariot from Egypt for 600 shekels[1] of silver, and a horse for 150. Likewise through them these were exported to all the kings of the Hittites and the kings of Syria.

Preparing to Build the Temple

2 [2] Now Solomon purposed to build a temple for the name of the Lord, and a royal palace for himself. [2][3] And Solomon assigned 70,000 men to bear burdens and 80,000 to quarry in the hill country, and 3,600 to oversee them. [3] And Solomon sent word to Hiram the king of Tyre: "As you dealt with David my father and sent him cedar to build himself a house to dwell in, so deal with me. [4] Behold, I am about to build a house for the name of the Lord my God and dedicate it to him for the burning of incense of sweet spices before him, and for the regular arrangement of the showbread, and for burnt offerings morning and evening, on the Sabbaths and the new moons and the appointed feasts of the Lord our God, as ordained forever for Israel. [5] The house that I am to build will be great, for our God is greater than all gods. [6] But who is able to build him a house, since heaven, even highest heaven, cannot contain him? Who am I to build a house for him, except as a place to make offerings before him? [7] So now send me a man skilled to work in gold, silver, bronze, and iron, and in purple, crimson, and blue fabrics, trained also in engraving, to be with the skilled workers who are with me in Judah and Jerusalem, whom David my father provided. [8] Send me also cedar, cypress, and algum timber from Lebanon, for I know that your servants know how to cut timber in Lebanon. And my servants will be with your servants, [9] to prepare timber for me in abundance, for the house I am to build will be great and wonderful. [10] I will give for your servants, the woodsmen who cut timber, 20,000 cors[4] of crushed wheat, 20,000 cors of barley, 20,000 baths[5] of wine, and 20,000 baths of oil."

[11] Then Hiram the king of Tyre answered in a letter that he sent to Solomon, "Because the Lord loves his people, he has made you king over them." [12] Hiram also said, "Blessed be the Lord God of Israel, who made heaven and

---

[1] A *shekel* was about 2/5 ounce or 11 grams [2] Ch 1:18 in Hebrew [3] Ch 2:1 in Hebrew [4] A *cor* was about 6 bushels or 220 liters [5] A *bath* was about 6 gallons or 22 liters

earth, who has given King David a wise son, who has discretion and understanding, who will build a temple for the Lord and a royal palace for himself.

¹³ "Now I have sent a skilled man, who has understanding, Huram-abi, ¹⁴ the son of a woman of the daughters of Dan, and his father was a man of Tyre. He is trained to work in gold, silver, bronze, iron, stone, and wood, and in purple, blue, and crimson fabrics and fine linen, and to do all sorts of engraving and execute any design that may be assigned him, with your craftsmen, the craftsmen of my lord, David your father. ¹⁵ Now therefore the wheat and barley, oil and wine, of which my lord has spoken, let him send to his servants. ¹⁶ And we will cut whatever timber you need from Lebanon and bring it to you in rafts by sea to Joppa, so that you may take it up to Jerusalem."

¹⁷ Then Solomon counted all the resident aliens who were in the land of Israel, after the census of them that David his father had taken, and there were found 153,600. ¹⁸ Seventy thousand of them he assigned to bear burdens, 80,000 to quarry in the hill country, and 3,600 as overseers to make the people work.

Solomon Builds the Temple

3 Then Solomon began to build the house of the Lord in Jerusalem on Mount Moriah, where the Lord[1] had appeared to David his father, at the place that David had appointed, on the threshing floor of Ornan the Jebusite. ² He began to build in the second month of the fourth year of his reign. ³ These are Solomon's measurements[2] for building the house of God: the length, in cubits[3] of the old standard, was sixty cubits, and the breadth twenty cubits. ⁴ The vestibule in front of the nave of the house was twenty cubits long, equal to the width of the house,[4] and its height was 120 cubits. He overlaid it on the inside with pure gold. ⁵ The nave he lined with cypress and covered it with fine gold and made palms and chains on it. ⁶ He adorned the house with settings of precious stones. The gold was gold of Parvaim. ⁷ So he lined the house with gold—its beams, its thresholds, its walls, and its doors—and he carved cherubim on the walls.

⁸ And he made the Most Holy Place. Its length, corresponding to the breadth of the house, was twenty cubits, and its breadth was twenty cubits. He overlaid it with 600 talents[5] of fine gold. ⁹ The weight of gold for the nails was fifty shekels.[6] And he overlaid the upper chambers with gold.

¹⁰ In the Most Holy Place he made two cherubim of wood[7] and overlaid[8] them with gold. ¹¹ The wings of the cherubim together extended twenty

---

[1] Septuagint; Hebrew lacks *the Lord* [2] Syriac; Hebrew *foundations* [3] A *cubit* was about 18 inches or 45 centimeters [4] Compare 1 Kings 6:3; the meaning of the Hebrew is uncertain [5] A *talent* was about 75 pounds or 34 kilograms [6] A *shekel* was about 2/5 ounce or 11 grams [7] Septuagint; the meaning of the Hebrew is uncertain [8] Hebrew *they overlaid*

cubits: one wing of the one, of five cubits, touched the wall of the house, and its other wing, of five cubits, touched the wing of the other cherub; [12] and of this cherub, one wing, of five cubits, touched the wall of the house, and the other wing, also of five cubits, was joined to the wing of the first cherub. [13] The wings of these cherubim extended twenty cubits. The cherubim[1] stood on their feet, facing the nave. [14] And he made the veil of blue and purple and crimson fabrics and fine linen, and he worked cherubim on it.

[15] In front of the house he made two pillars thirty-five cubits high, with a capital of five cubits on the top of each. [16] He made chains like a necklace[2] and put them on the tops of the pillars, and he made a hundred pomegranates and put them on the chains. [17] He set up the pillars in front of the temple, one on the south, the other on the north; that on the south he called Jachin, and that on the north Boaz.

The Temple's Furnishings

4 He made an altar of bronze, twenty cubits[3] long and twenty cubits wide and ten cubits high. [2] Then he made the sea of cast metal. It was round, ten cubits from brim to brim, and five cubits high, and a line of thirty cubits measured its circumference. [3] Under it were figures of gourds,[4] for ten cubits, compassing the sea all around. The gourds were in two rows, cast with it when it was cast. [4] It stood on twelve oxen, three facing north, three facing west, three facing south, and three facing east. The sea was set on them, and all their rear parts were inward. [5] Its thickness was a handbreadth.[5] And its brim was made like the brim of a cup, like the flower of a lily. It held 3,000 baths.[6] [6] He also made ten basins in which to wash, and set five on the south side, and five on the north side. In these they were to rinse off what was used for the burnt offering, and the sea was for the priests to wash in.

[7] And he made ten golden lampstands as prescribed, and set them in the temple, five on the south side and five on the north. [8] He also made ten tables and placed them in the temple, five on the south side and five on the north. And he made a hundred basins of gold. [9] He made the court of the priests and the great court and doors for the court and overlaid their doors with bronze. [10] And he set the sea at the southeast corner of the house.

[11] Hiram also made the pots, the shovels, and the basins. So Hiram finished the work that he did for King Solomon on the house of God: [12] the two pillars, the bowls, and the two capitals on the top of the pillars; and the two latticeworks to cover the two bowls of the capitals that were on the top of the pillars; [13] and the 400 pomegranates for the two latticeworks, two rows

---

[1] Hebrew *they* [2] Hebrew *chains in the inner sanctuary* [3] A *cubit* was about 18 inches or 45 centimeters [4] Hebrew *oxen*; twice in this verse; compare 1 Kings 7:24 [5] A *handbreadth* was about 3 inches or 7.5 centimeters [6] A *bath* was about 6 gallons or 22 liters

of pomegranates for each latticework, to cover the two bowls of the capitals that were on the pillars. ¹⁴ He made the stands also, and the basins on the stands, ¹⁵ and the one sea, and the twelve oxen underneath it. ¹⁶ The pots, the shovels, the forks, and all the equipment for these Huram-abi made of burnished bronze for King Solomon for the house of the Lord. ¹⁷ In the plain of the Jordan the king cast them, in the clay ground between Succoth and Zeredah.[1] ¹⁸ Solomon made all these things in great quantities, for the weight of the bronze was not sought.

¹⁹ So Solomon made all the vessels that were in the house of God: the golden altar, the tables for the bread of the Presence, ²⁰ the lampstands and their lamps of pure gold to burn before the inner sanctuary, as prescribed; ²¹ the flowers, the lamps, and the tongs, of purest gold; ²² the snuffers, basins, dishes for incense, and fire pans, of pure gold, and the sockets[2] of the temple, for the inner doors to the Most Holy Place and for the doors of the nave of the temple were of gold.

5 Thus all the work that Solomon did for the house of the Lord was finished. And Solomon brought in the things that David his father had dedicated, and stored the silver, the gold, and all the vessels in the treasuries of the house of God.

The Ark Brought to the Temple

² Then Solomon assembled the elders of Israel and all the heads of the tribes, the leaders of the fathers' houses of the people of Israel, in Jerusalem, to bring up the ark of the covenant of the Lord out of the city of David, which is Zion. ³ And all the men of Israel assembled before the king at the feast that is in the seventh month. ⁴ And all the elders of Israel came, and the Levites took up the ark. ⁵ And they brought up the ark, the tent of meeting, and all the holy vessels that were in the tent; the Levitical priests brought them up. ⁶ And King Solomon and all the congregation of Israel, who had assembled before him, were before the ark, sacrificing so many sheep and oxen that they could not be counted or numbered. ⁷ Then the priests brought the ark of the covenant of the Lord to its place, in the inner sanctuary of the house, in the Most Holy Place, underneath the wings of the cherubim. ⁸ The cherubim spread out their wings over the place of the ark, so that the cherubim made a covering above the ark and its poles. ⁹ And the poles were so long that the ends of the poles were seen from the Holy Place before the inner sanctuary, but they could not be seen from outside. And they are[3] there to this day. ¹⁰ There was nothing in the ark except the two tablets

---

[1] Spelled *Zarethan* in 1 Kings 7:46 [2] Compare 1 Kings 7:50; Hebrew *the entrance of the house* [3] Hebrew *it is*

that Moses put there at Horeb, where the Lord made a covenant with the people of Israel, when they came out of Egypt. ⁱⁱ And when the priests came out of the Holy Place (for all the priests who were present had consecrated themselves, without regard to their divisions, ¹² and all the Levitical singers, Asaph, Heman, and Jeduthun, their sons and kinsmen, arrayed in fine linen, with cymbals, harps, and lyres, stood east of the altar with 120 priests who were trumpeters; ¹³ and it was the duty of the trumpeters and singers to make themselves heard in unison in praise and thanksgiving to the Lord), and when the song was raised, with trumpets and cymbals and other musical instruments, in praise to the Lord,

"For he is good,
    for his steadfast love endures forever,"

the house, the house of the Lord, was filled with a cloud, ¹⁴ so that the priests could not stand to minister because of the cloud, for the glory of the Lord filled the house of God.

Solomon Blesses the People

6 Then Solomon said, "The Lord has said that he would dwell in thick darkness. ² But I have built you an exalted house, a place for you to dwell in forever." ³ Then the king turned around and blessed all the assembly of Israel, while all the assembly of Israel stood. ⁴ And he said, "Blessed be the Lord, the God of Israel, who with his hand has fulfilled what he promised with his mouth to David my father, saying, ⁵ 'Since the day that I brought my people out of the land of Egypt, I chose no city out of all the tribes of Israel in which to build a house, that my name might be there, and I chose no man as prince over my people Israel; ⁶ but I have chosen Jerusalem that my name may be there, and I have chosen David to be over my people Israel.' ⁷ Now it was in the heart of David my father to build a house for the name of the Lord, the God of Israel. ⁸ But the Lord said to David my father, 'Whereas it was in your heart to build a house for my name, you did well that it was in your heart. ⁹ Nevertheless, it is not you who shall build the house, but your son who shall be born to you shall build the house for my name.' ¹⁰ Now the Lord has fulfilled his promise that he made. For I have risen in the place of David my father and sit on the throne of Israel, as the Lord promised, and I have built the house for the name of the Lord, the God of Israel. ¹¹ And there I have set the ark, in which is the covenant of the Lord that he made with the people of Israel."

Solomon's Prayer of Dedication

[12] Then Solomon stood before the altar of the Lord in the presence of all the assembly of Israel and spread out his hands. [13] Solomon had made a bronze platform five cubits[1] long, five cubits wide, and three cubits high, and had set it in the court, and he stood on it. Then he knelt on his knees in the presence of all the assembly of Israel, and spread out his hands toward heaven, [14] and said, "O Lord, God of Israel, there is no God like you, in heaven or on earth, keeping covenant and showing steadfast love to your servants who walk before you with all their heart, [15] who have kept with your servant David my father what you declared to him. You spoke with your mouth, and with your hand have fulfilled it this day. [16] Now therefore, O Lord, God of Israel, keep for your servant David my father what you have promised him, saying, 'You shall not lack a man to sit before me on the throne of Israel, if only your sons pay close attention to their way, to walk in my law as you have walked before me.' [17] Now therefore, O Lord, God of Israel, let your word be confirmed, which you have spoken to your servant David.

[18] "But will God indeed dwell with man on the earth? Behold, heaven and the highest heaven cannot contain you, how much less this house that I have built! [19] Yet have regard to the prayer of your servant and to his plea, O Lord my God, listening to the cry and to the prayer that your servant prays before you, [20] that your eyes may be open day and night toward this house, the place where you have promised to set your name, that you may listen to the prayer that your servant offers toward this place. [21] And listen to the pleas of your servant and of your people Israel, when they pray toward this place. And listen from heaven your dwelling place, and when you hear, forgive.

[22] "If a man sins against his neighbor and is made to take an oath and comes and swears his oath before your altar in this house, [23] then hear from heaven and act and judge your servants, repaying the guilty by bringing his conduct on his own head, and vindicating the righteous by rewarding him according to his righteousness.

[24] "If your people Israel are defeated before the enemy because they have sinned against you, and they turn again and acknowledge your name and pray and plead with you in this house, [25] then hear from heaven and forgive the sin of your people Israel and bring them again to the land that you gave to them and to their fathers.

[26] "When heaven is shut up and there is no rain because they have sinned against you, if they pray toward this place and acknowledge your name and turn from their sin, when you afflict[2] them, [27] then hear in heaven and forgive

---

[1] A *cubit* was about 18 inches or 45 centimeters [2] Septuagint, Vulgate; Hebrew *answer*

the sin of your servants, your people Israel, when you teach them the good way[1] in which they should walk, and grant rain upon your land, which you have given to your people as an inheritance.

28 "If there is famine in the land, if there is pestilence or blight or mildew or locust or caterpillar, if their enemies besiege them in the land at their gates, whatever plague, whatever sickness there is, 29 whatever prayer, whatever plea is made by any man or by all your people Israel, each knowing his own affliction and his own sorrow and stretching out his hands toward this house, 30 then hear from heaven your dwelling place and forgive and render to each whose heart you know, according to all his ways, for you, you only, know the hearts of the children of mankind, 31 that they may fear you and walk in your ways all the days that they live in the land that you gave to our fathers.

32 "Likewise, when a foreigner, who is not of your people Israel, comes from a far country for the sake of your great name and your mighty hand and your outstretched arm, when he comes and prays toward this house, 33 hear from heaven your dwelling place and do according to all for which the foreigner calls to you, in order that all the peoples of the earth may know your name and fear you, as do your people Israel, and that they may know that this house that I have built is called by your name.

34 "If your people go out to battle against their enemies, by whatever way you shall send them, and they pray to you toward this city that you have chosen and the house that I have built for your name, 35 then hear from heaven their prayer and their plea, and maintain their cause.

36 "If they sin against you—for there is no one who does not sin—and you are angry with them and give them to an enemy, so that they are carried away captive to a land far or near, 37 yet if they turn their heart in the land to which they have been carried captive, and repent and plead with you in the land of their captivity, saying, 'We have sinned and have acted perversely and wickedly,' 38 if they repent with all their heart and with all their soul in the land of their captivity to which they were carried captive, and pray toward their land, which you gave to their fathers, the city that you have chosen and the house that I have built for your name, 39 then hear from heaven your dwelling place their prayer and their pleas, and maintain their cause and forgive your people who have sinned against you. 40 Now, O my God, let your eyes be open and your ears attentive to the prayer of this place.

41   "And now arise, O Lord God, and go to your resting place,
         you and the ark of your might.

---

[1] Septuagint, Syriac, Vulgate (compare 1 Kings 8:36); Hebrew *toward the good way*

Let your priests, O Lord God, be clothed with salvation,
>> and let your saints rejoice in your goodness.
42 O Lord God, do not turn away the face of your anointed one!
>> Remember your steadfast love for David your servant."

Fire from Heaven

7 As soon as Solomon finished his prayer, fire came down from heaven and consumed the burnt offering and the sacrifices, and the glory of the Lord filled the temple. ²And the priests could not enter the house of the Lord, because the glory of the Lord filled the Lord's house. ³When all the people of Israel saw the fire come down and the glory of the Lord on the temple, they bowed down with their faces to the ground on the pavement and worshiped and gave thanks to the Lord, saying, "For he is good, for his steadfast love endures forever."

The Dedication of the Temple

⁴Then the king and all the people offered sacrifice before the Lord. ⁵King Solomon offered as a sacrifice 22,000 oxen and 120,000 sheep. So the king and all the people dedicated the house of God. ⁶The priests stood at their posts; the Levites also, with the instruments for music to the Lord that King David had made for giving thanks to the Lord—for his steadfast love endures forever—whenever David offered praises by their ministry;¹ opposite them the priests sounded trumpets, and all Israel stood.

⁷And Solomon consecrated the middle of the court that was before the house of the Lord, for there he offered the burnt offering and the fat of the peace offerings, because the bronze altar Solomon had made could not hold the burnt offering and the grain offering and the fat.

⁸At that time Solomon held the feast for seven days, and all Israel with him, a very great assembly, from Lebo-hamath to the Brook of Egypt. ⁹And on the eighth day they held a solemn assembly, for they had kept the dedication of the altar seven days and the feast seven days. ¹⁰On the twenty-third day of the seventh month he sent the people away to their homes, joyful and glad of heart for the prosperity² that the Lord had granted to David and to Solomon and to Israel his people.

If My People Pray

¹¹Thus Solomon finished the house of the Lord and the king's house. All that Solomon had planned to do in the house of the Lord and in his own

---

¹ Hebrew *by their hand* ² Or *good*

house he successfully accomplished. ⁱ²Then the Lord appeared to Solomon in the night and said to him: "I have heard your prayer and have chosen this place for myself as a house of sacrifice. ¹³When I shut up the heavens so that there is no rain, or command the locust to devour the land, or send pestilence among my people, ¹⁴if my people who are called by my name humble themselves, and pray and seek my face and turn from their wicked ways, then I will hear from heaven and will forgive their sin and heal their land. ¹⁵Now my eyes will be open and my ears attentive to the prayer that is made in this place. ¹⁶For now I have chosen and consecrated this house that my name may be there forever. My eyes and my heart will be there for all time. ¹⁷And as for you, if you will walk before me as David your father walked, doing according to all that I have commanded you and keeping my statutes and my rules, ¹⁸then I will establish your royal throne, as I covenanted with David your father, saying, 'You shall not lack a man to rule Israel.'

¹⁹ "But if you[1] turn aside and forsake my statutes and my commandments that I have set before you, and go and serve other gods and worship them, ²⁰then I will pluck you[2] up from my land that I have given you, and this house that I have consecrated for my name, I will cast out of my sight, and I will make it a proverb and a byword among all peoples. ²¹And at this house, which was exalted, everyone passing by will be astonished and say, 'Why has the Lord done thus to this land and to this house?' ²²Then they will say, 'Because they abandoned the Lord, the God of their fathers who brought them out of the land of Egypt, and laid hold on other gods and worshiped them and served them. Therefore he has brought all this disaster on them.'"

Solomon's Accomplishments

8 At the end of twenty years, in which Solomon had built the house of the Lord and his own house, ²Solomon rebuilt the cities that Hiram had given to him, and settled the people of Israel in them.

³And Solomon went to Hamath-zobah and took it. ⁴He built Tadmor in the wilderness and all the store cities that he built in Hamath. ⁵He also built Upper Beth-horon and Lower Beth-horon, fortified cities with walls, gates, and bars, ⁶and Baalath, and all the store cities that Solomon had and all the cities for his chariots and the cities for his horsemen, and whatever Solomon desired to build in Jerusalem, in Lebanon, and in all the land of his dominion. ⁷All the people who were left of the Hittites, the Amorites, the Perizzites, the Hivites, and the Jebusites, who were not of Israel, ⁸from their descendants who were left after them in the land, whom the people of Israel

[1] The Hebrew for *you* is plural here [2] Hebrew *them*; twice in this verse

had not destroyed—these Solomon drafted as forced labor, and so they are to this day. ⁹But of the people of Israel Solomon made no slaves for his work; they were soldiers, and his officers, the commanders of his chariots, and his horsemen. ¹⁰And these were the chief officers of King Solomon, 250, who exercised authority over the people.

¹¹ Solomon brought Pharaoh's daughter up from the city of David to the house that he had built for her, for he said, "My wife shall not live in the house of David king of Israel, for the places to which the ark of the Lord has come are holy."

¹² Then Solomon offered up burnt offerings to the Lord on the altar of the Lord that he had built before the vestibule, ¹³ as the duty of each day required, offering according to the commandment of Moses for the Sabbaths, the new moons, and the three annual feasts—the Feast of Unleavened Bread, the Feast of Weeks, and the Feast of Booths. ¹⁴ According to the ruling of David his father, he appointed the divisions of the priests for their service, and the Levites for their offices of praise and ministry before the priests as the duty of each day required, and the gatekeepers in their divisions at each gate, for so David the man of God had commanded. ¹⁵ And they did not turn aside from what the king had commanded the priests and Levites concerning any matter and concerning the treasuries.

¹⁶ Thus was accomplished all the work of Solomon from[1] the day the foundation of the house of the Lord was laid until it was finished. So the house of the Lord was completed.

¹⁷ Then Solomon went to Ezion-geber and Eloth on the shore of the sea, in the land of Edom. ¹⁸ And Hiram sent to him by the hand of his servants ships and servants familiar with the sea, and they went to Ophir together with the servants of Solomon and brought from there 450 talents[2] of gold and brought it to King Solomon.

The Queen of Sheba

9 Now when the queen of Sheba heard of the fame of Solomon, she came to Jerusalem to test him with hard questions, having a very great retinue and camels bearing spices and very much gold and precious stones. And when she came to Solomon, she told him all that was on her mind. ² And Solomon answered all her questions. There was nothing hidden from Solomon that he could not explain to her. ³ And when the queen of Sheba had seen the wisdom of Solomon, the house that he had built, ⁴ the food of his table, the seating of his officials, and the attendance of his servants, and

---

[1] Septuagint, Syriac, Vulgate; Hebrew *to* [2] A *talent* was about 75 pounds or 34 kilograms

their clothing, his cupbearers, and their clothing, and his burnt offerings that he offered at the house of the LORD, there was no more breath in her.

⁵ And she said to the king, "The report was true that I heard in my own land of your words and of your wisdom, ⁶ but I did not believe the[1] reports until I came and my own eyes had seen it. And behold, half the greatness of your wisdom was not told me; you surpass the report that I heard. ⁷ Happy are your men! Happy are these your servants, who continually stand before you and hear your wisdom! ⁸ Blessed be the LORD your God, who has delighted in you and set you on his throne as king for the LORD your God! Because your God loved Israel and would establish them forever, he has made you king over them, that you may execute justice and righteousness." ⁹ Then she gave the king 120 talents[2] of gold, and a very great quantity of spices, and precious stones. There were no spices such as those that the queen of Sheba gave to King Solomon.

¹⁰ Moreover, the servants of Hiram and the servants of Solomon, who brought gold from Ophir, brought algum wood and precious stones. ¹¹ And the king made from the algum wood supports for the house of the LORD and for the king's house, lyres also and harps for the singers. There never was seen the like of them before in the land of Judah.

¹² And King Solomon gave to the queen of Sheba all that she desired, whatever she asked besides what she had brought to the king. So she turned and went back to her own land with her servants.

Solomon's Wealth

¹³ Now the weight of gold that came to Solomon in one year was 666 talents of gold, ¹⁴ besides that which the explorers and merchants brought. And all the kings of Arabia and the governors of the land brought gold and silver to Solomon. ¹⁵ King Solomon made 200 large shields of beaten gold; 600 shekels[3] of beaten gold went into each shield. ¹⁶ And he made 300 shields of beaten gold; 300 shekels of gold went into each shield; and the king put them in the House of the Forest of Lebanon. ¹⁷ The king also made a great ivory throne and overlaid it with pure gold. ¹⁸ The throne had six steps and a footstool of gold, which were attached to the throne, and on each side of the seat were armrests and two lions standing beside the armrests, ¹⁹ while twelve lions stood there, one on each end of a step on the six steps. Nothing like it was ever made for any kingdom. ²⁰ All King Solomon's drinking vessels were of gold, and all the vessels of the House of the Forest of Lebanon were of pure gold. Silver was not considered as anything in the days of Solomon.

[1] Hebrew *their* [2] A *talent* was about 75 pounds or 34 kilograms [3] A *shekel* was about 2/5 ounce or 11 grams

²¹ For the king's ships went to Tarshish with the servants of Hiram. Once every three years the ships of Tarshish used to come bringing gold, silver, ivory, apes, and peacocks.[1]

²² Thus King Solomon excelled all the kings of the earth in riches and in wisdom. ²³ And all the kings of the earth sought the presence of Solomon to hear his wisdom, which God had put into his mind. ²⁴ Every one of them brought his present, articles of silver and of gold, garments, myrrh,[2] spices, horses, and mules, so much year by year. ²⁵ And Solomon had 4,000 stalls for horses and chariots, and 12,000 horsemen, whom he stationed in the chariot cities and with the king in Jerusalem. ²⁶ And he ruled over all the kings from the Euphrates[3] to the land of the Philistines and to the border of Egypt. ²⁷ And the king made silver as common in Jerusalem as stone, and he made cedar as plentiful as the sycamore of the Shephelah. ²⁸ And horses were imported for Solomon from Egypt and from all lands.

Solomon's Death

²⁹ Now the rest of the acts of Solomon, from first to last, are they not written in the history of Nathan the prophet, and in the prophecy of Ahijah the Shilonite, and in the visions of Iddo the seer concerning Jeroboam the son of Nebat? ³⁰ Solomon reigned in Jerusalem over all Israel forty years. ³¹ And Solomon slept with his fathers and was buried in the city of David his father, and Rehoboam his son reigned in his place.

The Revolt Against Rehoboam

10 Rehoboam went to Shechem, for all Israel had come to Shechem to make him king. ² And as soon as Jeroboam the son of Nebat heard of it (for he was in Egypt, where he had fled from King Solomon), then Jeroboam returned from Egypt. ³ And they sent and called him. And Jeroboam and all Israel came and said to Rehoboam, ⁴ "Your father made our yoke heavy. Now therefore lighten the hard service of your father and his heavy yoke on us, and we will serve you." ⁵ He said to them, "Come to me again in three days." So the people went away.

⁶ Then King Rehoboam took counsel with the old men,[4] who had stood before Solomon his father while he was yet alive, saying, "How do you advise me to answer this people?" ⁷ And they said to him, "If you will be good to this people and please them and speak good words to them, then they will be your servants forever." ⁸ But he abandoned the counsel that the old men gave him, and took counsel with the young men who had grown up with

---

[1] Or *baboons* [2] Or *armor* [3] Hebrew *the River* [4] Or *the elders*; also verses 8, 13

him and stood before him. ⁹ And he said to them, "What do you advise that we answer this people who have said to me, 'Lighten the yoke that your father put on us'?" ¹⁰ And the young men who had grown up with him said to him, "Thus shall you speak to the people who said to you, 'Your father made our yoke heavy, but you lighten it for us'; thus shall you say to them, 'My little finger is thicker than my father's thighs. ¹¹ And now, whereas my father laid on you a heavy yoke, I will add to your yoke. My father disciplined you with whips, but I will discipline you with scorpions.'"

¹² So Jeroboam and all the people came to Rehoboam the third day, as the king said, "Come to me again the third day." ¹³ And the king answered them harshly; and forsaking the counsel of the old men, ¹⁴ King Rehoboam spoke to them according to the counsel of the young men, saying, "My father made your yoke heavy, but I will add to it. My father disciplined you with whips, but I will discipline you with scorpions." ¹⁵ So the king did not listen to the people, for it was a turn of affairs brought about by God that the Lord might fulfill his word, which he spoke by Ahijah the Shilonite to Jeroboam the son of Nebat.

¹⁶ And when all Israel saw that the king did not listen to them, the people answered the king, "What portion have we in David? We have no inheritance in the son of Jesse. Each of you to your tents, O Israel! Look now to your own house, David." So all Israel went to their tents. ¹⁷ But Rehoboam reigned over the people of Israel who lived in the cities of Judah. ¹⁸ Then King Rehoboam sent Hadoram,¹ who was taskmaster over the forced labor, and the people of Israel stoned him to death with stones. And King Rehoboam quickly mounted his chariot to flee to Jerusalem. ¹⁹ So Israel has been in rebellion against the house of David to this day.

Rehoboam Secures His Kingdom

11 When Rehoboam came to Jerusalem, he assembled the house of Judah and Benjamin, 180,000 chosen warriors, to fight against Israel, to restore the kingdom to Rehoboam. ² But the word of the Lord came to Shemaiah the man of God: ³ "Say to Rehoboam the son of Solomon, king of Judah, and to all Israel in Judah and Benjamin, ⁴ 'Thus says the Lord, You shall not go up or fight against your relatives. Return every man to his home, for this thing is from me.'" So they listened to the word of the Lord and returned and did not go against Jeroboam.

⁵ Rehoboam lived in Jerusalem, and he built cities for defense in Judah. ⁶ He built Bethlehem, Etam, Tekoa, ⁷ Beth-zur, Soco, Adullam, ⁸ Gath, Mareshah,

---
¹ Spelled *Adoram* in 1 Kings 12:18

Ziph, ⁹ Adoraim, Lachish, Azekah, ¹⁰ Zorah, Aijalon, and Hebron, fortified cities that are in Judah and in Benjamin. ¹¹ He made the fortresses strong, and put commanders in them, and stores of food, oil, and wine. ¹² And he put shields and spears in all the cities and made them very strong. So he held Judah and Benjamin.

Priests and Levites Come to Jerusalem

¹³ And the priests and the Levites who were in all Israel presented themselves to him from all places where they lived. ¹⁴ For the Levites left their common lands and their holdings and came to Judah and Jerusalem, because Jeroboam and his sons cast them out from serving as priests of the LORD, ¹⁵ and he appointed his own priests for the high places and for the goat idols and for the calves that he had made. ¹⁶ And those who had set their hearts to seek the LORD God of Israel came after them from all the tribes of Israel to Jerusalem to sacrifice to the LORD, the God of their fathers. ¹⁷ They strengthened the kingdom of Judah, and for three years they made Rehoboam the son of Solomon secure, for they walked for three years in the way of David and Solomon.

Rehoboam's Family

¹⁸ Rehoboam took as wife Mahalath the daughter of Jerimoth the son of David, and of Abihail the daughter of Eliab the son of Jesse, ¹⁹ and she bore him sons, Jeush, Shemariah, and Zaham. ²⁰ After her he took Maacah the daughter of Absalom, who bore him Abijah, Attai, Ziza, and Shelomith. ²¹ Rehoboam loved Maacah the daughter of Absalom above all his wives and concubines (he took eighteen wives and sixty concubines, and fathered twenty-eight sons and sixty daughters). ²² And Rehoboam appointed Abijah the son of Maacah as chief prince among his brothers, for he intended to make him king. ²³ And he dealt wisely and distributed some of his sons through all the districts of Judah and Benjamin, in all the fortified cities, and he gave them abundant provisions and procured wives for them.¹

Egypt Plunders Jerusalem

12 When the rule of Rehoboam was established and he was strong, he abandoned the law of the LORD, and all Israel with him. ² In the fifth year of King Rehoboam, because they had been unfaithful to the LORD, Shishak king of Egypt came up against Jerusalem ³ with 1,200 chariots and 60,000 horsemen. And the people were without number who came with him from Egypt—Libyans, Sukkiim, and Ethiopians. ⁴ And he took the

---

¹ Hebrew *and sought a multitude of wives*

fortified cities of Judah and came as far as Jerusalem. ⁵ Then Shemaiah the prophet came to Rehoboam and to the princes of Judah, who had gathered at Jerusalem because of Shishak, and said to them, "Thus says the Lord, 'You abandoned me, so I have abandoned you to the hand of Shishak.'" ⁶ Then the princes of Israel and the king humbled themselves and said, "The Lord is righteous." ⁷ When the Lord saw that they humbled themselves, the word of the Lord came to Shemaiah: "They have humbled themselves. I will not destroy them, but I will grant them some deliverance, and my wrath shall not be poured out on Jerusalem by the hand of Shishak. ⁸ Nevertheless, they shall be servants to him, that they may know my service and the service of the kingdoms of the countries."

⁹ So Shishak king of Egypt came up against Jerusalem. He took away the treasures of the house of the Lord and the treasures of the king's house. He took away everything. He also took away the shields of gold that Solomon had made, ¹⁰ and King Rehoboam made in their place shields of bronze and committed them to the hands of the officers of the guard, who kept the door of the king's house. ¹¹ And as often as the king went into the house of the Lord, the guard came and carried them and brought them back to the guardroom. ¹² And when he humbled himself the wrath of the Lord turned from him, so as not to make a complete destruction. Moreover, conditions were good¹ in Judah.

¹³ So King Rehoboam grew strong in Jerusalem and reigned. Rehoboam was forty-one years old when he began to reign, and he reigned seventeen years in Jerusalem, the city that the Lord had chosen out of all the tribes of Israel to put his name there. His mother's name was Naamah the Ammonite. ¹⁴ And he did evil, for he did not set his heart to seek the Lord.

¹⁵ Now the acts of Rehoboam, from first to last, are they not written in the chronicles of Shemaiah the prophet and of Iddo the seer?² There were continual wars between Rehoboam and Jeroboam. ¹⁶ And Rehoboam slept with his fathers and was buried in the city of David, and Abijah³ his son reigned in his place.

Abijah Reigns in Judah

13 In the eighteenth year of King Jeroboam, Abijah began to reign over Judah. ² He reigned for three years in Jerusalem. His mother's name was Micaiah⁴ the daughter of Uriel of Gibeah.

Now there was war between Abijah and Jeroboam. ³ Abijah went out to battle, having an army of valiant men of war, 400,000 chosen men. And Jeroboam drew up his line of battle against him with 800,000 chosen mighty warriors. ⁴ Then Abijah stood up on Mount Zemaraim that is in the hill

---

¹ Hebrew *good things were found* ² After *seer*, Hebrew adds *according to genealogy* ³ Spelled *Abijam* in 1 Kings 14:31 ⁴ Spelled *Maacah* in 1 Kings 15:2

country of Ephraim and said, "Hear me, O Jeroboam and all Israel! ⁵ Ought you not to know that the LORD God of Israel gave the kingship over Israel forever to David and his sons by a covenant of salt? ⁶ Yet Jeroboam the son of Nebat, a servant of Solomon the son of David, rose up and rebelled against his lord, ⁷ and certain worthless scoundrels¹ gathered about him and defied Rehoboam the son of Solomon, when Rehoboam was young and irresolute² and could not withstand them.

⁸ "And now you think to withstand the kingdom of the LORD in the hand of the sons of David, because you are a great multitude and have with you the golden calves that Jeroboam made you for gods. ⁹ Have you not driven out the priests of the LORD, the sons of Aaron, and the Levites, and made priests for yourselves like the peoples of other lands? Whoever comes for ordination³ with a young bull or seven rams becomes a priest of what are not gods. ¹⁰ But as for us, the LORD is our God, and we have not forsaken him. We have priests ministering to the LORD who are sons of Aaron, and Levites for their service. ¹¹ They offer to the LORD every morning and every evening burnt offerings and incense of sweet spices, set out the showbread on the table of pure gold, and care for the golden lampstand that its lamps may burn every evening. For we keep the charge of the LORD our God, but you have forsaken him. ¹² Behold, God is with us at our head, and his priests with their battle trumpets to sound the call to battle against you. O sons of Israel, do not fight against the LORD, the God of your fathers, for you cannot succeed."

¹³ Jeroboam had sent an ambush around to come upon them from behind. Thus his troops⁴ were in front of Judah, and the ambush was behind them. ¹⁴ And when Judah looked, behold, the battle was in front of and behind them. And they cried to the LORD, and the priests blew the trumpets. ¹⁵ Then the men of Judah raised the battle shout. And when the men of Judah shouted, God defeated Jeroboam and all Israel before Abijah and Judah. ¹⁶ The men of Israel fled before Judah, and God gave them into their hand. ¹⁷ Abijah and his people struck them with great force, so there fell slain of Israel 500,000 chosen men. ¹⁸ Thus the men of Israel were subdued at that time, and the men of Judah prevailed, because they relied on the LORD, the God of their fathers. ¹⁹ And Abijah pursued Jeroboam and took cities from him, Bethel with its villages and Jeshanah with its villages and Ephron⁵ with its villages. ²⁰ Jeroboam did not recover his power in the days of Abijah. And the LORD struck him down, and he died. ²¹ But Abijah grew mighty. And he took fourteen wives and had twenty-two sons and sixteen daughters. ²² The rest of the acts of Abijah, his ways and his sayings, are written in the story of the prophet Iddo.

¹ Hebrew *worthless men, sons of Belial* ² Hebrew *soft of heart* ³ Hebrew *to fill his hand* ⁴ Hebrew *they* ⁵ Or *Ephrain*

Asa Reigns in Judah

14 ¹ Abijah slept with his fathers, and they buried him in the city of David. And Asa his son reigned in his place. In his days the land had rest for ten years.² ² And Asa did what was good and right in the eyes of the Lord his God. ³ He took away the foreign altars and the high places and broke down the pillars and cut down the Asherim ⁴ and commanded Judah to seek the Lord, the God of their fathers, and to keep the law and the commandment. ⁵ He also took out of all the cities of Judah the high places and the incense altars. And the kingdom had rest under him. ⁶ He built fortified cities in Judah, for the land had rest. He had no war in those years, for the Lord gave him peace. ⁷ And he said to Judah, "Let us build these cities and surround them with walls and towers, gates and bars. The land is still ours, because we have sought the Lord our God. We have sought him, and he has given us peace on every side." So they built and prospered. ⁸ And Asa had an army of 300,000 from Judah, armed with large shields and spears, and 280,000 men from Benjamin that carried shields and drew bows. All these were mighty men of valor.

⁹ Zerah the Ethiopian came out against them with an army of a million men and 300 chariots, and came as far as Mareshah. ¹⁰ And Asa went out to meet him, and they drew up their lines of battle in the Valley of Zephathah at Mareshah. ¹¹ And Asa cried to the Lord his God, "O Lord, there is none like you to help, between the mighty and the weak. Help us, O Lord our God, for we rely on you, and in your name we have come against this multitude. O Lord, you are our God; let not man prevail against you." ¹² So the Lord defeated the Ethiopians before Asa and before Judah, and the Ethiopians fled. ¹³ Asa and the people who were with him pursued them as far as Gerar, and the Ethiopians fell until none remained alive, for they were broken before the Lord and his army. The men of Judah³ carried away very much spoil. ¹⁴ And they attacked all the cities around Gerar, for the fear of the Lord was upon them. They plundered all the cities, for there was much plunder in them. ¹⁵ And they struck down the tents of those who had livestock and carried away sheep in abundance and camels. Then they returned to Jerusalem.

Asa's Religious Reforms

15 The Spirit of God came⁴ upon Azariah the son of Oded, ² and he went out to meet Asa and said to him, "Hear me, Asa, and all Judah and Benjamin: The Lord is with you while you are with him. If you seek him, he will be found by you, but if you forsake him, he will forsake you.

¹ Ch 13:23 in Hebrew ² Ch 14:1 in Hebrew ³ Hebrew *They* ⁴ Or *was*

³ For a long time Israel was without the true God, and without a teaching priest and without law, ⁴ but when in their distress they turned to the Lord, the God of Israel, and sought him, he was found by them. ⁵ In those times there was no peace to him who went out or to him who came in, for great disturbances afflicted all the inhabitants of the lands. ⁶ They were broken in pieces. Nation was crushed by nation and city by city, for God troubled them with every sort of distress. ⁷ But you, take courage! Do not let your hands be weak, for your work shall be rewarded."

⁸ As soon as Asa heard these words, the prophecy of Azariah the son of Oded, he took courage and put away the detestable idols from all the land of Judah and Benjamin and from the cities that he had taken in the hill country of Ephraim, and he repaired the altar of the Lord that was in front of the vestibule of the house of the Lord.[1] ⁹ And he gathered all Judah and Benjamin, and those from Ephraim, Manasseh, and Simeon who were residing with them, for great numbers had deserted to him from Israel when they saw that the Lord his God was with him. ¹⁰ They were gathered at Jerusalem in the third month of the fifteenth year of the reign of Asa. ¹¹ They sacrificed to the Lord on that day from the spoil that they had brought 700 oxen and 7,000 sheep. ¹² And they entered into a covenant to seek the Lord, the God of their fathers, with all their heart and with all their soul, ¹³ but that whoever would not seek the Lord, the God of Israel, should be put to death, whether young or old, man or woman. ¹⁴ They swore an oath to the Lord with a loud voice and with shouting and with trumpets and with horns. ¹⁵ And all Judah rejoiced over the oath, for they had sworn with all their heart and had sought him with their whole desire, and he was found by them, and the Lord gave them rest all around.

¹⁶ Even Maacah, his mother, King Asa removed from being queen mother because she had made a detestable image for Asherah. Asa cut down her image, crushed it, and burned it at the brook Kidron. ¹⁷ But the high places were not taken out of Israel. Nevertheless, the heart of Asa was wholly true all his days. ¹⁸ And he brought into the house of God the sacred gifts of his father and his own sacred gifts, silver, and gold, and vessels. ¹⁹ And there was no more war until the thirty-fifth year of the reign of Asa.

Asa's Last Years

16 In the thirty-sixth year of the reign of Asa, Baasha king of Israel went up against Judah and built Ramah, that he might permit no one to go out or come in to Asa king of Judah. ² Then Asa took silver and gold

---

[1] Hebrew *the vestibule of the Lord*

from the treasures of the house of the Lord and the king's house and sent them to Ben-hadad king of Syria, who lived in Damascus, saying, ³ "There is a covenant[1] between me and you, as there was between my father and your father. Behold, I am sending to you silver and gold. Go, break your covenant with Baasha king of Israel, that he may withdraw from me." ⁴ And Ben-hadad listened to King Asa and sent the commanders of his armies against the cities of Israel, and they conquered Ijon, Dan, Abel-maim, and all the store cities of Naphtali. ⁵ And when Baasha heard of it, he stopped building Ramah and let his work cease. ⁶ Then King Asa took all Judah, and they carried away the stones of Ramah and its timber, with which Baasha had been building, and with them he built Geba and Mizpah.

⁷ At that time Hanani the seer came to Asa king of Judah and said to him, "Because you relied on the king of Syria, and did not rely on the Lord your God, the army of the king of Syria has escaped you. ⁸ Were not the Ethiopians and the Libyans a huge army with very many chariots and horsemen? Yet because you relied on the Lord, he gave them into your hand. ⁹ For the eyes of the Lord run to and fro throughout the whole earth, to give strong support to those whose heart is blameless[2] toward him. You have done foolishly in this, for from now on you will have wars." ¹⁰ Then Asa was angry with the seer and put him in the stocks in prison, for he was in a rage with him because of this. And Asa inflicted cruelties upon some of the people at the same time.

¹¹ The acts of Asa, from first to last, are written in the Book of the Kings of Judah and Israel. ¹² In the thirty-ninth year of his reign Asa was diseased in his feet, and his disease became severe. Yet even in his disease he did not seek the Lord, but sought help from physicians. ¹³ And Asa slept with his fathers, dying in the forty-first year of his reign. ¹⁴ They buried him in the tomb that he had cut for himself in the city of David. They laid him on a bier that had been filled with various kinds of spices prepared by the perfumer's art, and they made a very great fire in his honor.

Jehoshaphat Reigns in Judah

17 Jehoshaphat his son reigned in his place and strengthened himself against Israel. ² He placed forces in all the fortified cities of Judah and set garrisons in the land of Judah, and in the cities of Ephraim that Asa his father had captured. ³ The Lord was with Jehoshaphat, because he walked in the earlier ways of his father David. He did not seek the Baals, ⁴ but sought the God of his father and walked in his commandments, and not according to the practices of Israel. ⁵ Therefore the Lord established the kingdom in

[1] Or *treaty*; twice in this verse [2] Or *whole*

his hand. And all Judah brought tribute to Jehoshaphat, and he had great riches and honor. ⁶ His heart was courageous in the ways of the Lord. And furthermore, he took the high places and the Asherim out of Judah.

⁷ In the third year of his reign he sent his officials, Ben-hail, Obadiah, Zechariah, Nethanel, and Micaiah, to teach in the cities of Judah; ⁸ and with them the Levites, Shemaiah, Nethaniah, Zebadiah, Asahel, Shemiramoth, Jehonathan, Adonijah, Tobijah, and Tobadonijah; and with these Levites, the priests Elishama and Jehoram. ⁹ And they taught in Judah, having the Book of the Law of the Lord with them. They went about through all the cities of Judah and taught among the people.

¹⁰ And the fear of the Lord fell upon all the kingdoms of the lands that were around Judah, and they made no war against Jehoshaphat. ¹¹ Some of the Philistines brought Jehoshaphat presents and silver for tribute, and the Arabians also brought him 7,700 rams and 7,700 goats. ¹² And Jehoshaphat grew steadily greater. He built in Judah fortresses and store cities, ¹³ and he had large supplies in the cities of Judah. He had soldiers, mighty men of valor, in Jerusalem. ¹⁴ This was the muster of them by fathers' houses: Of Judah, the commanders of thousands: Adnah the commander, with 300,000 mighty men of valor; ¹⁵ and next to him Jehohanan the commander, with 280,000; ¹⁶ and next to him Amasiah the son of Zichri, a volunteer for the service of the Lord, with 200,000 mighty men of valor. ¹⁷ Of Benjamin: Eliada, a mighty man of valor, with 200,000 men armed with bow and shield; ¹⁸ and next to him Jehozabad with 180,000 armed for war. ¹⁹ These were in the service of the king, besides those whom the king had placed in the fortified cities throughout all Judah.

Jehoshaphat Allies with Ahab

18 Now Jehoshaphat had great riches and honor, and he made a marriage alliance with Ahab. ² After some years he went down to Ahab in Samaria. And Ahab killed an abundance of sheep and oxen for him and for the people who were with him, and induced him to go up against Ramoth-gilead. ³ Ahab king of Israel said to Jehoshaphat king of Judah, "Will you go with me to Ramoth-gilead?" He answered him, "I am as you are, my people as your people. We will be with you in the war."

⁴ And Jehoshaphat said to the king of Israel, "Inquire first for the word of the Lord." ⁵ Then the king of Israel gathered the prophets together, four hundred men, and said to them, "Shall we go to battle against Ramoth-gilead, or shall I refrain?" And they said, "Go up, for God will give it into the hand of the king." ⁶ But Jehoshaphat said, "Is there not here another prophet of the

Lord of whom we may inquire?" ⁷And the king of Israel said to Jehoshaphat, "There is yet one man by whom we may inquire of the Lord, Micaiah the son of Imlah; but I hate him, for he never prophesies good concerning me, but always evil." And Jehoshaphat said, "Let not the king say so." ⁸Then the king of Israel summoned an officer and said, "Bring quickly Micaiah the son of Imlah." ⁹Now the king of Israel and Jehoshaphat the king of Judah were sitting on their thrones, arrayed in their robes. And they were sitting at the threshing floor at the entrance of the gate of Samaria, and all the prophets were prophesying before them. ¹⁰And Zedekiah the son of Chenaanah made for himself horns of iron and said, "Thus says the Lord, 'With these you shall push the Syrians until they are destroyed.'" ¹¹And all the prophets prophesied so and said, "Go up to Ramoth-gilead and triumph. The Lord will give it into the hand of the king."

¹²And the messenger who went to summon Micaiah said to him, "Behold, the words of the prophets with one accord are favorable to the king. Let your word be like the word of one of them, and speak favorably." ¹³But Micaiah said, "As the Lord lives, what my God says, that I will speak." ¹⁴And when he had come to the king, the king said to him, "Micaiah, shall we go to Ramoth-gilead to battle, or shall I refrain?" And he answered, "Go up and triumph; they will be given into your hand." ¹⁵But the king said to him, "How many times shall I make you swear that you speak to me nothing but the truth in the name of the Lord?" ¹⁶And he said, "I saw all Israel scattered on the mountains, as sheep that have no shepherd. And the Lord said, 'These have no master; let each return to his home in peace.'" ¹⁷And the king of Israel said to Jehoshaphat, "Did I not tell you that he would not prophesy good concerning me, but evil?" ¹⁸And Micaiah said, "Therefore hear the word of the Lord: I saw the Lord sitting on his throne, and all the host of heaven standing on his right hand and on his left. ¹⁹And the Lord said, 'Who will entice Ahab the king of Israel, that he may go up and fall at Ramoth-gilead?' And one said one thing, and another said another. ²⁰Then a spirit came forward and stood before the Lord, saying, 'I will entice him.' And the Lord said to him, 'By what means?' ²¹And he said, 'I will go out, and will be a lying spirit in the mouth of all his prophets.' And he said, 'You are to entice him, and you shall succeed; go out and do so.' ²²Now therefore behold, the Lord has put a lying spirit in the mouth of these your prophets. The Lord has declared disaster concerning you."

²³Then Zedekiah the son of Chenaanah came near and struck Micaiah on the cheek and said, "Which way did the Spirit of the Lord go from me to speak to you?" ²⁴And Micaiah said, "Behold, you shall see on that day when

you go into an inner chamber to hide yourself." ²⁵ And the king of Israel said, "Seize Micaiah and take him back to Amon the governor of the city and to Joash the king's son, ²⁶ and say, 'Thus says the king, Put this fellow in prison and feed him with meager rations of bread and water until I return in peace.'" ²⁷ And Micaiah said, "If you return in peace, the Lord has not spoken by me." And he said, "Hear, all you peoples!"

The Defeat and Death of Ahab

²⁸ So the king of Israel and Jehoshaphat the king of Judah went up to Ramoth-gilead. ²⁹ And the king of Israel said to Jehoshaphat, "I will disguise myself and go into battle, but you wear your robes." And the king of Israel disguised himself, and they went into battle. ³⁰ Now the king of Syria had commanded the captains of his chariots, "Fight with neither small nor great, but only with the king of Israel." ³¹ As soon as the captains of the chariots saw Jehoshaphat, they said, "It is the king of Israel." So they turned to fight against him. And Jehoshaphat cried out, and the Lord helped him; God drew them away from him. ³² For as soon as the captains of the chariots saw that it was not the king of Israel, they turned back from pursuing him. ³³ But a certain man drew his bow at random¹ and struck the king of Israel between the scale armor and the breastplate. Therefore he said to the driver of his chariot, "Turn around and carry me out of the battle, for I am wounded." ³⁴ And the battle continued that day, and the king of Israel was propped up in his chariot facing the Syrians until evening. Then at sunset he died.

Jehoshaphat's Reforms

19 Jehoshaphat the king of Judah returned in safety to his house in Jerusalem. ² But Jehu the son of Hanani the seer went out to meet him and said to King Jehoshaphat, "Should you help the wicked and love those who hate the Lord? Because of this, wrath has gone out against you from the Lord. ³ Nevertheless, some good is found in you, for you destroyed the Asheroth out of the land, and have set your heart to seek God."

⁴ Jehoshaphat lived at Jerusalem. And he went out again among the people, from Beersheba to the hill country of Ephraim, and brought them back to the Lord, the God of their fathers. ⁵ He appointed judges in the land in all the fortified cities of Judah, city by city, ⁶ and said to the judges, "Consider what you do, for you judge not for man but for the Lord. He is with you in giving judgment. ⁷ Now then, let the fear of the Lord be upon you. Be careful what you do, for there is no injustice with the Lord our God, or partiality or taking bribes."

¹ Hebrew *in his innocence*

⁸ Moreover, in Jerusalem Jehoshaphat appointed certain Levites and priests and heads of families of Israel, to give judgment for the Lord and to decide disputed cases. They had their seat at Jerusalem. ⁹ And he charged them: "Thus you shall do in the fear of the Lord, in faithfulness, and with your whole heart: ¹⁰ whenever a case comes to you from your brothers who live in their cities, concerning bloodshed, law or commandment, statutes or rules, then you shall warn them, that they may not incur guilt before the Lord and wrath may not come upon you and your brothers. Thus you shall do, and you will not incur guilt. ¹¹ And behold, Amariah the chief priest is over you in all matters of the Lord; and Zebadiah the son of Ishmael, the governor of the house of Judah, in all the king's matters, and the Levites will serve you as officers. Deal courageously, and may the Lord be with the upright!"[1]

Jehoshaphat's Prayer

20 After this the Moabites and Ammonites, and with them some of the Meunites,[2] came against Jehoshaphat for battle. ² Some men came and told Jehoshaphat, "A great multitude is coming against you from Edom,[3] from beyond the sea; and, behold, they are in Hazazon-tamar" (that is, Engedi). ³ Then Jehoshaphat was afraid and set his face to seek the Lord, and proclaimed a fast throughout all Judah. ⁴ And Judah assembled to seek help from the Lord; from all the cities of Judah they came to seek the Lord.

⁵ And Jehoshaphat stood in the assembly of Judah and Jerusalem, in the house of the Lord, before the new court, ⁶ and said, "O Lord, God of our fathers, are you not God in heaven? You rule over all the kingdoms of the nations. In your hand are power and might, so that none is able to withstand you. ⁷ Did you not, our God, drive out the inhabitants of this land before your people Israel, and give it forever to the descendants of Abraham your friend? ⁸ And they have lived in it and have built for you in it a sanctuary for your name, saying, ⁹ 'If disaster comes upon us, the sword, judgment,[4] or pestilence, or famine, we will stand before this house and before you—for your name is in this house—and cry out to you in our affliction, and you will hear and save.' ¹⁰ And now behold, the men of Ammon and Moab and Mount Seir, whom you would not let Israel invade when they came from the land of Egypt, and whom they avoided and did not destroy— ¹¹ behold, they reward us by coming to drive us out of your possession, which you have given us to inherit. ¹² O our God, will you not execute judgment on them?

---

[1] Hebrew *the good* [2] Compare 26:7; Hebrew *Ammonites* [3] One Hebrew manuscript; most Hebrew manuscripts *Aram* (Syria) [4] Or *the sword of judgment*

For we are powerless against this great horde that is coming against us. We do not know what to do, but our eyes are on you."

¹³ Meanwhile all Judah stood before the Lord, with their little ones, their wives, and their children. ¹⁴ And the Spirit of the Lord came[1] upon Jahaziel the son of Zechariah, son of Benaiah, son of Jeiel, son of Mattaniah, a Levite of the sons of Asaph, in the midst of the assembly. ¹⁵ And he said, "Listen, all Judah and inhabitants of Jerusalem and King Jehoshaphat: Thus says the Lord to you, 'Do not be afraid and do not be dismayed at this great horde, for the battle is not yours but God's. ¹⁶ Tomorrow go down against them. Behold, they will come up by the ascent of Ziz. You will find them at the end of the valley, east of the wilderness of Jeruel. ¹⁷ You will not need to fight in this battle. Stand firm, hold your position, and see the salvation of the Lord on your behalf, O Judah and Jerusalem.' Do not be afraid and do not be dismayed. Tomorrow go out against them, and the Lord will be with you."

¹⁸ Then Jehoshaphat bowed his head with his face to the ground, and all Judah and the inhabitants of Jerusalem fell down before the Lord, worshiping the Lord. ¹⁹ And the Levites, of the Kohathites and the Korahites, stood up to praise the Lord, the God of Israel, with a very loud voice.

²⁰ And they rose early in the morning and went out into the wilderness of Tekoa. And when they went out, Jehoshaphat stood and said, "Hear me, Judah and inhabitants of Jerusalem! Believe in the Lord your God, and you will be established; believe his prophets, and you will succeed." ²¹ And when he had taken counsel with the people, he appointed those who were to sing to the Lord and praise him in holy attire, as they went before the army, and say,

"Give thanks to the Lord,
 for his steadfast love endures forever."

²² And when they began to sing and praise, the Lord set an ambush against the men of Ammon, Moab, and Mount Seir, who had come against Judah, so that they were routed. ²³ For the men of Ammon and Moab rose against the inhabitants of Mount Seir, devoting them to destruction, and when they had made an end of the inhabitants of Seir, they all helped to destroy one another.

The Lord Delivers Judah

²⁴ When Judah came to the watchtower of the wilderness, they looked toward the horde, and behold, there[2] were dead bodies lying on the ground; none had escaped. ²⁵ When Jehoshaphat and his people came to take their

[1] Or *was* [2] Hebrew *they*

spoil, they found among them, in great numbers, goods, clothing, and precious things, which they took for themselves until they could carry no more. They were three days in taking the spoil, it was so much. ²⁶ On the fourth day they assembled in the Valley of Beracah,¹ for there they blessed the Lord. Therefore the name of that place has been called the Valley of Beracah to this day. ²⁷ Then they returned, every man of Judah and Jerusalem, and Jehoshaphat at their head, returning to Jerusalem with joy, for the Lord had made them rejoice over their enemies. ²⁸ They came to Jerusalem with harps and lyres and trumpets, to the house of the Lord. ²⁹ And the fear of God came on all the kingdoms of the countries when they heard that the Lord had fought against the enemies of Israel. ³⁰ So the realm of Jehoshaphat was quiet, for his God gave him rest all around.

³¹ Thus Jehoshaphat reigned over Judah. He was thirty-five years old when he began to reign, and he reigned twenty-five years in Jerusalem. His mother's name was Azubah the daughter of Shilhi. ³² He walked in the way of Asa his father and did not turn aside from it, doing what was right in the sight of the Lord. ³³ The high places, however, were not taken away; the people had not yet set their hearts upon the God of their fathers.

³⁴ Now the rest of the acts of Jehoshaphat, from first to last, are written in the chronicles of Jehu the son of Hanani, which are recorded in the Book of the Kings of Israel.

The End of Jehoshaphat's Reign

³⁵ After this Jehoshaphat king of Judah joined with Ahaziah king of Israel, who acted wickedly. ³⁶ He joined him in building ships to go to Tarshish, and they built the ships in Ezion-geber. ³⁷ Then Eliezer the son of Dodavahu of Mareshah prophesied against Jehoshaphat, saying, "Because you have joined with Ahaziah, the Lord will destroy what you have made." And the ships were wrecked and were not able to go to Tarshish.

Jehoram Reigns in Judah

21 Jehoshaphat slept with his fathers and was buried with his fathers in the city of David, and Jehoram his son reigned in his place. ² He had brothers, the sons of Jehoshaphat: Azariah, Jehiel, Zechariah, Azariah, Michael, and Shephatiah; all these were the sons of Jehoshaphat king of Israel.² ³ Their father gave them great gifts of silver, gold, and valuable possessions, together with fortified cities in Judah, but he gave the kingdom to Jehoram, because he was the firstborn. ⁴ When Jehoram had ascended the

¹ *Beracah* means *blessing* ² That is, Judah

throne of his father and was established, he killed all his brothers with the sword, and also some of the princes of Israel. ⁵ Jehoram was thirty-two years old when he became king, and he reigned eight years in Jerusalem. ⁶ And he walked in the way of the kings of Israel, as the house of Ahab had done, for the daughter of Ahab was his wife. And he did what was evil in the sight of the LORD. ⁷ Yet the LORD was not willing to destroy the house of David, because of the covenant that he had made with David, and since he had promised to give a lamp to him and to his sons forever.

⁸ In his days Edom revolted from the rule of Judah and set up a king of their own. ⁹ Then Jehoram passed over with his commanders and all his chariots, and he rose by night and struck the Edomites who had surrounded him and his chariot commanders. ¹⁰ So Edom revolted from the rule of Judah to this day. At that time Libnah also revolted from his rule, because he had forsaken the LORD, the God of his fathers.

¹¹ Moreover, he made high places in the hill country of Judah and led the inhabitants of Jerusalem into whoredom and made Judah go astray. ¹² And a letter came to him from Elijah the prophet, saying, "Thus says the LORD, the God of David your father, 'Because you have not walked in the ways of Jehoshaphat your father, or in the ways of Asa king of Judah, ¹³ but have walked in the way of the kings of Israel and have enticed Judah and the inhabitants of Jerusalem into whoredom, as the house of Ahab led Israel into whoredom, and also you have killed your brothers, of your father's house, who were better than you, ¹⁴ behold, the LORD will bring a great plague on your people, your children, your wives, and all your possessions, ¹⁵ and you yourself will have a severe sickness with a disease of your bowels, until your bowels come out because of the disease, day by day.'"

¹⁶ And the LORD stirred up against Jehoram the anger[1] of the Philistines and of the Arabians who are near the Ethiopians. ¹⁷ And they came up against Judah and invaded it and carried away all the possessions they found that belonged to the king's house, and also his sons and his wives, so that no son was left to him except Jehoahaz, his youngest son.

¹⁸ And after all this the LORD struck him in his bowels with an incurable disease. ¹⁹ In the course of time, at the end of two years, his bowels came out because of the disease, and he died in great agony. His people made no fire in his honor, like the fires made for his fathers. ²⁰ He was thirty-two years old when he began to reign, and he reigned eight years in Jerusalem. And he departed with no one's regret. They buried him in the city of David, but not in the tombs of the kings.

[1] Hebrew *spirit*

Ahaziah Reigns in Judah

22 And the inhabitants of Jerusalem made Ahaziah, his youngest son, king in his place, for the band of men that came with the Arabians to the camp had killed all the older sons. So Ahaziah the son of Jehoram king of Judah reigned. ² Ahaziah was twenty-two[1] years old when he began to reign, and he reigned one year in Jerusalem. His mother's name was Athaliah, the granddaughter of Omri. ³ He also walked in the ways of the house of Ahab, for his mother was his counselor in doing wickedly. ⁴ He did what was evil in the sight of the LORD, as the house of Ahab had done. For after the death of his father they were his counselors, to his undoing. ⁵ He even followed their counsel and went with Jehoram the son of Ahab king of Israel to make war against Hazael king of Syria at Ramoth-gilead. And the Syrians wounded Joram, ⁶ and he returned to be healed in Jezreel of the wounds that he had received at Ramah, when he fought against Hazael king of Syria. And Ahaziah the son of Jehoram king of Judah went down to see Joram the son of Ahab in Jezreel, because he was wounded.

⁷ But it was ordained by[2] God that the downfall of Ahaziah should come about through his going to visit Joram. For when he came there, he went out with Jehoram to meet Jehu the son of Nimshi, whom the LORD had anointed to destroy the house of Ahab. ⁸ And when Jehu was executing judgment on the house of Ahab, he met the princes of Judah and the sons of Ahaziah's brothers, who attended Ahaziah, and he killed them. ⁹ He searched for Ahaziah, and he was captured while hiding in Samaria, and he was brought to Jehu and put to death. They buried him, for they said, "He is the grandson of Jehoshaphat, who sought the LORD with all his heart." And the house of Ahaziah had no one able to rule the kingdom.

Athaliah Reigns in Judah

¹⁰ Now when Athaliah the mother of Ahaziah saw that her son was dead, she arose and destroyed all the royal family of the house of Judah. ¹¹ But Jehoshabeath,[3] the daughter of the king, took Joash the son of Ahaziah and stole him away from among the king's sons who were about to be put to death, and she put him and his nurse in a bedroom. Thus Jehoshabeath, the daughter of King Jehoram and wife of Jehoiada the priest, because she was a sister of Ahaziah, hid him[4] from Athaliah, so that she did not put him to death. ¹² And he remained with them six years, hidden in the house of God, while Athaliah reigned over the land.

---

[1] See 2 Kings 8:26; Hebrew *forty-two*; Septuagint *twenty* [2] Hebrew *was from* [3] Spelled *Jehosheba* in 2 Kings 11:2 [4] That is, Joash

Joash Made King

23 But in the seventh year Jehoiada took courage and entered into a covenant with the commanders of hundreds, Azariah the son of Jeroham, Ishmael the son of Jehohanan, Azariah the son of Obed, Maaseiah the son of Adaiah, and Elishaphat the son of Zichri. ² And they went about through Judah and gathered the Levites from all the cities of Judah, and the heads of fathers' houses of Israel, and they came to Jerusalem. ³ And all the assembly made a covenant with the king in the house of God. And Jehoiada[1] said to them, "Behold, the king's son! Let him reign, as the LORD spoke concerning the sons of David. ⁴ This is the thing that you shall do: of you priests and Levites who come off duty on the Sabbath, one third shall be gatekeepers, ⁵ and one third shall be at the king's house and one third at the Gate of the Foundation. And all the people shall be in the courts of the house of the LORD. ⁶ Let no one enter the house of the LORD except the priests and ministering Levites. They may enter, for they are holy, but all the people shall keep the charge of the LORD. ⁷ The Levites shall surround the king, each with his weapons in his hand. And whoever enters the house shall be put to death. Be with the king when he comes in and when he goes out."

⁸ The Levites and all Judah did according to all that Jehoiada the priest commanded, and they each brought his men, who were to go off duty on the Sabbath, with those who were to come on duty on the Sabbath, for Jehoiada the priest did not dismiss the divisions. ⁹ And Jehoiada the priest gave to the captains the spears and the large and small shields that had been King David's, which were in the house of God. ¹⁰ And he set all the people as a guard for the king, every man with his weapon in his hand, from the south side of the house to the north side of the house, around the altar and the house. ¹¹ Then they brought out the king's son and put the crown on him and gave him the testimony. And they proclaimed him king, and Jehoiada and his sons anointed him, and they said, "Long live the king."

Athaliah Executed

¹² When Athaliah heard the noise of the people running and praising the king, she went into the house of the LORD to the people. ¹³ And when she looked, there was the king standing by his pillar at the entrance, and the captains and the trumpeters beside the king, and all the people of the land rejoicing and blowing trumpets, and the singers with their musical instruments leading in the celebration. And Athaliah tore her clothes and cried, "Treason! Treason!" ¹⁴ Then Jehoiada the priest brought out the captains who

---

[1] Hebrew *he*

were set over the army, saying to them, "Bring her out between the ranks, and anyone who follows her is to be put to death with the sword." For the priest said, "Do not put her to death in the house of the Lord." ⁱ⁵ So they laid hands on her,¹ and she went into the entrance of the horse gate of the king's house, and they put her to death there.

Jehoiada's Reforms

¹⁶ And Jehoiada made a covenant between himself and all the people and the king that they should be the Lord's people. ¹⁷ Then all the people went to the house of Baal and tore it down; his altars and his images they broke in pieces, and they killed Mattan the priest of Baal before the altars. ¹⁸ And Jehoiada posted watchmen for the house of the Lord under the direction of the Levitical priests and the Levites whom David had organized to be in charge of the house of the Lord, to offer burnt offerings to the Lord, as it is written in the Law of Moses, with rejoicing and with singing, according to the order of David. ¹⁹ He stationed the gatekeepers at the gates of the house of the Lord so that no one should enter who was in any way unclean. ²⁰ And he took the captains, the nobles, the governors of the people, and all the people of the land, and they brought the king down from the house of the Lord, marching through the upper gate to the king's house. And they set the king on the royal throne. ²¹ So all the people of the land rejoiced, and the city was quiet after Athaliah had been put to death with the sword.

Joash Repairs the Temple

24 Joash² was seven years old when he began to reign, and he reigned forty years in Jerusalem. His mother's name was Zibiah of Beersheba. ² And Joash did what was right in the eyes of the Lord all the days of Jehoiada the priest. ³ Jehoiada got for him two wives, and he had sons and daughters.

⁴ After this Joash decided to restore the house of the Lord. ⁵ And he gathered the priests and the Levites and said to them, "Go out to the cities of Judah and gather from all Israel money to repair the house of your God from year to year, and see that you act quickly." But the Levites did not act quickly. ⁶ So the king summoned Jehoiada the chief and said to him, "Why have you not required the Levites to bring in from Judah and Jerusalem the tax levied by Moses, the servant of the Lord, and the congregation of Israel for the tent of testimony?" ⁷ For the sons of Athaliah, that wicked woman, had broken into the house of God, and had also used all the dedicated things of the house of the Lord for the Baals.

¹ Or *they made a passage for her* ² Spelled *Jehoash* in 2 Kings 12:1

⁸ So the king commanded, and they made a chest and set it outside the gate of the house of the Lord. ⁹ And proclamation was made throughout Judah and Jerusalem to bring in for the Lord the tax that Moses the servant of God laid on Israel in the wilderness. ¹⁰ And all the princes and all the people rejoiced and brought their tax and dropped it into the chest until they had finished.¹ ¹¹ And whenever the chest was brought to the king's officers by the Levites, when they saw that there was much money in it, the king's secretary and the officer of the chief priest would come and empty the chest and take it and return it to its place. Thus they did day after day, and collected money in abundance. ¹² And the king and Jehoiada gave it to those who had charge of the work of the house of the Lord, and they hired masons and carpenters to restore the house of the Lord, and also workers in iron and bronze to repair the house of the Lord. ¹³ So those who were engaged in the work labored, and the repairing went forward in their hands, and they restored the house of God to its proper condition and strengthened it. ¹⁴ And when they had finished, they brought the rest of the money before the king and Jehoiada, and with it were made utensils for the house of the Lord, both for the service and for the burnt offerings, and dishes for incense and vessels of gold and silver. And they offered burnt offerings in the house of the Lord regularly all the days of Jehoiada.

¹⁵ But Jehoiada grew old and full of days, and died. He was 130 years old at his death. ¹⁶ And they buried him in the city of David among the kings, because he had done good in Israel, and toward God and his house.

¹⁷ Now after the death of Jehoiada the princes of Judah came and paid homage to the king. Then the king listened to them. ¹⁸ And they abandoned the house of the Lord, the God of their fathers, and served the Asherim and the idols. And wrath came upon Judah and Jerusalem for this guilt of theirs. ¹⁹ Yet he sent prophets among them to bring them back to the Lord. These testified against them, but they would not pay attention.

Joash's Treachery

²⁰ Then the Spirit of God clothed Zechariah the son of Jehoiada the priest, and he stood above the people, and said to them, "Thus says God, 'Why do you break the commandments of the Lord, so that you cannot prosper? Because you have forsaken the Lord, he has forsaken you.'" ²¹ But they conspired against him, and by command of the king they stoned him with stones in the court of the house of the Lord. ²² Thus Joash the king did not remember the kindness that Jehoiada, Zechariah's father, had shown

---

¹ Or *until it was full*

him, but killed his son. And when he was dying, he said, "May the LORD see and avenge!"[1]

Joash Assassinated

[23] At the end of the year the army of the Syrians came up against Joash. They came to Judah and Jerusalem and destroyed all the princes of the people from among the people and sent all their spoil to the king of Damascus. [24] Though the army of the Syrians had come with few men, the LORD delivered into their hand a very great army, because Judah[2] had forsaken the LORD, the God of their fathers. Thus they executed judgment on Joash.

[25] When they had departed from him, leaving him severely wounded, his servants conspired against him because of the blood of the son[3] of Jehoiada the priest, and killed him on his bed. So he died, and they buried him in the city of David, but they did not bury him in the tombs of the kings. [26] Those who conspired against him were Zabad the son of Shimeath the Ammonite, and Jehozabad the son of Shimrith the Moabite. [27] Accounts of his sons and of the many oracles against him and of the rebuilding[4] of the house of God are written in the Story[5] of the Book of the Kings. And Amaziah his son reigned in his place.

Amaziah Reigns in Judah

25 Amaziah was twenty-five years old when he began to reign, and he reigned twenty-nine years in Jerusalem. His mother's name was Jehoaddan of Jerusalem. [2] And he did what was right in the eyes of the LORD, yet not with a whole heart. [3] And as soon as the royal power was firmly his, he killed his servants who had struck down the king his father. [4] But he did not put their children to death, according to what is written in the Law, in the Book of Moses, where the LORD commanded, "Fathers shall not die because of their children, nor children die because of their fathers, but each one shall die for his own sin."

Amaziah's Victories

[5] Then Amaziah assembled the men of Judah and set them by fathers' houses under commanders of thousands and of hundreds for all Judah and Benjamin. He mustered those twenty years old and upward, and found that they were 300,000 choice men, fit for war, able to handle spear and shield. [6] He hired also 100,000 mighty men of valor from Israel for 100 talents[6] of silver. [7] But a man of God came to him and said, "O king, do not let the

---

[1] Or *and require it* [2] Hebrew *they* [3] Septuagint, Vulgate; Hebrew *sons* [4] Hebrew *founding* [5] Or *Exposition*
[6] A *talent* was about 75 pounds or 34 kilograms

army of Israel go with you, for the LORD is not with Israel, with all these Ephraimites. ⁸ But go, act, be strong for the battle. Why should you suppose that God will cast you down before the enemy? For God has power to help or to cast down." ⁹ And Amaziah said to the man of God, "But what shall we do about the hundred talents that I have given to the army of Israel?" The man of God answered, "The LORD is able to give you much more than this." ¹⁰ Then Amaziah discharged the army that had come to him from Ephraim to go home again. And they became very angry with Judah and returned home in fierce anger. ¹¹ But Amaziah took courage and led out his people and went to the Valley of Salt and struck down 10,000 men of Seir. ¹² The men of Judah captured another 10,000 alive and took them to the top of a rock and threw them down from the top of the rock, and they were all dashed to pieces. ¹³ But the men of the army whom Amaziah sent back, not letting them go with him to battle, raided the cities of Judah, from Samaria to Beth-horon, and struck down 3,000 people in them and took much spoil.

Amaziah's Idolatry

¹⁴ After Amaziah came from striking down the Edomites, he brought the gods of the men of Seir and set them up as his gods and worshiped them, making offerings to them. ¹⁵ Therefore the LORD was angry with Amaziah and sent to him a prophet, who said to him, "Why have you sought the gods of a people who did not deliver their own people from your hand?" ¹⁶ But as he was speaking, the king said to him, "Have we made you a royal counselor? Stop! Why should you be struck down?" So the prophet stopped, but said, "I know that God has determined to destroy you, because you have done this and have not listened to my counsel."

Israel Defeats Amaziah

¹⁷ Then Amaziah king of Judah took counsel and sent to Joash the son of Jehoahaz, son of Jehu, king of Israel, saying, "Come, let us look one another in the face." ¹⁸ And Joash the king of Israel sent word to Amaziah king of Judah, "A thistle on Lebanon sent to a cedar on Lebanon, saying, 'Give your daughter to my son for a wife,' and a wild beast of Lebanon passed by and trampled down the thistle. ¹⁹ You say, 'See, I¹ have struck down Edom,' and your heart has lifted you up in boastfulness. But now stay at home. Why should you provoke trouble so that you fall, you and Judah with you?"

²⁰ But Amaziah would not listen, for it was of God, in order that he might give them into the hand of their enemies, because they had sought the gods

---

¹ Hebrew *you*

of Edom. ²¹ So Joash king of Israel went up, and he and Amaziah king of Judah faced one another in battle at Beth-shemesh, which belongs to Judah. ²² And Judah was defeated by Israel, and every man fled to his home. ²³ And Joash king of Israel captured Amaziah king of Judah, the son of Joash, son of Ahaziah, at Beth-shemesh, and brought him to Jerusalem and broke down the wall of Jerusalem for 400 cubits,[1] from the Ephraim Gate to the Corner Gate. ²⁴ And he seized all the gold and silver, and all the vessels that were found in the house of God, in the care of Obed-edom. He seized also the treasuries of the king's house, also hostages, and he returned to Samaria.

²⁵ Amaziah the son of Joash, king of Judah, lived fifteen years after the death of Joash the son of Jehoahaz, king of Israel. ²⁶ Now the rest of the deeds of Amaziah, from first to last, are they not written in the Book of the Kings of Judah and Israel? ²⁷ From the time when he turned away from the LORD they made a conspiracy against him in Jerusalem, and he fled to Lachish. But they sent after him to Lachish and put him to death there. ²⁸ And they brought him upon horses, and he was buried with his fathers in the city of David.[2]

Uzziah Reigns in Judah

26 And all the people of Judah took Uzziah, who was sixteen years old, and made him king instead of his father Amaziah. ² He built Eloth and restored it to Judah, after the king slept with his fathers. ³ Uzziah was sixteen years old when he began to reign, and he reigned fifty-two years in Jerusalem. His mother's name was Jecoliah of Jerusalem. ⁴ And he did what was right in the eyes of the LORD, according to all that his father Amaziah had done. ⁵ He set himself to seek God in the days of Zechariah, who instructed him in the fear of God, and as long as he sought the LORD, God made him prosper.

⁶ He went out and made war against the Philistines and broke through the wall of Gath and the wall of Jabneh and the wall of Ashdod, and he built cities in the territory of Ashdod and elsewhere among the Philistines. ⁷ God helped him against the Philistines and against the Arabians who lived in Gurbaal and against the Meunites. ⁸ The Ammonites paid tribute to Uzziah, and his fame spread even to the border of Egypt, for he became very strong. ⁹ Moreover, Uzziah built towers in Jerusalem at the Corner Gate and at the Valley Gate and at the Angle, and fortified them. ¹⁰ And he built towers in the wilderness and cut out many cisterns, for he had large herds, both in the Shephelah and in the plain, and he had farmers and vinedressers in the hills and in the fertile lands, for he loved the soil. ¹¹ Moreover, Uzziah had an army

---

[1] A *cubit* was about 18 inches or 45 centimeters [2] Hebrew *of Judah*

of soldiers, fit for war, in divisions according to the numbers in the muster made by Jeiel the secretary and Maaseiah the officer, under the direction of Hananiah, one of the king's commanders. ¹²The whole number of the heads of fathers' houses of mighty men of valor was 2,600. ¹³Under their command was an army of 307,500, who could make war with mighty power, to help the king against the enemy. ¹⁴And Uzziah prepared for all the army shields, spears, helmets, coats of mail, bows, and stones for slinging. ¹⁵In Jerusalem he made machines, invented by skillful men, to be on the towers and the corners, to shoot arrows and great stones. And his fame spread far, for he was marvelously helped, till he was strong.

Uzziah's Pride and Punishment

¹⁶But when he was strong, he grew proud, to his destruction. For he was unfaithful to the Lord his God and entered the temple of the Lord to burn incense on the altar of incense. ¹⁷But Azariah the priest went in after him, with eighty priests of the Lord who were men of valor, ¹⁸and they withstood King Uzziah and said to him, "It is not for you, Uzziah, to burn incense to the Lord, but for the priests, the sons of Aaron, who are consecrated to burn incense. Go out of the sanctuary, for you have done wrong, and it will bring you no honor from the Lord God." ¹⁹Then Uzziah was angry. Now he had a censer in his hand to burn incense, and when he became angry with the priests, leprosy[1] broke out on his forehead in the presence of the priests in the house of the Lord, by the altar of incense. ²⁰And Azariah the chief priest and all the priests looked at him, and behold, he was leprous in his forehead! And they rushed him out quickly, and he himself hurried to go out, because the Lord had struck him. ²¹And King Uzziah was a leper to the day of his death, and being a leper lived in a separate house, for he was excluded from the house of the Lord. And Jotham his son was over the king's household, governing the people of the land.

²²Now the rest of the acts of Uzziah, from first to last, Isaiah the prophet the son of Amoz wrote. ²³And Uzziah slept with his fathers, and they buried him with his fathers in the burial field that belonged to the kings, for they said, "He is a leper." And Jotham his son reigned in his place.

Jotham Reigns in Judah

27 Jotham was twenty-five years old when he began to reign, and he reigned sixteen years in Jerusalem. His mother's name was Jerushah the daughter of Zadok. ²And he did what was right in the eyes of

---

[1] *Leprosy* was a term for several skin diseases; see Leviticus 13

the Lord according to all that his father Uzziah had done, except he did not enter the temple of the Lord. But the people still followed corrupt practices. ³ He built the upper gate of the house of the Lord and did much building on the wall of Ophel. ⁴ Moreover, he built cities in the hill country of Judah, and forts and towers on the wooded hills. ⁵ He fought with the king of the Ammonites and prevailed against them. And the Ammonites gave him that year 100 talents[1] of silver, and 10,000 cors[2] of wheat and 10,000 of barley. The Ammonites paid him the same amount in the second and the third years. ⁶ So Jotham became mighty, because he ordered his ways before the Lord his God. ⁷ Now the rest of the acts of Jotham, and all his wars and his ways, behold, they are written in the Book of the Kings of Israel and Judah. ⁸ He was twenty-five years old when he began to reign, and he reigned sixteen years in Jerusalem. ⁹ And Jotham slept with his fathers, and they buried him in the city of David, and Ahaz his son reigned in his place.

Ahaz Reigns in Judah

28 Ahaz was twenty years old when he began to reign, and he reigned sixteen years in Jerusalem. And he did not do what was right in the eyes of the Lord, as his father David had done, ² but he walked in the ways of the kings of Israel. He even made metal images for the Baals, ³ and he made offerings in the Valley of the Son of Hinnom and burned his sons as an offering,[3] according to the abominations of the nations whom the Lord drove out before the people of Israel. ⁴ And he sacrificed and made offerings on the high places and on the hills and under every green tree.

Judah Defeated

⁵ Therefore the Lord his God gave him into the hand of the king of Syria, who defeated him and took captive a great number of his people and brought them to Damascus. He was also given into the hand of the king of Israel, who struck him with great force. ⁶ For Pekah the son of Remaliah killed 120,000 from Judah in one day, all of them men of valor, because they had forsaken the Lord, the God of their fathers. ⁷ And Zichri, a mighty man of Ephraim, killed Maaseiah the king's son and Azrikam the commander of the palace and Elkanah the next in authority to the king.

⁸ The men of Israel took captive 200,000 of their relatives, women, sons, and daughters. They also took much spoil from them and brought the spoil to Samaria. ⁹ But a prophet of the Lord was there, whose name was Oded, and he went out to meet the army that came to Samaria and said to them,

---

[1] A *talent* was about 75 pounds or 34 kilograms [2] A *cor* was about 6 bushels or 220 liters [3] Hebrew *made his sons pass through the fire*

"Behold, because the LORD, the God of your fathers, was angry with Judah, he gave them into your hand, but you have killed them in a rage that has reached up to heaven. ⁱ⁰ And now you intend to subjugate the people of Judah and Jerusalem, male and female, as your slaves. Have you not sins of your own against the LORD your God? ¹¹ Now hear me, and send back the captives from your relatives whom you have taken, for the fierce wrath of the LORD is upon you."

¹² Certain chiefs also of the men of Ephraim, Azariah the son of Johanan, Berechiah the son of Meshillemoth, Jehizkiah the son of Shallum, and Amasa the son of Hadlai, stood up against those who were coming from the war ¹³ and said to them, "You shall not bring the captives in here, for you propose to bring upon us guilt against the LORD in addition to our present sins and guilt. For our guilt is already great, and there is fierce wrath against Israel." ¹⁴ So the armed men left the captives and the spoil before the princes and all the assembly. ¹⁵ And the men who have been mentioned by name rose and took the captives, and with the spoil they clothed all who were naked among them. They clothed them, gave them sandals, provided them with food and drink, and anointed them, and carrying all the feeble among them on donkeys, they brought them to their kinsfolk at Jericho, the city of palm trees. Then they returned to Samaria.

¹⁶ At that time King Ahaz sent to the king[1] of Assyria for help. ¹⁷ For the Edomites had again invaded and defeated Judah and carried away captives. ¹⁸ And the Philistines had made raids on the cities in the Shephelah and the Negeb of Judah, and had taken Beth-shemesh, Aijalon, Gederoth, Soco with its villages, Timnah with its villages, and Gimzo with its villages. And they settled there. ¹⁹ For the LORD humbled Judah because of Ahaz king of Israel, for he had made Judah act sinfully[2] and had been very unfaithful to the LORD. ²⁰ So Tiglath-pileser[3] king of Assyria came against him and afflicted him instead of strengthening him. ²¹ For Ahaz took a portion from the house of the LORD and the house of the king and of the princes, and gave tribute to the king of Assyria, but it did not help him.

Ahaz's Idolatry

²² In the time of his distress he became yet more faithless to the LORD—this same King Ahaz. ²³ For he sacrificed to the gods of Damascus that had defeated him and said, "Because the gods of the kings of Syria helped them, I will sacrifice to them that they may help me." But they were the ruin of him and of all Israel. ²⁴ And Ahaz gathered together the vessels of the house

---

[1] Septuagint, Syriac, Vulgate (compare 2 Kings 16:7); Hebrew *kings* [2] Or *wildly* [3] Hebrew *Tilgath-pilneser*

of God and cut in pieces the vessels of the house of God, and he shut up the doors of the house of the Lord, and he made himself altars in every corner of Jerusalem. ²⁵ In every city of Judah he made high places to make offerings to other gods, provoking to anger the Lord, the God of his fathers. ²⁶ Now the rest of his acts and all his ways, from first to last, behold, they are written in the Book of the Kings of Judah and Israel. ²⁷ And Ahaz slept with his fathers, and they buried him in the city, in Jerusalem, for they did not bring him into the tombs of the kings of Israel. And Hezekiah his son reigned in his place.

Hezekiah Reigns in Judah

29 Hezekiah began to reign when he was twenty-five years old, and he reigned twenty-nine years in Jerusalem. His mother's name was Abijah[1] the daughter of Zechariah. ² And he did what was right in the eyes of the Lord, according to all that David his father had done.

Hezekiah Cleanses the Temple

³ In the first year of his reign, in the first month, he opened the doors of the house of the Lord and repaired them. ⁴ He brought in the priests and the Levites and assembled them in the square on the east ⁵ and said to them, "Hear me, Levites! Now consecrate yourselves, and consecrate the house of the Lord, the God of your fathers, and carry out the filth[2] from the Holy Place. ⁶ For our fathers have been unfaithful and have done what was evil in the sight of the Lord our God. They have forsaken him and have turned away their faces from the habitation of the Lord and turned their backs. ⁷ They also shut the doors of the vestibule and put out the lamps and have not burned incense or offered burnt offerings in the Holy Place to the God of Israel. ⁸ Therefore the wrath of the Lord came on Judah and Jerusalem, and he has made them an object of horror, of astonishment, and of hissing, as you see with your own eyes. ⁹ For behold, our fathers have fallen by the sword, and our sons and our daughters and our wives are in captivity for this. ¹⁰ Now it is in my heart to make a covenant with the Lord, the God of Israel, in order that his fierce anger may turn away from us. ¹¹ My sons, do not now be negligent, for the Lord has chosen you to stand in his presence, to minister to him and to be his ministers and make offerings to him."

¹² Then the Levites arose, Mahath the son of Amasai, and Joel the son of Azariah, of the sons of the Kohathites; and of the sons of Merari, Kish the son of Abdi, and Azariah the son of Jehallelel; and of the Gershonites, Joah the son of Zimmah, and Eden the son of Joah; ¹³ and of the sons of Elizaphan,

[1] Spelled *Abi* in 2 Kings 18:2 [2] Hebrew *impurity*

Shimri and Jeuel; and of the sons of Asaph, Zechariah and Mattaniah; ¹⁴ and of the sons of Heman, Jehuel and Shimei; and of the sons of Jeduthun, Shemaiah and Uzziel. ¹⁵ They gathered their brothers and consecrated themselves and went in as the king had commanded, by the words of the Lord, to cleanse the house of the Lord. ¹⁶ The priests went into the inner part of the house of the Lord to cleanse it, and they brought out all the uncleanness that they found in the temple of the Lord into the court of the house of the Lord. And the Levites took it and carried it out to the brook Kidron. ¹⁷ They began to consecrate on the first day of the first month, and on the eighth day of the month they came to the vestibule of the Lord. Then for eight days they consecrated the house of the Lord, and on the sixteenth day of the first month they finished. ¹⁸ Then they went in to Hezekiah the king and said, "We have cleansed all the house of the Lord, the altar of burnt offering and all its utensils, and the table for the showbread and all its utensils. ¹⁹ All the utensils that King Ahaz discarded in his reign when he was faithless, we have made ready and consecrated, and behold, they are before the altar of the Lord."

Hezekiah Restores Temple Worship

²⁰ Then Hezekiah the king rose early and gathered the officials of the city and went up to the house of the Lord. ²¹ And they brought seven bulls, seven rams, seven lambs, and seven male goats for a sin offering for the kingdom and for the sanctuary and for Judah. And he commanded the priests, the sons of Aaron, to offer them on the altar of the Lord. ²² So they slaughtered the bulls, and the priests received the blood and threw it against the altar. And they slaughtered the rams, and their blood was thrown against the altar. And they slaughtered the lambs, and their blood was thrown against the altar. ²³ Then the goats for the sin offering were brought to the king and the assembly, and they laid their hands on them, ²⁴ and the priests slaughtered them and made a sin offering with their blood on the altar, to make atonement for all Israel. For the king commanded that the burnt offering and the sin offering should be made for all Israel.

²⁵ And he stationed the Levites in the house of the Lord with cymbals, harps, and lyres, according to the commandment of David and of Gad the king's seer and of Nathan the prophet, for the commandment was from the Lord through his prophets. ²⁶ The Levites stood with the instruments of David, and the priests with the trumpets. ²⁷ Then Hezekiah commanded that the burnt offering be offered on the altar. And when the burnt offering began, the song to the Lord began also, and the trumpets, accompanied by the instruments of David king of Israel. ²⁸ The whole assembly worshiped,

and the singers sang, and the trumpeters sounded. All this continued until the burnt offering was finished. ²⁹ When the offering was finished, the king and all who were present with him bowed themselves and worshiped. ³⁰ And Hezekiah the king and the officials commanded the Levites to sing praises to the Lord with the words of David and of Asaph the seer. And they sang praises with gladness, and they bowed down and worshiped.

³¹ Then Hezekiah said, "You have now consecrated yourselves to¹ the Lord. Come near; bring sacrifices and thank offerings to the house of the Lord." And the assembly brought sacrifices and thank offerings, and all who were of a willing heart brought burnt offerings. ³² The number of the burnt offerings that the assembly brought was 70 bulls, 100 rams, and 200 lambs; all these were for a burnt offering to the Lord. ³³ And the consecrated offerings were 600 bulls and 3,000 sheep. ³⁴ But the priests were too few and could not flay all the burnt offerings, so until other priests had consecrated themselves, their brothers the Levites helped them, until the work was finished—for the Levites were more upright in heart than the priests in consecrating themselves. ³⁵ Besides the great number of burnt offerings, there was the fat of the peace offerings, and there were the drink offerings for the burnt offerings. Thus the service of the house of the Lord was restored. ³⁶ And Hezekiah and all the people rejoiced because God had provided for the people, for the thing came about suddenly.

Passover Celebrated

30 Hezekiah sent to all Israel and Judah, and wrote letters also to Ephraim and Manasseh, that they should come to the house of the Lord at Jerusalem to keep the Passover to the Lord, the God of Israel. ² For the king and his princes and all the assembly in Jerusalem had taken counsel to keep the Passover in the second month— ³ for they could not keep it at that time because the priests had not consecrated themselves in sufficient number, nor had the people assembled in Jerusalem— ⁴ and the plan seemed right to the king and all the assembly. ⁵ So they decreed to make a proclamation throughout all Israel, from Beersheba to Dan, that the people should come and keep the Passover to the Lord, the God of Israel, at Jerusalem, for they had not kept it as often as prescribed. ⁶ So couriers went throughout all Israel and Judah with letters from the king and his princes, as the king had commanded, saying, "O people of Israel, return to the Lord, the God of Abraham, Isaac, and Israel, that he may turn again to the remnant of you who have escaped from the hand of the kings of Assyria. ⁷ Do not be

¹ Hebrew *filled your hand for*

like your fathers and your brothers, who were faithless to the Lord God of their fathers, so that he made them a desolation, as you see. ⁸ Do not now be stiff-necked as your fathers were, but yield yourselves to the Lord and come to his sanctuary, which he has consecrated forever, and serve the Lord your God, that his fierce anger may turn away from you. ⁹ For if you return to the Lord, your brothers and your children will find compassion with their captors and return to this land. For the Lord your God is gracious and merciful and will not turn away his face from you, if you return to him."

¹⁰ So the couriers went from city to city through the country of Ephraim and Manasseh, and as far as Zebulun, but they laughed them to scorn and mocked them. ¹¹ However, some men of Asher, of Manasseh, and of Zebulun humbled themselves and came to Jerusalem. ¹² The hand of God was also on Judah to give them one heart to do what the king and the princes commanded by the word of the Lord.

¹³ And many people came together in Jerusalem to keep the Feast of Unleavened Bread in the second month, a very great assembly. ¹⁴ They set to work and removed the altars that were in Jerusalem, and all the altars for burning incense they took away and threw into the brook Kidron. ¹⁵ And they slaughtered the Passover lamb on the fourteenth day of the second month. And the priests and the Levites were ashamed, so that they consecrated themselves and brought burnt offerings into the house of the Lord. ¹⁶ They took their accustomed posts according to the Law of Moses the man of God. The priests threw the blood that they received from the hand of the Levites. ¹⁷ For there were many in the assembly who had not consecrated themselves. Therefore the Levites had to slaughter the Passover lamb for everyone who was not clean, to consecrate it to the Lord. ¹⁸ For a majority of the people, many of them from Ephraim, Manasseh, Issachar, and Zebulun, had not cleansed themselves, yet they ate the Passover otherwise than as prescribed. For Hezekiah had prayed for them, saying, "May the good Lord pardon everyone ¹⁹ who sets his heart to seek God, the Lord, the God of his fathers, even though not according to the sanctuary's rules of cleanness."¹ ²⁰ And the Lord heard Hezekiah and healed the people. ²¹ And the people of Israel who were present at Jerusalem kept the Feast of Unleavened Bread seven days with great gladness, and the Levites and the priests praised the Lord day by day, singing with all their might² to the Lord. ²² And Hezekiah spoke encouragingly to all the Levites who showed good skill in the service of the Lord. So they ate the food of the festival for seven days, sacrificing peace offerings and giving thanks to the Lord, the God of their fathers.

¹ Hebrew *not according to the cleanness of holiness* ² Compare 1 Chronicles 13:8; Hebrew *with instruments of might*

²³ Then the whole assembly agreed together to keep the feast for another seven days. So they kept it for another seven days with gladness. ²⁴ For Hezekiah king of Judah gave the assembly 1,000 bulls and 7,000 sheep for offerings, and the princes gave the assembly 1,000 bulls and 10,000 sheep. And the priests consecrated themselves in great numbers. ²⁵ The whole assembly of Judah, and the priests and the Levites, and the whole assembly that came out of Israel, and the sojourners who came out of the land of Israel, and the sojourners who lived in Judah, rejoiced. ²⁶ So there was great joy in Jerusalem, for since the time of Solomon the son of David king of Israel there had been nothing like this in Jerusalem. ²⁷ Then the priests and the Levites arose and blessed the people, and their voice was heard, and their prayer came to his holy habitation in heaven.

Hezekiah Organizes the Priests

31 Now when all this was finished, all Israel who were present went out to the cities of Judah and broke in pieces the pillars and cut down the Asherim and broke down the high places and the altars throughout all Judah and Benjamin, and in Ephraim and Manasseh, until they had destroyed them all. Then all the people of Israel returned to their cities, every man to his possession.

² And Hezekiah appointed the divisions of the priests and of the Levites, division by division, each according to his service, the priests and the Levites, for burnt offerings and peace offerings, to minister in the gates of the camp of the Lord and to give thanks and praise. ³ The contribution of the king from his own possessions was for the burnt offerings: the burnt offerings of morning and evening, and the burnt offerings for the Sabbaths, the new moons, and the appointed feasts, as it is written in the Law of the Lord. ⁴ And he commanded the people who lived in Jerusalem to give the portion due to the priests and the Levites, that they might give themselves to the Law of the Lord. ⁵ As soon as the command was spread abroad, the people of Israel gave in abundance the firstfruits of grain, wine, oil, honey, and of all the produce of the field. And they brought in abundantly the tithe of everything. ⁶ And the people of Israel and Judah who lived in the cities of Judah also brought in the tithe of cattle and sheep, and the tithe of the dedicated things that had been dedicated to the Lord their God, and laid them in heaps. ⁷ In the third month they began to pile up the heaps, and finished them in the seventh month. ⁸ When Hezekiah and the princes came and saw the heaps, they blessed the Lord and his people Israel. ⁹ And Hezekiah questioned the priests and the Levites about the heaps. ¹⁰ Azariah the chief priest, who was of the house

of Zadok, answered him, "Since they began to bring the contributions into the house of the Lord, we have eaten and had enough and have plenty left, for the Lord has blessed his people, so that we have this large amount left."

¹¹ Then Hezekiah commanded them to prepare chambers in the house of the Lord, and they prepared them. ¹² And they faithfully brought in the contributions, the tithes, and the dedicated things. The chief officer in charge of them was Conaniah the Levite, with Shimei his brother as second, ¹³ while Jehiel, Azaziah, Nahath, Asahel, Jerimoth, Jozabad, Eliel, Ismachiah, Mahath, and Benaiah were overseers assisting Conaniah and Shimei his brother, by the appointment of Hezekiah the king and Azariah the chief officer of the house of God. ¹⁴ And Kore the son of Imnah the Levite, keeper of the east gate, was over the freewill offerings to God, to apportion the contribution reserved for the Lord and the most holy offerings. ¹⁵ Eden, Miniamin, Jeshua, Shemaiah, Amariah, and Shecaniah were faithfully assisting him in the cities of the priests, to distribute the portions to their brothers, old and young alike, by divisions, ¹⁶ except those enrolled by genealogy, males from three years old and upward—all who entered the house of the Lord as the duty of each day required—for their service according to their offices, by their divisions. ¹⁷ The enrollment of the priests was according to their fathers' houses; that of the Levites from twenty years old and upward was according to their offices, by their divisions. ¹⁸ They were enrolled with all their little children, their wives, their sons, and their daughters, the whole assembly, for they were faithful in keeping themselves holy. ¹⁹ And for the sons of Aaron, the priests, who were in the fields of common land belonging to their cities, there were men in the several cities who were designated by name to distribute portions to every male among the priests and to everyone among the Levites who was enrolled.

²⁰ Thus Hezekiah did throughout all Judah, and he did what was good and right and faithful before the Lord his God. ²¹ And every work that he undertook in the service of the house of God and in accordance with the law and the commandments, seeking his God, he did with all his heart, and prospered.

Sennacherib Invades Judah

32 After these things and these acts of faithfulness, Sennacherib king of Assyria came and invaded Judah and encamped against the fortified cities, thinking to win them for himself. ² And when Hezekiah saw that Sennacherib had come and intended to fight against Jerusalem, ³ he planned with his officers and his mighty men to stop the water of the springs that were outside the city; and they helped him. ⁴ A great many people were gathered, and they stopped all the springs and the brook that flowed through the land, saying, "Why should the kings of Assyria come and find much water?" ⁵ He set to work resolutely and built up all the wall that was broken down and raised towers upon it,¹ and outside it he built another wall, and he strengthened the Millo in the city of David. He also made weapons and shields in abundance. ⁶ And he set combat commanders over the people and gathered them together to him in the square at the gate of the city and spoke encouragingly to them, saying, ⁷ "Be strong and courageous. Do not be afraid or dismayed before the king of Assyria and all the horde that is with him, for there are more with us than with him. ⁸ With him is an arm of flesh, but with us is the Lord our God, to help us and to fight our battles." And the people took confidence from the words of Hezekiah king of Judah.

Sennacherib Blasphemes

⁹ After this, Sennacherib king of Assyria, who was besieging Lachish with all his forces, sent his servants to Jerusalem to Hezekiah king of Judah and to all the people of Judah who were in Jerusalem, saying, ¹⁰ "Thus says Sennacherib king of Assyria, 'On what are you trusting, that you endure the siege in Jerusalem? ¹¹ Is not Hezekiah misleading you, that he may give you over to die by famine and by thirst, when he tells you, "The Lord our God will deliver us from the hand of the king of Assyria"? ¹² Has not this same Hezekiah taken away his high places and his altars and commanded Judah and Jerusalem, "Before one altar you shall worship, and on it you shall burn your sacrifices"? ¹³ Do you not know what I and my fathers have done to all the peoples of other lands? Were the gods of the nations of those lands at all able to deliver their lands out of my hand? ¹⁴ Who among all the gods of those nations that my fathers devoted to destruction was able to deliver his people from my hand, that your God should be able to deliver you from my hand? ¹⁵ Now, therefore, do not let Hezekiah deceive you or mislead you in this fashion, and do not believe him, for no god of any nation or kingdom has been able to deliver his people from my hand or from the hand of my fathers. How much less will your God deliver you out of my hand!'"

¹⁶ And his servants said still more against the Lord God and against his servant Hezekiah. ¹⁷ And he wrote letters to cast contempt on the Lord, the God of Israel, and to speak against him, saying, "Like the gods of the nations of the lands who have not delivered their people from my hands, so the God of Hezekiah will not deliver his people from my hand." ¹⁸ And they shouted

---

¹ Vulgate; Hebrew *and raised upon the towers*

it with a loud voice in the language of Judah to the people of Jerusalem who were on the wall, to frighten and terrify them, in order that they might take the city. ¹⁹ And they spoke of the God of Jerusalem as they spoke of the gods of the peoples of the earth, which are the work of men's hands.

The Lord Delivers Jerusalem

²⁰ Then Hezekiah the king and Isaiah the prophet, the son of Amoz, prayed because of this and cried to heaven. ²¹ And the Lord sent an angel, who cut off all the mighty warriors and commanders and officers in the camp of the king of Assyria. So he returned with shame of face to his own land. And when he came into the house of his god, some of his own sons struck him down there with the sword. ²² So the Lord saved Hezekiah and the inhabitants of Jerusalem from the hand of Sennacherib king of Assyria and from the hand of all his enemies, and he provided for them on every side. ²³ And many brought gifts to the Lord to Jerusalem and precious things to Hezekiah king of Judah, so that he was exalted in the sight of all nations from that time onward.

Hezekiah's Pride and Achievements

²⁴ In those days Hezekiah became sick and was at the point of death, and he prayed to the Lord, and he answered him and gave him a sign. ²⁵ But Hezekiah did not make return according to the benefit done to him, for his heart was proud. Therefore wrath came upon him and Judah and Jerusalem. ²⁶ But Hezekiah humbled himself for the pride of his heart, both he and the inhabitants of Jerusalem, so that the wrath of the Lord did not come upon them in the days of Hezekiah.

²⁷ And Hezekiah had very great riches and honor, and he made for himself treasuries for silver, for gold, for precious stones, for spices, for shields, and for all kinds of costly vessels; ²⁸ storehouses also for the yield of grain, wine, and oil; and stalls for all kinds of cattle, and sheepfolds. ²⁹ He likewise provided cities for himself, and flocks and herds in abundance, for God had given him very great possessions. ³⁰ This same Hezekiah closed the upper outlet of the waters of Gihon and directed them down to the west side of the city of David. And Hezekiah prospered in all his works. ³¹ And so in the matter of the envoys of the princes of Babylon, who had been sent to him to inquire about the sign that had been done in the land, God left him to himself, in order to test him and to know all that was in his heart.

³² Now the rest of the acts of Hezekiah and his good deeds, behold, they are written in the vision of Isaiah the prophet, the son of Amoz, in the Book of

the Kings of Judah and Israel. ³³ And Hezekiah slept with his fathers, and they buried him in the upper part of the tombs of the sons of David, and all Judah and the inhabitants of Jerusalem did him honor at his death. And Manasseh his son reigned in his place.

Manasseh Reigns in Judah

33 Manasseh was twelve years old when he began to reign, and he reigned fifty-five years in Jerusalem. ² And he did what was evil in the sight of the Lord, according to the abominations of the nations whom the Lord drove out before the people of Israel. ³ For he rebuilt the high places that his father Hezekiah had broken down, and he erected altars to the Baals, and made Asheroth, and worshiped all the host of heaven and served them. ⁴ And he built altars in the house of the Lord, of which the Lord had said, "In Jerusalem shall my name be forever." ⁵ And he built altars for all the host of heaven in the two courts of the house of the Lord. ⁶ And he burned his sons as an offering in the Valley of the Son of Hinnom, and used fortune-telling and omens and sorcery, and dealt with mediums and with necromancers. He did much evil in the sight of the Lord, provoking him to anger. ⁷ And the carved image of the idol that he had made he set in the house of God, of which God said to David and to Solomon his son, "In this house, and in Jerusalem, which I have chosen out of all the tribes of Israel, I will put my name forever, ⁸ and I will no more remove the foot of Israel from the land that I appointed for your fathers, if only they will be careful to do all that I have commanded them, all the law, the statutes, and the rules given through Moses." ⁹ Manasseh led Judah and the inhabitants of Jerusalem astray, to do more evil than the nations whom the Lord destroyed before the people of Israel.

Manasseh's Repentance

¹⁰ The Lord spoke to Manasseh and to his people, but they paid no attention. ¹¹ Therefore the Lord brought upon them the commanders of the army of the king of Assyria, who captured Manasseh with hooks and bound him with chains of bronze and brought him to Babylon. ¹² And when he was in distress, he entreated the favor of the Lord his God and humbled himself greatly before the God of his fathers. ¹³ He prayed to him, and God was moved by his entreaty and heard his plea and brought him again to Jerusalem into his kingdom. Then Manasseh knew that the Lord was God.

¹⁴ Afterward he built an outer wall for the city of David west of Gihon, in the valley, and for the entrance into the Fish Gate, and carried it around Ophel, and raised it to a very great height. He also put commanders of the

army in all the fortified cities in Judah. ¹⁵ And he took away the foreign gods and the idol from the house of the Lord, and all the altars that he had built on the mountain of the house of the Lord and in Jerusalem, and he threw them outside of the city. ¹⁶ He also restored the altar of the Lord and offered on it sacrifices of peace offerings and of thanksgiving, and he commanded Judah to serve the Lord, the God of Israel. ¹⁷ Nevertheless, the people still sacrificed at the high places, but only to the Lord their God.

¹⁸ Now the rest of the acts of Manasseh, and his prayer to his God, and the words of the seers who spoke to him in the name of the Lord, the God of Israel, behold, they are in the Chronicles of the Kings of Israel. ¹⁹ And his prayer, and how God was moved by his entreaty, and all his sin and his faithlessness, and the sites on which he built high places and set up the Asherim and the images, before he humbled himself, behold, they are written in the Chronicles of the Seers.[1] ²⁰ So Manasseh slept with his fathers, and they buried him in his house, and Amon his son reigned in his place.

Amon's Reign and Death

²¹ Amon was twenty-two years old when he began to reign, and he reigned two years in Jerusalem. ²² And he did what was evil in the sight of the Lord, as Manasseh his father had done. Amon sacrificed to all the images that Manasseh his father had made, and served them. ²³ And he did not humble himself before the Lord, as Manasseh his father had humbled himself, but this Amon incurred guilt more and more. ²⁴ And his servants conspired against him and put him to death in his house. ²⁵ But the people of the land struck down all those who had conspired against King Amon. And the people of the land made Josiah his son king in his place.

Josiah Reigns in Judah

34 Josiah was eight years old when he began to reign, and he reigned thirty-one years in Jerusalem. ² And he did what was right in the eyes of the Lord, and walked in the ways of David his father; and he did not turn aside to the right hand or to the left. ³ For in the eighth year of his reign, while he was yet a boy, he began to seek the God of David his father, and in the twelfth year he began to purge Judah and Jerusalem of the high places, the Asherim, and the carved and the metal images. ⁴ And they chopped down the altars of the Baals in his presence, and he cut down the incense altars that stood above them. And he broke in pieces the Asherim and the carved and the metal images, and he made dust of them and scattered it over

---
[1] One Hebrew manuscript, Septuagint; most Hebrew manuscripts *of Hozai*

the graves of those who had sacrificed to them. ⁵ He also burned the bones of the priests on their altars and cleansed Judah and Jerusalem. ⁶ And in the cities of Manasseh, Ephraim, and Simeon, and as far as Naphtali, in their ruins¹ all around, ⁷ he broke down the altars and beat the Asherim and the images into powder and cut down all the incense altars throughout all the land of Israel. Then he returned to Jerusalem.

The Book of the Law Found

⁸ Now in the eighteenth year of his reign, when he had cleansed the land and the house, he sent Shaphan the son of Azaliah, and Maaseiah the governor of the city, and Joah the son of Joahaz, the recorder, to repair the house of the LORD his God. ⁹ They came to Hilkiah the high priest and gave him the money that had been brought into the house of God, which the Levites, the keepers of the threshold, had collected from Manasseh and Ephraim and from all the remnant of Israel and from all Judah and Benjamin and from the inhabitants of Jerusalem. ¹⁰ And they gave it to the workmen who were working in the house of the LORD. And the workmen who were working in the house of the LORD gave it for repairing and restoring the house. ¹¹ They gave it to the carpenters and the builders to buy quarried stone, and timber for binders and beams for the buildings that the kings of Judah had let go to ruin. ¹² And the men did the work faithfully. Over them were set Jahath and Obadiah the Levites, of the sons of Merari, and Zechariah and Meshullam, of the sons of the Kohathites, to have oversight. The Levites, all who were skillful with instruments of music, ¹³ were over the burden-bearers and directed all who did work in every kind of service, and some of the Levites were scribes and officials and gatekeepers.

¹⁴ While they were bringing out the money that had been brought into the house of the LORD, Hilkiah the priest found the Book of the Law of the LORD given through² Moses. ¹⁵ Then Hilkiah answered and said to Shaphan the secretary, "I have found the Book of the Law in the house of the LORD." And Hilkiah gave the book to Shaphan. ¹⁶ Shaphan brought the book to the king, and further reported to the king, "All that was committed to your servants they are doing. ¹⁷ They have emptied out the money that was found in the house of the LORD and have given it into the hand of the overseers and the workmen." ¹⁸ Then Shaphan the secretary told the king, "Hilkiah the priest has given me a book." And Shaphan read from it before the king.

¹⁹ And when the king heard the words of the Law, he tore his clothes. ²⁰ And the king commanded Hilkiah, Ahikam the son of Shaphan, Abdon the son

¹ The meaning of the Hebrew is uncertain ² Hebrew *by the hand of*

of Micah, Shaphan the secretary, and Asaiah the king's servant, saying, ²¹ "Go, inquire of the Lord for me and for those who are left in Israel and in Judah, concerning the words of the book that has been found. For great is the wrath of the Lord that is poured out on us, because our fathers have not kept the word of the Lord, to do according to all that is written in this book."

Huldah Prophesies Disaster

²² So Hilkiah and those whom the king had sent[1] went to Huldah the prophetess, the wife of Shallum the son of Tokhath, son of Hasrah, keeper of the wardrobe (now she lived in Jerusalem in the Second Quarter) and spoke to her to that effect. ²³ And she said to them, "Thus says the Lord, the God of Israel: 'Tell the man who sent you to me, ²⁴ Thus says the Lord, Behold, I will bring disaster upon this place and upon its inhabitants, all the curses that are written in the book that was read before the king of Judah. ²⁵ Because they have forsaken me and have made offerings to other gods, that they might provoke me to anger with all the works of their hands, therefore my wrath will be poured out on this place and will not be quenched. ²⁶ But to the king of Judah, who sent you to inquire of the Lord, thus shall you say to him, Thus says the Lord, the God of Israel: Regarding the words that you have heard, ²⁷ because your heart was tender and you humbled yourself before God when you heard his words against this place and its inhabitants, and you have humbled yourself before me and have torn your clothes and wept before me, I also have heard you, declares the Lord. ²⁸ Behold, I will gather you to your fathers, and you shall be gathered to your grave in peace, and your eyes shall not see all the disaster that I will bring upon this place and its inhabitants.'" And they brought back word to the king.

²⁹ Then the king sent and gathered together all the elders of Judah and Jerusalem. ³⁰ And the king went up to the house of the Lord, with all the men of Judah and the inhabitants of Jerusalem and the priests and the Levites, all the people both great and small. And he read in their hearing all the words of the Book of the Covenant that had been found in the house of the Lord. ³¹ And the king stood in his place and made a covenant before the Lord, to walk after the Lord and to keep his commandments and his testimonies and his statutes, with all his heart and all his soul, to perform the words of the covenant that were written in this book. ³² Then he made all who were present in Jerusalem and in Benjamin join in it. And the inhabitants of Jerusalem did according to the covenant of God, the God of their fathers. ³³ And Josiah took away all the abominations from all the territory that belonged to the people of

---

[1] Syriac, Vulgate; Hebrew lacks *had sent*

Israel and made all who were present in Israel serve the LORD their God. All his days they did not turn away from following the LORD, the God of their fathers.

Josiah Keeps the Passover

35 Josiah kept a Passover to the LORD in Jerusalem. And they slaughtered the Passover lamb on the fourteenth day of the first month. ² He appointed the priests to their offices and encouraged them in the service of the house of the LORD. ³ And he said to the Levites who taught all Israel and who were holy to the LORD, "Put the holy ark in the house that Solomon the son of David, king of Israel, built. You need not carry it on your shoulders. Now serve the LORD your God and his people Israel. ⁴ Prepare yourselves according to your fathers' houses by your divisions, as prescribed in the writing of David king of Israel and the document of Solomon his son. ⁵ And stand in the Holy Place according to the groupings of the fathers' houses of your brothers the lay people, and according to the division of the Levites by fathers' household. ⁶ And slaughter the Passover lamb, and consecrate yourselves, and prepare for your brothers, to do according to the word of the LORD by[1] Moses."

⁷ Then Josiah contributed to the lay people, as Passover offerings for all who were present, lambs and young goats from the flock to the number of 30,000, and 3,000 bulls; these were from the king's possessions. ⁸ And his officials contributed willingly to the people, to the priests, and to the Levites. Hilkiah, Zechariah, and Jehiel, the chief officers of the house of God, gave to the priests for the Passover offerings 2,600 Passover lambs and 300 bulls. ⁹ Conaniah also, and Shemaiah and Nethanel his brothers, and Hashabiah and Jeiel and Jozabad, the chiefs of the Levites, gave to the Levites for the Passover offerings 5,000 lambs and young goats and 500 bulls.

¹⁰ When the service had been prepared for, the priests stood in their place, and the Levites in their divisions according to the king's command. ¹¹ And they slaughtered the Passover lamb, and the priests threw the blood that they received from them while the Levites flayed the sacrifices. ¹² And they set aside the burnt offerings that they might distribute them according to the groupings of the fathers' houses of the lay people, to offer to the LORD, as it is written in the Book of Moses. And so they did with the bulls. ¹³ And they roasted the Passover lamb with fire according to the rule; and they boiled the holy offerings in pots, in cauldrons, and in pans, and carried them quickly to all the lay people. ¹⁴ And afterward they prepared for themselves and for the priests, because the priests, the sons of Aaron, were offering the burnt offerings and the fat parts until night; so the Levites prepared for themselves and for the

---

[1] Hebrew *by the hand of*

priests, the sons of Aaron. ¹⁵ The singers, the sons of Asaph, were in their place according to the command of David, and Asaph, and Heman, and Jeduthun the king's seer; and the gatekeepers were at each gate. They did not need to depart from their service, for their brothers the Levites prepared for them.

¹⁶ So all the service of the LORD was prepared that day, to keep the Passover and to offer burnt offerings on the altar of the LORD, according to the command of King Josiah. ¹⁷ And the people of Israel who were present kept the Passover at that time, and the Feast of Unleavened Bread seven days. ¹⁸ No Passover like it had been kept in Israel since the days of Samuel the prophet. None of the kings of Israel had kept such a Passover as was kept by Josiah, and the priests and the Levites, and all Judah and Israel who were present, and the inhabitants of Jerusalem. ¹⁹ In the eighteenth year of the reign of Josiah this Passover was kept.

Josiah Killed in Battle

²⁰ After all this, when Josiah had prepared the temple, Neco king of Egypt went up to fight at Carchemish on the Euphrates, and Josiah went out to meet him. ²¹ But he sent envoys to him, saying, "What have we to do with each other, king of Judah? I am not coming against you this day, but against the house with which I am at war. And God has commanded me to hurry. Cease opposing God, who is with me, lest he destroy you." ²² Nevertheless, Josiah did not turn away from him, but disguised himself in order to fight with him. He did not listen to the words of Neco from the mouth of God, but came to fight in the plain of Megiddo. ²³ And the archers shot King Josiah. And the king said to his servants, "Take me away, for I am badly wounded." ²⁴ So his servants took him out of the chariot and carried him in his second chariot and brought him to Jerusalem. And he died and was buried in the tombs of his fathers. All Judah and Jerusalem mourned for Josiah. ²⁵ Jeremiah also uttered a lament for Josiah; and all the singing men and singing women have spoken of Josiah in their laments to this day. They made these a rule in Israel; behold, they are written in the Laments. ²⁶ Now the rest of the acts of Josiah, and his good deeds according to what is written in the Law of the LORD, ²⁷ and his acts, first and last, behold, they are written in the Book of the Kings of Israel and Judah.

Judah's Decline

36 The people of the land took Jehoahaz the son of Josiah and made him king in his father's place in Jerusalem. ² Jehoahaz was twenty-three years old when he began to reign, and he reigned three months in

Jerusalem. ³ Then the king of Egypt deposed him in Jerusalem and laid on the land a tribute of a hundred talents of silver and a talent[1] of gold. ⁴ And the king of Egypt made Eliakim his brother king over Judah and Jerusalem, and changed his name to Jehoiakim. But Neco took Jehoahaz his brother and carried him to Egypt.

⁵ Jehoiakim was twenty-five years old when he began to reign, and he reigned eleven years in Jerusalem. He did what was evil in the sight of the Lord his God. ⁶ Against him came up Nebuchadnezzar king of Babylon and bound him in chains to take him to Babylon. ⁷ Nebuchadnezzar also carried part of the vessels of the house of the Lord to Babylon and put them in his palace in Babylon. ⁸ Now the rest of the acts of Jehoiakim, and the abominations that he did, and what was found against him, behold, they are written in the Book of the Kings of Israel and Judah. And Jehoiachin his son reigned in his place.

⁹ Jehoiachin was eighteen[2] years old when he became king, and he reigned three months and ten days in Jerusalem. He did what was evil in the sight of the Lord. ¹⁰ In the spring of the year King Nebuchadnezzar sent and brought him to Babylon, with the precious vessels of the house of the Lord, and made his brother Zedekiah king over Judah and Jerusalem.

¹¹ Zedekiah was twenty-one years old when he began to reign, and he reigned eleven years in Jerusalem. ¹² He did what was evil in the sight of the Lord his God. He did not humble himself before Jeremiah the prophet, who spoke from the mouth of the Lord. ¹³ He also rebelled against King Nebuchadnezzar, who had made him swear by God. He stiffened his neck and hardened his heart against turning to the Lord, the God of Israel. ¹⁴ All the officers of the priests and the people likewise were exceedingly unfaithful, following all the abominations of the nations. And they polluted the house of the Lord that he had made holy in Jerusalem.

¹⁵ The Lord, the God of their fathers, sent persistently to them by his messengers, because he had compassion on his people and on his dwelling place. ¹⁶ But they kept mocking the messengers of God, despising his words and scoffing at his prophets, until the wrath of the Lord rose against his people, until there was no remedy.

Jerusalem Captured and Burned

¹⁷ Therefore he brought up against them the king of the Chaldeans, who killed their young men with the sword in the house of their sanctuary and had no compassion on young man or virgin, old man or aged. He gave

---

[1] A *talent* was about 75 pounds or 34 kilograms [2] Septuagint (compare 2 Kings 24:8); most Hebrew manuscripts *eight*

them all into his hand. ⁱ⁸ And all the vessels of the house of God, great and small, and the treasures of the house of the Lord, and the treasures of the king and of his princes, all these he brought to Babylon. ⁱ⁹ And they burned the house of God and broke down the wall of Jerusalem and burned all its palaces with fire and destroyed all its precious vessels. ²⁰ He took into exile in Babylon those who had escaped from the sword, and they became servants to him and to his sons until the establishment of the kingdom of Persia, ²¹ to fulfill the word of the Lord by the mouth of Jeremiah, until the land had enjoyed its Sabbaths. All the days that it lay desolate it kept Sabbath, to fulfill seventy years.

The Proclamation of Cyrus

²² Now in the first year of Cyrus king of Persia, that the word of the Lord by the mouth of Jeremiah might be fulfilled, the Lord stirred up the spirit of Cyrus king of Persia, so that he made a proclamation throughout all his kingdom and also put it in writing: ²³ "Thus says Cyrus king of Persia, 'The Lord, the God of heaven, has given me all the kingdoms of the earth, and he has charged me to build him a house at Jerusalem, which is in Judah. Whoever is among you of all his people, may the Lord his God be with him. Let him go up.'"

EZRA

The Proclamation of Cyrus

1 In the first year of Cyrus king of Persia, that the word of the Lord by the mouth of Jeremiah might be fulfilled, the Lord stirred up the spirit of Cyrus king of Persia, so that he made a proclamation throughout all his kingdom and also put it in writing:

² "Thus says Cyrus king of Persia: The Lord, the God of heaven, has given me all the kingdoms of the earth, and he has charged me to build him a house at Jerusalem, which is in Judah. ³ Whoever is among you of all his people, may his God be with him, and let him go up to Jerusalem, which is in Judah, and rebuild the house of the Lord, the God of Israel—he is the God who is in Jerusalem. ⁴ And let each survivor, in whatever place he sojourns, be assisted by the men of his place with silver and gold, with goods and with beasts, besides freewill offerings for the house of God that is in Jerusalem."

⁵ Then rose up the heads of the fathers' houses of Judah and Benjamin, and the priests and the Levites, everyone whose spirit God had stirred to go up to rebuild the house of the Lord that is in Jerusalem. ⁶ And all who were about them aided them with vessels of silver, with gold, with goods, with beasts, and with costly wares, besides all that was freely offered. ⁷ Cyrus the king also brought out the vessels of the house of the Lord that Nebuchadnezzar had carried away from Jerusalem and placed in the house of his gods. ⁸ Cyrus king of Persia brought these out in the charge of Mithredath the treasurer, who counted them out to Sheshbazzar the prince of Judah. ⁹ And this was the number of them: 30 basins of gold, 1,000 basins of silver, 29 censers, ¹⁰ 30 bowls of gold, 410 bowls of silver, and 1,000 other vessels; ¹¹ all the vessels of gold and of silver were 5,400. All these did Sheshbazzar bring up, when the exiles were brought up from Babylonia to Jerusalem.

The Exiles Return

2 Now these were the people of the province who came up out of the captivity of those exiles whom Nebuchadnezzar the king of Babylon had carried captive to Babylonia. They returned to Jerusalem and Judah, each

to his own town. ² They came with Zerubbabel, Jeshua, Nehemiah, Seraiah, Reelaiah, Mordecai, Bilshan, Mispar, Bigvai, Rehum, and Baanah.

The number of the men of the people of Israel: ³ the sons of Parosh, 2,172. ⁴ The sons of Shephatiah, 372. ⁵ The sons of Arah, 775. ⁶ The sons of Pahath-moab, namely the sons of Jeshua and Joab, 2,812. ⁷ The sons of Elam, 1,254. ⁸ The sons of Zattu, 945. ⁹ The sons of Zaccai, 760. ¹⁰ The sons of Bani, 642. ¹¹ The sons of Bebai, 623. ¹² The sons of Azgad, 1,222. ¹³ The sons of Adonikam, 666. ¹⁴ The sons of Bigvai, 2,056. ¹⁵ The sons of Adin, 454. ¹⁶ The sons of Ater, namely of Hezekiah, 98. ¹⁷ The sons of Bezai, 323. ¹⁸ The sons of Jorah, 112. ¹⁹ The sons of Hashum, 223. ²⁰ The sons of Gibbar, 95. ²¹ The sons of Bethlehem, 123. ²² The men of Netophah, 56. ²³ The men of Anathoth, 128. ²⁴ The sons of Azmaveth, 42. ²⁵ The sons of Kiriath-arim, Chephirah, and Beeroth, 743. ²⁶ The sons of Ramah and Geba, 621. ²⁷ The men of Michmas, 122. ²⁸ The men of Bethel and Ai, 223. ²⁹ The sons of Nebo, 52. ³⁰ The sons of Magbish, 156. ³¹ The sons of the other Elam, 1,254. ³² The sons of Harim, 320. ³³ The sons of Lod, Hadid, and Ono, 725. ³⁴ The sons of Jericho, 345. ³⁵ The sons of Senaah, 3,630.

³⁶ The priests: the sons of Jedaiah, of the house of Jeshua, 973. ³⁷ The sons of Immer, 1,052. ³⁸ The sons of Pashhur, 1,247. ³⁹ The sons of Harim, 1,017.

⁴⁰ The Levites: the sons of Jeshua and Kadmiel, of the sons of Hodaviah, 74. ⁴¹ The singers: the sons of Asaph, 128. ⁴² The sons of the gatekeepers: the sons of Shallum, the sons of Ater, the sons of Talmon, the sons of Akkub, the sons of Hatita, and the sons of Shobai, in all 139.

⁴³ The temple servants: the sons of Ziha, the sons of Hasupha, the sons of Tabbaoth, ⁴⁴ the sons of Keros, the sons of Siaha, the sons of Padon, ⁴⁵ the sons of Lebanah, the sons of Hagabah, the sons of Akkub, ⁴⁶ the sons of Hagab, the sons of Shamlai, the sons of Hanan, ⁴⁷ the sons of Giddel, the sons of Gahar, the sons of Reaiah, ⁴⁸ the sons of Rezin, the sons of Nekoda, the sons of Gazzam, ⁴⁹ the sons of Uzza, the sons of Paseah, the sons of Besai, ⁵⁰ the sons of Asnah, the sons of Meunim, the sons of Nephisim, ⁵¹ the sons of Bakbuk, the sons of Hakupha, the sons of Harhur, ⁵² the sons of Bazluth, the sons of Mehida, the sons of Harsha, ⁵³ the sons of Barkos, the sons of Sisera, the sons of Temah, ⁵⁴ the sons of Neziah, and the sons of Hatipha.

⁵⁵ The sons of Solomon's servants: the sons of Sotai, the sons of Hassophereth, the sons of Peruda, ⁵⁶ the sons of Jaalah, the sons of Darkon, the sons of Giddel, ⁵⁷ the sons of Shephatiah, the sons of Hattil, the sons of Pochereth-hazzebaim, and the sons of Ami.

⁵⁸ All the temple servants and the sons of Solomon's servants were 392.

⁵⁹ The following were those who came up from Tel-melah, Tel-harsha, Cherub, Addan, and Immer, though they could not prove their fathers'

houses or their descent, whether they belonged to Israel: ⁶⁰ the sons of Delaiah, the sons of Tobiah, and the sons of Nekoda, 652. ⁶¹ Also, of the sons of the priests: the sons of Habaiah, the sons of Hakkoz, and the sons of Barzillai (who had taken a wife from the daughters of Barzillai the Gileadite, and was called by their name). ⁶² These sought their registration among those enrolled in the genealogies, but they were not found there, and so they were excluded from the priesthood as unclean. ⁶³ The governor told them that they were not to partake of the most holy food, until there should be a priest to consult Urim and Thummim.

⁶⁴ The whole assembly together was 42,360, ⁶⁵ besides their male and female servants, of whom there were 7,337, and they had 200 male and female singers. ⁶⁶ Their horses were 736, their mules were 245, ⁶⁷ their camels were 435, and their donkeys were 6,720.

⁶⁸ Some of the heads of families, when they came to the house of the LORD that is in Jerusalem, made freewill offerings for the house of God, to erect it on its site. ⁶⁹ According to their ability they gave to the treasury of the work 61,000 darics¹ of gold, 5,000 minas² of silver, and 100 priests' garments.

⁷⁰ Now the priests, the Levites, some of the people, the singers, the gatekeepers, and the temple servants lived in their towns, and all the rest of Israel³ in their towns.

Rebuilding the Altar

3 When the seventh month came, and the children of Israel were in the towns, the people gathered as one man to Jerusalem. ² Then arose Jeshua the son of Jozadak, with his fellow priests, and Zerubbabel the son of Shealtiel with his kinsmen, and they built the altar of the God of Israel, to offer burnt offerings on it, as it is written in the Law of Moses the man of God. ³ They set the altar in its place, for fear was on them because of the peoples of the lands, and they offered burnt offerings on it to the LORD, burnt offerings morning and evening. ⁴ And they kept the Feast of Booths, as it is written, and offered the daily burnt offerings by number according to the rule, as each day required, ⁵ and after that the regular burnt offerings, the offerings at the new moon and at all the appointed feasts of the LORD, and the offerings of everyone who made a freewill offering to the LORD. ⁶ From the first day of the seventh month they began to offer burnt offerings to the LORD. But the foundation of the temple of the LORD was not yet laid. ⁷ So they gave money to the masons and the carpenters, and food, drink, and oil to the Sidonians and the Tyrians to bring cedar trees

---

¹ A *daric* was a coin weighing about 1/4 ounce or 8.5 grams ² A *mina* was about 1 1/4 pounds or 0.6 kilogram
³ Hebrew *all Israel*

from Lebanon to the sea, to Joppa, according to the grant that they had from Cyrus king of Persia.

Rebuilding the Temple

⁸ Now in the second year after their coming to the house of God at Jerusalem, in the second month, Zerubbabel the son of Shealtiel and Jeshua the son of Jozadak made a beginning, together with the rest of their kinsmen, the priests and the Levites and all who had come to Jerusalem from the captivity. They appointed the Levites, from twenty years old and upward, to supervise the work of the house of the Lord. ⁹ And Jeshua with his sons and his brothers, and Kadmiel and his sons, the sons of Judah, together supervised the workmen in the house of God, along with the sons of Henadad and the Levites, their sons and brothers.

¹⁰ And when the builders laid the foundation of the temple of the Lord, the priests in their vestments came forward with trumpets, and the Levites, the sons of Asaph, with cymbals, to praise the Lord, according to the directions of David king of Israel. ¹¹ And they sang responsively, praising and giving thanks to the Lord,

"For he is good,
   for his steadfast love endures forever toward Israel."

And all the people shouted with a great shout when they praised the Lord, because the foundation of the house of the Lord was laid. ¹² But many of the priests and Levites and heads of fathers' houses, old men who had seen the first house, wept with a loud voice when they saw the foundation of this house being laid, though many shouted aloud for joy, ¹³ so that the people could not distinguish the sound of the joyful shout from the sound of the people's weeping, for the people shouted with a great shout, and the sound was heard far away.

Adversaries Oppose the Rebuilding

4 Now when the adversaries of Judah and Benjamin heard that the returned exiles were building a temple to the Lord, the God of Israel, ² they approached Zerubbabel and the heads of fathers' houses and said to them, "Let us build with you, for we worship your God as you do, and we have been sacrificing to him ever since the days of Esarhaddon king of Assyria who brought us here." ³ But Zerubbabel, Jeshua, and the rest of the heads of fathers' houses in Israel said to them, "You have nothing to do with us in

building a house to our God; but we alone will build to the Lord, the God of Israel, as King Cyrus the king of Persia has commanded us."

⁴ Then the people of the land discouraged the people of Judah and made them afraid to build ⁵ and bribed counselors against them to frustrate their purpose, all the days of Cyrus king of Persia, even until the reign of Darius king of Persia.

⁶ And in the reign of Ahasuerus, in the beginning of his reign, they wrote an accusation against the inhabitants of Judah and Jerusalem.

The Letter to King Artaxerxes

⁷ In the days of Artaxerxes, Bishlam and Mithredath and Tabeel and the rest of their associates wrote to Artaxerxes king of Persia. The letter was written in Aramaic and translated.[1] ⁸ Rehum the commander and Shimshai the scribe wrote a letter against Jerusalem to Artaxerxes the king as follows: ⁹ Rehum the commander, Shimshai the scribe, and the rest of their associates, the judges, the governors, the officials, the Persians, the men of Erech, the Babylonians, the men of Susa, that is, the Elamites, ¹⁰ and the rest of the nations whom the great and noble Osnappar deported and settled in the cities of Samaria and in the rest of the province Beyond the River. ¹¹ (This is a copy of the letter that they sent.) "To Artaxerxes the king: Your servants, the men of the province Beyond the River, send greeting. And now ¹² be it known to the king that the Jews who came up from you to us have gone to Jerusalem. They are rebuilding that rebellious and wicked city. They are finishing the walls and repairing the foundations. ¹³ Now be it known to the king that if this city is rebuilt and the walls finished, they will not pay tribute, custom, or toll, and the royal revenue will be impaired. ¹⁴ Now because we eat the salt of the palace[2] and it is not fitting for us to witness the king's dishonor, therefore we send and inform the king, ¹⁵ in order that search may be made in the book of the records of your fathers. You will find in the book of the records and learn that this city is a rebellious city, hurtful to kings and provinces, and that sedition was stirred up in it from of old. That was why this city was laid waste. ¹⁶ We make known to the king that if this city is rebuilt and its walls finished, you will then have no possession in the province Beyond the River."

The King Orders the Work to Cease

¹⁷ The king sent an answer: "To Rehum the commander and Shimshai the scribe and the rest of their associates who live in Samaria and in the rest of

---

[1] Hebrew *written in Aramaic and translated in Aramaic*, indicating that 4:8–6:18 is in Aramaic; another interpretation is *The letter was written in the Aramaic script and set forth in the Aramaic language* [2] Aramaic *because the salt of the palace is our salt*

the province Beyond the River, greeting. And now ¹⁸ the letter that you sent to us has been plainly read before me. ¹⁹ And I made a decree, and search has been made, and it has been found that this city from of old has risen against kings, and that rebellion and sedition have been made in it. ²⁰ And mighty kings have been over Jerusalem, who ruled over the whole province Beyond the River, to whom tribute, custom, and toll were paid. ²¹ Therefore make a decree that these men be made to cease, and that this city be not rebuilt, until a decree is made by me. ²² And take care not to be slack in this matter. Why should damage grow to the hurt of the king?"

²³ Then, when the copy of King Artaxerxes' letter was read before Rehum and Shimshai the scribe and their associates, they went in haste to the Jews at Jerusalem and by force and power made them cease. ²⁴ Then the work on the house of God that is in Jerusalem stopped, and it ceased until the second year of the reign of Darius king of Persia.

Rebuilding Begins Anew

5 Now the prophets, Haggai and Zechariah the son of Iddo, prophesied to the Jews who were in Judah and Jerusalem, in the name of the God of Israel who was over them. ² Then Zerubbabel the son of Shealtiel and Jeshua the son of Jozadak arose and began to rebuild the house of God that is in Jerusalem, and the prophets of God were with them, supporting them.

³ At the same time Tattenai the governor of the province Beyond the River and Shethar-bozenai and their associates came to them and spoke to them thus: "Who gave you a decree to build this house and to finish this structure?" ⁴ They also asked them this:[1] "What are the names of the men who are building this building?" ⁵ But the eye of their God was on the elders of the Jews, and they did not stop them until the report should reach Darius and then an answer be returned by letter concerning it.

Tattenai's Letter to King Darius

⁶ This is a copy of the letter that Tattenai the governor of the province Beyond the River and Shethar-bozenai and his associates, the governors who were in the province Beyond the River, sent to Darius the king. ⁷ They sent him a report, in which was written as follows: "To Darius the king, all peace. ⁸ Be it known to the king that we went to the province of Judah, to the house of the great God. It is being built with huge stones, and timber is laid in the walls. This work goes on diligently and prospers in their hands. ⁹ Then we asked those elders and spoke to them thus: 'Who gave you a decree to build

---

[1] Septuagint, Syriac; Aramaic *Then we said to them,*

this house and to finish this structure?' ¹⁰ We also asked them their names, for your information, that we might write down the names of their leaders.¹ ¹¹ And this was their reply to us: 'We are the servants of the God of heaven and earth, and we are rebuilding the house that was built many years ago, which a great king of Israel built and finished. ¹² But because our fathers had angered the God of heaven, he gave them into the hand of Nebuchadnezzar king of Babylon, the Chaldean, who destroyed this house and carried away the people to Babylonia. ¹³ However, in the first year of Cyrus king of Babylon, Cyrus the king made a decree that this house of God should be rebuilt. ¹⁴ And the gold and silver vessels of the house of God, which Nebuchadnezzar had taken out of the temple that was in Jerusalem and brought into the temple of Babylon, these Cyrus the king took out of the temple of Babylon, and they were delivered to one whose name was Sheshbazzar, whom he had made governor; ¹⁵ and he said to him, "Take these vessels, go and put them in the temple that is in Jerusalem, and let the house of God be rebuilt on its site." ¹⁶ Then this Sheshbazzar came and laid the foundations of the house of God that is in Jerusalem, and from that time until now it has been in building, and it is not yet finished.' ¹⁷ Therefore, if it seems good to the king, let search be made in the royal archives there in Babylon, to see whether a decree was issued by Cyrus the king for the rebuilding of this house of God in Jerusalem. And let the king send us his pleasure in this matter."

The Decree of Darius

6 Then Darius the king made a decree, and search was made in Babylonia, in the house of the archives where the documents were stored. ² And in Ecbatana, the citadel that is in the province of Media, a scroll was found on which this was written: "A record. ³ In the first year of Cyrus the king, Cyrus the king issued a decree: Concerning the house of God at Jerusalem, let the house be rebuilt, the place where sacrifices were offered, and let its foundations be retained. Its height shall be sixty cubits² and its breadth sixty cubits, ⁴ with three layers of great stones and one layer of timber. Let the cost be paid from the royal treasury. ⁵ And also let the gold and silver vessels of the house of God, which Nebuchadnezzar took out of the temple that is in Jerusalem and brought to Babylon, be restored and brought back to the temple that is in Jerusalem, each to its place. You shall put them in the house of God."

⁶ "Now therefore, Tattenai, governor of the province Beyond the River, Shethar-bozenai, and your³ associates the governors who are in the province Beyond the River, keep away. ⁷ Let the work on this house of God alone. Let

---

¹ Aramaic *of the men at their heads* ² A *cubit* was about 18 inches or 45 centimeters ³ Aramaic *their*

the governor of the Jews and the elders of the Jews rebuild this house of God on its site. ⁸ Moreover, I make a decree regarding what you shall do for these elders of the Jews for the rebuilding of this house of God. The cost is to be paid to these men in full and without delay from the royal revenue, the tribute of the province from Beyond the River. ⁹ And whatever is needed—bulls, rams, or sheep for burnt offerings to the God of heaven, wheat, salt, wine, or oil, as the priests at Jerusalem require—let that be given to them day by day without fail, ¹⁰ that they may offer pleasing sacrifices to the God of heaven and pray for the life of the king and his sons. ¹¹ Also I make a decree that if anyone alters this edict, a beam shall be pulled out of his house, and he shall be impaled on it, and his house shall be made a dunghill. ¹² May the God who has caused his name to dwell there overthrow any king or people who shall put out a hand to alter this, or to destroy this house of God that is in Jerusalem. I Darius make a decree; let it be done with all diligence."

The Temple Finished and Dedicated

¹³ Then, according to the word sent by Darius the king, Tattenai, the governor of the province Beyond the River, Shethar-bozenai, and their associates did with all diligence what Darius the king had ordered. ¹⁴ And the elders of the Jews built and prospered through the prophesying of Haggai the prophet and Zechariah the son of Iddo. They finished their building by decree of the God of Israel and by decree of Cyrus and Darius and Artaxerxes king of Persia; ¹⁵ and this house was finished on the third day of the month of Adar, in the sixth year of the reign of Darius the king.

¹⁶ And the people of Israel, the priests and the Levites, and the rest of the returned exiles, celebrated the dedication of this house of God with joy. ¹⁷ They offered at the dedication of this house of God 100 bulls, 200 rams, 400 lambs, and as a sin offering for all Israel 12 male goats, according to the number of the tribes of Israel. ¹⁸ And they set the priests in their divisions and the Levites in their divisions, for the service of God at Jerusalem, as it is written in the Book of Moses.

Passover Celebrated

¹⁹ On the fourteenth day of the first month, the returned exiles kept the Passover. ²⁰ For the priests and the Levites had purified themselves together; all of them were clean. So they slaughtered the Passover lamb for all the returned exiles, for their fellow priests, and for themselves. ²¹ It was eaten by the people of Israel who had returned from exile, and also by every one who had joined them and separated himself from the uncleanness of the

peoples of the land to worship the LORD, the God of Israel. ²² And they kept the Feast of Unleavened Bread seven days with joy, for the LORD had made them joyful and had turned the heart of the king of Assyria to them, so that he aided them in the work of the house of God, the God of Israel.

Ezra Sent to Teach the People

7 Now after this, in the reign of Artaxerxes king of Persia, Ezra the son of Seraiah, son of Azariah, son of Hilkiah, ² son of Shallum, son of Zadok, son of Ahitub, ³ son of Amariah, son of Azariah, son of Meraioth, ⁴ son of Zerahiah, son of Uzzi, son of Bukki, ⁵ son of Abishua, son of Phinehas, son of Eleazar, son of Aaron the chief priest— ⁶ this Ezra went up from Babylonia. He was a scribe skilled in the Law of Moses that the LORD, the God of Israel, had given, and the king granted him all that he asked, for the hand of the LORD his God was on him.

⁷ And there went up also to Jerusalem, in the seventh year of Artaxerxes the king, some of the people of Israel, and some of the priests and Levites, the singers and gatekeepers, and the temple servants. ⁸ And Ezra[1] came to Jerusalem in the fifth month, which was in the seventh year of the king. ⁹ For on the first day of the first month he began to go up from Babylonia, and on the first day of the fifth month he came to Jerusalem, for the good hand of his God was on him. ¹⁰ For Ezra had set his heart to study the Law of the LORD, and to do it and to teach his statutes and rules in Israel.

¹¹ This is a copy of the letter that King Artaxerxes gave to Ezra the priest, the scribe, a man learned in matters of the commandments of the LORD and his statutes for Israel:[2] ¹² "Artaxerxes, king of kings, to Ezra the priest, the scribe of the Law of the God of heaven. Peace.[3] And now ¹³ I make a decree that anyone of the people of Israel or their priests or Levites in my kingdom, who freely offers to go to Jerusalem, may go with you. ¹⁴ For you are sent by the king and his seven counselors to make inquiries about Judah and Jerusalem according to the Law of your God, which is in your hand, ¹⁵ and also to carry the silver and gold that the king and his counselors have freely offered to the God of Israel, whose dwelling is in Jerusalem, ¹⁶ with all the silver and gold that you shall find in the whole province of Babylonia, and with the freewill offerings of the people and the priests, vowed willingly for the house of their God that is in Jerusalem. ¹⁷ With this money, then, you shall with all diligence buy bulls, rams, and lambs, with their grain offerings and their drink offerings, and you shall offer them on the altar of the house of your God that is in Jerusalem. ¹⁸ Whatever seems good to you and your

[1] Hebrew *he* [2] The text of Ezra 7:12–26 is in Aramaic [3] Aramaic *Perfect* (probably a greeting)

brothers to do with the rest of the silver and gold, you may do, according to the will of your God. ⁱ⁹ The vessels that have been given you for the service of the house of your God, you shall deliver before the God of Jerusalem. ²⁰ And whatever else is required for the house of your God, which it falls to you to provide, you may provide it out of the king's treasury.

²¹ "And I, Artaxerxes the king, make a decree to all the treasurers in the province Beyond the River: Whatever Ezra the priest, the scribe of the Law of the God of heaven, requires of you, let it be done with all diligence, ²² up to 100 talents[1] of silver, 100 cors[2] of wheat, 100 baths[3] of wine, 100 baths of oil, and salt without prescribing how much. ²³ Whatever is decreed by the God of heaven, let it be done in full for the house of the God of heaven, lest his wrath be against the realm of the king and his sons. ²⁴ We also notify you that it shall not be lawful to impose tribute, custom, or toll on anyone of the priests, the Levites, the singers, the doorkeepers, the temple servants, or other servants of this house of God.

²⁵ "And you, Ezra, according to the wisdom of your God that is in your hand, appoint magistrates and judges who may judge all the people in the province Beyond the River, all such as know the laws of your God. And those who do not know them, you shall teach. ²⁶ Whoever will not obey the law of your God and the law of the king, let judgment be strictly executed on him, whether for death or for banishment or for confiscation of his goods or for imprisonment."

²⁷ Blessed be the LORD, the God of our fathers, who put such a thing as this into the heart of the king, to beautify the house of the LORD that is in Jerusalem, ²⁸ and who extended to me his steadfast love before the king and his counselors, and before all the king's mighty officers. I took courage, for the hand of the LORD my God was on me, and I gathered leading men from Israel to go up with me.

Genealogy of Those Who Returned with Ezra

8 These are the heads of their fathers' houses, and this is the genealogy of those who went up with me from Babylonia, in the reign of Artaxerxes the king: ² Of the sons of Phinehas, Gershom. Of the sons of Ithamar, Daniel. Of the sons of David, Hattush. ³ Of the sons of Shecaniah, who was of the sons of Parosh, Zechariah, with whom were registered 150 men. ⁴ Of the sons of Pahath-moab, Eliehoenai the son of Zerahiah, and with him 200 men. ⁵ Of the sons of Zattu,[4] Shecaniah the son of Jahaziel, and with him 300 men. ⁶ Of the sons of Adin, Ebed the son of Jonathan, and with him 50 men. ⁷ Of the sons of Elam, Jeshaiah the son of Athaliah, and with him 70 men. ⁸ Of the sons

---

[1] A *talent* was about 75 pounds or 34 kilograms [2] A *cor* was about 6 bushels or 220 liters [3] A *bath* was about 6 gallons or 22 liters [4] Septuagint; Hebrew lacks *of Zattu*

of Shephatiah, Zebadiah the son of Michael, and with him 80 men. ⁹ Of the sons of Joab, Obadiah the son of Jehiel, and with him 218 men. ¹⁰ Of the sons of Bani,¹ Shelomith the son of Josiphiah, and with him 160 men. ¹¹ Of the sons of Bebai, Zechariah, the son of Bebai, and with him 28 men. ¹² Of the sons of Azgad, Johanan the son of Hakkatan, and with him 110 men. ¹³ Of the sons of Adonikam, those who came later, their names being Eliphelet, Jeuel, and Shemaiah, and with them 60 men. ¹⁴ Of the sons of Bigvai, Uthai and Zaccur, and with them 70 men.

Ezra Sends for Levites

¹⁵ I gathered them to the river that runs to Ahava, and there we camped three days. As I reviewed the people and the priests, I found there none of the sons of Levi. ¹⁶ Then I sent for Eliezer, Ariel, Shemaiah, Elnathan, Jarib, Elnathan, Nathan, Zechariah, and Meshullam, leading men, and for Joiarib and Elnathan, who were men of insight, ¹⁷ and sent them to Iddo, the leading man at the place Casiphia, telling them what to say to Iddo and his brothers and² the temple servants at the place Casiphia, namely, to send us ministers for the house of our God. ¹⁸ And by the good hand of our God on us, they brought us a man of discretion, of the sons of Mahli the son of Levi, son of Israel, namely Sherebiah with his sons and kinsmen, 18; ¹⁹ also Hashabiah, and with him Jeshaiah of the sons of Merari, with his kinsmen and their sons, 20; ²⁰ besides 220 of the temple servants, whom David and his officials had set apart to attend the Levites. These were all mentioned by name.

Fasting and Prayer for Protection

²¹ Then I proclaimed a fast there, at the river Ahava, that we might humble ourselves before our God, to seek from him a safe journey for ourselves, our children, and all our goods. ²² For I was ashamed to ask the king for a band of soldiers and horsemen to protect us against the enemy on our way, since we had told the king, "The hand of our God is for good on all who seek him, and the power of his wrath is against all who forsake him." ²³ So we fasted and implored our God for this, and he listened to our entreaty.

Priests to Guard Offerings

²⁴ Then I set apart twelve of the leading priests: Sherebiah, Hashabiah, and ten of their kinsmen with them. ²⁵ And I weighed out to them the silver and the gold and the vessels, the offering for the house of our God that the king and his counselors and his lords and all Israel there present had offered.

---

¹ Septuagint; Hebrew lacks *Bani* ² Hebrew lacks *and*

²⁶ I weighed out into their hand 650 talents[1] of silver, and silver vessels worth 200 talents,[2] and 100 talents of gold, ²⁷ 20 bowls of gold worth 1,000 darics,[3] and two vessels of fine bright bronze as precious as gold. ²⁸ And I said to them, "You are holy to the LORD, and the vessels are holy, and the silver and the gold are a freewill offering to the LORD, the God of your fathers. ²⁹ Guard them and keep them until you weigh them before the chief priests and the Levites and the heads of fathers' houses in Israel at Jerusalem, within the chambers of the house of the LORD." ³⁰ So the priests and the Levites took over the weight of the silver and the gold and the vessels, to bring them to Jerusalem, to the house of our God.

³¹ Then we departed from the river Ahava on the twelfth day of the first month, to go to Jerusalem. The hand of our God was on us, and he delivered us from the hand of the enemy and from ambushes by the way. ³² We came to Jerusalem, and there we remained three days. ³³ On the fourth day, within the house of our God, the silver and the gold and the vessels were weighed into the hands of Meremoth the priest, son of Uriah, and with him was Eleazar the son of Phinehas, and with them were the Levites, Jozabad the son of Jeshua and Noadiah the son of Binnui. ³⁴ The whole was counted and weighed, and the weight of everything was recorded.

³⁵ At that time those who had come from captivity, the returned exiles, offered burnt offerings to the God of Israel, twelve bulls for all Israel, ninety-six rams, seventy-seven lambs, and as a sin offering twelve male goats. All this was a burnt offering to the LORD. ³⁶ They also delivered the king's commissions to the king's satraps[4] and to the governors of the province Beyond the River, and they aided the people and the house of God.

Ezra Prays About Intermarriage

9 After these things had been done, the officials approached me and said, "The people of Israel and the priests and the Levites have not separated themselves from the peoples of the lands with their abominations, from the Canaanites, the Hittites, the Perizzites, the Jebusites, the Ammonites, the Moabites, the Egyptians, and the Amorites. ² For they have taken some of their daughters to be wives for themselves and for their sons, so that the holy race[5] has mixed itself with the peoples of the lands. And in this faithlessness the hand of the officials and chief men has been foremost." ³ As soon as I heard this, I tore my garment and my cloak and pulled hair from my head and beard and sat appalled. ⁴ Then all who trembled at the words of the God of Israel, because of the faithlessness of the returned exiles, gathered around me

---

[1] A *talent* was about 75 pounds or 34 kilograms [2] Revocalization; the number is missing in the Masoretic Text
[3] A *daric* was a coin weighing about 1/4 ounce or 8.5 grams [4] A *satrap* was a Persian official [5] Hebrew *offspring*

while I sat appalled until the evening sacrifice. ⁵ And at the evening sacrifice I rose from my fasting, with my garment and my cloak torn, and fell upon my knees and spread out my hands to the Lord my God, ⁶ saying:

"O my God, I am ashamed and blush to lift my face to you, my God, for our iniquities have risen higher than our heads, and our guilt has mounted up to the heavens. ⁷ From the days of our fathers to this day we have been in great guilt. And for our iniquities we, our kings, and our priests have been given into the hand of the kings of the lands, to the sword, to captivity, to plundering, and to utter shame, as it is today. ⁸ But now for a brief moment favor has been shown by the Lord our God, to leave us a remnant and to give us a secure hold[1] within his holy place, that our God may brighten our eyes and grant us a little reviving in our slavery. ⁹ For we are slaves. Yet our God has not forsaken us in our slavery, but has extended to us his steadfast love before the kings of Persia, to grant us some reviving to set up the house of our God, to repair its ruins, and to give us protection[2] in Judea and Jerusalem.

¹⁰ "And now, O our God, what shall we say after this? For we have forsaken your commandments, ¹¹ which you commanded by your servants the prophets, saying, 'The land that you are entering, to take possession of it, is a land impure with the impurity of the peoples of the lands, with their abominations that have filled it from end to end with their uncleanness. ¹² Therefore do not give your daughters to their sons, neither take their daughters for your sons, and never seek their peace or prosperity, that you may be strong and eat the good of the land and leave it for an inheritance to your children forever.' ¹³ And after all that has come upon us for our evil deeds and for our great guilt, seeing that you, our God, have punished us less than our iniquities deserved and have given us such a remnant as this, ¹⁴ shall we break your commandments again and intermarry with the peoples who practice these abominations? Would you not be angry with us until you consumed us, so that there should be no remnant, nor any to escape? ¹⁵ O Lord, the God of Israel, you are just, for we are left a remnant that has escaped, as it is today. Behold, we are before you in our guilt, for none can stand before you because of this."

The People Confess Their Sin

10 While Ezra prayed and made confession, weeping and casting himself down before the house of God, a very great assembly of men, women, and children, gathered to him out of Israel, for the people wept bitterly. ² And Shecaniah the son of Jehiel, of the sons of Elam, addressed

---
[1] Hebrew *nail, or tent-pin* [2] Hebrew *a wall*

Ezra: "We have broken faith with our God and have married foreign women from the peoples of the land, but even now there is hope for Israel in spite of this. ³ Therefore let us make a covenant with our God to put away all these wives and their children, according to the counsel of my lord[1] and of those who tremble at the commandment of our God, and let it be done according to the Law. ⁴ Arise, for it is your task, and we are with you; be strong and do it." ⁵ Then Ezra arose and made the leading priests and Levites and all Israel take an oath that they would do as had been said. So they took the oath.

⁶ Then Ezra withdrew from before the house of God and went to the chamber of Jehohanan the son of Eliashib, where he spent the night,[2] neither eating bread nor drinking water, for he was mourning over the faithlessness of the exiles. ⁷ And a proclamation was made throughout Judah and Jerusalem to all the returned exiles that they should assemble at Jerusalem, ⁸ and that if anyone did not come within three days, by order of the officials and the elders all his property should be forfeited, and he himself banned from the congregation of the exiles.

⁹ Then all the men of Judah and Benjamin assembled at Jerusalem within the three days. It was the ninth month, on the twentieth day of the month. And all the people sat in the open square before the house of God, trembling because of this matter and because of the heavy rain. ¹⁰ And Ezra the priest stood up and said to them, "You have broken faith and married foreign women, and so increased the guilt of Israel. ¹¹ Now then make confession to the LORD, the God of your fathers and do his will. Separate yourselves from the peoples of the land and from the foreign wives." ¹² Then all the assembly answered with a loud voice, "It is so; we must do as you have said. ¹³ But the people are many, and it is a time of heavy rain; we cannot stand in the open. Nor is this a task for one day or for two, for we have greatly transgressed in this matter. ¹⁴ Let our officials stand for the whole assembly. Let all in our cities who have taken foreign wives come at appointed times, and with them the elders and judges of every city, until the fierce wrath of our God over this matter is turned away from us." ¹⁵ Only Jonathan the son of Asahel and Jahzeiah the son of Tikvah opposed this, and Meshullam and Shabbethai the Levite supported them.

¹⁶ Then the returned exiles did so. Ezra the priest selected men,[3] heads of fathers' houses, according to their fathers' houses, each of them designated by name. On the first day of the tenth month they sat down to examine the matter; ¹⁷ and by the first day of the first month they had come to the end of all the men who had married foreign women.

[1] Or *of the Lord* [2] Probable reading; Hebrew *where he went* [3] Syriac; Hebrew *And there were selected Ezra...*

Those Guilty of Intermarriage

[18] Now there were found some of the sons of the priests who had married foreign women: Maaseiah, Eliezer, Jarib, and Gedaliah, some of the sons of Jeshua the son of Jozadak and his brothers. [19] They pledged themselves to put away their wives, and their guilt offering was a ram of the flock for their guilt.[1] [20] Of the sons of Immer: Hanani and Zebadiah. [21] Of the sons of Harim: Maaseiah, Elijah, Shemaiah, Jehiel, and Uzziah. [22] Of the sons of Pashhur: Elioenai, Maaseiah, Ishmael, Nethanel, Jozabad, and Elasah.

[23] Of the Levites: Jozabad, Shimei, Kelaiah (that is, Kelita), Pethahiah, Judah, and Eliezer. [24] Of the singers: Eliashib. Of the gatekeepers: Shallum, Telem, and Uri.

[25] And of Israel: of the sons of Parosh: Ramiah, Izziah, Malchijah, Mijamin, Eleazar, Hashabiah,[2] and Benaiah. [26] Of the sons of Elam: Mattaniah, Zechariah, Jehiel, Abdi, Jeremoth, and Elijah. [27] Of the sons of Zattu: Elioenai, Eliashib, Mattaniah, Jeremoth, Zabad, and Aziza. [28] Of the sons of Bebai were Jehohanan, Hananiah, Zabbai, and Athlai. [29] Of the sons of Bani were Meshullam, Malluch, Adaiah, Jashub, Sheal, and Jeremoth. [30] Of the sons of Pahath-moab: Adna, Chelal, Benaiah, Maaseiah, Mattaniah, Bezalel, Binnui, and Manasseh. [31] Of the sons of Harim: Eliezer, Isshijah, Malchijah, Shemaiah, Shimeon, [32] Benjamin, Malluch, and Shemariah. [33] Of the sons of Hashum: Mattenai, Mattattah, Zabad, Eliphelet, Jeremai, Manasseh, and Shimei. [34] Of the sons of Bani: Maadai, Amram, Uel, [35] Benaiah, Bedeiah, Cheluhi, [36] Vaniah, Meremoth, Eliashib, [37] Mattaniah, Mattenai, Jaasu. [38] Of the sons of Binnui:[3] Shimei, [39] Shelemiah, Nathan, Adaiah, [40] Machnadebai, Shashai, Sharai, [41] Azarel, Shelemiah, Shemariah, [42] Shallum, Amariah, and Joseph. [43] Of the sons of Nebo: Jeiel, Mattithiah, Zabad, Zebina, Jaddai, Joel, and Benaiah. [44] All these had married foreign women, and some of the women had even borne children.[4]

---

[1] Or *as their reparation* [2] Septuagint; Hebrew *Malchijah* [3] Septuagint; Hebrew *Bani, Binnui* [4] Or *and they put them away with their children*

NEHEMIAH

Report from Jerusalem

1 The words of Nehemiah the son of Hacaliah.

Now it happened in the month of Chislev, in the twentieth year, as I was in Susa the citadel, ²that Hanani, one of my brothers, came with certain men from Judah. And I asked them concerning the Jews who escaped, who had survived the exile, and concerning Jerusalem. ³And they said to me, "The remnant there in the province who had survived the exile is in great trouble and shame. The wall of Jerusalem is broken down, and its gates are destroyed by fire."

Nehemiah's Prayer

⁴As soon as I heard these words I sat down and wept and mourned for days, and I continued fasting and praying before the God of heaven. ⁵And I said, "O Lord God of heaven, the great and awesome God who keeps covenant and steadfast love with those who love him and keep his commandments, ⁶let your ear be attentive and your eyes open, to hear the prayer of your servant that I now pray before you day and night for the people of Israel your servants, confessing the sins of the people of Israel, which we have sinned against you. Even I and my father's house have sinned. ⁷We have acted very corruptly against you and have not kept the commandments, the statutes, and the rules that you commanded your servant Moses. ⁸Remember the word that you commanded your servant Moses, saying, 'If you are unfaithful, I will scatter you among the peoples, ⁹but if you return to me and keep my commandments and do them, though your outcasts are in the uttermost parts of heaven, from there I will gather them and bring them to the place that I have chosen, to make my name dwell there.' ¹⁰They are your servants and your people, whom you have redeemed by your great power and by your strong hand. ¹¹O Lord, let your ear be attentive to the prayer of your servant, and to the prayer of your servants who delight to fear your name, and give success to your servant today, and grant him mercy in the sight of this man."

Now I was cupbearer to the king.

Nehemiah Sent to Judah

2 In the month of Nisan, in the twentieth year of King Artaxerxes, when wine was before him, I took up the wine and gave it to the king. Now I had not been sad in his presence. ²And the king said to me, "Why is your face sad, seeing you are not sick? This is nothing but sadness of the heart." Then I was very much afraid. ³I said to the king, "Let the king live forever! Why should not my face be sad, when the city, the place of my fathers' graves, lies in ruins, and its gates have been destroyed by fire?" ⁴Then the king said to me, "What are you requesting?" So I prayed to the God of heaven. ⁵And I said to the king, "If it pleases the king, and if your servant has found favor in your sight, that you send me to Judah, to the city of my fathers' graves, that I may rebuild it." ⁶And the king said to me (the queen sitting beside him), "How long will you be gone, and when will you return?" So it pleased the king to send me when I had given him a time. ⁷And I said to the king, "If it pleases the king, let letters be given me to the governors of the province Beyond the River, that they may let me pass through until I come to Judah, ⁸and a letter to Asaph, the keeper of the king's forest, that he may give me timber to make beams for the gates of the fortress of the temple, and for the wall of the city, and for the house that I shall occupy." And the king granted me what I asked, for the good hand of my God was upon me.

Nehemiah Inspects Jerusalem's Walls

⁹Then I came to the governors of the province Beyond the River and gave them the king's letters. Now the king had sent with me officers of the army and horsemen. ¹⁰But when Sanballat the Horonite and Tobiah the Ammonite servant heard this, it displeased them greatly that someone had come to seek the welfare of the people of Israel.

¹¹So I went to Jerusalem and was there three days. ¹²Then I arose in the night, I and a few men with me. And I told no one what my God had put into my heart to do for Jerusalem. There was no animal with me but the one on which I rode. ¹³I went out by night by the Valley Gate to the Dragon Spring and to the Dung Gate, and I inspected the walls of Jerusalem that were broken down and its gates that had been destroyed by fire. ¹⁴Then I went on to the Fountain Gate and to the King's Pool, but there was no room for the animal that was under me to pass. ¹⁵Then I went up in the night by the valley and inspected the wall, and I turned back and entered by the Valley Gate, and so returned. ¹⁶And the officials did not know where I had gone or what I was doing, and I had not yet told the Jews, the priests, the nobles, the officials, and the rest who were to do the work.

¹⁷ Then I said to them, "You see the trouble we are in, how Jerusalem lies in ruins with its gates burned. Come, let us build the wall of Jerusalem, that we may no longer suffer derision." ¹⁸ And I told them of the hand of my God that had been upon me for good, and also of the words that the king had spoken to me. And they said, "Let us rise up and build." So they strengthened their hands for the good work. ¹⁹ But when Sanballat the Horonite and Tobiah the Ammonite servant and Geshem the Arab heard of it, they jeered at us and despised us and said, "What is this thing that you are doing? Are you rebelling against the king?" ²⁰ Then I replied to them, "The God of heaven will make us prosper, and we his servants will arise and build, but you have no portion or right or claim[1] in Jerusalem."

Rebuilding the Wall

3 Then Eliashib the high priest rose up with his brothers the priests, and they built the Sheep Gate. They consecrated it and set its doors. They consecrated it as far as the Tower of the Hundred, as far as the Tower of Hananel. ² And next to him the men of Jericho built. And next to them[2] Zaccur the son of Imri built.

³ The sons of Hassenaah built the Fish Gate. They laid its beams and set its doors, its bolts, and its bars. ⁴ And next to them Meremoth the son of Uriah, son of Hakkoz repaired. And next to them Meshullam the son of Berechiah, son of Meshezabel repaired. And next to them Zadok the son of Baana repaired. ⁵ And next to them the Tekoites repaired, but their nobles would not stoop to serve their Lord.[3]

⁶ Joiada the son of Paseah and Meshullam the son of Besodeiah repaired the Gate of Yeshanah.[4] They laid its beams and set its doors, its bolts, and its bars. ⁷ And next to them repaired Melatiah the Gibeonite and Jadon the Meronothite, the men of Gibeon and of Mizpah, the seat of the governor of the province Beyond the River. ⁸ Next to them Uzziel the son of Harhaiah, goldsmiths, repaired. Next to him Hananiah, one of the perfumers, repaired, and they restored Jerusalem as far as the Broad Wall. ⁹ Next to them Rephaiah the son of Hur, ruler of half the district of[5] Jerusalem, repaired. ¹⁰ Next to them Jedaiah the son of Harumaph repaired opposite his house. And next to him Hattush the son of Hashabneiah repaired. ¹¹ Malchijah the son of Harim and Hasshub the son of Pahath-moab repaired another section and the Tower of the Ovens. ¹² Next to him Shallum the son of Hallohesh, ruler of half the district of Jerusalem, repaired, he and his daughters.

---

[1] Or *memorial* [2] Hebrew *him* [3] Or *lords* [4] Or *of the old city* [5] Or *foreman of half the portion assigned to*; also verses 12, 14, 15, 16, 17, 18

¹³ Hanun and the inhabitants of Zanoah repaired the Valley Gate. They rebuilt it and set its doors, its bolts, and its bars, and repaired a thousand cubits[1] of the wall, as far as the Dung Gate.

¹⁴ Malchijah the son of Rechab, ruler of the district of Beth-haccherem, repaired the Dung Gate. He rebuilt it and set its doors, its bolts, and its bars.

¹⁵ And Shallum the son of Col-hozeh, ruler of the district of Mizpah, repaired the Fountain Gate. He rebuilt it and covered it and set its doors, its bolts, and its bars. And he built the wall of the Pool of Shelah of the king's garden, as far as the stairs that go down from the city of David. ¹⁶ After him Nehemiah the son of Azbuk, ruler of half the district of Beth-zur, repaired to a point opposite the tombs of David, as far as the artificial pool, and as far as the house of the mighty men. ¹⁷ After him the Levites repaired: Rehum the son of Bani. Next to him Hashabiah, ruler of half the district of Keilah, repaired for his district. ¹⁸ After him their brothers repaired: Bavvai the son of Henadad, ruler of half the district of Keilah. ¹⁹ Next to him Ezer the son of Jeshua, ruler of Mizpah, repaired another section opposite the ascent to the armory at the buttress.[2] ²⁰ After him Baruch the son of Zabbai repaired[3] another section from the buttress to the door of the house of Eliashib the high priest. ²¹ After him Meremoth the son of Uriah, son of Hakkoz repaired another section from the door of the house of Eliashib to the end of the house of Eliashib. ²² After him the priests, the men of the surrounding area, repaired. ²³ After them Benjamin and Hasshub repaired opposite their house. After them Azariah the son of Maaseiah, son of Ananiah repaired beside his own house. ²⁴ After him Binnui the son of Henadad repaired another section, from the house of Azariah to the buttress and to the corner. ²⁵ Palal the son of Uzai repaired opposite the buttress and the tower projecting from the upper house of the king at the court of the guard. After him Pedaiah the son of Parosh ²⁶ and the temple servants living on Ophel repaired to a point opposite the Water Gate on the east and the projecting tower. ²⁷ After him the Tekoites repaired another section opposite the great projecting tower as far as the wall of Ophel.

²⁸ Above the Horse Gate the priests repaired, each one opposite his own house. ²⁹ After them Zadok the son of Immer repaired opposite his own house. After him Shemaiah the son of Shecaniah, the keeper of the East Gate, repaired. ³⁰ After him Hananiah the son of Shelemiah and Hanun the sixth son of Zalaph repaired another section. After him Meshullam the son of Berechiah repaired opposite his chamber. ³¹ After him Malchijah, one of the goldsmiths, repaired as far as the house of the temple servants and of the merchants, opposite the Muster Gate,[4] and to the upper chamber of the

---

[1] A *cubit* was about 18 inches or 45 centimeters [2] Or *corner*; also verses 20, 24, 25 [3] Some manuscripts *vigorously repaired* [4] Or *Hammiphkad Gate*

corner. ³² And between the upper chamber of the corner and the Sheep Gate the goldsmiths and the merchants repaired.

Opposition to the Work

4 ¹ Now when Sanballat heard that we were building the wall, he was angry and greatly enraged, and he jeered at the Jews. ² And he said in the presence of his brothers and of the army of Samaria, "What are these feeble Jews doing? Will they restore it for themselves?² Will they sacrifice? Will they finish up in a day? Will they revive the stones out of the heaps of rubbish, and burned ones at that?" ³ Tobiah the Ammonite was beside him, and he said, "Yes, what they are building—if a fox goes up on it he will break down their stone wall!" ⁴ Hear, O our God, for we are despised. Turn back their taunt on their own heads and give them up to be plundered in a land where they are captives. ⁵ Do not cover their guilt, and let not their sin be blotted out from your sight, for they have provoked you to anger in the presence of the builders.

⁶ So we built the wall. And all the wall was joined together to half its height, for the people had a mind to work.

⁷ ³ But when Sanballat and Tobiah and the Arabs and the Ammonites and the Ashdodites heard that the repairing of the walls of Jerusalem was going forward and that the breaches were beginning to be closed, they were very angry. ⁸ And they all plotted together to come and fight against Jerusalem and to cause confusion in it. ⁹ And we prayed to our God and set a guard as a protection against them day and night.

¹⁰ In Judah it was said,⁴ "The strength of those who bear the burdens is failing. There is too much rubble. By ourselves we will not be able to rebuild the wall." ¹¹ And our enemies said, "They will not know or see till we come among them and kill them and stop the work." ¹² At that time the Jews who lived near them came from all directions and said to us ten times, "You must return to us."⁵ ¹³ So in the lowest parts of the space behind the wall, in open places, I stationed the people by their clans, with their swords, their spears, and their bows. ¹⁴ And I looked and arose and said to the nobles and to the officials and to the rest of the people, "Do not be afraid of them. Remember the Lord, who is great and awesome, and fight for your brothers, your sons, your daughters, your wives, and your homes."

The Work Resumes

¹⁵ When our enemies heard that it was known to us and that God had frustrated their plan, we all returned to the wall, each to his work. ¹⁶ From

¹ Ch 3:33 in Hebrew ² Or *Will they commit themselves to God?* ³ Ch 4:1 in Hebrew ⁴ Hebrew *Judah said*
⁵ The meaning of the Hebrew is uncertain

that day on, half of my servants worked on construction, and half held the spears, shields, bows, and coats of mail. And the leaders stood behind the whole house of Judah, ¹⁷ who were building on the wall. Those who carried burdens were loaded in such a way that each labored on the work with one hand and held his weapon with the other. ¹⁸ And each of the builders had his sword strapped at his side while he built. The man who sounded the trumpet was beside me. ¹⁹ And I said to the nobles and to the officials and to the rest of the people, "The work is great and widely spread, and we are separated on the wall, far from one another. ²⁰ In the place where you hear the sound of the trumpet, rally to us there. Our God will fight for us."

²¹ So we labored at the work, and half of them held the spears from the break of dawn until the stars came out. ²² I also said to the people at that time, "Let every man and his servant pass the night within Jerusalem, that they may be a guard for us by night and may labor by day." ²³ So neither I nor my brothers nor my servants nor the men of the guard who followed me, none of us took off our clothes; each kept his weapon at his right hand.¹

Nehemiah Stops Oppression of the Poor

5 Now there arose a great outcry of the people and of their wives against their Jewish brothers. ² For there were those who said, "With our sons and our daughters, we are many. So let us get grain, that we may eat and keep alive." ³ There were also those who said, "We are mortgaging our fields, our vineyards, and our houses to get grain because of the famine." ⁴ And there were those who said, "We have borrowed money for the king's tax on our fields and our vineyards. ⁵ Now our flesh is as the flesh of our brothers, our children are as their children. Yet we are forcing our sons and our daughters to be slaves, and some of our daughters have already been enslaved, but it is not in our power to help it, for other men have our fields and our vineyards."

⁶ I was very angry when I heard their outcry and these words. ⁷ I took counsel with myself, and I brought charges against the nobles and the officials. I said to them, "You are exacting interest, each from his brother." And I held a great assembly against them ⁸ and said to them, "We, as far as we are able, have bought back our Jewish brothers who have been sold to the nations, but you even sell your brothers that they may be sold to us!" They were silent and could not find a word to say. ⁹ So I said, "The thing that you are doing is not good. Ought you not to walk in the fear of our God to prevent the taunts of the nations our enemies? ¹⁰ Moreover, I and my brothers and my servants are lending them money and grain. Let us abandon this exacting of interest. ¹¹ Return to them

¹ Or *his weapon when drinking*

this very day their fields, their vineyards, their olive orchards, and their houses, and the percentage of money, grain, wine, and oil that you have been exacting from them." ¹²Then they said, "We will restore these and require nothing from them. We will do as you say." And I called the priests and made them swear to do as they had promised. ¹³I also shook out the fold[1] of my garment and said, "So may God shake out every man from his house and from his labor who does not keep this promise. So may he be shaken out and emptied." And all the assembly said "Amen" and praised the LORD. And the people did as they had promised.

Nehemiah's Generosity

¹⁴ Moreover, from the time that I was appointed to be their governor in the land of Judah, from the twentieth year to the thirty-second year of Artaxerxes the king, twelve years, neither I nor my brothers ate the food allowance of the governor. ¹⁵ The former governors who were before me laid heavy burdens on the people and took from them for their daily ration[2] forty shekels[3] of silver. Even their servants lorded it over the people. But I did not do so, because of the fear of God. ¹⁶ I also persevered in the work on this wall, and we acquired no land, and all my servants were gathered there for the work. ¹⁷ Moreover, there were at my table 150 men, Jews and officials, besides those who came to us from the nations that were around us. ¹⁸ Now what was prepared at my expense[4] for each day was one ox and six choice sheep and birds, and every ten days all kinds of wine in abundance. Yet for all this I did not demand the food allowance of the governor, because the service was too heavy on this people. ¹⁹ Remember for my good, O my God, all that I have done for this people.

Conspiracy Against Nehemiah

6 Now when Sanballat and Tobiah and Geshem the Arab and the rest of our enemies heard that I had built the wall and that there was no breach left in it (although up to that time I had not set up the doors in the gates), ²Sanballat and Geshem sent to me, saying, "Come and let us meet together at Hakkephirim in the plain of Ono." But they intended to do me harm. ³And I sent messengers to them, saying, "I am doing a great work and I cannot come down. Why should the work stop while I leave it and come down to you?" ⁴And they sent to me four times in this way, and I answered them in the same manner. ⁵In the same way Sanballat for the fifth time sent his servant to me with an open letter in his hand. ⁶In it was written, "It is reported among the nations, and Geshem[5] also says it, that you and the Jews intend to rebel; that is why you are building

---

[1] Hebrew *bosom* [2] Compare Vulgate; Hebrew *took from them for food and wine after* [3] A *shekel* was about 2/5 ounce or 11 grams [4] Or *prepared for me* [5] Hebrew *Gashmu*

the wall. And according to these reports you wish to become their king. ⁷ And you have also set up prophets to proclaim concerning you in Jerusalem, 'There is a king in Judah.' And now the king will hear of these reports. So now come and let us take counsel together." ⁸ Then I sent to him, saying, "No such things as you say have been done, for you are inventing them out of your own mind." ⁹ For they all wanted to frighten us, thinking, "Their hands will drop from the work, and it will not be done." But now, O God,¹ strengthen my hands.

¹⁰ Now when I went into the house of Shemaiah the son of Delaiah, son of Mehetabel, who was confined to his home, he said, "Let us meet together in the house of God, within the temple. Let us close the doors of the temple, for they are coming to kill you. They are coming to kill you by night." ¹¹ But I said, "Should such a man as I run away? And what man such as I could go into the temple and live?² I will not go in." ¹² And I understood and saw that God had not sent him, but he had pronounced the prophecy against me because Tobiah and Sanballat had hired him. ¹³ For this purpose he was hired, that I should be afraid and act in this way and sin, and so they could give me a bad name in order to taunt me. ¹⁴ Remember Tobiah and Sanballat, O my God, according to these things that they did, and also the prophetess Noadiah and the rest of the prophets who wanted to make me afraid.

The Wall Is Finished

¹⁵ So the wall was finished on the twenty-fifth day of the month Elul, in fifty-two days. ¹⁶ And when all our enemies heard of it, all the nations around us were afraid and fell greatly in their own esteem, for they perceived that this work had been accomplished with the help of our God. ¹⁷ Moreover, in those days the nobles of Judah sent many letters to Tobiah, and Tobiah's letters came to them. ¹⁸ For many in Judah were bound by oath to him, because he was the son-in-law of Shecaniah the son of Arah: and his son Jehohanan had taken the daughter of Meshullam the son of Berechiah as his wife. ¹⁹ Also they spoke of his good deeds in my presence and reported my words to him. And Tobiah sent letters to make me afraid.

7 Now when the wall had been built and I had set up the doors, and the gatekeepers, the singers, and the Levites had been appointed, ² I gave my brother Hanani and Hananiah the governor of the castle charge over Jerusalem, for he was a more faithful and God-fearing man than many. ³ And I said to them, "Let not the gates of Jerusalem be opened until the sun is hot. And while they are still standing guard, let them shut and bar the doors. Appoint guards from among the inhabitants of Jerusalem, some at their

---

¹ Hebrew lacks *O God* ² Or *would go into the temple to save his life*

guard posts and some in front of their own homes." ⁴ The city was wide and large, but the people within it were few, and no houses had been rebuilt.

Lists of Returned Exiles

⁵ Then my God put it into my heart to assemble the nobles and the officials and the people to be enrolled by genealogy. And I found the book of the genealogy of those who came up at the first, and I found written in it:

⁶ These were the people of the province who came up out of the captivity of those exiles whom Nebuchadnezzar the king of Babylon had carried into exile. They returned to Jerusalem and Judah, each to his town. ⁷ They came with Zerubbabel, Jeshua, Nehemiah, Azariah, Raamiah, Nahamani, Mordecai, Bilshan, Mispereth, Bigvai, Nehum, Baanah.

The number of the men of the people of Israel: ⁸ the sons of Parosh, 2,172. ⁹ The sons of Shephatiah, 372. ¹⁰ The sons of Arah, 652. ¹¹ The sons of Pahath-moab, namely the sons of Jeshua and Joab, 2,818. ¹² The sons of Elam, 1,254. ¹³ The sons of Zattu, 845. ¹⁴ The sons of Zaccai, 760. ¹⁵ The sons of Binnui, 648. ¹⁶ The sons of Bebai, 628. ¹⁷ The sons of Azgad, 2,322. ¹⁸ The sons of Adonikam, 667. ¹⁹ The sons of Bigvai, 2,067. ²⁰ The sons of Adin, 655. ²¹ The sons of Ater, namely of Hezekiah, 98. ²² The sons of Hashum, 328. ²³ The sons of Bezai, 324. ²⁴ The sons of Hariph, 112. ²⁵ The sons of Gibeon, 95. ²⁶ The men of Bethlehem and Netophah, 188. ²⁷ The men of Anathoth, 128. ²⁸ The men of Beth-azmaveth, 42. ²⁹ The men of Kiriath-jearim, Chephirah, and Beeroth, 743. ³⁰ The men of Ramah and Geba, 621. ³¹ The men of Michmas, 122. ³² The men of Bethel and Ai, 123. ³³ The men of the other Nebo, 52. ³⁴ The sons of the other Elam, 1,254. ³⁵ The sons of Harim, 320. ³⁶ The sons of Jericho, 345. ³⁷ The sons of Lod, Hadid, and Ono, 721. ³⁸ The sons of Senaah, 3,930.

³⁹ The priests: the sons of Jedaiah, namely the house of Jeshua, 973. ⁴⁰ The sons of Immer, 1,052. ⁴¹ The sons of Pashhur, 1,247. ⁴² The sons of Harim, 1,017.

⁴³ The Levites: the sons of Jeshua, namely of Kadmiel of the sons of Hodevah, 74. ⁴⁴ The singers: the sons of Asaph, 148. ⁴⁵ The gatekeepers: the sons of Shallum, the sons of Ater, the sons of Talmon, the sons of Akkub, the sons of Hatita, the sons of Shobai, 138.

⁴⁶ The temple servants: the sons of Ziha, the sons of Hasupha, the sons of Tabbaoth, ⁴⁷ the sons of Keros, the sons of Sia, the sons of Padon, ⁴⁸ the sons of Lebana, the sons of Hagaba, the sons of Shalmai, ⁴⁹ the sons of Hanan, the sons of Giddel, the sons of Gahar, ⁵⁰ the sons of Reaiah, the sons of Rezin, the sons of Nekoda, ⁵¹ the sons of Gazzam, the sons of Uzza, the sons of Paseah, ⁵² the sons of Besai, the sons of Meunim, the sons of Nephushesim, ⁵³ the sons of Bakbuk, the sons of Hakupha, the sons of Harhur, ⁵⁴ the sons of Bazlith, the

sons of Mehida, the sons of Harsha, ⁵⁵ the sons of Barkos, the sons of Sisera, the sons of Temah, ⁵⁶ the sons of Neziah, the sons of Hatipha.

⁵⁷ The sons of Solomon's servants: the sons of Sotai, the sons of Sophereth, the sons of Perida, ⁵⁸ the sons of Jaala, the sons of Darkon, the sons of Giddel, ⁵⁹ the sons of Shephatiah, the sons of Hattil, the sons of Pochereth-hazzebaim, the sons of Amon.

⁶⁰ All the temple servants and the sons of Solomon's servants were 392.

⁶¹ The following were those who came up from Tel-melah, Tel-harsha, Cherub, Addon, and Immer, but they could not prove their fathers' houses nor their descent, whether they belonged to Israel: ⁶² the sons of Delaiah, the sons of Tobiah, the sons of Nekoda, 642. ⁶³ Also, of the priests: the sons of Hobaiah, the sons of Hakkoz, the sons of Barzillai (who had taken a wife of the daughters of Barzillai the Gileadite and was called by their name). ⁶⁴ These sought their registration among those enrolled in the genealogies, but it was not found there, so they were excluded from the priesthood as unclean. ⁶⁵ The governor told them that they were not to partake of the most holy food until a priest with Urim and Thummim should arise.

Totals of People and Gifts

⁶⁶ The whole assembly together was 42,360, ⁶⁷ besides their male and female servants, of whom there were 7,337. And they had 245 singers, male and female. ⁶⁸ Their horses were 736, their mules 245,¹ ⁶⁹ their camels 435, and their donkeys 6,720.

⁷⁰ Now some of the heads of fathers' houses gave to the work. The governor gave to the treasury 1,000 darics² of gold, 50 basins, 30 priests' garments and 500 minas³ of silver.⁴ ⁷¹ And some of the heads of fathers' houses gave into the treasury of the work 20,000 darics of gold and 2,200 minas of silver. ⁷² And what the rest of the people gave was 20,000 darics of gold, 2,000 minas of silver, and 67 priests' garments.

⁷³ So the priests, the Levites, the gatekeepers, the singers, some of the people, the temple servants, and all Israel, lived in their towns.

And when the seventh month had come, the people of Israel were in their towns.

Ezra Reads the Law

8

And all the people gathered as one man into the square before the Water Gate. And they told Ezra the scribe to bring the Book of the Law of Moses that the Lord had commanded Israel. ² So Ezra the priest brought

---

¹ Compare Ezra 2:66 and the margins of some Hebrew manuscripts; Hebrew lacks *Their horses... 245* ² A *daric* was a coin weighing about 1/4 ounce or 8.5 grams ³ A *mina* was about 1 1/4 pounds or 0.6 kilogram ⁴ Probable reading; Hebrew lacks *minas of silver*

the Law before the assembly, both men and women and all who could understand what they heard, on the first day of the seventh month. ³ And he read from it facing the square before the Water Gate from early morning until midday, in the presence of the men and the women and those who could understand. And the ears of all the people were attentive to the Book of the Law. ⁴ And Ezra the scribe stood on a wooden platform that they had made for the purpose. And beside him stood Mattithiah, Shema, Anaiah, Uriah, Hilkiah, and Maaseiah on his right hand, and Pedaiah, Mishael, Malchijah, Hashum, Hashbaddanah, Zechariah, and Meshullam on his left hand. ⁵ And Ezra opened the book in the sight of all the people, for he was above all the people, and as he opened it all the people stood. ⁶ And Ezra blessed the Lord, the great God, and all the people answered, "Amen, Amen," lifting up their hands. And they bowed their heads and worshiped the Lord with their faces to the ground. ⁷ Also Jeshua, Bani, Sherebiah, Jamin, Akkub, Shabbethai, Hodiah, Maaseiah, Kelita, Azariah, Jozabad, Hanan, Pelaiah, the Levites,[1] helped the people to understand the Law, while the people remained in their places. ⁸ They read from the book, from the Law of God, clearly,[2] and they gave the sense, so that the people understood the reading.

This Day Is Holy

⁹ And Nehemiah, who was the governor, and Ezra the priest and scribe, and the Levites who taught the people said to all the people, "This day is holy to the Lord your God; do not mourn or weep." For all the people wept as they heard the words of the Law. ¹⁰ Then he said to them, "Go your way. Eat the fat and drink sweet wine and send portions to anyone who has nothing ready, for this day is holy to our Lord. And do not be grieved, for the joy of the Lord is your strength." ¹¹ So the Levites calmed all the people, saying, "Be quiet, for this day is holy; do not be grieved." ¹² And all the people went their way to eat and drink and to send portions and to make great rejoicing, because they had understood the words that were declared to them.

Feast of Booths Celebrated

¹³ On the second day the heads of fathers' houses of all the people, with the priests and the Levites, came together to Ezra the scribe in order to study the words of the Law. ¹⁴ And they found it written in the Law that the Lord had commanded by Moses that the people of Israel should dwell in booths[3] during the feast of the seventh month, ¹⁵ and that they should proclaim it and publish it in all their towns and in Jerusalem, "Go out to the hills and

---

[1] Vulgate; Hebrew *and the Levites* [2] Or *with interpretation*, or *paragraph by paragraph* [3] Or *temporary shelters*

bring branches of olive, wild olive, myrtle, palm, and other leafy trees to make booths, as it is written." ⁱ⁶ So the people went out and brought them and made booths for themselves, each on his roof, and in their courts and in the courts of the house of God, and in the square at the Water Gate and in the square at the Gate of Ephraim. ¹⁷ And all the assembly of those who had returned from the captivity made booths and lived in the booths, for from the days of Jeshua the son of Nun to that day the people of Israel had not done so. And there was very great rejoicing. ¹⁸ And day by day, from the first day to the last day, he read from the Book of the Law of God. They kept the feast seven days, and on the eighth day there was a solemn assembly, according to the rule.

The People of Israel Confess Their Sin

9 Now on the twenty-fourth day of this month the people of Israel were assembled with fasting and in sackcloth, and with earth on their heads. ² And the Israelites¹ separated themselves from all foreigners and stood and confessed their sins and the iniquities of their fathers. ³ And they stood up in their place and read from the Book of the Law of the Lord their God for a quarter of the day; for another quarter of it they made confession and worshiped the Lord their God. ⁴ On the stairs of the Levites stood Jeshua, Bani, Kadmiel, Shebaniah, Bunni, Sherebiah, Bani, and Chenani; and they cried with a loud voice to the Lord their God. ⁵ Then the Levites, Jeshua, Kadmiel, Bani, Hashabneiah, Sherebiah, Hodiah, Shebaniah, and Pethahiah, said, "Stand up and bless the Lord your God from everlasting to everlasting. Blessed be your glorious name, which is exalted above all blessing and praise.

⁶ ² "You are the Lord, you alone. You have made heaven, the heaven of heavens, with all their host, the earth and all that is on it, the seas and all that is in them; and you preserve all of them; and the host of heaven worships you. ⁷ You are the Lord, the God who chose Abram and brought him out of Ur of the Chaldeans and gave him the name Abraham. ⁸ You found his heart faithful before you, and made with him the covenant to give to his offspring the land of the Canaanite, the Hittite, the Amorite, the Perizzite, the Jebusite, and the Girgashite. And you have kept your promise, for you are righteous.

⁹ "And you saw the affliction of our fathers in Egypt and heard their cry at the Red Sea, ¹⁰ and performed signs and wonders against Pharaoh and all his servants and all the people of his land, for you knew that they acted arrogantly against our fathers. And you made a name for yourself, as it is to this day. ¹¹ And you divided the sea before them, so that they went through the

---

¹ Hebrew *the offspring of Israel* ² Septuagint adds *And Ezra said*

midst of the sea on dry land, and you cast their pursuers into the depths, as a stone into mighty waters. ¹²By a pillar of cloud you led them in the day, and by a pillar of fire in the night to light for them the way in which they should go. ¹³You came down on Mount Sinai and spoke with them from heaven and gave them right rules and true laws, good statutes and commandments, ¹⁴and you made known to them your holy Sabbath and commanded them commandments and statutes and a law by Moses your servant. ¹⁵You gave them bread from heaven for their hunger and brought water for them out of the rock for their thirst, and you told them to go in to possess the land that you had sworn to give them.

¹⁶"But they and our fathers acted presumptuously and stiffened their neck and did not obey your commandments. ¹⁷They refused to obey and were not mindful of the wonders that you performed among them, but they stiffened their neck and appointed a leader to return to their slavery in Egypt.[1] But you are a God ready to forgive, gracious and merciful, slow to anger and abounding in steadfast love, and did not forsake them. ¹⁸Even when they had made for themselves a golden[2] calf and said, 'This is your God who brought you up out of Egypt,' and had committed great blasphemies, ¹⁹you in your great mercies did not forsake them in the wilderness. The pillar of cloud to lead them in the way did not depart from them by day, nor the pillar of fire by night to light for them the way by which they should go. ²⁰You gave your good Spirit to instruct them and did not withhold your manna from their mouth and gave them water for their thirst. ²¹Forty years you sustained them in the wilderness, and they lacked nothing. Their clothes did not wear out and their feet did not swell.

²²"And you gave them kingdoms and peoples and allotted to them every corner. So they took possession of the land of Sihon king of Heshbon and the land of Og king of Bashan. ²³You multiplied their children as the stars of heaven, and you brought them into the land that you had told their fathers to enter and possess. ²⁴So the descendants went in and possessed the land, and you subdued before them the inhabitants of the land, the Canaanites, and gave them into their hand, with their kings and the peoples of the land, that they might do with them as they would. ²⁵And they captured fortified cities and a rich land, and took possession of houses full of all good things, cisterns already hewn, vineyards, olive orchards and fruit trees in abundance. So they ate and were filled and became fat and delighted themselves in your great goodness.

²⁶"Nevertheless, they were disobedient and rebelled against you and cast your law behind their back and killed your prophets, who had warned them in order to turn them back to you, and they committed great blasphemies.

---

[1] Some Hebrew manuscripts; many Hebrew manuscripts *and in their rebellion appointed a leader to return to their slavery* [2] Hebrew *metal*

⁲⁷ Therefore you gave them into the hand of their enemies, who made them suffer. And in the time of their suffering they cried out to you and you heard them from heaven, and according to your great mercies you gave them saviors who saved them from the hand of their enemies. ²⁸ But after they had rest they did evil again before you, and you abandoned them to the hand of their enemies, so that they had dominion over them. Yet when they turned and cried to you, you heard from heaven, and many times you delivered them according to your mercies. ²⁹ And you warned them in order to turn them back to your law. Yet they acted presumptuously and did not obey your commandments, but sinned against your rules, which if a person does them, he shall live by them, and they turned a stubborn shoulder and stiffened their neck and would not obey. ³⁰ Many years you bore with them and warned them by your Spirit through your prophets. Yet they would not give ear. Therefore you gave them into the hand of the peoples of the lands. ³¹ Nevertheless, in your great mercies you did not make an end of them or forsake them, for you are a gracious and merciful God.

³² "Now, therefore, our God, the great, the mighty, and the awesome God, who keeps covenant and steadfast love, let not all the hardship seem little to you that has come upon us, upon our kings, our princes, our priests, our prophets, our fathers, and all your people, since the time of the kings of Assyria until this day. ³³ Yet you have been righteous in all that has come upon us, for you have dealt faithfully and we have acted wickedly. ³⁴ Our kings, our princes, our priests, and our fathers have not kept your law or paid attention to your commandments and your warnings that you gave them. ³⁵ Even in their own kingdom, and amid your great goodness that you gave them, and in the large and rich land that you set before them, they did not serve you or turn from their wicked works. ³⁶ Behold, we are slaves this day; in the land that you gave to our fathers to enjoy its fruit and its good gifts, behold, we are slaves. ³⁷ And its rich yield goes to the kings whom you have set over us because of our sins. They rule over our bodies and over our livestock as they please, and we are in great distress.

³⁸ [1] "Because of all this we make a firm covenant in writing; on the sealed document are the names of[2] our princes, our Levites, and our priests.

The People Who Sealed the Covenant

10 [3] "On the seals are the names of[4] Nehemiah the governor, the son of Hacaliah, Zedekiah, ² Seraiah, Azariah, Jeremiah, ³ Pashhur, Amariah, Malchijah, ⁴ Hattush, Shebaniah, Malluch, ⁵ Harim, Meremoth,

[1] Ch 10:1 in Hebrew [2] Hebrew lacks *the names of* [3] Ch 10:2 in Hebrew [4] Hebrew lacks *the names of*

Obadiah, ⁶ Daniel, Ginnethon, Baruch, ⁷ Meshullam, Abijah, Mijamin, ⁸ Maaziah, Bilgai, Shemaiah; these are the priests. ⁹ And the Levites: Jeshua the son of Azaniah, Binnui of the sons of Henadad, Kadmiel; ¹⁰ and their brothers, Shebaniah, Hodiah, Kelita, Pelaiah, Hanan, ¹¹ Mica, Rehob, Hashabiah, ¹² Zaccur, Sherebiah, Shebaniah, ¹³ Hodiah, Bani, Beninu. ¹⁴ The chiefs of the people: Parosh, Pahath-moab, Elam, Zattu, Bani, ¹⁵ Bunni, Azgad, Bebai, ¹⁶ Adonijah, Bigvai, Adin, ¹⁷ Ater, Hezekiah, Azzur, ¹⁸ Hodiah, Hashum, Bezai, ¹⁹ Hariph, Anathoth, Nebai, ²⁰ Magpiash, Meshullam, Hezir, ²¹ Meshezabel, Zadok, Jaddua, ²² Pelatiah, Hanan, Anaiah, ²³ Hoshea, Hananiah, Hasshub, ²⁴ Hallohesh, Pilha, Shobek, ²⁵ Rehum, Hashabnah, Maaseiah, ²⁶ Ahiah, Hanan, Anan, ²⁷ Malluch, Harim, Baanah.

The Obligations of the Covenant

²⁸ "The rest of the people, the priests, the Levites, the gatekeepers, the singers, the temple servants, and all who have separated themselves from the peoples of the lands to the Law of God, their wives, their sons, their daughters, all who have knowledge and understanding, ²⁹ join with their brothers, their nobles, and enter into a curse and an oath to walk in God's Law that was given by Moses the servant of God, and to observe and do all the commandments of the LORD our Lord and his rules and his statutes. ³⁰ We will not give our daughters to the peoples of the land or take their daughters for our sons. ³¹ And if the peoples of the land bring in goods or any grain on the Sabbath day to sell, we will not buy from them on the Sabbath or on a holy day. And we will forgo the crops of the seventh year and the exaction of every debt.

³² "We also take on ourselves the obligation to give yearly a third part of a shekel[1] for the service of the house of our God: ³³ for the showbread, the regular grain offering, the regular burnt offering, the Sabbaths, the new moons, the appointed feasts, the holy things, and the sin offerings to make atonement for Israel, and for all the work of the house of our God. ³⁴ We, the priests, the Levites, and the people, have likewise cast lots for the wood offering, to bring it into the house of our God, according to our fathers' houses, at times appointed, year by year, to burn on the altar of the LORD our God, as it is written in the Law. ³⁵ We obligate ourselves to bring the firstfruits of our ground and the firstfruits of all fruit of every tree, year by year, to the house of the LORD; ³⁶ also to bring to the house of our God, to the priests who minister in the house of our God, the firstborn of our sons and of our cattle, as it is written in the Law, and the firstborn of our herds and of our flocks; ³⁷ and to bring the first of our dough, and our contributions, the fruit of every tree, the

---

[1] A *shekel* was about 2/5 ounce or 11 grams

wine and the oil, to the priests, to the chambers of the house of our God; and to bring to the Levites the tithes from our ground, for it is the Levites who collect the tithes in all our towns where we labor. ³⁸ And the priest, the son of Aaron, shall be with the Levites when the Levites receive the tithes. And the Levites shall bring up the tithe of the tithes to the house of our God, to the chambers of the storehouse. ³⁹ For the people of Israel and the sons of Levi shall bring the contribution of grain, wine, and oil to the chambers, where the vessels of the sanctuary are, as well as the priests who minister, and the gatekeepers and the singers. We will not neglect the house of our God."

The Leaders in Jerusalem

11 Now the leaders of the people lived in Jerusalem. And the rest of the people cast lots to bring one out of ten to live in Jerusalem the holy city, while nine out of ten[1] remained in the other towns. ² And the people blessed all the men who willingly offered to live in Jerusalem.

³ These are the chiefs of the province who lived in Jerusalem; but in the towns of Judah everyone lived on his property in their towns: Israel, the priests, the Levites, the temple servants, and the descendants of Solomon's servants. ⁴ And in Jerusalem lived certain of the sons of Judah and of the sons of Benjamin. Of the sons of Judah: Athaiah the son of Uzziah, son of Zechariah, son of Amariah, son of Shephatiah, son of Mahalalel, of the sons of Perez; ⁵ and Maaseiah the son of Baruch, son of Col-hozeh, son of Hazaiah, son of Adaiah, son of Joiarib, son of Zechariah, son of the Shilonite. ⁶ All the sons of Perez who lived in Jerusalem were 468 valiant men.

⁷ And these are the sons of Benjamin: Sallu the son of Meshullam, son of Joed, son of Pedaiah, son of Kolaiah, son of Maaseiah, son of Ithiel, son of Jeshaiah, ⁸ and his brothers, men of valor, 928.[2] ⁹ Joel the son of Zichri was their overseer; and Judah the son of Hassenuah was second over the city.

¹⁰ Of the priests: Jedaiah the son of Joiarib, Jachin, ¹¹ Seraiah the son of Hilkiah, son of Meshullam, son of Zadok, son of Meraioth, son of Ahitub, ruler of the house of God, ¹² and their brothers who did the work of the house, 822; and Adaiah the son of Jeroham, son of Pelaliah, son of Amzi, son of Zechariah, son of Pashhur, son of Malchijah, ¹³ and his brothers, heads of fathers' houses, 242; and Amashsai, the son of Azarel, son of Ahzai, son of Meshillemoth, son of Immer, ¹⁴ and their brothers, mighty men of valor, 128; their overseer was Zabdiel the son of Haggedolim.

¹⁵ And of the Levites: Shemaiah the son of Hasshub, son of Azrikam, son of Hashabiah, son of Bunni; ¹⁶ and Shabbethai and Jozabad, of the chiefs

[1] Hebrew *nine hands* [2] Compare Septuagint; Hebrew *Jeshaiah, and after him Gabbai, Sallai, 928*

of the Levites, who were over the outside work of the house of God; ¹⁷ and Mattaniah the son of Mica, son of Zabdi, son of Asaph, who was the leader of the praise,¹ who gave thanks, and Bakbukiah, the second among his brothers; and Abda the son of Shammua, son of Galal, son of Jeduthun. ¹⁸ All the Levites in the holy city were 284.

¹⁹ The gatekeepers, Akkub, Talmon and their brothers, who kept watch at the gates, were 172. ²⁰ And the rest of Israel, and of the priests and the Levites, were in all the towns of Judah, every one in his inheritance. ²¹ But the temple servants lived on Ophel; and Ziha and Gishpa were over the temple servants.

²² The overseer of the Levites in Jerusalem was Uzzi the son of Bani, son of Hashabiah, son of Mattaniah, son of Mica, of the sons of Asaph, the singers, over the work of the house of God. ²³ For there was a command from the king concerning them, and a fixed provision for the singers, as every day required. ²⁴ And Pethahiah the son of Meshezabel, of the sons of Zerah the son of Judah, was at the king's side² in all matters concerning the people.

Villages Outside Jerusalem

²⁵ And as for the villages, with their fields, some of the people of Judah lived in Kiriath-arba and its villages, and in Dibon and its villages, and in Jekabzeel and its villages, ²⁶ and in Jeshua and in Moladah and Beth-pelet, ²⁷ in Hazar-shual, in Beersheba and its villages, ²⁸ in Ziklag, in Meconah and its villages, ²⁹ in En-rimmon, in Zorah, in Jarmuth, ³⁰ Zanoah, Adullam, and their villages, Lachish and its fields, and Azekah and its villages. So they encamped from Beersheba to the Valley of Hinnom. ³¹ The people of Benjamin also lived from Geba onward, at Michmash, Aija, Bethel and its villages, ³² Anathoth, Nob, Ananiah, ³³ Hazor, Ramah, Gittaim, ³⁴ Hadid, Zeboim, Neballat, ³⁵ Lod, and Ono, the valley of craftsmen. ³⁶ And certain divisions of the Levites in Judah were assigned to Benjamin.

Priests and Levites

12 These are the priests and the Levites who came up with Zerubbabel the son of Shealtiel, and Jeshua: Seraiah, Jeremiah, Ezra, ² Amariah, Malluch, Hattush, ³ Shecaniah, Rehum, Meremoth, ⁴ Iddo, Ginnethoi, Abijah, ⁵ Mijamin, Maadiah, Bilgah, ⁶ Shemaiah, Joiarib, Jedaiah, ⁷ Sallu, Amok, Hilkiah, Jedaiah. These were the chiefs of the priests and of their brothers in the days of Jeshua.

⁸ And the Levites: Jeshua, Binnui, Kadmiel, Sherebiah, Judah, and Mattaniah, who with his brothers was in charge of the songs of thanksgiving.

¹ Compare Septuagint, Vulgate; Hebrew *beginning* ² Hebrew *hand*

⁹ And Bakbukiah and Unni and their brothers stood opposite them in the service. ¹⁰ And Jeshua was the father of Joiakim, Joiakim the father of Eliashib, Eliashib the father of Joiada, ¹¹ Joiada the father of Jonathan, and Jonathan the father of Jaddua.

¹² And in the days of Joiakim were priests, heads of fathers' houses: of Seraiah, Meraiah; of Jeremiah, Hananiah; ¹³ of Ezra, Meshullam; of Amariah, Jehohanan; ¹⁴ of Malluchi, Jonathan; of Shebaniah, Joseph; ¹⁵ of Harim, Adna; of Meraioth, Helkai; ¹⁶ of Iddo, Zechariah; of Ginnethon, Meshullam; ¹⁷ of Abijah, Zichri; of Miniamin, of Moadiah, Piltai; ¹⁸ of Bilgah, Shammua; of Shemaiah, Jehonathan; ¹⁹ of Joiarib, Mattenai; of Jedaiah, Uzzi; ²⁰ of Sallai, Kallai; of Amok, Eber; ²¹ of Hilkiah, Hashabiah; of Jedaiah, Nethanel.

²² In the days of Eliashib, Joiada, Johanan, and Jaddua, the Levites were recorded as heads of fathers' houses; so too were the priests in the reign of Darius the Persian. ²³ As for the sons of Levi, their heads of fathers' houses were written in the Book of the Chronicles until the days of Johanan the son of Eliashib. ²⁴ And the chiefs of the Levites: Hashabiah, Sherebiah, and Jeshua the son of Kadmiel, with their brothers who stood opposite them, to praise and to give thanks, according to the commandment of David the man of God, watch by watch. ²⁵ Mattaniah, Bakbukiah, Obadiah, Meshullam, Talmon, and Akkub were gatekeepers standing guard at the storehouses of the gates. ²⁶ These were in the days of Joiakim the son of Jeshua son of Jozadak, and in the days of Nehemiah the governor and of Ezra, the priest and scribe.

Dedication of the Wall

²⁷ And at the dedication of the wall of Jerusalem they sought the Levites in all their places, to bring them to Jerusalem to celebrate the dedication with gladness, with thanksgivings and with singing, with cymbals, harps, and lyres. ²⁸ And the sons of the singers gathered together from the district surrounding Jerusalem and from the villages of the Netophathites; ²⁹ also from Beth-gilgal and from the region of Geba and Azmaveth, for the singers had built for themselves villages around Jerusalem. ³⁰ And the priests and the Levites purified themselves, and they purified the people and the gates and the wall.

³¹ Then I brought the leaders of Judah up onto the wall and appointed two great choirs that gave thanks. One went to the south on the wall to the Dung Gate. ³² And after them went Hoshaiah and half of the leaders of Judah, ³³ and Azariah, Ezra, Meshullam, ³⁴ Judah, Benjamin, Shemaiah, and Jeremiah, ³⁵ and certain of the priests' sons with trumpets: Zechariah the son of Jonathan, son of Shemaiah, son of Mattaniah, son of Micaiah, son of

Zaccur, son of Asaph; ³⁶ and his relatives, Shemaiah, Azarel, Milalai, Gilalai, Maai, Nethanel, Judah, and Hanani, with the musical instruments of David the man of God. And Ezra the scribe went before them. ³⁷ At the Fountain Gate they went up straight before them by the stairs of the city of David, at the ascent of the wall, above the house of David, to the Water Gate on the east.

³⁸ The other choir of those who gave thanks went to the north, and I followed them with half of the people, on the wall, above the Tower of the Ovens, to the Broad Wall, ³⁹ and above the Gate of Ephraim, and by the Gate of Yeshanah,¹ and by the Fish Gate and the Tower of Hananel and the Tower of the Hundred, to the Sheep Gate; and they came to a halt at the Gate of the Guard. ⁴⁰ So both choirs of those who gave thanks stood in the house of God, and I and half of the officials with me; ⁴¹ and the priests Eliakim, Maaseiah, Miniamin, Micaiah, Elioenai, Zechariah, and Hananiah, with trumpets; ⁴² and Maaseiah, Shemaiah, Eleazar, Uzzi, Jehohanan, Malchijah, Elam, and Ezer. And the singers sang with Jezrahiah as their leader. ⁴³ And they offered great sacrifices that day and rejoiced, for God had made them rejoice with great joy; the women and children also rejoiced. And the joy of Jerusalem was heard far away.

Service at the Temple

⁴⁴ On that day men were appointed over the storerooms, the contributions, the firstfruits, and the tithes, to gather into them the portions required by the Law for the priests and for the Levites according to the fields of the towns, for Judah rejoiced over the priests and the Levites who ministered. ⁴⁵ And they performed the service of their God and the service of purification, as did the singers and the gatekeepers, according to the command of David and his son Solomon. ⁴⁶ For long ago in the days of David and Asaph there were directors of the singers, and there were songs² of praise and thanksgiving to God. ⁴⁷ And all Israel in the days of Zerubbabel and in the days of Nehemiah gave the daily portions for the singers and the gatekeepers; and they set apart that which was for the Levites; and the Levites set apart that which was for the sons of Aaron.

Nehemiah's Final Reforms

13 On that day they read from the Book of Moses in the hearing of the people. And in it was found written that no Ammonite or Moabite should ever enter the assembly of God, ² for they did not meet the people of Israel with bread and water, but hired Balaam against them to curse

¹ Or *of the old city* ² Or *leaders*

them—yet our God turned the curse into a blessing. ³ As soon as the people heard the law, they separated from Israel all those of foreign descent.

⁴ Now before this, Eliashib the priest, who was appointed over the chambers of the house of our God, and who was related to Tobiah, ⁵ prepared for Tobiah a large chamber where they had previously put the grain offering, the frankincense, the vessels, and the tithes of grain, wine, and oil, which were given by commandment to the Levites, singers, and gatekeepers, and the contributions for the priests. ⁶ While this was taking place, I was not in Jerusalem, for in the thirty-second year of Artaxerxes king of Babylon I went to the king. And after some time I asked leave of the king ⁷ and came to Jerusalem, and I then discovered the evil that Eliashib had done for Tobiah, preparing for him a chamber in the courts of the house of God. ⁸ And I was very angry, and I threw all the household furniture of Tobiah out of the chamber. ⁹ Then I gave orders, and they cleansed the chambers, and I brought back there the vessels of the house of God, with the grain offering and the frankincense.

¹⁰ I also found out that the portions of the Levites had not been given to them, so that the Levites and the singers, who did the work, had fled each to his field. ¹¹ So I confronted the officials and said, "Why is the house of God forsaken?" And I gathered them together and set them in their stations. ¹² Then all Judah brought the tithe of the grain, wine, and oil into the storehouses. ¹³ And I appointed as treasurers over the storehouses Shelemiah the priest, Zadok the scribe, and Pedaiah of the Levites, and as their assistant Hanan the son of Zaccur, son of Mattaniah, for they were considered reliable, and their duty was to distribute to their brothers. ¹⁴ Remember me, O my God, concerning this, and do not wipe out my good deeds that I have done for the house of my God and for his service.

¹⁵ In those days I saw in Judah people treading winepresses on the Sabbath, and bringing in heaps of grain and loading them on donkeys, and also wine, grapes, figs, and all kinds of loads, which they brought into Jerusalem on the Sabbath day. And I warned them on the day when they sold food. ¹⁶ Tyrians also, who lived in the city, brought in fish and all kinds of goods and sold them on the Sabbath to the people of Judah, in Jerusalem itself! ¹⁷ Then I confronted the nobles of Judah and said to them, "What is this evil thing that you are doing, profaning the Sabbath day? ¹⁸ Did not your fathers act in this way, and did not our God bring all this disaster[1] on us and on this city? Now you are bringing more wrath on Israel by profaning the Sabbath."

¹⁹ As soon as it began to grow dark at the gates of Jerusalem before the Sabbath, I commanded that the doors should be shut and gave orders that

---

[1] The Hebrew word can mean *evil*, *harm*, or *disaster*, depending on the context

they should not be opened until after the Sabbath. And I stationed some of my servants at the gates, that no load might be brought in on the Sabbath day. ²⁰ Then the merchants and sellers of all kinds of wares lodged outside Jerusalem once or twice. ²¹ But I warned them and said to them, "Why do you lodge outside the wall? If you do so again, I will lay hands on you." From that time on they did not come on the Sabbath. ²² Then I commanded the Levites that they should purify themselves and come and guard the gates, to keep the Sabbath day holy. Remember this also in my favor, O my God, and spare me according to the greatness of your steadfast love.

²³ In those days also I saw the Jews who had married women of Ashdod, Ammon, and Moab. ²⁴ And half of their children spoke the language of Ashdod, and they could not speak the language of Judah, but only the language of each people. ²⁵ And I confronted them and cursed them and beat some of them and pulled out their hair. And I made them take an oath in the name of God, saying, "You shall not give your daughters to their sons, or take their daughters for your sons or for yourselves. ²⁶ Did not Solomon king of Israel sin on account of such women? Among the many nations there was no king like him, and he was beloved by his God, and God made him king over all Israel. Nevertheless, foreign women made even him to sin. ²⁷ Shall we then listen to you and do all this great evil and act treacherously against our God by marrying foreign women?"

²⁸ And one of the sons of Jehoiada, the son of Eliashib the high priest, was the son-in-law of Sanballat the Horonite. Therefore I chased him from me. ²⁹ Remember them, O my God, because they have desecrated the priesthood and the covenant of the priesthood and the Levites.

³⁰ Thus I cleansed them from everything foreign, and I established the duties of the priests and Levites, each in his work; ³¹ and I provided for the wood offering at appointed times, and for the firstfruits.

Remember me, O my God, for good.

ESTHER

The King's Banquets

1 Now in the days of Ahasuerus, the Ahasuerus who reigned from India to Ethiopia over 127 provinces, ² in those days when King Ahasuerus sat on his royal throne in Susa, the citadel, ³ in the third year of his reign he gave a feast for all his officials and servants. The army of Persia and Media and the nobles and governors of the provinces were before him, ⁴ while he showed the riches of his royal glory and the splendor and pomp of his greatness for many days, 180 days. ⁵ And when these days were completed, the king gave for all the people present in Susa the citadel, both great and small, a feast lasting for seven days in the court of the garden of the king's palace. ⁶ There were white cotton curtains and violet hangings fastened with cords of fine linen and purple to silver rods[1] and marble pillars, and also couches of gold and silver on a mosaic pavement of porphyry, marble, mother-of-pearl, and precious stones. ⁷ Drinks were served in golden vessels, vessels of different kinds, and the royal wine was lavished according to the bounty of the king. ⁸ And drinking was according to this edict: "There is no compulsion." For the king had given orders to all the staff of his palace to do as each man desired. ⁹ Queen Vashti also gave a feast for the women in the palace that belonged to King Ahasuerus.

Queen Vashti's Refusal

¹⁰ On the seventh day, when the heart of the king was merry with wine, he commanded Mehuman, Biztha, Harbona, Bigtha and Abagtha, Zethar and Carkas, the seven eunuchs who served in the presence of King Ahasuerus, ¹¹ to bring Queen Vashti before the king with her royal crown,[2] in order to show the peoples and the princes her beauty, for she was lovely to look at. ¹² But Queen Vashti refused to come at the king's command delivered by the eunuchs. At this the king became enraged, and his anger burned within him.

¹³ Then the king said to the wise men who knew the times (for this was the king's procedure toward all who were versed in law and judgment, ¹⁴ the men next to him being Carshena, Shethar, Admatha, Tarshish, Meres,

---
[1] Or *rings* [2] Or *headdress*

Marsena, and Memucan, the seven princes of Persia and Media, who saw the king's face, and sat first in the kingdom): ¹⁵ "According to the law, what is to be done to Queen Vashti, because she has not performed the command of King Ahasuerus delivered by the eunuchs?" ¹⁶ Then Memucan said in the presence of the king and the officials, "Not only against the king has Queen Vashti done wrong, but also against all the officials and all the peoples who are in all the provinces of King Ahasuerus. ¹⁷ For the queen's behavior will be made known to all women, causing them to look at their husbands with contempt,[1] since they will say, 'King Ahasuerus commanded Queen Vashti to be brought before him, and she did not come.' ¹⁸ This very day the noble women of Persia and Media who have heard of the queen's behavior will say the same to all the king's officials, and there will be contempt and wrath in plenty. ¹⁹ If it please the king, let a royal order go out from him, and let it be written among the laws of the Persians and the Medes so that it may not be repealed, that Vashti is never again to come before King Ahasuerus. And let the king give her royal position to another who is better than she. ²⁰ So when the decree made by the king is proclaimed throughout all his kingdom, for it is vast, all women will give honor to their husbands, high and low alike."

²¹ This advice pleased the king and the princes, and the king did as Memucan proposed. ²² He sent letters to all the royal provinces, to every province in its own script and to every people in its own language, that every man be master in his own household and speak according to the language of his people.

Esther Chosen Queen

2 After these things, when the anger of King Ahasuerus had abated, he remembered Vashti and what she had done and what had been decreed against her. ² Then the king's young men who attended him said, "Let beautiful young virgins be sought out for the king. ³ And let the king appoint officers in all the provinces of his kingdom to gather all the beautiful young virgins to the harem in Susa the citadel, under custody of Hegai, the king's eunuch, who is in charge of the women. Let their cosmetics be given them. ⁴ And let the young woman who pleases the king[2] be queen instead of Vashti." This pleased the king, and he did so.

⁵ Now there was a Jew in Susa the citadel whose name was Mordecai, the son of Jair, son of Shimei, son of Kish, a Benjaminite, ⁶ who had been carried away from Jerusalem among the captives carried away with Jeconiah king of Judah, whom Nebuchadnezzar king of Babylon had carried away. ⁷ He was bringing up Hadassah, that is Esther, the daughter of his uncle, for she had

---

[1] Hebrew *to disdain their husbands in their eyes* [2] Hebrew *who is good in the eyes of the king*

neither father nor mother. The young woman had a beautiful figure and was lovely to look at, and when her father and her mother died, Mordecai took her as his own daughter. [8] So when the king's order and his edict were proclaimed, and when many young women were gathered in Susa the citadel in custody of Hegai, Esther also was taken into the king's palace and put in custody of Hegai, who had charge of the women. [9] And the young woman pleased him and won his favor. And he quickly provided her with her cosmetics and her portion of food, and with seven chosen young women from the king's palace, and advanced her and her young women to the best place in the harem. [10] Esther had not made known her people or kindred, for Mordecai had commanded her not to make it known. [11] And every day Mordecai walked in front of the court of the harem to learn how Esther was and what was happening to her.

[12] Now when the turn came for each young woman to go in to King Ahasuerus, after being twelve months under the regulations for the women, since this was the regular period of their beautifying, six months with oil of myrrh and six months with spices and ointments for women— [13] when the young woman went in to the king in this way, she was given whatever she desired to take with her from the harem to the king's palace. [14] In the evening she would go in, and in the morning she would return to the second harem in custody of Shaashgaz, the king's eunuch, who was in charge of the concubines. She would not go in to the king again, unless the king delighted in her and she was summoned by name.

[15] When the turn came for Esther the daughter of Abihail the uncle of Mordecai, who had taken her as his own daughter, to go in to the king, she asked for nothing except what Hegai the king's eunuch, who had charge of the women, advised. Now Esther was winning favor in the eyes of all who saw her. [16] And when Esther was taken to King Ahasuerus, into his royal palace, in the tenth month, which is the month of Tebeth, in the seventh year of his reign, [17] the king loved Esther more than all the women, and she won grace and favor in his sight more than all the virgins, so that he set the royal crown[1] on her head and made her queen instead of Vashti. [18] Then the king gave a great feast for all his officials and servants; it was Esther's feast. He also granted a remission of taxes to the provinces and gave gifts with royal generosity.

Mordecai Discovers a Plot

[19] Now when the virgins were gathered together the second time, Mordecai was sitting at the king's gate. [20] Esther had not made known her kindred or her

[1] Or *headdress*

people, as Mordecai had commanded her, for Esther obeyed Mordecai just as when she was brought up by him. ²¹ In those days, as Mordecai was sitting at the king's gate, Bigthan and Teresh, two of the king's eunuchs, who guarded the threshold, became angry and sought to lay hands on King Ahasuerus. ²² And this came to the knowledge of Mordecai, and he told it to Queen Esther, and Esther told the king in the name of Mordecai. ²³ When the affair was investigated and found to be so, the men were both hanged on the gallows.[1] And it was recorded in the book of the chronicles in the presence of the king.

Haman Plots Against the Jews

3 After these things King Ahasuerus promoted Haman the Agagite, the son of Hammedatha, and advanced him and set his throne above all the officials who were with him. ² And all the king's servants who were at the king's gate bowed down and paid homage to Haman, for the king had so commanded concerning him. But Mordecai did not bow down or pay homage. ³ Then the king's servants who were at the king's gate said to Mordecai, "Why do you transgress the king's command?" ⁴ And when they spoke to him day after day and he would not listen to them, they told Haman, in order to see whether Mordecai's words would stand, for he had told them that he was a Jew. ⁵ And when Haman saw that Mordecai did not bow down or pay homage to him, Haman was filled with fury. ⁶ But he disdained[2] to lay hands on Mordecai alone. So, as they had made known to him the people of Mordecai, Haman sought to destroy[3] all the Jews, the people of Mordecai, throughout the whole kingdom of Ahasuerus.

⁷ In the first month, which is the month of Nisan, in the twelfth year of King Ahasuerus, they cast Pur (that is, they cast lots) before Haman day after day; and they cast it month after month till the twelfth month, which is the month of Adar. ⁸ Then Haman said to King Ahasuerus, "There is a certain people scattered abroad and dispersed among the peoples in all the provinces of your kingdom. Their laws are different from those of every other people, and they do not keep the king's laws, so that it is not to the king's profit to tolerate them. ⁹ If it please the king, let it be decreed that they be destroyed, and I will pay 10,000 talents[4] of silver into the hands of those who have charge of the king's business, that they may put it into the king's treasuries." ¹⁰ So the king took his signet ring from his hand and gave it to Haman the Agagite, the son of Hammedatha, the enemy of the Jews. ¹¹ And the king said to Haman, "The money is given to you, the people also, to do with them as it seems good to you."

---

[1] Or *wooden beam* or *stake*; Hebrew *tree* or *wood*. This Persian execution practice involved affixing or impaling a person on a stake or pole (compare Ezra 6:11) [2] Hebrew *disdained in his eyes* [3] Or *annihilate* [4] A *talent* was about 75 pounds or 34 kilograms

¹²Then the king's scribes were summoned on the thirteenth day of the first month, and an edict, according to all that Haman commanded, was written to the king's satraps and to the governors over all the provinces and to the officials of all the peoples, to every province in its own script and every people in its own language. It was written in the name of King Ahasuerus and sealed with the king's signet ring. ¹³Letters were sent by couriers to all the king's provinces with instruction to destroy, to kill, and to annihilate all Jews, young and old, women and children, in one day, the thirteenth day of the twelfth month, which is the month of Adar, and to plunder their goods. ¹⁴A copy of the document was to be issued as a decree in every province by proclamation to all the peoples to be ready for that day. ¹⁵The couriers went out hurriedly by order of the king, and the decree was issued in Susa the citadel. And the king and Haman sat down to drink, but the city of Susa was thrown into confusion.

Esther Agrees to Help the Jews

4 When Mordecai learned all that had been done, Mordecai tore his clothes and put on sackcloth and ashes, and went out into the midst of the city, and he cried out with a loud and bitter cry. ²He went up to the entrance of the king's gate, for no one was allowed to enter the king's gate clothed in sackcloth. ³And in every province, wherever the king's command and his decree reached, there was great mourning among the Jews, with fasting and weeping and lamenting, and many of them lay in sackcloth and ashes.

⁴When Esther's young women and her eunuchs came and told her, the queen was deeply distressed. She sent garments to clothe Mordecai, so that he might take off his sackcloth, but he would not accept them. ⁵Then Esther called for Hathach, one of the king's eunuchs, who had been appointed to attend her, and ordered him to go to Mordecai to learn what this was and why it was. ⁶Hathach went out to Mordecai in the open square of the city in front of the king's gate, ⁷and Mordecai told him all that had happened to him, and the exact sum of money that Haman had promised to pay into the king's treasuries for the destruction of the Jews. ⁸Mordecai also gave him a copy of the written decree issued in Susa for their destruction,¹ that he might show it to Esther and explain it to her and command her to go to the king to beg his favor and plead with him² on behalf of her people. ⁹And Hathach went and told Esther what Mordecai had said. ¹⁰Then Esther spoke to Hathach and commanded him to go to Mordecai and say, ¹¹"All the king's servants and the people of the king's provinces know that if any man or woman goes to the king inside the inner court without being called, there

---
¹ Or *annihilation* ² Hebrew *and seek from before his face*

is but one law—to be put to death, except the one to whom the king holds out the golden scepter so that he may live. But as for me, I have not been called to come in to the king these thirty days."

ⁱ² And they told Mordecai what Esther had said. ¹³ Then Mordecai told them to reply to Esther, "Do not think to yourself that in the king's palace you will escape any more than all the other Jews. ¹⁴ For if you keep silent at this time, relief and deliverance will rise for the Jews from another place, but you and your father's house will perish. And who knows whether you have not come to the kingdom for such a time as this?" ¹⁵ Then Esther told them to reply to Mordecai, ¹⁶ "Go, gather all the Jews to be found in Susa, and hold a fast on my behalf, and do not eat or drink for three days, night or day. I and my young women will also fast as you do. Then I will go to the king, though it is against the law, and if I perish, I perish."[1] ¹⁷ Mordecai then went away and did everything as Esther had ordered him.

Esther Prepares a Banquet

5 On the third day Esther put on her royal robes and stood in the inner court of the king's palace, in front of the king's quarters, while the king was sitting on his royal throne inside the throne room opposite the entrance to the palace. ² And when the king saw Queen Esther standing in the court, she won favor in his sight, and he held out to Esther the golden scepter that was in his hand. Then Esther approached and touched the tip of the scepter. ³ And the king said to her, "What is it, Queen Esther? What is your request? It shall be given you, even to the half of my kingdom." ⁴ And Esther said, "If it please the king,[2] let the king and Haman come today to a feast that I have prepared for the king." ⁵ Then the king said, "Bring Haman quickly, so that we may do as Esther has asked." So the king and Haman came to the feast that Esther had prepared. ⁶ And as they were drinking wine after the feast, the king said to Esther, "What is your wish? It shall be granted you. And what is your request? Even to the half of my kingdom, it shall be fulfilled."[3] ⁷ Then Esther answered, "My wish and my request is: ⁸ If I have found favor in the sight of the king, and if it please the king[4] to grant my wish and fulfill my request, let the king and Haman come to the feast that I will prepare for them, and tomorrow I will do as the king has said."

Haman Plans to Hang Mordecai

⁹ And Haman went out that day joyful and glad of heart. But when Haman saw Mordecai in the king's gate, that he neither rose nor trembled before

---

[1] Hebrew *if I am destroyed, then I will be destroyed* [2] Hebrew *If it is good to the king* [3] Or *done* [4] Hebrew *if it is good to the king*

him, he was filled with wrath against Mordecai. ¹⁰ Nevertheless, Haman restrained himself and went home, and he sent and brought his friends and his wife Zeresh. ¹¹ And Haman recounted to them the splendor of his riches, the number of his sons, all the promotions with which the king had honored him, and how he had advanced him above the officials and the servants of the king. ¹² Then Haman said, "Even Queen Esther let no one but me come with the king to the feast she prepared. And tomorrow also I am invited by her together with the king. ¹³ Yet all this is worth nothing to me, so long as I see Mordecai the Jew sitting at the king's gate." ¹⁴ Then his wife Zeresh and all his friends said to him, "Let a gallows¹ fifty cubits² high be made, and in the morning tell the king to have Mordecai hanged upon it. Then go joyfully with the king to the feast." This idea pleased Haman, and he had the gallows made.

The King Honors Mordecai

6 On that night the king could not sleep. And he gave orders to bring the book of memorable deeds, the chronicles, and they were read before the king. ² And it was found written how Mordecai had told about Bigthana³ and Teresh, two of the king's eunuchs, who guarded the threshold, and who had sought to lay hands on King Ahasuerus. ³ And the king said, "What honor or distinction has been bestowed on Mordecai for this?" The king's young men who attended him said, "Nothing has been done for him." ⁴ And the king said, "Who is in the court?" Now Haman had just entered the outer court of the king's palace to speak to the king about having Mordecai hanged on the gallows⁴ that he had prepared for him. ⁵ And the king's young men told him, "Haman is there, standing in the court." And the king said, "Let him come in." ⁶ So Haman came in, and the king said to him, "What should be done to the man whom the king delights to honor?" And Haman said to himself, "Whom would the king delight to honor more than me?" ⁷ And Haman said to the king, "For the man whom the king delights to honor, ⁸ let royal robes be brought, which the king has worn, and the horse that the king has ridden, and on whose head a royal crown⁵ is set. ⁹ And let the robes and the horse be handed over to one of the king's most noble officials. Let them dress the man whom the king delights to honor, and let them lead him on the horse through the square of the city, proclaiming before him: 'Thus shall it be done to the man whom the king delights to honor.'" ¹⁰ Then the king said to Haman, "Hurry; take the robes and the horse, as you have said, and do so to Mordecai the Jew, who sits at the king's gate. Leave out nothing that you

---

¹ Or *wooden beam*; twice in this verse (see note on 2:23) ² A *cubit* was about 18 inches or 45 centimeters
³ *Bigthana* is an alternate spelling of *Bigthan* (see 2:21) ⁴ Or *wooden beam* (see note on 2:23) ⁵ Or *headdress*

have mentioned." ¹¹ So Haman took the robes and the horse, and he dressed Mordecai and led him through the square of the city, proclaiming before him, "Thus shall it be done to the man whom the king delights to honor."

¹² Then Mordecai returned to the king's gate. But Haman hurried to his house, mourning and with his head covered. ¹³ And Haman told his wife Zeresh and all his friends everything that had happened to him. Then his wise men and his wife Zeresh said to him, "If Mordecai, before whom you have begun to fall, is of the Jewish people, you will not overcome him but will surely fall before him."

Esther Reveals Haman's Plot

¹⁴ While they were yet talking with him, the king's eunuchs arrived and hurried to bring Haman to the feast that Esther had prepared.

7 So the king and Haman went in to feast with Queen Esther. ² And on the second day, as they were drinking wine after the feast, the king again said to Esther, "What is your wish, Queen Esther? It shall be granted you. And what is your request? Even to the half of my kingdom, it shall be fulfilled." ³ Then Queen Esther answered, "If I have found favor in your sight, O king, and if it please the king, let my life be granted me for my wish, and my people for my request. ⁴ For we have been sold, I and my people, to be destroyed, to be killed, and to be annihilated. If we had been sold merely as slaves, men and women, I would have been silent, for our affliction is not to be compared with the loss to the king." ⁵ Then King Ahasuerus said to Queen Esther, "Who is he, and where is he, who has dared[1] to do this?" ⁶ And Esther said, "A foe and enemy! This wicked Haman!" Then Haman was terrified before the king and the queen.

Haman Is Hanged

⁷ And the king arose in his wrath from the wine-drinking and went into the palace garden, but Haman stayed to beg for his life from Queen Esther, for he saw that harm was determined against him by the king. ⁸ And the king returned from the palace garden to the place where they were drinking wine, as Haman was falling on the couch where Esther was. And the king said, "Will he even assault the queen in my presence, in my own house?" As the word left the mouth of the king, they covered Haman's face. ⁹ Then Harbona, one of the eunuchs in attendance on the king, said, "Moreover, the gallows[2] that Haman has prepared for Mordecai, whose word saved the king, is standing at Haman's house, fifty cubits[3] high." And the king said, "Hang him on that."

---

[1] Hebrew *whose heart has filled him* [2] Or *wooden beam*; also verse 10 (see note on 2:23) [3] A *cubit* was about 18 inches or 45 centimeters

¹⁰ So they hanged Haman on the gallows that he had prepared for Mordecai. Then the wrath of the king abated.

Esther Saves the Jews

8 On that day King Ahasuerus gave to Queen Esther the house of Haman, the enemy of the Jews. And Mordecai came before the king, for Esther had told what he was to her. ² And the king took off his signet ring, which he had taken from Haman, and gave it to Mordecai. And Esther set Mordecai over the house of Haman.

³ Then Esther spoke again to the king. She fell at his feet and wept and pleaded with him to avert the evil plan of Haman the Agagite and the plot that he had devised against the Jews. ⁴ When the king held out the golden scepter to Esther, Esther rose and stood before the king. ⁵ And she said, "If it please the king, and if I have found favor in his sight, and if the thing seems right before the king, and I am pleasing in his eyes, let an order be written to revoke the letters devised by Haman the Agagite, the son of Hammedatha, which he wrote to destroy the Jews who are in all the provinces of the king. ⁶ For how can I bear to see the calamity that is coming to my people? Or how can I bear to see the destruction of my kindred?" ⁷ Then King Ahasuerus said to Queen Esther and to Mordecai the Jew, "Behold, I have given Esther the house of Haman, and they have hanged him on the gallows,¹ because he intended to lay hands on the Jews. ⁸ But you may write as you please with regard to the Jews, in the name of the king, and seal it with the king's ring, for an edict written in the name of the king and sealed with the king's ring cannot be revoked."

⁹ The king's scribes were summoned at that time, in the third month, which is the month of Sivan, on the twenty-third day. And an edict was written, according to all that Mordecai commanded concerning the Jews, to the satraps and the governors and the officials of the provinces from India to Ethiopia, 127 provinces, to each province in its own script and to each people in its own language, and also to the Jews in their script and their language. ¹⁰ And he wrote in the name of King Ahasuerus and sealed it with the king's signet ring. Then he sent the letters by mounted couriers riding on swift horses that were used in the king's service, bred from the royal stud, ¹¹ saying that the king allowed the Jews who were in every city to gather and defend their lives, to destroy, to kill, and to annihilate any armed force of any people or province that might attack them, children and women included, and to plunder their goods, ¹² on one day throughout all the provinces of King

---

¹ Or *wooden beam* (see note on 2:23)

Ahasuerus, on the thirteenth day of the twelfth month, which is the month of Adar. ¹³ A copy of what was written was to be issued as a decree in every province, being publicly displayed to all peoples, and the Jews were to be ready on that day to take vengeance on their enemies. ¹⁴ So the couriers, mounted on their swift horses that were used in the king's service, rode out hurriedly, urged by the king's command. And the decree was issued in Susa the citadel.

¹⁵ Then Mordecai went out from the presence of the king in royal robes of blue and white, with a great golden crown¹ and a robe of fine linen and purple, and the city of Susa shouted and rejoiced. ¹⁶ The Jews had light and gladness and joy and honor. ¹⁷ And in every province and in every city, wherever the king's command and his edict reached, there was gladness and joy among the Jews, a feast and a holiday. And many from the peoples of the country declared themselves Jews, for fear of the Jews had fallen on them.

The Jews Destroy Their Enemies

9 Now in the twelfth month, which is the month of Adar, on the thirteenth day of the same, when the king's command and edict were about to be carried out, on the very day when the enemies of the Jews hoped to gain the mastery over them, the reverse occurred: the Jews gained mastery over those who hated them. ² The Jews gathered in their cities throughout all the provinces of King Ahasuerus to lay hands on those who sought their harm. And no one could stand against them, for the fear of them had fallen on all peoples. ³ All the officials of the provinces and the satraps and the governors and the royal agents also helped the Jews, for the fear of Mordecai had fallen on them. ⁴ For Mordecai was great in the king's house, and his fame spread throughout all the provinces, for the man Mordecai grew more and more powerful. ⁵ The Jews struck all their enemies with the sword, killing and destroying them, and did as they pleased to those who hated them. ⁶ In Susa the citadel itself the Jews killed and destroyed 500 men, ⁷ and also killed Parshandatha and Dalphon and Aspatha ⁸ and Poratha and Adalia and Aridatha ⁹ and Parmashta and Arisai and Aridai and Vaizatha, ¹⁰ the ten sons of Haman the son of Hammedatha, the enemy of the Jews, but they laid no hand on the plunder.

¹¹ That very day the number of those killed in Susa the citadel was reported to the king. ¹² And the king said to Queen Esther, "In Susa the citadel the Jews have killed and destroyed 500 men and also the ten sons of Haman. What then have they done in the rest of the king's provinces! Now what is your wish? It shall be granted you. And what further is your request? It shall be

---

¹ Or *headdress*

fulfilled." ¹³ And Esther said, "If it please the king, let the Jews who are in Susa be allowed tomorrow also to do according to this day's edict. And let the ten sons of Haman be hanged on the gallows."¹ ¹⁴ So the king commanded this to be done. A decree was issued in Susa, and the ten sons of Haman were hanged. ¹⁵ The Jews who were in Susa gathered also on the fourteenth day of the month of Adar and they killed 300 men in Susa, but they laid no hands on the plunder.

¹⁶ Now the rest of the Jews who were in the king's provinces also gathered to defend their lives, and got relief from their enemies and killed 75,000 of those who hated them, but they laid no hands on the plunder. ¹⁷ This was on the thirteenth day of the month of Adar, and on the fourteenth day they rested and made that a day of feasting and gladness. ¹⁸ But the Jews who were in Susa gathered on the thirteenth day and on the fourteenth, and rested on the fifteenth day, making that a day of feasting and gladness. ¹⁹ Therefore the Jews of the villages, who live in the rural towns, hold the fourteenth day of the month of Adar as a day for gladness and feasting, as a holiday, and as a day on which they send gifts of food to one another.

The Feast of Purim Inaugurated

²⁰ And Mordecai recorded these things and sent letters to all the Jews who were in all the provinces of King Ahasuerus, both near and far, ²¹ obliging them to keep the fourteenth day of the month Adar and also the fifteenth day of the same, year by year, ²² as the days on which the Jews got relief from their enemies, and as the month that had been turned for them from sorrow into gladness and from mourning into a holiday; that they should make them days of feasting and gladness, days for sending gifts of food to one another and gifts to the poor.

²³ So the Jews accepted what they had started to do, and what Mordecai had written to them. ²⁴ For Haman the Agagite, the son of Hammedatha, the enemy of all the Jews, had plotted against the Jews to destroy them, and had cast Pur (that is, cast lots), to crush and to destroy them. ²⁵ But when it came before the king, he gave orders in writing that his evil plan that he had devised against the Jews should return on his own head, and that he and his sons should be hanged on the gallows. ²⁶ Therefore they called these days Purim, after the term Pur. Therefore, because of all that was written in this letter, and of what they had faced in this matter, and of what had happened to them, ²⁷ the Jews firmly obligated themselves and their offspring and all who joined them, that without fail they would keep these two days

---

¹ Or *wooden beam*; also verse 25 (see note on 2:23)

according to what was written and at the time appointed every year, ²⁸ that these days should be remembered and kept throughout every generation, in every clan, province, and city, and that these days of Purim should never fall into disuse among the Jews, nor should the commemoration of these days cease among their descendants.

²⁹ Then Queen Esther, the daughter of Abihail, and Mordecai the Jew gave full written authority, confirming this second letter about Purim. ³⁰ Letters were sent to all the Jews, to the 127 provinces of the kingdom of Ahasuerus, in words of peace and truth, ³¹ that these days of Purim should be observed at their appointed seasons, as Mordecai the Jew and Queen Esther obligated them, and as they had obligated themselves and their offspring, with regard to their fasts and their lamenting. ³² The command of Esther confirmed these practices of Purim, and it was recorded in writing.

The Greatness of Mordecai

10 King Ahasuerus imposed tax on the land and on the coastlands of the sea. ² And all the acts of his power and might, and the full account of the high honor of Mordecai, to which the king advanced him, are they not written in the Book of the Chronicles of the kings of Media and Persia? ³ For Mordecai the Jew was second in rank to King Ahasuerus, and he was great among the Jews and popular with the multitude of his brothers, for he sought the welfare of his people and spoke peace to all his people.

TABLE OF
WEIGHTS AND MEASURES
AND MONETARY UNITS

The following table is based on the best generally accepted information available for biblical weights, measures, and monetary units. All equivalents are approximate. Weights and measures also varied somewhat in different times and places in the ancient world. Most weights, measures, and monetary units are also explained in footnotes on the pages where they occur in the ESV text.

Biblical Unit	Approximate American and Metric Equivalents	Biblical Equivalent
bath	A *bath* was about 6 gallons or 22 liters	1 ephah
beka	A *beka* was about 1/5 ounce or 5.5 grams	10 gerahs
cor	A *cor* was about 6 bushels or 220 liters	10 ephahs
cubit	A *cubit* was about 18 inches or 45 centimeters	6 handbreadths
daric	A *daric* was a coin of about 1/4 ounce or 8.5 grams	
denarius	A *denarius* was a day's wage for a laborer	
ephah	An *ephah* was about 3/5 bushel or 22 liters	10 omers
gerah	A *gerah* was about 1/50 ounce or 0.6 gram	1/10 beka
handbreadth	A *handbreadth* was about 3 inches or 7.5 centimeters	1/6 cubit
hin	A *hin* was about 4 quarts or 3.5 liters	1/6 bath
homer	A *homer* was about 6 bushels or 220 liters	10 ephahs
kab	A *kab* was about 1 quart or 1 liter	1/22 ephah
lethech	A *lethech* was about 3 bushels or 110 liters	5 ephahs
log	A *log* was about 1/3 quart or 0.3 liter	1/72 bath
mina	A *mina* was about 1 1/4 pounds or 0.6 kilogram	50 shekels
omer	An *omer* was about 2 quarts or 2 liters	1/10 ephah
pim	A *pim* was about 1/3 ounce or 7.5 grams	2/3 shekel
seah	A *seah* was about 7.7 quarts or 7.3 liters	1/3 ephah
shekel	A *shekel* was about 2/5 ounce or 11 grams	2 bekas
span	A *span* was about 9 inches or 22 centimeters	3 handbreadths
stadion	A *stadion* was about 607 feet or 185 meters	
talent	A *talent* was about 75 pounds or 34 kilograms	60 minas